NEW
CONCISE

PROJECT
MATHS 5

FOR LEAVING CERT HIGHER LEVEL

GEORGE HUMPHREY, BRENDAN GUILDEA, GEOFFREY REEVES

g GILL EDUCATION

Gill Education
Hume Avenue
Park West
Dublin 12
www.gilleducation.ie

Gill Education is an imprint of M.H. Gill & Co.

978 07171 5429 6

Print origination by MPS Limited

For permission to reproduce photographs, the authors and publisher
gratefully acknowledge the following:

© Alamy: 173, 225, 314, 318, 329, 340T, 351B, 357, 379, 385, 398, 397,
415, 416; © Getty Images: 191, 340B, 351T, 352; © William Warby: 431.

The authors and publisher have made every effort to trace all copyright
holders, but if any has been inadvertently overlooked we would be pleased
to make the necessary arrangement at the first opportunity.

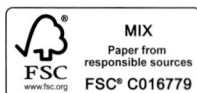

MIX
Paper from
responsible sources
FSC
www.fsc.org   FSC® C016779

Contents

Acknowledgements		iv
Preface		v
1	Integration	1
2	Complex Numbers	33
3	Statistics	80
4	Patterns, Sequences and Series	216
5	Theorems	259
6	Geometry	270
7	Geometry Constructions	303
8	Financial Maths I	324
9	Financial Maths II	343
10	Methods of Proof	371
11	Induction	380
12	Perimeter, Area, Nets and Volume	389
13	Sample Exam Revision Questions	417
Glossary of Statistical Terms		457
Answers		464

Acknowledgements

The authors would like to thank Colman Humphrey, Jessica Hayden and Michael Brennan who helped with proof reading, checking the answers and making many valuable suggestions that are included in the final text. They also would like to thank Stacey Carter in Our Lady's College Greenhills, Drogheda and Mark Lynch in Monkstown CBC for all their help.

The authors also wish to express their thanks to the staff of Gill Education, and special thanks to Kristin Jensen, for her advice, guidance and untiring assistance in the preparation and presentation of the book.

Preface

New Concise Project Maths 5 is one of two books covering the Leaving Certificate Higher Level course. The second book is *New Concise Project Maths 4*.

Additional teachers' resources, including a **Digital Flipbook**, are provided online at www.gillexplore.ie.

An excellent resource for teachers and students is the dynamic software package GeoGebra. The package is of particular use for co-ordinate geometry, geometry and graphing functions. It can be accessed at www.geogebra.org.

George Humphrey
Brendan Guildea
Geoffrey Reeves
Louise Boylan

Estimating the area under a curve

Area of a trapezium

Our definition of a trapezium is a quadrilateral with at least two sides parallel. We will usually deal with the case where there is just one pair of parallel lines.

The sides marked a and b are called the bases and h represents the (perpendicular) height of the trapezium.

The area is given by $A = \left(\dfrac{a + b}{2}\right)h.$

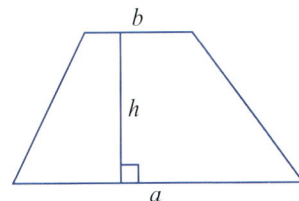

Notes: 1. It may be convenient to interpret this formula as the average of the widths (bases) multiplied by the height.
2. The formula can be found in the booklet of formulae and tables.

Using trapeziums to estimate area

The diagram shows a curve. The area under the curve between $x = 1$ and $x = 3$ has been shaded. Three vertical lines are also shown with the heights marked 2, 6 and 20.

This creates two trapeziums whose bases are represented by the *vertical* lines. Each has height 1.

The area under the curve can be estimated by adding the areas of the two trapeziums.

This would result in an overestimation of the actual area.

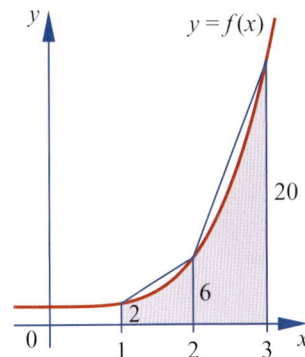

The area under this curve can be estimated by adding the areas of the two outer triangles and rectangle in the centre.

It can also be estimated by treating the first triangle as a trapezium with bases 0 and 2 and with height 1.

In this case, we would have underestimated the actual area.

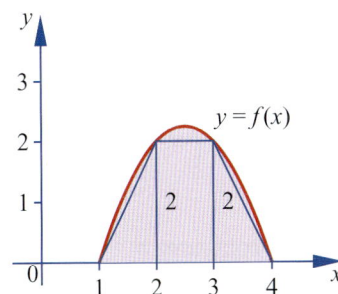

Improving the estimation of area

To improve our estimation of the area under a curve, we could use narrower trapeziums.

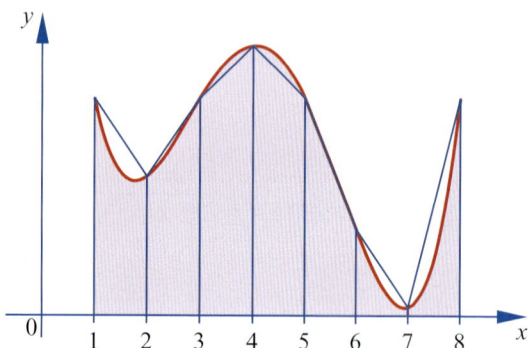

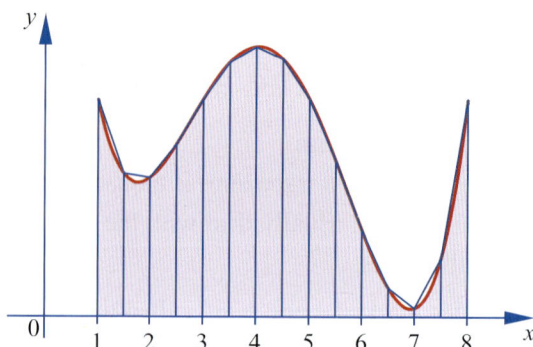

Without a sketch, it is difficult to predict how inaccurate our estimation will be. Even with the sketch, the diagram on the left shows that the trapezium between $x = 1$ and $x = 2$ has a greater area than the corresponding shaded part. That would be partially compensated by the trapeziums between $x = 3$ and $x = 4$ suggesting that the extra work in using narrower widths (in the diagram on the right) may not always significantly improve our estimation.

EXAMPLE

Estimate the area under the curve $y = x^2$ between $x = 2$ and $x = 4$ by using trapeziums of width 1 unit.

Solution:

Make out a table using $2 \leq x \leq 4$ and hence draw a rough sketch.

x	2	3	4
y	4	9	16

You may notice that the area found using trapeziums will be slightly bigger than the actual area.

$$A_1 = \left(\frac{4 + 9}{2}\right)(1) = \frac{13}{2}$$

$$A_2 = \left(\frac{9 + 16}{2}\right)(1) = \frac{25}{2}$$

Total area $= \dfrac{13}{2} + \dfrac{25}{2} = 19.$

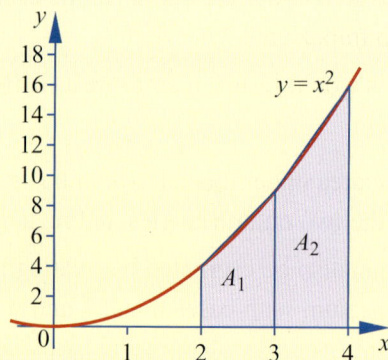

Note: Later you will be able to show that the actual area is $\dfrac{56}{3} = 18\dfrac{2}{3}$.

Exercise 1.1

1. Find the area of the following shapes.

(i)

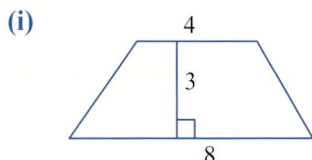

(ii)

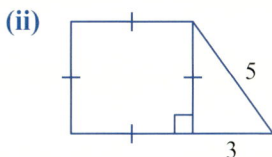

(iii)

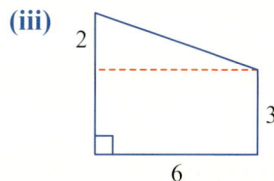

2. Use suitable trapeziums to estimate the shaded area. In each case, indicate whether your area is an underestimate or an overestimate of the actual area.

(i)

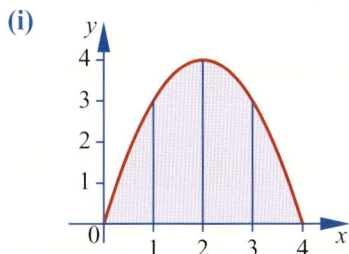

(ii)

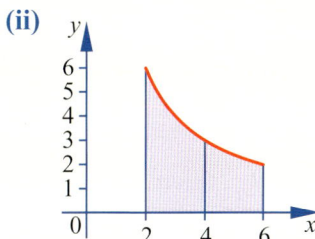

(iii)

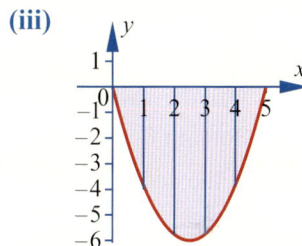

The trapezoidal rule

To improve our method and speed up the process of estimating the area under a curve, we need to look for a pattern or rule.

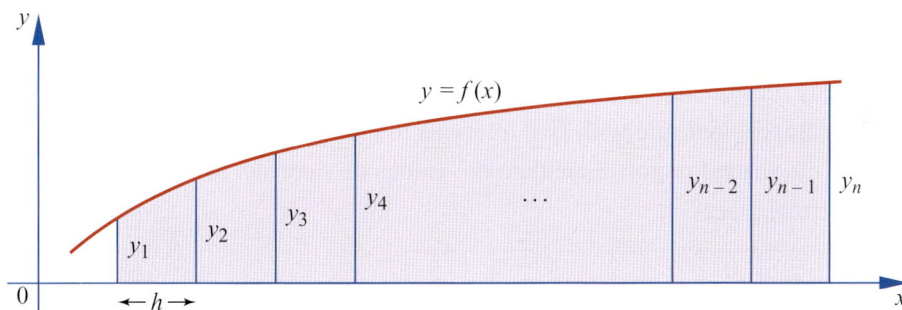

The shaded area can be estimated by:

$$A = \left(\frac{y_1 + y_2}{2}\right)h + \left(\frac{y_2 + y_3}{2}\right)h + \left(\frac{y_3 + y_4}{2}\right)h + \cdots + \left(\frac{y_{n-1} + y_n}{2}\right)h$$

$$= \frac{h}{2}\left[y_1 + y_2 + y_2 + y_3 + y_3 + y_4 + \cdots + y_{n-1} + y_n\right]$$

$$A = \frac{h}{2}\left[y_1 + y_n + 2(y_2 + y_3 + y_4 + \cdots + y_{n-1})\right]$$

$$\boxed{A = \frac{h}{2}\left[y_1 + y_n + 2(y_2 + y_3 + y_4 + \cdots + y_{n-1})\right]}$$

This can be read as:

$$\text{Area} = \frac{\text{width of strip}}{2}\left[\text{first} + \text{last} + 2(\text{sum of middles})\right]$$

Exercise 1.2

1. **(i)** Draw a sketch of the curve represented by the points in the table.

x	0	1	2	3	4	5	6
y	0	15	16	9	0	−5	0

(ii) Use the values in the table to estimate the area between the curve and the x-axis in the domain $0 \le x \le 6$.

(iii) If the actual area is $\frac{148}{3}$ or $49\frac{1}{3}$, calculate the percentage error correct to one decimal place.

2. The diagram shows part of the curve $y = \frac{x^2}{2^x}$.

Using four strips, estimate the area of the shaded region, giving your answer as a fraction.

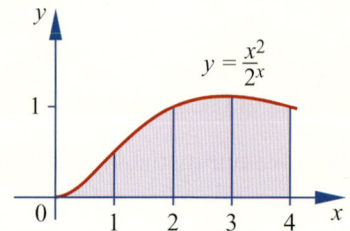

3. The diagram shows part of a circle with centre $(0, 0)$. The curve is represented by the equation $y = \sqrt{25 - x^2}$.

(i) Use the trapezoidal rule with five intervals to estimate the area of the shaded region. Calculate the values of y correct to two decimal places.

x	0	1	2	3	4	5
y	5			4		0

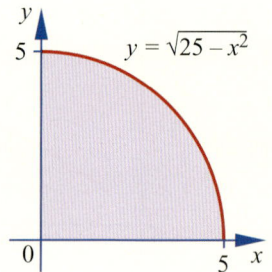

(ii) Is this an overestimation or an underestimation?

(iii) Use the trapezoidal rule with 10 intervals to estimate the shaded area. Calculate the values of y correct to two decimal places.

x	0	0·5	1	1·5	2	2·5	3	3·5	4	4·5	5
y	5						4				0

(iv) Find the exact area of the shaded region.

(v) Use your answers from parts **(iii)** and **(iv)** to estimate π to one decimal place.

4. Estimate the area under the curve $y = x^2 + 1$ between $x = 1$ and $x = 5$.

5. Estimate the area under the curve $f(x) = x^3$ between $x = 1$ and $x = 4$.

6. The curve $y = \sin x$ is shown in the domain $0 \le x \le \pi$.

   (i) Estimate the shaded area using the trapezoidal rule. Give your answer in surd form.

   (ii) If the actual area is 2 units^2, find the percentage error in your estimation.

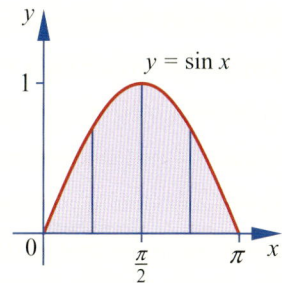

7. The curve $y = \dfrac{1}{1 + x^2}$ is shown in the domain $-3 \le x \le 3$.

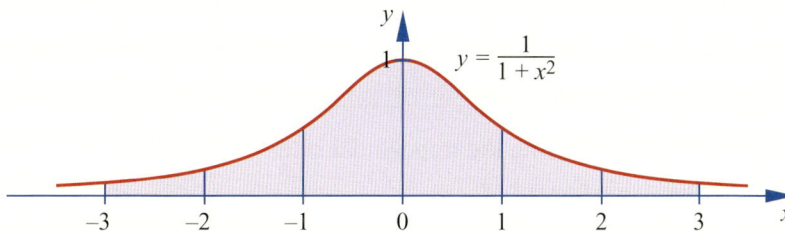

   (i) Estimate the area of the shaded region using the trapezoidal rule. Give your answer as a fraction.

   (ii) If the actual area of the shaded region is $2 \tan^{-1} 3$ units^2, find the percentage error in your estimation, giving your answer correct to two decimal places.

   (iii) Comment on the accuracy of the estimation.

   (iv) The total area under the curve is π units^2. Find the percentage error, correct to two decimal places, if you use your answer from (i) as an estimate for the total area.

8. A car journey of 30 minutes was monitored every 5 minutes and the speed recorded.

Time	0	5	10	15	20	25	30
Speed	0	40	60	100	100	70	0

   (i) Estimate the time spent on the motorway section of journey.

   (ii) Represent the information on a graph, using curved and straight sections as appropriate.

   (iii) Explain why the area under the graph represents the distance travelled.

   (iv) Estimate the distance travelled and hence estimate the average speed.

9. The normal curve is represented by $y = \dfrac{1}{\sqrt{2\pi}} e^{-\frac{1}{2}x^2}$. A section of it is shown below.

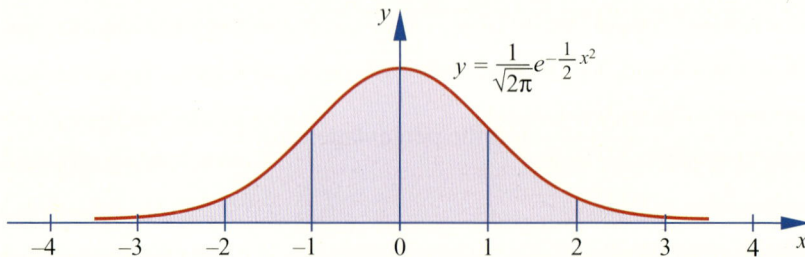

$$y = \dfrac{1}{\sqrt{2\pi}} e^{-\frac{1}{2}x^2}$$

(i) If the complete graph was shown, what would be the total area between the curve and the x-axis?

(ii) Copy and complete the table with values accurate to three decimal places.

x	−3	−2	−1	0	1	2	3
y							

(iii) Estimate the shaded area using the trapezoidal rule.

(iv) What should this shaded area be?

(v) Find the percentage error in your estimation.

Exact area under a curve

The following diagrams suggest a pattern which would give us a method to calculate the exact area under a curve. The first has a rectangular area while the second has a triangular shaded area. It is known that the area shown under part of a parabola is $\dfrac{1}{3}$ of the rectangle enclosing that area.

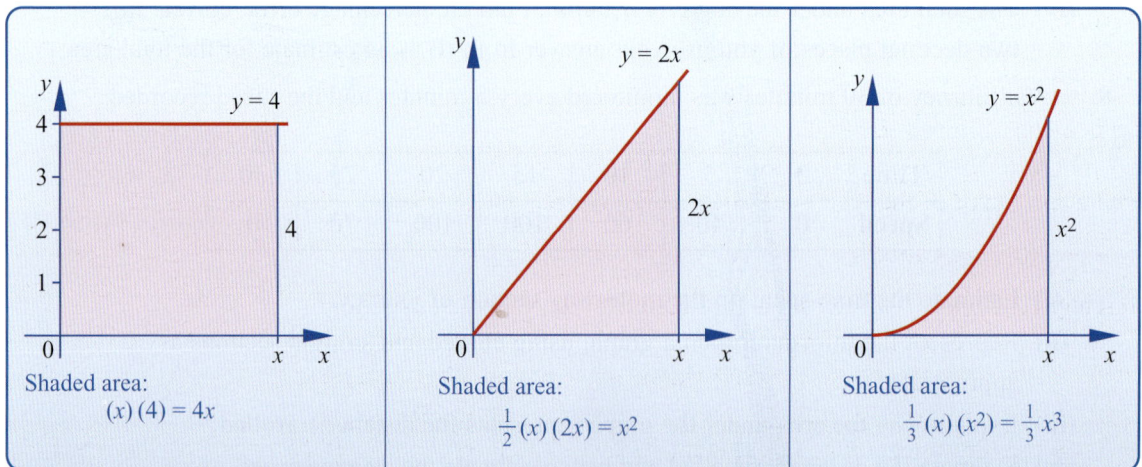

Shaded area:
$(x)(4) = 4x$

Shaded area:
$\dfrac{1}{2}(x)(2x) = x^2$

Shaded area:
$\dfrac{1}{3}(x)(x^2) = \dfrac{1}{3}x^3$

It is either a remarkable coincidence or a provable fact that in each case, the differentiation of the area is the expression for the graph.

It is beyond this course to prove that the anti-differentiation of a curve will yield an expression for the area under that curve, but we must now study that process more closely.

The indefinite integral

The process of finding a function from its derivative is called **anti-differentiation.**

It is more often referred to as **integration.**

For example, we know that if $f(x) = x^2$, then $f'(x) = 2x$.
Now suppose that we are given $f'(x) = 2x$ and asked to find $f(x)$.
In other words, we start with the derivative and work backwards to the original function.
However, if $f(x) = x^2 + 10$, then $f'(x) = 2x$ and if $f(x) = x^2 - 3$, then $f'(x) = 2x$.
In fact, if $f(x) = x^2 + c$, then $f'(x) = 2x$, where c is a constant.
In other words, we do not know whether the original function contained a constant term or not. Notation:

$$\int f'(x)\,dx = f(x) + c$$

The symbol for integration is $\int$, an elongated S.

dx indicates that the integration is with respect to the variable x. c is called the **constant of integration.**

Note: $\int 2x\,dx$ is read as 'the integral of $2x\,dx$' or 'the integral of $2x$ with respect to x'.

Integrals of the form x^n, $n \neq -1$

$$\int x^n\,dx = \frac{x^{n+1}}{n+1} + c \quad (n \neq -1)$$

In words: Increase the power by 1 and divide by the new power or 'up and over'.

Constant factors

If a is a constant, $\int ax^n\,dx = a\int x^n\,dx = a\frac{x^{n+1}}{n+1} + c, n \neq -1$.

A constant factor of the integrand can be taken outside the symbol of integration.

Sum or difference of terms

To integrate a sum or difference, add or subtract the individual integrals.

$$\int (f(x) \pm g(x))\,dx = \int f(x)\,dx \pm \pm \int g(x)\,dx$$

Notes: 1. Before integrating, all items must be written in the form x^n or ax^n, where a is a constant.
2. There is no product rule, quotient rule or chain rule in integration.
3. It is possible to check your answer in integration by differentiating your answer and seeing whether you get back to the original integral.

EXAMPLE 1

Find: **(i)** $\int 3x^2\,dx$ **(ii)** $\int \dfrac{1}{x^3}\,dx$ **(iii)** $\int \dfrac{1}{\sqrt{x}}\,dx$

Solution:

(i) $\int 3x^2\,dx$

$= \dfrac{3x^3}{3} + c$

$= x^3 + c$

(ii) $\int \dfrac{1}{x^3}\,dx$

$= \int x^{-3}\,dx$

$= \dfrac{x^{-2}}{-2} + c$

$= -\dfrac{2}{x^2} + c$

(iii) $\int \dfrac{1}{\sqrt{x}}\,dx$

$= \int x^{-\frac{1}{2}}\,dx$

$= \dfrac{x^{\frac{1}{2}}}{\frac{1}{2}} + c$

$= 2x^{\frac{1}{2}} + c \text{ or } 2\sqrt{x} + c$

Sometimes it is necessary to manipulate the integrand to write each part in the form ax^n.

EXAMPLE 2

Find: **(i)** $\int \left(x + \dfrac{1}{x}\right)^2 dx$ **(ii)** $\int \dfrac{3 + x}{\sqrt{x}}\,dx$

Solution:

(i) $\int \left(x + \dfrac{1}{x}\right)^2 dx$

$= \int \left(x^2 + 2 + \dfrac{1}{x^2}\right) dx$

$= \int (x^2 + 2 + x^{-2})\,dx$

$= \dfrac{x^3}{3} + 2x + \dfrac{x^{-1}}{-1} + c$

$= \dfrac{1}{3}x^3 + 2x - \dfrac{1}{x} + c$

(ii) $\int \dfrac{3 + x}{\sqrt{x}}\,dx$

$= \int \left(\dfrac{3}{\sqrt{x}} + \dfrac{x}{\sqrt{x}}\right) dx$

$= \int \left(\dfrac{3}{x^{\frac{1}{2}}} + \dfrac{x}{x^{\frac{1}{2}}}\right) dx$

$= \int \left(3x^{-\frac{1}{2}} + x^{\frac{1}{2}}\right) dx$

$= \dfrac{3x^{\frac{1}{2}}}{\frac{1}{2}} + \dfrac{x^{\frac{3}{2}}}{\frac{3}{2}} + c$

$= 6x^{\frac{1}{2}} + \dfrac{2}{3}x^{\frac{3}{2}} + c$

Sometimes if we are given some extra information, we may be asked to find the constant of integration or an expression for $f(x)$.

EXAMPLE 3

Find the constant of integration, given that $\int (3x^2 + 1)\,dx = 6$ when $x = 2$.

Solution:

Use integration to find the original function.

$$\int (3x^2 + 1)\,dx$$

$$= \frac{3x^3}{3} + x + c$$

$$= x^3 + x + c$$

This expression equals 6 when $x = 2$.

$$\therefore \quad 2^3 + 2 + c = 6$$

$$8 + 2 + c = 6$$

$$c = 6 - 10$$

$$c = -4$$

Thus, the constant of integration is -4.

EXAMPLE 4

Find the function $y = f(x)$, given that $\dfrac{dy}{dx} = 5 - 2x$ and that the graph of $y = f(x)$ passes through the point $(1, 7)$.

Solution:

Use integration to find the original function.

$$\frac{dy}{dx} = 5 - 2x$$

$$dy = (5 - 2x)dx$$

$$\int 1\,dy = \int (5 - 2x)\,dx$$

$$y = 5x - x^2 + c$$

Use the point $(1, 7)$ to find the value of c.

$$y = 5x - x^2 + c$$

$$7 = 5(1) - (1)^2 + c$$

$$7 = 5 - 1 + c$$

$$7 - 4 = c$$

$$c = 3$$

Thus, $y = 3 + 5x - x^2$.

Exercise 1.3

In questions 1–25, find the integral.

1. $\int x^3 dx$ 2. $\int x^2 dx$ 3. $\int 5x^4 dx$ 4. $\int -x\, dx$ 5. $\int -2x^2 dx$

6. $\int 5\, dx$ 7. $\int -2\, dx$ 8. $\int \dfrac{1}{x^2} dx$ 9. $\int \sqrt{x}\, dx$ 10. $\int \dfrac{2}{\sqrt{x}} dx$

11. $\int (3x^2 + 8x)\, dx$ 12. $\int (x^2 + 2x)\, dx$ 13. $\int (2x^2 - 5x)\, dx$

14. $\int \left(x^2 - \dfrac{1}{x^2} \right) dx$ 15. $\int \left(4x^3 - \dfrac{2}{x^3} \right) dx$ 16. $\int \left(\sqrt{x} - \dfrac{1}{\sqrt{x}} \right) dx$

17. $\int x(2 + x)\, dx$ 18. $\int x^2(x + 5)\, dx$ 19. $\int \sqrt{x}(x + 1)\, dx$

20. $\int \left(\dfrac{x^2 + 3}{x^2} \right) dx$ 21. $\int \left(\dfrac{x + 1}{x^3} \right) dx$ 22. $\int \left(\dfrac{3x^2 - 5}{\sqrt{x}} \right) dx$

23. $\int \left(\dfrac{x^4 - 2x^3 + x^2}{x} \right) dx$ 24. $\int \left(x - \dfrac{1}{x} \right)^2 dx$ 25. $\int \left(x^2 + \dfrac{1}{x} \right)^2 dx$

26. If $f'(x) = 3x^2 - 2x$ and $f(2) = 9$, find $f(x)$.

27. If $f'(x) = 3x^2 - \sqrt{x}$ and $f(0) = 4$, find $f(x)$.

28. If $f'(t) = 4t^3 - 6t$ and $f(-2) = 8$, find $f(t)$.

29. A curve contains the point $\left(\dfrac{1}{2}, 3 \right)$ and its slope at any point (x, y) on the curve is given by $f'(x) = 16x^3 + 2x + 1$. Find $f(x)$.

30. A curve contains the point $(1, 7)$ and its slope at any point (x, y) on the curve is given by $\dfrac{dy}{dx} = 3x^2 + 4$. Find the equation of the curve.

The definite integral

$$\int_a^b f'(x)\, dx = \Big[f(x) \Big]_a^b = f(b) - f(a)$$

We call $\displaystyle\int_a^b f(x)\, dx$ a definite integral, as it gives a definite answer.

The dx indicates that the limits a and b are the limits of x.

The constant a is called the lower limit of the integral.

The constant b is called upper limit of the integral.

Notes:

1. $\int_a^b f(x)\,dx$ is read as 'the integral from $x = a$ to b of $f(x)\,dx$'.

2. There is no constant of integration when we evaluate definite integrals.

3. If the limits are swapped, the sign of the definite integral is changed.

$$\int_a^b f'(x)\,dx = -\int_b^a f'(x)\,dx$$

4. Definite integrals can be used to find the area beneath a curve.

EXAMPLE

Evaluate: **(i)** $\int_1^3 (x^2 + 2x)\,dx$ **(ii)** $\int_1^4 \left(\sqrt{x} - \dfrac{3}{x}\right)^2 dx$

Solution:

(i) $\int_1^3 (x^2 + 2x)\,dx$

$= \left[\dfrac{x^3}{3} + x^2\right]_1^3$

$= \left[\dfrac{3^3}{3} + 3^2\right] - \left[\dfrac{1^3}{3} + 1^2\right]$

$= \dfrac{50}{3}$ or $16\dfrac{2}{3}$

(ii) $\int_1^4 \left(\sqrt{x} - \dfrac{3}{x}\right)^2 dx$

$= \int_1^4 \left(x - \dfrac{6}{\sqrt{x}} + \dfrac{9}{x^2}\right)dx$

$= \int_1^4 \left(x - 6x^{-\frac{1}{2}} + 9x^{-2}\right)dx$

$= \left[\dfrac{x^2}{2} - \dfrac{6x^{\frac{1}{2}}}{\frac{1}{2}} + \dfrac{9x^{-1}}{-1}\right]_1^4$

$= \left[\dfrac{x^2}{2} - 12\sqrt{x} - \dfrac{9}{x}\right]_1^4$

$= \left[\dfrac{4^2}{2} - 12\sqrt{4} - \dfrac{9}{4}\right] - \left[\dfrac{1^2}{2} - 12\sqrt{1} - \dfrac{9}{1}\right]$

$= \dfrac{9}{4}$ or $2\dfrac{1}{4}$

Exercise 1.4

In questions 1–16, evaluate the definite integral.

1. $\int_1^2 3x^2 dx$

2. $\int_0^2 4x^3 dx$

3. $\int_1^2 x^3 dx$

4. $\int_1^4 \sqrt{x}\, dx$

5. $\int_1^2 (4x - x^2) dx$

6. $\int_0^2 x(2 - 3x) dx$

7. $\int_{-2}^2 x(x + 4) dx$

8. $\int_1^4 \frac{1}{\sqrt{x}} dx$

9. $\int_{-1}^1 \frac{1}{x^3} dx$

10. $\int_2^4 \left(\frac{1}{x^2} + 3\right) dx$

11. $\int_4^9 \left(1 - \frac{3}{\sqrt{x}}\right) dx$

12. $\int_1^4 \left(3 - \frac{1}{\sqrt{x}}\right) dx$

13. $\int_1^2 \left(x + \frac{1}{x}\right)^2 dx$

14. $\int_1^{16} \left(\frac{\sqrt{x} - 4}{\sqrt{x}}\right) dx$

15. $\int_1^2 \frac{x^2 + x}{x^4} dx$

16. $\int_1^4 \frac{3x - 2\sqrt{x}}{x} dx$

17. Express $\frac{4x^2 - 9}{4x - 6}$ in the form $\frac{1}{a}(ax + b)$ and hence evaluate $\int_0^2 \frac{4x^2 - 9}{4x - 6} dx$.

18. Express $\frac{x^3 - 8}{x - 2}$ in the form $x^2 + px + q$ and hence evaluate $\int_0^1 \frac{x^3 - 8}{x - 2} dx$.

In questions 19–21, find the value of $k > 0$.

19. $\int_0^k x^2 dx = 9$

20. $\int_1^k (2x + 3) dx = 6$

21. $\int_0^9 \frac{k}{\sqrt{x}} dx = 30$

22. Verify that $\int_{4-k}^{4+k} (x - 4) dx = 0$.

Integrals leading to a logarithmic function

The general rule for integrating x^n had an exception for $n = 1$. This case requires a new rule:

$$\int \frac{1}{x} dx = \ln x + c \qquad \text{or} \qquad \int \frac{1}{ax + b} dx = \frac{1}{a}\ln(ax + b) + c$$

We sometimes use the laws of logarithms when we are tidying up an answer to a definite integral involving $\frac{1}{x}$. For example, it would be quite natural to simplify:

$$\ln 6 - \ln 2 = \ln \frac{6}{2} = \ln 3$$

Remember also that $\ln 1 = 0$ and $\ln e = 1$.

EXAMPLE

(i) Find $\int \dfrac{x+2}{x}\,dx$.   (ii) Evaluate $\int_1^5 \dfrac{dx}{2x}$.

Solution:

(i)
$$\int \dfrac{x+2}{x}\,dx$$

$$= \int \left[\dfrac{x}{x} + \dfrac{2}{x} \right] dx$$

$$= \int \left[1 + \dfrac{2}{x} \right] dx$$

$$= \int \left[1 + 2\left(\dfrac{1}{x}\right) \right] dx$$

$$= x + 2 \ln |x| + c$$

(ii)
$$\int_1^5 \dfrac{dx}{2x}$$

$$= \dfrac{1}{2} \int_1^5 \dfrac{1}{x}\,dx$$

$$= \dfrac{1}{2} \Big[\ln x \Big]_1^5$$

$$= \dfrac{1}{2} \Big[\ln 5 - \ln 1 \Big]$$

$$= \dfrac{1}{2} \ln 5$$

Note: When $x > 0$ (x is positive), we can write $\ln x$ instead of $\ln |x|$.

Exercise 1.5

Find each of the following.

1. $\int \dfrac{2}{x}\,dx$

2. $\int 3x - \dfrac{5}{x}\,dx$

3. $\int x^2 + \dfrac{7}{2x}\,dx$

4. $\int \dfrac{1}{3x+5}\,dx$

5. $\int \dfrac{5}{4x-5}\,dx$

6. $\int \dfrac{3}{5x+7}\,dx$

Evaluate the following.

7. $\int_1^5 \dfrac{x^3+6}{2x}\,dx$

8. $\int_2^7 \dfrac{3x^2-x}{x^2}\,dx$

9. $\int_1^4 \dfrac{4-2\sqrt{x}}{\sqrt{x^3}}\,dx$

Integrating trigonometric functions

$$\int \cos ax \, dx = \dfrac{1}{a} \sin ax + c$$

$$\int \sin ax \, dx = -\dfrac{1}{a} \cos ax + c$$

These integrals can be written down directly although they are not included in the booklet of formulae and tables.

Note: When integrating, the angle must be in **radians.**

EXAMPLE 1

(i) Find $\int \cos 3x \, dx$.   (ii) Evaluate. $\int_0^{\frac{\pi}{2}} \sin 5x \, dx$.

Solution:

(i) $\int \cos 3x \, dx = \dfrac{\sin 3x}{3} + c$

(ii) $\int_0^{\frac{\pi}{2}} \sin 5x \, dx = \left[-\dfrac{\cos 5x}{5} \right]_0^{\frac{\pi}{2}} = \left[-\dfrac{\cos \frac{5\pi}{2}}{5} \right] - \left[-\dfrac{\cos 0}{5} \right] = \left[-\dfrac{0}{5} \right] - \left[-\dfrac{1}{5} \right] = \dfrac{1}{5}$

EXAMPLE 2

(i) Express $\cos 2\theta \sin 4\theta$ as a sum of two trigonometrical functions.

(ii) Hence, evaluate $\int_0^{\frac{\pi}{6}} \cos 2\theta \sin 4\theta \, d\theta$.

Solution:

(i) $\cos 2\theta \sin 4\theta$

   $= \sin 4\theta \cos 2\theta$ (swap the terms so that the bigger angle is first)

   $= \dfrac{1}{2} [\sin(4\theta + 2\theta) + \sin(4\theta - 2\theta)]$ (booklet of formulae and tables, page 15)

   $= \dfrac{1}{2} (\sin 6\theta + \sin 2\theta)$

(ii) $\int_0^{\frac{\pi}{6}} \cos 2\theta \sin 4\theta \, d\theta$

   $= \dfrac{1}{2} \int_0^{\frac{\pi}{6}} (\sin 6\theta + \sin 2\theta) d\theta$

   $= \dfrac{1}{2} \left[-\dfrac{\cos 6\theta}{6} - \dfrac{\cos 2\theta}{2} \right]_0^{\frac{\pi}{6}}$

   $= -\dfrac{1}{2} \left[\dfrac{\cos 6\theta}{6} + \dfrac{\cos 2\theta}{2} \right]_0^{\frac{\pi}{6}}$

   $= -\dfrac{1}{2} \left(\left[\dfrac{\cos \pi}{6} + \dfrac{\cos \frac{\pi}{3}}{2} \right] - \left[\dfrac{\cos 0}{6} + \dfrac{\cos 0}{2} \right] \right)$

   $= \dfrac{7}{24}$

Exercise 1.6

In questions 1–6, find the integral.

1. $\displaystyle\int \cos 2x \, dx$ 2. $\displaystyle\int \sin 4x \, dx$ 3. $3\displaystyle\int \cos 3x \, dx$ 4. $\displaystyle\int (\cos 4\theta - \sin 2\theta) \, d\theta$

5. $8\displaystyle\int (\cos 2\theta - \sin 8\theta) \, d\theta$ 6. $\displaystyle\int (\sin 5\theta + \cos 7\theta) \, d\theta$

In questions 7–10, write the expression as a sum or difference and hence find the integral.

7. $\displaystyle\int 2 \sin 4x \cos 2x \, dx$ 8. $\displaystyle\int 2 \cos 6x \sin x \, dx$

9. $\displaystyle\int \sin 3x \sin 5x \, dx$ 10. $\displaystyle\int \cos 2x \cos 3x \, dx$

In questions 11–13, evaluate the integral.

11. $\displaystyle\int_0^{\frac{\pi}{4}} \cos \theta \, d\theta$ 12. $\displaystyle\int_0^{\frac{\pi}{2}} \cos 2x \, dx$ 13. $3\displaystyle\int_0^{\frac{\pi}{4}} \sin 4x \, dx$

14. (i) Express $\cos 3x \cos 2x$ as the sum of two trigonometrical functions.

   (ii) Hence, evaluate $\displaystyle\int_0^{\frac{\pi}{2}} \cos 3x \cos 2x \, dx$.

15. (i) Express $\cos 2x \sin 4x$ as the sum or difference of two trigonometrical functions.

   (ii) Hence, evaluate $\displaystyle\int_0^{\frac{\pi}{6}} \cos 2x \sin 4x \, dx$.

Integration of exponential functions

$$\int e^{ax} \, dx = \frac{1}{a} e^{ax} + c \quad \text{or} \quad \int e^{ax+b} \, dx = \frac{1}{a} e^{ax+b} + c$$

These integrals can be written down directly without substitution.

> ### EXAMPLE

Find $\int e^{4x+1}\,dx$.

Solution:

Method 1: Using the basic rule only

$$\int e^{4x+1}dx = \int e^{4x} \times e^1\,dx = e\int e^{4x}\,dx = \frac{1}{4}(e)e^{4x} + c = \frac{1}{4}e^{4x+1} + c$$

Method 2: Using the more general rule

$$\int e^{4x+1}\,dx = \frac{1}{4}e^{4x+1} + c$$

Integrals of the form a^x

We have already dealt with the special case of e^x, but a more general rule is:

$$\int a^x\,dx = \frac{a^x}{\ln a} + c \text{ where } a > 0 \text{ and } a \neq 1$$

> ### EXAMPLE

(i) Evaluate $\int_2^4 2^x dx.$ (ii) Find $\int 3^{x-2}dx.$

Solution:

(i) $\displaystyle\int_2^4 2^x dx$

$= \left[\dfrac{2^x}{\ln 2}\right]_2^4$

$= \left[\dfrac{2^4}{\ln 2}\right] - \left[\dfrac{2^2}{\ln 2}\right]$

$= \dfrac{16}{\ln 2} - \dfrac{4}{\ln 2}$

$= \dfrac{12}{\ln 2}$

(ii) $\displaystyle\int 3^{x-2}dx$

$= \int (3^x \times 3^{-2})dx$

$= 3^{-2}\int 3^x dx$

$= 3^{-2} \times \dfrac{3^x}{\ln 3} + c$

$= \dfrac{3^{x-2}}{\ln 3} + c$

Exercise 1.7

In questions 1–8, find the integral.

1. $\int e^{3x}\,dx$

2. $\int e^{2x+3}\,dx$

3. $\int e^{-4x}\,dx$

4. $\int e^{1-3x}\,dx$

5. $\int \dfrac{1}{e^{2x}}\,dx$

6. $2\int e^{\frac{x}{2}}\,dx$

7. $\int (e^{2x}+e^{x})\,dx$

8. $\int \left(e^{3x}-\dfrac{1}{e^{3x}}\right)dx$

In questions 9–11, evaluate the integral.

9. $\displaystyle\int_{0}^{1} e^{2x}\,dx$

10. $\displaystyle\int_{-1}^{1} e^{3x-1}\,dx$

11. $\displaystyle\int_{0}^{2} e^{4x-1}\,dx$

In questions 12–15, find the integral.

12. $\int 4^{x}\,dx$

13. $\int 7^{x+3}\,dx$

14. $\int 6^{x}\,dx$

15. $\int 2^{x-2}\,dx$

In questions 16–18, evaluate the integral.

16. $\displaystyle\int_{0}^{2} 5^{x}\,dx$

17. $\displaystyle\int_{1}^{3} 10^{x}\,dx$

18. $\displaystyle\int_{0}^{2} 2^{x-3}\,dx$

Area under a curve

While it is beyond this course to show exactly how the method of integration calculates the exact area, the following diagram and overview may go some way to explain the *notation*.

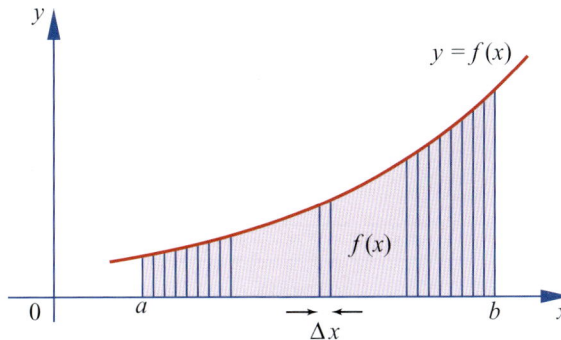

To get the area under a curve, it was cut into very thin strips; so thin that they could be considered as rectangles rather than trapeziums. This thin width was denoted by Δx. Summing up these strips would approximate the area: $\sum f(x)\Delta x$ or $\sum y\Delta x$.

Further study which involved making the widths infinitesimally small (which infinitely increased the number of strips) arrived at the notation we use today:

$$\text{Area} = \int_{a}^{b} y\,dx$$

Area between a curve and the *x*-axis

The area, A, of the region bounded by the curve $y = f(x)$, the *x*-axis and the lines $x = a$ and $x = b$ is given by:

$$A = \int_a^b y \, dx \quad \text{or} \quad A = \int_a^b f(x) \, dx$$

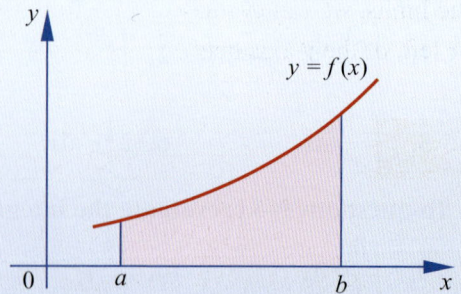

This is positive if the area is above the *x*-axis.
This is negative if the area is below the *x*-axis.

If the curve cuts the *x*-axis between the limits, then:

(i) Find the areas above and below the *x*-axis separately.

(ii) Add these two values together.

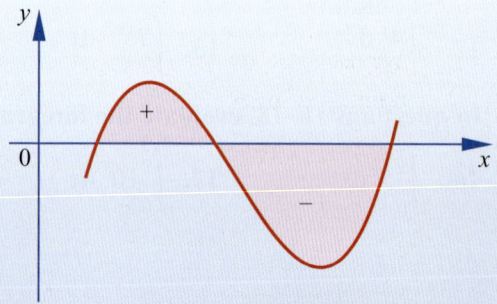

Area between a curve and the *y*-axis

The area, A, bounded by the curve $y = f(x)$, the *y*-axis and the lines $y = a$ and $y = b$ is given by:

$$A = \int_a^b x \, dy$$

In this case, x must be expressed as a function of y before we can integrate.

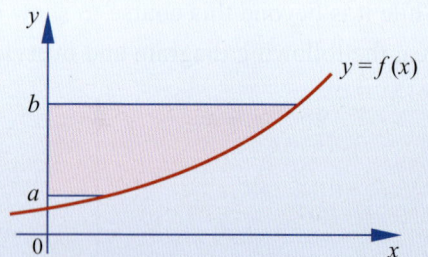

This is positive if the area is to the right of the *y*-axis.
This is negative if the area is to the left of the *y*-axis.

If the curve cuts the *y*-axis between the limits, then:

(i) Find the areas to the right and the left of the *y*-axis separately.

(ii) Add these two values together.

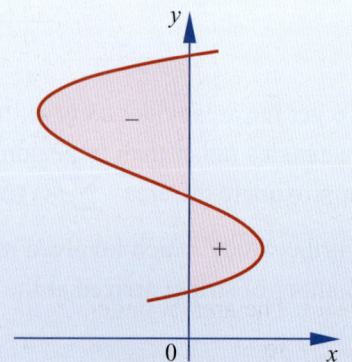

If not given, it is good practice to draw a sketch of the function and check to see if the curve cuts the x-axis or y-axis between the given limits. If the curve is completely above, or below, the x-axis between the limits, we can evaluate the integral between the limits given. If the curve is completely to the right, or left, of the y-axis between the limits, we can evaluate the integral between the limits given.

EXAMPLE 1

c: $y = 3x - x^2$ and l: $y = x$ represent a curve and a line respectively. Find the coordinates of the points where the curve and line intersect and draw a rough sketch of c and l. Find the area bounded by the curve c, the line l and the x-axis.

Solution:

We use simultaneous equations to find the point(s) of intersection of the line and curve.

$$3x - x^2 = x$$
$$-x^2 + 2x = 0$$
$$x^2 - 2x = 0$$
$$x(x - 2) = 0$$
$$x = 0 \text{ or } x = 2$$

As $y = x$, when $x = 0$, $y = 0$ and when $x = 2$, $y = 2$.

The points of intersection are $(0, 0)$ and $(2, 2)$.

We also need to find where the curve cuts the x-axis.

On the x-axis, $y = 0$

$$\therefore \quad 3x - x^2 = 0$$
$$x^2 - 3x = 0$$
$$x(x - 3) = 0$$
$$x = 0 \text{ or } x = 3$$

The curve cuts the x-axis at $x = 0$ and $x = 3$.

Now we can draw a good sketch and shade the appropriate region.

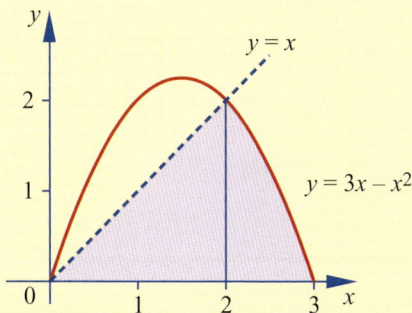

$$\text{Area} = \int_0^2 (\text{line}) \, dx + \int_2^3 (\text{curve}) \, dx$$

$$= \int_0^2 x \, dx + \int_2^3 (3x - x^2) \, dx$$

$$= \left[\frac{x^2}{2}\right]_0^2 + \left[\frac{3x^2}{2} - \frac{x^3}{3}\right]_2^3$$

$$= \left[\frac{4}{2} - 0\right] + \left[\left(\frac{27}{2} - \frac{27}{3}\right) - \left(\frac{12}{2} - \frac{8}{3}\right)\right]$$

$$= \frac{19}{6}$$

Note: The area bounded by the line and the x-axis between $x = 0$ and $x = 2$ could also have been found by calculating the area of a triangle.

EXAMPLE 2

Find the area bounded by the curve $y = x^2 - 2x - 8$, the x-axis and the lines $x = 1$ and $x = 5$.

Solution:

First make a sketch of the curve $y = x^2 - 2x - 8$.

It cuts the x-axis at $y = 0$.

$$\text{Thus,} \quad x^2 - 2x - 8 = 0$$
$$(x - 4)(x + 2) = 0$$
$$x = 4 \text{ or } x = -2$$

The graph is shown on the right.

The sketch shows that the required area is in two parts.

One part lies below the x-axis, A_1, and is negative; the other part lies above the x-axis, A_2, and is positive.

Thus, we calculate the two areas separately.

To ensure we get a positive area for A_1, we get the negative of the integral. We then swap the limits for convenience.

$$A_1 = -\int_1^4 (x^2 - 2x - 8)\, dx \qquad\qquad A_2 = \int_4^5 (x^2 - 2x - 8)\, dx$$

$$= \int_4^1 (x^2 - 2x - 8)\, dx \qquad\qquad = \left[\frac{x^3}{3} - x^2 - 8x\right]_4^5$$

$$= \left[\frac{x^3}{3} - x^2 - 8x\right]_4^1 \qquad\qquad = \left[\frac{125}{3} - 25 - 40\right] - \left[\frac{64}{3} - 16 - 32\right]$$

$$= \left[\frac{1}{3} - 1 - 8\right] - \left[\frac{64}{3} - 16 - 32\right] \qquad\qquad = \frac{10}{3}$$

$$= 18$$

$$\text{Thus, area} = A_1 + A_2 = 18 + \frac{10}{3} = \frac{64}{3}.$$

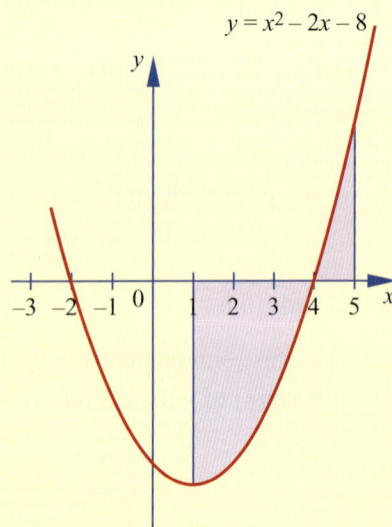

Area between two curves

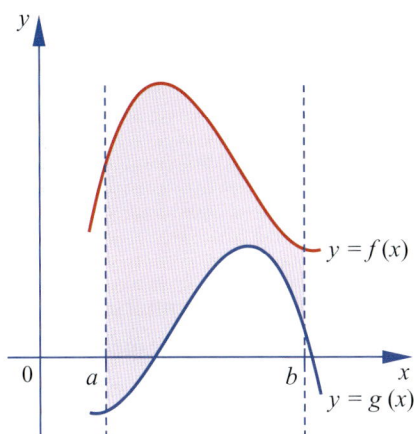

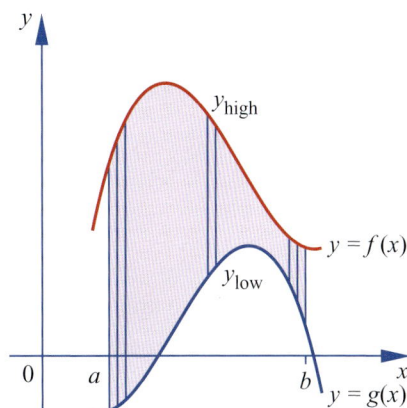

Recalling the overview given earlier, where we split the area into a large number of very thin strips, we extend our previous notation to read:

$$\text{Area} = \int_a^b (\text{height of strip})\, dx$$

In the diagram above this becomes:

$$\text{Area} = \int_a^b \left[f(x) - g(x) \right] dx$$

Once we have a sketch, it might be easier to use:

$$\text{Area} = \int_a^b \left[y_{high} - y_{low} \right] dx$$

The simplicity of this approach is that once one curve is always above the other within the given interval, we will always get a positive area. This is true even if one (or both) of the curves go below the x-axis, as $y_{high} - y_{low}$ *must* be a positive height.

If the graphs intersect within the interval, then it will be necessary to calculate more than one integral. This is the same problem as when a curve lies above *and* below the x-axis.

1. Draw a sketch of both curves.
2. If necessary, find where the curves intersect.
3. Between each pair of points of intersection, calculate $\int_a^b [y_{high} - y_{low}]\, dx.$

An alternative approach

It is easy to see why the area between two curves would be:

$$\text{Area} = \int_a^b \left[f(x) - g(x) \right] dx$$

However, some people use this version:

$$\text{Area} = \int_a^b f(x)\,dx - \int_a^b g(x)\,dx$$

This is interpreted as getting the area under each curve between the points of intersection and subtracting the areas. It is not immediately clear how this works on a diagram, especially when one of the curves goes above and below the x-axis. With this method, if an area is negative, it must not be changed to a positive. However, if the subtraction of the areas is negative, then that should be changed to a positive.

1. If necessary, find where the curves intersect.
2. Between each pair of points of intersection, subtract the areas under the curves.

EXAMPLE

The diagram shows part of the curve
$c: y = 3 + 6x - x^2$ and the line $l : y = 15 - 2x$.

(i) Find the x coordinates of P and Q.

(ii) Calculate the area bounded by c and l.

Solution:

(i) We need to find the x coordinates where the
curve and line intersect.

$c : y = 3 + 6x - x^2$ $\quad l : y = 15 - 2x$

Thus,

$$3 + 6x - x^2 = 15 - 2x$$
$$-x^2 + 8x - 12 = 0$$
$$x^2 - 8x + 12 = 0$$
$$(x - 2)(x - 6) = 0$$
$$x = 2 \text{ or } x = 6$$

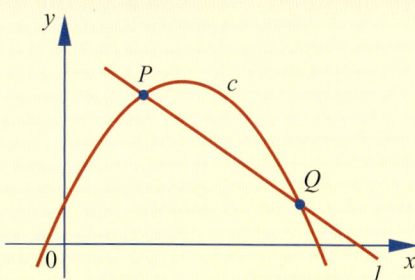

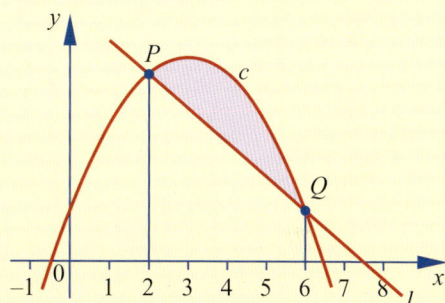

(ii) The shaded region represents the area bounded by the curve, c, and the line, l,
between the limits $x = 2$ and $x = 6$.

$$\text{Shaded area} = \int_2^6 \left[y_{\text{high}} - y_{\text{low}} \right] dx$$

$$= \int_2^6 \left[3 + 6x - x^2 - (15 - 2x) \right] dx$$

$$= \int_2^6 \left[3 + 6x - x^2 - 15 + 2x \right] dx$$

$$= \int_2^6 (-12 + 8x - x^2) \, dx$$

$$= \left[-12x + 4x^2 - \frac{x^3}{3} \right]_2^6$$

$$= \left[-12(6) + 4(6)^2 - \frac{6^3}{3} \right] - \left[-12(2) + 4(2)^2 - \frac{2^3}{3} \right]$$

$$= \frac{32}{3} \text{ or } 10\frac{2}{3}$$

Exercise 1.8

In questions 1–10, calculate the area of the shaded region.

1.

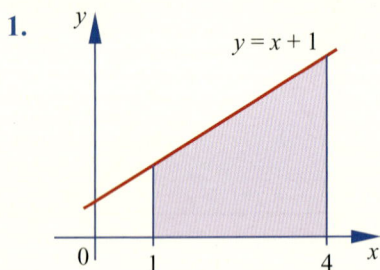

$y = x + 1$

2.

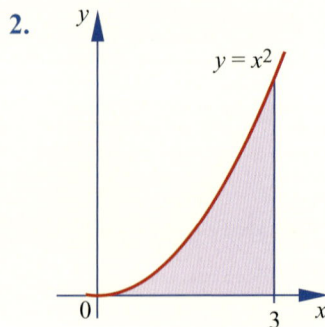

$y = x^2$

3.

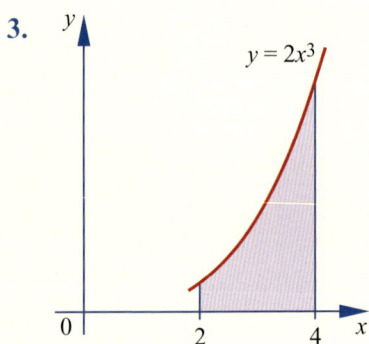

$y = 2x^3$

4.

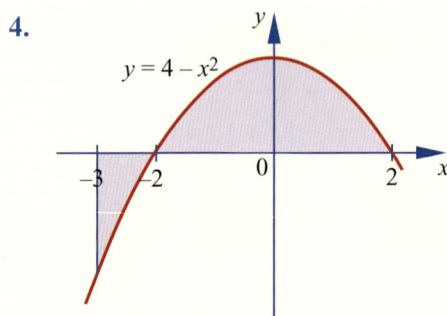

$y = 4 - x^2$

5.

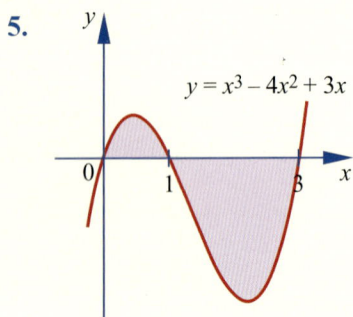

$y = x^3 - 4x^2 + 3x$

6.

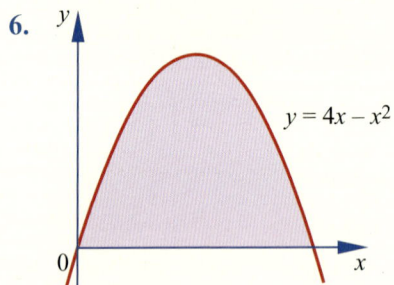

$y = 4x - x^2$

7.

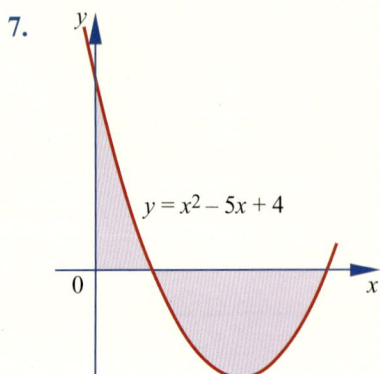

$y = x^2 - 5x + 4$

8.

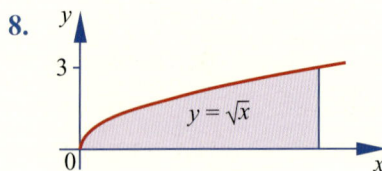

$y = \sqrt{x}$

9.

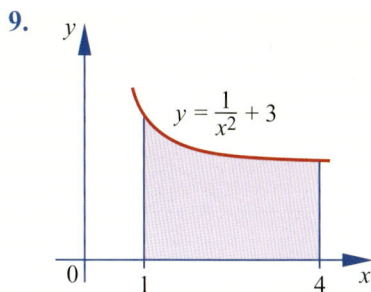

$y = \dfrac{1}{x^2} + 3$

10.

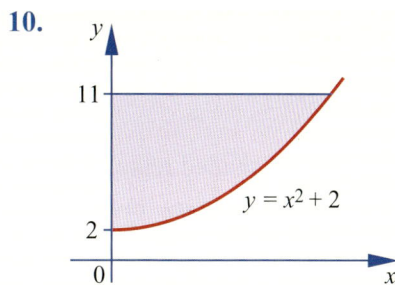

$y = x^2 + 2$

In questions 11–12, calculate the area enclosed by the line and the curve.

11.

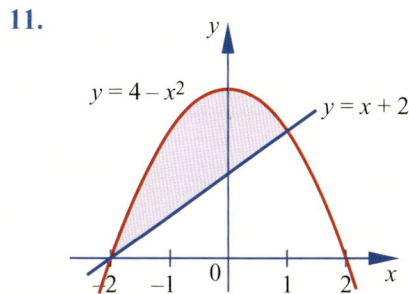

$y = 4 - x^2$

$y = x + 2$

12.

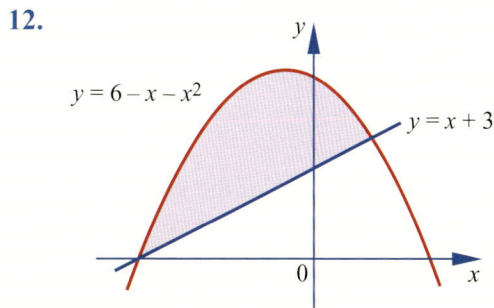

$y = 6 - x - x^2$

$y = x + 3$

13. The diagram shows part of the curve

$$c : y = 5x - x^2 \text{ and the line } l : y = 8 - x.$$

(i) Find the x coordinates of P and Q.

(ii) Calculate the area bounded by c and l.

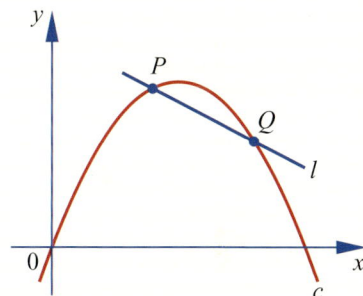

14. $f(x) = x^2 + 3$ and $g(x) = 3x + 1$. $f(x)$ and $g(x)$ meet at the points A and B.

(i) Find the coordinates of A and B.

(ii) Sketch $f(x)$ and $g(x)$ on the same axes and scales.

(iii) Find the area of the bounded region enclosed by $f(x)$ and $g(x)$.

15. Find the area of the bounded region enclosed by the curve $y = 4x - x^2$ and the lines $x = 0$ and $x = 5$.

16. Find the area of the bounded region enclosed by the curve $y = 5x - 2x^2$ and the line $y = x$.

17. Find the area of the bounded region enclosed by the curve $y = x^2 - 3x + 3$ and the line $y = 2x - 1$.

18. Find the area enclosed by the curve $y = x^2 + 1$ and the line $y = 5$.

19. Find the area enclosed by the curve $y = x^2$ and the y-axis from $y = 1$ to $y = 4$.

20. The diagram shows part of the graph of the function

$$f(x) = \frac{x^2 - 1}{x}.$$

Calculate the area of the shaded region.
Write your answer in the form $a - \ln b$.

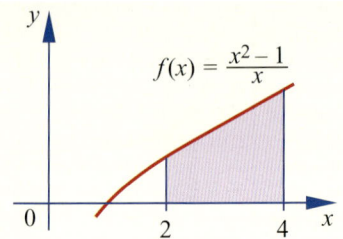

21. The diagram shows part of the graph of the curve

$$f(x) = \frac{12}{x^2}.$$

If the region bounded by $f(x)$, the x-axis and lines
$x = 2$ and $x = k$, $k > 2$, is 4, find the value of k.

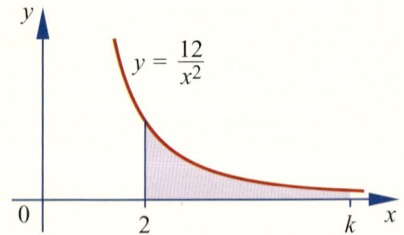

22. The diagram shows part of the graph of the function

$$f(x) = 4x - x^2.$$

If the areas of the two shaded regions are equal, find the
value of p, $p > 0$.

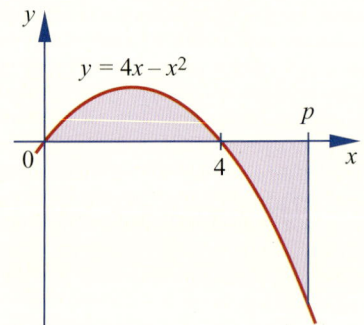

23. The diagram shows a sketch of the functions

$$f(x) = x^2 - 2x \text{ and } g(x) = 2x.$$

$f(x)$ cuts the x-axis at the origin and point A.
$f(x)$ and $g(x)$ meet at the point B.
   (i) Find the coordinates of A and B.
   (ii) Find the area of the shaded region.

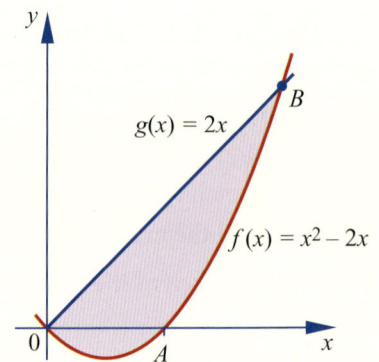

24. The diagram shows part of the curve $y = x^3 - 12x^2 + 36x$.
It touches the x-axis at $(6, 0)$.
   (i) Find the coordinates of the local maximum point.
   (ii) Use the trapezoidal rule to estimate the area of the
       shaded region.
   (iii) Use integration to find the exact area.

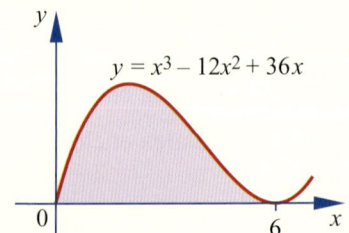

25. **(i)** If $y = x^3$, express x as a function of y.

   (ii) The region bounded by the y-axis, the curve $y = x^3$ and the line $y = 8$ is divided into two regions of equal area by the line $y = k$.

   Show that $k^4 = 512$.

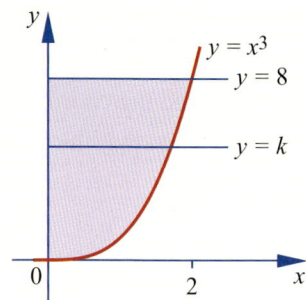

26. Sally's Sweet Shop uses the logo of a wrapped sweet on all its merchandise.

   Find the area of the logo (the shaded area on the diagram).

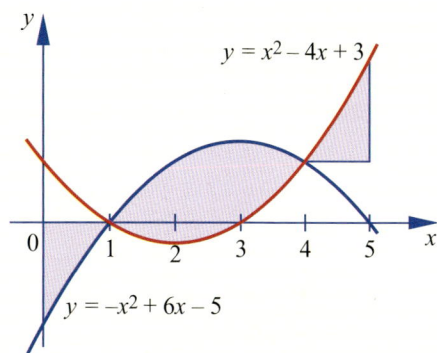

27. Find the area of the region bounded by the line $x + y = 5$ and the curve $y = \dfrac{1}{x}$ in the first quadrant.

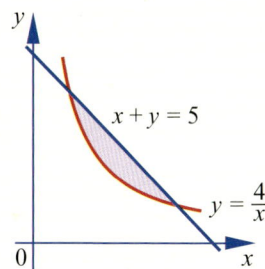

28. Freddie's Fish and Chip Shop uses the logo shown. The curves used are
$$y = -x^2 + 4x$$
and
$$y = x^2 - 4x + 6$$
from $x = 2$ to $x = 4$. Find the area of this logo.

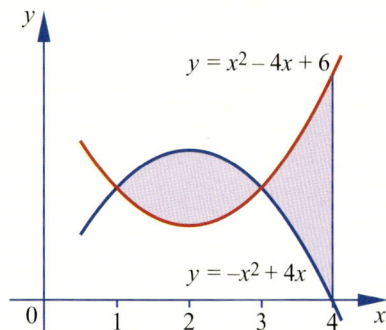

29. The diagram shows two parabolic curves:

$y = 2x^2 - 4x - 16$ and $y = -x^2 + 2x + 8$.

   (i) Find the coordinates of the points A and B.

   (ii) Show that the area of the shaded region is given by

$$\int_{-2}^{4} (-3x^2 + 6x + 24)\, dx.$$

   (iii) Hence or otherwise, show that the area is 108.

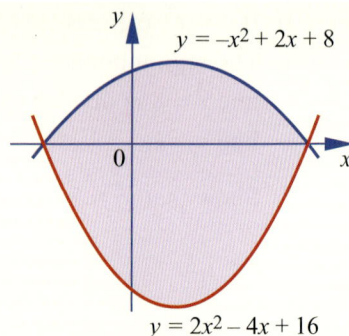

30. The graph of sin x is shown for $0 \leq x \leq \pi$.
    Verify that the area of the shaded region is 2.

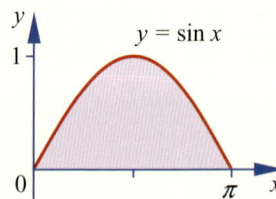

31. The graphs of $y = \sin x$ and $y = \cos x$ are shown in the domain $0 \leq x \leq \frac{\pi}{2}$.

    Calculate the area of the shaded region.

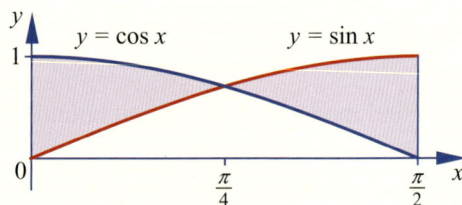

32. The graphs of $f(x) = \left(\dfrac{1}{2}\right)^x$ and $g(x) = -3x - 1$

    are shown in the domain $-3 \leq x \leq -1$.

   (i) Find the points of intersection from the graph.
       Verify their correctness.

   (ii) Find the area enclosed by the curves, correct to two
        decimal places.

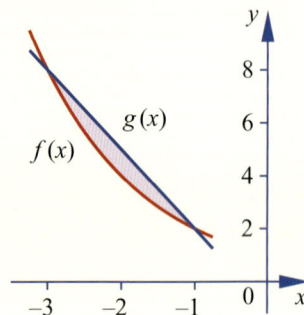

Average value of a function over an interval

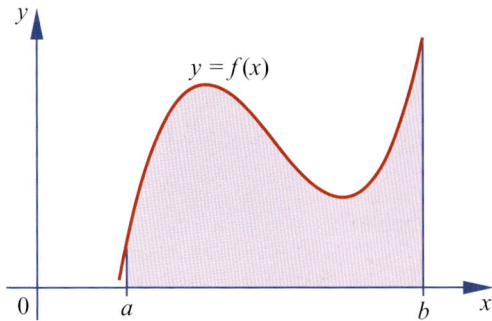

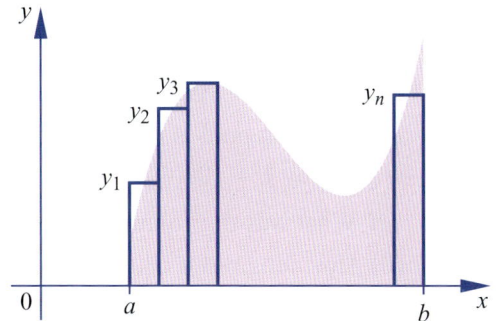

The first diagram shows a region under the graph $y = f(x)$ between $x = a$ and $x = b$. We can calculate the exact area using integration.

The second diagram shows an approximation using n rectangles of equal width.

The width of each rectangle is $\dfrac{b - a}{n}$, so the area can be approximated as the sum of the areas of the n rectangles.

$$\text{Area} = \frac{b - a}{n} \times y_1 + \frac{b - a}{n} \times y_2 + \frac{b - a}{n} \times y_3 + \cdots \frac{b - a}{n} \times y_n$$

$$= \frac{b - a}{n} \left[y_1 + y_2 + y_3 + \cdots y_n \right]$$

$$= (b - a) \frac{y_1 + y_2 + y_3 + \cdots y_n}{n}$$

$$\text{Area} = (b - a) \text{ (average value of } y \text{ over the interval)}$$

This approximation would approach the actual area as the number of strips increased and the width of the rectangles approached zero, so we can write:

$$(b - a) \text{ (average value of } y \text{ over the interval)} = \int_a^b y \, dx$$

$$\therefore \qquad \text{Average value of } y \text{ over the interval} = \frac{1}{b - a} \int_a^b y \, dx$$

$$\boxed{\text{Average value of } f(x) \text{ over the interval } [a, b] = \frac{1}{b - a} \int_a^b f(x) \, dx}$$

Note: In geometry, $[AB]$ represents all the points between A and B, including the endpoints. We can also use $[a, b]$ to represent all the values between a and b, including a and b.

Exercise 1.9

In questions 1–4, calculate the average value of $f(x)$ in the given interval.

1. $f(x) = 2x + 3$; $[2, 6]$
2. $f(x) = 3x^2 - 1$; $[1, 4]$
3. $f(x) = \sin x$; $[0, \pi]$
4. $f(x) = e^x$; $[0, 3]$

5. A swimming pool is being drained such that the volume of water remaining after t minutes is given by $V = 100(40 - t)^2 \text{ m}^3$.

    (i) What was the volume of the water just as the draining began?

    (ii) How long did it take to fully drain the pool?

    (iii) What was the average volume of water in the pool while it was being drained?

6. The velocity, in metres per second, of a particle is given by $v = 3t^2 - 18t + 15$.

    (i) At which times is the particle at rest?

    (ii) What is the average velocity during the times when it is stopped?

7. **(i)** Sketch the curve $y = 4x - x^2$ in the domain $0 \le x \le 4$.

    (ii) Find the maximum value of y.

    (iii) From your graph, write down the minimum value of y within the given domain.

    (iv) Calculate the average value of y in the interval $[0, 4]$.

    (v) Verify that the average value of y lies between its minimum and maximum values.

8. The temperature, $T°$ Celsius, on a certain day at a time t hours relative to midday can be represented by:

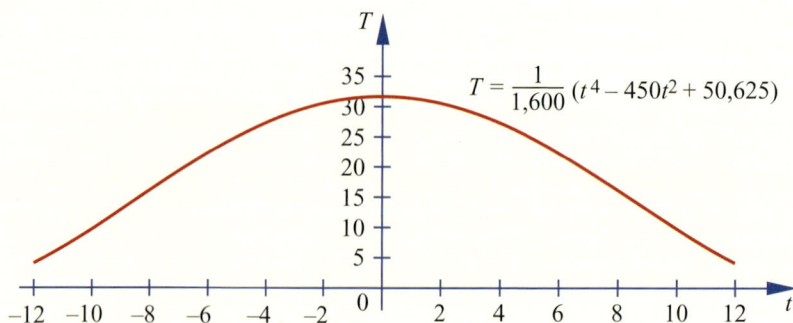

$$T = \frac{1}{1,600}(t^4 - 450t^2 + 50,625)$$

    (i) What time is represented at $t = -8$?

    (ii) Calculate the average temperature during the day.

Applications of integration

Recall that displacement, velocity and acceleration are linked together by the process of differentiation with respect to time. If s represents displacement, in terms of t:

$$V = \text{Velocity} = \frac{ds}{dt} \quad \text{and} \quad \text{Acceleration} = \frac{dv}{dt}$$

In reverse order acceleration, velocity and displacement are linked together by integration.

$$\frac{ds}{dt} = velocity \quad \rightarrow \quad s = \int velocity \cdot dt$$

$$\frac{dv}{dt} = acceleration \quad \rightarrow \quad v = \int acceleration \cdot dt$$

EXAMPLE

The acceleration of a body is given by $a = 6t - 12$.

(i) Find the velocity, v, in terms of t

(ii) Find the displacement, s, in terms of t

Solution

(i) $a = \dfrac{dv}{dt} = 6t - 12$

$dv = (6t - 12)\, dt$

$v = \int (6t - 12)\, dt$

$v = \dfrac{6t^2}{2} - 12t + c$

$v = 3t^2 - 12t + c$

(ii) $v = \dfrac{ds}{dt} = 3t^2 - 12t + 4$

$ds = (3t^2 - 12t + 4)\, dt$

$s = \int (3t^2 - 12t + 4)\, dt$

$s = \dfrac{3t^3}{3} - \dfrac{12t^2}{2} + 4t + c$

$s = t^3 - 6t^2 + 4t + c$

Exercise 1.10

1. An object is travelling with a velocity, $v = 3t^2 + 4t - 5$.

   (i) Find the acceleration when $t = 3$ seconds.

   (ii) If s is the distance travelled, express s in terms of t, given that $s = 4$ when $t = 1$.

   (iii) Find the displacement when $t = 3$.

2. $\dfrac{dN}{dt} = 6e^{3t} - 5$ represents the rate of growth of a culture of bacteria, where N is the number of bacteria and t is measured in hours.

   (i) Find N in terms of t.

   (ii) If there were 35 bacteria in the initial culture, find the number of bacteria present after 3 minutes, correct to the nearest whole number.

3. An object is shot upwards from ground level with an initial velocity of 100 m/s. It is subject only to the force of gravity (no air resistance). This results in the object experiencing a deceleration, due to gravity, of 9·8 m/s². Find:

   (i) The maximum altitude reached by the object

   (ii) The time at which the object hits the ground

Anti-derivatives

Note: $\int (x^3 + x^2)\,dx = \int x^3\,dx + \int x^2\,dx$

EXAMPLE

Let $f(x) = \sin x$.　　**(i)** Find $f'(x)$.　　**(ii)** Hence, find $\int x \cos x\,dx$.

Solution

(i) $f(x) = x \sin x$

$f'(x) = (x)(\cos x) + (\sin x)(1)$

$f'(x) = x \cos x + \sin x$

(ii) $f'(x) = x \cos x + \sin x$

$\therefore \int f'(x)\,dx = \int x \cos x\,dx + \int \sin x\,dx$

$f(x) = \int x \cos x\,dx - \cos x$

$x \sin x = \int x \cos x\,dx - \cos x$

$x \sin x + \cos x = \int x \cos x\,dx$

$\therefore \int x \cos x\,dx = x \sin x + \cos x + c$

Exercise 1.11

1. Let $f(x) = e^{x^2}$.　　**(i)** Find $f'(x)$.　　**(ii)** Hence, find $\int 2xe^{x^2}\,dx$.

2. Let $g(x) = x\,e^x$.　　**(i)** Find $g'(x)$.　　**(ii)** Hence, find $\int xe^x\,dx$.

3. Let $h(x) = x \ln x$.　　**(i)** Find $h'(x)$.　　**(ii)** Hence, evaluate $\displaystyle\int_{1}^{e} \ln x\,dx$.

4. Let $k(x) = 4x\,e^{2x}$.　　**(i)** Find $k'(x)$.　　**(ii)** Hence, evaluate $\displaystyle\int_{0}^{1} 8x\,e^{2x}\,dx$.

5. Let $f(x) = 3x \sin 3x$.　　**(i)** Find $f'(x)$.　　**(ii)** Hence, evaluate $\displaystyle\int_{0}^{\frac{\pi}{6}} 9x \cos 3x\,dx$.

6. Let $g(x) = xe^x - e^x$. Find $g'(x)$ and hence evaluate $\displaystyle\int_{0}^{1} 2x\,e^x\,dx$.

7. Let $h(x) = (x^2 - 1)^5$. Find $h'(x)$ and hence evaluate $\displaystyle\int_{0}^{1} 20x(x^2 - 1)^4\,dx$.

8. **(i)** Solve for x, $\sin 2x = 0$, for $0 \le x \le 2$ and $x \in \mathbb{R}$.

   (ii) Let $h(x) = 2x \cos 2x$. Find $h'(x)$ and hence $\int 4x \sin 2x\,dx$.

   (iii) The diagram shows part of the function $f : x \to 4x \sin 2x$.

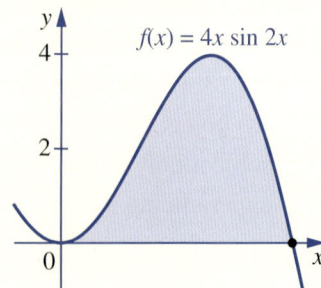

$f(x) = 4x \sin 2x$

Imaginary numbers, the symbol i

Consider the equations **(i)** $x^2 - 1 = 0$ and **(ii)** $x^2 + 1 = 0$.

(i) $x^2 - 1 = 0$	**(ii)** $x^2 + 1 = 0$
$x^2 = 1$	$x^2 = -1$
$x = \pm \sqrt{1}$	$x = \pm \sqrt{-1}$
$x = \pm 1$	

The solution to the second equation, $x^2 + 1 = 0$, requires finding $\sqrt{-1}$. With real numbers this cannot be done.

To overcome this, mathematicians invented a new number. They defined:

$$\boxed{i = \sqrt{-1} \quad \text{or} \quad i^2 = -1}$$

$$x^2 + 1 = 0$$
$$i^2 + 1 = 0 \qquad \text{(replace } x \text{ with } i\text{)}$$
$$-1 + 1 = 0 \qquad \text{(true, where } i^2 = -1\text{)}$$

The square root of a negative number is called an **imaginary** number, e.g. $\sqrt{-4}, \sqrt{-9}, \sqrt{-64}, \sqrt{-100}$ are imaginary numbers.

Imaginary numbers cannot be represented by a real number, as there is no real number whose square is a negative number.

All imaginary numbers can now be expressed in terms of i. For example:

$$\sqrt{-36} = \sqrt{36 \times -1} = \sqrt{36}\sqrt{-1} = 6i$$
$$\sqrt{-81} = \sqrt{81 \times -1} = \sqrt{81}\sqrt{-1} = 9i$$
$$\sqrt{-50} = \sqrt{50 \times -1} = \sqrt{25 \times 2 \times -1} = \sqrt{25}\sqrt{2}\sqrt{-1} = 5\sqrt{2}i$$

Integer powers of i

Every integer power of i is a member of the set $\{1, -1, i, -i\}$.

$$i = \sqrt{-1}$$
$$i^2 = -1$$
$$i^3 = i^2 \times i = (-1)i = -i$$
$$i^4 = i^2 \times i^2 = (-1)(-1) = 1$$

$$\boxed{\begin{aligned} i &= \sqrt{-1} \\ i^2 &= -1 \\ i^3 &= -i \\ i^4 &= 1 \end{aligned}}$$

EXAMPLE

Simplify: **(i)** i^{21} **(ii)** i^{10} **(iii)** i^{-13}

Solution:

(i) i^{21}

$= i^4 \times i^4 \times i^4 \times i^4 \times i^4 \times i$

$= (1)(1)(1)(1)(1)i$

$= i$

Alternatively,

$i^{21} = i^{20} \times i$

$= (i^4)^5 \times i$

$= (1)^5 \times i = i$

(ii) i^{10}

$= i^{10}$

$= i^4 \times i^4 \times i^2$

$= (1)(1)(-1)$

$= -1$

Alternatively,

$i^{10} = i^8 \times i^2$

$= (i^4)^2 \times i^2$

$= (1)^2 \times (-1)$

$= -1$

(iii) i^{-13}

$= \dfrac{1}{i^{13}}$

$= \dfrac{1}{i^{13}} \times \dfrac{i^3}{i^3}$

$= \dfrac{i^3}{i^{16}}$

$= \dfrac{i^3}{1}$

$= i^3 = -i$

Complex numbers

A complex number has two parts, a **real** part and an **imaginary** part.

Some examples are $3 + 4i$, $2 - 5i$, $-6 + 0i$, $0 - i$.

Consider the complex number $4 + 3i$:

   4 is called the **real** part. 3 is called the **imaginary** part.

Note: $3i$ is **not** the imaginary part.

> Complex number = (real part) + (imaginary part) i

The set of complex numbers is denoted by $\mathbb{C}$.

The letter z is usually used to represent a complex number. For example:

$$z_1 = 2 + 3i \qquad z_2 = -2 - i \qquad z_3 = -5i$$

If $z = a + bi$, then:

 (i) a is called the real part of z and is written $\mathrm{Re}(z) = a$.

 (ii) b is called the imaginary part of z and is written $\mathrm{Im}(z) = b$.

Note: u, v and w are also often used to denote complex numbers.

EXAMPLE 1

Write down the real and imaginary parts of each of the following complex numbers.

(i) $5 - 4i$ (ii) $-3 + 2i$ (iii) 6 (iv) $-5i$

Solution:

z	Real part (Re(z))	Imaginary part (Im(z))
(i) $5 - 4i$	5	-4
(ii) $-3 + 2i$	-3	2
(iii) $6 = 6 + 0i$	6	0
(iv) $-5i = 0 - 5i$	0	-5

Notes: i **never** appears in the imaginary part.

If Im(z) = 0, then z is a **real** number.

If Re(z) = 0, then z is a **purely imaginary** number.

Addition and subtraction of complex numbers

To add or subtract complex numbers, do the following:

> Add or subtract the real and the imaginary parts separately.

For example:

$(3 + 5i) - (2 - 3i) = 3 + 5i - 2 + 3i = 1 + 8i$

$2(-1 + 3i) - 3(1 + 4i) = -2 + 6i - 3 - 12i = -5 - 6i$

Multiplication of complex numbers

Multiplication of complex numbers is performed using the usual algebraic method, except that:

$$i^2 \text{ is replaced with } -1.$$

For example:

$$
\begin{aligned}
(3 - 2i)(-4 + 5i) &= 3(-4 + 5i) - 2i(-4 + 5i) \\
&= -12 + 15i + 8i - 10i^2 \\
&= -12 + 15i + 8i - 10(-1) \quad (i^2 = -1) \\
&= -12 + 15i + 8i + 10 \\
&= -2 + 23i
\end{aligned}
$$

EXAMPLE 2

If $z_1 = 3 + 2i$ and $z_2 = -1 + 5i$, express the following in the form $a + bi$, where $a, b \in \mathbb{R}$.

(i) $2z_1 - iz_2$ (ii) z_1z_2 (iii) z_1^2 (iv) z_1^3

Solution:

(i) $2z_1 - iz_2$
$= 2(3 + 2i) - i(-1 + 5i)$
$= 6 + 4i + i - 5i^2$
$= 6 + 4i + i + 5$ $(i^2 = -1)$
$= 11 + 5i$

(ii) z_1z_2
$= (3 + 2i)(-1 + 5i)$
$= 3(-1 + 5i) + 2i(-1 + 5i)$
$= -3 + 15i - 2i + 10i^2$
$= -3 + 15i - 2i - 10$ $(i^2 = -1)$
$= -13 + 13i$

(iii) z_1^2
$= (3 + 2i)^2$
$= (3 + 2i)(3 + 2i)$
$= 3(3 + 2i) + 2i(3 + 2i)$
$= 9 + 6i + 6i + 4i^2$
$= 9 + 6i + 6i - 4$ $(i^2 = -1)$
$= 5 + 12i$

(iv) z_1^3
$= z_1 z_1^2$
$= (3 + 2i)(5 + 12i)$
$= 3(5 + 12i) + 2i(5 + 12i)$
$= 15 + 36i + 10i + 24i^2$
$= 15 + 36i + 10i - 24$ $(i^2 = -1)$
$= -9 + 46i$

EXAMPLE 3

Given that $z = 1 - \sqrt{3}i$, find the real number k such that $z^2 + kz$ is:

(i) real   (ii) purely imaginary.

Solution:

$z = 1 - \sqrt{3}i$
$z^2 = (1 - \sqrt{3}i)^2$
$= (1 - \sqrt{3}i)(1 - \sqrt{3}i)$
$= 1(1 - \sqrt{3}i) - \sqrt{3}i(1 - \sqrt{3}i)$
$= 1 - \sqrt{3}i - \sqrt{3}i + 3i^2$
$= 1 - \sqrt{3}i - \sqrt{3}i - 3$
$= -2 - 2\sqrt{3}i$

(i) If $z^2 + kz$ is real, then the imaginary part is zero,
$\therefore -2\sqrt{3} - k\sqrt{3} = 0$
$-2 - k = 0$
$k = -2$

$z^2 + kz$
$= (-2 - 2\sqrt{3}i) + k(1 - \sqrt{3}i)$
$= -2 - 2\sqrt{3}i + k - k\sqrt{3}i$
$= (-2 + k) + (-2\sqrt{3} - k\sqrt{3})i$

(Group real and imaginary parts together)

(ii) If $z^2 + kz$ is imaginary, then the real part is zero,
$\therefore -2 + k = 0$
$k = 2$

Note: $\sqrt{3}i$ is often written as $i\sqrt{3}$ to avoid the error $\sqrt{3i}$.

Exercise 2.1

Express questions 1–12 in the form *ai*, where $a \in \mathbb{N}$.

1. $\sqrt{-4}$　　2. $\sqrt{-25}$　　3. $\sqrt{-49}$　　4. $\sqrt{-100}$　　5. $\sqrt{-16}$　　6. $\sqrt{-144}$

7. $\sqrt{-9}$　　8. $\sqrt{-121}$　　9. $\sqrt{-400}$　　10. $\sqrt{-196}$　　11. $\sqrt{-169}$　　12. $\sqrt{-289}$

Express questions 13–18 in the form $a\sqrt{bi}$, where $a, b \in \mathbb{N}$ and *b* is prime.

13. $\sqrt{-8}$　　14. $\sqrt{-12}$　　15. $\sqrt{-18}$　　16. $\sqrt{-50}$　　17. $\sqrt{-80}$　　18. $\sqrt{-63}$

Express questions 19–30 as an element of the set $\{1, -1, i, -i\}$.

19. i^6　　20. i^7　　21. i^8　　22. i^{13}　　23. i^{20}　　24. i^{22}

25. i^{27}　　26. i^{102}　　27. i^{-3}　　28. i^{-2}　　29. i^{-1}　　30. i^{-20}

31. Simplify **(i)** i^{4n} **(ii)** i^{4n+1} **(iii)** i^{4n+2} **(iv)** i^{4n+3}, where $n \in \mathbb{N}$.

32. Express each of the following in the form $a + bi$, where $a, b \in \mathbb{R}$.
    (i) $i^2 + 4i^3$ **(ii)** $i^{30} - 2i^{11}$ **(iii)** $4i^3 - 3i^6$

33. Write down the real part and imaginary parts of *z* if:
    (i) $z = 2 + 5i$ **(ii)** $z = -3 - 4i$ **(iii)** $z = -7 - \sqrt{3}i$ **(iv)** $z = -7i$

Express questions 34–43 in the form $a + bi$, where $a, b \in \mathbb{R}$ and $i^2 = -1$.

34. $(3 + 2i) - 2(5 - 4i)$　　　　35. $2(2 - 3i) - 3(2 - 7i)$

36. $(2 + 3i)(-3 + 4i)$　　　　37. $(3 + i)(-2 - 5i)$

38. $3 + 2i(3 + 4i) - i$　　　　39. $i(-2 + 5i) - 5(-1 + 2i)$

40. $i(3 - 5i)(4 + i)$　　　　41. $4i(2 - 3i)(-2 - 4i)$

42. $(1 + 2i)^2 - 2(5 - 3i)$　　　　43. $(1 + \sqrt{3}i)^2 - \sqrt{3}(-\sqrt{3} + 2i)$

44. If $z = 1 - 3i$, where $i^2 = -1$, evaluate $z^2 - 3z$.

45. If $z_1 = 5 - 2i$, $z_2 = -2 - 3i$, express the following in the form $a + bi$, where $a, b \in \mathbb{R}$ and $i^2 = -1$.
    (i) $z_1 z_2$ **(ii)** z_2^2 **(iii)** iz_1 **(iv)** $iz_1 z_2$

46. If $w = 2 + 3i$, show that $w^2 - 4w + 13 = 0$.

47. If $u = 1 + i$, show that $u^3 - 4u^2 + 6u - 4 = 0$.

48. Find the value of $k \in \mathbb{R}$ if $(1 - 3i)(k + 2i)$ is real, where $i^2 = -1$.

49. Find the value of $k \in \mathbb{R}$ if $(2 + i)(k - 5i)$ is purely imaginary, where $i^2 = -1$.

50. Given that $z = 1 + 3i$, find the real number *k* such that $z^2 + kz$ is real.

51. Given that $z = 1 + \sqrt{2}i$, find the real number *t* such that $z^2 + tz$ is:
    (i) real　**(ii)** purely imaginary.

52. Given that $z = (-1 + \sqrt{5}i)$, find the real number *k* such that $z^2 - kz + \sqrt{5}i$ is:
    (i) real　**(ii)** purely imaginary.

53. If z_1 and z_2 are complex numbers, solve the simultaneous equations:
$$2z_1 + z_2 = 5$$
$$z_1 + z_2 = 4 - i$$

Conjugate and division

Conjugate of a complex number

Two complex numbers which differ only in the sign of their imaginary parts are called **conjugate complex numbers**, each being the conjugate of the other.

Thus, $3 + 4i$ and $3 - 4i$ are conjugates, and $-2 - 3i$ is the conjugate of $-2 + 3i$ and vice versa.

In general, $a + bi$ and $a - bi$ are conjugates.

If $z = a + bi$, then its conjugate, $a - bi$, is denoted by $\bar{z}$.

$$z = a + bi \implies \bar{z} = a - bi$$

To find the conjugate, simply **change the sign** of the imaginary part only.

For example, if $z = -6 - 5i$, then $\bar{z} = -6 + 5i$.

EXAMPLE 1

If $z = -3 + 5i$, where $i^2 = -1$, simplify: **(i)** $z + \bar{z}$ **(ii)** $z - \bar{z}$ **(iii)** $z\bar{z}$

Solution:

If $z = -3 + 5i$, then $\bar{z} = -3 - 5i$ (change sign of the imaginary part only).

(i) $z + \bar{z}$
$$= (-3 + 5i) + (-3 - 5i)$$
$$= -3 + 5i - 3 - 5i$$
$$= -6 \quad \text{(a real number)}$$

(ii) $z - \bar{z}$
$$= (-3 + 5i) - (-3 - 5i)$$
$$= -3 + 5i + 3 + 5i$$
$$= 10i \quad \text{(a purely imaginary number)}$$

(iii) $z\bar{z}$
$$= (-3 + 5i)(-3 - 5i)$$
$$= -3(-3 - 5i) + 5i(-3 - 5i)$$
$$= 9 + \cancel{15i} - \cancel{15i} - 25i^2$$
$$= 9 + 25 \quad (i^2 = -1)$$
$$= 34 \quad \text{(a real number)}$$

Note: If a complex number is added to or multiplied by its conjugate, the result will **always** be a real number.

If $z = a + bi$, then:

> **1.** $z + \bar{z} = (a + bi) + (a - bi) = a + bi + a - bi = 2a$ (a real number)
>
> **2.** $z\bar{z} = (a + bi)(a - bi) = a^2 - abi + abi - b^2i^2 = a^2 + b^2$ (a real number)

Division by a complex number

> Multiply the top and bottom by the conjugate of the bottom.

This will convert the complex number on the bottom into a real number. The division is then performed by dividing the real number on the bottom into **each part** on the top.

EXAMPLE 2

If $z = \dfrac{2 + i}{1 - i}$, find the real part of z.

Solution:

First write z in the form $a + bi$:

$$z = \frac{2 + i}{1 - i}$$

$$= \frac{2 + i}{1 - i} \times \frac{1 + i}{1 - i} \qquad \left(\begin{array}{c}\text{multiply the top and bottom by } 1 + i,\\ \text{the conjugate of } 1 - i\end{array}\right)$$

$$= \frac{2 + 2i + i + i^2}{1 + i - i - i^2}$$

$$= \frac{2 + 2i + i - 1}{1 + i - i + 1} \qquad (i^2 = -1)$$

$$= \frac{1 + 3i}{2}$$

$$= \tfrac{1}{2} + \tfrac{3}{2}i \qquad \text{(divide \textbf{each} part on top by the bottom)}$$

Thus, the real part of z is $\tfrac{1}{2}$.

EXAMPLE 3

Simplify $\dfrac{4 + 3i}{3 - 4i}$ and hence evaluate $\left(\dfrac{4 + 3i}{3 - 4i}\right)^{10}$.

Solution:

$$\frac{4 + 3i}{3 - 4i}$$

$$= \frac{4 + 3i}{3 - 4i} \times \frac{3 + 4i}{3 + 4i}$$

$$= \frac{12 + 16i + 9i + 12i^2}{9 + 12i - 12i - 16i^2}$$

$$= \frac{25i}{25} \qquad (i^2 = -1)$$

$$= i$$

$$\frac{4 + 3i}{3 - 4i} = i$$

$$\therefore \left(\frac{4 + 3i}{3 - 4i}\right)^{10} = i^{10}$$

$$= i^4 \times i^4 \times i^2$$

$$= (1)(1)(-1)$$

$$= -1$$

Exercise 2.2

Express questions 1–8 in the form $a + bi$, where $a, b \in \mathbb{R}$ and $t^2 = -1$.

1. $\dfrac{3 + 4i}{2 + i}$

2. $\dfrac{7 + 4i}{2 - i}$

3. $\dfrac{1 + 5i}{3 + 2i}$

4. $\dfrac{7 - 17i}{5 - i}$

5. $\dfrac{1}{1 - i}$

6. $\dfrac{2 + i}{1 + 2i}$

7. $\dfrac{2 - i}{3 + 2i}$

8. $\dfrac{3 + 4i}{1 - i}$

9. If $a + bi = \dfrac{9 - 7i}{2 - 3i}$, find the value of a and the value of b, where $a, b \in \mathbb{R}$.

10. If $p + qi = \dfrac{2 - i}{1 - 2i}$, where $p, q \in \mathbb{R}$, evaluate $p^2 + q^2$.

11. Simplify $\left(\dfrac{5 + 2i}{2 - 5i}\right)$ and hence find the value of $\left(\dfrac{5 + 2i}{2 - 5i}\right)^4$, where $i^2 = -1$.

12. Simplify $\left(\dfrac{-2 + 3i}{3 + 2i}\right)$ and hence find the value of $\left(\dfrac{-2 + 3i}{3 + 2i}\right)^9$, where $i^2 = -1$.

13. Simplify $\left(\dfrac{2 + i}{1 - 2i}\right)$ and hence find the value of $3\left(\dfrac{2 + i}{1 - 2i}\right)^2$.

14. Simplify **(i)** $\left(\dfrac{-6 + 8i}{4 + 3i}\right)^3$ **(ii)** $\left(\dfrac{2 - 3i}{9 + 6i}\right)^2$ **(iii)** $\left(\dfrac{-1 + \sqrt{2}i}{\sqrt{2} + i}\right)^6$

15. Simplify $\dfrac{a + bi}{b - ai}$ and hence find the value of $\left(\dfrac{a + bi}{b - ai}\right)^4$.

16. $z_1 = -2 + 3i$ and $z_2 = 3 + 2i$. Evaluate $\left(\dfrac{z_1}{z_2}\right)^5$.

17. Write $i(i^4 + i^5 + i^6)$ in its simplest form.

18. Let $u = \dfrac{3 + 4i}{4 - 3i}$. Evaluate $u(u^6 + u^7 + u^8)$.

19. Evaluate **(i)** $\left(\dfrac{1}{2 + i} + \dfrac{2}{3 - i}\right)^{100}$ **(ii)** $\left(\dfrac{-1 + \sqrt{3}i}{\sqrt{3} + i}\right)^{102}$

20. If z_1 and z_2 are complex numbers, solve the simultaneous equations:
$$4z_1 + 3z_2 = 5 + 13i$$
$$z_1 + iz_2 = -1$$

21. $z_1 = a + bi$ and $z_2 = c + di$, where $i^2 = -1$.

    Prove that **(i)** $\bar{z}_1 + \bar{z}_2 = \overline{z_1 + z_2}$ **(ii)** $\bar{z}_1\bar{z}_2 = \overline{z_1 z_2}$ **(iii)** $z_1\bar{z}_2 + \bar{z}_1 z_2$ is a real number

Equality of complex numbers

If two complex numbers are equal, then **their real parts are equal and their imaginary parts are also equal.**

For example, if $a + bi = c + di$, then $a = c$ and $b = d$.

This definition is very useful when dealing with equations involving complex numbers.

Equations involving complex numbers are usually solved with the following steps:

1. Remove the brackets.

2. Put an R under the real parts and an I under the imaginary parts to identify them.

3. Let the real parts equal the real parts and the imaginary parts equal the imaginary parts.

4. Solve these resultant equations (usually simultaneous equations).

Note: If one side of the equation does not contain a real part or an imaginary part, it should be replaced with 0 or $0i$, respectively.

EXAMPLE 1

Let $z_1 = 4 - 2i$ and $z_2 = -2 - 6i$. If $z_2 - pz_1 = qi$, where $p, q \in \mathbb{R}$, find p and q.

Solution:

$z_2 - pz_1 = qi$

The right-hand side has no real part, hence a 0, representing the real part, should be placed on the right-hand side.

Now the equation is:

$$z_2 - pz_1 = 0 + qi \qquad \text{(put 0 in for the real part)}$$

$$(-2 - 6i) - p(4 - 2i) = 0 + qi \qquad \text{(substitute for } z_1 \text{ and } z_2\text{)}$$

$$\underset{R\ \ I\quad R\quad \ I\ \ R\ \ I}{-2 - 6i - 4p + 2pi = 0 + qi} \qquad \begin{array}{l}\text{(remove the brackets)}\\ \text{(identify real and imaginary parts)}\end{array}$$

Real parts = Real parts   **Imaginary parts = Imaginary parts**

$-2 - 4p = 0$ .... ① $-6 + 2p = q$ .... ②

Solve between the equations ① and ②:

$$-2 - 4p = 0 \qquad ①$$

$$-4p = 2$$

$$4p = -2$$

$$p = -\frac{2}{4} = -\frac{1}{2}$$

Substitute $p = -\frac{1}{2}$ into equation ②:

$$-6 + 2p = q \qquad ②$$

$$-6 + 2\left(-\frac{1}{2}\right) = q$$

$$-6 - 1 = q$$

$$-7 = q$$

Solution: $p = -\frac{1}{2}, q = -7$

EXAMPLE 2

$w = a + bi$ is a complex number such that $w\overline{w} - 2iw = 17 - 6i$.
Find the two possible values of w.

Solution:

$$w = a + bi \qquad \therefore \overline{w} = a - bi$$

Given:
$$w\overline{w} - 2iw = 17 - 6i$$

$$\therefore \qquad (a + bi)(a - bi) - 2i(a + bi) = 17 - 6i$$

$$a^2 - \cancel{abi} + \cancel{abi} - b^2i^2 - 2ai - 2bi^2 = 17 - 6i \qquad \text{(remove brackets)}$$

$$a^2 + b^2 - 2ai + 2b = 17 - 6i \qquad (i^2 = -1)$$

$$R \quad R \quad I \quad R \qquad R \quad I \qquad \text{(identify real and imaginary parts)}$$

Real parts = Real parts	**Imaginary parts = Imaginary parts**
$a^2 + b^2 + 2b = 17 \qquad ①$	$-2a = -6 \qquad ②$

Solve between equations ① and ②:

$$-2a = -6 \qquad ②$$

$$2a = 6$$

$$a = 3$$

$$a^2 + b^2 + 2b = 17$$

$$9 + b^2 + 2b = 17 \qquad (a = 3)$$

$$b^2 + 2b - 8 = 0$$

$$(b + 4)(b - 2) = 0$$

$$b = -4 \quad \text{or} \quad b = 2$$

$$w = a + bi$$

Thus, $w = 3 - 4i \quad$ or $\quad w = 3 + 2i$.

Exercise 2.3

In questions 1–4, solve for $x, y \in \mathbb{R}$.

1. $x(3 + 4i) + y(2 - 3i) = 8 + 5i$

2. $x(3 - 2i) + y(i - 2) = 5 - 4i$

3. $3x - i(x + y + 5) = (1 + 3i)i + 2(3 - y)$

4. $(x + y) - (xi - y) = (3 + 2i)^2 - 7i$

5. If $2(h - 2) - k + i = i(2k - h)$, find h and k, where $h, k \in \mathbb{R}$.

6. If $2p - q + i(7i + 3) = 2(2i - q) - i(p + 3q)$, find p and q, where $p, q \in \mathbb{R}$.

7. Let $z_1 = 4 - 3i$ and $z_2 = 5(1 + i)$. If $z_1 + tz_2 = k$, find t and k, where $t, k \in \mathbb{R}$.

8. Let $z_1 = 5 + 7i$ and $z_2 = 3 - i$. If $k(z_1 + z_2) = 16 + (t + 2)i$, find t and k, where $t, k \in \mathbb{R}$.

9. $z = 2 - 3i$. If $z + i + 3(a + bi) = iz - 5$, find a and b, where $a, b \in \mathbb{R}$.

10. Let $z_1 = 2 + 3i$ and $z_2 = -4 - 3i$. If $lz_1 - z_2 = ki$, find l and k, where $l, k \in \mathbb{R}$.

11. Let $z_1 = 6 - 8i$ and $z_2 = 4 - 3i$. If $pi = z_2 + lz_3$, find p and l, where $z_1 - z_3 = z_2$ and $p, l \in \mathbb{R}$.

12. Let $u = 1 + i$.

    (i) Write $\dfrac{6}{u}$ in the form $x + yi$.

    (ii) a and b are real numbers such that $a\left(\dfrac{6}{u}\right) - b(u + 1) = 3(u + 1)$.

    Find the value of a and the value of b.

13. $z = a + bi$ is a complex number such that $z + \bar{z} = 8$ and $z\bar{z} = 25$. Find two values of z.

14. $w = p + qi$ is a complex number such that $w\bar{w} - 2iw = 7 - 4i$. Find two possible values of w.

15. $z = p + qi$ is a complex number such that $z\bar{z} - i\bar{z} = 11 - 3i$. Find two values of z.

16. If $a(a + i) - bi(3 + bi) = 10(1 + i)$, find a, b, where $a, b \in \mathbb{R}$.

17. Let $u = 4 + 3i$, where $i^2 = -1$. If $uv = 10 - 5i$, express v in the form $a + bi$, where $a, b \in \mathbb{R}$.

18. Let $u_1 = \dfrac{a}{1 + 2i}$ and $u_2 = \dfrac{b}{1 + i}$, where $a, b \in \mathbb{R}$ and $i^2 = -1$.

    (i) Given that $u_1 + u_2 = 2$, find the value of a and the value of b.

    (ii) Find $u_1 u_2$.

19. k is a real number such that $\dfrac{-1 + \sqrt{3}i}{-5\sqrt{3} - 5i} = ki$. Find k.

20. If $(2 + \sqrt{3}i)^2 = a + bi + 2(1 + i)$, express $2(b - 2a)$ in the form $p\sqrt{q}$, where $p, q \in \mathbb{N}$ and q is prime.

21. (i) Find two numbers, a and b, whose sum is 10 and whose product is 34.

    (ii) Explain why a and b are not real numbers.

22. Let $u = 2 + ai$ and $v = b + i$, where $a, b \in \mathbb{R}$.

    Find the values of a and b that satisfy $u = \dfrac{2(3 - i)}{v}$.

Argand diagram and modulus

Argand diagram

An Argand diagram is used to plot complex numbers. It is very similar to the x- and y-axes used in coordinate geometry, except that the **horizontal** axis is called the **real axis**, Re(z) axis, and the **vertical** axis is called the imaginary axis, Im(z) axis. It is also called the **complex plane**.

To represent a complex number on an Argand diagram, it must be written in the form $a + bi$. The complex number $a + bi$ is represented by the point with coordinates (a, b).

EXAMPLE 1

If $z_1 = 2 - 3i$ and $z_2 = 6 - 5i$, represent the following on an Argand diagram.

(i) $\bar{z}_1$ (ii) $2z_1 - z_2$

Solution:

(i) $z_1 = 2 - 3i$

$\bar{z}_1 = 2 + 3i$

(ii) $2z_1 - z_2$

$= 2(2 - 3i) - (6 - 5i)$

$= 4 - 6i - 6 + 5i$

$= -2 - i$

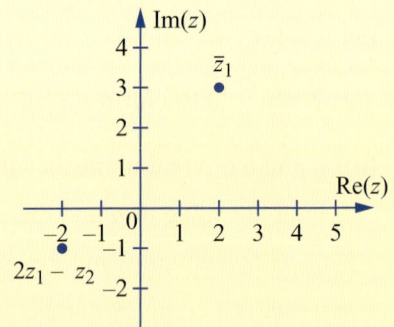

Modulus of a complex number

The **modulus** of a complex number is the **distance from the origin to the point representing the complex number on the Argand diagram.**

If $z = a + bi$, then the modulus of z is written $|z|$ or $|a + bi|$.

The point z represents the complex number $a + bi$.

The modulus of z is the distance from the origin, o, to the complex number $a + bi$.

Using the theorem of Pythagoras, $|z| = \sqrt{a^2 + b^2}$.

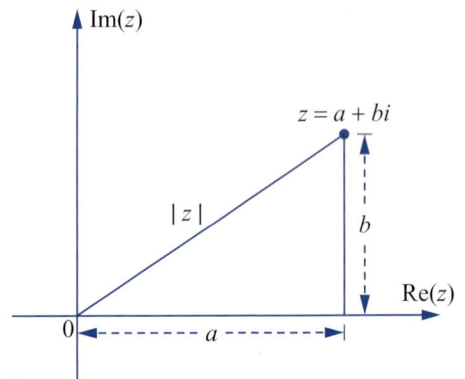

If $z = a + bi$, then
$$|z| = |a + bi| = \sqrt{a^2 + b^2}.$$

Notes:
1. i **never** appears when the modulus formula is used.
2. The modulus of a complex number is **always positive**.
3. Before using the formula, a complex number must be in the form $a + bi$.

For example, if $z = -2 + 5i$, then:

$$|z| = |-2 + 5i| = \sqrt{(-2)^2 + (5)^2} = \sqrt{4 + 25} = \sqrt{29}$$

EXAMPLE 2

Let $z = (k - 1) + 7i$ and $w = 8 - i$.
If $|z| = |w|$, find two values of k, where $k \in \mathbb{R}$.

Solution:

Given: $\qquad |z| = |w|$

$\therefore \qquad |(k - 1) + 7i| = |8 - i|$

$\sqrt{(k - 1)^2 + (7)^2} = \sqrt{8^2 + (-1)^2} \qquad \left(|a + bi| = \sqrt{a^2 + b^2}\right)$

$(k - 1)^2 + (7)^2 = 8^2 + (-1)^2 \qquad$ (square both sides)

$k^2 - 2k + 1 + 49 = 64 + 1$

$k^2 - 2k - 15 = 0$

$(k - 5)(k + 3) = 0$

$k = 5 \quad$ or $\quad k = -3$

Exercise 2.4

For questions 1–11, construct an Argand diagram from −6 to 6 on the real axis and −5 to 5 on the imaginary axis.

If $z = 1 + i$ and $w = -6 + 4i$, represent questions 1–10 on an Argand diagram.

1. z
2. $\bar{z}$
3. w
4. $\overline{w}$
5. $2\bar{z} + w$
6. $\frac{1}{2}z\overline{w}$
7. $\frac{w}{z}$
8. $\frac{\bar{z} - w + 3}{\bar{z} + 1}$
9. $\frac{i\overline{w}}{z}$
10. $\frac{w}{z^2}$

11. Let $w = 9 + 7i$ and $u = \dfrac{5 + i}{1 - i}$. Represent the following on an Argand diagram.

    (i) u
    (ii) $\dfrac{w}{u}$
    (iii) $\dfrac{w - 4(u - 1)}{3 - u}$

12. Evaluate each of the following.

    (i) $|3 + 4i|$
    (ii) $|12 - 5i|$
    (iii) $|-15 + 8i|$
    (iv) $|-7 - 24i|$
    (v) $|1 + \sqrt{3}i|$
    (vi) $|-2 + 2\sqrt{3}i|$
    (vii) $|-8\sqrt{3} - 8i|$
    (viii) $|-i|$
    (ix) $|1|$
    (x) $|1 + i|$
    (xi) $|-2 + 3i|$
    (xii) $\left|\dfrac{1}{2} + \dfrac{\sqrt{3}}{2}i\right|$

13. Given that $z = 2 - i$, calculate $|z^2 - z + 3|$ where $i^2 = -1$.

14. Let $w = \dfrac{4 - 2i}{2 + i}$.

    (i) Express w in the form $a + bi$, where $a, b \in \mathbb{R}$.   (ii) Evaluate $|w|$.

15. Let $z_1 = 1 + 2i$ and $z_2 = 2 - 3i$. Show that $|z_1||z_2| = |z_1 z_2|$.

16. Let $z = 4 - 3i$ and $w = \dfrac{1 - \sqrt{3}i}{1 + \sqrt{3}i}$. Evaluate: (i) $\left|\dfrac{1}{z}\right|$ (ii) $|w|$

17. Let $z = 1 + 7i$ and $w = -1 + i$. Express $\dfrac{z}{w}$ in the form $a + bi$, where $a, b \in \mathbb{R}$ and $i^2 = -1$.

    (i) Verify that (a) $|z||w| = |zw|$ (b) $\dfrac{|z|}{|w|} = \left|\dfrac{z}{w}\right|$.

    (ii) Solve, for real h and k: $hz = \left|\dfrac{z}{w}\right| kw + 16i$.

18. If $|8 + ki| = 10$, where $k \in \mathbb{R}$, find two possible values of k.

19. If $|a + ai| = |1 - 7i|$, where $a \in \mathbb{R}$, find two possible values of a.

20. Let $z = (k - 1) - 5i$ and $w = -2 + 11i$.
    If $|z| = |w|$, find two possible values of k, where $k \in \mathbb{R}$.

21. Let $z = a + bi$, where $a, b \in \mathbb{R}$.
    If $z - \bar{z} + |z| = 17 + 16i$, find two values of z.

22. Let $w = a + bi$. Find the complex number w such that $\sqrt{3}|w| + iw = 2 + \sqrt{2}i$.

23. If $u = 3 + 2i$ and $v = 1 - ki$, where $k \in \mathbb{R}$, find the possible values of k for which $|uv| = \sqrt{65}$.

24. Let $z = x + yi$. Show that if $|z - 1| = |z - 2i|$, then $2x - 4y + 3 = 0$.

25. (i) Solve for real s and real t, $s(2 - i) + ti(4 + 2i) = 1 + s + ti$.
    (ii) If $z = x + yi$, where $x, y \in \mathbb{R}$, describe the curve $|z| = |s + ti|$.

Quadratic equations with complex roots

The equation $az^2 + bz + c = 0$ has roots given by:
$$z = \frac{-b \pm \sqrt{b^2 - 4ac}}{2a}.$$

If $b^2 - 4ac < 0$, then the number under the square root sign will be negative, and so the solutions will be complex numbers.

EXAMPLE 1

Solve the equations: **(i)** $z^2 - 4z + 13 = 0$ **(ii)** $2z^2 + 2z + 1 = 0$

Solution:

(i) $z^2 - 4z + 13 = 0$

$az^2 + bz + c = 0$

$a = 1, b = -4, c = 13$

$$z = \frac{-b \pm \sqrt{b^2 - 4ac}}{2a}$$

$$z = \frac{4 \pm \sqrt{(-4)^2 - 4(1)(13)}}{2(1)}$$

$$z = \frac{4 \pm \sqrt{16 - 52}}{2}$$

$$z = \frac{4 \pm \sqrt{-36}}{2}$$

$$z = \frac{4 \pm 6i}{2}$$

$$z = 2 \pm 3i$$

∴ The roots are $2 + 3i$ and $2 - 3i$.

(ii) $2z^2 + 2z + 1 = 0$

$az^2 + bz + c = 0$

$a = 2, b = 2, c = 1$

$$z = \frac{-b \pm \sqrt{b^2 - 4ac}}{2a}$$

$$z = \frac{-2 \pm \sqrt{(2)^2 - 4(2)(1)}}{2(2)}$$

$$z = \frac{-2 \pm \sqrt{4 - 8}}{4}$$

$$z = \frac{-2 \pm \sqrt{-4}}{4}$$

$$z = \frac{-2 \pm 2i}{4} = \frac{-1 \pm i}{2}$$

$$z = -\tfrac{1}{2} \pm \tfrac{1}{2}i$$

∴ The roots are $-\tfrac{1}{2} + \tfrac{1}{2}i$ and $-\tfrac{1}{2} - \tfrac{1}{2}i$.

Note: Notice that in both solutions, the roots occur in conjugate pairs. If one root of a quadratic equation, with **real coefficients**, is a complex number, then the other root must also be complex and the conjugate of the first. For example:

if $3 - 4i$ is a root, then $3 + 4i$ is also a root

if $-2 - 5i$ is a root, then $-2 + 5i$ is also a root

if $a + bi$ is a root, then $a - bi$ is also a root

Conjugate roots theorem

> If all the coefficients of a polynomial equation are **real**, then all complex roots occur as conjugate pairs.

In other words, if one root is a complex number, then its conjugate is also a root. The conjugate roots theorem can be used only if all the coefficients in the equation are **real**. If even one coefficient is nonreal (contains an i), then the conjugate roots theorem cannot be used.

The roots of the equation $z^2 - 2z + 10 = 0$ are $1 + 3i$ and $1 - 3i$.

The complex roots occur as conjugate pairs, since all the coefficients, 1, −2 and 10, are real.

The roots of the equation $z^2 + (i - 2)z + (3 - i) = 0$ are $1 + i$ and $1 - 2i$.

The complex roots do not occur as conjugate pairs because the coefficients, 1, $i - 2$ and $3 - i$, are **not** all real numbers.

EXAMPLE 2

Solve $z^2 - (2 - i)z + 7 - i = 0$. Explain why the roots do not occur in conjugate pairs.

Solution:

$$z^2 - (2 - i)z + 7 - i = 0$$

$$z^2 + (-2 + i)z + (7 - i) = 0 \qquad \text{(write in the form } az^2 + bz + c = 0\text{)}$$

$$z = \frac{-b \pm \sqrt{b^2 - 4ac}}{2a}$$

$$= \frac{-(-2 + i) \pm \sqrt{(-2 + i)^2 - 4(1)(7 - i)}}{2(1)}$$

$$= \frac{2 - i \pm \sqrt{4 - 4i - 1 - 28 + 4i}}{2}$$

$$= \frac{2 - i \pm \sqrt{-25}}{2} = \frac{2 - i \pm 5i}{2}$$

$$z_1 = \frac{2 - i + 5i}{2} = \frac{2 + 4i}{2} = 1 + 2i$$

$$z_2 = \frac{2 - i - 5i}{2} = \frac{2 - 6i}{2} = 1 - 3i$$

Thus, the roots are $1 + 2i$ and $1 - 3i$.

They are not complex conjugates because **not** all the coefficient are real.

EXAMPLE 3

If $-3 - 2i$ is a root of the equation $z^2 + pz + q = 0$, where $p, q \in \mathbb{R}$, write down the other root and hence find the value of p and the value of q.

Solution:

All the coefficients are real (given). Thus, we can use the conjugate root theorem.

Therefore, as $-3 - 2i$ is a root, then $-3 + 2i$ is also a root (roots occur in conjugate pairs).

Method 1: Form a quadratic equation with roots $-3 - 2i$ and $-3 + 2i$.

$$\text{Let } z = -3 - 2i \quad \text{and} \quad z = -3 + 2i.$$

$$\therefore \qquad z + 3 + 2i = 0 \quad \text{and} \quad z + 3 - 2i = 0$$

$$\text{and} \qquad (z + 3 + 2i)(z + 3 - 2i) = 0 \qquad (0 \times 0 = 0)$$

$$z(z + 3 - 2i) + 3(z + 3 - 2i) + 2i(z + 3 - 2i) = 0$$

$$z^2 + 3z - 2zi + 3z + 9 - 6i + 2zi + 6i - 4i^2 = 0$$

$$z^2 + 6z + 9 - 4(-1) = 0 \qquad (i^2 = -1)$$
$$z^2 + 6z + 9 + 4 = 0$$
$$z^2 + 6z + 13 = 0$$

By comparing $z^2 + pz + q = 0$ to $z^2 + 6z + 13 = 0$,
$$p = 6 \quad \text{and} \quad q = 13.$$

Method 2: Substitute $z = -3 - 2i$ into $z^2 + pz + q = 0$ and equate coefficients.

$$z^2 + pz + q = 0$$
$$(-3 - 2i)^2 + p(-3 - 2i) + q = 0 \qquad \text{(put in } (-3 - 2i) \text{ for } z)$$
$$5 + 12i - 3p - 2pi + q = 0 \qquad ((-3 - 2i)^2 = 5 + 12i)$$
$$(-3p + q + 5) + (-2p + 12)i = 0 \qquad \text{(group real and imaginary parts together)}$$
$$\therefore \ -3p + q + 5 = 0 \quad \text{①} \quad \text{and} \qquad \text{(equate coefficients)}$$
$$-2p + 12 = 0 \quad \text{②}$$

Solving the simultaneous equations ① and ② gives $p = 6$ and $q = 13$.

Exercise 2.5

In questions 1–9, solve for z.

1. $z^2 - 2z + 2 = 0$
2. $z^2 - 2z + 5 = 0$
3. $z^2 + 10z + 34 = 0$
4. $2z^2 - 2z + 1 = 0$
5. $2z^2 + 6z + 5 = 0$
6. $5z^2 - 2z + 10 = 0$
7. $z^2 + 4 = 0$
8. $z^2 + 9 = 0$
9. $z^2 + 100 = 0$

10. p and k are real numbers such that $p(2 + i) + 8 - ki = 5k - 3 - i$.

   (i) Find the value of p and the value of k.

   (ii) Investigate if $p + ki$ is a root of the equation $z^2 - 4z + 13 = 0$.

11. Express $\dfrac{1 + 7i}{1 - 3i}$ in the form $p + qi$. Hence, show that $\dfrac{1 + 7i}{1 - 3i}$ is a root of the equation

   $z^2 + 4z + 5 = 0$ and write down the other root in the form $a + bi$, where $a, b \in \mathbb{R}$.

12. Solve the quadratic equation $z^2 - 2(1 + i)z + (4 + 2i) = 0$ and explain why the roots do not occur in conjugate pairs.

In questions 13–15, solve the quadratic equation.

13. $z^2 - (1 + 4i)z - 2(3 - i) = 0$
14. $z^2 - (3 - 2i)z - (1 + 3i) = 0$
15. $z^2 - (2 + 5i)z + 5(i - 1) = 0$

In questions 16–23, form a quadratic equation with the given roots.

16. $-2 \pm i$
17. $3 \pm 2i$
18. $-1 \pm 5i$
19. $\pm 3i$
20. $-1 \pm \sqrt{2}i$
21. $2 \pm \sqrt{5}i$
22. $\frac{1}{2} \pm \frac{1}{2}i$
23. $-\frac{1}{3} \pm \frac{2}{3}i$

24. If $3 + 5i$ is a root of $z^2 + pz + q = 0$, where $p, q \in \mathbb{R}$, find p and q.

25. If $-3 - 3i$ is a root of $x^2 + mx + n = 0$, where $m, n \in \mathbb{R}$, find the value of m and n.

26. If $-1 + 5i$ is a root of $x^2 + 2x + k = 0$, where $k \in \mathbb{R}$, find the value of k.

27. If $\dfrac{7 - 17i}{5 - i}$ is a root of $z^2 + az + b = 0$, where $a, b \in \mathbb{R}$, find the values of a and b.

28. (i) If $z = \dfrac{19 - 4i}{3 - 2i} = a + bi$, find the value of a and the value of b, where $a, b \in \mathbb{R}$.

    (ii) Verify that $z^2 - 10z + 29 = 0$.

    (iii) Hence, find two complex numbers, u, such that $(u + 3i)^2 - 10(u + 3i) + 29 = 0$.

29. Find the value of $k \in \mathbb{R}$ if $1 + 2i$ is a root of the equation $z^2 + kz + 7 + 4i = 0$.

30. Find the value of $\lambda \in \mathbb{R}$ if $3 - 2i$ is a root of the equation $z^2 + (1 - i)z - 6 + \lambda i = 0$.

31. One root of the quadratic equation $z^2 - (p - i)z + (q - i) = 0$ is $1 + 2i$ where $p, q \in \mathbb{R}$. Find the value of p and q and the other root.

32. Solve the quadratic equation $2iz^2 + (6 + 2i)z + (3 - 6i)$. Write your answers in the form $a + bi$, where $a, b \in \mathbb{Q}$.

Square roots and quadratic equations with complex roots

In some problems we have to find the square root of a complex number in order to find the roots of a quadratic equation.

EXAMPLE

(i) Express $\sqrt{5 + 12i}$ in the form $a + bi$, where $a, b \in \mathbb{R}$.

(ii) Hence, determine the two roots of the equation $z^2 - (1 + 4i)z - 5 - i = 0$.

Solution:

(i)   Let $a + bi = \sqrt{5 + 12i}$, where $a, b \in \mathbb{R}$.

$(a + bi)^2 = (\sqrt{5 + 12i})^2$ (square both sides)

$a^2 + 2abi - b^2 = 5 + 12i$ (remove brackets)

$ R \quad I \quad R \quad R \quad I$ (identify real and imaginary parts)

Real parts = Real parts   **Imaginary parts = Imaginary parts**

$\qquad a^2 - b^2 = 5 \qquad ①$ $2ab = 12 \qquad ②$

Solve between equations ① and ②:

$$2ab = 12 \quad ② \qquad\qquad a^2 - b^2 = 5 \quad ①$$

$$ab = 6 \qquad\qquad a^2 - \left(\dfrac{6}{a}\right)^2 = 5 \quad \left(\text{replace } b \text{ with } \dfrac{6}{a}\right)$$

$$b = \left(\dfrac{6}{a}\right) \qquad\qquad a^2 - \dfrac{36}{a^2} = 5$$

put this into equation ① $a^4 - 36 = 5a^2$

$$a^4 - 5a^2 - 36 = 0$$

$$(a^2 - 9)(a^2 + 4) = 0$$
$$a^2 - 9 = 0 \quad \text{or} \quad a^2 + 4 = 0$$
$$a^2 = 9 \quad \text{or} \quad a^2 = -4$$
$$a = \pm 3 \quad \text{or} \quad a = \pm 2i$$

As $a, b \in \mathbb{R}$, the result $a = \pm 2i$ is rejected.

$$b = \frac{6}{a}$$

$a = 3$	$a = -3$
$b = \dfrac{6}{3}$	$b = \dfrac{6}{-3}$
$= 2$	$= -2$
$a = 3, b = 2$	$a = -3, b = -2$

Thus, $\sqrt{5 + 12i} = 3 + 2i$

or $\quad \sqrt{5 + 12i} = -3 - 2i$

(i.e. $\pm(3 + 2i)$)

(ii) $\quad z^2 - (1 + 4i)z - 5 - i = 0$

$z^2 + (-1 - 4i)z + (-5 - i) = 0$ $\qquad$ (write in the form $az^2 + bz + c = 0$)

$$z = \frac{-b \pm \sqrt{b^2 - 4ac}}{2a}$$

$$= \frac{-(-1 - 4i) \pm \sqrt{(-1 - 4i)^2 - 4(1)(-5 - i)}}{2(1)}$$

$$= \frac{1 + 4i \pm \sqrt{1 + 8i - 16 + 20 + 4i}}{2}$$

$$= \frac{1 + 4i \pm \sqrt{5 + 12i}}{2}$$

$$= \frac{1 + 4i \pm (3 + 2i)}{2} \qquad \text{(put in } (3 + 2i) \text{ for } \sqrt{5 + 12i})$$

$$z_1 = \frac{1 + 4i + (3 + 2i)}{2} = \frac{1 + 4i + 3 + 2i}{2} = \frac{4 + 6i}{2} = 2 + 3i$$

$$z_2 = \frac{1 + 4i - (3 + 2i)}{2} = \frac{1 + 4i - 3 - 2i}{2} = \frac{-2 + 2i}{2} = -1 + i$$

Thus, the roots of $z^2 - (1 + 4i)z - 5 - i = 0$ are $2 + 3i$ and $-1 + i$.

Note: It makes no difference if we substitute $3 + 2i$ or $-3 - 2i$ for $\sqrt{5 + 12i}$.

Note: Another way of asking for $\sqrt{5 + 12i}$ to be expressed in the form $a + bi$ is:

1. If $(a + bi)^2 = 5 + 12i$, find the values of a and b, where $a, b \in \mathbb{R}$.
2. If $z^2 = 5 + 12i$ or $z = \sqrt{5 + 12i}$, find all the values of z.

Exercise 2.6

1. Find two complex numbers $a + bi$ such that $(a + bi)^2 = -15 + 8i$, where $a, b \in \mathbb{R}$.

Express questions 2–9 in the form $a + bi$, where $a, b \in \mathbb{R}$ and $i^2 = -1$.

2. $\sqrt{-3 - 4i}$ 3. $\sqrt{8 - 6i}$ 4. $\sqrt{-5 + 12i}$ 5. $\sqrt{15 - 8i}$

6. $\sqrt{-21 + 20i}$ 7. $\sqrt{-7 - 24i}$ 8. $\sqrt{-9 - 40i}$ 9. $\sqrt{2i}$

10. (i) Find the two complex numbers $a + bi$ for which $(a + bi)^2 = -3 + 4i$.
    (ii) Hence, determine the two roots of the equations:
        (a) $z^2 - 3z + (3 - i) = 0$ (b) $x^2 + x + 1 - i = 0$.

11. (i) Find the two complex numbers $p + qi$ for which $(p + qi)^2 = -24 + 10i$.
    (ii) Hence, determine the two roots of the equation $z^2 - 3(1 + i)z + 2(3 + i) = 0$.

12. (i) Find the two complex numbers $x + yi$ for which $(x + yi)^2 = 15 + 8i$.
    (ii) Hence, show that one of the roots of the equation $z^2 + (2 + i)z - (3 + i) = 0$ is a real number and the other is a complex number.

13. (i) Find the two complex numbers $a + bi$ for which $(a + bi)^2 = 3 + 4i$.
    (ii) Hence, show that one of the roots of the equation $z^2 + (2 - i)z - 2i = 0$ is a real number and the other is a complex number.

14. (i) Find the two complex numbers $p + qi$ for which $(p + qi)^2 = 5 - 12i$.
    (ii) Hence, determine the two roots of the equations:
        (a) $z^2 + z + (3i - 1) = 0$ (b) $z^2 - 2(1 + i)z + 5(1 - 2i) = 0$.

15. (i) Find the two complex numbers $a + bi$ for which $(a + bi)^2 = 15 + 8i$.
    (ii) Solve the equation $iz^2 + (2 - 3i)z + (-5 + 5i) = 0$.

16. Find the two complex numbers $x + yi$ such that $(x + yi)^2 = 2 - 2\sqrt{3}i$.

17. (i) Find the two complex numbers $a + bi$ such that:
        (a) $(a + bi)^2 = 3 + 4i$ (b) $(a + bi)^2 = 3 - 4i$.
    (ii) Hence, determine the four roots of the equation $z^4 - 6z^2 + 25 = 0$. (Hint: Let $y = z^2$.)

Cubic equations with complex roots

The conjugate root theorem also applies to cubic equations.

Conjugate root theorem

> If all the coefficients of a polynomial equation are **real**, then all complex roots occur as conjugate pairs.

In other words, if one root is a complex number, then its conjugate is also a root, provided all the coefficients are real.

EXAMPLE 1

Show that $-1 + 2i$ is a root of $z^3 - 2z^2 - 3z - 20 = 0$ and find the other two roots.

Solution:

Put in $(-1 + 2i)$ for z:

$z^3 - 2z^2 - 3z - 20$

$(-1 + 2i)^3 - 2(-1 + 2i)^2 - 3(-1 + 2i) - 20$

$= (11 - 2i) - 2(-3 - 4i) - 3(-1 + 2i) - 20$

$= 11 - 2i + 6 + 8i + 3 - 6i - 20$

$= 20 - 20 + 8i - 8i$

$= 0$

$\therefore -1 + 2i$ is a root.

$\therefore -1 - 2i$ is also a root (roots occur in conjugate pairs, as all the coefficients are real).

$$(-1 + 2i)^2$$
$$= (-1 + 2i)(-1 + 2i)$$
$$= -3 - 4i$$

$$(-1 + 2i)^3$$
$$= (-1 + 2i)^2(-1 + 2i)$$
$$= (-3 - 4i)(-1 + 2i)$$
$$= 11 - 2i$$

We now need to construct the quadratic factor.

$z = -1 + 2i$ and $z = -1 - 2i$

$\therefore z + 1 - 2i = 0$ and $z + 1 + 2i = 0$

The quadratic factor is given by $(z + 1 - 2i)(z + 1 + 2i)$.

$(z + 1 - 2i)(z + 1 + 2i)$

$= z(z + 1 + 2i) + 1(z + 1 + 2i) - 2i(z + 1 + 2i)$

$= z^2 + z + 2zi + z + 1 + 2i - 2zi - 2i - 4i^2$

$= z^2 + 2z + 1 + 4$ $(i^2 = -1)$

$= z^2 + 2z + 5$

Dividing $z^3 - 2z^2 - 3z - 20$ by $z^2 + 2z + 5$ gives $z - 4$.

$\therefore$ The third factor is $z - 4$.

Let $z - 4 = 0$.

$\therefore \qquad z = 4$

Thus, the other two roots are $-1 - 2i$ and 4.

Division:

$$
\begin{array}{r}
z - 4 \\
z^2 + 2z + 5 \overline{\smash{\big)}\ z^3 - 2z^2 - 3z - 20} \\
\underline{z^3 + 2z^2 + 5z} \\
-4z^2 - 8z - 20 \\
\underline{-4z^2 - 8z - 20} \\
0
\end{array}
$$

Note 1: We did not have to use long division to get the third factor.

Let the third factor be $z + k$.

$\therefore (z + k)(z^2 + 2z + 5) = z^3 - 2z^2 - 3z - 20$

Comparing constants on both sides, we get:

$\qquad 5k = -20$

$\qquad \therefore \quad k = -4$

Thus, the third factor is $z - 4$.

However, this option is not always available.

Note 2: A shortcut to find the quadratic factor is to use

z^2 − (sum of roots) z + (product of the roots)

z^2 − (−1 + 2i − 1 − 2i) z + (−1 + 2i)(−1 − 2i)

z^2 − (−2) z + (1 + 2i − 2i − 4i²)

z^2 + 2z + 5   ($i^2 = -1$)

EXAMPLE 2

One root of the equation $z^3 + az^2 + bz - 52 = 0$, where $a, b \in \mathbb{R}$, is $2 - 3i$.

Find the value of a and the value of b.

Solution:

$(2 - 3i)^2 = (2 - 3i)(2 - 3i) = -5 - 12i$

$(2 - 3i)^3 = (2 - 3i)^2(2 - 3i) = (-5 - 12i)(2 - 3i) = -46 - 9i$

$z^3 + az^2 + bz - 52 = 0$

$(2 - 3i)^3 + a(2 - 3i)^2 + b(2 - 3i) - 52 = 0$ (put in $(2 - 3i)$ for z)

$(-46 - 9i) + a(-5 - 12i) + b(2 - 3i) - 52 = 0$

$-46 - 9i - 5a - 12ai + 2b - 3bi - 52 = 0$

$(-5a + 2b - 98) + (-12a - 3b - 9)i = 0$ (group real and imaginary parts together)

∴ $-5a + 2b - 98 = 0$ ①   and $-12a - 3b - 9 = 0$ ②

Solving the simultaneous equations ① and ② gives $a = -8$ and $b = 29$.

Exercise 2.7

1. $f(z) = z^3 - 5z^2 + 4z + 10$

   (i) Verify that $p(-1) = 0$.

   (ii) Find the two complex roots of $f(z) = 0$.

2. $p(z) = z^3 + z^2 + z - 39$

   (i) Verify that $p(3) = 0$.

   (ii) Find the two complex roots of $p(z) = 0$.

3. (i) The cubic function $f : x \rightarrow x^3 + 7x^2 + 17x + 15$ has one integer root and two complex roots. Find all three roots.

   (ii) Using part (i) or otherwise, solve the equation $(x - 2)^3 + 7(x - 2)^2 + 17(x - 2) + 15 = 0$.

4. (i) Express in the form $a + bi$: **(a)** $(1 + i)^2$ **(b)** $(1 + i)^3$.

   (ii) Show that $1 + i$ is a root of $z^3 - 5z^2 + 8z - 6 = 0$ and find the other two roots.

5. $p(z) = z^3 + 2z^2 - 3z + 20$. If $p(1 + 2i) = 0$, find the three roots of $p(z) = 0$.

6. $f(z) = z^3 - z^2 - 7z - 65$. If $f(-2 + 3i) = 0$, find the three roots of $f(z) = 0$.

7. Solve the equation $x^3 + 2x^2 + 2x = 0$.

8. **(i)** $p(z) = z^3 - 11z + 20$. Verify that $p(2 - i) = 0$ and solve $p(z) = 0$.

    (ii) Hence, using part **(i)** or otherwise, solve the equation $(z + 3i)^3 - 11(z + 3i) + 20 = 0$.

    (iii) Verify one of your answers to part **(ii)**.

9. $f(x) = x^3 - 4x^2 + 6x + k$, where $k \in \mathbb{R}$ and $f(1 - i) = 0$.

    (i) Find k.   **(ii)** Solve $f(x) = 0$.   **(iii)** Hence, solve $f(x + 2) = 0$.

10. $p(z) = z^3 + kz^2 + 7z + k - 2$, where $k \in \mathbb{R}$ and $p(1 - 2i) = 0$.

    (i) Find k.   **(ii)** Solve $p(z) = 0$.   **(iii)** Hence, solve $p(z - 2i) = 0$.

11. **(i)** $p(z) = z^3 - iz^2 - 9z + 9i = 0$. Verify that $p(i) = 0$ and solve $p(z) = 0$.

    (ii) Hence, using part **(i)** or otherwise, solve the equation
$$(z - 2i)^3 - i(z - 2i)^2 - 9(z - 2i) + 9i = 0.$$

12. $p(z) = z^3 + az^2 + bz - 4$, where $a, b \in \mathbb{R}$ and $p(1 + i) = 0$.

    (i) Find the values of a and b.   **(ii)** Solve **(a)** $p(z) = 0$ **(b)** $p(z + 1) = 0$.

13. $f(x) = x^3 + px^2 + x + q$, where $p, q \in \mathbb{R}$ and $f(4 - i) = 0$.

    (i) Find the values of p and q.   **(ii)** Solve **(a)** $f(x) = 0$ **(b)** $f(x - 2i) = 0$.

14. $(z - 2)(z^2 + az + b) = z^3 - 4z^2 + 6z - 4$, where $a, b \in \mathbb{Z}$.

    (i) Find the values of a and b.

    (ii) Solve $z^3 - 4z^2 + 6z - 4 = 0$.

15. Let $p(z) = z^3 - (4 - 2i)z^2 + (5 - 8i) z - 10i$, where $i^2 = -1$.
Determine the real numbers a and b if $p(z) = (z - 2i)(z^2 + az + b)$.

16. Let $p(z) = z^3 - (10 + i)z^2 + (29 + 10i)z - 29i$, where $i^2 = -1$.
Determine the real numbers a and b if $p(z) = (z - i)(z^2 + az + b)$.

17. **(i)** Factorise $z^2 - 5z + 6$ and hence solve the equation $z^2 - 5z + 6 = 0$.

    (ii) Show that $z^2 - 5z + 6$ is a factor of $z^3 + (-4 + i)z^2 + (1 - 5i)z + 6(1 + i)$.

    (iii) Find the three roots of the equation $z^3 + (-4 + i)z^2 + (1 - 5i)z + 6(1 + i) = 0$.

18. **(i)** Factorise $z^2 - 4$ and hence or otherwise, solve the equation $z^2 - 4 = 0$.

    (ii) Show that $z^2 - 4$ is a factor of $z^3 + (3 + i)z^2 - 4z - 4(3 + i)$.

    (iii) Find the three roots of the equation $z^3 + (3 + i)z^2 - 4z - 4(3 + i) = 0$.

19. Show that $z^2 - 16$ is a factor of $z^3 + (1 + i)z^2 - 16z - 16(1 + i)$ and hence find the three roots of $z^3 + (1 + i)z^2 - 16z - 16(1 + i) = 0$.

20. **(i)** Find a quadratic equation whose roots are $3 + i$ and $3 - i$, where $i^2 = -1$.

    (ii) Let $p(z) = z^3 - kz^2 + 22z - 20$, where $k \in \mathbb{R}$.

        (a) $3 + i$ is a root of the equation $p(z) = 0$. Find the value of k.

        (b) Find the other two roots of the equation $p(z) = 0$.

21. Part of the graph of the function
    $f(z) = z^3 + 3z^2 + kz - 8$ is shown here.
    (i) Write down the coordinates of the two
        points where the graph of $f(z)$ crosses the
        axes.
    (ii) Write down the real root of $f(z) = 0$.
    (iii) Find the value of k, where $k \in \mathbb{N}$.
    (iv) $f(z) = (z - a)(z^2 + bz + c)$.
        Find the value of a, b and c.
    (v) Solve $f(z) = 0$.

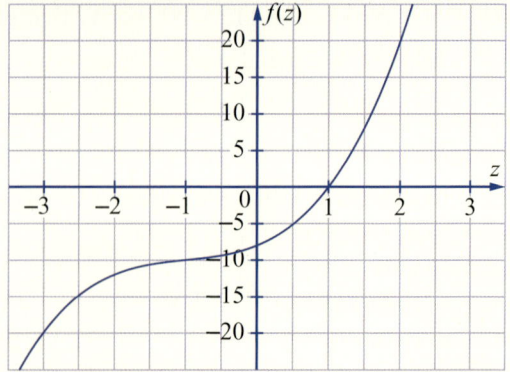

22. Part of the graph of the function
    $f(z) = z^3 + kz^2 + kz - 15$ is shown here.
    (i) Write down the real root of $f(z) = 0$.
    (ii) Find the value of k, where $k \in \mathbb{N}$.
    (iii) $f(z) = (z - a)(z^2 + bz + c)$.
        Find the value of a, b and c.
    (iv) Solve $f(z) = 0$.

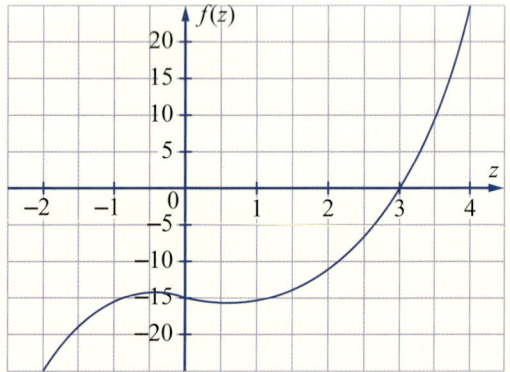

23. Part of the graph of the function
    $f(z) = z^4 - 2z^3 + z^2 - 8z - 12$ is shown here.
    (i) $f(z) = 0$ has two integer roots. Using the
        graph, write down the integer roots.
    (ii) Show that $g(z) = z^2 - 2z - 3$ is a factor of
        $f(z)$.
    (iii) Hence, find the two complex roots of
        $f(z) = 0$.

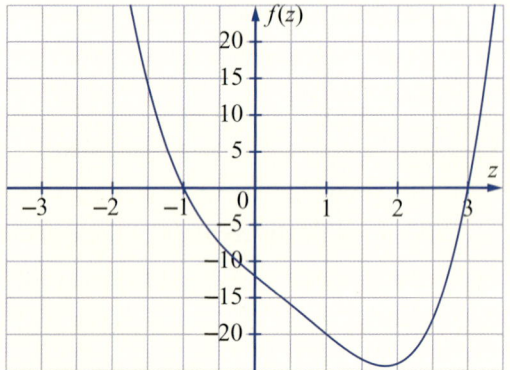

24. ki is a root of the equation $2z^3 - z^2 + 18z - 9 = 0$, where $k \in \mathbb{R}$.
    Find the values of k and the three roots of the equation $2z^3 - z^2 + 18z - 9 = 0$.

Polar coordinates and the polar form of a complex number

Polar coordinates

Consider the complex number $z = x + yi$. The position of z on the Argand diagram can be given by Cartesian, or rectangular, coordinates, (x, y). An alternative way of describing the position of z is to give its modulus, r, and its **argument**, θ.

(r, θ) are called the polar coordinates of the complex number.

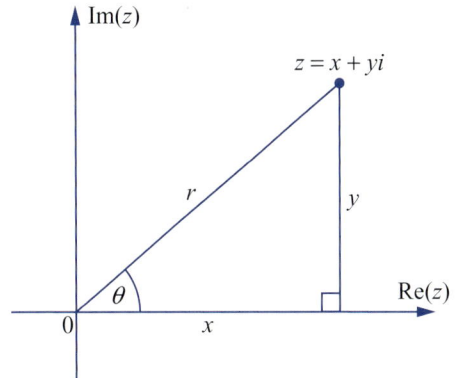

1. Modulus	**2. Argument**
The modulus $= r = \|z\| = \sqrt{x^2 + y^2}$.	The argument $= \theta$.
The modulus is the distance from the origin to the point representing the complex number on the Argand diagram.	The argument, θ, is the angle between the positive real-axis and the line from the origin to the point $z = x + yi$.

Note: Drawing a diagram can be a very good aid in calculating θ.

Polar form

Having calculated r and θ, there is a simple connection between the Cartesian coordinates (x, y) and the polar coordinates (r, θ).

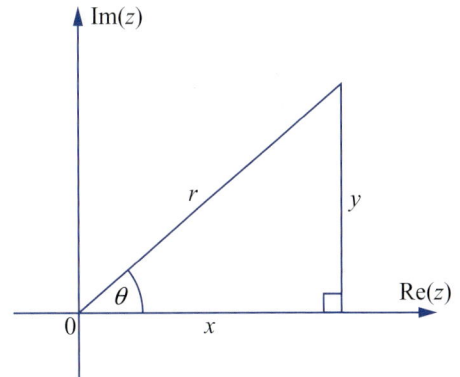

$$\frac{x}{r} = \cos \theta \qquad \frac{y}{r} = \sin \theta$$
$$x = r \cos \theta \qquad y = r \sin \theta$$

Now we can write $z = x + yi$ in terms of r and θ.

$$z = x + yi$$
$$z = (r \cos \theta) + (r \sin \theta)i$$
$$z = r(\cos \theta + i \sin \theta)$$

This is called the **polar form** of the complex number.

> The polar form of the complex number $z = x + yi$ is
> $$z = r(\cos \theta + i \sin \theta).$$

Note: It is conventional to write i before $\sin \theta$.
In other words, $i \sin \theta$ is preferable to $\sin \theta i$.

EXAMPLE 1

Express each of these complex numbers in the form $r(\cos\theta + i\sin\theta)$, where $i^2 = -1$.

(i) $-1 + i$ **(ii)** $-\sqrt{3} - i$ **(iii)** $\dfrac{1}{2} + \dfrac{\sqrt{3}}{2}i$ **(iv)** $-6i$

Solution:

(i) $-1 + i = (-1, 1)$

$$r = |-1 + i| = \sqrt{(-1)^2 + (1)^2} = \sqrt{1+1} = \sqrt{2}$$

$$\tan\alpha = \frac{1}{1} = 1, \quad \alpha = \tan^{-1}1 = 45°$$

$$\therefore \theta = 180° - 45° = 135°$$

$$\therefore -1 + i = \sqrt{2}(\cos 135° + i\sin 135°)$$

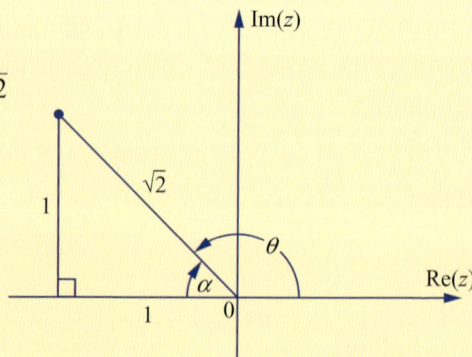

(ii) $-\sqrt{3} - i = (-\sqrt{3}, -1)$

$$r = |-\sqrt{3} - i| = \sqrt{(-\sqrt{3})^2 + (-1)^2}$$

$$= \sqrt{3+1} = \sqrt{4} = 2$$

$$\tan\alpha = \frac{1}{\sqrt{3}}, \quad \alpha = \tan^{-1}\left(\frac{1}{\sqrt{3}}\right) = 30°$$

$$\therefore \theta = 180° + 30° = 210°$$

$$\therefore -\sqrt{3} - i = 2(\cos 210° + i\sin 210°)$$

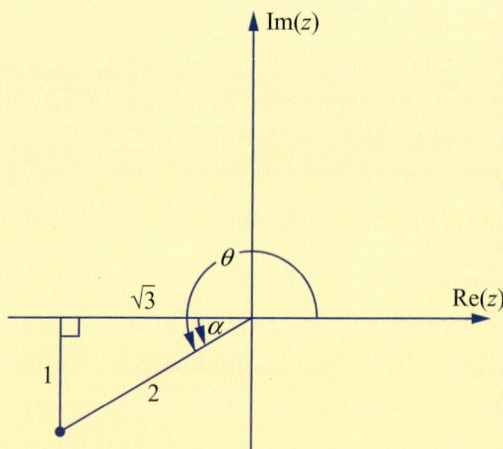

(iii) $\dfrac{1}{2} + \dfrac{\sqrt{3}}{2}i = \left(\dfrac{1}{2}, \dfrac{\sqrt{3}}{2}\right)$

$$r = \left|\frac{1}{2} + \frac{\sqrt{3}}{2}\right| = \sqrt{\left(\frac{1}{2}\right)^2 + \left(\frac{\sqrt{3}}{2}\right)^2}$$

$$= \sqrt{\frac{1}{4} + \frac{3}{4}} = \sqrt{1} = 1$$

$$\tan\theta = \frac{\frac{\sqrt{3}}{2}}{\frac{1}{2}} = \sqrt{3}, \quad \theta = \tan^{-1}\sqrt{3} = 60°$$

$$\therefore \frac{1}{2} + \frac{\sqrt{3}}{2}i = \cos 60° + i\sin 60°$$

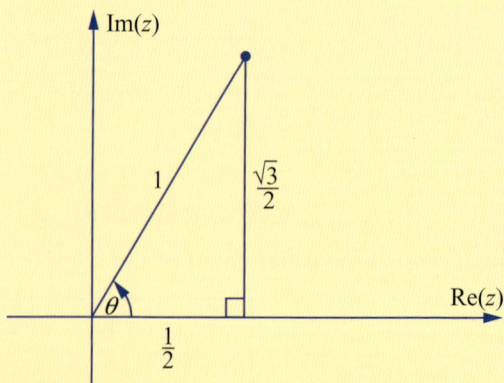

(iv) $-6i = 0 - 6i = (0, -6)$

$$r = |0 - 6i| = \sqrt{0^2 + (-6)^2} = \sqrt{0 + 36}$$

$$= \sqrt{36} = 6$$

$$\theta = 270°$$

$$\therefore -6i = 6(\cos 270° + i \sin 270°)$$

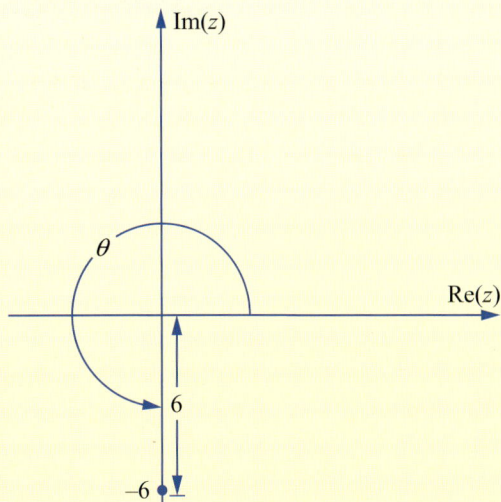

Sometimes we are given a number in polar form, $r(\cos \theta + i \sin \theta)$, and asked to write it in Cartesian form, $x + yi$. Again, it is good practice to draw a diagram.

EXAMPLE 2

Express $4\left(\cos \dfrac{5\pi}{6} + i \sin \dfrac{5\pi}{6}\right)$ in the form $x + yi$.

Solution:

$$\frac{5\pi}{6} = \frac{5(180°)}{6} = 150°$$

$$\cos 150° = -\frac{\sqrt{3}}{2}$$

$$\sin 150° = \frac{1}{2}$$

$$\therefore 4\left(\cos \frac{5\pi}{6} + i \sin \frac{5\pi}{6}\right)$$

$$= 4\cos 150° + i \sin 150° = 4\left(-\frac{\sqrt{3}}{2} + \frac{1}{2}i\right) = -2\sqrt{3} + 2i$$

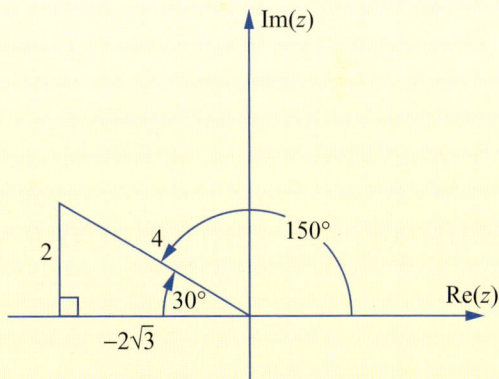

Note: If your calculator is in radian mode ($\mathbb{R}$), you do not have to change the radians into degrees.

$$\cos \frac{5\pi}{6} = -\frac{\sqrt{3}}{2} \quad \text{and} \quad \sin \frac{5\pi}{6} = \frac{1}{2}.$$

Exercise 2.8

In questions 1–16, express the complex number in polar form $[r(\cos\theta + i\sin\theta)]$.

1. $1 + i$
2. $\sqrt{3} + i$
3. $2 + 2\sqrt{3}i$
4. i

5. 2
6. $1 - \sqrt{3}i$
7. $1 - i$
8. $-\sqrt{2} + \sqrt{2}i$

9. $-2 - 2i$
10. $-2\sqrt{3} + 2i$
11. $-4 - 4\sqrt{3}i$
12. $\sqrt{3} - i$

13. $(1 + i)^2$
14. $\dfrac{2}{1 - i}$
15. $\dfrac{4}{-\sqrt{3} + i}$
16. $\dfrac{1}{2} + \dfrac{\sqrt{3}}{2}i$

In questions 17–22, express each in rectangular form $(a + bi)$.

17. $\cos\dfrac{\pi}{2} + i\sin\dfrac{\pi}{2}$

18. $\sqrt{2}(\cos 45° + i\sin 45°)$

19. $6\left(\cos\dfrac{2\pi}{3} + i\sin\dfrac{2\pi}{3}\right)$

20. $10(\cos 510° + i\sin 510°)$

21. $4\left(\cos\dfrac{4\pi}{3} + i\sin\dfrac{4\pi}{3}\right)$

22. $2\sqrt{2}(\cos 315° + i\sin 315°)$

23. If $z = 2 - 2i$, evaluate **(i)** $\arg(z)$ **(ii)** $\arg\left(\dfrac{4}{z}\right)$.

24. Let $u = \sqrt{3} + i$ and $w = -1 + \sqrt{3}i$. Show that $\arg(u) + \arg(w) = \arg(uw)$.

25. Let $z = 5 + ki$. If $\arg(z) = \dfrac{\pi}{4}$, find **(i)** k **(ii)** $|z|$.

26. Let $z_1 = a + 8i$, $z_2 = -3 + bi$, $z_3 = c - i$ and $z_4 = 2\sqrt{3} + di$.

If $\arg(z_1) = \dfrac{3\pi}{4}$, $\arg(z_2) = 225°$, $\arg(z_3) = \dfrac{7\pi}{6}$ and $\arg(z_4) = 300°$, find:

(i) (a) a **(b)** $|z_1|$ **(ii) (a)** b **(b)** $|z_2|$

(iii) (a) c **(b)** $|z_3|$ **(iv) (a)** d **(b)** $|z_4|$

27. Let $w = 2\sqrt{3} + ki$, where $k \in \mathbb{R}$. If $|w| = 4$, find $\arg(w)$.

Multiplying and dividing numbers in polar form

If $z_1 = r_1(\cos A + i\sin A)$ and $z_2 = r_2(\cos B + i\sin B)$, then:

1. $z_1z_2 = r_1r_2[\cos(A + B) + i\sin(A + B)]$

$\therefore |z_1z_2| = |z_1| \times |z_2|$ and $\arg(z_1z_2) = \arg(z_1) + \arg(z_2)$

2. $\dfrac{z_1}{z_2} = \dfrac{r_1}{r_2}[\cos(A - B) + i\sin(A - B)]$

$\therefore \left|\dfrac{z_1}{z_2}\right| = \dfrac{|z_1|}{|z_2|}$ and $\arg\left(\dfrac{z_1}{z_2}\right) = \arg(z_1) - \arg(z_2)$

EXAMPLE

(i) Evaluate $[5(\cos 243° + i \sin 243°)][2(\cos 27° + i \sin 27°)]$

(ii) If $u = 8(\cos 81° + i \sin 81°)$ and $v = 2(\cos 21° + i \sin 21°)$, express $\dfrac{u}{v}$ in rectangular form.

Solution:

(i) $[5(\cos 243° + i \sin 243°)][2(\cos 27° + i \sin 27°)]$

$= 5 \times 2[\cos(243° + 27°) + i \sin(243° + 27°)]$

$= 10[\cos 270° + i \sin 270°]$

$= 10[0 + i(-1)] = 10(0 - i) = -10i$

(ii) $u = 8(\cos 81° + i \sin 81°)$ and $v = 2(\cos 21° + i \sin 21°)$

$\dfrac{u}{v} = \dfrac{8(\cos 81° + i \sin 81°)}{2(\cos 21° + i \sin 21°)}$

$= \dfrac{8}{2}[\cos(81° - 21°) + i \sin(81° - 21°)]$

$= 4(\cos 60° + i \sin 60°) = 4\left(\dfrac{1}{2} + \dfrac{\sqrt{3}}{2} i\right) = 2 + 2\sqrt{3}\, i$

Exercise 2.9

Evaluate each of the following in questions 1–11.

1. $(\cos 33° + i \sin 33°)(\cos 57° + i \sin 57°)$

2. $(\cos 139° + i \sin 139°)(\cos 41° + i \sin 41°)$

3. $\left[2\left(\cos \dfrac{\pi}{3} + i \sin \dfrac{\pi}{3}\right)\right]\left[4\left(\cos \dfrac{\pi}{6} + i \sin \dfrac{\pi}{6}\right)\right]$

4. $\left[3\left(\cos \dfrac{4\pi}{3} + i \sin \dfrac{4\pi}{3}\right)\right]\left[5\left(\cos \dfrac{2\pi}{3} + i \sin \dfrac{2\pi}{3}\right)\right]$

5. $[4(\cos 240° + i \sin 240°)][3(\cos 30° + i \sin 30°)]$

6. $\left[2\left(\cos \dfrac{3\pi}{10} + i \sin \dfrac{3\pi}{10}\right)\right]\left[8\left(\cos \dfrac{\pi}{5} + i \sin \dfrac{\pi}{5}\right)\right]$

7. $[10(\cos 300° + i \sin 300°)][2(\cos 150° + i \sin 150°)]$

8. $\left[3\left(\cos \dfrac{9\pi}{4} + i \sin \dfrac{9\pi}{4}\right)\right]\left[2\left(\cos \dfrac{3\pi}{4} + i \sin \dfrac{3\pi}{4}\right)\right]$

9. $\dfrac{\cos 110° + i \sin 110°}{\cos 20° + i \sin 20°}$

10. $\dfrac{8\left(\cos \dfrac{3\pi}{2} + i \sin \dfrac{3\pi}{2}\right)}{4\left(\cos \dfrac{\pi}{2} + i \sin \dfrac{\pi}{2}\right)}$

11. $\dfrac{24(\cos 303° + i \sin 303°)}{8(\cos 33° + i \sin 33°)}$

In questions 12–16, express each in rectangular form.

12. $[4(\cos 150° + i \sin 150°)][2(\cos 60° + i \sin 60°)]$

13. $\left[2\left(\cos \dfrac{\pi}{9} + i \sin \dfrac{\pi}{9}\right)\right]\left[5\left(\cos \dfrac{2\pi}{9} + i \sin \dfrac{2\pi}{9}\right)\right]$

14. $\dfrac{\cos 130° + i \sin 130°}{\cos 40° + i \sin 40°}$

15. $\dfrac{6\left(\cos \dfrac{7\pi}{6} + i \sin \dfrac{7\pi}{6}\right)}{3\left(\cos \dfrac{\pi}{6} + i \sin \dfrac{\pi}{6}\right)}$

16. $\dfrac{15(\cos 312° + i \sin 312°)}{5(\cos 42° + i \sin 42°)}$

17. **(i)** If $u = \cos 5x + i \sin 5x$ and $v = \cos 4x + i \sin 4x$, express:

    (a) uv **(b)** $\dfrac{u}{v}$ in the form $\cos kx + i \sin kx$, where $k \in \mathbb{R}$.

    (ii) If $x = \dfrac{\pi}{6}$, evaluate **(a)** uv **(b)** $\dfrac{u}{v}$.

18. Let $z_1 = 3\left(\cos \dfrac{\pi}{6} + i \sin \dfrac{\pi}{6}\right)$ and $z_2 = 2\sqrt{3} - 2i$. Evaluate $z_1 z_2$.

19. $z_1 = 2\left(\cos \dfrac{\pi}{6} + i \sin \dfrac{\pi}{6}\right)$ and $z_2 = 3\left(\cos \dfrac{\pi}{3} + i \sin \dfrac{\pi}{3}\right)$, where $i^2 = -1$.

    (i) If $z_3 = z_1 z_2$, express z_3 in the form $a + bi$, where $a, b \in \mathbb{R}$.

    (ii) Form a quadratic equation with roots z_3 and $\bar{z}_3$.

20. $u = (\cos A + i \sin A)$ and $v = (\cos B + i \sin B)$. Prove:

    (i) $uv = \cos(A + B) + i \sin(A + B)$ **(ii)** $\dfrac{u}{v} = \cos(A - B) + i \sin(A - B)$

    (iii) $u^2 = \cos 2A + i \sin 2A$

    (iv) Suggest an answer for u^3, u^4, u^5, u^n, where $n \in \mathbb{N}$.

De Moivre's theorem

$$[r(\cos \theta + i \sin \theta)]^n = r^n(\cos n\theta + i \sin n\theta)], \text{ where } n \in \mathbb{Q}.$$

There are three applications of De Moivre's theorem:

1. Finding powers of complex numbers.
2. Proving trigonometric identities.
3. Finding roots of complex numbers.

Finding powers of complex numbers

Method:

1. Write the number in polar form.
2. Apply De Moivre's theorem.
3. Simplify the result.

Note: After applying De Moivre's theorem, the angle can be very large. However, we can keep subtracting 360° until the angle is in the range $0° \le \theta \le 360°$. If using radians, keep subtracting 2π until the angle is in the range $0 \le \theta \le 2\pi$.

EXAMPLE 1

Express $(-1 + i)^{10}$ in the form $x + yi$, where $x, y \in \mathbb{R}$ and $i^2 = -1$.

Solution:

1. $r = |-1 + i| = \sqrt{(-1)^2 + 1^2} = \sqrt{1 + 1} = \sqrt{2}$

   $\tan \alpha = \frac{1}{1} = 1, \quad \alpha = \tan^{-1} 1 = 45°$

   $\theta = 180° - 45° = 135°$

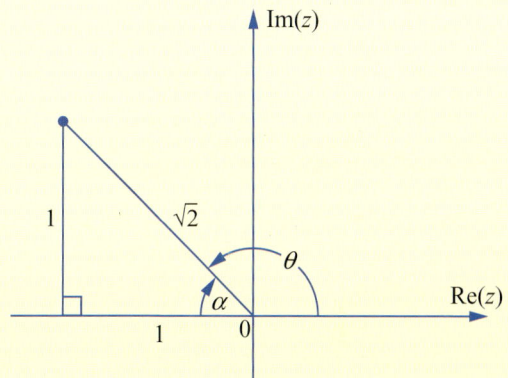

$\therefore (-1 + i) = \sqrt{2}(\cos 135° + i \sin 135°)$ (rectangular form to polar form)

2. $\therefore (-1 + i)^{10} = \left[\sqrt{2}(\cos 135° + i \sin 135°)\right]^{10}$ (raise both sides to the power of 10)

   $= (\sqrt{2})^{10}[\cos 10(135°) + i \sin 10(135°)]$ (apply De Moivre's theorem)

3. $= 32(\cos 1350° + i \sin 1350°)$ $\left((\sqrt{2})^{10} = (2^{\frac{1}{2}})^{10} = 2^5 = 32\right)$

   $= 32(\cos 270° + i \sin 270°)$

   $= 32(0 + i(-1))$

   $= 32(0 - i) = 0 - 32i$

$\therefore (-1 + i)^{10} = 0 - 32i$

Note: $\cos 1350° = \cos(1350° - 360° - 360° - 360°) = \cos 270° = 0$

$\sin 1350° = \sin(1350° - 360° - 360° - 360°) = \sin 270° = -1$

EXAMPLE 2

(i) Express $\cos 18° - i \sin 18°$ in the form $\cos \theta + i \sin \theta$.

(ii) Hence, evaluate $\dfrac{(\cos 36° + i \sin 36°)^2}{\cos 18° - i \sin 18°}$.

Solution:

(i) $\cos(-A) = \cos A$ and $\sin(-A) = -\sin A$

$\therefore \quad \cos 18° - i \sin 18°$

$\quad = \cos(-18°) - i \times -\sin(-18°)$ $\qquad\qquad$ $(-\sin(-18°) = \sin 18°)$

$\quad = \cos(-18°) + i \sin(-18°)$ $\qquad\qquad$ $(\cos \theta + i \sin \theta)$

(ii) $\dfrac{(\cos 36° + i \sin 36°)^2}{\cos 18° - i \sin 18°}$

$= \dfrac{(\cos 36° + i \sin 36°)^2}{\cos(-18°) + i \sin(-18°)}$

$= \dfrac{(\cos 36° + i \sin 36°)^2}{(\cos(-18°) + i \sin(-18°))^1}$ $\qquad\qquad$ $(x = x^1)$

$= (\cos 36° + i \sin 36°)^2 \, (\cos(-18°) + i \sin(-18°))^{-1}$ $\qquad$ $\left(\dfrac{1}{x^1} = x^{-1}\right)$

$= [\cos(2 \times 36°) + i \sin(2 \times 36°)][\cos(-1 \times -18°) + i \sin(-1 \times -18°)]$

$\qquad\qquad\qquad\qquad\qquad\qquad\qquad\qquad$ (using De Moivre's theorem)

$= (\cos 72° + i \sin 72°)(\cos 18° + i \sin 18°)$

$= \cos(72° + 18°) + i \sin(72° + 18°)$

$= \cos 90° + i \sin 90° = 0 + i(1) = 0 + i = i$

Exercise 2.10

In questions 1–9, use De Moivre's theorem to write each in the form $a + bi$ (rectangular form).

1. $\left(\cos \dfrac{\pi}{3} + i \sin \dfrac{\pi}{3}\right)^6$

2. $(\cos 36° + i \sin 36°)^5$

3. $\left(\cos \dfrac{\pi}{4} + i \sin \dfrac{\pi}{4}\right)^{10}$

4. $(\cos 15° + i \sin 15°)^{12}$

5. $\left[2\left(\cos \dfrac{\pi}{6} + i \sin \dfrac{\pi}{6}\right)\right]^6$

6. $\left[\sqrt{2}\left(\cos 45° + i \sin 45°\right)\right]^6$

7. $\left[2\left(\cos \dfrac{\pi}{3} + i \sin \dfrac{\pi}{3}\right)\right]^5$

8. $(\cos 22\cdot5° + i \sin 22\cdot5°)^8$

9. $\left[2\left(\cos \dfrac{\pi}{4} + i \sin \dfrac{\pi}{4}\right)\right]^5$

10. The complex number $z = \sqrt{3} + i$ is shown on the Argand diagram.

   (i) The polar coordinates of z are (r, θ).
      Find (a) r (b) θ.
   (ii) Write z in polar form.
   (iii) Evaluate z^3.

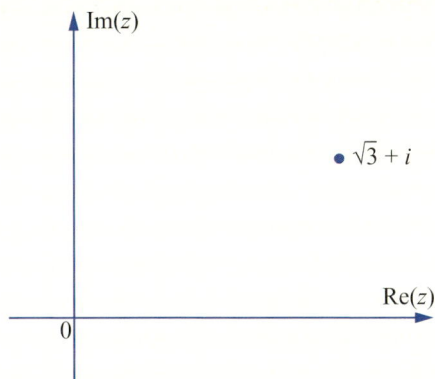

In questions 11–18, use De Moivre's theorem to write each in the form $x + yi$ (rectangular form).

11. $(1 + i)^8$

12. $(-1 + i)^4$

13. $(-\sqrt{3} - i)^3$

14. $(-2 - 2i)^5$

15. $(\sqrt{2} - \sqrt{2}i)^6$

16. $(2 - 2\sqrt{3}i)^4$

17. $\left(\dfrac{\sqrt{3}}{2} + \dfrac{1}{2}i\right)^9$

18. $\left(\dfrac{1}{2} - \dfrac{\sqrt{3}}{2}i\right)^{20}$

19. (i) Express $\dfrac{1 + 3i}{2 + i}$ in the form $r(\cos\theta + i\sin\theta)$, where $i^2 = -1$.

   (ii) Hence, evaluate $\left(\dfrac{1 + 3i}{2 + i}\right)^{10}$.

20. Let $z = \dfrac{5}{2 + i} - 1$, where $i^2 = -1$.

   (i) Express z in the form $a + bi$.
   (ii) Use De Moivre's theorem to evaluate z^6.

21. Let $z = -1 + i$.

   (i) Find the polar coordinates of z and hence express z in polar form.
   (ii) Use De Moivre's theorem to show that $z^5 + z^9 = 12z$.

22. $(2 + 3i)(a + ib) = -1 + 5i$. Express $a + ib$ in the form $r(\cos\theta + i\sin\theta)$ and hence or otherwise, calculate $(a + ib)^{11}$.

23. Use De Moivre's theorem to express $(-\sqrt{3} - i)^{10}$ in the form $2^n(1 - i\sqrt{k})$ where $n, k \in \mathbb{N}$.

24. Evaluate: (i) $\left(\dfrac{\sqrt{3} + i}{-1 + \sqrt{3}i}\right)^6$ (ii) $(-1 + i)^{-4}$

25. Let $z_1 = \cos\dfrac{\pi}{3} + i\sin\dfrac{\pi}{3}$ and $z_2 = \cos\dfrac{4\pi}{3} + i\sin\dfrac{4\pi}{3}$. Express $z_1^2\, z_2^4$ in the form $a + bi$.

26. Evaluate: (i) $\dfrac{\cos\dfrac{2\pi}{3} + i\sin\dfrac{2\pi}{3}}{\cos\dfrac{\pi}{3} - i\sin\dfrac{\pi}{3}}$ (ii) $\dfrac{(\cos 28° + i\sin 28°)(\cos 15° + i\sin 15°)}{(\cos 47° - i\sin 47°)}$

27. Let $w_1 = \cos \dfrac{\pi}{3} + i \sin \dfrac{\pi}{3}$ and $w_2 = \cos \dfrac{\pi}{6} - i \sin \dfrac{\pi}{6}$, where $i^2 = -1$.

   Use De Moivre's theorem to show that $\left(\dfrac{w_1}{w_2}\right)^4$ is real.

28. Express the following in the form $p + qi$, where $p, q \in \mathbb{R}$ and $i^2 = -1$.

   (i) $\left(\cos \dfrac{\pi}{3} + i \sin \dfrac{\pi}{3}\right)^2 \left(\cos \dfrac{\pi}{6} + i \sin \dfrac{\pi}{6}\right)$ **(ii)** $\dfrac{\left(\cos \frac{2\pi}{5} + i \sin \frac{2\pi}{5}\right)^8}{\left(\cos \frac{3\pi}{5} - i \sin \frac{3\pi}{5}\right)^3}$

29. $z = \dfrac{[\sqrt{3}\,(\cos\theta + i \sin\theta)]^4}{\cos 2\theta - i \sin 2\theta}$. Find **(i)** $|z|$ **(ii)** arg z.

30. Let $z = \log_2 2 - i\sqrt{\log_2 8}$. Evaluate z^3.

Proving trigonometric identities

De Moivre's theorem can be used to prove trigonometric identities by expressing cos $n\theta$ and sin $n\theta$ as polynomials in cos θ and sin θ, respectively.

EXAMPLE

Using De Moivre's theorem, prove that $\cos 3\theta = 4\cos^3\theta - 3\cos\theta$.

Solution:
De Moivre's theorem: $(\cos\theta + i \sin\theta)^n = \cos n\theta + i \sin n\theta$.
Therefore, by De Moivre's theorem:
$\cos 3\theta + i \sin 3\theta = (\cos\theta + i \sin\theta)^3$ (put in 3 for n on both sides)

$$= \binom{3}{0}\cos^3\theta + \binom{3}{1}\cos^2\theta(i\sin\theta) + \binom{3}{2}\cos\theta(i\sin\theta)^2 + \binom{3}{3}(i\sin\theta)^3$$

$$= \cos^3\theta + 3\cos^2\theta(i\sin\theta) + 3\cos\theta(i^2\sin^2\theta) + i^3\sin^3\theta$$

$\cos 3\theta + i \sin 3\theta = \cos^3\theta + i\,3\cos^2\theta\sin\theta - 3\cos\theta\sin^2\theta - i\sin^3\theta$ $(i^2 = -1,\ i^3 = -i)$

        R I R I R I

Equating the real parts:
$\cos 3\theta = \cos^3\theta - 3\cos\theta\sin^2\theta$
$\cos 3\theta = \cos^3\theta - 3\cos\theta(1 - \cos^2\theta)$ $(\sin^2\theta = 1 - \cos^2\theta)$
$\cos 3\theta = \cos^3\theta - 3\cos\theta + 3\cos^3\theta$
$\cos 3\theta = 4\cos^3\theta - 3\cos\theta$

Exercise 2.11

1. (i) Using De Moivre's theorem, prove that:

    (a) $\sin 2\theta = 2 \sin \theta \cos \theta$ (b) $\cos 2\theta = \cos^2 \theta - \sin^2 \theta$

    (ii) Hence, express $\tan 2\theta$ in terms of $\tan \theta$.

2. (i) Using De Moivre's theorem, prove that:

    (a) $\sin 3\theta = 3 \cos^2 \theta \sin \theta - \sin^3 \theta = 3 \sin \theta - 4 \sin^3 \theta$

    (b) $\cos 3\theta = \cos^3 \theta - 3 \cos \theta \sin^2 \theta = 4 \cos^3 \theta - 3 \cos \theta$

    (ii) Hence, express $\tan 3\theta$ in terms of $\tan \theta$.

3. (i) Using De Moivre's theorem, prove that:

    (a) $\cos 4\theta = 8 \cos^4 \theta - 8 \cos^2 \theta + 1$

    (b) $\sin 4\theta = 4 \cos^3 \theta \sin \theta - 4 \cos \theta \sin^3 \theta$

    (ii) Hence, express $\tan 4\theta$ in terms of $\tan \theta$.

4. Using De Moivre's theorem, prove that:

    (i) $\sin 5\theta = 16 \sin^5 \theta - 20 \sin^3 \theta + 5 \sin \theta$

    (ii) $\cos 5\theta = 16 \cos^5 \theta - 20 \cos^3 \theta + 5 \cos \theta$

5. (i) Prove by induction that $(\cos \theta + i \sin \theta)^n = \cos n\theta + i \sin n\theta$, for $n \in \mathbb{N}$ and $i^2 = -1$.

    (ii) Deduce that $(\cos \theta + i \sin \theta)^{-n} = \cos n\theta - i \sin n\theta$.

    (iii) If $z = \cos \theta + i \sin \theta$, show that $\dfrac{1}{z} = \cos \theta - i \sin \theta$.

    (Hint: $\cos(-A) = \cos A$ and $\sin(-A) = -\sin A$.)

    (iv) Show that:

    (a) $z^n + \dfrac{1}{z^n} = 2 \cos n\theta$ (b) $z^n - \dfrac{1}{z^n} = 2i \sin n\theta$

    (c) $z + \dfrac{1}{z} = 2 \cos \theta$ (d) $z - \dfrac{1}{z} = 2i \sin \theta$

    (e) By expanding $\left(z + \dfrac{1}{z} \right)^3$, show that $\cos^3 \theta = \dfrac{1}{4} \cos 3\theta + \dfrac{3}{4} \cos \theta$.

    (f) By expanding $\left(z - \dfrac{1}{z} \right)^4$, express $\sin^4 \theta$ in terms of $\cos 4\theta$ and $\cos 2\theta$.

Finding roots of complex numbers

From trigonometry, we know that:

$$\cos \theta = \cos(\theta + n(360°)) = \cos(\theta + 2n\pi), \text{ where } n \in \mathbb{Z}.$$
$$\sin \theta = \sin(\theta + n(360°)) = \sin(\theta + 2n\pi), \text{ where } n \in \mathbb{Z}.$$

That is, when 360°, 720°, 1080° or 2π, 4π, 6π is added to or subtracted from an angle θ, the value of $\cos\theta$ and $\sin\theta$ is unchanged. In other words, we can add any whole number of rotations to an angle or subtract any whole number of rotations from an angle without changing the value of sine or cosine.

Thus, we can write, for $n \in \mathbb{Z}$:

$$r(\cos\theta + i\sin\theta) = r[\cos(\theta + n(360°)) + i\sin\theta + n(360°)] = r[\cos(\theta + 2n\pi) + i\sin(\theta + 2n\pi)]$$

When a complex number is written in the form $r[\cos(\theta + n(360°)) + i\sin(\theta + n(360°))]$, the complex number is said to be written in **general polar form**.

Method for finding roots of a complex number

> 1. Write the number in polar form.
> 2. Write the number in general polar form.
> 3. Apply De Moivre's theorem.
> 4. Let $n = 0, 1, 2, \ldots$ (as required).

EXAMPLE 1

Use De Moivre's theorem to find the three roots of the equation $z^3 - 8i = 0$.

Solution:

$z^3 - 8i = 0$

$\quad z^3 = 8i$

$\quad z^3 = 0 + 8i$ (rectangular form)

1. Write $0 + 8i$ in polar form.

   $0 + 8i = (0, 8)$

   $r = 8$ and $\theta = 90°$

   Polar form: $0 + 8i = 8(\cos 90° + i\sin 90°)$

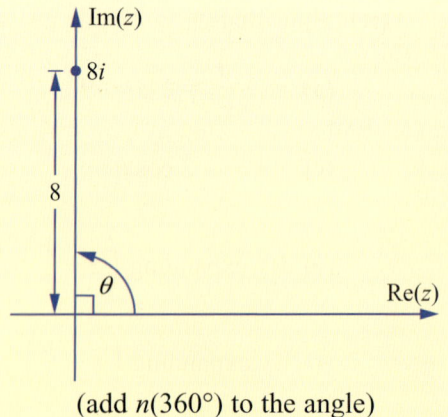

2. Write in general polar form.

   $8[\cos(90° + n(360°)) + i\sin(90° + n(360°))]$ (add $n(360°)$ to the angle)

3. Apply De Moivre's theorem.

   $z^3 = 0 + 8i$

   $z^3 = 8[\cos(90° + n(360°)) + i\sin(90° + n(360°))]$ (general polar form)

   $z = [8[\cos(90° + n(360°)) + i\sin(90° + n(360°))]]^{\frac{1}{3}}$ (take the cube root of both sides)

   $z = 8^{\frac{1}{3}}[\cos\frac{1}{3}(90° + n(360°)) + i\sin\frac{1}{3}(90° + n(360°))]$ (apply De Moivre's theorem)

   $z = 2[\cos(30° + n(120°)) + i\sin(30° + n(120°))]$

4. Let $n = 0$, 1 and 2 to get the three different roots.

$n = 0$: $z = 2(\cos 30° + i \sin 30°) = 2\left(\dfrac{\sqrt{3}}{2} + \dfrac{1}{2}i\right) = \sqrt{3} + i$

$n = 1$: $z = 2(\cos 150° + i \sin 150°) = 2\left(-\dfrac{\sqrt{3}}{2} + \dfrac{1}{2}i\right) = -\sqrt{3} + i$

$n = 2$: $z = 2(\cos 270° + i \sin 270°) = 2(0 - i) = -2i$

(**Note:** Letting $n = 3, 4, 5, \ldots$ merely regenerates the same roots.)

The diagram shows the position of the three roots. Notice that the three roots lie on a circle with centre at the origin and radius 2. Its equation is $x^2 + y^2 = 4$. The points $(\sqrt{3}, 1)$, $(-\sqrt{3}, 1)$ and $(0, -2)$ all satisfy the equation $x^2 + y^2 = 4$. Each root is equally spaced on the circle.

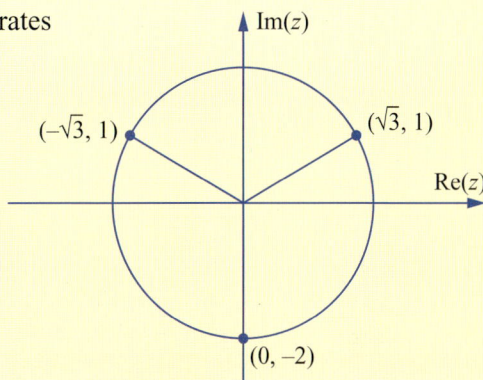

Notes: 1. The same method is used if the index is a rational number (fraction). For example, $(1 - \sqrt{3}i)^{\frac{3}{2}}$.

2. The number of different roots is the same as the bottom number in the fraction. Thus, $(1 - \sqrt{3}i)^{\frac{3}{2}}$ will have two different roots.

EXAMPLE 2

Express $-\dfrac{1}{2} + \dfrac{\sqrt{3}}{2}i$ in the form $r(\cos \theta + i \sin \theta)$ where $i^2 = -1$.

Using De Moivre's theorem, find two values of $\left(-\dfrac{1}{2} + \dfrac{\sqrt{3}}{2}i\right)^{\frac{3}{2}}$.

Solution:

1. Write $\left(-\dfrac{1}{2} + \dfrac{\sqrt{3}}{2}i\right)$ in polar form.

$-\dfrac{1}{2} + \dfrac{\sqrt{3}}{2}i = \left(-\dfrac{1}{2}, \dfrac{\sqrt{3}}{2}\right)$

$r = \left|-\dfrac{1}{2} + \dfrac{\sqrt{3}}{2}i\right|$

$= \sqrt{\left(-\dfrac{1}{2}\right)^2 + \left(\dfrac{\sqrt{3}}{2}\right)^2} = \sqrt{\dfrac{1}{4} + \dfrac{3}{4}} = \sqrt{1} = 1$

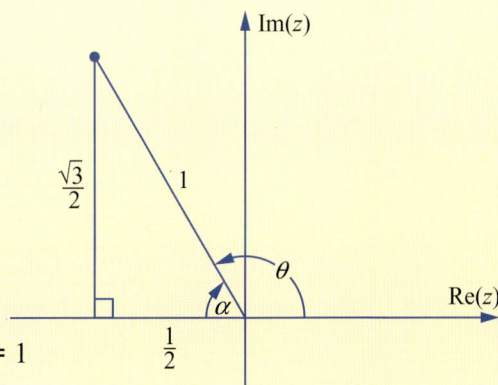

$$\tan \alpha = \frac{\frac{\sqrt{3}}{2}}{\frac{1}{2}} = \sqrt{3}, \qquad \alpha = \tan^{-1}\sqrt{3} = 60°$$

$$\therefore \theta = 180° - 60° = 120°$$

$$\therefore -\frac{1}{2} + \frac{\sqrt{3}}{2}i = 1(\cos 120° + i \sin 120°) = \cos 120° + i \sin 120°$$

2. Write in general polar form.
$$\cos(120° + n(360°)) + i \sin(120° + n(360°)) \qquad \text{(add } n(360°) \text{ to the angle)}$$

3. Apply De Moivre's theorem:

$$-\frac{1}{2} + \frac{\sqrt{3}}{2}i = \cos(120° + n(360°)) + i \sin(120° + n(360°)) \qquad \text{(general polar form)}$$

$$\left(-\frac{1}{2} + \frac{\sqrt{3}}{2}\right)^{\frac{3}{2}} = [\cos(120° + n(360°)) + i \sin(120° + n(360°))]^{\frac{3}{2}} \qquad \left(\begin{array}{c}\text{raise both sides to}\\ \text{the power of } \frac{3}{2}\end{array}\right)$$

$$= [\cos\tfrac{3}{2}(120° + n(360°)) + i \sin\tfrac{3}{2}(120° + n(360°))] \qquad \text{(apply De Moivre's}$$

$$= [\cos(180° + n(540°)) + i \sin(180° + n(540°))] \qquad \text{theorem)}$$

4. Let $n = 0$ and 1 to find the two roots.
$n = 0$: $\cos 180° + i \sin 180° = -1 + i(0) = -1$
$n = 1$: $\cos 720° + i \sin 720° = 1 + i(0) = 1$

(**Note:** Letting $n = 2, 3, 4, \ldots$ merely regenerates the same roots.)

Exercise 2.12

1. (i) Express $-2i$ in the form $r(\cos \theta + i \sin \theta)$, where $i^2 = -1$.
   (ii) Use De Moivre's theorem to find the two roots of the equation $z^2 = -2i$.
   (iii) If the roots are α and β, show that $\alpha + \beta = 0$.

2. (i) Express $z = 1$ in the form $(\cos \theta + i \sin \theta)$.
   (ii) Use De Moivre's theorem to find the four roots of the equation $z^4 - 1 = 0$.
   (iii) If $1, z_1, z_2$ and z_3 are the roots of the equation $z^4 - 1 = 0$, evaluate $(1 - z_1)(1 - z_2)(1 - z_3)$.

3. (i) Express $-8i$ in the form $r(\cos \theta + i \sin \theta)$, where $i^2 = -1$.
   (ii) Use De Moivre's theorem to find the three roots of the equation $z^3 + 8i = 0$.
   (iii) Hence, write down the three roots of the equation $(z - i)^3 = -8i$.

4. **(i)** Express $-64i$ in the form **(a)** $r(\cos\theta + i\sin\theta)$
   (b) $r(\cos(\theta + n(360°)) + i\sin(\theta + n(360°)))$.

   (ii) Use De Moivre's theorem to find the three roots of the equation $z^3 + 64i = 0$.

   (iii) If the three roots are z_1, z_2 and z_3, evaluate $\sum\limits_{r=1}^{3} z_r$.

   (iv) Represent the three roots on an Argand diagram.

5. **(i)** Express $2 - 2\sqrt{3}i$ in the form $r(\cos\theta + i\sin\theta)$.
   (ii) Hence, use De Moivre's theorem to find the two roots of the equation $z^2 - 2 + 2\sqrt{3}i = 0$.

6. **(i)** Express $-8 - 8\sqrt{3}i$ in the form $r(\cos\theta + i\sin\theta)$.
   (ii) Hence, find $(-8 - 8\sqrt{3}i)^3$.
   (iii) Find the four complex numbers z such that $z^4 = -8 - 8\sqrt{3}i$.

   Give your answers in the form $a + bi$, with a and b fully evaluated.

   (iv) When plotted on an Argand diagram, the four complex numbers lie on a curve. Find the equation of this curve.

   (v) Draw this curve and plot the four complex numbers on the curve.

   (vi) Label the four complex numbers, in cyclic order, z_1, z_2, z_3 and z_4. Name the shape $z_1 z_2 z_3 z_4$.

7. Use De Moivre's theorem to find the six roots of the equation $z^6 + 64 = 0$.

8. **(i)** Use De Moivre's theorem to find, in polar form, the five roots of the equation $z^5 = 1$.
   (ii) Choose one of the roots w, where $w \neq 1$. Prove that $w^2 + w^3$ is real.

   (iii) If 1, w_1, w_2, w_3 and w_4 are the roots of $z^5 = 1$, calculate $\sum\limits_{n=0}^{4}\left(\cos\dfrac{2n\pi}{5} + i\sin\dfrac{2n\pi}{5}\right)$.

9. **(i)** Write $\dfrac{1}{2} - \dfrac{\sqrt{3}}{2}i$ in the form $r(\cos\theta + i\sin\theta)$, where $i^2 = -1$.

   (ii) Using De Moivre's theorem, find the two values of $\left(\dfrac{1}{2} - \dfrac{\sqrt{3}}{2}i\right)^{\frac{3}{2}}$.

10. **(i)** Write $2(-1 + \sqrt{3}i)$ in the form $r(\cos\theta + i\sin\theta)$, where $i^2 = -1$.
    (ii) Using De Moivre's theorem, find the two values of $[2(-1 + \sqrt{3}i)]^{\frac{3}{2}}$.

11. **(i)** Write $4i$ in the form $r(\cos\theta + i\sin\theta)$, where $i^2 = -1$.
    (ii) Using De Moivre's theorem, find the two values of $(4i)^{\frac{5}{2}}$.

12. **(i)** Express -27 in the form $r(\cos\theta + i\sin\theta)$, where $i^2 = -1$.

    (ii) Use De Moivre's theorem to find the three roots of the equation $z^3 + 27 = 0$.

    (iii) When plotted on an Argand diagram, the three roots lie on a curve. Find the equation of this curve.

    (iv) Draw this curve and plot the three roots on the curve.

    (v) Verify that the three roots form an equilateral triangle.

13. The complex number z has modulus $5\frac{1}{16}$ and argument $\dfrac{4\pi}{9}$. Find in polar form, the four

complex fourth roots of z. (That is, find the four values of w for which $w^4 = z$.)

14. **(i)** Use De Moivre's theorem to find the three roots of the equation $z^3 - 1 = 0$.

   (ii) If w is one of the non-real roots, show that the roots can be written $1, w, w^2$.

   (iii) Show that:

   (a) $1 + w + w^2 = 0$ **(b)** $w^3 = 1$ **(c)** $(1 - w + w^2)(1 + w - w^2) = 4$
   (d) $(1 + w^2)^6 = 1$

   (iv) Evaluate: **(a)** $(1 + w)^6$ **(b)** $(1 - w - w^2)^5$

   (v) If $x = a + b$, $y = aw + bw^2$ and $z = aw^2 + bw^4$, show that $x^2 + y^2 + z^2 = 6ab$.

15. The complex number z is such that $z = (1 + 3i)(a + bi)$.

   If the polar form of z is $10\sqrt{2}\left(\cos \dfrac{\pi}{4} + i \sin \dfrac{\pi}{4} \right)$, find the values of a and b.

Further geometrical properties of complex numbers

Rotations

A **rotation** turns a point through an angle about a fixed point.

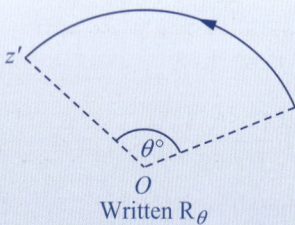

An **anticlockwise** turn is described as a **positive rotation**.	A **clockwise** turn is described as a **negative rotation**.
z' $\theta°$ O Written R_θ	u u' $\theta°$ O Written $R_{-\theta}$

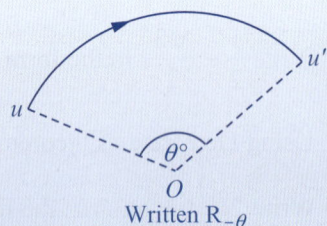

Successive multiplication by i on an Argand diagram:

Multiplication by i rotates a complex number by $+90°$ ($R_{90°}$).

Multiplication by i^2 rotates a complex number by $+180°$ ($R_{180°}$).

Multiplication by i^3 rotates a complex number by $+270°$ ($R_{270°}$).

Multiplication by i^4 rotates a complex number by $+360°$ ($R_{360°}$).

All these rotations are about the origin. Multiplication by i^{-1}, i^{-2}, i^{-3} and i^{-4} results in a clockwise (negative) rotation.

Note: $i^{-1} = -i$, $i^{-2} = -i^2$, $i^{-3} = -i^3$ and $i^{-4} = -i^4$.

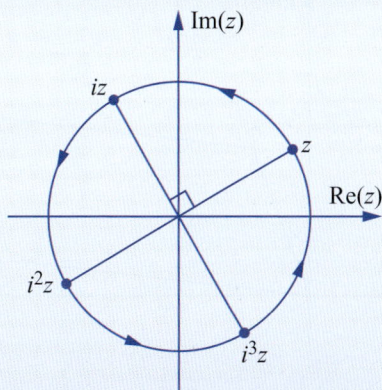

$$z = i^4z = i^8z = i^{12}z = \dots$$
$$iz = i^5z = i^9z = i^{13}z = \dots$$
$$i^2z = i^6z = i^{10}z = i^{14}z = \dots$$
$$i^3z = i^7z = i^{11}z = i^{15}z = \dots$$

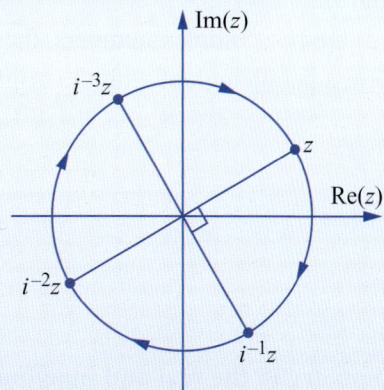

$$z = i^{-4}z = i^{-8}z = i^{-12}z = \dots$$
$$i^{-1}z = i^{-5}z = i^{-9}z = i^{-13}z = \dots$$
$$i^{-2}z = i^{-6}z = i^{-10}z = i^{-14}z = \dots$$
$$i^{-3}z = i^{-7}z = i^{-11}z = i^{-15}z = \dots$$

Dilations

If a complex number is multiplied by k, where $k \in \mathbb{R}$ (a real number), then its modulus (distance from the origin) will be multiplied by k. This is called a dilation (enlargement) and is a dilation of factor k about the origin. In other words, if a complex number is multiplied by 3 (dilation by a factor of 3), then its distance from the origin will be three times as far from the origin as the original complex number. If a complex number is multiplied by $\frac{1}{2}$ (dilation by a factor of $\frac{1}{2}$), then its distance from the origin will be half the distance from the origin as the original complex number. If $k < 0$, then the original complex number will also undergo a central symmetry in the origin (a rotation of 180°).

If a complex number is multiplied by ki, where $k \in \mathbb{R}$, its modulus (distance from the origin) will be multiplied by k **and** it will also be rotated by 90°. This is called a composition of a dilation and a rotation. In other words, if a complex number is multiplied by $2i$, then its distance from the origin will be twice the distance from the origin as the original complex number **and** also rotated by 90°. If a complex number is multiplied by $\frac{1}{3}i$, then its distance from the origin will be one-third the distance from the origin as the original complex number **and** also rotated by 90°.

If a non-zero complex number, z_1, is multiplied by another non-zero complex number, z_2, the result is a composition of a dilation and a rotation. This leads to:

1. Dilation (enlargement) by a factor of $|z_2|$ about the origin.
2. A rotation of $\arg(z_2)$ about the origin.

Parallelogram

If z_1 and z_2 are two complex numbers, then z_1, z_2 and $z_1 + z_2$ form a parallelogram with the origin.

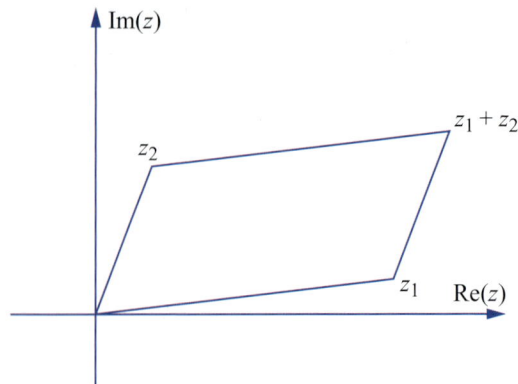

Axial symmetry in the real and imaginary axis

Let $z = a + bi$ be a complex number.

(i) Under an axial symmetry in the real axis, $a + bi$ is mapped onto $a - bi$. In other words, change the sign of the imaginary part (z is mapped onto $\bar{z}$).

(ii) Under an axial symmetry in the imaginary axis, $a + bi$ is mapped onto $-a + bi$. In other words, change the sign of the real part.

Using De Moivre's theorem for repeated multiplication

If $z = r(\cos\theta + i\sin\theta)$, then $z^n = r^n(\cos n\theta + i\sin n\theta)$.

If $|z| > 1$, then when a complex number is repeatedly multiplied by itself, it will spiral outwards (from the origin).

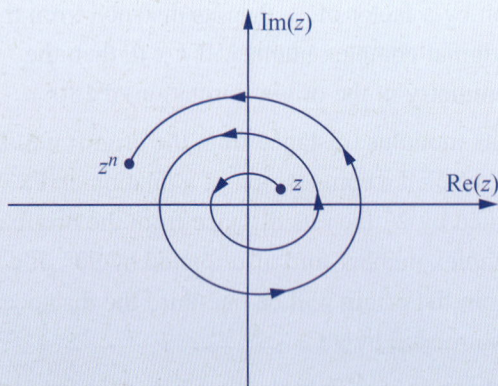

If $|z| < 1$, then when a complex number is repeatedly multiplied by itself, it will spiral inwards (towards the origin).

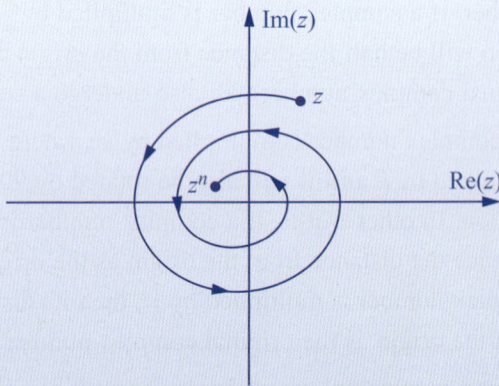

Note: If $|z| = 1$, then when a complex is repeatedly multiplied by itself, it will always stay on a circle of radius 1.

EXAMPLE

A complex number, z, has a modulus greater than 1.
The three numbers z, z^2 and z^3 are shown on the
Argand diagram. One of them lies on the imaginary
axis, as shown.

(i) Label the points on the diagram to show which
point corresponds to which number.
(ii) Find θ_1, the argument of z, and θ_2, the argument
of z^2.

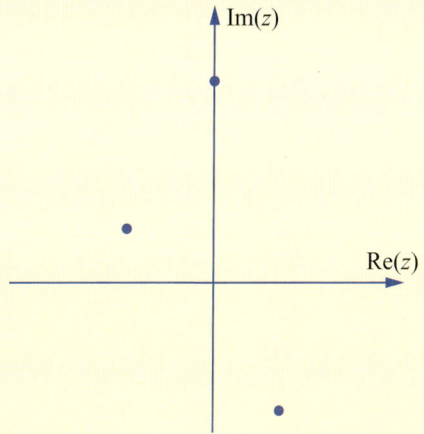

Solution:

(i) Given that the modulus of z is greater than 1.
Thus, as we repeatedly multiply z by itself, it
spirals away from the origin. This means
that:

z is nearest to the origin,
z^2 is further from the origin than z
and z^3 is furthest from the origin.

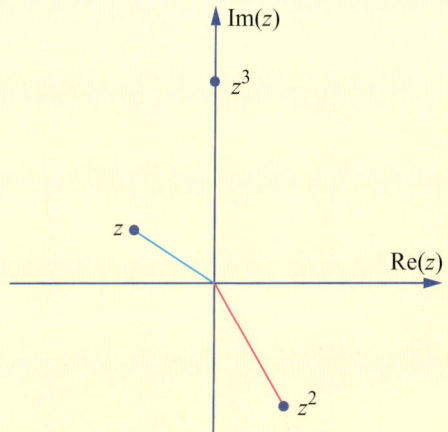

(ii) z^3 is z multiplied by itself three times and is
on the imaginary axis.
Remember:
$[r(\cos\theta + i\sin\theta)]^n = r^n(\cos n\theta + i\sin n\theta)$
Therefore, z^3 has argument:
$\theta_3 = 3\theta_1 = 90° + n(360°)$
$\theta_1 = 30° + n(120°)$
z is in the second quadrant.

$\therefore \theta_1 = 150°$ or $\dfrac{5\pi}{6}$

$\theta_2 = 2(150°) = 300°$ or $\dfrac{5\pi}{3}$

$\left(\text{Alternatively, } \theta_2 = -60° \text{ or } -\dfrac{\pi}{3}.\right)$

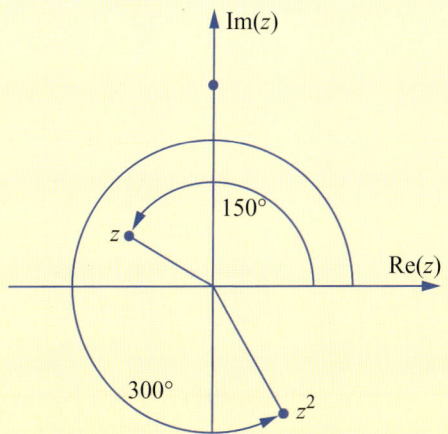

Exercise 2.13

1. $z = 3 + 4i$. Investigate whether $|z| = |iz|$. Give a geometrical interpretation for your answer.

2. $z = 2 + i$ and $u = -4 + 3i$.

   (i) On the Argand diagram, plot:

       (a) z, iz, i^2z and i^3z

       (b) u, iu, i^2u and i^3u

   (ii) Describe the position of i^4z.

   (iii) Describe a transformation, which is not a rotation, that maps iz onto i^3z.

   (iv) Name the image of u under a central symmetry in iz.

   (v) Explain why iz and i^5z can be represented by the same point on the Argand diagram.

   (vi) $w = 2iu$. Give a geometrical interpretation of how to find the position of w on the Argand diagram.

   (vii) Using the diagram, explain why $|u| > |z|$.

3. (i) Let $z = 7 + i$, $w = 3 - i$, $u = z - w$ and $v = \dfrac{z}{w}$.

   Express u and v in the form $a + bi$ and plot u and v on an Argand diagram.

   (ii) $u = kv$, where $k \in \mathbb{N}$. Find the value of k.

   (iii) $v = lu$, where $l \in \mathbb{Q}$. Find the value of l.

   (iv) On your Argand diagram, plot $2i^3v$ and $-iv$. Comment on the position of $2i^3v$ and $-iv$.

4. (i) $w = 3 - 2i$. On an Argand diagram, plot w, $-iw$, $-i^2w$, $-i^3w$ and $-i^4w$.

   (ii) Explain why w and i^4w have the same position on the Argand diagram.

   (iii) Is $i^2w = -i^2w$? Justify your answer.

   (iv) $u = 3iw$. Give a geometrical interpretation of u.

5. $z_1 = -1 + 10i$, $z_2 = 3 + 2i$ and $z_3 = 4$ are three complex numbers.

   (i) Are z_1, z_2 and z_3 collinear? Justify your answer.

   (ii) Find a complex number z_4 which is collinear with z_1, z_2 and z_3.

6. (i) Let $z = 2 + i$ and $w = -1 - 3i$.
   Plot z and w on the Argand diagram.

   (ii) Verify that $|w - z| = 5$.

   (iii) Draw the set k of all complex numbers such that each is a distance of 5 from z.

   (iv) What geometrical figure is represented by k?

   (v) Let $u = -2 + 4i$. Investigate whether $u \in k$.

   (vi) Write the image of w under a central symmetry in z in the form $a + bi$.

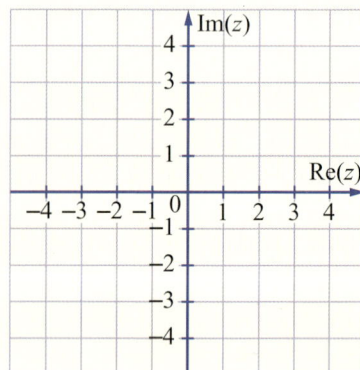

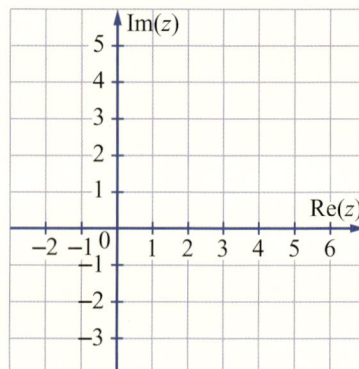

7. **(i)** z is the complex number $1 + i$, where $i^2 = -1$. Find z^2 and z^3.

   (ii) Verify that $z^4 = -4$.   **(iii)** Show z, z^2, z^3 and z^4 on the Argand diagram.

   (iv) Make one observation about the pattern of points on the diagram.

   (v) Using the value of z^4 or otherwise, find the values of z^8, z^{12} and z^{16}.

   (vi) Based on the pattern of values in part **(v)** or otherwise, state whether z^{40} is positive or negative. Explain how you got your answer.

   (vii) Write z^{40} as a power of 2. **(viii)** Find z^{41}.

   (ix) On an Argand diagram, how far from the origin is z^{41}?

8. **(i)** $z_1 = 3 + 4i$. Write down   **(a)** $\text{Re}(z_1)$ **(b)** $\text{Im}(z_1)$.

   (ii) John thinks $\text{Im}(z_1)$ is an imaginary number. Mary thinks $\text{Im}(z_1)$ is a real number.

   (a) Who is correct?   **(b)** Justify your answer.

   (iii) z_2 is a complex number where $z_2 = \text{Im}(z_1)$. Plot z_2 on an Argand diagram.

9. Five complex numbers, z_1, z_2, z_3, z_4 and z_5, are shown on the Argand diagram where the same scale is used on both axes. They satisfy the following conditions:

   $z_2 = 3z_1$ $z_3 = \bar{z}_1$

   $z_4 = iz_2$ $z_5 = z_1 + z_3$

   Identify each number on the diagram.

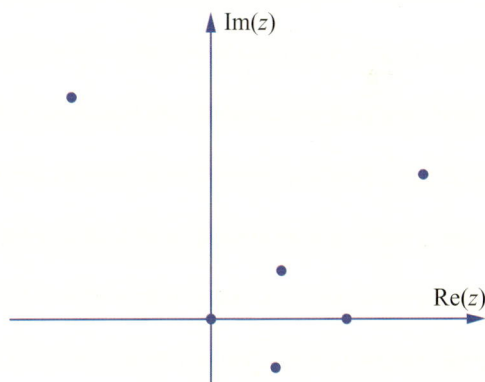

10. Six complex numbers z_1, z_2, z_3, z_4, z_5 and z_6, are shown on the Argand diagram where the same scale is used on both axes. They satisfy the following conditions:

   $z_2 = -2z_1$ $\text{Re}(z_3) = \text{Re}(z_2)$

   $\text{Im}(z_4) = \text{Im}(z_2)$ $z_5 = z_2 + z_4$

   $z_6 = \text{Im}(z_4)$

   Identify each number on the diagram.

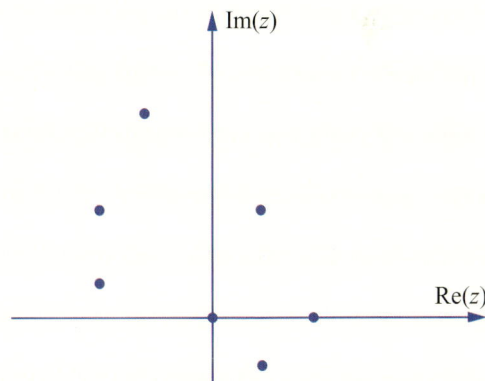

11. Four complex numbers, z_1, z_2, z_3 and z_4, are shown on the Argand diagram where the same scale is used on both axes. They satisfy the following conditions:

$z_2 = iz_1$

$z_3 = kz_1$, where $k \in \mathbb{R}$

$z_4 = z_2 + z_3$

   (i) Identify each number on the diagram.

   (ii) Write down the approximate value of k.

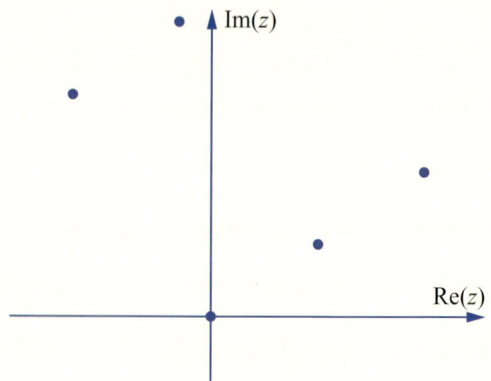

12. Three complex numbers, z, z^2 and z^3, are shown on the Argand diagram where the same scale is used on both axes. They satisfy the following conditions:

$|z| > 1$

   One of them lies on the real axis.

   (i) Identify each number on the diagram.

   (ii) Find θ_1, the argument of z, θ_2, the argument of z^2, and θ_3, the argument of z^3.

   (iii) If $|z| = 2$, express z, z^2 and z^3 in the form $a + bi$.

   (iv) If $z^4 = kz$, find the value of k.

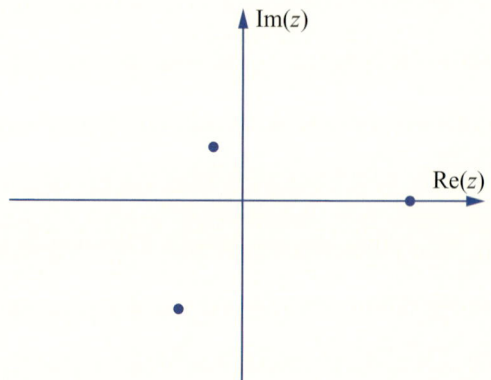

13. Four complex numbers, z, u, v and w, are shown on the Argand diagram where the same scale is used on both axes.

   (i) u, v and w and the origin are collinear. What does this mean?

   (ii) If $v = z^2$, find $|z|$.

   (iii) If $|z| < 1$, identify the point z^2. Justify your answer.

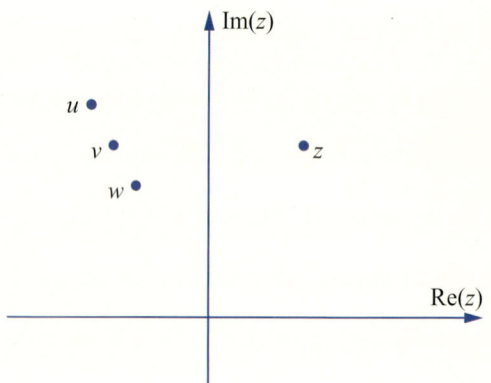

14. The diagram shows the complex numbers z_n, where $0 \leq n \leq 7$ and $n \in \mathbb{Z}$.

The transformation $z_n \rightarrow z_{n+1}$ is a positive rotation of $\dfrac{\pi}{4}$ radians.

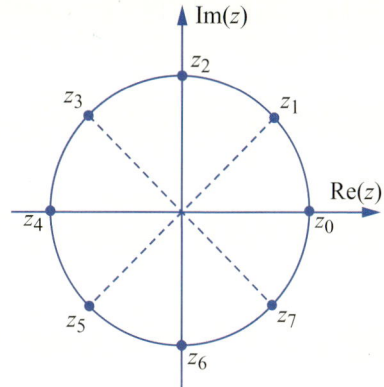

   (i) Write down **(a)** arg (z_3) **(b)** arg (z_7)
   (ii) If $|z_0| = 1$, express in the form $a + bi$
      (a) z_2 **(b)** z_4 **(c)** z_1 **(d)** z_5
   (iii) Verify that arg (z_1) + arg (z_5) = arg $(z_1 z_5)$
   (iv) Express in polar form **(a)** z_0 **(b)** z_1 **(c)** z_2 **(d)** z_3
   (v) Express z_n in polar form and, hence, verify your answers to part (ii).
   (vi) Evaluate $\displaystyle\sum_{n=0}^{7} z_n$.
   (vii) If $z_7 = z_n$, where $n \in \mathbb{N}$ and $n \neq 7$. Write down the minimum value of n. Justify your answer.

15. The complex number $z = x + yi$ satisfies the equation $|z| = |z + 2|$.
   (i) Show that the real part of z is -1.
   (ii) The complex number z also satisfies $|z| = 2$. Find the two possible values of the imaginary part of z. Plot these two possible complex numbers z_1 and z_2, on an Argand diagram.
   (iii) Write these two values of z in polar form. **(iv)** Hence, evaluate $z_1 z_2$.
   (v) Find the minimum value of $n \in \mathbb{N}$ for which $z_1{}^n = z_2{}^n$. Justify your answer.

16. Let $z = x + yi$, where $x, y \in \mathbb{R}$ and $i^2 = -1$. Indicate by shading on an Argand diagram the set of points where $1 \leq |z| \leq 2$.

17. Let $z = a + bi$, where $a, b \in \mathbb{R}$ and $i^2 = -1$.
   (i) If z is real, find arg (z). **(ii)** If z is purely imaginary, find arg (z).

18. Let $z = p + qi$, where $p, q \in \mathbb{R}$ and $i^2 = -1$.
   If $|z| = \sqrt{2}$ and arg $(z) = \dfrac{3\pi}{4}$, find the values of p and q.

19. Let $z = x + yi$, where $x, y \in \mathbb{R}$ and $i^2 = -1$.
   (i) Find the locus of the set of points $z \in \mathbb{C}$ such that arg $(z) = \dfrac{\pi}{4}$.
   (ii) If arg $(z) = \dfrac{\pi}{6}$, express x in terms of y.
   (iii) Find the set of points $z \in \mathbb{C}$ such that $|z - 2| = 4$.

20. Let $z = x + yi$, where $x, y \in \mathbb{R}$ and $i^2 = -1$.
   (i) Show on an Argand diagram the set of points such that $|z - 1 - 4i| = |z - 5|$.
   (ii) Let $f(z) = \frac{1}{2}(z + \bar{z}) + \frac{1}{2} i(z - \bar{z})$. Find $f(z)$ and explain the result.
   (iii) Find **(a)** $f(3 - 4i)$ **(b)** $f(5 + 2i)$.

Statistics deal with the collection, presentation, analysis and interpretation of data. Insurance (of people and property), which now dominates many aspects of our lives, utilises statistical methodology. Social scientists, psychologists, pollsters, medical researchers, governments and many others use statistical methodology to study behaviours of populations.

You need to know the following statistical terms.

A **variable** is a characteristic of interest in each element of the sample or population. For example, we may be interested in the age of each of the seven dwarfs.

An **observation** is the value of a variable for one particular element of the sample or population, for example the age of the dwarf called Bashful (= 619 years).

A **data set** is all the observations of a particular variable for the elements of the sample, for example a complete list of the ages of the seven dwarfs {685, 702, 498, 539, 402, 685, 619}.

Collecting data

Census

The **population** is the complete set of data under consideration. For example, a population may be all the females in Ireland between the ages of 12 and 18, all the sixth year students in your school or the number of red cars in Ireland. A **census** is a collection of data relating to a population. A list of every item in a population is called a **sampling frame**.

Sample

A **sample** is a small part of the population selected. A **random sample** is a sample in which every member of the population has an equal chance of being selected. Data gathered from a sample are called **statistics**. Conclusions drawn from a sample can then be applied to the whole population (this is called **statistical inference**). However, it is very important that the sample chosen is representative of that population to avoid bias.

Bias

Bias (unfairness) is anything that distorts the data so that they will not give a representative sample. Bias can occur in sampling due to:

1. Failing to identify the correct population.
2. A sample size that is too small or using a sample that is not representative.
3. Careless or dishonest answers to questions.
4. Using questions that are misleading or ambiguous.
5. Failure to respond to a survey.
6. Errors in recording the data, for example recording 23 as 32.
7. The data can go out of date, for example conclusions drawn from an opinion poll can change over a period of time.

Reasons for using samples:

1. They are fast and cheap.
2. It is essential when the sampling units are destroyed (called destructive sampling). For example, we cannot test the lifetimes of every light bulb manufactured until they fail.
3. Quality of information gained is more manageable and better controlled, leading to better accuracy. (More time and money can be spent on the sample.)
4. It is often very difficult to gather data on a whole population.

Sample survey

A survey collects data (information). A **sample survey** is a survey that collects data from a sample of the population, usually using a questionnaire. Questionnaires are well-designed forms that are used to conduct sample surveys.

The main survey methods are:

- **Personal interview:** People are asked questions directly. This is regularly used in market research.
- **Telephone survey:** Often used for a personal interview.
- **Postal survey:** A survey is sent to someone's address.
- **Online questionnaires:** People fill out the questionnaire online.

Advantages and disadvantages of surveys are as follows.

Method	Advantages	Disadvantages
Personal interview (face to face)	• High response rate. • Can ask many questions. • Can ask more personal questions.	• Can be expensive. • Interviewer can influence response.
Telephone survey	• High response rate. • Can ask many questions. • Can ask more personal questions.	• Can be expensive. • Interviewer can influence response. • Easier to tell lies.
Postal survey	• Relatively cheap. • Can ask many questions. • Can ask more personal questions.	• Poor response rate. • Partly completed. • Limited in the type of data collected. • No way of clarifying any questions.
Online questionnaires	• Cheap and fast to collect large volumes of data. • More flexible design. • Ease of editing. • Can be sent directly to a database such as Microsoft Excel. • No interviewer bias. • Anonymity. • No geographical problems.	• Limited to those with access to an online computer. This leads to sample bias. • Technical problems (crashes, freezes). • Protecting privacy is an ethical issue.

Other methods for collecting data

Experiment
An **experiment** is a **controlled study** in which the researcher understands cause-and-effect relationships. The study is controlled. This method of collecting data is very popular with drug companies testing a new drug.

Observational studies
Data obtained by making observations are called **observational studies**. The data are collected by counting, measuring or noting things that happen. For example, a traffic survey might be done in this way to reveal the number of vehicles passing over a bridge. Important factors are place, time of day and the amount of time spent collecting the data. Observational studies can be laborious and time consuming.

Designed experiments
Data obtained by an experiment are called **designed experiments**. The data are collected by counting or measuring, e.g. throwing a die or tossing two coins a number of times and recording the results. The

key things to remember are that the experiment must be repeated a number of times and that the experiment must be capable of being repeated by other people. **Data capture** is the process by which data are transferred from a paper copy, e.g. a questionnaire, to an electronic file, usually on a computer. Also, in an experiment, we can measure the effects, if any, that result from changes in the situation.

Descriptive statistics is the use of graphs, charts, tables, various measurements and calculations to organise and summarise information (data). It attempts to focus our information and reduce it to a manageable size.

Inferential statistics is when a portion or a sample of a population is studied and conclusions are reached about the entire population. The table below gives examples of sampling a particular population and how it might be carried out.

Population	Sample
30 million actual voters in a UK general election	An exit poll of 16,500 actual voters who were asked who they voted for.
All owners of dogs	A telephone survey of 1,000 dog owners.
All prison inmates	A criminal justice study of 200 prison inmates.
The CEOs of all private companies	Results from surveys sent to 120 CEOs of private companies.
Legal aliens living in Ireland	A sociological study conducted by a university researcher of 250 legal aliens.
Adult children of drug addicts	A psychological study of 75 such individuals.

In our course, we consider:

Quantitative data	Qualitative data
Which can be counted or measured	Which cannot be measured

We divide quantitative data into	We divide qualitative data into
(i) Discrete data	**(i)** Categorical data
(ii) Continuous data	**(ii)** Ordinal data

Quantitative data

Discrete and continuous data

Data which can only have certain individual values are called **discrete data**. Discrete variables usually result from counting.

Discrete variable	Possible values for the variable
Number of students in a class of 30 with blood type A	0, 1, 2 30
The number of times a coin is tossed before a tail appears	1, 2, 3 .... This has no upper limit since a tail might never appear!

Data which are measured on some scale and can take any value on that scale are called **continuous data**. A continuous variable usually results from making a measurement of some type.

Continuous variable	Possible values for the variable
The amount of time (t) in hours spent on one day by certain individuals on Facebook	All real numbers between 0 and 24 inclusive, i.e. $0 \leq t \leq 24$, where $t \in \mathbb{R}$.
The heights for those individuals having heights equal to or greater than 178 cm	All real numbers between 178 and W where W is the tallest height of all such individuals.

Qualitative data

Categorical and ordinal data

Data which fit into a group or category are called **categorical data**. If the categories have an obvious order, the data are said to be **ordinal**.

Categorical variable	Possible ordinal level data values associated with the variable
Restaurant service	Poor, good, excellent.
Pain level	None, low, moderate, severe.
County of residence	Wicklow, Dublin, Cork, Sligo, etc. No ordinal values in this case.
Blood type	O, A, B, AB No ordinal values here.

> ### EXAMPLE
>
> A class test in English poetry consists of 20 questions. The resulting score reflects the work rate and aptitude in English poetry of the test candidate.
>
> How could the score be reported?
>
> What are the possible values for the scores?
>
> Describe the variable in terms of discrete, continuous, categorical, ordinal.
>
> **Solution:**
>
> This is an interesting question and solution. It illustrates different answers, yet all are correct. It shows how important it is for the examination candidate to be creative.
>
> The score reported would likely be the number or percentage of correct answers. In other words, the number of correct answers would give a whole number score from 0 to 20, presuming equal credit per question (0 incorrect, 1 correct). Similarly, the percentage correct would yield a score from 0 to 100 in steps of five. Here the scores would be discrete. The position is complicated if each question does not have equal credit.
>
> However, if the teacher considered not only the answer but the reasoning process used to arrive at the answers and assigned partial credit for each problem, the score could be any real number between 0 and 20 or any real number between 0 and 100 per cent continuously, i.e. the data would be continuous.
>
> Alternatively, the teacher might allocate a grade of A, B, C, D, E, F and NG to each candidate based on a scale deemed suitable at the time. In this case, the data would be ordinal.

Univariate data

When **one item** of information is collected from each member of a group, the data collected are called **univariate data**.

Examples of univariate data include:

(i) Height in centimetres.

(ii) Eye colour.

(iii) Number of siblings.

Bivariate data

When **two items** of information are collected, e.g. a person's height and weight, this is called **bivariate data** (or paired data).

Examples of bivariate data include:

(i) Starting salary and years of education.

(ii) Hair colour and gender.

(iii) The amount of milk and number of eggs required to make scrambled eggs.

(iv) The number of people in a house and the number of rooms in a house.

Notes:

Example **(i)** is bivariate continuous data.

Example **(ii)** is bivariate categorical data.

Example **(iii)** is continuous, then discrete bivariate data.

Example **(iv)** is bivariate discrete data.

Exercise 3.1

1. Classify each of the following as either inferential statistics or descriptive statistics.

   (i) Eleven per cent of the packets of crisps sampled by a quality inspector are found to be below the labelled weight. Based on this finding, the filling machine is adjusted to increase the amount of fill.

   (ii) *The Irish Times* gives a full page of numerical quantities concerning stocks listed in Dublin, New York and London as well as conversion rates for the euro (€) against the major world currencies.

   (iii) Based on a survey of 140 prisoners by the Department of Justice, a magazine reports that 92% of prisoners did not attend third-level education.

2. A data set lists apartments and villas available for tourists to rent. Information provided includes the weekly rent, whether or not electricity is included free of charge, whether or not pets are allowed, the number of rooms and the distance to the beach.

   (i) Describe the elements in the data set.

   (ii) Give the number of variables and specify if each variable is categorical, discrete or continuous.

3. Make up your own survey with at least six questions. Include at least two categorical variables, at least one discrete variable and at least two continuous variables. State which variables are categorical, discrete and continuous. Give reasons for your answers.

4. You are planning a survey to collect information about the study habits of secondary students. Describe one categorical variable, one discrete variable and one continuous variable that you might measure for each student. Give the units of measurement where relevant.

5. Identify the sample and the population in each of the following scenarios.

   (i) Eight hundred individuals who watch soccer on TV are selected and information concerning their income level, age, place of residence and so forth is recorded.

(ii) Two hundred and ten athletes at a major track and field event are selected to give a blood sample to check for substance abuse.

(iii) In order to study the response times for emergency fire brigade calls in Cork city and county, 40 emergency fire brigade calls in progress are selected randomly over a three-month period and the response times are recorded.

6. For each of the following, state how many observations are in the data set and state the variable.

(i) In a sociological study involving 40 households, the number of children per household attending primary school was recorded for each household.

(ii) In a school with 660 students, the number of hours spent studying per student was recorded. The minimum was zero hours studying and the maximum was 25 hours studying.

(iii) A survey was mailed to 6,000 households and one question asked for the number of pets per household. Two thousand eight hundred and five of the surveys were completed and returned.

7. Classify the variables in parts **(i)**, **(ii)** and **(iii)** of question 6 as continuous or discrete.

8. Garda checkpoints are used to identify and arrest motorists driving over the legal blood alcohol limit. Let x represent the number of motorists stopped before the first drunk driver is identified.

(i) What are the possible values for x?

(ii) Classify x as discrete or continuous.

Surveys

Designing a questionnaire

A **questionnaire** is a set of questions used to obtain data from a population. Anyone who answers a questionnaire is called a **respondent**.

Always have a clear aim for your survey and ask questions in a logical order.

The questionnaire should:

Be clear about who is to complete it.	Be as brief as possible.
Start with simple questions.	Be able to be answered quickly.
Be clear how the answers are to be recorded.	Be clear where the answers are to be recorded.

The questions should:

Be short and use simple language.	Not be leading in any way, as this can influence the answer.
Provide tick boxes.	Not cause embarrassment or offend.
Be clear about what is asked.	Be relevant to the survey.
Allow a 'yes' or 'no' answer, a number or a response from a choice of answers.	Not be open-ended, which might produce long or rambling answers that are difficult to analyse.

Question	Comment
Gender: Male ☐ Female ☐	Good clear question.
How old are you?	Personal question, as people may be embarrassed to give their age. No indication of accuracy.
A better question would be: Which is your age group, in years? Under 18 18–40 41–60 Over 60 ☐ ☐ ☐ ☐	Only one response required. No gaps and no overlapping of boxes.
You prefer to go out on Saturdays, don't you?	A leading question. It forces an opinion on the person being surveyed.
A better question is: On which day do you prefer to go out? Mon Tue Wed Thu Fri Sat Sun ☐ ☐ ☐ ☐ ☐ ☐ ☐	A much better question. Respondents have a choice. Better accuracy for the survey.
How much TV do you watch on a school weeknight? A lot ☐ A bit ☐ Very little ☐	This question is too vague.
A better question is: How many hours of TV, to the nearest hour, do you watch on a school weeknight? 0 1 2 3 4 or more ☐ ☐ ☐ ☐ ☐	This is more precise. Better accuracy for the survey.

Samples

A sample is a small part of the population selected for surveying. A random sample is a sample in which every member of the population has an equal chance of being selected, and the selections are made independently. Notice this is sampling with replacement. When a population is very large compared with the size of the sample, the difference between sampling with and without replacement is negligible. Random sampling without replacement is considered to be a modification to random sampling with replacement.

Sampling methods

There are various ways of actually selecting a sample.

1. **Simple random sampling.** Sometimes called the lottery method, this is the best method (from a theoretical viewpoint) of selecting a truly random sample. All the items in a population are given a number and pieces of paper, each with one number on it, are placed in a drum or hat. The numbers are selected one at a time until the required sample size is reached. This method is very tedious, particularly for very large populations. You must bear in mind that although the method of selection is free from personal bias, there is no guarantee that the resulting sample is unbiased. Sometimes a computer simulation may be used instead.

2. **Stratified sampling.** This method uses the natural divisions of a population, such as gender, age, weight, occupation or colour. These are the strata and they can be used to ensure all sections of the population are adequately represented in any sample. It is essential when using this method to know in advance the proportion of the population in each natural stratum and to take account of this when selecting the sample. The strata chosen must be readily determinable. They should be exhaustive and mutually exclusive (that is, covering the whole population and each item in the population belongs to one and only one stratum).

3. **Systematic sampling.** Sometimes called the constant skip method. As the name implies, some type of system is used for selecting a sample. For example, select a person at random and then select every eightieth name onwards (and/or backwards) until the required sample size has been reached. Thus, only the first item in the sample is chosen randomly and this considerably reduces the work involved. Problems can arise for example, if we consider items on a production line being sampled at regular intervals of time. The starting time for measurement each day should be varied, since fluctuations of attention by the workers could change in a regular pattern during the day.

4. **Cluster sampling.** This consists of a list of groups of individuals rather than individuals themselves. A random sample of these groups or clusters is taken and then observations are made on every individual within these selected group. Cluster samples are popular with biologists, agricultural scientists and geographers. Their technique is to cover the survey area with a grid of numbered squares. A random sample of the squares is taken and a complete study/investigation is made of the selected squares, whether it be plant species, incidence of disease or number of bacteria. It is preferable to divide the population/area into a large number of small clusters rather than a small number of large clusters.

5. **Multi-stage sampling.** This method is designed to reduce the time and cost of surveying samples from very large populations. Suppose we wanted to survey 1,000 members of the population of Ireland at random. We could select five counties at random, then select four towns at random from each of these counties and finally select 50 people at random within each of the four towns. This gives us $5 \times 4 \times 50 = 1,000$ random members. The advantage of this is that the data are collected in 20 relatively small areas instead of having to visit 1,000 scattered locations.

6. **Quota sampling.** This method allows the interviewer a certain amount of discretion when collecting the data. Quotas for different sections of the population are set and the interviewer is allowed to select the sample according to these quotas, for example 30 teenagers, 15 female pensioners, 20 farmers, etc. Quota sampling is used to ensure that the sample contains members of the population in the desired proportions. As a result, the interviewer can be a source of bias, as only the views of those chosen by the interviewer are recorded. Quota sampling is an example of non-random sampling. Its main advantage is it reduces survey time and cost.

7. **Panel sampling.** This type of survey collects data from the same sample on more than one occasion. The initial sample can be chosen by any of the earlier methods. This can easily monitor long-term trends, measure changes in behaviour/opinions and is relatively cheap. Problems include replacing dropout members, sample initially enthusiastic becoming tired and panel members 'learning' responses, which can all lead to bias. The BBC World Panel where members are invited to participate in surveys at least twice a month is an example of non-random panel sampling.

Exercise 3.2

Comment critically on questions 1–7. If necessary, suggest how the question could be improved, either by rewriting the question and/or by giving a choice of answers.

1. Do you have a computer at home?   Yes ☐   No ☐

2. Saturday is the best day to have a disco, wouldn't you agree?

3. How many emails did you send today?   0–5 ☐   6–10 ☐   10 or more ☐

4. The waiter service in this restaurant is: Excellent ☐   Very good ☐

5. What do you think of our new and improved apple juice?

6. Sweets are bad for your teeth. Do you eat many sweets?

7. The new supermarket seems to be a great success. Do you agree?

8. Frank wants to find out how much time people spend playing computer games each week. Design a questionnaire he could use. Include tick boxes for a response.

9. Design a questionnaire with five questions you might include in a survey on school uniforms.

10. Draw up a short questionnaire to find out how students spend their leisure time. Briefly describe how you collect the data.

11. Brian wants to use a questionnaire to find out what kind of music the students at his school like. He also wants to find out if the boys and girls in his school like the same type of music and if there is a difference between year groups. Write down four questions that Brian might include in his questionnaire.

12. A company that makes toothpaste says the new brand is better than the old brand. A dentist wants to investigate this claim. He chooses 40 boys and 40 girls at random from his patients. The boys are given the new brand and the girls are given the old brand. After four months the dentist compares the boys' and girls' teeth.

    (i) Write down two reasons why this is not a reliable experiment.

    (ii) Give two ways in which this experiment could be improved.

13. Anne and Brendan carried out a sample survey of householders to see if they prefer to shop locally or in an out-of-town supermarket. They recorded their results in the following two-way table.

	Local shop	Out-of-town supermarket	Total
Men aged 25 or younger	18	12	30
Men older than 25	23	7	30
Women aged 25 or younger	6	24	30
Women older than 25	13	17	30
Total	60	60	120

Anne says, 'Sixty people prefer the local shop and 60 people prefer the out-of-town supermarket, so there is no difference in people's preferences.' Brendan says, 'I don't agree with you.' Explain why Brendan does not agree with Anne.

14. A company wants to find out what the public thinks of their products and services. To collect the data, they intend to use a questionnaire.

    (i) Write down three important points that should be remembered when designing the questionnaire.

    (ii) The company is going to post the questionnaire to people's homes. Give one advantage and one disadvantage of using the postal system.

15. Prepare a data capture sheet for surveys to find out the following by observation.

    (i) The colours of cars at a road intersection

    (ii) The gender and approximate age of people entering a supermarket

16. Mary goes to an all-girls school. She decided to do a sample survey to find out the time students spent studying. Mary chose 40 students randomly from her own school register and

asked each of these students the time, to the nearest hour, they spent studying per week. The raw data were recorded as follows.

7 9 14   6 1 10 2 6   7 11 10   1 10 2 6   3 5   3 0 5
11 7 13 10 1   9 5 2 15   6   6 11   6 4 0 12 9 13 4 8

Complete the following grouped frequency table.

Time spent studying, in hours	0–3	4–7	8–11	12–15
Tally				
Number of students				

   (i) Is this primary or secondary data? Give a reason for your answer.
  (ii) Is the data discrete or continuous? Explain your answer.
 (iii) Give two reasons why this may be a biased sample.
  (iv) Suggest two ways Mary could improve her sample to make it more representative.

17. John carried out a survey to find out people's opinion on attending sports events in his local area. He stood outside the local sports stadium and asked a random sample of people their opinions on attending sports events as they entered the stadium.

   (i) Is the data that John collects primary or secondary? Justify your answer.
  (ii) Give two reasons why this sample may be biased.
 (iii) Make two suggestions to John to improve the accuracy of his survey.

18. A soccer club with 300 members has 10 tickets to give to its members to attend an international soccer match. All 300 members want a ticket for the international match. Describe two fair methods that the club could use in choosing the 10 members at random to receive these international match tickets.

Averages

There are many types of averages. Three that we meet initially are called the **mean**, the **mode** and the **median**. They are also known as measures of central tendency.

Mean

The **mean** is the proper name for what most people call the average.

> The **mean** of a set of values is defined as **the sum of all the values divided by the number of values**.

That is:

$$\text{Mean} = \frac{\text{Sum of all the values}}{\text{Number of values}}$$

The formula is often written as:

$$\mu = \frac{\Sigma x}{n}$$

where:

(i) μ, pronounced 'mu', is the symbol for the mean.

Note: Strictly speaking, μ should be called the **arithmetic mean**.

(ii) Σ, the Greek capital letter sigma, means 'the sum of' (i.e. Σx means 'add up all the x-values').

(iii) n is the number of values of x.

(iv) You can use your calculator to add up a list of numbers, i.e. Σx is very easy to do on a calculator.

Mode

> The **mode** of a set of items is the **item that occurs most often**. If there are no repeated items, then the mode does not exist.

Median

> When the values are arranged in ascending or descending order of size, then the **median** is the middle value. If the number of values is even, then the median is the average of the two middle values.

Note: Half the values lie below the median and half the values lie above the median. The median is also called the second quartile (Q_2).

A measure of spread

The **range** is the difference between the highest data value and the lowest data value.

> Range = highest value − lowest value

EXAMPLE

The ages of the seven dwarfs are as follows.

Name	Happy	Doc	Sleepy	Sneezy	Dopey	Grumpy	Bashful
Age	685	702	498	539	402	685	619

   (i) Find the mean age.

  (ii) Find the (mode) modal age.

 (iii) Find the median age.

 (iv) State the age range of the seven dwarfs.

  (v) When Snow White is included with the seven dwarfs, their mean age is 518·5 years. Find Snow White's age.

 (vi) State the age range of Snow White and the seven dwarfs.

Solution:

(i) Mean age $= \dfrac{\Sigma x}{n} = \dfrac{\text{Sum of all their ages}}{\text{Number of dwarfs}}$

$$= \frac{685 + 702 + 498 + 539 + 402 + 685 + 619}{7} = \frac{4{,}130}{7} = 590 \text{ years}$$

(ii) Mode = 685 years, the number that occurs most often (Happy and Grumpy are twins).

(iii) Median = Middle value, when values are arranged in ascending or descending order.

$$402, \ 498, \ 539, \ \textcircled{619}, \ 685, \ 685, \ 702$$

Median = 619 years

(iv) Dwarfs' age range = oldest − youngest = 702 − 402 = 300 years.

(v) Mean = 518·5 years (including Snow White's age)

Let x = Snow White's age in years

$$\therefore \ \frac{485 + 702 + 498 + 539 + 402 + 685 + 619 + x}{8} = 518 \cdot 5$$

$$\frac{4{,}130 + x}{8} = 518 \cdot 5$$

$$4{,}130 + x = 4{,}148$$

$$x = 18$$

$\therefore$ Snow White's age is 18 years.

(vi) Snow White and dwarfs' age range = oldest − youngest = 702 − 18 = 684 years.

A note on averages

Average	Advantages	Disadvantages
Mean	• Useful for further analysis. • Uses all the data. • Easy to calculate.	• Distorted by extreme results. • Mean is not always a given data value.
Mode	• Easy to find. • Not influenced by extreme values. • Good with nominal data.	• Not very useful for further analysis. • May not exist. • Can be more than one mode.
Median	• Useful for further analysis. • Unaffected by extremes. • Easy to calculate if data are ordered. • Considered to be a typical value.	• Not always a given data value. • Can be difficult to calculate. • Does not take actual data into account, only its ordered position.

Exercise 3.3

1. Jack has six cards, each of which has a positive whole number printed on it. Four of the cards each have the number 8 on it.

   (i) Without knowing the numbers on the other two cards, can you give the value of the
      (a) median (b) mode (c) range? Explain your reasoning.

  (ii) You are told that the six cards have a mean of 8. Write down some possible whole
      numbers that could be on the other two cards. Hence, find the greatest range.

 (iii) If the six cards have a mean of 8 and a range of 6, how many answers can you now
      find for the numbers on the remaining two cards? Explain your answer.

2. Four girls and six boys received text messages. The mean number of messages received by the four girls was 31. The mean number of messages received by the six boys was 27. Decide whether the following statements are true (T) or false (F) and justify your answer in each case.

   (i) The person who received the most messages must have been a girl.

  (ii) The mean number of messages for the 10 people was 29.

3. A set of numbers arranged in ascending order reads as follows:

$$2 \quad 3 \quad 7 \quad 12 \quad x \quad 18 \quad 21 \quad 27 \quad y \quad 36$$

What are the values of x and y if the median of these numbers is 16 and the mean is 17?

4. The mode of the nine numbers 2, 3, 7, 4, 9, 2, x, 3, 5 is x.

   (i) How many different values of x are possible?

  (ii) Given that x is also the median of the nine values, what is the exact value of x?

5. Dani sat a Maths test every week for five weeks. Her marks (out of 10) were recorded.

Week	One	Two	Three	Four	Five
Test result	2	7	9	2	8

Which of the three measures of average (mean, mode, median) would Dani use to describe her results to her parents if she wants to show her results in the best possible light? Give a reason for your answer.

6. Ten people state their approximate annual incomes.

$$€150 \text{ k} \quad €35 \text{ k} \quad €500 \text{ k} \quad €35 \text{ k} \quad €200 \text{ k}$$
$$€35 \text{ k} \quad €50 \text{ k} \quad €100 \text{ k} \quad €28 \text{ k} \quad €80 \text{ k}$$

   (i) What is the mode? Why is it not a very meaningful average?

   (ii) What is the mean? Why is it not a very meaningful average?

   (iii) What is the median?

7. Four numbers are 7, 18, W, 10.

   (i) If their median is 12, find the value of W.

   (ii) If their mean is 12, find the value of W.

   (iii) If their range is 17, find the possible values of W.

8. The mean height of a group of students is 181 cm. Another student whose height is 163 cm joins the group. The mean height of the group is now reduced to 179 cm. What was the number of students in the original group?

9. Four numbers are 9, P, Q, 17 in ascending order of size. The mean of the four numbers is 12. Find the median.

10. The table shows the Mathematics grades for a group of students.

Grade	1	2	3	4	5	6
Frequency	1	3	5	6	W	2

   (i) If $W = 3$, find the median grade.

   (ii) If the median grade was 5, what can you say about the value of W?

   (iii) Find, in terms of W, the mean grade.

   (iv) If 37·5% of the students obtained grades 5 or 6, find the value of W. Hence, find the mean grade.

11. Consider the four numbers P, Q, R, S with $P \leq Q \leq R \leq S$ where P, Q, R, $S \in \mathbb{N}$. The mean of the four numbers is 11, the mode is 10, the median is 10 and the range is 6. Find the value of P, Q, R and S.

12. 45 students in a class each recorded the number of whole minutes, x, spent doing experiments on Monday. The results are $\sum_{i=1}^{45} x_i = 2{,}232$.

   (i) Find the mean number of minutes the students spent doing experiments on Monday.

   (ii) Two new students joined the class and reported that they spent 37 minutes and 34 minutes, respectively. Calculate the new mean including these two students.

Frequency distribution table for discrete (countable) data

If the values in a distribution are arranged in ascending or descending order, showing their corresponding frequencies, the distribution is called a **frequency distribution**.

Note: If the values and frequencies are given in a table, it is called a **frequency distribution table**.

EXAMPLE

A casino owner tested a new six-sided die by throwing it 36 times and recording the results.

$$\begin{array}{cccccccccccc}
4 & 3 & 2 & 6 & 3 & 1 & 2 & 5 & 6 & 1 & 1 & 3 \\
2 & 2 & 5 & 6 & 4 & 5 & 1 & 5 & 5 & 3 & 6 & 2 \\
1 & 1 & 6 & 4 & 5 & 3 & 2 & 2 & 3 & 5 & 6 & 1
\end{array}$$

  (i) Show these results on a frequency distribution table.
 (ii) What conclusions, if any, might the casino owner draw from the results?
(iii) What further action, if any, might the casino owner take?
Justify your statements.

Solution:

(i)

Score on die	1	2	3	4	5	6
Tally	卌 ‖	卌 ‖	卌 │	‖‖	卌 ‖	卌 │
Frequency	7	7	6	3	7	6

 (ii) In making 36 throws of the die, the casino owner might expect each score to appear six times (36 throws ÷ 6 numbers = 6 times each). Since the score of 4 appears only three times, it might be concluded the die is not fair (**biased**). Hence, the new six-sided die would be rejected.

(iii) However, the casino owner might decide that 36 throws is not enough. The experiment might be repeated with another 36 (or more) throws. This course of action would give a more accurate description of the situation.

Mean, mode, median for discrete or continuous grouped frequency distributions

Sometimes the range of the values is very wide and it is not suitable to show all the values individually. When this happens, we arrange the values into suitable groups called **class intervals**, such as 0–10, 10–20, etc. When the information is arranged in class intervals it is not possible to calculate the exact value of the mean. However, it is possible to estimate it by using the **mid-interval value** of each class interval. The easiest way to find the mid-interval value is to add the two extreme values and divide by 2.

For example, in the class interval 30–50, add 30 and 50 and divide by 2.

$$\frac{30 + 50}{2} = \frac{80}{2} = 40 \qquad \therefore \text{40 is the mid-interval value.}$$

To find the mean, do the following.

1. Multiply each value (or where relevant, the mid-interval value) by its corresponding frequency.
2. Sum all these products.
3. Divide this sum by the total number of frequencies.

That is:

$$\mu = \frac{\Sigma fx}{\Sigma f}$$

(i) x is the value of each measurement or the mid-interval value of each group measurement

(ii) f is the frequency of each measurement

(iii) Σfx is the sum of all the fx values

(iv) Σf is the sum of all the frequencies

Note: You can use your calculator to calculate the mean, μ.

$\mu = \bar{x}$ on many calculators. You may need to consult your calculator manual.

Mode

To find the mode of a frequency distribution, check the frequency distribution table. The mode is the number (score) with the largest frequency, i.e. the most common number (score) in the distribution.

Median

As the values are arranged in order of size, the median can be read directly from a frequency distribution table by looking for the middle value, or the average of the two middle values if there is an even number of values.

The frequency distribution below shows the time per week spent watching television by 37 people.

Time in hours	0−2	2−6	6−12	12−20	20−30
Number of people	5	9	12	6	5

Note: 0−2 means 0 is included but 2 is not, etc.

  (i) Estimate the mean time spent per week watching television.

 (ii) In which class interval does the median lie?

(iii) What is the modal class (mode)?

 (iv) State the range of the data.

  (v) Is the data discrete or continuous? Justify your answer.

Solution:

We assume the data to be at mid-interval values.

It is good practice to rewrite the table using these mid-interval values.

New table:

Time in hours (mid-interval values)	1	4	9	16	25
Number of people	5	9	12	6	5

(i) Mean $= \mu = \dfrac{\Sigma fx}{\Sigma f} = \dfrac{5(1) + 9(4) + 12(9) + 6(16) + 5(25)}{5 + 9 + 12 + 6 + 5} = \dfrac{370}{37} = 10$

∴ The mean number of hours spent watching television per week is 10 hours.

(ii) There are 37 people altogether. The middle one is the 19th person. Therefore, we require the class interval in which the 19th person lies.

By looking at the table, we find that the time spent watching television by the 19th person lies in the 6−12 hour class interval.

∴ The median lies in the 6−12 hour class interval.

(iii) The mode or modal class is 6−12 hours, with 12 people spending such times watching television. Twelve is the largest number of people watching TV in the five class intervals.

(iv) The range for grouped data is given by the difference between the upper boundary of the class with the largest values minus the lower boundary of the class with the smallest values.

Range $= 30 - 0 = 30$

(v) As time is measurable, we could conclude that a person could spend 1·25 hours or 1·26 hours watching TV.

∴ You could conclude that the time (hours) in this example is continuous.

Given the mean of a frequency distribution

We are often given the mean of a frequency distribution and need to find one of the values or frequencies. Essentially, we are given an equation in disguise, and by solving this equation we can calculate the missing value or frequency.

EXAMPLE

The table below shows the ages of children in a crèche.

Age	1	2	3	4	5
Number of children	4	7	9	x	5

If the mean age is 3, find the value of x.

Solution:

Equation given in disguise: mean = 3.

$$\therefore \frac{4(1) + 7(2) + 9(3) + x(4) + 5(5)}{4 + 7 + 9 + x + 5} = 3$$

$$\frac{4 + 14 + 27 + 4x + 25}{x + 25} = 3$$

$$\frac{4x + 70}{x + 25} = 3$$

$$4x + 70 = 3(x + 25) \quad \text{(multiply both sides by } (x + 25))$$

$$4x + 70 = 3x + 75$$

$$4x - 3x = 75 - 70$$

$$x = 5$$

Exercise 3.4

1. A die was thrown 40 times and the frequency of each score was as follows.

Value	1	2	3	4	5	6
Frequency	7	7	8	9	5	4

   (i) Find the median score.

   (ii) Find the modal (mode) score.

   (iii) Find the range.

   (iv) Calculate the mean of these scores.

   (v) The die was then thrown another 10 times. The mean of these 10 throws was 3·5. Calculate the overall mean for all 50 throws.

2. A test consisting of eight questions was given to 40 pupils. One mark was awarded per question for a correct solution and no marks for an incorrect solution. The results were as follows.

$$
\begin{array}{cccccccccc}
3 & 2 & 5 & 6 & 1 & 3 & 5 & 7 & 1 & 4 \\
2 & 4 & 3 & 7 & 4 & 8 & 6 & 3 & 2 & 3 \\
6 & 5 & 6 & 1 & 5 & 5 & 2 & 4 & 5 & 4 \\
5 & 4 & 2 & 3 & 4 & 3 & 4 & 5 & 3 & 5
\end{array}
$$

   (i) Represent the information in a frequency distribution table.
   (ii) Calculate the mean mark per pupil.
   (iii) Calculate the median mark.
   (iv) What is the mode?
   (v) If the pass mark was 4, what percentage of the pupils failed the test?
   (vi) Ten other pupils did the same test. The mean mark then for the 50 pupils was unchanged. Calculate the sum of the marks for the 50 pupils.
   (vii) A second set of 50 pupils did the same test and the mean for the 100 pupils was increased by one mark. Calculate the mean mark for the second set of 50 pupils.

3. A survey of 80 students gave the amount of money spent per month in the school canteen.

Amount in €	0−8	8−16	16−24	24−32	32−40
Number of students	8	12	20	24	16

   Note: 0−8 means 0 is included but 8 is not, etc.

   (i) Taking the amounts at the mid-interval values, show that the mean amount of money spent per student was €22·80.
   (ii) 'The money amount in euro is a continuous variable.' Do you agree or disagree with this statement? Justify your answer.

4. A department store carried out a survey on the length of time a number of people spent shopping in their store. The table shows the length of time spent shopping, in 10-minute intervals.

Time interval in minutes	0−10	10−20	20−30	30−40	40−50	50−60	60−70
Number of shoppers	30	x	24	30	40	20	10

   Note: 0−10 means 0 is included but 10 is not, etc.

   (i) If the average number of shoppers for the first, second and third intervals was 30, calculate the value of x.
   (ii) Using mid-interval values, calculate the average shopping time in the store.

    (iii) What is the least number of shoppers who completed their shopping within 35 minutes?

    (iv) In which class interval does the median lie?

    (v) Name the modal class.

    (vi) Comment on the mean, mode and median values you found. Do you consider that any one of the three averages is better or worse than the others to help describe the situation? Explain your reasoning.

    (vii) Describe two difficulties the store may have encountered when carrying out this survey.

5. The result of a survey of the number of passengers carried by taxi in a town was recorded as follows.

Number of passengers	1	2	3	4	5
Number of taxis	3	t	9	6	4

    (i) If the mean number of passengers carried per taxis was 3, find the value of t.

    (ii) How many taxis were in the survey?

    (iii) Is the given data discrete or continuous?

6. The following grouped frequency distribution table shows the number of hours secondary school students spent watching TV in one particular week.

Time in hours	4−6	6−8	8−10	10−12	12−14
Number of students	2	8	5	x	3

    Note: 4−6 means 4 is included but 6 is not, etc.

    (i) Using the mid-interval values, the mean time spent watching TV was calculated to be 9 hours. Find the value of x.

    (ii) A comment was made that this frequency distribution table was not representative of the time spent by secondary school students watching TV. By doing a survey in your own class or otherwise, make a statement in response to the comment.

7. People attending a course were asked to choose one of the whole numbers from 1 to 12. The results were recorded as follows.

Number	1−3	4−6	7−9	10−12
Number of people	4	7	x	8

    (i) Using mid-interval values, 7 was calculated as the mean of the numbers chosen. Find the value of x.

    (ii) Is the given data discrete or continuous?

    (iii) Carry out a similar class survey. Construct a suitable frequency distribution table and find **(a)** the mean **(b)** the mode **(c)** the median.

Variability of data

Each of these sets of numbers has a mean of 4, but the spread of each set is different:

(a) 4, 4, 4, 4, 4   **(b)** 1, 3, $3\frac{1}{2}$, 4·2, 8·3   **(c)** −196, −49, 25, 66, 174

There is no variability in set **(a)**, while the numbers in set **(c)** are much more spread out than in set **(b)**.

We have three ways of measuring the variability or spread of a distribution: the **range**, the **interquartile range** and the **standard deviation**.

The range

The range is based on the extreme values of the distribution.

Range = highest value − lowest value.

- In **(a)** the range = 4 − 4 = 0.
- In **(b)** the range = 8·3 − 1 = 7·3.
- In **(c)** the range = 174 − (−196) = 370.

What is the chief advantage and the chief disadvantage of the range as a measure of dispersion?

The chief advantage is the simplicity of computation of the range and the chief disadvantage is that it is insensitive to the values between the extremes.

Interquartile range

We will discuss the interquartile range ($Q_3 - Q_1$) later in this chapter.

The standard deviation (σ)

The standard deviation (σ, pronounced 'sigma') is an important and useful measure of spread. It gives a measure of the deviations from the mean, μ. It is calculated using all the values in the distribution.

To calculate σ:

- For each reading x, calculate $x - \mu$, its deviation from the mean.
- Square this deviation to give $(x - \mu)^2$. Note that irrespective of whether the deviation was positive or negative, this is now positive.
- Find $\Sigma (x - \mu)^2$, the sum of all these values.
- Find the average by dividing the sum by n, the number of readings. This gives $\dfrac{\Sigma(x - \mu)^2}{n}$.
- Finally, take the positive square root of $\dfrac{\Sigma(x - \mu)^2}{n}$ to obtain the standard deviation, σ.

The standard deviation, σ, of a set of n numbers with mean μ is given by:

$$\sigma = \sqrt{\frac{\Sigma(x - \mu)^2}{n}} \qquad \text{(see the formulae and tables booklet)}$$

Note: The square root ensures that the x values and the standard deviation are in the same units.

Let's return to **(a)** from before.

For the set 4, 4, 4, 4, 4, find the standard deviation, σ.

Since $x - \mu = 4 - 4 = 0$ for every reading, then $\sigma = \sqrt{\dfrac{0 + 0 + 0 + 0 + 0}{5}}$.

Hence, $\sigma = 0$, indicating that there is no deviation from the mean.

Let's return to **(b)** from before.

For the set 1, 3, 3·5, 4·2, 8·3, find the standard deviation, σ.

$$\Sigma(x - \mu)^2 = (1 - 4)^2 + (3 - 4)^2 + (3·5 - 4)^2 + (4·2 - 4)^2 + (8·3 - 4)^2$$
$$= 9 + 1 + 0·25 + 0·04 + 18·49$$
$$= 28·78$$

$$\sigma = \sqrt{\dfrac{\Sigma(x - \mu)^2}{n}} = \sqrt{\dfrac{28·78}{5}} = 2·39916 \approx 2·4$$

Finally, let's return to **(c)** from before.

For the set −196, −49, 25, 66, 174, find the standard deviation, σ.

$$\Sigma(x - \mu)^2 = (-196 - 4)^2 + (-49 - 4)^2 + (25 - 4)^2 + (66 - 4)^2 + (174 - 4)^2$$
$$= 75{,}994$$

$$\sigma = \sqrt{\dfrac{\Sigma(x - \mu)^2}{n}} = \sqrt{\dfrac{75{,}994}{5}} = 123·3, \text{ correct to one decimal place}$$

Note: Set **(c)** has a much higher standard deviation than set **(b)**, confirming that **(c)** is much more spread about the mean.

Properties of the standard deviation

- σ measures spread about the mean and should be used only when the mean is chosen as the measure of centre.
- $\sigma = 0$ only when there is *no spread*. This happens only when all observations have the same value. Otherwise, $\sigma > 0$. As the observations become more spread out about their mean, σ gets larger. We can say the higher the standard deviation, the greater the variability in the data.
- σ, like the mean, μ, is affected by extreme values.
- Standard deviation units are the same as the units of data.
- You can use your calculator to calculate the standard deviation, σ. The statistical mode (SD or STAT) on your calculator makes calculating standard deviation easy and routine. However, you may need to consult your calculator manual to learn this.

Empirical rule (68%, 95% or 99·7%)

For many large populations, the **empirical rule** provides an estimate of the approximate percentage of observations that are contained within one, two or three standard deviations of the mean:

- Approximately 68% of the observations are in the interval $\mu \pm 1\sigma$.
- Approximately 95% of the observations are in the interval $\mu \pm 2\sigma$.
- Approximately 99·7% of the observations are in the interval $\mu \pm 3\sigma$.

EXAMPLE

Consider a very large number of students taking a college entrance exam such as the SAT. Suppose the mean score on the mathematics section of the SAT is 550, with a standard deviation of 50.

- $\mu \pm 1\sigma = 550 \pm 50$ Covers 68% of students
- $\mu \pm 2\sigma = 550 \pm 100$ Covers 95% of students
- $\mu \pm 3\sigma = 550 \pm 150$ Covers 99·7% of students

Exercise 3.5

Calculate the standard deviation of each of the following arrays of numbers in questions 1–9 (give your answers correct to two decimal places).

1. 1, 2, 3, 4, 5
2. 2, 5, 6, 8, 10, 11
3. 4, 5, 6, 9
4. 1, 2, 2, 3, 4, 6
5. 4, 8, 10, 10, 11, 11
6. 5, 8, 11, 14, 17
7. 2, 4, 5, 7, 11, 13
8. 9, 12, 4, 6, 10, 7
9. 12, 4, 9, 8, 7, 11, 5

10. The standard deviation of the array of numbers 2, 3, 4, 5, 6, 7, 8 is k. Calculate the value of k.

11. Show that the following arrays of numbers have the same standard deviation.
    (i) 3, 4, 6, 8, 9   (ii) 7, 8, 10, 12, 13

12. The array of numbers 1, 2, 4, 5, 8, 16 has mean μ and standard deviation σ. Verify that $\mu - \sigma = 1$.

13. The array of numbers 1·8, 2·6, 4·8, 7·2 has mean μ and standard deviation σ. Verify that $\mu - \sigma = 2$.

14. Two machines, X and Y, are used to pack biscuits. A random sample of 10 packets was taken from each machine and the mass of each packet was measured to the nearest gram.
    (i) Find the standard deviation of the masses of the packets taken in the sample from each machine.

| Machine X (mass in g) | 195 | 197 | 197 | 198 | 199 | 199 | 200 | 200 | 201 | 204 |
| Machine Y (mass in g) | 191 | 193 | 194 | 197 | 199 | 200 | 202 | 203 | 205 | 206 |

    (ii) By comparing the results for the standard deviations, comment on which machine is more reliable.

15. The size, mean and standard deviation of three different data sets are given in the table below.

	P	Q	R
Size (N)	62	203	11
Mean (μ)	10	5	4
Standard deviation (σ)	9	3	0

Complete the sentences below by inserting the relevent letter or numbers in each space.

   (i) The biggest data set is ———— and the smallest is ————.

   (ii) In general, the data in set ———— are the biggest.

   (iii) The data in set ———— are more spread out than the data in other sets.

   (iv) List the elements in set R. { ———— }

   (v) If the sets P and R are combined, the mode is most likely to be ————.

16. In a school there are two fifth year Mathematics teachers called Sir and Miss. Over the last 10 years the mean mark achieved by Sir's students on the Leaving Certificate Mathematics exam was 60%, with a standard deviation of 2%. During the same period, Miss's students also have a mean mark of 60%, but the standard deviation of these students' marks is 10%.

Students in this school have a choice of teacher when entering fifth year. Which teacher should a student who is good at Mathematics choose? Which teacher should a student who is weak at Mathematics choose? Justify your answers.

17. In each case, construct a set of data with six elements where:

   (i) $\mu = 9$ **(ii)** $\sigma = 0$ **(iii)** $\mu = 9$ and $\sigma = 0$

18. The ages and incomes, in €1,000s, of the 10 employees at a city centre department store are recorded in the table below.

Age (next birthday)	28	30	40	55	29	45	42	55	37	39
Income (in €1,000s)	24	26	30	48	35	38	32	53	40	44

   (i) Compute the standard deviation of ages and incomes for these employees.

   (ii) Assuming that all employees remain with the company for five years and that each income is multiplied by 1·5 over that period, what will the standard deviation of ages and incomes equal five years from now?

Standard deviation of a frequency distribution

To calculate the standard deviation, σ, of a frequency distribution, we use the following formula.

$$\sigma = \sqrt{\frac{\Sigma f(x - \mu)^2}{\Sigma f}}$$ (see the formulae and tables booklet)

- x represents the values, or mid-interval values.
- f represents the frequency of the values.
- μ represents the mean value.
- Σ means 'add up'.

As before, you can use your calculator to calculate the standard deviation, σ.

EXAMPLE

Fifty boxes of matches were taken and a record made of the number of matches per box. The results were as follows.

Number of matches per box	47	48	49	50	51
Frequency	6	9	18	13	4

(i) Find the mean number of matches per box and the standard deviation, correct to two decimal places. Do this question (a) without using SD mode (b) using SD mode on your calculator.

(ii) Hence, estimate the number of matchboxes that are within the range $(\mu - \sigma, \mu + \sigma)$. Comment on your reasoning.

(iii) If the number of matches per box was doubled, write down (a) the mean (b) the standard deviation.

Solution:

(i)

f	x	fx	$x - \mu$	$(x - \mu)^2$	$f(x - \mu)^2$
6	47	282	$47 - 49$	$(-2)^2 = 4$	24
9	48	432	$48 - 49$	$(-1)^2 = 1$	9
18	49	882	$49 - 49$	$(0)^2 = 0$	0
13	50	650	$50 - 49$	$(1)^2 = 1$	13
4	51	204	$51 - 49$	$(2)^2 = 4$	16
$\Sigma f = 50$		$\Sigma fx = 2{,}450$			$\Sigma f(x - \mu)^2 = 62$

$$\text{Mean} = \mu = \frac{\Sigma fx}{\Sigma f} = \frac{2450}{50} = 49$$

$$\sigma = \sqrt{\frac{\Sigma f(x - \mu)^2}{\Sigma f}} = \sqrt{\frac{62}{50}} = 1{\cdot}11, \text{ correct to two decimal places}$$

Using SD mode on your calculator quickly gives the same answers. Check your operating manual if you are not sure how to proceed. If you do not have the manual, ask for help from a friend or a teacher.

(ii) We now calculate $\mu - \sigma$ and $\mu + \sigma$.

$\mu - \sigma = 49 - 1\cdot11 = 47\cdot89$

$\mu + \sigma = 49 + 1\cdot11 = 50\cdot11$

Hence, estimate the number of matchboxes that are within the range $(47\cdot89, 50\cdot11)$.

Number of matches per box	47	48	49	50	51
Frequency	6	9	18	13	4

Our answer counts the number of matchboxes that have 48 or 49 or 50 matches within the range $(47\cdot89, 50\cdot11)$.

The number of matchboxes within the range $= 9 + 18 + 13 = 40$.

The reasoning is based on the fact that boxes with 47 matches are lower than the required range, while boxes with 51 matches are above the required range.

(iii) If the number of matches per box was doubled, the new table would be as follows.

Number of matches per box	94	96	98	100	102
Frequency (number of boxes)	6	9	18	13	4

We can calculate the mean and standard deviation as before.

However, when we double the number of matches per box, we also double the mean and standard deviation.

(a) New mean $= 2 \times 49 = 98$

(b) New standard deviation $= 2 \times 1\cdot11 = 2\cdot22$

Note: If we just added, say, five matches to every box of matches, then the mean would increase by 5 but the standard deviation would remain the same.

For grouped frequency distributions, the mean and standard deviation are calculated in exactly the same way, except that x stands for the mid-interval value.

Exercise 3.6

Find the mean and standard deviation, correct to two decimal places, of each of the following frequency distributions in questions 1–4.

1.

Value	1	2	3	4	5
Frequency	2	3	5	3	2

2.

Value	2	6	8	9	10	13
Frequency	3	4	2	6	5	2

3.

Value	0–4	4–8	8–12	12–16	16–20
Frequency	2	3	9	7	3

4.

Value	0–20	20–40	40–60	60–80
Frequency	11	14	9	6

5. An intelligence test was taken by 120 candidates. For each candidate, the time taken to complete the test was recorded and the times were summarised in a pie chart (see diagram).

    (i) Write down the frequency for each of the class intervals 0–1, 1–2, 2–3, 3–5 and 5–10 minutes.

Note: The interval 2–3, for example, represents
    $2 \leq \text{time} < 3$.

  (ii) Calculate: **(a)** The mean time, correct to the nearest integer

               (b) The standard deviation, correct to one decimal place

 (iii) The times were recorded in four different centres in Cork, Sligo, Athlone and Dublin. The timing was carried out by one researcher in each centre, using a stopwatch. Comment on the validity or otherwise of the data collection method.

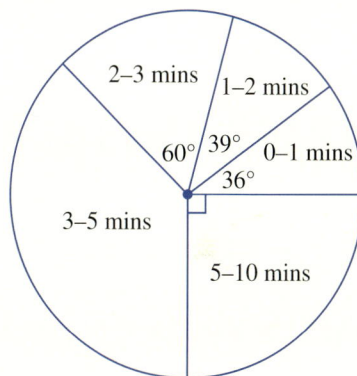

6. The table below shows the number of text messages a student sent each day over a period of three weeks.

Text messages sent	5	6	7	8	9
Frequency	2	6	10	2	1

    (i) Find the mean (μ) number of text messages sent.
   (ii) Find the standard deviation (σ) of the number of text messages sent.
  (iii) Evaluate $\mu + 2\sigma$ and $\mu - 2\sigma$. On what percentage of days is the number of texts sent $\pm$ two standard deviations from the mean?

7.

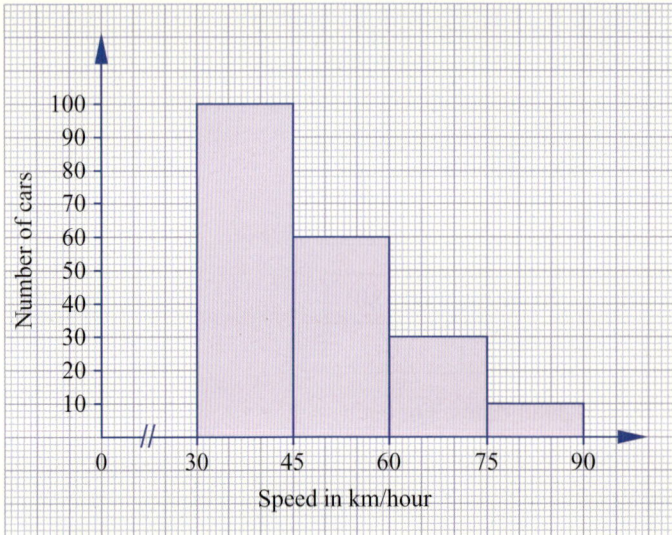

(i) The speeds of cars passing a speed camera are shown in the histogram. Calculate estimates for the mean speed (μ) and the standard deviation (σ).

(ii) The speed limit in operation is 75 km/hour. A motorist caught on camera at a speed of 76 km/hour makes a case in front of a judge that he was not speeding but simply keeping up with the other traffic. By considering the empirical rule for $\mu + 2\sigma$, what conclusion might the judge arrive at? Speeding or not speeding? Explain your decision.

8. The owner of a small clothes shop records the number of customers she has during a typical six-day week in June. The number of customers each day were:

Monday 15, Tuesday 12, Wednesday 15, Thursday 14, Friday 21, Saturday 31

(i) Calculate μ, the mean number of customers per day.

(ii) Calculate σ, the standard deviation, correct to one decimal place.

(iii) Calculate $\mu + \sigma$ and $\mu - \sigma$.

(iv) On how many days is the number of customers within one standard deviation of the mean?

(v) On what percentage of the days is the number of customers within ± one standard deviation of the mean?

Later during a week in July the number of customers was:

Monday 17, Tuesday 14, Wednesday 17, Thursday 16, Friday 23, Saturday 33

Notice there are +2 customers on each day when compared to the previous week.

(vi) Write down the mean number of customers for the July week.

(vii) Write down the standard deviation for the July week.

9. On 1 September 2010 the mean age of the first year students in a school was 12·4 years and the standard deviation was 0·6 years. One year later, all of these students had moved into second year and no other students had joined them.

   (i) State the mean and the standard deviation of the ages of these students on 1 September 2011. Give a reason for each answer.

   A new group of first year students began on 1 September 2011. This group had a similar age distribution and was of a similar size to the first year group of September 2010.

   (ii) State the mean age of the combined group of the first year and second year students on 1 September 2011.

   (iii) State whether the standard deviation of the ages of this combined group is less than, equal to or greater than 0·6 years. Give a reason for your answer.

10. The times taken to get to school on seven consecutive mornings were (in minutes) 22, 37, 28, 62, 44, 24, 56.

    (i) Calculate the mean and standard deviation of these journey times.

    (ii) How many of these journeys were shorter than the mean time by more than one standard deviation?

11. The following table shows the length of time for which 120 people have been unemployed.

Time in months	0−2	2−4	4−6	6−8	8−10	10−12
Number of people	14	17	24	36	18	11

    Note: The interval 4−6, for example, represents $4 \leq$ time < 6.

    (i) Write down the modal class.

    (ii) Are the data discrete or continuous?

    (iii) Calculate the mean time and the standard deviation, correct to one decimal place, using the mid-interval values.

    (iv) Hence, estimate the number of people who have been unemployed for a time which is within one standard deviation of the mean time.

12. Do men or women have more friends? To answer this question, a researcher asked 15 men and 15 women to list the names of friends they had spent time with during the past year. The researcher then counted the number of friends for each man and each woman. The results are given below.

    Men: 5, 9, 10, 4, 22, 13, 19, 21, 28, 17, 11, 13, 17, 16, 20

    Women: 35, 21, 10, 18, 9, 23, 39, 33, 29, 18, 20, 17, 15, 14, 29

    (i) Verify that $\mu_{men} = 15$ and $\mu_{women} = 22$.

    (ii) Using your calculator or otherwise, find the standard deviations σ_{men} and σ_{women}, correct to one decimal place.

(iii) By considering $\mu \pm \sigma$, construct a minimum and maximum value of friends for both men and women.

(iv) Use your answers to comment on the question: Do men or women have more friends?

13. Two numbers have a mean of zero and a standard deviation of two. Two other numbers have a mean of zero and a standard deviation of one. Taking the four numbers together, find:

(i) Their mean

(ii) Their standard deviation in the form $\sqrt{w}$, where $w \in \mathbb{R}$

14. In a school with 125 girls, each student is tested to see how many sit-up exercises (sit-ups) she can do in one minute. The results are given in the table below.

Number of sit-ups	Number of students	Cumulative number of students
15	11	11
16	21	32
17	33	p
18	q	99
19	18	117
20	8	125

(i) (a) Write down the value of q.

(b) Find the value of p.

(ii) Find the median number of sit-ups.

(iii) Find the mean number of sit-ups, correct to the nearest integer.

Histogram

A histogram is often used to display information contained in a frequency distribution. It is similar to a bar chart with no gaps between the bars, and the two are often confused. It is worth remembering that bar charts can only represent discrete data, while histograms can represent discrete or continuous data. The essential characteristic of a histogram is that the **area of each rectangle represents the frequency**, and the sum of the areas of the rectangles is equal to the sum of the frequencies.

Drawing a histogram is straightforward.

1. Decide on the length of the base for each rectangle in the diagram. Make sure all rectangles have the same width.

2. Draw each rectangle the correct height (or length) to represent the information it displays.

3. Each rectangle must touch its neighbour.

4. Label each axis.

5. Label each rectangle clearly.

6. Give the histogram a title to describe the information.

Note: For the sake of drawing a histogram or using a histogram to work out frequencies, we say the area of the rectangle represents the frequency. However, mathematically we say that the **area of each rectangle is proportional to the frequency** of the corresponding class, i.e. if one class has a frequency twice that of another, then the area of the rectangle representing this class will have twice the area of the rectangle representing the other class, etc.

EXAMPLE

The following frequency distribution gives the number of marks obtained by students in an examination.

Mark	0–20	20–40	40–60	60–80	80–100
Number of students	8	21	8	10	24

Note: 0–20 means 0 is included but 20 is not, etc.

(i) Represent the data with a histogram. Name the modal class. In which class interval does the median lie?

(ii) On your histogram, indicate clearly where the median lies. Write down your value for the median.

Solution:

(i) There are five divisions: 0–20, 20–40, 40–60, 60–80, 80–100.

∴ We require five rectangles, all with the same width.

The heights of each rectangle are 8, 21, 8, 10, 24.

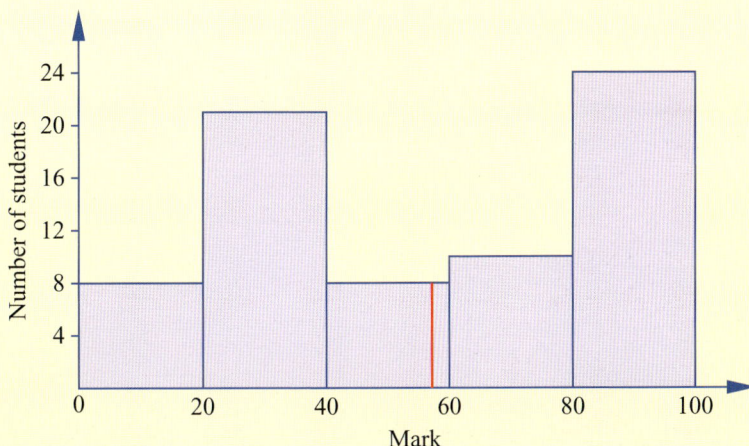

The modal class is the class with the greatest number of students in it.

∴ Modal class = (80–100), where $80 \leq$ mark < 100.

The median is associated with the 'middle' student.

Notice that $8 + 21 + 8 + 10 + 24 = 71$, the total number of students.

The median is thus associated with the 36th student.

Hence, $8 + 21 + 8 = 37$ students tells us the median is in the class 40–60 mark.

(ii) We note that $8 + 21 + 7 = 36$ and $8 + 21 + 8 = 37$.

Thus, the median is $\frac{7}{8}$ along the interval $40 - 60$.

This interval is 20.

$\frac{7}{8}$ of $20 = 17 \cdot 5$

$40 + 17\frac{1}{2} = 57 \cdot 5$

Hence, the red line on the histogram gives us a median value of approximately $57 \cdot 5$.

Given the histogram

Sometimes we are given the histogram already drawn and we need to calculate the frequencies represented by the rectangles. We are usually given the area of one of the rectangles (which represents the frequency) and its height (read directly from the diagram). We can then work out the remaining frequencies from the information given.

In histograms, it is useful to know that:

$$\text{Frequency} = \text{area of rectangle} = \text{base} \times \text{height}$$

EXAMPLE

The distribution of the distances, in km, that a group of people have to travel to work each day is shown in the histogram.

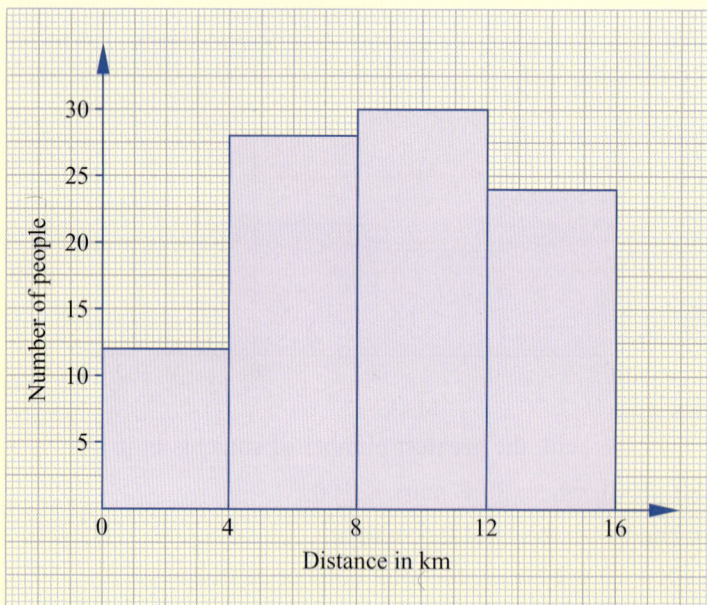

(i) Complete the corresponding frequency distribution table.

Distance (km)	0−4	4−8	8−12	12−16
Number of people		28		

(ii) Given that the distribution has mean $\mu = 8\cdot4$ km and standard deviation $\sigma = 4$ km, mark on the histogram $\mu - \sigma$ and $\mu + \sigma$.

(iii) Hence, estimate the number of people in the interval $(\mu - \sigma, \mu + \sigma)$.

Solution:

(i)

Distance (km)	0−4	4−8	8−12	12−16
Number of people	12	28	30	24

(ii) We have $\mu - \sigma = 8\cdot4 - 4 = 4\cdot4$

and $\mu + \sigma = 8\cdot4 + 4 = 12\cdot4$

Now return to the original graph.

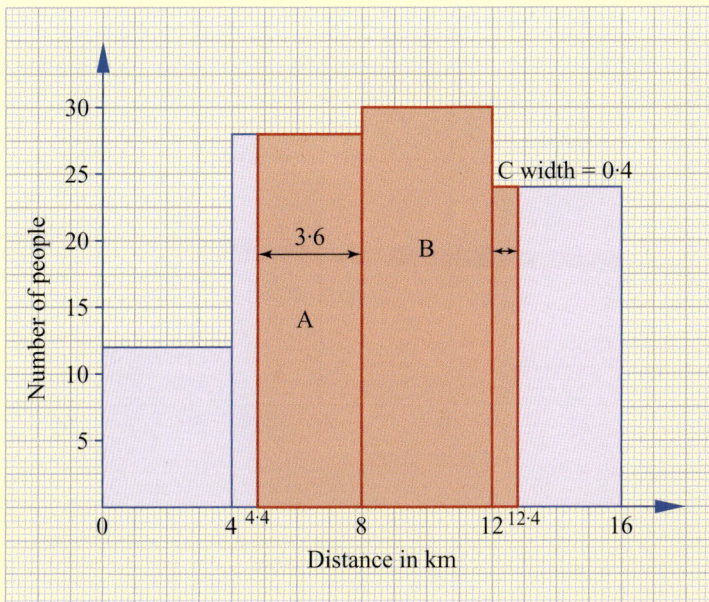

(iii) To find the number of people who travelled between 4·4 km and 12·4 km, we find area A + area B + area C.

$$= \left(\frac{3\cdot6}{4}\right)(28) + \left(\frac{4}{4}\right)(30) + \left(\frac{0\cdot4}{4}\right)(24)$$
$$= 25\cdot2 + 30 + 2\cdot4$$
$$= 57\cdot6$$

Whatever answer we give will be an approximation.

56, 57, 58 or 59 people would also be acceptable here.

Exercise 3.7

1. The distribution of the ages of people at a meeting is shown in the histogram.

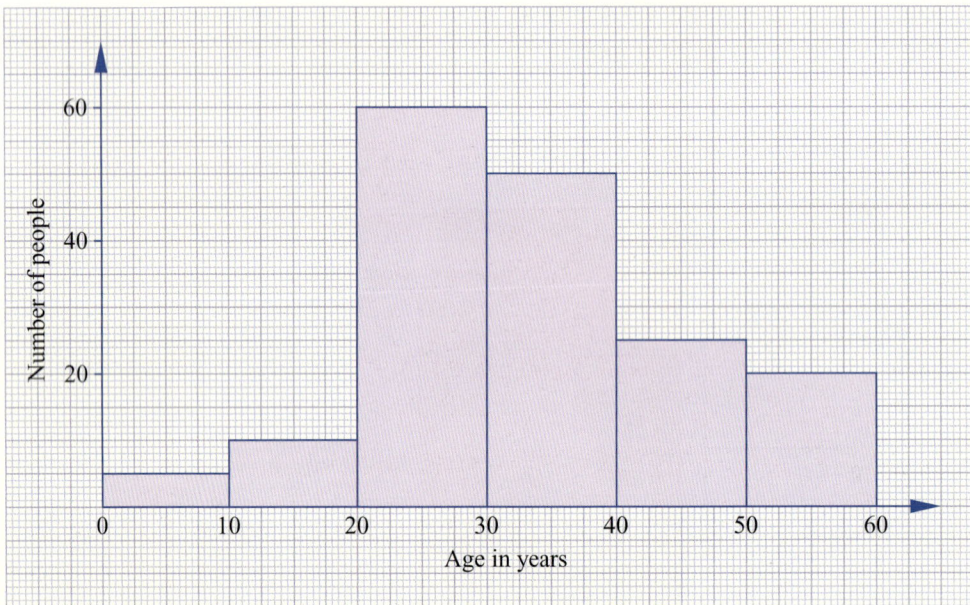

(i) Complete the corresponding frequency distribution table.

Age (years)	0–10	10–20	20–30	30–40	40–50	50–60
Number of people			60			

(ii) How many people were at the meeting?

(iii) Given that the distribution has mean $\mu = 43$ years and standard deviation $\sigma = 15$ years, mark on the histogram $\mu - \sigma$ and $\mu + \sigma$. Hence, estimate the number of people in the interval $(\mu - \sigma, \mu + \sigma)$.

2. The claims made against an insurance company for a certain year is shown in the histogram.

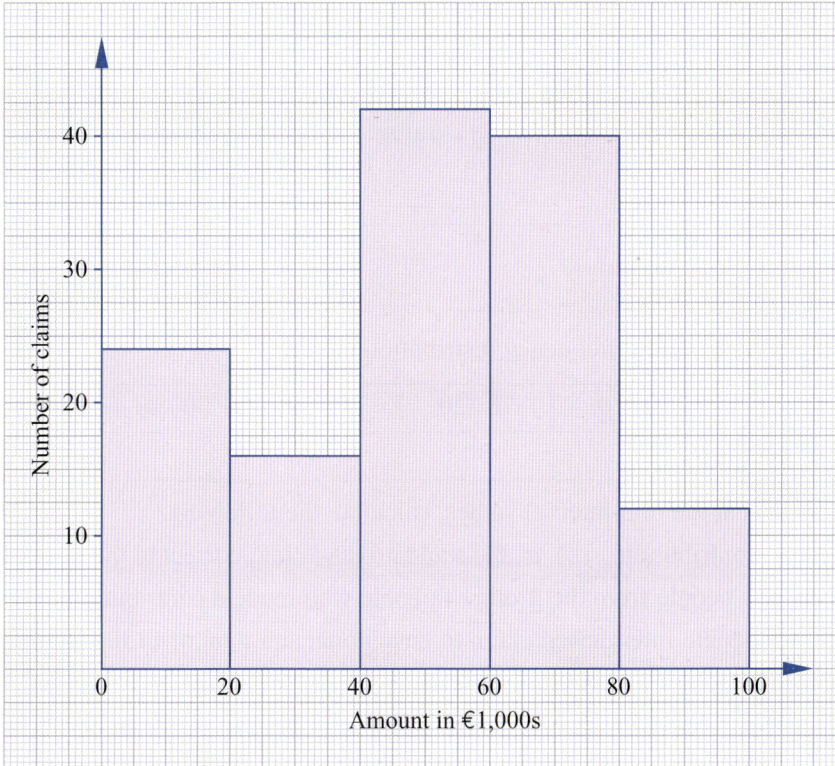

(i) Complete the corresponding frequency distribution table.

Amount (€1,000s)	0–20	20–40	40–60	60–80	80–100
Number of claims			42		

(ii) In which interval does the median lie?

(iii) By taking the mid-interval value of the median score in euro, find an estimate for the total amount paid out by the company in the year.

3. The distribution of contributions, in euro, given to a charity by a number of people is shown in the histogram below.

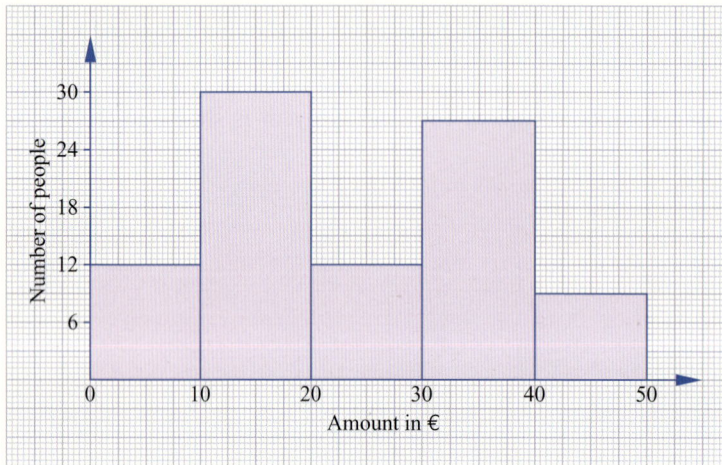

(i) Complete the corresponding frequency distribution table.

Amount in €	0–10	10–20	20–30	30–40	40–50
Number of people		30			

(ii) By taking the data at the mid-interval values, calculate the following.
  (a) μ, the mean contribution   (b) σ, the standard deviation, correct to the nearest euro

(iii) You interview two people from the group of people who made a contribution to the charity. The two people interviewed claim to have donated a total of €150. Would you be surprised by this claim? Justify your answer.

(iv) You interview a different three people from the group. Using $\mu + \sigma$ from above, what is the maximum amount you might expect these three people to claim to have contributed in total?

4. Study each of the pairs of graphs that follow. The mean for each graph (μ) is given above each histogram.

In each case, the mid-interval value was used to calculate μ. In other situations, with continuous data, μ may have slightly different values to the values given here.
For each pair of graphs presented below:
  (i) Indicate whether one of the graphs has a larger standard deviation than the other or if the two graphs have the same standard deviation by ticking the relevant box provided.
  (ii) Identify the characteristics of the graphs that make the standard deviation larger or smaller.
    Hint: While the relative shapes of the histograms can provide the answer, if it is not clear to you with any particular pair of histograms, you could consider calculating the standard deviation (σ) using the mid-interval values. This method, while not ideal, could help you arrive at the correct conclusion and also deepen your understanding of standard deviation.

(a)

P
$\mu = 3$

Q
$\mu = 3$

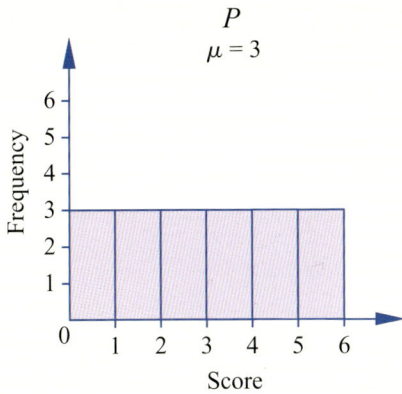

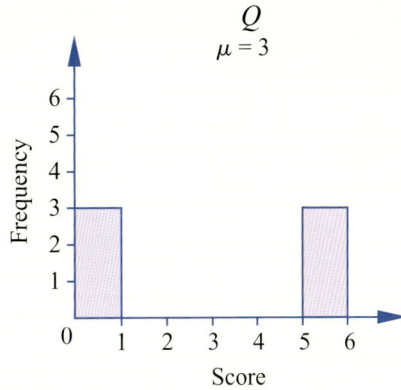

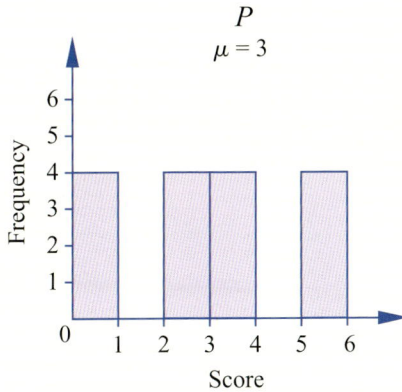

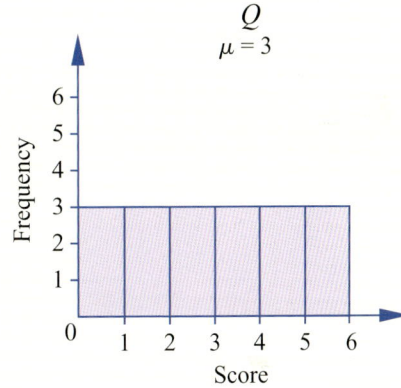

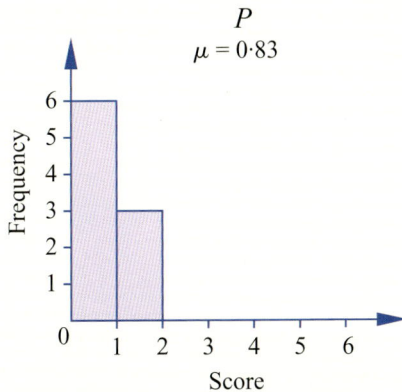

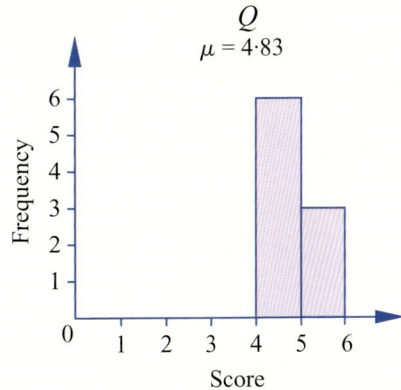

1. P has a larger standard deviation than Q ☐
2. Q has a larger standard deviation than P ☐
3. Both graphs have the same standard deviation ☐

(b)

P
$\mu = 3$

Q
$\mu = 3$

1. P has a larger standard deviation than Q ☐
2. Q has a larger standard deviation than P ☐
3. Both graphs have the same standard deviation ☐

(c)

P
$\mu = 0{\cdot}83$

Q
$\mu = 4{\cdot}83$

1. P has a larger standard deviation than Q ☐
2. Q has a larger standard deviation than P ☐
3. Both graphs have the same standard deviation ☐

(d)

P
$\mu = 2\cdot83$

Q
$\mu = 3\cdot83$

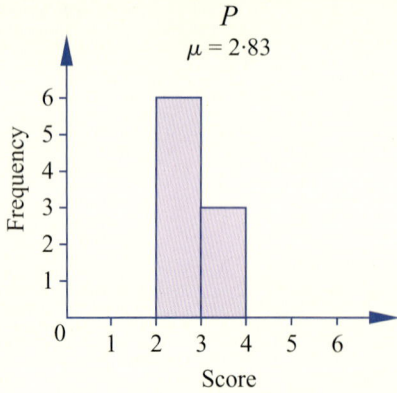

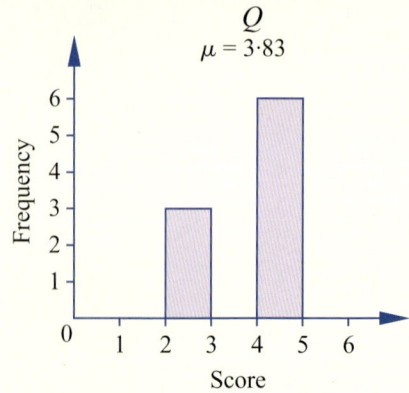

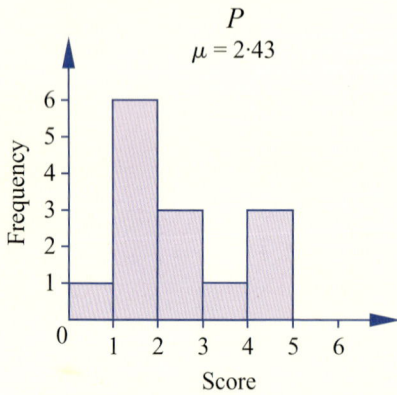

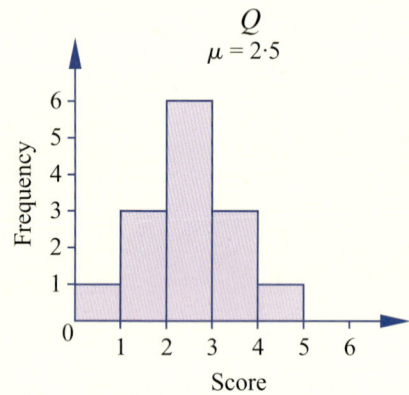

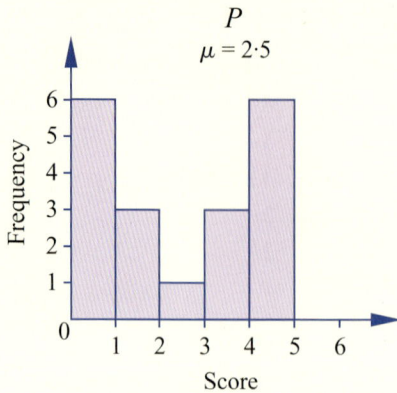

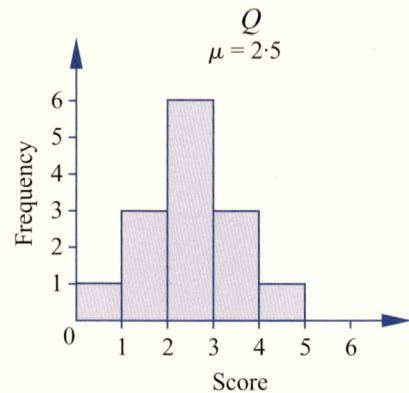

1. *P* has a larger standard deviation than *Q* ☐
2. *Q* has a larger standard deviation than *P* ☐
3. Both graphs have the same standard deviation ☐

(e)

P
$\mu = 2\cdot43$

Q
$\mu = 2\cdot5$

1. *P* has a larger standard deviation than *Q* ☐
2. *Q* has a larger standard deviation than *P* ☐
3. Both graphs have the same standard deviation ☐

(f)

P
$\mu = 2\cdot5$

Q
$\mu = 2\cdot5$

1. *P* has a larger standard deviation than *Q* ☐
2. *Q* has a larger standard deviation than *P* ☐
3. Both graphs have the same standard deviation ☐

EXAMPLE

This data shows the ages of people attending a school concert (numbers are rounded to the nearest 10).

Age	0–10	10–20	20–30	30–40	40–50	50–60	60–70
Frequency	20	190	180	140	90	70	10

Note: 0–10 means 0 is included but 10 is not, etc.

Draw a histogram and hence a frequency polygon to illustrate this data.

Solution:

To draw a frequency histogram, first work out the best scale to use.

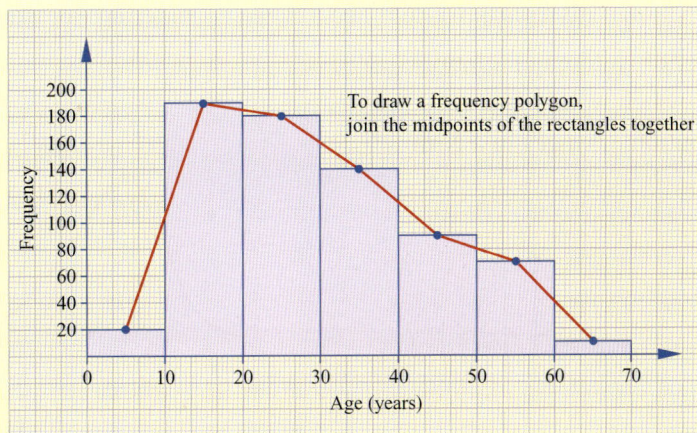

To draw a frequency polygon, join the midpoints of the rectangles together

Frequency curves

When the number of intervals is large, the frequency polygon consists of a large number of line segments. The frequency polygon approaches a smooth curve, known as a frequency curve.

The shape of a distribution

If distributions represented by a vertical line graph or a histogram are illustrated using a frequency curve, it is easier to see the general 'shape' of the distribution. For example:

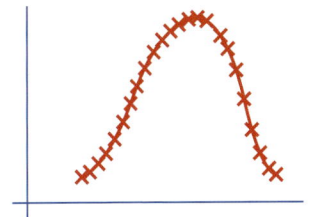

(i) **Uniform or rectangular**

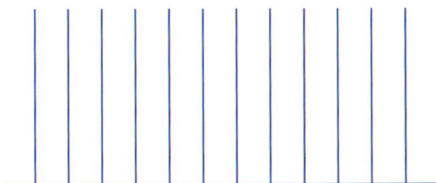

In a **uniform or rectangular distribution**, the data are evenly spread throughout the range.

(ii) The normal distribution

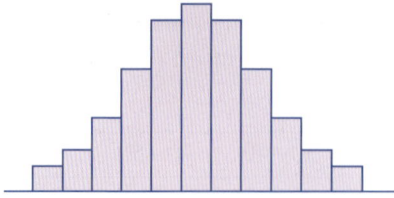

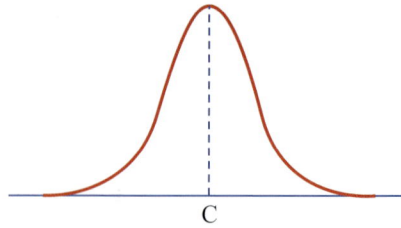

C

In this type of curve, mean = median = mode.

This symmetrical, bell-shaped distribution is known as a normal distribution.

An approximately normal distribution occurs when measuring quantities such as heights, masses or examination marks.

(iii) Positive skew

A **positively skewed distribution** could occur when considering, for example:

- The number of children in a family
- The age at which women marry
- The distribution of wages in a firm

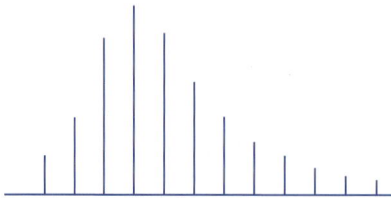

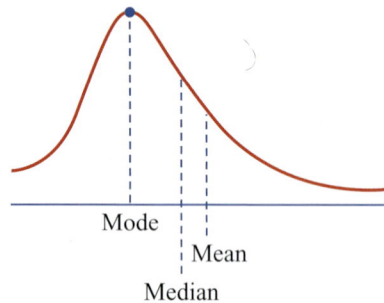

Mode
Mean
Median

In this type of curve, mean $>$ median.

In a positively skewed distribution, there is a long tail at the *positive* end of the distribution.

We also could say the distribution is skewed to the right.

(iv) Negative skew

A **negatively skewed distribution** could occur when considering, for example:

- Reaction times for an experiment
- Daily maximum temperatures for a month in the summer

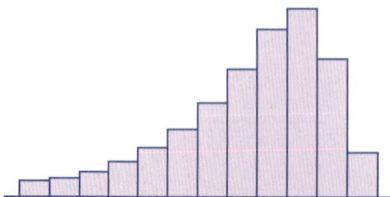

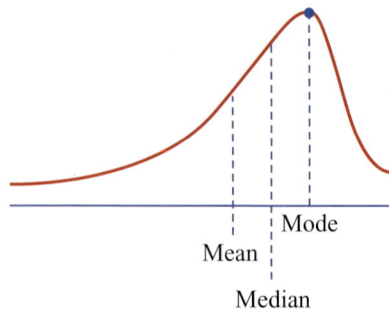

Mode
Mean
Median

In this type of curve, mean $<$ median.

In a negatively skewed distribution, there is a long tail at the *negative* end of the distribution. We also could say the distribution is skewed to the left.

(v) Reverse J-shape

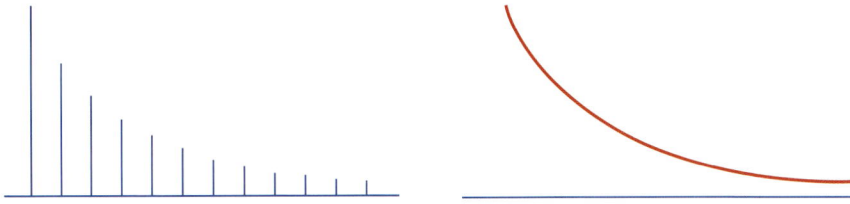

In a **J-shaped (reverse) distribution**, an initial 'bulge' is followed by a long tail.

A special note on 'tail' in statistics and probability:

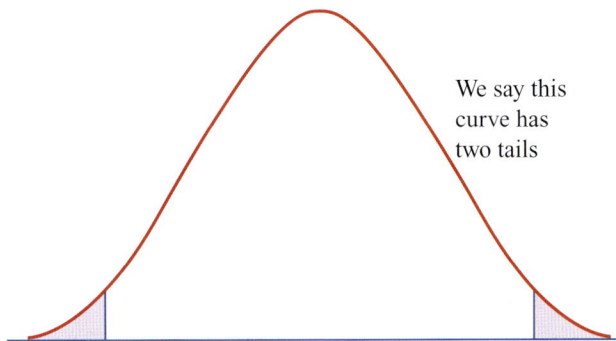

We say this curve has two tails

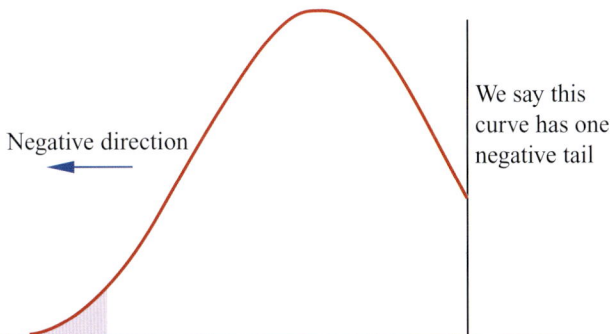

Negative direction

We say this curve has one negative tail

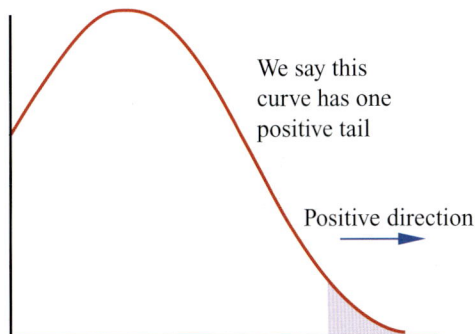

We say this curve has one positive tail

Positive direction

Distributions and shapes of histograms

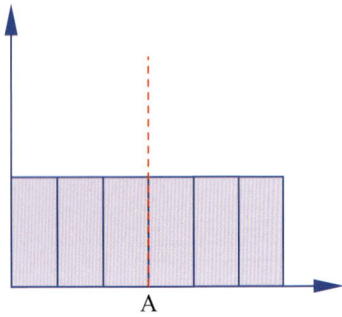

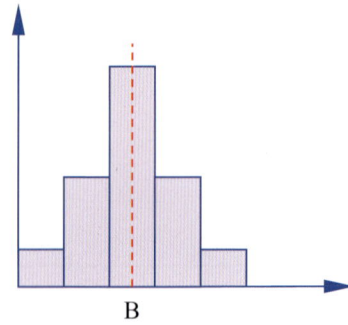

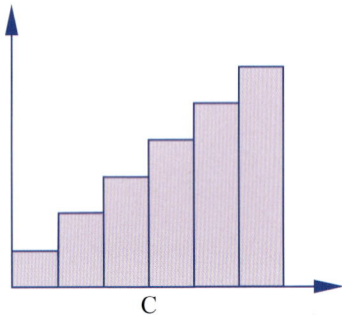

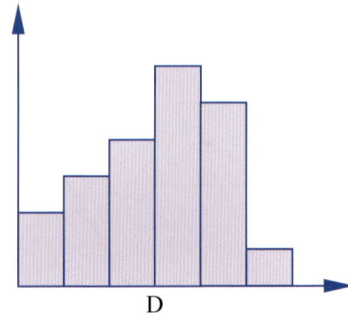

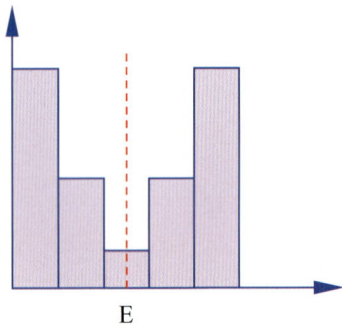

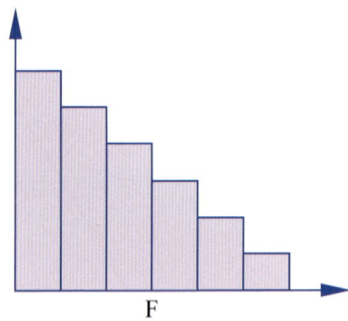

Histograms come in many shapes. Above we have six histograms, all with different shapes.

- A, B and E have an axis of symmetry, i.e. they are balanced.
- C, D and F have no axis of symmetry, i.e. they are less balanced or skewed in some way.

Histograms are a shape of the distribution.

- A has a totally uniform distribution.
- C has the distribution concentrated at the higher values.
- F has the distribution concentrated at the lower values.

Exercise 3.8

1. From the list of the following five curve descriptions, match each one with the correct common shape.

    (i) Normal curve/bell shape

    (ii) Uniform/rectangular

    (iii) Reverse J-shape

    (iv) Positively skewed

    (v) Negatively skewed

(a)

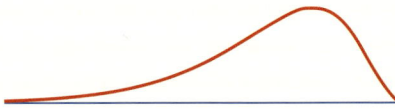

(b)

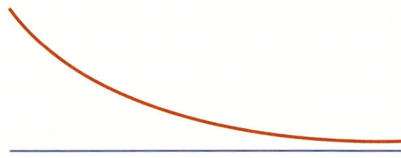

(c)

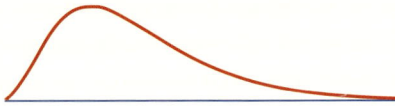

(d)

(e)

2. The yearly income of workers in the Netherlands is given in the following table.

Yearly income (€)	0–40,000	40,000–80,000	80,000–120,000	120,000–160,000	160,000–200,000	200,000–240,000	240,000–280,000
% of workers	30%	40%	15%	8%	4%	2%	1%

    (i) Draw a histogram and hence a frequency polygon to illustrate this data.

    (ii) How would you describe the shape of this distribution?

    (iii) Is the distribution skewed? If so, which way is it skewed?

3. A research physician obtained the following histogram with a sample of 400 diabetics.

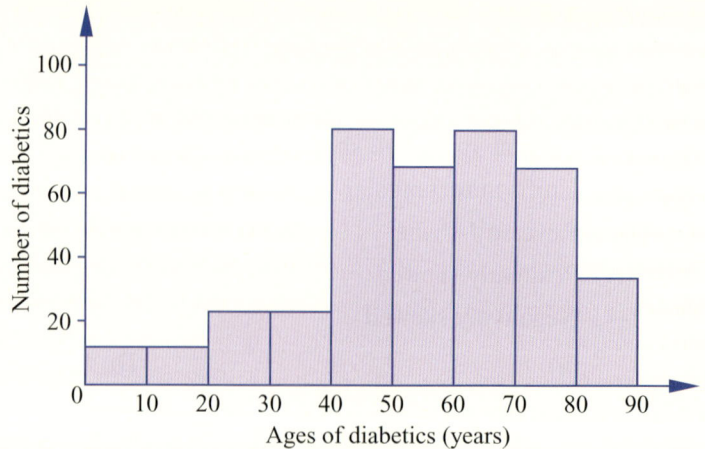

   (i) Identify the overall shape of the distribution, including whether the distribution is (approximately) symmetric, positively skewed or negatively skewed.

   (ii) In considering the shape of a distribution, it is helpful to observe the number of peaks (highest points). A distribution is said to be **unimodal** if it has one peak, **bimodal** if it has two peaks and **multimodal** if it has three or more peaks.

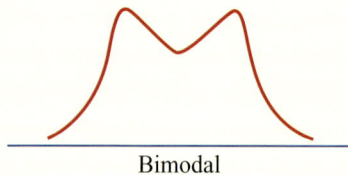

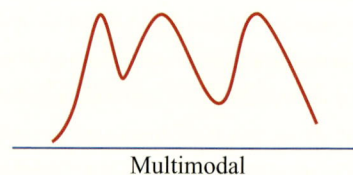

   Bimodal   Multimodal

   State whether the distribution above is:

   (a) Unimodal   **(b)** Bimodal   **(c)** Multimodal

4. The following is a frequency histogram for the number of questions answered incorrectly on an eight-question fraction quiz by each of the 50 students in a sixth class from primary school.

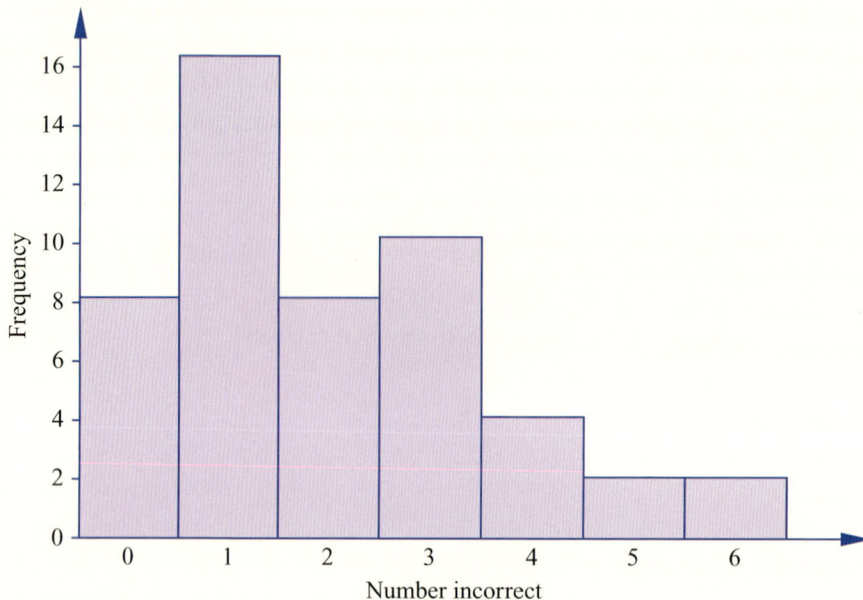

(i) Identify the overall shape of the distribution.

(ii) State whether the distribution is:

    (a) Unimodal   (b) Bimodal   (c) Multimodal

5. A transition year class carried out a survey on the age of a sample of people who use email.

Age	$10 < t \leq 18$	$18 < t \leq 26$	$26 < t \leq 34$	$34 < t \leq 42$	$42 < t \leq 50$	$50 < t \leq 58$	$58 < t \leq 66$
Frequency	8	35	53	44	33	17	10

(i) Draw a histogram of the data and calculate the mean and the median age of the email users.

(ii) How are the data distributed? Explain your reasoning.

(iii) Do you think this survey gives a result that is representative of email use in Ireland today?

(iv) How might such a survey have been carried out?

6. The following data represent the ages, to the nearest year, of 27 first year university students in the university gym.

$$22 \quad 18 \quad 22 \quad 24 \quad 20 \quad 28 \quad 19 \quad 21 \quad 29$$
$$34 \quad 19 \quad 22 \quad 25 \quad 33 \quad 26 \quad 20 \quad 23 \quad 28$$
$$41 \quad 19 \quad 30 \quad 23 \quad 21 \quad 33 \quad 29 \quad 22 \quad 24$$

(i) Determine the mean, median and mode for the data set.

(ii) Do you think the data are normally distributed? Give a reason for your answer.

(iii) Determine the standard deviation of the data.

(iv) Do you think these 27 students would be representative of first year students from the university? Justify your answer.

7. (i) Draw a rough histogram of a data set that is skewed to the right.

(ii) A data set consists of the salaries in a company employing 200 factory workers and three highly paid executives. For this data set, which is higher, the mean or median, or are they about equal?

(iii) Would the range or the median be more heavily influenced by extreme values?

8. Using the mean, median and mode, sketch the shape of the frequency curve with the following characteristics.

(i) Mean = 8·5, median = 7, mode = 6·7

(ii) Mean = 5, median = 5, mode = 5

(iii) Mean = 8·8, median = 8·8, mode = 10, 12

(iv) Mean = 10, median = 12, mode = 13

9. The shapes of the histograms of four different sets of data are shown below.

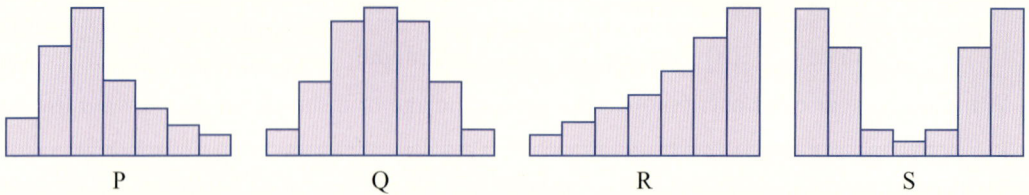

	P	Q	R	S
The data are positively skewed				
The data are negatively skewed				
The mean is equal to the median				
The mean is greater than the median				
There is a single mode				

(i) Complete the table below, indicating whether the statement is correct (✓) or incorrect (✗) with respect to each data set.

(ii) Assume that the four histograms are drawn on the same scale.
State which of them has the largest standard deviation and justify your answer.

Stem and leaf diagrams

Histograms provide an easy-to-understand summary of the distribution of data. However, they do not show the data values themselves. Below is a histogram of the time taken by 24 students to complete an exercise.

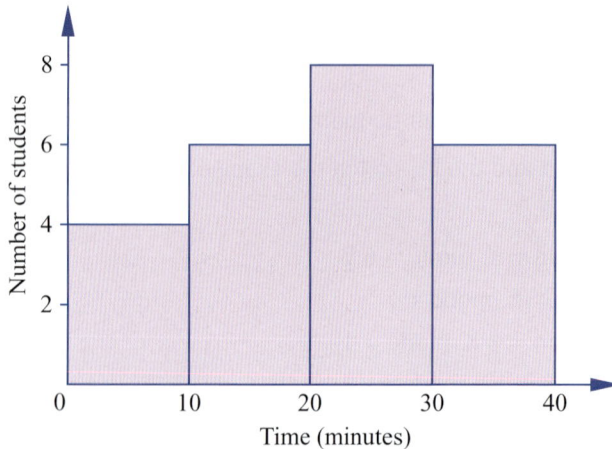

To look at this data in more detail, consider the following example.

EXAMPLE 1

The number of minutes taken to complete an exercise was recorded for 24 students in a class. The results were as follows.

20 9 36 24 17 32 25 21 14 8 26 38
18 15 21 8 11 23 6 37 25 32 17 36

Represent the data with a stem and leaf plot.

Solution:

The smallest value is 6 and the largest value is 38.

Let the intervals be 0–9, 10–19, 20–29, 30–39.

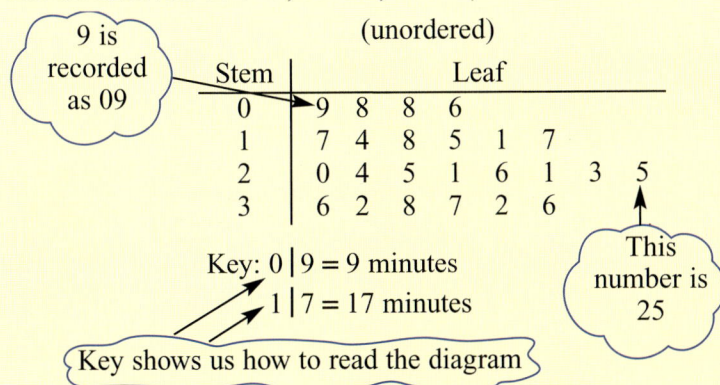

9 is recorded as 09

(unordered)

Stem	Leaf
0	9 8 8 6
1	7 4 8 5 1 7
2	0 4 5 1 6 1 3 5
3	6 2 8 7 2 6

Key: 0|9 = 9 minutes
1|7 = 17 minutes

Key shows us how to read the diagram

This number is 25

Number of minutes taken to complete an exercise.

(ordered)

Stem	Leaf
0	6 8 8 9
1	1 4 5 7 7 8
2	0 1 1 3 4 5 5 6
3	2 2 6 6 7 8

Key: 0|9 = 9 minutes
1|7 = 17 minutes

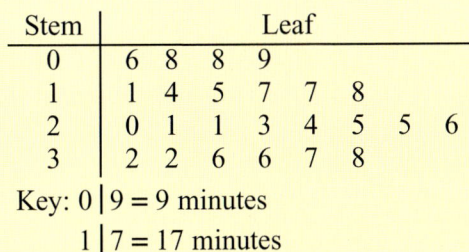

Enter the leaves, crossing out the values as you record them. This is called an **unordered** stem and leaf plot. Then create a new stem and leaf plot so that the leaves are in increasing order. This is called an **ordered** stem and leaf plot.

If you turn the stem and leaf diagram on its side, it has the same shape as the original histogram but with individual values shown.

EXAMPLE 2

The ordered stem and leaf plot shows the times taken by 24 students to complete an exercise.

Stem	Leaf
0	6 8 8 9
1	1 4 5 7 7 8
2	0 1 1 3 4 5 5 6
3	2 2 6 6 7 8

Key: $0\,|\,9 = 9$ minutes

$\quad\;\,1\,|\,7 = 17$ minutes

Use this stem and leaf plot to calculate the following.

  (i) The range   **(ii)** The median   **(iii)** The lower quartile

(iv) The upper quartile   **(v)** The interquartile range

Solution:

  (i) Range = largest value − smallest value = $38 - 6 = 32$ minutes.

 (ii) The median mark (Q_2) is the time value halfway through the distribution.

      The halfway value is between the 12th and 13th values

      $= \frac{1}{2}[21 + 21] = 21$

      $\therefore$ The median = 21 minutes.

(iii) The lower quartile (Q_1) is the value one-quarter of the way through the distribution.

      This one-quarter value is between the 6th and 7th values.

      $= \frac{1}{2}[14 + 15] = 14\frac{1}{2}$

      $\therefore$ The lower quartile (Q_1) = $14\frac{1}{2}$ minutes.

 (iv) The upper quartile (Q_3) is the value three-quarters of the way through the distribution.

      This three-quarters value is between the 18th and 19th values.

      $= \frac{1}{2}[26 + 32] = 29$

      $\therefore$ The upper quartile (Q_3) = 29 minutes.

  (v) The interquartile range

      $= Q_3 - Q_1 = 29 - 14\frac{1}{2} = 14\frac{1}{2}$ minutes.

Note: The interquartile range is more useful than the range.

Here is a diagram to help clarify the situation.

The median (Q_2) is the value that subdivides the ordered data into two halves.

The quartiles (Q_1 and Q_3) subdivide the data into quarters.

EXAMPLE 3

Use a back-to-back stem and leaf diagram to compare the examination marks in History and Geography for a class of 20 primary school students.

History	75	69	58	58	46	44	32	50	57	77
	81	61	61	45	31	44	53	66	48	53
Geography	52	58	68	77	38	85	43	44	55	66
	65	79	44	71	84	72	63	69	79	72

(i) Use the stemplots to find the median mark for History and the median mark for Geography.

(ii) By comparing the medians, state which subject had the highest marks.

Solution:

(i) The completed diagram before rearranging:

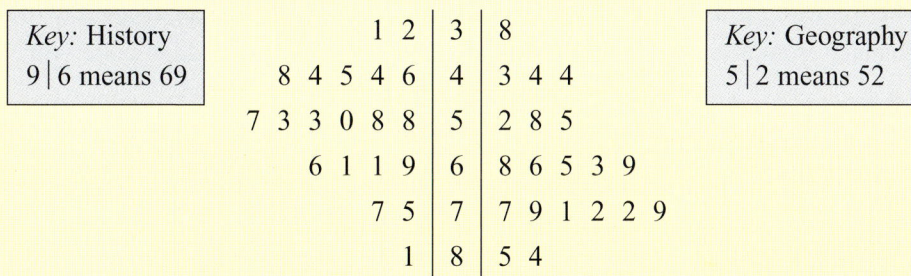

Key: History 9 | 6 means 69					Key: Geography 5 | 2 means 52

```
          1 2 | 3 | 8
      8 4 5 4 6 | 4 | 3 4 4
    7 3 3 0 8 8 | 5 | 2 8 5
        6 1 1 9 | 6 | 8 6 5 3 9
            7 5 | 7 | 7 9 1 2 2 9
              1 | 8 | 5 4
```

The final diagram, arranged in order:

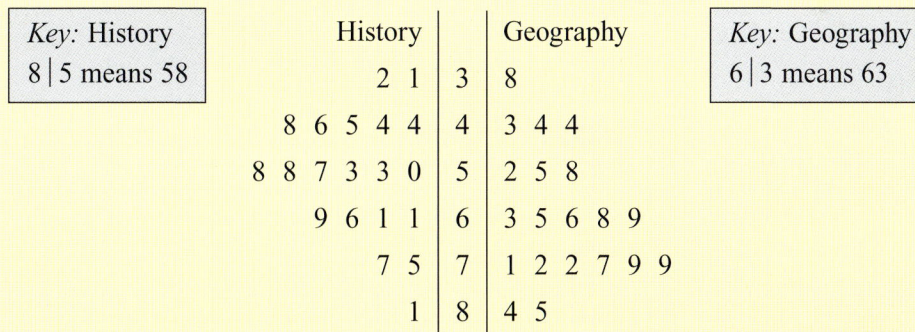

Key: History 8 | 5 means 58		History	Geography		Key: Geography 6 | 3 means 63

```
          2 1 | 3 | 8
      8 6 5 4 4 | 4 | 3 4 4
    8 8 7 3 3 0 | 5 | 2 5 8
        9 6 1 1 | 6 | 3 5 6 8 9
            7 5 | 7 | 1 2 2 7 9 9
              1 | 8 | 4 5
```

From the diagram, it is clear that the class had higher marks in Geography than in History and it appears that they performed better in Geography. However, this would depend on the standard of marking used in the two examinations. It would also depend on the standards of questions used in the two examinations.

The median for both subjects is associated with the middle result when the results are written in order.

The median for both subjects is the average of the 10th and 11th results in the final diagram.

History	Geography
53 and 57	66 and 68
are the relevant results.	are the relevant results.
$\therefore$ Median for History	$\therefore$ Median for Geography
$= \dfrac{53 + 57}{2}$	$= \dfrac{66 + 68}{2}$
$= 55$ marks	$= 67$ marks

(ii) A comparison of the medians reinforces our notion that the marks for Geography are greater than the marks for History.

Exercise 3.9

1. The following is a stem and leaf diagram (unordered) for the lengths of stay in Ireland obtained from a sample of 36 Australian residents who travelled here one year.

```
0 | 5 3 3 1 6 2 1 1 8 5 3 3
1 | 6 3 1 5 4 0 2 7 8 0 2 2
2 | 1 0 1 7 1
3 | 1 2
4 | 1 4 8
5 | 6
6 | 4
```

Key: $3|1 = 31$ days

(i) Identify the overall shape of the distribution.

(ii) State whether the distribution is:
   (a) Unimodal (b) Bimodal (c) Multimodal

(iii) Find the median (Q_2).

(iv) Find the interquartile range.

2. (i) Complete the following table for the height and weight of the seven dwarfs.

	Values	Mode	Median	Mean	Standard deviation
Height (cm)	101, 110, 121, 134, 113, 121, 98			114	12·1
Weight (kg)	63, 71, 68, 92, 55, 77, 92	92	71		

(ii) Represent **(a)** the heights and **(b)** the weights of the dwarfs on two separate stem and leaf plots.

(iii) Comment on the usefulness or otherwise of the two stemplots drawn.

(iv) If the ages in years of the seven dwarfs are 685, 702, 498, 539, 402, 685 and 619, comment on how useful it would be to construct a stem and leaf plot for the ages of the seven dwarfs.

3. Twenty refrigerator motors were run to destruction under advanced stress conditions and the times to failure (to the nearest day) were recorded in the ordered stemplot, as follows.

Key: 0 | 8 = 8 days	**0**	4
2 | 4 = 24 days	**0**	6 *x* 8 8 8
	1	0 2 2 3 *y*
	1	5 5 5 *k* 9
	2	0 4
	2	5 *w*

Find the value of the following.

(i) *w*, given the range is 24

(ii) *x*, given the mode is 8

(iii) *y*, given the median is 13·5

(iv) *k*, given the mean is 14

4. The ages of 12 workers (to the nearest year) in a government department in ascending order are 25, 26, 27, 27, 29, 29, *A*, 30, *B*, 33, 33, *C*. The median age is 29·5 and the upper quartile (Q_3) is 33.

(i) Write down the value of *A*.

(ii) Write down the value of *B*.

(iii) Calculate the value of *C* if the mean age is 30.

5. In soccer careers extending over 15 seasons, Pelubio (1948–62) and Maraldinho (1986–2000) were the top players in their respective eras. The ordered back-to-back stem and leaf diagram that follows shows the number of goals scored by both players during their respective 15-year careers.

Key: 6 | 3 = 36 goals scored	Pelubio				Maraldinho	*Key:* 2 | 1 = 21 goals scored
		7	0	4 9		
	9 5	1	*x* *x* *x*			
8 3 *y* *y* *y* 1		2	0 1 *B* 5 6 *V*			
7 6 5 *R* 0		3	2 3 7 *Q*			
W		4				

(i) Given that the range of scores for both players was equal to 34 goals, find the value of W and the value of Q.

(ii) If Maraldinho's modal (mode) score of 16 goals was six lower than Pelubio's modal score, write down the value of x and the value of y.

(iii) If the median score of both players was equal, write down the value of B.

(iv) Pelubio's total goals was 390 and Maraldinho's total goals was 345. Calculate the value of R and the value of V.

(v) Suggest two reasons why Pelubio scored more goals in his career than Maraldinho.

6. The pulse rates of 30 workers in a factory were measured before and after taking exercise.

Before: 110, 93, 81, 75, 73, 73, 48, 53, 69, 69, 66, 111, 100, 93, 90, 50, 57, 64, 90, 111, 91, 70, 70, 51, 79, 93, 105, 51, 66, 98

After: 117, 84, 77, 108, 130, 69, 77, 84, 84, 86, 95, 125, 96, 104, 104, 137, 143, 70, 80, 131, 145, 106, 130, 109, 137, 75, 104, 72, 97, 80

(i) Display the data in an ordered back-to-back stemplot. (Use class intervals 40–49, 50–59, 60–69, etc.)

(ii) Calculate the median value for **(a)** before and **(b)** after taking exercise.

(iii) Calculate the range of values of pulse rates for **(a)** before and **(b)** after taking exercise.

(iv) By analysing your answers to **(i)**, **(ii)** and **(iii)**, what conclusions can you draw?

(v) This investigation of the factory workers' pulse rates arose from comments that these workers were unusually athletic. State **one** additional piece of information that you would need in order to decide whether that is true.

7. A teacher recorded the times taken by 20 boys to swim one length of the pool. The times are given to the nearest second.

(i) Using the intervals 24–25, 26–27, etc., draw a stem and leaf diagram to illustrate the results.

32 31 26 27 27 32 29 26 25 25
29 31 32 26 30 24 32 27 26 31

(ii) The teacher later recorded the times taken by 20 girls to swim one length of the pool. The times are given to the nearest second. Display the data for boys and girls in an ordered back-to-back stemplot. (Use the intervals 24–25, 26–27, etc.)

25 34 29 26 27 27 33 28 26 24
30 31 33 25 29 25 33 26 26 32

(iii) By considering any two statistical terms, e.g. range, median, mean, mode, etc., what conclusions can you draw when comparing the times for the two groups?

8. The population of Ireland is ageing, though less rapidly than in other developed countries. Here is a stemplot of the per cents of residents aged 65 and over in the 32 counties according to a recent census. The stems are whole per cents and the leaves are tenths of a per cent.

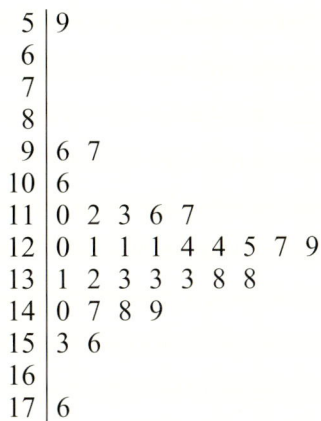

```
 5 | 9
 6 |
 7 |
 8 |
 9 | 6 7
10 | 6
11 | 0 2 3 6 7
12 | 0 1 1 1 4 4 5 7 9
13 | 1 2 3 3 3 8 8
14 | 0 7 8 9
15 | 3 6
16 |
17 | 6
```

(i) There are two outliers: County Leitrim has the highest percent of older residents and County Dublin has the lowest. What are the per cents for these two counties?

(ii) Ignoring Leitrim and Dublin, describe the shape, centre and spread of this distribution.

9. An educator believes that Project Maths methods will help Leaving Certificate students improve their maths grades. She arranges for a Leaving Cert class of 21 students to take part in Project Maths methods for a one-year period. A control class of 24 Leaving Cert students follows the traditional maths methods. At the end of the year, a maths test is given to all students. The results in percentages are given on the ordered back-to-back stem and leaf plot.

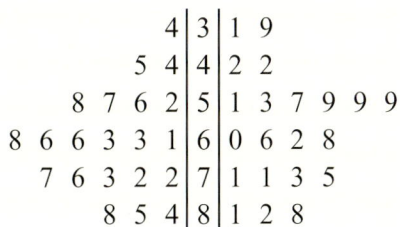

```
            4 | 3 | 1 9
          5 4 | 4 | 2 2
      8 7 6 2 | 5 | 1 3 7 9 9 9
    8 6 6 3 3 1 | 6 | 0 6 2 8
      7 6 3 2 2 | 7 | 1 1 3 5
          8 5 4 | 8 | 1 2 8
```

Write down four errors in the above ordered back-to-back stem and leaf plot.

Scatter plots (scatter graphs)

Is the number of cigarettes smoked by an individual related to the age of their death?

Are your overall Leaving Certificate results related to the number of hours you spend at your part-time job?

To look at the relationship between two sets of quantitative data, we plot the points on a graph (similar to x-axis/y-axis). Data that come in pairs are called **bivariate data**.

EXAMPLE 1

A car salesman recorded the age (to the nearest year) and the total distance travelled as measured on the cars' odometer (to the nearest thousand kilometres) of 16 cars in the salesroom.

Does the distance travelled by a car increase over the lifespan of the car? If so, is this increase consistent?

Here we show the total distance travelled by the car plotted against the age of the car.

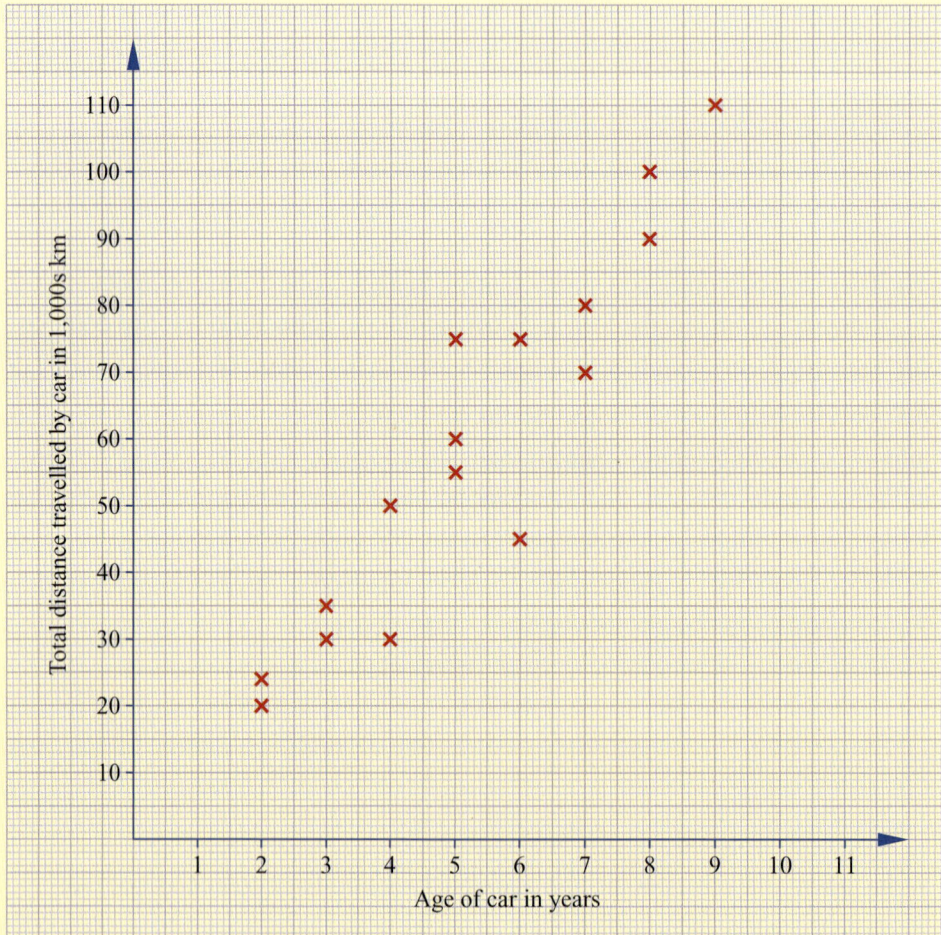

The scatter plot (scatter graph) shows a consistent and steady increase.

The advantage of scatter plots is that simply by looking at them we can see patterns, trends, relationships and even the ocassional extraordinary value sitting apart from the others. Scatter plots are the best way to start observing the relationship between two **quantitative** variables.

Questions scatter plots can help us answer:

- Has the number and intensity of storms/hurricanes increased due to global warming in the past 100 years?
- Does weight at birth determine the eventual height of an adult?

EXAMPLE 2

A class of students takes examinations in English and French. The marks they obtained are as follows.

Student	1	2	3	4	5	6	7	8
English	70	55	40	60	70	80	65	50
French	65	60	40	70	80	85	30	55

  (i) Plot the data on a scatter diagram.

 (ii) Comment on the diagram in the context of the question.

Solution:

(i)

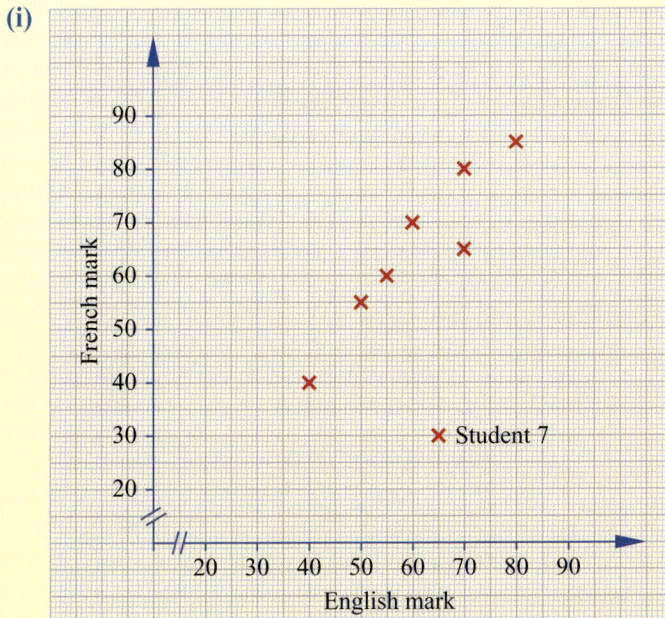

 (ii) With the exception of student 7, there is a very strong correspondence between the two sets of marks.

Note: Always look for the unexpected. An example of something unexpected would be student 7 in the scatter plot above. A point standing away from the overall pattern is called an **outlier**.

Scatter plot patterns

Here are five scatter diagrams that are typical of what we meet.

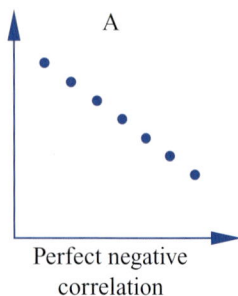

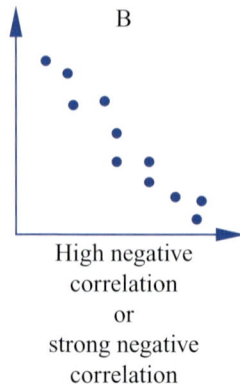

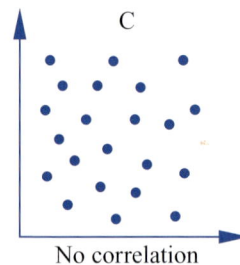

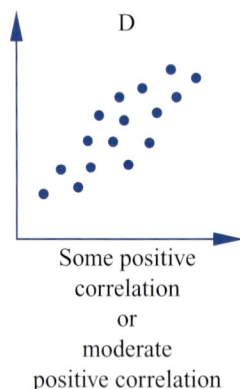

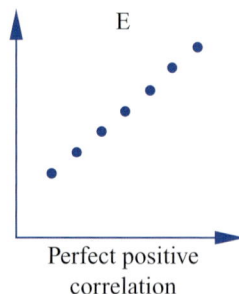

A — Perfect negative correlation

B — High negative correlation or strong negative correlation

C — No correlation

D — Some positive correlation or moderate positive correlation

E — Perfect positive correlation

We get negative correlation where increasing values of one variable are associated with generally decreasing values of the other variable (case A and B above).

We get positive correlation where increasing values of one variable are associated with generally increasing values of the other variable (case D and E above).

We have no correlation when the points are randomly and widely spaced out (case C above).

Note: Correlation measures the strength of the linear association between two quantitative variables. Before using correlation, check the following.

1. Are both variables quantitative?
2. Check the scatter plot for evidence of 'straightness', i.e. can you visualise a straight line passing through the plot and representing the relationship? We call this the line of best fit, by eye.
3. Check for outliers and extreme values (stragglers). Outliers are very important and always deserve special attention. Outliers can make a weak correlation look strong or can hide a strong correlation.

EXAMPLE 1

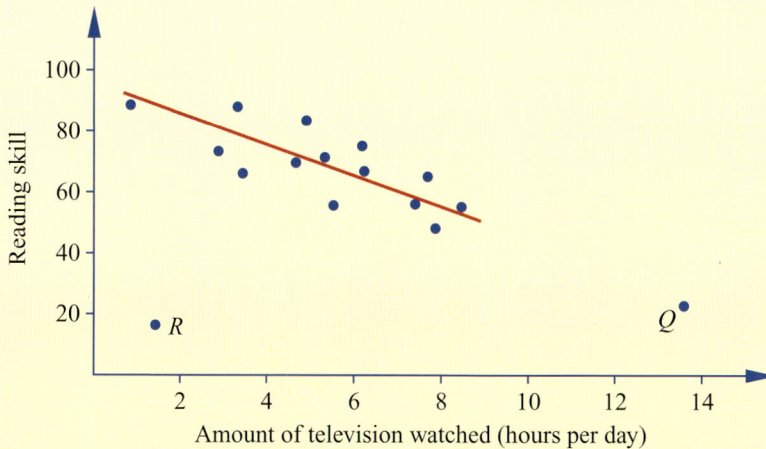

The scatter plot shows the reading skill and amount of television watched by 16 fifth class students selected from primary schools in Co. Meath.

Notes: 1. Both variables are quantitative.

2. A line of best fit, by eye, is drawn.

3. R is a definite outlier. Q is an extreme point (straggler) but seems to lie on the extended line of best fit.

EXAMPLE 2

Seven students took an exam in Statistics and an exam in Mathematics. The examination placings of the seven students were as follows.

Student	Statistics placing	Mathematics placing
A	2	1
B	1	3
C	4	7
D	6	5
E	5	6
F	3	2
G	7	4

(i) Illustrate the placings on a scatter diagram.

(ii) Classify the correlation from the diagram using two words from the following list:

Positive   Negative   None

Weak   Strong   Moderate

(iii) Would you consider any points on the diagram to be outliers? Explain.

(iv) 'A small number of data points can make it difficult to claim strong correlation.' Discuss.

Solution:

(i)

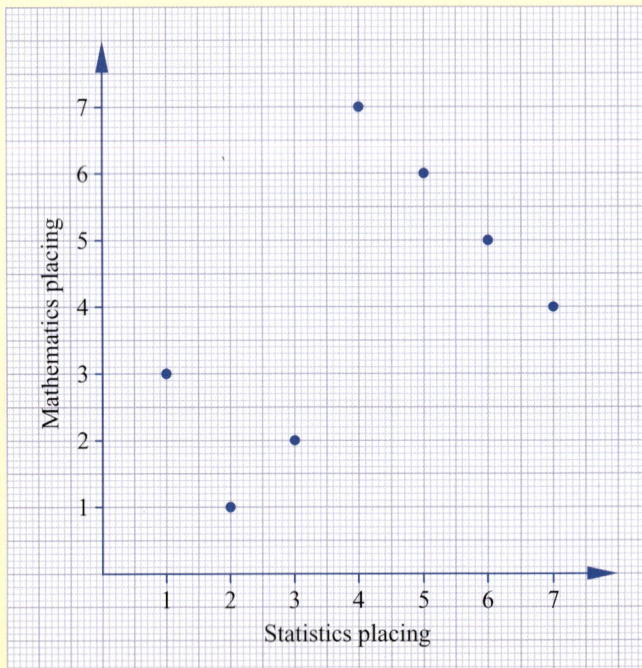

(ii) Weak positive.

Using two words to describe the correlation seems to hint that the word 'none' in the list is not required here.

We often find ambiguous/unclear results and we simply do our best to answer the question.

(iii) Some observers might suggest that (7, 4) and (4, 7) are outliers. However, my answer is that there are no obvious outliers: all pairs seem OK.

(iv) I agree with the statement. My intuition tells me there is possibly a strong positive correlation between Statistics placings and Mathematics placings.

A bigger number of students, 12 or even 20, would clarify the situation. Seven students is too few for a clear correlation (if it exists) to become apparent.

Note: The examiner may not agree with this discussion. However, the argument is logical and makes sense, and that is what will be required in the examination.

Exercise 3.10

1. Is the correlation between the following pairs of variables likely to be strong, moderate, weak or none? Is it likely to be positive, negative or zero?

   (i) Daily sunshine in Los Angeles and Cork

   (ii) Daily rainfall in Athlone and Mullingar

   (iii) Engine size of a car and its petrol consumption

   (iv) The weight of a randomly selected person and the amount of time they spend in a gym

   (v) The depth and the visibility when scuba diving

   (vi) Students' shoe size and CAO points gained

   (vii) Drivers' blood alcohol level and reaction time

   (viii) Number of firemen called out to a fire and the amount of the insurance claim

2. An economics student wants to find out whether the length of time people spend in education affects the income they earn. The student carries out a small study. Fifteen adults are asked to state their annual income and the number of years they spent in full-time education. The data are given in the table below, as well as a partially completed scatter diagram.

Years of education	Income (€1,000s)
11	65
11	28
12	30
13	35
13	43
14	55
15	38
16	45
16	38
17	55
17	60
17	30
17	58
17	65
19	70

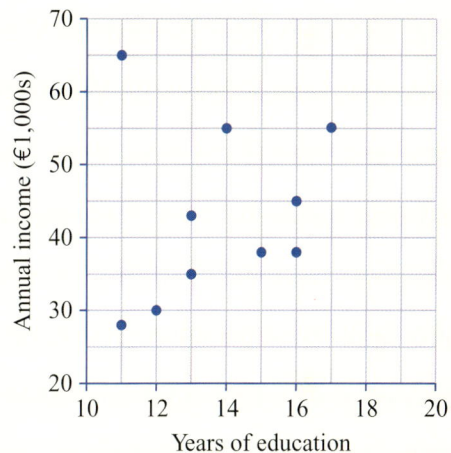

   (i) The last five rows of data have not been included on the scatter plot. Insert them now.

   (ii) Highlight outliers (if any). Justify your reasoning.

(iii) What can you conclude from the scatter plot?

(iv) Suggest two problems that could be associated with carrying out such a study.

3. Ray makes and sells ice cream and he wants to predict how much he needs to make each day. He believes he sells more when the weather is hotter. He recorded the maximum temperature and the ice cream sales every day for eight days. His results are summarised in the table.

Temperature (°C)	16	15	18	14	21	25	23	24
Sales in €	80	70	80	60	100	150	130	130

(i) Draw a scatter diagram of this data.

(ii) Do you agree with Ray's claim?

(iii) Ray can use the graph to predict sales depending on the temperature. Can you estimate what his expected sales would be on a day with a maximum temperature of 22°C?

(iv) Ray's friend, Chris, suggests that the day of the week could also affect sales and that Ray should include this in his analysis. Is Chris correct? Justify your answer.

4. One measure of personal fitness is the time taken for an individual's pulse rate to return to normal after strenuous exercise; the greater the fitness, the shorter the time. Pat and Nora have the same normal pulse rates. Following a short programme of strenuous exercise, both recorded their pulse rates P at time t minutes after they had stopped exercising. Nora's results are given in the table below.

Time (minutes)	t	0·5	1·0	1·5	2·0	3·0	4·0	5·0
Pulse rate for Nora	P	125	113	102	94	81	83	71

(i) Draw a scatter diagram to show Nora's data.

(ii) Pat's results are given in the table below.

Time (minutes)	t	0·5	1·0	1·5	2·0	3·0	4·0	5·0
Pulse rate for Pat	P	122	118	111	108	96	88	77

Using a different colour pen, plot the scatter points for Pat on the same diagram as Nora's data.

(iii) Giving a reason, state who you consider to be fitter.

(iv) Are there any outliers in either set of data? Explain.

5. Statements A, B, C, D and E represent descriptions of the correlation between two variables.

   A High positive linear correlation
   B Low positive linear correlation
   C No correlation
   D Low negative linear correlation
   E High negative linear correlation

   Which statement **best** represents the relationship between the two variables shown in each of the scatter diagrams below?

(i)

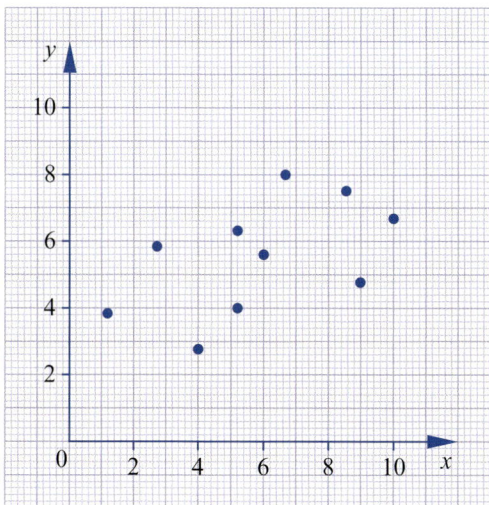

(ii)

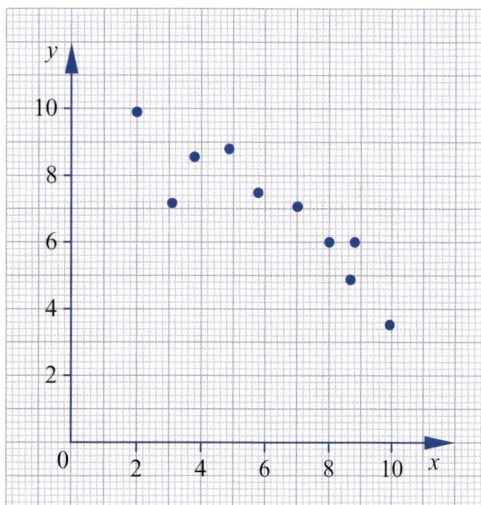

(iii)

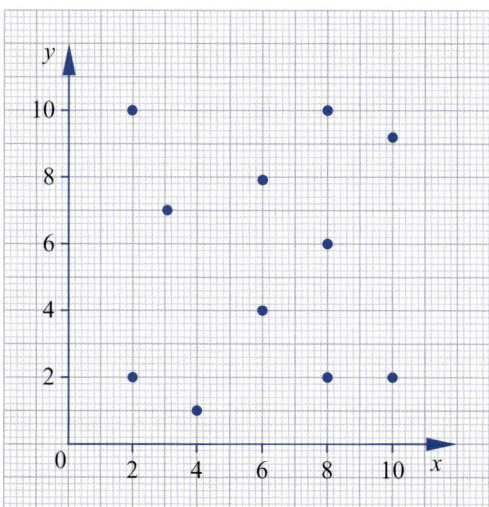

(iv)

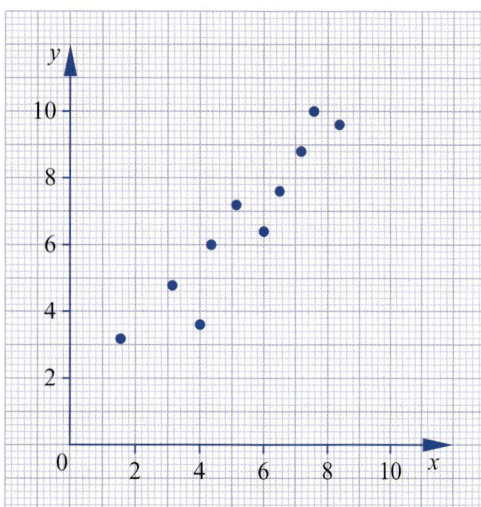

6.

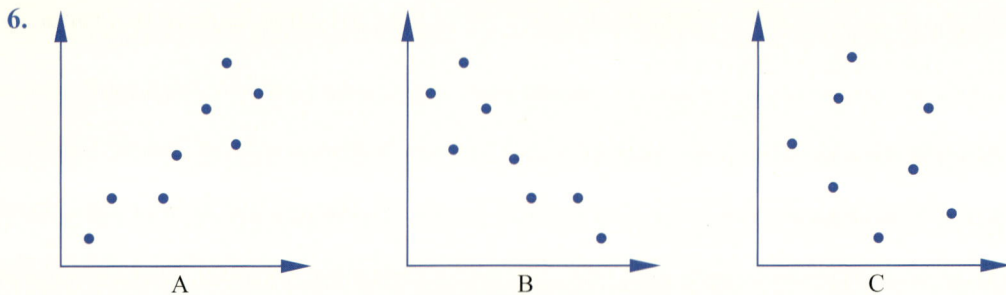

A   B   C

Match the scatter diagrams A, B, C with the statements P, Q, R.

P   As you get older, your eyesight disimproves.

Q   Students who are good at maths are usually good at physics.

R   There is no connection between height and intelligence.

7. A school owns a minibus, which is used for transporting students to sports fixtures and on school visits. It is the practice that for each trip the mileage and the petrol consumption are recorded. The tank is topped up with petrol at the end of each trip.

A teacher decides to record, for each trip, the number of students transported, x, and the petrol consumption, y, in km per litre. The following table shows the data recorded for a number of trips.

Trip	A	B	C	D	E	F	G	H	I	J
x	14	2	16	9	12	5	7	7	15	11
y	8·07	8·98	8·02	8·42	8·39	8·21	8·69	8·85	8·13	8·19

(i)   Draw a scatter diagram of the data.

(ii)   'The scatter diagram shows a strong positive correlation for the data.' Discuss.

(iii) On one of the trips, a large amount of heavy equipment was carried in addition to the students. Identify the most likely trip, giving a reason.

(iv)   Suggest two possible errors the teacher might make gathering and recording the data. For example, does the distance travelled matter?

Measuring correlation of scatter plots (scatter graphs)

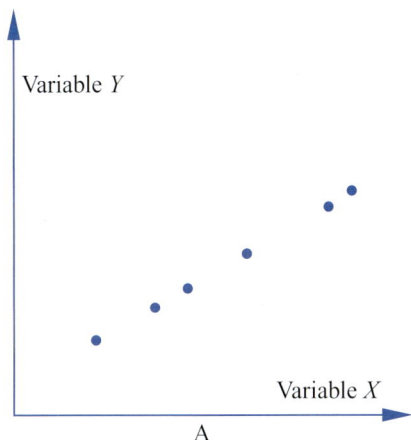

A

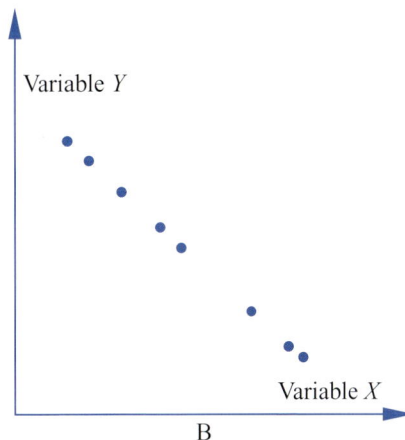

B

The points on scatter graph A are in a straight line. In this case we say there is **perfect positive correlation** between the two variables, X and Y.

We use the letter r to represent the correlation. We say that $r = 1$ when we have perfect positive correlation.

The points on scatter graph B are in a straight line. In this case we say there is **perfect negative correlation** between the two variables, X and Y.

We say that $r = -1$ when we have perfect negative correlation.

How the correlation, r, measures the direction and strength of a linear association

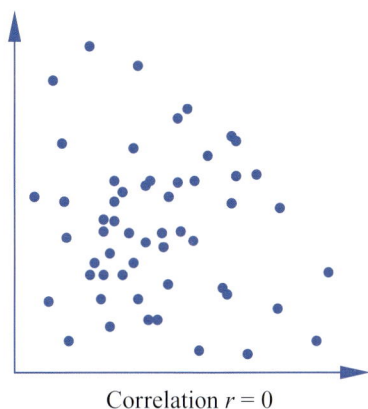

Correlation $r = 0$

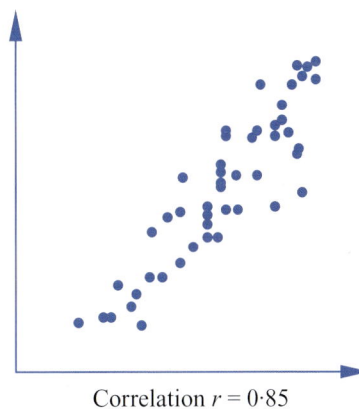

Correlation $r = 0.85$

145

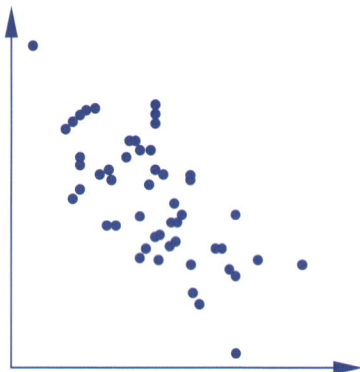
Correlation $r = -0.6$

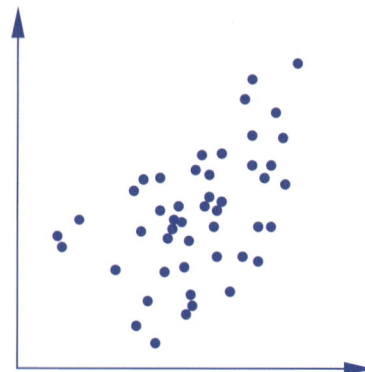
Correlation $r = 0.5$

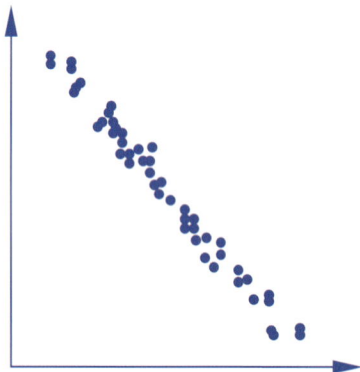
Correlation $r = -0.95$

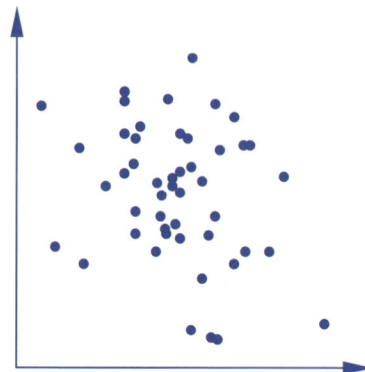
Correlation $r = -0.25$

To calculate the correlation coefficient

The first step is to establish that a linear (straight line) relationship exists between two variables, x and y. To do this, we draw and then examine a scatter plot.

When we see a straight line relationship on the scatter plot, we then proceed to measure the strength of the relationship between the two variables.

There are several ways of doing this. The most common measure is the **Pearson product moment correlation coefficient**, usually known as the correlation coefficient, r.

Usually we estimate the value of the population correlation coefficient using samples from the populations. That is, when looking for a correlation between the age of a car and the distance travelled, we do not consider every car, only the samples of cars given in the question.

This sample correlation coefficient is called r and it measures the linearity of the relationship between x and y for a sample of n points.

$$(x_1, y_1), (x_2, y_2), (x_3, y_3) \ldots\ldots\ldots\ldots (x_n, y_n)$$

EXAMPLE 1

Sally decides to buy her first car. She has an idea that the value of a car decreases with age. Sally checks the age and price of nine cars in her local garage.

Age (years)	2	3	5	9	5	7	8	4	2
Price (€1,000s)	24	19	16	4	18	10	6	15	23

(i) Graph the data on a scatter plot.

(ii) Calculate the correlation coefficient, r.

(iii) As a result of her investigation, Sally concludes that the price of cars decreases consistently as they age. Do you agree with Sally? Explain your answer.

Solution:

(i)

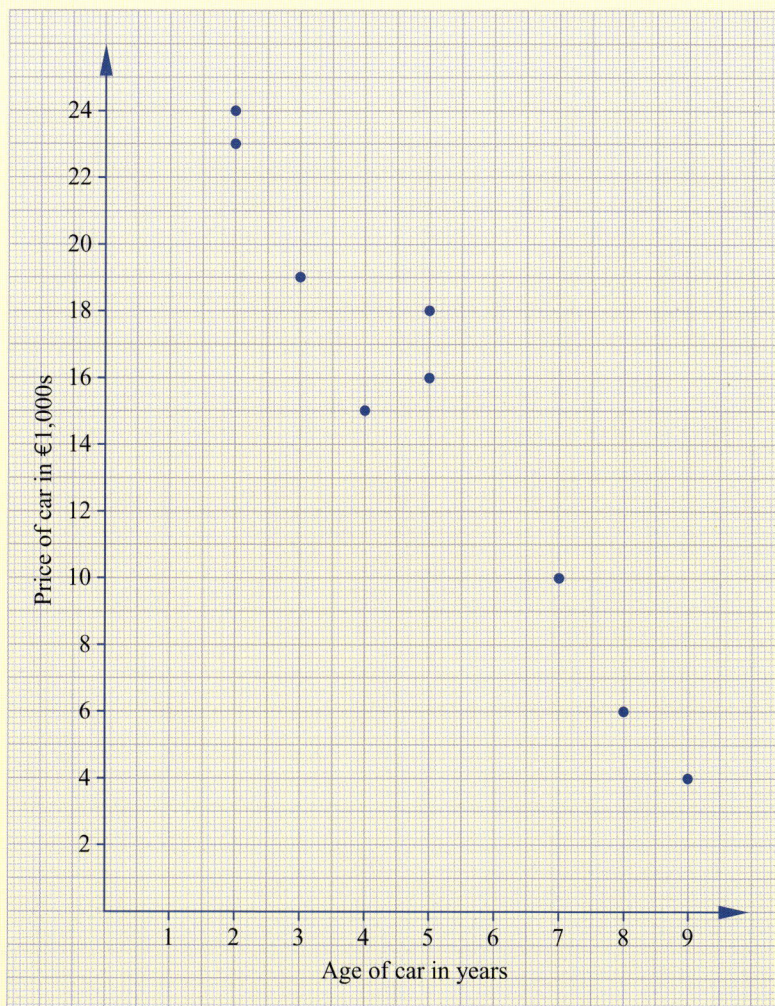

(ii) The scatter plot indicates a strong negative correlation between age and price. It makes sense to calculate the coefficient of correlation, r.

Using technology is a fast, efficient way to calculate r.

You must be able to input the data on your calculator and know how to find r $(= -0.97$ in this case).

(iii) $r = -0.97$ indicates a massive negative correlation with the data. It seems certain that Sally's conclusion is correct. Yes, we agree with Sally.

EXAMPLE 2

Sally decides to buy her first car. She has an idea that the value of a car decreases with age. Sally checks the age and price of nine cars in her local garage.

Age (years)	2	3	5	9	5	7	8	4	2
Price (€1,000s)	24	19	16	4	18	10	6	15	23

Sally asks if she could use the scatter plot of her data to estimate the price of a six-year-old car. Her brother, Drew, suggests it would be useful to have a line to read off. Where would they draw it?

Drew suggests they calculate $\bar{x}$, the mean age of the cars in Sally's data, and $\bar{y}$, the mean price per car.

$$\bar{x} = \frac{2 + 3 + 5 + 9 + 5 + 7 + 8 + 4 + 2}{9} = \frac{45}{9} = 5 \text{ years}$$

$$\bar{y} = \frac{24 + 19 + 16 + 4 + 18 + 10 + 6 + 15 + 23}{9} = \frac{135}{9} = 15 \times €1,000$$

Now they redraw the original scatter plot, including the $(\bar{x}, \bar{y})$ point.

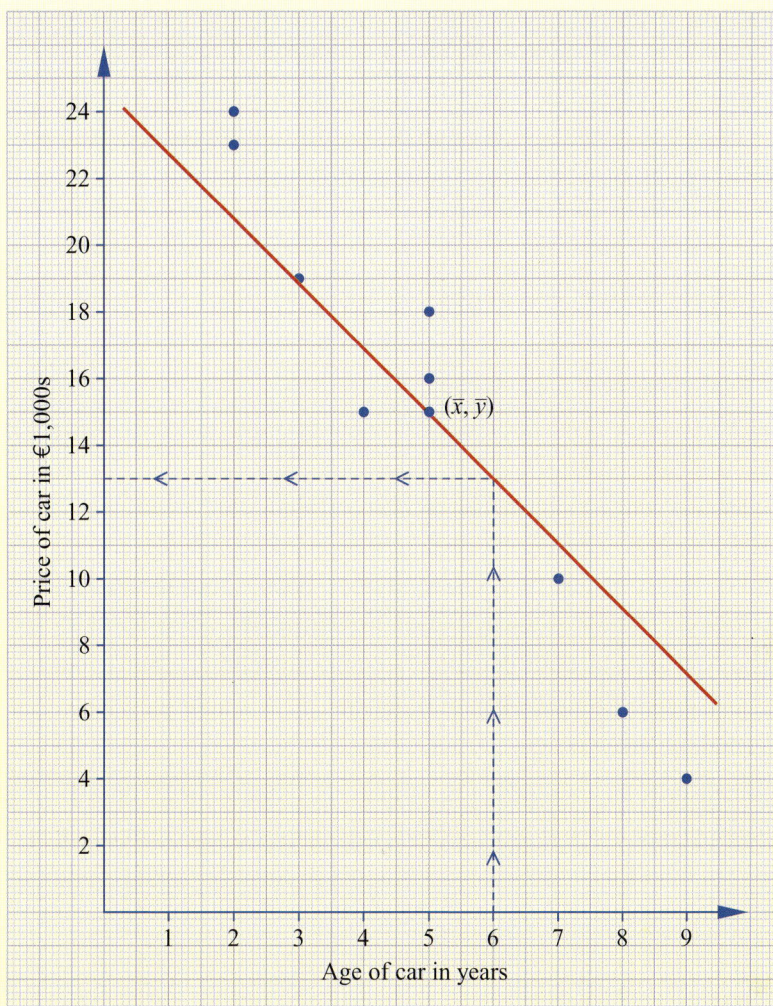

With $r = -0.97$ from Example 1, it is sensible for Sally and Drew to find a model for this relationship (age/price) in the form of a line.

We call this line the **line of best fit**. This line should go through $(\bar{x}, \bar{y})$, the means of the two data sets. In addition, the line should be drawn so that there are as many points above the line as below it.

Note: The slope of the line of best fit $\neq r$, the correlation coefficient.

From the line of best fit on the graph, we estimate the price of a six-year-old car as €13,000.

Exercise

(i) Suggest one possible flaw or error in Sally's collection of the data.

(ii) Make one suggestion that might improve her data collection information.

(iii) If Sally has €8,000 to spend, use the line of best fit to estimate the expected age of the car she might buy. Give your answer correct to the nearest year.

Summary

Properties of *r*, the correlation coefficient

- *r* is positive when there is a positive association between the variables, e.g. between the age of a car and the total distance it has travelled.
- *r* is negative when there is a negative association between the variables, e.g. between the age of a car and the price of a car.
- Correlation treats *x* and *y* symmetrically. The correlation of *x* with *y* is the same as the correlation of *y* with *x*.
- *r* has no unit of measurement, it is just a number. It's best not to write *r* as a percentage.
- $-1 \leq r \leq 1$. The correlation is always a number between −1 and 1.
- Like the mean (μ) and standard deviation (σ), the correlation coefficient (*r*) is strongly affected by outliers. Use *r* with caution when outliers appear. A single outlying value can make a large correlation small or vice versa.
- Correlation measures the strength of the **linear** association between two variables. Variables can be strongly associated but still have a small correlation if the association is not linear.
- Correlations are not affected by changes in units of measurement (centimetres to inches, Centigrade to Fahrenheit).

What *r* is not

- *r* is not the slope of the line of best fit.
- *r* is not resistant. This means *r* is strongly affected by outliers.
- *r* is never a value above 1.
- *r* is never a value below −1.
- *r* does not describe curved relationships.
- An *r* value of +0·58 is not better than an *r* value of −0·75. Do not assume a positive value of *r* is good or a negative value of *r* is not good.

Exercise 3.11

1. **(i)** Make a scatter plot of the following data.

x	1	2	3	4	10	10
y	1	3	3	5	1	10

  (ii) Show that the correlation coefficient, r, is about 0·5.

  (iii) What feature of the data is responsible for reducing the correlation to this value despite a strong straight line association between x and y in most of the observations?

2. A teacher asked a random sample of eight students to record their study times. She then made a table for total hours studied, t, over four weeks and class exam score, y, at the end of four weeks. The results are given in the table below.

Study time (t)	25	35	29	45	21	37	33	47
Exam score (y)	92	81	84	74	85	80	84	80

  (i) Draw a scatter plot of the data.

  (ii) Describe the apparent relationship between study time and test score. Does it surprise you?

  (iii) Identify outliers and potential influential variables.

  (iv) Compute the linear correlation coefficient, r.

3. Siobhan wonders if tall women tend to date taller men than short women do. She measures herself and five of her friends. They measure the heights of the next man each woman dates. The results are given in the table below.

Women's height in cm (x)	168	163	168	165	178	165
Men's height in cm (y)	183	173	178	173	180	165

  (i) Make a scatter plot of the data. Based on the scatter plot, do you expect the correlation to be:

    (a) Positive or negative?

    (b) Near ±1 or not?

  (ii) Find the correlation, r, between the heights of the men and women.

  (iii) Does the correlation tell us whether women tend to date men taller than themselves?

  (iv) If every woman dated a man exactly 7 cm taller than herself, what would be the correlation between female and male heights?

4. Each of the following statements contains a blunder. Explain in each case what is wrong.

   (i) There is a high correlation between the gender of Irish workers and income.

  (ii) The correlation between planting rate and yield of potatoes was found to be 0·55 tons.

 (iii) A high correlation was found ($r = 2·03$) between students' ratings of their teachers and ratings made by the students' parents.

5. Models of cars are classified according to their engine capacity, measured in cubic centimetres (cc).

  Seven new cars are tested to find the distance they will travel, from rest, during the first 10 seconds. The results are given in the table below.

Engine capacity (cc)	800	1,000	1,200	1,500	2,000	2,400	3,000
Distance (m)	85	120	140	175	190	235	280

   (i) Draw a scatter plot for these results.

  (ii) **(a)** Calculate the mean engine capacity.

     (b) Calculate the mean distance.

     (c) Plot and label the point M (mean engine capacity, mean distance) on the scatter diagram.

     (d) Draw a line of best fit through the point M.

 (iii) By using the scatter diagram and showing your method clearly, estimate the following.

     (a) The distance that a car with an engine capacity of 1,800 cc will travel in the first 10 seconds

     (b) The engine capacity of a car that will travel a distance of 125 m in the first 10 seconds

 (iv) Which new car in the table do you think performs best for its engine capacity? Give a reason for your choice.

  (v) A car for invalids has an engine capacity of 400 cc. Estimate the distance it will travel in the first 10 seconds from your line of best fit. Give one reason why this answer might be unreliable.

6. The table below shows the height (in cm) and the mass (in kg) of seven adults.

	A	B	C	D	E	F	G
Height (x)	180	168	158	162	170	174	178
Mass (y)	94	68	60	66	78	60	78

   (i) Construct a scatter plot for $150 \le x \le 180$.

(ii) Find $\bar{x}$ and $\bar{y}$, then mark the point $(\bar{x}, \bar{y})$ on your graph. Draw by eye the line of best fit passing through $(\bar{x}, \bar{y})$.

(iii) Body mass index (BMI) is defined as $\dfrac{\text{Mass in kg}}{(\text{Height in m})^2}$. For example, B has a BMI of

$\dfrac{68}{1\cdot68^2} = 24\cdot1$. This lies within the healthy range ($20 \leq$ BMI ≤ 25). Find the BMIs of

A and F and comment on the results with reference to your scatter graph.

7. (i) Nine cartoon characters have their heights and nose lengths measured. One of the characters is Pinocchio (P). From the plot, write down the bivariate data (couple) for Pinocchio.

(ii) Verify that the correlation coefficient for the eight characters excluding Pinocchio is $r = 0\cdot76$.

(iii) Calculate the value of r when Pinocchio is included. Comment on the difference between the two values of r and the extent to which the outlier dominates the correlation value.

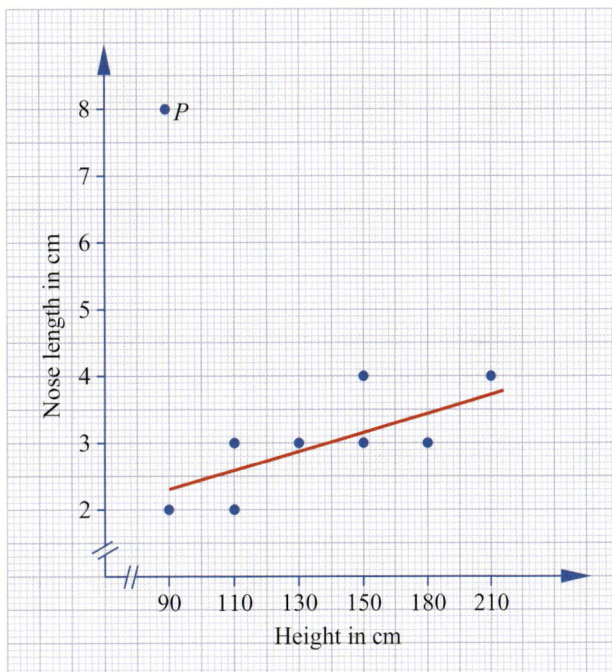

Note: If the sample is a large random sample, an extreme value usually will not greatly alter the size of the correlation. However, if the sample is a small one, an extreme score can have a large effect.

8. The scatter diagram shows the scores obtained by four candidates, A, C, D and E, on Test 1 and Test 2. The scores for a fifth candidate, B, have not been plotted. $M(9, 11)$ represents the *mean scores* of Test 1 and Test 2 for the five candidates.

   (i) Find the scores for candidate B on Test 1 and Test 2.

   (ii) The line of best fit passes through the points A and M. A sixth candidate obtained a score of 4 on Test 1. Estimate from the line of best fit the score he would have obtained on Test 2.

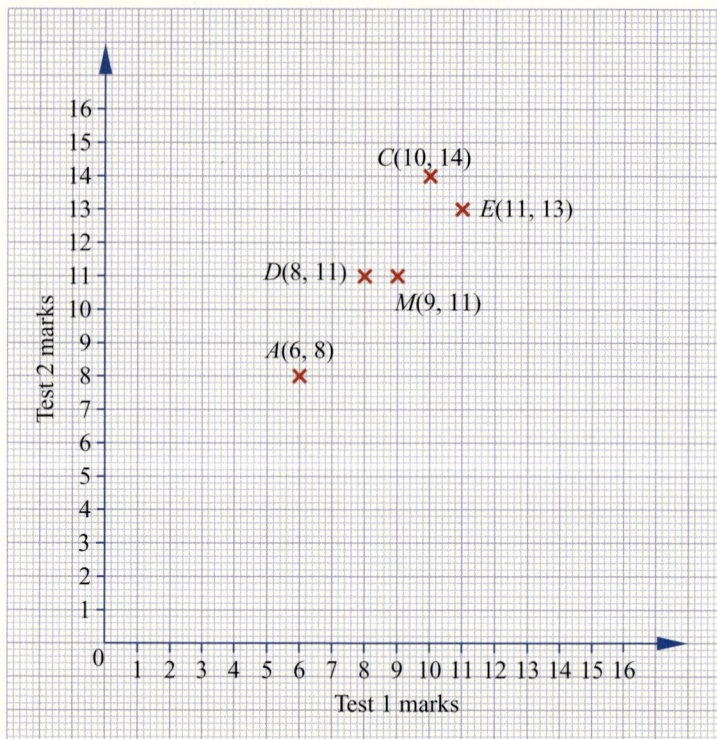

9. (i) Calculate the correlation coefficient, r, for the bivariate data $(0, 4) = A$, $(1, 3)$ $(2, 9)$ $(3, 12)$ $(4, 7)$ $(5, 16)$ and $(6, 16) = B$ on the graph marked $\bullet$. Calculate the slope of the line AB.

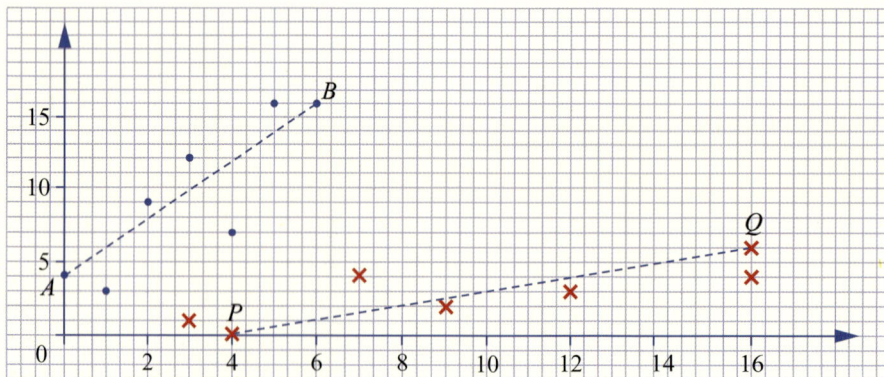

   (ii) Hence or otherwise, calculate the correlation coefficient, r, for the bivariate data $(4, 0) = P$, $(3, 1)$ $(9, 2)$ $(12, 3)$ $(7, 4)$ $(16, 5)$ and $(16, 6) = Q$ on the graph marked ×. Calculate the slope of the line PQ.

Correlation and causality

> **Correlation** implies a connection between two variables.

For example, people who are good at maths are usually good at physics. This is a general trend to which there will often be exceptions.

> **Causality** implies a direct link between two variables. One variable causes the change in the other variable.

For example, consider the outside temperature and the amount of oil used for central heating. The lower the temperature, the greater the amount of oil used: one variable directly causes the other to change.

Sometimes there is no direct link between two variables, but they are connected by a third variable.

For example, in the past generation the number of microwave ovens and the number of mobile phones have both increased. One is not directly related to the other, but they are both related to changes in technology.

The number of people attending music festivals in Europe is constantly increasing, while the number of people worldwide suffering from malnutrition is constantly increasing.

Can we assume going to music festivals is causing malnutrition? The link to both increases is probably the growth of world population. Hence, the apparent link between an increase in numbers attending music festivals and numbers suffering from malnutrition is not an actual link.

EXAMPLE

Association vs. causality

The more churches in an area, the higher the crime rate.

A police chief in England observed that in many medium to large city centres, the crime rate was higher in areas with more churches. When he measured both, he found a direct positive relationship, meaning the more churches in an area, the higher the crime rate (and the fewer churches in an area, the lower the crime rate).

Clearly, the two variables must have something in common with one another. It must relate to both the number of churches and level of crime rate. What is it?

Urban decay and development are what they both have in common. Historically, churches were built in town and city centres. When the main populations the churches served moved away, the churches remained. The replacement population was not like the original population. The new population was transient, poor and disadvantaged. The original populations were generally church-going and law-abiding citizens, while the new population are less so.

In some cities the churches were knocked down and massive developments of office blocks/financial services replaced the original building and their populations. Consequently, there would be fewer people living in the area, no churches and very little crime.

'Knock down the churches and the crime rate will go down' might seem like a sensible solution from the original information. However, on closer examination, it makes no sense at all. This is because of the principle that correlations express the association that exists between two variables; they have nothing to do with causality. In other words, just because a high number of churches is linked to a high crime rate (and vice versa) does not mean a change in one results in a change in the other.

For example, if all the churches were knocked down, do you think the crime rate would decrease? Of course not. However, that's often how associations are interpreted, and complex issues in the social and behavioral sciences are ignored. Do not make that mistake.

Exercise on correlation/causality

Attracta said, 'We had a fire in our house recently. Five firemen and one fire engine were called to deal with it. The insurance company paid the claim of €17,000 for the damage.'

Her friend Noreen replied, 'We had a fire in our house last year. Eighteen firemen and two fire engines were called to deal with it. The insurance company paid the claim of €235,000 for the damage. Those firemen caused a frightful mess.'

'In the event of a fire, do not call the fire brigade.' Discuss.

Exercise 3.12

1. A manager of a large store selling women's clothing does a survey of 10 customers and finds the following.

Woman's age (years)	18	21	36	45	23	53	25	37	30	32
Annual expenditure on clothes (€)	330	300	180	120	310	200	200	150	250	190

(i) Show the data on a scatter plot.

(ii) The manager expected to find a strong negative correlation. Was he correct? Explain your answer.

(iii) Calculate the mean age of the women in years.

(iv) Calculate the mean annual expenditure on clothes in euro.

(v) Plot the mean age and mean annual expenditure point on the scatter plot. Label this point K.

(vi) Draw a line of best fit through the point K. Use this line of best fit to estimate the following.

    (a) The expected age of a woman with annual expenditure on clothes of €225

    (b) The expected amount of annual expenditure in euro of a 40-year-old woman

(vii) Are your answers to (a) and (b) above reliable? Give a reason.

2. Vincent had a collection of old pennies. The following table shows how old each coin was and how much it weighed.

Age (years) x	51	47	53	33	39	46	42	48	28	36
Weight (grams) y	7·3	9·5	6	11·1	10·4	8·5	9·7	7·4	11·5	11·6

  (i) Find the mean age of the coins.

  (ii) Find the mean weight of the coins.

  (iii) Draw a scatter graph to represent the data.

  (iv) Comment on the type of correlation (if any).

  (v) Plot the mean age and mean weight point (x, y) and label it K.

  (vi) Draw a line of best fit through the mean age and mean weight point, K.

  (vii) Use this line of best fit to estimate the following.

    (a) The expected weight of a 75-year-old coin

    (b) The expected age of a coin with a weight of 13·7 grams

  (viii) Are your answers to (a) and (b) reliable? Justify your answers.

3. The scatter graph, complete with a line of best fit, shows the ages and the number of road traffic accidents for men.

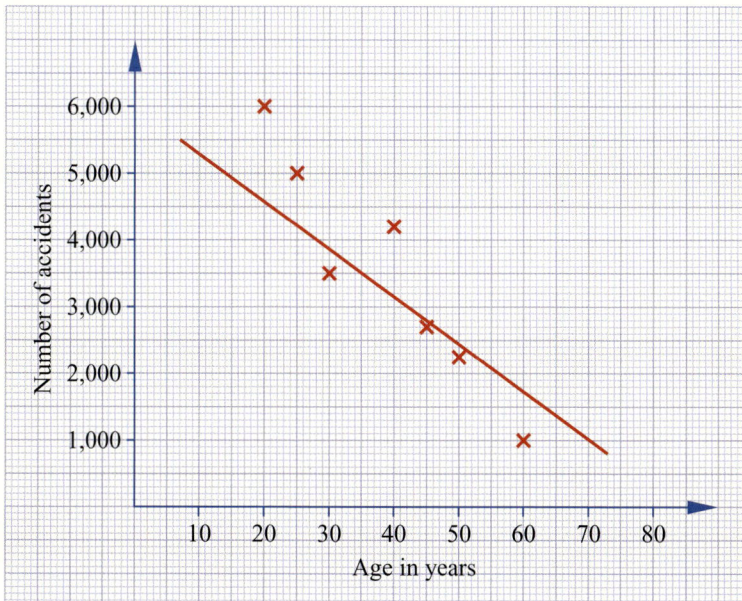

(i) Is the correlation shown positive or negative? Justify your answer.

(ii) Estimate the number of accidents for 35-year-olds.

(iii) Estimate the number of accidents for 80-year-olds.

(iv) Estimate the number of accidents for 15-year-olds.

(v) Which of (ii), (iii) or (iv), if any, would be most reliable? Justify your answer.

4. The scatter graph, complete with a line of best fit, shows the amount in euro gambled on a fruit machine and the amount in euro paid out to 12 different gamblers.

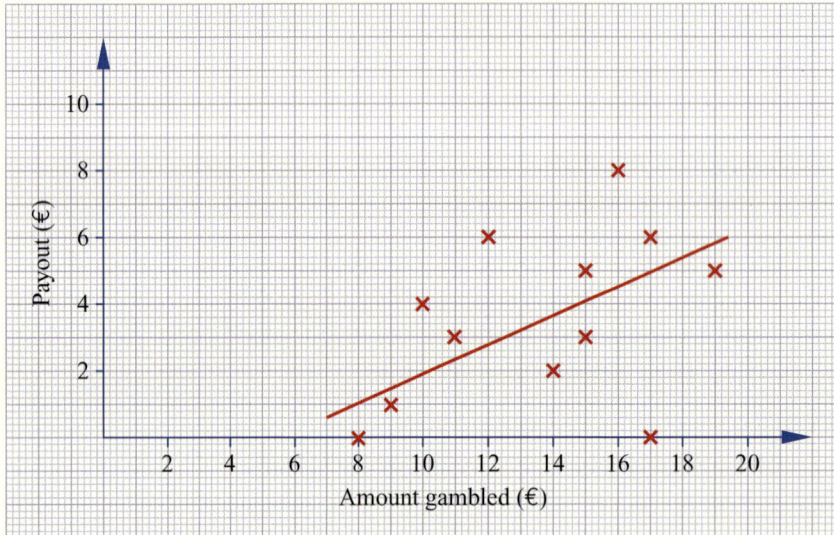

(i) What was the greatest amount lost by any one gambler?

(ii) A new player decides to gamble €13. How much could that player expect the machine to pay out?

(iii) Eamonn has €5 to gamble. What could he reasonably expect his payout to be? Explain your answer.

(iv) Shaun claims to have received a payout of €10. Do you believe him? Justify your answer.

(v) Olly gambled €16 and was paid out €8. Find and indicate Olly on the plot and describe his position relative to the other gamblers.

5. When two variables are correlated (such as strength and running speed), it also means that they are associated with one another. But if they are associated with one another, then why doesn't one cause the other?

6. A student newspaper produced data showing the percentage of Leaving Certificate students owning a mobile phone and the percentage of Leaving Certificate students scoring an A grade in Higher Level Mathematics over an eight-year period.

% of students owning mobile phones (x-value)	40	45	55	60	85	90	90	95
% of students A grade in Maths (y-value)	18	14	14	20	22	24	30	26

    (i) Show the data on a scatter plot.

   (ii) Evaluate $(\bar{x}, \bar{y})$ and include them on a scatter plot.

  (iii) Draw a line of best fit.

  (iv) From the scatter plot, describe the correlation.

   (v) Calculate the correlation coefficient, r.

  (vi) If mobile phone ownership decreased to 70%, what might be the percentage of students getting an A grade?

 (vii) Comment on the correlation identified here. What do the variables share in common? (You may use the word 'illusion' in your answer.)

The normal curve and the standard deviation as a ruler

When characteristics such as height, IQ, mass or test results of a large number of individuals are arranged in order from lowest to highest in a frequency distribution, the same pattern shows up repeatedly. (The large numbers cluster near the middle of the distribution and are symmetrical.)

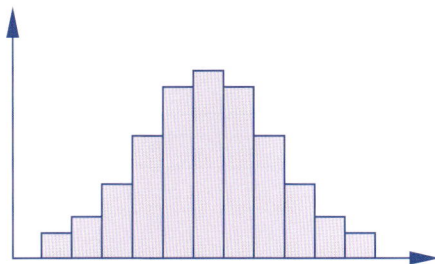

If the distribution is very large and continuous and the class intervals become sufficiently small, the distribution forms a symmetrical, bell-shaped smooth curve called the **curve of normal distribution** or simply the **normal curve**.

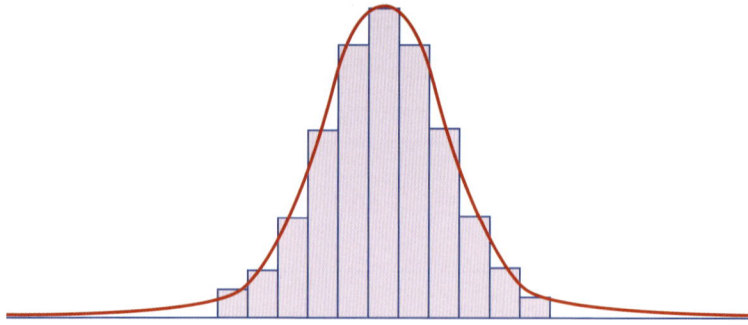

The standard normal distribution

There are many different normal distributions, all with the same bell shape, but with different means and standard deviations. To avoid needing separate tables for each normal curve, we convert the units in a given curve to **standard units** to get the standard normal distribution. The standard units are often referred to as z-units.

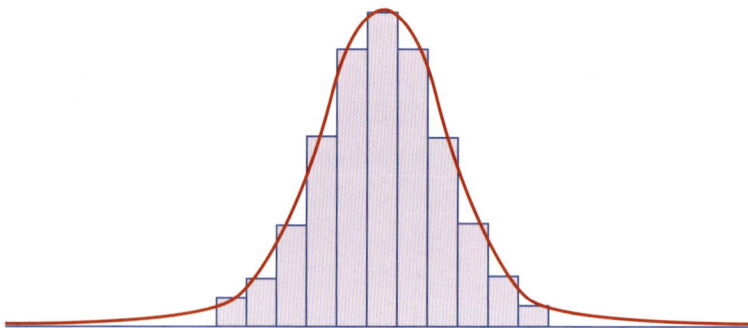

becomes

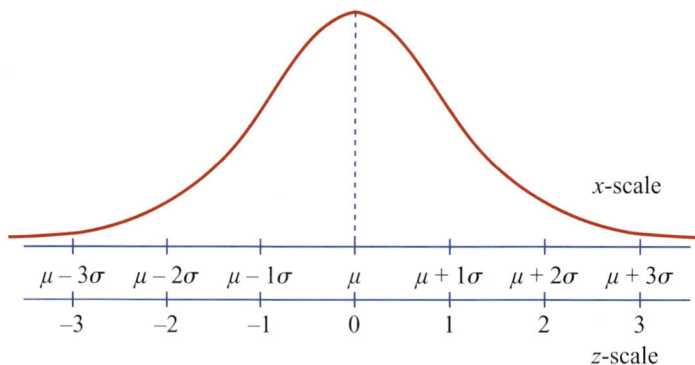

The formula that changes the given units (x-units) into z-units is:

$$z = \frac{x - \mu}{\sigma}$$

(See page 36 in the formulae and tables booklet.)

where μ is the given mean

σ is the given standard deviation

and x is the given variable.

In any normal distribution:

- Approximately 68% of the distribution lies within one standard deviation of the mean, i.e. 68% lies between $\mu - \sigma$ and $\mu + \sigma$.
- 95% lies between $\mu - 2\sigma$ and $\mu + 2\sigma$.
- 99·7% lies between $\mu - 3\sigma$ and $\mu + 3\sigma$.

Note: A value of z tells us how many standard deviations the corresponding x-value lies above or below the mean.

We always use the letter z to denote values that have been standardised with the mean and standard deviation.

EXAMPLE

Suppose it takes you 30 minutes on average for your journey to school, with a standard deviation of 4 minutes. Given that the distribution of these journey times is normal, that is, approximates the normal curve, then using the empirical rule, find the percentage of journeys you will arrive at school taking:

  (i) Less than 34 minutes

 (ii) More than 34 minutes

(iii) Less than 22 minutes

(iv) More than 22 minutes

Solution:

We make use of this graph illustrating the empirical rule.

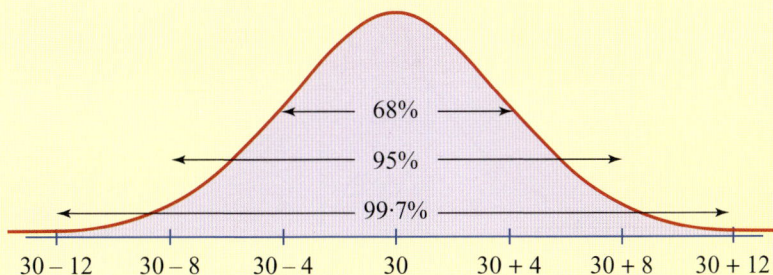

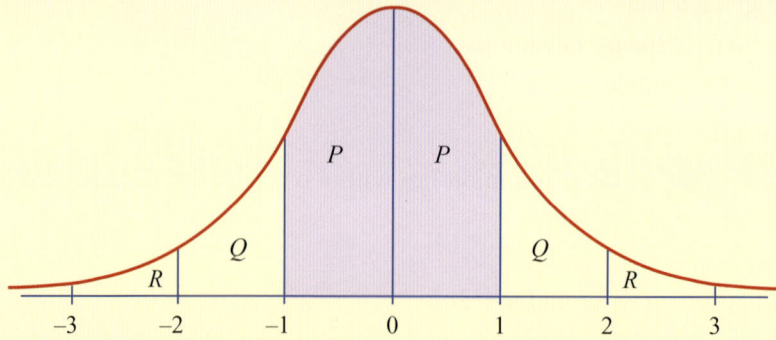

Using the empirical rule:

$\Rightarrow$ Area P + area $P = 68\%$

 2 area $P = 68\%$

 area $P = 34\%$

Also $\Rightarrow$ area Q + area P + area P + area $Q = 95\%$

 2 area Q + 2 area $P = 95\%$

 2 area $Q + 68\% = 95\%$

 2 area $Q = 27\%$

 area $Q = 13 \cdot 5\%$

And $\Rightarrow$ (area R + area Q + area P)2 = 99·7%

 (area $R + 13\frac{1}{2}\% + 34\%$)2 = 99·7%

 2 area $R + 95\% = 99 \cdot 7\%$

 2 area $R = \ 4 \cdot 7\%$

 area $R = 2 \cdot 35\%$

Hence:

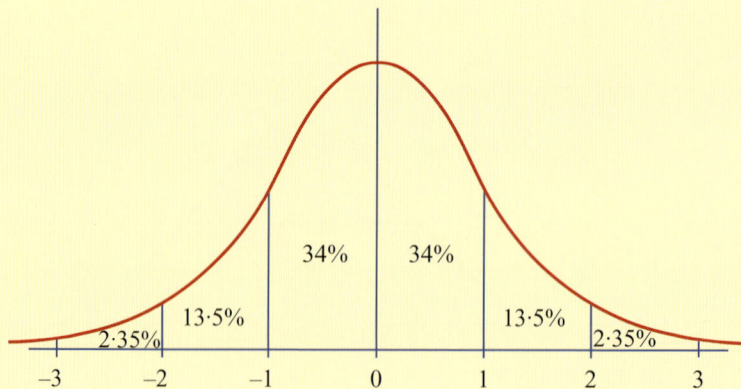

Now answer the questions using the empirical rule.

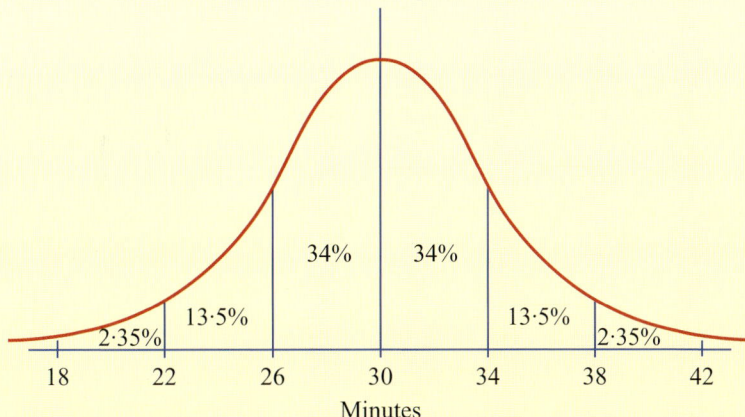

Note: In this example, using the empirical rule, for convenience we ignore
(100% − 99·7% =) 0·3% of the curve.

(i) Less than 34 minutes = 34% + 34% + 13·5% + 2·35%
= 83·85% of the journeys

(ii) More than 34 minutes = 13·5% + 2·35% = 15·85% of the journeys

(iii) Less than 22 minutes = 2·35% of the journeys

(iv) More than 22 minutes = 13·5% + 34% + 34% + 13·5% + 2·35% = 97·25% of the
journeys

Shifting data (transforming data)

We have already seen what happens when we shift data.

When we shift data by adding (or subtracting)

When we add (or subtract) a constant to all the data values, all measures of position (such as the
mean, mode, median) are increased (or decreased) by that constant, while measures of spread (such as
the range, the standard deviation, interquartile range) are unchanged.

When we shift data by multiplying (or dividing)

When we multiply (or divide) all the data values by any constant, all measures of position (such as the
mean, median and percentiles) and measures of spread (such as the range, the interquartile range and
the standard deviation) are multiplied (or divided) by that same constant.

Standardising scores

When standardising data into *z*-scores:

(i) We subtract the mean of the data from every data value. This shifts the mean to 0. As we already know, such subtraction does not change the standard deviation.

(ii) We divide each of these shifted values by the standard deviation. This shifts the standard deviation to 1. Such division does not change the mean when the mean is 0.

The overall result is:

- Standardising into *z*-scores changes the *centre* by making the mean 0.
- Standardising into *z*-scores changes the *spread* by making the standard deviation 1.
- Standardising into *z*-scores does not change the *shape* of the distribution of a variable.

EXAMPLE

Bert and Ernie study Mathematics in two separate classes with a large number of students in each class. The two groups sit a different class test in Mathematics. Both tests are at a similar level but are set and corrected by two different teachers of Mathematics.

Bert scored 90% and Ernie scored 80%. It seems clear that Bert's result is best. However, for comparison purposes, the teachers grade on the normal curve and the scores are standardised using $z = \dfrac{x - \mu}{\sigma}$.

Given that $\mu = 88$ and $\sigma = 4$ for Bert's class and $\mu = 75$ and $\sigma = 5$ for Ernie's class, who did best?

Solution:

For Bert, $z = \dfrac{x - \mu}{\sigma} = \dfrac{90 - 88}{4} = \dfrac{1}{2}$

For Ernie, $z = \dfrac{x - \mu}{\sigma} = \dfrac{80 - 75}{5} = 1$

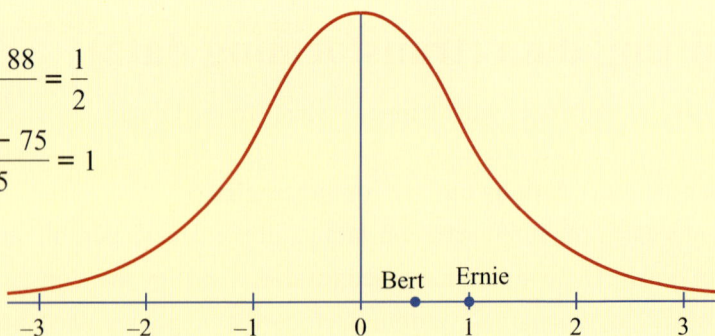

The result shows: Bert's score $\frac{1}{2}$ standard deviation above the mean

Ernie's score 1 standard deviation above the mean

∴ Ernie did best.

Exercise

Discuss this example in class. Does this z-score seem fair?

Finding normal percentiles by hand

In our example with Bert and Ernie, Ernie's score of $z = 1$ was easy to evaluate using the empirical rule.

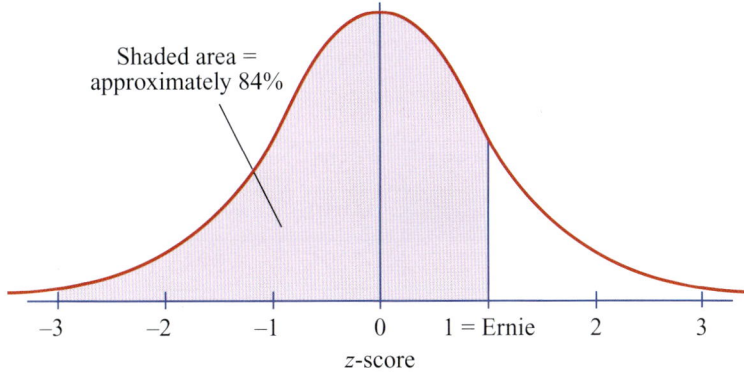

Shaded area = approximately 84%

z-score

This tells us that Ernie's score was higher than 84% of candidates. We could say Ernie's score put him in the 84th percentile, i.e. 84% of the candidates in that test are below Ernie's score.

However, evaluating Bert's score of $z = \frac{1}{2} = 0.50$ is not as easy to evaluate.
$z = 0.50$ indicates Bert is $+\frac{1}{2}$ (standard deviation) above the mean.

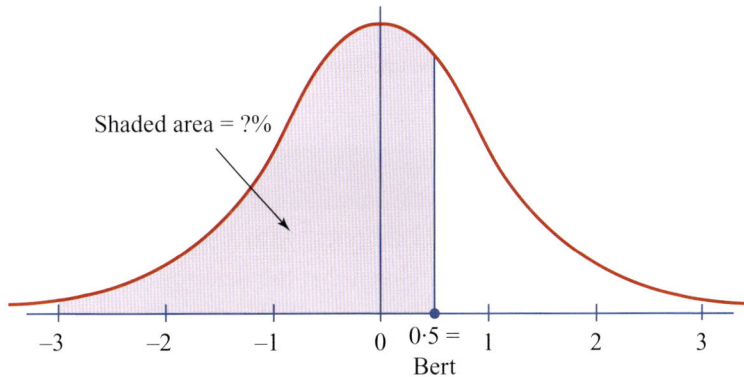

Shaded area = ?%

When the value of z does not fall exactly one, two or three standard deviations from the mean, we can look it up in the formulae and tables booklet, pages 36−7.

z	**0·00**	**0·01**	**0·02**
0·0	0·5000	·5040	·5080
0·1	0·5398	·5438	·5478
0·2	0·5793	·5832	·5871
0·3	0·6179	·6217	·6255
0·4	0·6554	·6591	·6628
0·5	0·6915	·6950	·6985
0·6	0·7257	·7291	·7324

The table lets us find the percentage (expressed as a decimal) of individuals in a standard normal distribution falling below any specified z-score value.

In the extract of the table shown above, we find Bert's z-score by looking down the left column for the first two digits (0·5) and across the top row for the third digit (0).

The table gives us 0·6915 = 69·15 percentile.

This means that 69·15% of the z-scores are less than Bert's score of 0·50.

This also tells us that (100% − 69·15% =) 30·85% of candidates scored higher than Bert in this test.

EXAMPLE 1

The mean time to complete a race is 22 minutes, with a standard deviation of 1·6 minutes. Sue completes the race in 20 minutes. Given that the data for the race and the runners follow the normal model, calculate Sue's percentile for the race.

Solution:
Standardising Sue's time:
$$z = \frac{x - \mu}{\sigma} = \frac{20 - 22}{1·6} = -1·25$$

Note: z-score of 'minus' numbers is not in the formulae and tables booklet.

However, because the normal curve is symmetric, −1·25 is 'linked' with +1·25.

Note: Sue's standard z-score is negative. However, we know that in running, a lower time is superior to a higher time.

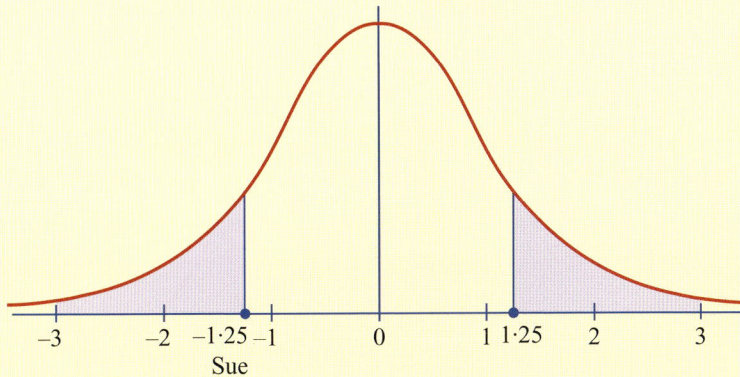

Sue

z	0·00	0·01	0·02	0·03	0·04	0·05	0·06
1·1	0·8643	·8665	·8686	·8708	·8729	·8749	·8770
1·2	0·8849	·8869	·8888	·8907	·8925	·8944	·8962
1·3	0·9032	·9049	·9066				

In the extract of the z-score table above, we find that $0·8944 = 89·44$ percentile are below +1·25.

Remember to find the score above +1·25: $100\% - 89·44\% = 10·56\%$.

Finally, looking at the graph of the normal curve, we observe that 10·56% of standardised race times are faster than Sue's.

∴ Sue's percentile is 89·44.

EXAMPLE 2

You are told that Leaving Certificate CAO points are approximately normally distributed with mean 380 and standard deviation 60. Find the proportion of scores that fall between 290 and 425 points.

Solution:
Let x = Leaving Certificate CAO points score.

Use $z = \dfrac{x - \mu}{\sigma}$ twice to get

$$z = \frac{290 - 380}{60} = -1\cdot5$$

$$z = \frac{425 - 380}{60} = 0\cdot75$$

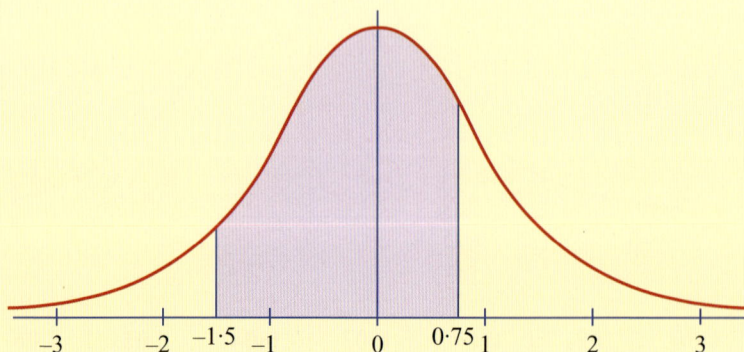

From tables: area $(z < 0\cdot75) = 0\cdot7734$

area $(z < -1\cdot5) = 1 - 0\cdot9332$

$= 0\cdot0668$

∴ Proportion of scores between $-1\cdot5$ and $0\cdot75$

$= 0\cdot7734 - 0\cdot0668$

$= 0\cdot7066$

This normal model estimates that about 71% of Leaving Certificate CAO points scores fall between 290 and 425 points for the mean and standard deviation scores given in this question.

From percentiles to scores or finding z in reverse

In some circumstances we start with areas and are required to work backwards to find the corresponding z-score or even the original data value.

EXAMPLE

A university decides to apply CAO points achieved plus an interview to accept candidates for a Business degree course. To be called for interview, candidates must be in the top quartile of the Leaving Certificate CAO points score. What z-score would represent this?

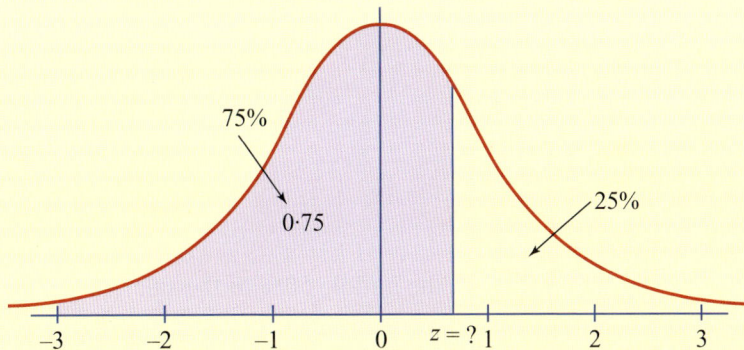

Remember, the top quartile (Q_3) is associated with 75%.

We require a value of z to give us 0.75 (= 75%).

Look at the tables for z in the formulae and tables booklet, page 36.

Notice $z = 0.6 \Rightarrow 0.7257$

$$\left. \begin{array}{l} z = 0.67 \Rightarrow 0.7485 \\ z = 0.68 \Rightarrow 0.7517 \end{array} \right\} \ ?$$

There is no exact value of z in the tables to give 0.75: either $z = 0.67$ or $z = 0.68$.

The university applied the upper quartile score $z = 0.68$ as the minimum score required for an interview. Find the real minimum Leaving Certificate CAO points required in a year with mean $\mu = 360$ and standard deviation $\sigma = 65$.

Use $z = \dfrac{x - \mu}{\sigma}$.

$$0.68 = \frac{x - 360}{65}$$

$$44.2 = x - 360$$

$$404.2 = x$$

$\therefore$ A minimum of 405 CAO points are required for interview, as CAO points are scored in units of 5.

Exercise: If the university applied $z = 0.67$, what would the corresponding points score be?

Exercise 3.13

Note: Whether we use the empirical rule or the standard normal tables (z-scores) in solving
    questions, our answers will vary slightly.

1. The summary statistics for the monthly payroll of a city corporation are as follows.

    Lowest salary   = €1,400
    Mean salary   = €3,000
    Median salary   = €2,200
    Range   = €5,000
    Interquartile range = €2,600
    First quartile   = €1,600
    Standard deviation = €1,600

    (i) Between what two values are the middle 50% of the salaries found?

    (ii) Is the distribution of salaries symmetric, positively skewed or negatively skewed?

    (iii) The city corporation receives a large increase in revenue. As a result, every employee is given a €200 per month raise. Write down the new value of each of the summary statistics.

    (iv) Suppose the city corporation gives each employee a 15% raise. Write down the new value of each of the summary statistics.

2. The masses of a group of students were found to be approximately normal with a mean of 62 kilograms and a standard deviation of 6 kilograms.

    On the normal curve, the arrows indicate intervals of one standard deviation.

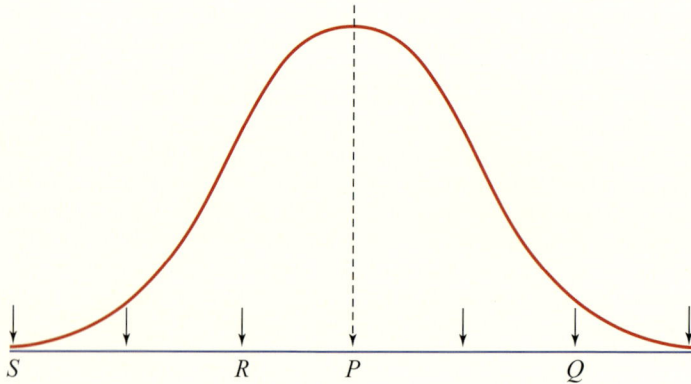

    What is the approximate value of the mass at the following?

    (i) *P*   **(ii)** *Q*   **(iii)** *R*   **(iv)** *S*

3. The distribution of scores in a competition is normally distributed with a mean of 50 and a standard deviation of 2. The diagram shows the distribution, with arrows indicating intervals of one standard deviation.

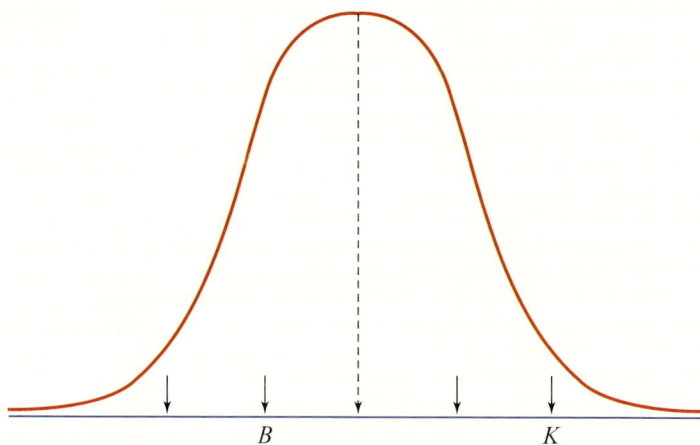

(i) Write down the value of the score shown at (a) B (b) K.

(ii) If there were 8,800 competition entries, how many had a score greater than 54?

4. The graph shows a normal curve for the random variable X, with mean μ and standard deviation σ.

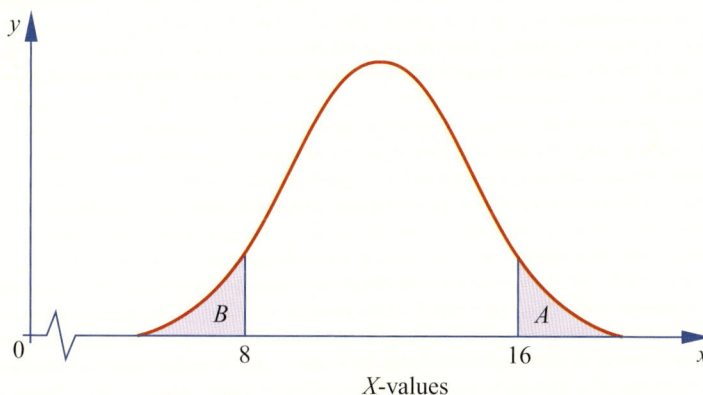

X-values

(i) Given that the area of $A = 0{\cdot}10 =$ area of B, write down the X-value of μ.

(ii) Explain how you arrived at this value.

5. The heights of certain plants are normally distributed. The plants are classified into three categories:

- The shortest 12·92% are in category P.
- The tallest 10·38% are in category Q.
- All the other plants are in category R.

Complete the following diagram to represent this information.

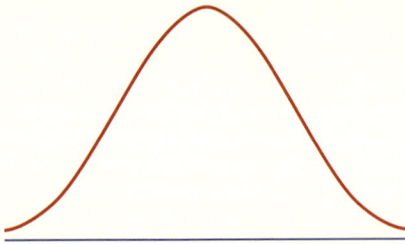

6.

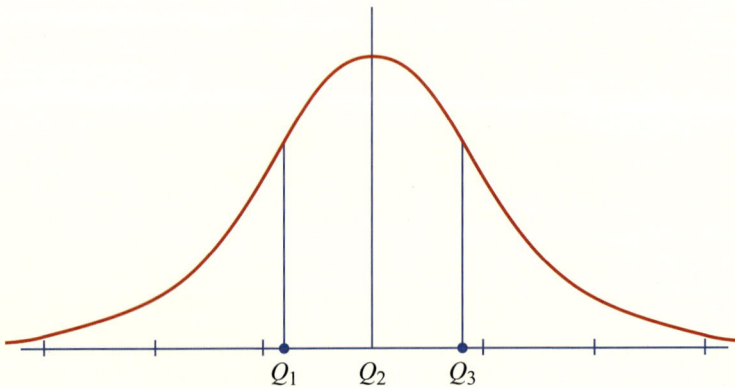

The normal curve shown has a mean value of $\mu = 80$ with a standard deviation $\sigma = 4$. Find:

   (i) The value of Q_2, the median value

  (ii) The value of Q_1, the first quartile value

 (iii) The value of Q_3, the third quartile value

 (iv) The interquartile range

7. Find the shaded areas.

(i)

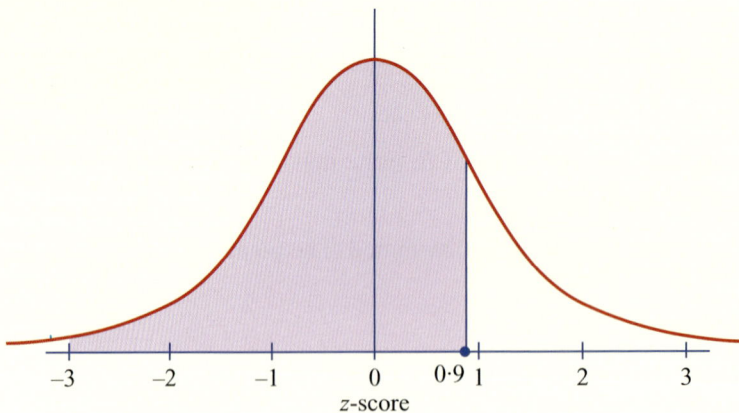

(ii)

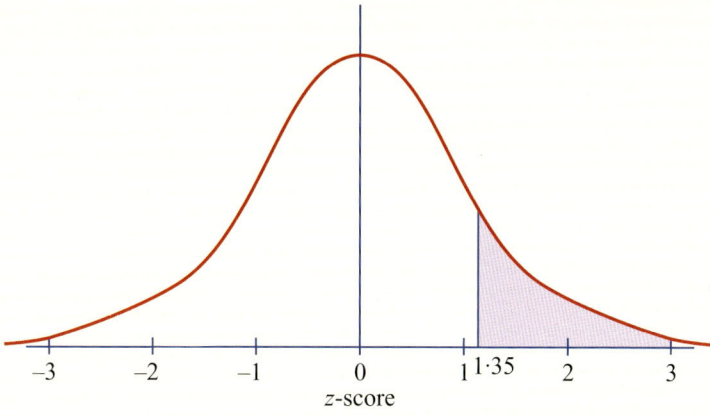

(iii)

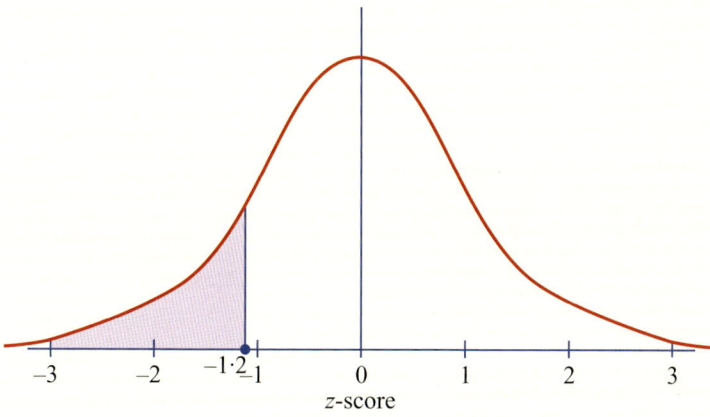

(iv)

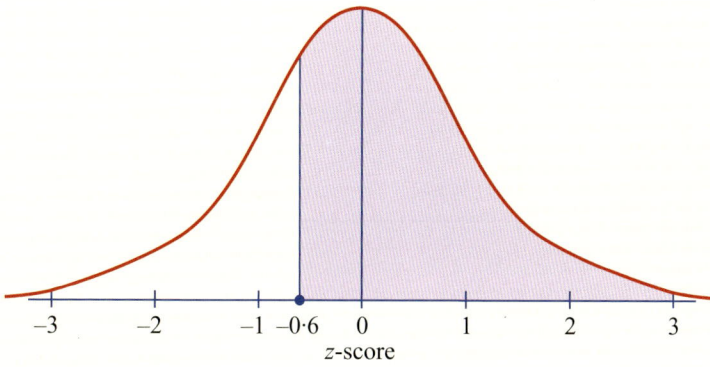

8. Find the *z*-score associated with each area.

(i)

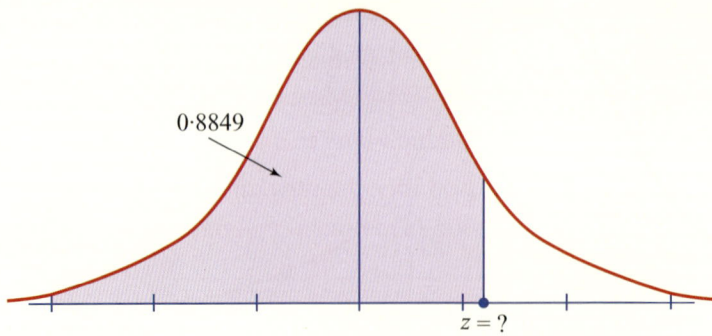

0·8849

$z = ?$

(ii)

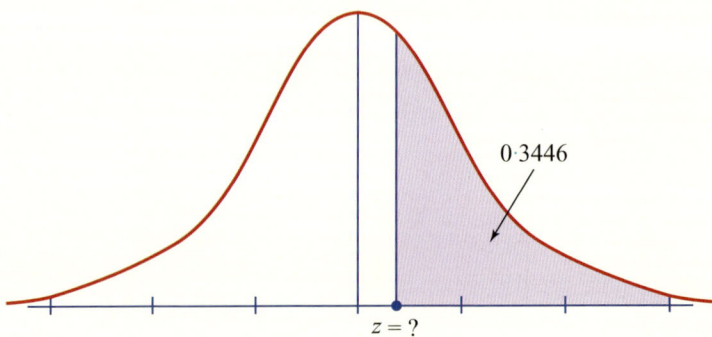

0·3446

$z = ?$

(iii)

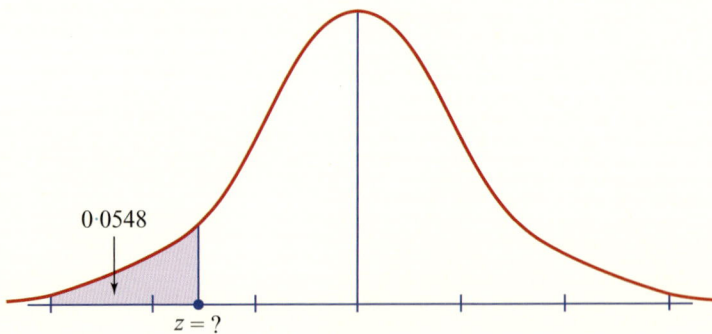

0·0548

$z = ?$

(iv)

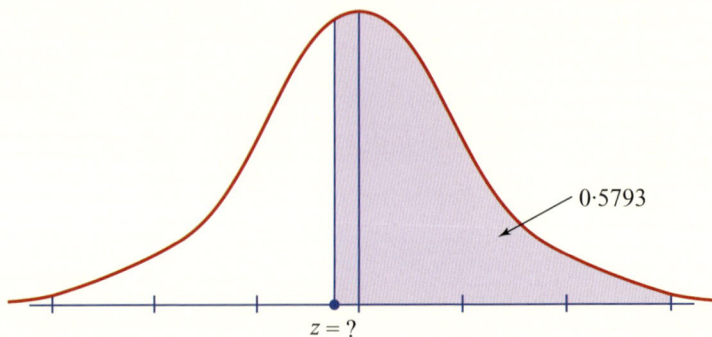

0·5793

$z = ?$

9. Croke Park is one of the largest stadiums in Europe. Wikipedia states that the maximum capacity of the stadium for a match is 82,300 fans. The average attendance for major matches is calculated at 61,400 spectators. Which of these values do you think is most likely to be the correct one for standard deviation: 60, 600, 6,000 or 60,000 fans? Explain the reasoning behind your choice.

10. Some IQ tests are standardised to a normal model with a mean of 100 and standard deviation of 16.

   (i) Using the empirical rule, draw the model for these IQ scores. Clearly label the drawing. Show what the emperical rule predicts about the scores.

   (ii) From the diagram, what percentage of people should have a score:
      (a) below 100   (b) below 132   (c) below 84   (d) above 84   (e) above 68?

11. Joan took her final university examination in Music and Home Economics. In Music she scored 88% and in Home Economics she scored 82%. The overall results on the Music exam had a mean of 78 and a standard deviation of 7, while the mean Home Economics score was 70 with a standard deviation of 7.

   Given that the examination results were standard normal, calculate both z-scores to identify which result was best when compared to other candidates in the final examinations.

12. Two brands of battery are available to owners of personal music players. Never Stop batteries are known to have a mean life of 10 hours, while Always Go have 11 hours.

   (i) Explain why we would also like to know the standard deviations of the battery lifetimes before deciding which brand to buy.

   (ii) Suppose the standard deviations are 1·8 hours for Never Stop and 2·8 for Always Go. You are headed out for 8 hours at the beach. Which battery is most likely to last all day? Justify your answer.

13. A company produces calculator batteries. The diameter of the batteries is supposed to be 20 mm. The tolerance is 0·25 mm. Any batteries outside this tolerance are rejected. You may assume that this is the only reason for rejecting the batteries.

   (i) The company has a machine that produces batteries with diameters that are normally distributed with mean 20 mm and standard deviation 0·1 mm. Out of every 10,000 batteries produced by this machine, how many, on average, are rejected?

   (ii) A setting on the machine slips, so that the mean diameter of the batteries increases to 20·05 mm, while the standard deviation remains unchanged. Find the percentage increase in the rejection rate for batteries from this machine, given the tolerance is maintained as in (i), correct to the nearest per cent.

14. The life of a certain make of electric light bulb is known to be normally distributed with a mean life of 2,000 hours and a standard deviation of 120 hours.

The quality control department in the factory that manufactures the light bulbs tests a random selection of 600 bulbs to destruction. How many of those bulbs would you expect to last:
   (i) Less than 1,800 hours
   (ii) More than 2,200 hours
   (iii) Between 1,800 hours and 2,200 hours

15. The manufacturer of a new model of car states that when travelling at 90 kilometres per hour, the petrol consumption has a mean value of 11 kilometres per litre with a standard deviation of 0·5.
   (i) How many standard deviations from the mean is a car with a mean value of 11·75 km per litre?
   (ii) Which would be more unusual: a car with a mean value of 11·75 km per litre or a car with a mean value of 10·25 km per litre?

16. The Department of Forestry carried out a survey on the diameter of trees in a large woodland. The survey found that the mean diameter was 38·5 cm and a standard deviation of 11·75 cm. The survey provided an accurate description of the entire woodland and the standard normal model applied.
   (i) Approximately what percentage of trees would be less than 10 cm in diameter?
   (ii) About what percentage of trees would be over 40 cm in diameter?
   (iii) What percentage of trees should be between 20 and 60 cm in diameter? Give this answer correct to the nearest whole number.

17. Six thousand eggs in a large consignment have masses that are normally distributed. The mean mass of the eggs is 42 grams with a standard deviation of 5·5 grams.
   (i) Show that the number of eggs in the consignment with a mass greater than 50 grams is approximately 440.
   (ii) Four thousand of the 6,000 eggs have masses greater than W grams. Estimate the value of W, correct to one decimal place.

18. Marks obtained on a national test (Test K1) are normally distributed with a mean of 100 and a standard deviation of 16.
   (i) (a) Draw a large, neat diagram showing the distribution of marks. Label the points which show marks of 100, 116, 132 and 148.
       (b) What percentage of the students who took Test K1 obtained marks greater than 116?
       (c) What is the probability that a randomly selected student who took the test obtained a mark of less than 68?
       (d) What are the end points of the interval which has its centre at the mean and within which 95% of the marks lie?

A new national test (Test K2) was constructed to have marks ranging from 100 to 250 and to be normally distributed for this range.

(ii) (a) What is the mean mark on Test K2?

(b) What is the median mark?

(c) If 83·85% of students obtained marks of less than 196 on Test K2, estimate the standard deviation of marks for this test.

Hypothesis testing

A hypothesis is a statement (or theory) whose truth has yet to be proven or disproven.

Examples of hypotheses:

- More than half the population is satisfied with EU membership.
- Drinking fizzy drinks causes tooth decay.
- The age at marriage has increased over the past 20 years.

Null Hypothesis

The statement being tested in a test of significance is called the **null hypothesis**. The test of significance is designed to assess the strength of the evidence against the null hypothesis. Usually the null hypothesis is a statement of 'no effect' or 'no difference.'

We abbreviate 'null hypothesis' as H_0.

Statistics help to make decisions

We can use statistics to accept or reject claims.

1. Is global temperature increasing?
   The null hypothesis, H_0, is that global temperature is not increasing, i.e. no difference in temperature.
   The alternative hypothesis, H_A, is that global temperature is increasing.

2. Is a new drug effective for treating HIV/AIDS?
   The null hypothesis, H_0, is the new drug is not effective.
   The alternative hypothesis, H_A, is the new drug is effective.

3. Is a survey on left-handed people biased if it indicates 24% of people are left handed?
   The null hypothesis, H_0, is that 24% of people are left handed, i.e. survey not biased.
   The alternative hypothesis, H_A, is the survey is biased.

Note 1: At time of writing, H_A, the alternative hypothesis, is not on our course.

Note 2: Often the people investigating the data hope to reject H_0. They hope:

- Their new drug is better than the old one

  or

- The new ad campaign is better than the old one etc.

However, in statistics, it is essential that our attitude is one of skepticism. Until we are convinced otherwise we accept H_0. In other words, we cling to the idea that there is no change, no improvement, no deterioration, no effect.

The reasoning behind hypothesis testing is that we usually prefer to think about getting things right rather than getting them wrong. A similar logic applies in trials by jury, where the defendant is considered innocent until it is shown otherwise.

In testing a hypothesis, data may be given or collected.

With given data in this course, we accept the information at face value and proceed to analyse the data and answer the question.

To **collect data**, a questionnaire could be used to carry out a survey.

A survey is a valuable assessment tool in which a sample is selected and information from the sample can then be generalised to a larger population. Surveying has been likened to taste-testing soup – a few spoonfuls indicate what the whole pot tastes like.

The key to the validity of any survey is randomness. Just as the soup must be stirred in order for the few spoonfuls to represent the whole pot, when sampling a population, the group must be stirred before respondents are selected. It is critical that respondents are chosen randomly so that the survey results can be generalised to the whole population.

Consider the statement

'EU membership is a massive advantage for Ireland.'

To test the statement, we could decide to survey a random sample of 80 people. There are many problems associated with getting a random sample.

Using the section on surveys already covered in this chapter or otherwise, discuss how a survey might be conducted to investigate whether or not the hypothesis 'EU membership is a massive advantage for Ireland' is accepted by Irish people.

If 80 Irish people selected at random were asked if they agree with the statement, how many of them would we require to agree with the statement in order for us to claim the statement is accepted?

Is it 40 ☐ or ☐ 45 ☐ or ☐ 50 . . . ?

There is no one correct answer. This is where margins of error and confidence levels come in.

EXAMPLE

A marketing manager investigates the effect of advertising expenditure on company sales. He has a hypothesis that an increase in advertising expenditure results in an increase in company sales. The company accounts department provides the following information.

Advertising expenditure in € (x)	800	1,000	1,200	1,200	1,500	1,600	1,800	1,900	2,000	2,200	2,600
Company sales in € (y)	20,000	20,000	25,000	22,000	26,000	26,000	32,000	31,000	30,000	34,000	32,000

 (i) Draw a scatter diagram to illustrate the data.
 (ii) Does the scatter diagram verify the hypothesis? Explain your answer.
(iii) The marketing manager's daughter, Elaine, is studying statistics in school. She calculates the correlation coefficient, r. Find this value. Does Elaine's value for r verify the hypothesis?

Solution:

(i)

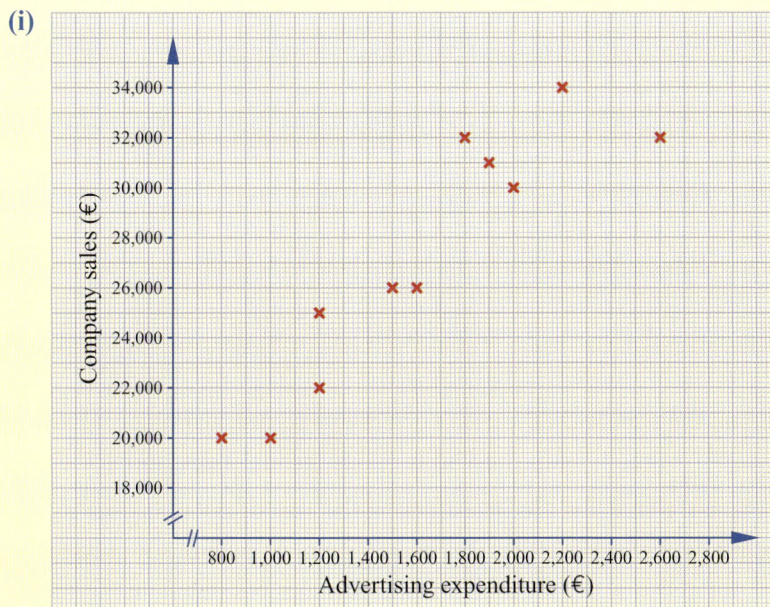

 (ii) Yes, the scatter diagram shows a clear positive correlation between advertising expenditure and company sales.

(iii) Elaine calculates r, the correlation coefficient, using her calculator.

   She calculates $r = 0.92$, confirming a very strong positive correlation for the data.

   This high positive value of r verifies the hypothesis.

Exercise 3.14

1. In a Maths test, 50 students in transition year obtained the results given on the following stem and leaf plot.

```
0 | 8 7 5
1 | 6 8 4 5 1 1 7 8 9 7 9
2 | 7 1 8 9 2 7 3 3 1 8 7 2 6 7 3 8 9 8 1 5 9
3 | 1 5 7 8 1 1 3 5 7
4 | 2 3 5 1 8 4
```

Key 1|6 = Score 16

By analysing the above information, test the hypothesis that a majority of students scored more than 28.

2. In a furniture factory, 20 pieces of material are cut into the following lengths.

169	169	172	170
172	170	169	171
169	174	169	169
171	170	171	165
170	165	165	174

(i) Complete the following frequency table.

Length	165	169	170	171	172	174
Tally						
Frequency						

(ii) Find the mean and the standard deviation correct to one decimal place. Hence, test the hypothesis that 90% of the lengths are within ± one standard deviation of the mean.

3. Some Agricultural Science students are investigating the size of potatoes in 5 kg bags. They are investigating the hypothesis that the median mass of potatoes in a bag correlates with the number of potatoes in it. They weigh some potatoes and tabulate their results.

Median mass of potatoes (to nearest gram)	72	87	96	105	110	125	136	142	147	159	174	192
Number of potatoes per bag	50	51	36	40	45	35	35	36	40	28	32	25

(i) Draw a scatter plot to illustrate the data.

(ii) Which does the scatter plot show? Explain your answer.

(a) No correlation

(b) Positive correlation

(c) Negative correlation

(iii) Would you accept or reject the hypotheses from your observation of the scatter plot?

(iv) Use your calculator to evaluate r, the correlation coefficient of the data. Write down the value of r.

(v) Would you accept or reject the hypothesis based on your calculation of r? Explain your answer.

4. The following information was obtained from the accounts department of a local authority in the UK. Each household in the local area had a water consumption meter installed. The recorded weekly consumption of water in litres from the size of the household was as follows.

Household size	2	7	9	4	10	6	8	3	3	2
Recorded water used	650	1,200	1,300	450	1,400	900	1,800	650	800	900

(i) Construct a scatter plot of this data and determine whether there is a relationship between household size and recorded water consumption.

(ii) Compute the correlation coefficient for this data set. Does the computed correlation coefficient match your previous conclusion?

(iii) Interpret the value of the correlation coefficient that you computed. Suppose that instead of measuring the water consumption in litres, the engineers had measured the water consumption in gallons. If you were to convert the values in the table above from litres to gallons, what effect would this have on the correlation coefficient?

(One gallon = 4·55 litres)

(iv) The local authority has a tenant, Mr Frank Gallagher. Mr Gallagher's household size is known to be 12 and the recorded water used was 1,100 litres per week.

The local authority manager has a hypothesis that Mr Gallagher's water meter is under-recording the amount of water used. To test this, she includes Mr Gallagher's data (i) on the scatter plot (ii) in the calculation of the coefficient correlation, r.

By refering to (i) and (ii), do you think the manager would accept or reject her hypothesis? Explain your reasoning.

5. Lisa sits a nationwide examination in Mathematics. The examination is designed to identify mathematically gifted children under 10 years of age. Lisa scores 55 marks out of a possible total of 80 marks. She is very disappointed with her result. Lisa explains the situation to her dad, Homer.

Homer assures Lisa that she is one of the brightest students of Mathematics for her age group in the nation.

Lisa decides to check Homer's statement as a hypothesis: 'Lisa is one of the brightest students for her age in the nation.' Lisa requests, and receives, the mean national score, $\mu = 48$, and the standard deviation, $\sigma = 3$, for the examination from the authorities. She is also told that the results are approximately standard normal. Test Homer's and Lisa's hypothesis by finding z, the standard normal score.

Margin of error and confidence intervals for population proportions

Many statistical studies are concerned with obtaining the proportion (percentage) of a population that has a specified attribute. In most cases the population under consideration will be large and hence it would be impractical, if not impossible, to obtain the population proportion by taking a census. Thus, we generally employ sampling and use the sample data to make inferences about the population. The key to the validity of any survey is randomness. It is important that the sample be chosen randomly so that the survey results can be generalised to the whole population. The results of a survey are only an estimate of the quantity of interest. When results of surveys are reported in the media, they often include a statement like: '**35% of respondents favour Mr Smith in the upcoming election. However, there is a margin of error of 3 percentage points**.' What this means is that the people who carried out the survey are reasonably confident that in the real election, the percentage of votes for Mr Smith will be 35% ± 3%. In other words, they are confident that if the election was held now, Mr Smith will receive somewhere between 32% and 38% of the vote. Such intervals are called **confidence intervals**. An estimate from a survey should be treated with caution. Sampling errors mean that the results in the sample differ to the true results due to the 'luck of the draw'. However, it is important to remember that sampling errors do not render surveys useless.

Notation
We use the letter p to denote the **population proportion** and it is this value that is to be estimated. We use $\hat{p}$ (pronounced 'p hat') to denote the **sample proportion**. $\hat{p}$ is the statistic that will be used to estimate the unknown population proportion, p.

$$p = \text{population proportion} \qquad \hat{p} = \text{sample proportion}$$

The population proportion, p, although unknown, is a fixed number. On the other hand, the sample proportion, $\hat{p}$, is a random variable and its value depends on chance.

Suppose we wanted to know the proportion (percentage) of people in Ireland who are left-handed. We randomly selected 400 people and found that 64 of them are left-handed.

$$\hat{p} = \frac{\text{Number of people in the sample who are left-handed}}{\text{The number of people sampled}} = \frac{64}{400} = 0.16 \ (16\%)$$

If 60 of 400 people sampled were left-handed, then:

$$\hat{p} = \frac{60}{400} = 0 \cdot 15 \ (15\%)$$

If 72 of 400 people sampled were left-handed, then:

$$\hat{p} = \frac{72}{400} = 0 \cdot 18 \ (18\%)$$

Notice that the value of $\hat{p}$, the sample proportion, changes depending on the sample chosen. If the sample chosen is a good representation of the population, then $\hat{p}$, the sample proportion, will be a good estimate of the true population proportion, p.

Margin of error for the estimate of p

How should we summarise the strength of the data in a survey? This is where the role of the margin of error comes in. The margin of error is a number that represents the accuracy of a survey. It is a statistic expressing the amount of random sampling error in a survey's results. The margin of error is denoted by E. On our course, the margin of error, at the 95% level of confidence, is given by:

$$\text{Margin of error} = E = \frac{1}{\sqrt{n}}$$

where n is the size of the sample

If $n = 100$: $\quad E = \dfrac{1}{\sqrt{100}} = 0 \cdot 1 = 10\%$

If $n = 400$: $\quad E = \dfrac{1}{\sqrt{400}} = 0 \cdot 05 = 5\%$

If $n = 1{,}000$: $\quad E = \dfrac{1}{\sqrt{1{,}000}} = 0 \cdot 0316227766 = 3 \cdot 16\%$ (correct to two decimal places)

If $n = 10{,}000$: $\quad E = \dfrac{1}{\sqrt{10{,}000}} = 0 \cdot 01 = 1\%$

There is an inverse relationship between the sample size, n, and the margin of error, E. The smaller the sample size, the larger the margin of error. However, there are diminishing returns. Going from a sample size of 100 to a sample size of 1,000, a tenfold increase, will decrease the margin of error from 10% to 3·16%. Going from a sample size of 1,000 to a sample size of 10,000, also a tenfold increase, will decrease the margin of error from 3·16% to 1%.

Note: One factor that generally has little effect on the margin of error is the population size. For example, a sample size of 100 in a population of 10,000 will have almost the same margin of error as a sample size of 100 in a population of 1,000,000.

EXAMPLE

At the 95% confidence level, calculate the sample size, n, to have a margin of error of:
(i) 1·25%   **(ii)** 3%

Solution:

$$\frac{1}{\sqrt{n}} = \text{margin of error}$$

(i)   1·25% = 0·0125

$$\frac{1}{\sqrt{n}} = 0.0125$$

$$1 = 0.0125 \sqrt{n}$$

(multiply both sides by $\sqrt{n}$)

$$\frac{1}{0.0125} = \sqrt{n}$$

(divide both sides by 0·0125)

$$\frac{1}{(0.0125)^2} = n$$

(square both sides)

$$6{,}400 = n$$

(ii)   3% = 0·03

$$\frac{1}{\sqrt{n}} = 0.03$$

$$1 = 0.03 \sqrt{n}$$

(multiply both sides by $\sqrt{n}$)

$$\frac{1}{0.03} = \sqrt{n}$$

(divide both sides by 0·03)

$$\frac{1}{(0.03)^2} = n$$

(square both sides)

$$1111 \cdot 111111 = n$$

$$1{,}112 = n$$

Note: Always use the next whole number value of n, not to the nearest whole number.

Confidence interval

The estimated proportion plus or minus its margin of error is called a **confidence interval** for the true proportion. The 95% confidence for a proportion is given by:

sample proportion − margin of error ≤ true proportion ≤ sample proportion + margin of error

$$\hat{p} - \frac{1}{\sqrt{n}} \le p \le \hat{p} + \frac{1}{\sqrt{n}}$$

Where n is the sample size, p is the population proportion and $\hat{p}$ is the sample proportion.

We can state with 95% confidence that the true population, p, lies inside this interval. What this means is that if the same population was surveyed on numerous occasions and the confidence interval was calculated, then about 95% of these confidence intervals **would** contain the true proportion and about 5% of these confidence intervals would **not** contain the true proportion.

The end points of the 95% confidence are given by $\hat{p} \pm \dfrac{1}{\sqrt{n}}$.

Population parameters and sample statistics

It is important to distinguish between a **population parameter** and a **sample statistic**. A population parameter is a numerical measure from the entire population. A sample statistic is a numerical measure from a sample of the population. To distinguish between population parameters and sample statistics, different symbols are used. In general, Greek letters are used for population parameters and Roman letters for sample statistics. Remember that sample statistics are only **estimates** of the corresponding population parameters. The science of statistics is to evaluate how well the sample statistic estimates the true population parameter. If the sample statistic is a good estimate of the true population parameter, then it can be used to make inferences about the population.

Parallels between means and proportions

	Population parameter	Sample statistic
Means	μ	$\bar{x}$
Proportions	p	$\hat{p}$

A sample mean, $\bar{x}$, can be used to make inferences about a population mean, μ. Similarly, a sample proportion, $\hat{p}$, can be used to make inferences about a population proportion, p.

There is a connection between the 95% confidence interval for the population proportion, p, and the 95% confidence interval for the population mean, μ.

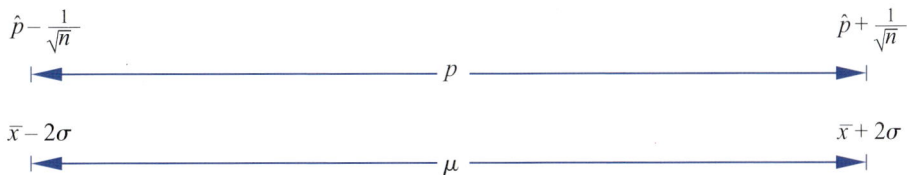

$$\hat{p} - \frac{1}{\sqrt{n}} \qquad\qquad p \qquad\qquad \hat{p} + \frac{1}{\sqrt{n}}$$

$$\bar{x} - 2\sigma \qquad\qquad \mu \qquad\qquad \bar{x} + 2\sigma$$

EXAMPLE

A survey was carried out on 1,600 randomly selected people and the result was that 960 were in favour of holding an election now. At the 95% confidence level, calculate:

(i) The margin of error

(ii) The confidence interval for the proportion of the people that want an election now

(iii) Four weeks later, a similar survey was carried out on 1,200 randomly selected people to see if there was a change in support for an election. The result was that 696 are now in favour of a change of government.

The null hypothesis, H_0, is there is no change in the support for the government.

The alternative hypothesis, H_A, is there is a change in the support for the government.

At the 95% level of confidence for this second survey, would you accept the null hypothesis? Give a reason for your answer.

Solution:

(i) At the 95% level of confidence, the margin of error $= \dfrac{1}{\sqrt{n}} = \dfrac{1}{\sqrt{1,600}} = 0.025$ (2·5%).

(ii) The sample proportion $= \hat{p} = \dfrac{960}{1,600} = 0.6$ (60%).

The 95% confidence interval for the proportion of people, p, who want an election now is:

$$\hat{p} - \frac{1}{\sqrt{n}} \leq p \leq \hat{p} + \frac{1}{\sqrt{n}}$$

$$0.6 - 0.025 \leq p \leq 0.6 + 0.025$$

$$0.575 \leq p \leq 0.625$$

Thus, the 95% confidence level for the proportion of people who want an election now is between 57·5% and 62·5%, inclusive.

Answers can also be given in brackets: [0·575, 0·625] or [57·5%, 62·5%].

(iii) Null hypothesis $= H_0 =$ there is no change in support for an election now.
Alternative hypothesis $= H_A =$ there is a change in support for an election now.

In the second survey, $\hat{p} = \dfrac{696}{1,200} = 0.58$ (58%)

This is **inside** the 95% confidence interval in the first survey. Thus, we **accept** the null hypothesis and **reject** the alternative hypothesis.

Note: If the second sample proportion was outside the 95% confidence interval, 57·5 to 62·5, we would reject the null hypothesis and accept the alternative hypothesis.

Exercise 3.15

In this exercise, where necessary, give all decimal answers correct to four decimal places and all percentages correct to two decimal places.

1. For each given random sample of size n, calculate the margin of error at the 95% confidence level.

    (i) $n = 10,000$ (ii) $n = 1,890$ (iii) $n = 976$ (iv) $n = 816$ (v) $n = 434$

2. For each of the following, calculate the sample size n at the 95% confidence level to have a margin of error of:

    (i) 5%   (ii) 4%   (iii) 2%   (iv) 1·5%   (v) 1·2%

    Comment on the relationship between the margin of error and the sample size.

3. During the making of a movie, it was found that out of 400 extras, only 120 were suitable for parts in a major movie. Find the 95% confidence interval for the proportion of all film extras that may be suitable for parts in major movies.

4. In a survey carried out in a large city, 450 households out of a random sample of 625 owned at least one pet. Calculate the 95% confidence interval for the proportion of households that own at least one pet.

5. In a market research survey, 34 people out of a random sample of 100 from a certain area said that they use a particular brand of toothpaste. Find the 95% confidence interval for the proportion of people in this area who use this brand of toothpaste.

6. Out of 276 cars parked in a car park, 207 were fitted with an anti-theft device. Assuming that the cars form a random sample of parked cars, construct the 95% confidence interval for the population of parked cars fitted with an anti-theft device.

7. Out of a random sample of 400 apples, 92 apples had sticky labels that were difficult to remove. All the other apples had sticky labels that were easily removed. Calculate the 95% confidence interval for the proportion of apples that have sticky labels that are difficult to remove.

8. In an opinion poll carried out before a local election, 513 people out of a random sample of 950 declare that they will vote for a particular one of the two candidates contesting the election. Construct the 95% limits for the true proportion of all voters that will vote for this candidate. In your opinion, is there significant evidence that this candidate will win the election?

9. (i) A random sample of 100 students in a university was asked to calculate how much money they had earned during their last summer break. The mean of the sample was €3,500. Can we say that the mean amount of money earned by the students during the last summer break in this university was €3,500? Justify your answer.
   (ii) Calculate the margin of error if the confidence level is cited at 95%.
   (iii) Construct a 95% confidence interval for the proportion of students who earned €3,500 in summer earnings in this university.
   (iv) If the margin of error is required to be 5%, calculate the sample size.

10. When designing a large auditorium for a university, an architect made the assumption that 12% of the students in the university are left handed. As a result, he wanted to design the auditorium so that 12% of the built-in desks in the auditorium were suitable for left-handed people. Before the auditorium was built, the head of the university commissioned a survey to see if the architect's assumption was reasonable. Four hundred students were randomly selected from the student register and 72 identified as left handed.
    (i) At the 95% confidence level: (a) calculate the margin of error
       (b) construct the confidence interval.
    (ii) Using the results of the survey, would you accept the architect's assumption? Justify your answer.

Inferential statistics is the branch of statistics that uses probability and statistics to draw conclusions from data that are affected by random variation. To work on inferential statistics, we should be able to:

1. Estimate the value of a population proportion
2. Calculate the margin of error for a sample
3. Construct a confidence interval
4. Test a hypothesis about a population proportion
5. Apply sampling theory to hypothesis questions
6. Use *p*-value as an alternative to hypothesis testing

Margin of error and confidence intervals for population proportions

Many statistical studies want to obtain the proportion (percentage) of a population that has a specified attribute. In most cases the population under consideration will be large and hence it would be impractical, if not impossible, to obtain the population proportion by taking a census. Thus, we generally employ sampling and use the sample data to make inferences about the population.

The key to the validity of any survey is randomness. It is important that the sample be chosen randomly so that the survey results can be generalised to the whole population.

The results of a survey are only an estimate of the quantity of interest. When results of surveys are reported in the media, they often include a statement like: **'35% of respondents favour Mr Smith in the upcoming election. However, there is a margin of error of 3 percentage points.'** What this means is that the people who carried out the survey are reasonably confident that in the real election, the percentage of votes for Mr Smith will be 35% $\pm$ 3%. In other words, they are confident that if the election was held now, Mr Smith would receive somewhere between 32% and 38% of the vote. Such intervals are called **confidence intervals**.

An estimate from a survey should be treated with caution. Sampling errors mean that the results in the sample differ from the true results due to the 'luck of the draw.' However, it is important to remember that sampling errors do not make surveys useless.

Notation

We use the letter p to denote the **population proportion**. It is this value that is to be estimated. We use $\hat{p}$ (pronounced 'p hat') to denote the **sample proportion**. $\hat{p}$ is the statistic that will be used to estimate the unknown population proportion, p.

$$p = \text{population proportion} \qquad \hat{p} = \text{sample proportion}$$

The population proportion, p, although unknown, is a fixed number. On the other hand, the sample proportion, $\hat{p}$, is a random variable and its value depends on chance.

Suppose we wanted to know the proportion (percentage) of people in Ireland who are left-handed. We randomly selected 400 people and found that 64 of them are left-handed.

$$\hat{p} = \frac{\text{Number of people in the sample who are left-handed}}{\text{The number of people sampled}} = \frac{64}{400} = 0\cdot16\ (16\%)$$

If 60 out of 400 people sampled were left-handed, then:

$$\hat{p} = \frac{60}{400} = 0\cdot15\ (15\%)$$

Notice that the value of $\hat{p}$, the sample proportion, changes depending on the sample chosen. If the sample chosen is a good representation of the population, then $\hat{p}$, the sample proportion, will be a good estimate of the true population proportion, p.

Confidence interval for population proportion using the standard normal tables

How should we summarise the strength of the data in a sample survey? This is where the role of the **standard error (SE) of the proportion**, written $\sigma_{\hat{p}}$, comes in. The standard error is a number that represents the accuracy of a sample survey. It is a statistic expressing the amount of random sampling error in the results of a sample survey. The most commonly used level of confidence is 95%, but others you may meet include 90%, 98% and 99%. On our course, the 95% confidence level for the standard error (SE) is given by

$$\sigma_{\hat{p}} = \sqrt{\frac{p(1-p)}{n}} \qquad \text{(see the formulae and tables booklet)}$$

where $\sigma_{\hat{p}}$ is called the **standard error** (SE),
n is the size of the samples where $n \geq 30$
and p is the true proportion of the population (or $\hat{p}$ instead of p if p is unknown).

To calculate the margin of error (ME) at the 95% level of confidence, we need to know the associated z-value from the normal curve.

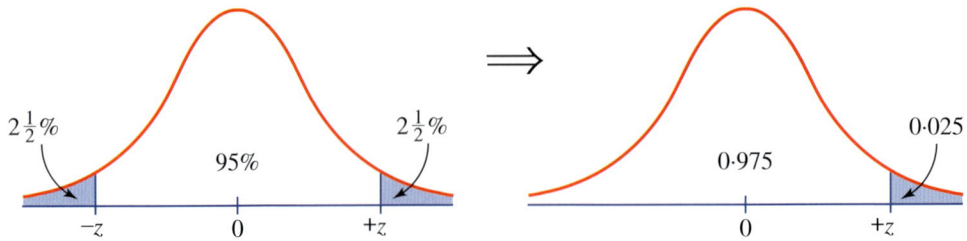

From the standard normal tables, $z = 1.96$.

Now z is the number of standard deviation that the margin of error is from the mean. Thus, the margin of error, E, is given by:

$$E = z\,\sigma_{\hat{p}}$$
$$E = 1.96\,\sigma_{\hat{p}}$$

Confidence interval

The estimated proportion plus or minus its margin of error is called a confidence interval for the true proportion. The 95% confidence for a proportion is given by:

sample proportion $-$ margin of error $\leq$ true proportion $\leq$ sample proportion + margin of error

$$\hat{p} - z\sigma_{\hat{p}} \leq p \leq \hat{p} + z\sigma_{\hat{p}}$$

$$\hat{p} - 1.96\sigma_{\hat{p}} \leq p \leq \hat{p} + 1.96\sigma_{\hat{p}}$$

$$\hat{p} - 1.96\sqrt{\frac{\hat{p}(1-\hat{p})}{n}} \leq p \leq \hat{p} + 1.96\sqrt{\frac{\hat{p}(1-\hat{p})}{n}}$$

Where n is the sample size, p is the population proportion and $\hat{p}$ is the sample proportion.

We can state with 95% confidence that the true population, p, lies inside this interval. What this means is that if the same population was surveyed on numerous occasions and the confidence interval was calculated, then about 95% of these confidence intervals would contain the true proportion and about 5% of these confidence intervals would not contain the true proportion.

The end points of the 95% confidence are given by $\hat{p} \pm 1.96\sigma_{\hat{p}}$:

The 95% confidence interval

$\hat{p} - 1.96\,\sigma_{\hat{p}}$ $\hat{p} + 1.96\,\sigma_{\hat{p}}$

It is worth noting that when p (or $\hat{p}$ instead of p if p is unknown) is close to $\dfrac{1}{2}$, a good approximation

to the margin of error, at the 95% confidence level, is given by $E = z\sigma_p = \dfrac{1}{\sqrt{n}}$.

EXAMPLE 1

A poll was taken of 2,020 workers in a city. The workers sampled were asked whether they take a 'duvet day', that is, call in sick, at least once a year when they simply need time to relax. 404 workers responded yes. Use these data to obtain a 95% confidence interval for the proportion, p, of all employees in the city who take a 'duvet day'.

Solution
Step 1: Calculate the standard error.

$$\text{SE} = \sigma_{\hat{p}} = \sqrt{\dfrac{\hat{p}(1-\hat{p})}{n}} \quad \text{where } n = 2{,}020$$

$$\text{and } \hat{p} = \dfrac{404}{2{,}020} = 0.2.$$

$$\text{Then } \sigma_{\hat{p}} = \sqrt{\dfrac{(0.2)(1-0.2)}{2{,}020}} = 0.008899 = 0.009.$$

Step 2: The margin of error, E, at the 95% confidence interval is given by

$$E = 1.96\sigma_{\hat{p}} = 1.96(0.009) = 0.0176.$$

Step 3: The 95% confidence interval for the true proportion, p, is then:

$$\hat{p} - E \leq p \leq \hat{p} + E$$
$$0\cdot 2 - 0\cdot 0176 \leq p \leq 0\cdot 2 + 0\cdot 0176$$
$$0\cdot 1824 \leq p \leq 0\cdot 2176$$
$$18\cdot 24\% \leq p \leq 21\cdot 76\%$$

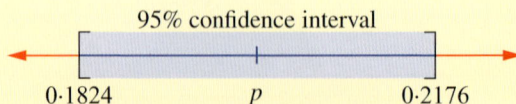

95% confidence interval

0·1824 p 0·2176

We are 95% confident that the percentage of all the city's employees who take a duvet day is somewhere between 18·24% and 21·76%.

It is worth noting that the margin of error, E, is half the length of the confidence interval.

EXAMPLE 2

In a by-election, a random sample of 900 voters suggests that 35% will vote for candidate A.

(i) Find the standard error at the 95% confidence level.

(ii) If a random sample of 400 voters was used, would the standard error (at the 95% confidence level) be greater than or less than 1·6%? Justify your answer.

(iii) Candidate A is a billionaire who wishes to determine his level of support to within $\pm\frac{1}{2}\%$. What sample size should be taken at the 95% confidence level?

Solution

(i) Standard error $= \sigma_{\hat{p}} = \sqrt{\dfrac{\hat{p}(1 - \hat{p})}{n}} = \sqrt{\dfrac{(0\cdot 35)(1 - 0\cdot 35)}{900}} = 0\cdot 016 = 1\cdot 6\%$

(ii) Since the sample size, $n = 400$, is less than the sample size $n = 900$ from part **(i)**, we state:

Method 1

Standard error $= \sigma_{\hat{p}} = \sqrt{\dfrac{\hat{p}(1 - \hat{p})}{n}} = \sqrt{\dfrac{(0\cdot 35)(0\cdot 65)}{400}} = 0\cdot 024 = 2\cdot 4\%$

Hence, standard error is greater than 1·6%.

Method 2

Since $n = 900$ in part **(i)** is greater than $n = 400$ in part **(ii)**, this means the answer in part **(i)** is more accurate than the answer to part **(ii)**.

$\therefore n = 400$ has a standard error > 1·6%.

(iii) Note: To within $\pm\frac{1}{2}\%$ means that the margin of error should be $\frac{1}{2}\%$.

Let n = size of the random sample

$$E = \frac{1}{2}\% = 0\cdot005$$

$$\hat{p} = 0\cdot35$$

Then $E = 1\cdot96 = \sqrt{\dfrac{\hat{p}(1-\hat{p})}{n}}$

becomes $\quad 0\cdot005 = 1\cdot96\sqrt{\dfrac{(0\cdot35)(0\cdot65)}{n}}$

$$0\cdot000025 = 3\cdot8416\dfrac{0\cdot2275}{n} \quad \text{(square both sides)}$$

$$0\cdot000025n = 0\cdot873964$$

$$n = 34{,}959$$

A sample size of 34,959 would be required to obtain a margin of error of $\frac{1}{2}\%$.

Some notes on margin of error

- On our course, the margin of error is **always** at the 95% level of confidence.
- As the sample size increases the margin of error decreases.
- At the 95% level of confidence a sample of about
  (i) 80 has a margin of error approximately $\pm11\%$
  (ii) 1,000 has a margin of error approximately $\pm3\cdot2\%$.
- The size of the (original) population does not matter.
- If the sample size, m, is doubled (say 500 to 1,000) the margin of error, E, is **not** halved.
- The margin of error estimates how accurately the results of a poll reflect the true feelings of the population.

Exercise 3.16

1. Show on separate diagrams the following confidence intervals.

   (i) In a survey, 52% of voters supported a certain candidate with a margin of error of 5%.

   (ii) $0\cdot18 \leq p \leq 0\cdot26$

   (iii) $62\% \leq p \leq 67\%$

   (iv) $\dfrac{5}{18} \leq p \leq \dfrac{1}{2}$

   (v) In a clinical study, 86% of patients reported relief after taking a new drug. The margin of error was calculated as $4\cdot5\%$.

2. In a study on UFOs (unidentified flying objects), 34% of those surveyed reported at least one UFO sighting. The margin of error was plus or minus 2·6 percentage points (for a 95% confidence level). Use this information to obtain a 95% confidence interval for the percentage of those surveyed who reported at least one UFO sighting.

3. The results of two polls on the government's budget plan appeared in a national newspaper. Poll A stated that 79% supported the budget plan; the margin of error was plus or minus 5%. Poll B stated that 74% supported the budget plan; the margin of error was plus or minus 4%. Is it possible that both of these polls were correct in their conclusion?

4. A poll was taken of 825 self-employed workers. The workers sampled were asked if they contribute to a pension scheme to provide for retirement. 462 workers responded yes. Use these data to obtain a 95% confidence interval for the proportion, p, of all self-employed workers who contribute to a pension scheme.

5. A survey on the drinking habits of Europeans, carried out by the EU, estimated the percentage of adults across the EU who drink beer, wine or spirits at least occasionally. Of the 4,548 adults interviewed, 2,955 said they drank at least occasionally.

    (i) Determine a 95% confidence interval for the proportion, p, of all EU citizens who drink beer, wine or spirits at least occasionally.

    (ii) Interpret your results from part **(i)**.

6. A government department wants to estimate the proportion, p, of its employees who went on sick leave during the past year. A random sample of 64 employees was taken. 36 of the sample went on sick leave during the past year.

    (i) Find the standard error at the 95% confidence level.

    (ii) If a random sample of 100 employees was taken, how would the standard error compare to the answer for part **(i)**? Explain your answer.

    (iii) The CEO of the department wants to determine the annual proportion of employees who went on sick leave to within 2%. What sample size should be taken at the 95% level of confidence?

7. High-visibility vests come in five different sizes: 1, 2, 3, 4 and 5. A road maintenance company issued vests to 40 randomly selected employees. The sizes issued to these 40 employees were as follows.

    1 3 2 3 5 4 3 2 4 5 5 3 3 2 1 3 4 3 2 3

    3 2 3 4 3 3 2 1 2 3 4 3 5 3 2 1 5 3 4 4

    (i) Find $\hat{p}$, the proportion in the sample of employees that were issued with size 3.

    (ii) Calculate the 95% confidence interval for the proportion of all employees in the company that require size 3.

    (iii) How could the company find a more precise 95% confidence interval?

(iv) The estimate of p is $\hat{p}$. How large a sample would be needed in order to obtain an approximate 95% confidence interval of the form $\hat{p} \pm 0.1$?

8. **(i)** A catalogue sales company promises to deliver orders placed on the internet within five days. Follow-up calls to n randomly selected customers show that a 95% confidence interval for the proposition that all orders arrive on time (within five days) is 88% ± 6%. Find the value of n.

(ii) Which, if any, of the following conclusions is correct? (In each case, justify your answer.)

   (a) Between 82% and 94% of all orders arrive on time.

   (b) 95% of all random samples of customers will show that 88% of all orders will arrive on time.

   (c) On 95% of the days, between 82% and 94% of the orders will arrive on time.

9. Consider each situation described below.
Identify the population and the sample, explain what p and $\hat{p}$ represent and state whether we can construct a 95% confidence interval for each situation and justify your statement.

   (i) A university admits 1,916 students to first year, and three years later 1,798 of them graduated on time. The university wants to estimate the percentage of all their first years who graduate on time.

   (ii) A radio talk show asks listeners to register their opinions on prayer in schools by logging on to a website. Of the 702 people who voted, 588 favoured prayer in schools. Can we estimate from this opinion poll the level of support among the general public?

   (iii) In a poll of 11 secondary school students, four students expected to get maximum CAO points in their Leaving Certificate. Is it possible to estimate the percentage of all Leaving Certificate students who would expect to get maximum CAO points based on this poll?

   (iv) The gardaí set up a motor vehicle checkpoint at which drivers are stopped and their vehicles inspected for safety problems. They find that 12 of the 126 cars stopped have at least one safety violation. They want to estimate the percentage of all motor vehicles that may be unsafe.

   (v) A school is considering changing the type of school uniform. The Parents Association surveys parent opinion by sending a questionaire home with all 1,143 students. 299 surveys are returned, with 201 surveys in favour of the change. What conclusions can the Parents Association draw?

Hypothesis testing

A **hypothesis** is a statement or conjecture whose truth has yet to be proven or disproven. Examples of hypotheses:

- More than half the population is satisfied with EU membership
- Drinking fizzy drinks causes tooth decay
- The age at marriage has increased over the past 20 years.

> ### Null hypothesis
> The statement being tested in a test of significance is called the **null hypothesis**. The test of significance is designed to assess the strength of the evidence against the null hypothesis.
> Usually the null hypothesis is a statement of 'no effect' or 'no difference.'
> We abbreviate 'null hypothesis' as H_0.

Statistics help to make decisions

We can use statistics to accept or reject claims.

1. Is global temperature increasing?
   The null hypothesis, H_0, is that global temperature is not increasing, i.e. there is no difference in temperature.
   The alternative hypothesis, H_A, is that global temperature is increasing.

2. Is a new drug effective for treating HIV/AIDS?
   The null hypothesis, H_0, is that the new drug is not effective.
   The alternative hypothesis, H_A, is that the new drug is effective.

3. Is a survey on left-handed people biased if it indicates that 24% of people are left-handed?
   The null hypothesis, H_0, is that 24% of people are left-handed, i.e. the survey is not biased.
   The alternative hypothesis, H_A, is that the survey is biased.

Often the people investigating the data hope to reject H_0. They hope:

- Their new drug is better than the old one

  or

- The new ad campaign is better than the old one, etc.

However, in statistics, it is essential that our attitude is one of skepticism. Until we are convinced otherwise, we accept H_0. In other words, we cling to the idea that there is no change, no improvement, no deterioration, no effect.

In a courtroom, the null hypothesis is that the defendant did *not* commit a crime.

A verdict of guilty means we reject the null hypothesis, that is to say, the defendant committed a crime.

However, a verdict of not guilty does not mean the defendant did not commit a crime, but simply that the case has not been proven.

Applying this logic to hypothesis testing, we either reject H_0 or fail to reject H_0.

The reasoning behind hypothesis testing is that we usually prefer to think about getting things right rather than getting them wrong.

In testing a hypothesis, data may be given or collected.

With given data in this course, we accept the information at face value and proceed to analyse the data and answer the question.

To collect data, a questionnaire could be used to carry out a survey. The key to the validity of any survey is randomness.

Procedure for carrying out a hypothesis test

The procedure for carrying out a hypothesis test will involve the following steps:

1. Write down H_0, the null hypothesis, and H_A, the alternative hypothesis.

2. Write down or calculate the sample proportion, $\hat{p}$.

3. Find the 95% margin of error.

4. Write down the 95% confidence interval for p, using

$$\hat{p} - 1{\cdot}96\sqrt{\frac{\hat{p}(1 - \hat{p})}{n}} \leq p \leq \hat{p} + 1{\cdot}96\sqrt{\frac{\hat{p}(1 - \hat{p})}{n}}.$$

   In addition, we can illustrate the confidence interval with a diagram.

5. (i) If the value of the population proportion stated is within the confidence interval, we fail to reject H_0.

   (ii) If the value of the population proportion is outside the confidence interval, reject the null hypothesis, H_0.

6. State your conclusion in words.

EXAMPLE

A poll carried out by a newspaper indicated that 48% of the voting population would support a candidate in a presidential election. Three weeks later, a rival newspaper surveyed 1,800 voters and 918 said they would support the candidate. Investigate at the 5% level of significance whether support for the candidate changed.

Solution

1. State H_0 and H_A.

   H_0: The support for the candidate has remained at 48%. $\mu = 48\%$.

   H_A: The support for the candidate is not at 48%. $\mu \neq 48\%$, i.e. the support has changed.

2. Sample proportion $\hat{p} = \dfrac{918}{1,800} = 0{\cdot}51$

3. 95% margin of error $= E = 1{\cdot}96\sigma_{\hat{p}} = 1{\cdot}96\sqrt{\dfrac{\hat{p}(1 - \hat{p})}{n}} = 1{\cdot}96\sqrt{\dfrac{(0{\cdot}51)(0{\cdot}49)}{1,800}}$

   $E = 0{\cdot}023\ (=2{\cdot}3\%)$

4. Confidence interval

$$\hat{p} - E \leq p \leq \hat{p} + E$$

$$0\cdot51 - 0\cdot023 \leq p \leq 0\cdot51 + 0\cdot023$$

$$0\cdot487 \leq p \leq 0\cdot523$$

$$48\cdot7\% \leq p \leq 52\cdot3\%$$

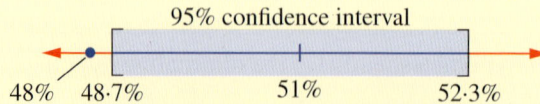

5. The claimed voter support of 48% is not within the confidence interval, so we reject the null hypothesis, H_0.

6. We conclude that voter support has changed.

Note: When working with the terms *levels of significance* or *levels of confidence*, statisticians use percentages ambiguously. In particular, the 5% level of significance and the 95% level of confidence refer to the same region.

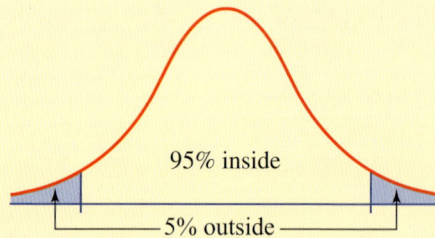

Exercise 3.17

1. A drugs company produced a new pain-relieving drug for migraine sufferers and claimed that the drug had an 80% success rate. A group of doctors doubted the company's claim. They prescribed the drug for a group of 1,600 patients. After one year 1,232 of these patients said that their migraine symptoms had been relieved by the drug.

Calculate:

(i) The sample proportion

(ii) The margin of error at the 95% level of confidence

(iii) The 95% confidence interval for the proportion of patients in the sample who had their migraine symptoms relieved

(iv) State the null hypothesis, H_0

(v) Is this result consistent with the company's claim at the 95% level of confidence? Justify your answer.

2. A national newspaper is investigating a claim made by the CEO of a large multinational company. The CEO claims that 90% of the company's one million customers are satisfied with the service they receive. Using simple random sampling, the newspaper surveyed 300 customers. Among the sampled customers, 261 said they were satisfied with the company's service.
    (i) Construct a 95% confidence interval for the proportion of satisfied customers.
    (ii) Explain what the 95% confidence interval means in the context of the question.
    (iii) State the null hypothesis, H_0, and the alternative hypothesis, H_A.
    (iv) Based on these findings, can we reject the CEO's claim?
    (v) How could the investigation be made more accurate? Explain your reasoning.

3. An insurance company conducted a survey of 14,000 car crashes. It found that 8,330 of the crashes occurred within 8 km of the driver's home. The company claims that 60% of car crashes occur within 8 km of home.
    (i) State the null hypothesis, H_0, and the alternative hypothesis, H_A.
    (ii) Use a hypothesis test at the 5% level of significance to decide whether there is sufficient evidence to justify the company's claim. State your conclusion clearly.

4. Jack tosses his lucky coin 1,000 times and a head occurs 450 times. Jack claims his coin is biased.

    Use a hypothesis test at the 5% level of significance to decide whether there is sufficient evidence to justify Jack's claim. State the null hypothesis and state your conclusion clearly.

5. A pharmaceutical company has developed and tested a new pain-killing drug. The company's records show that the old drug provided relief for 72% of all patients who were administered it. A random sample of 1,225 were administered the new drug and 900 of these claimed that the new drug provided relief.
    (i) State the null hypothesis, H_0, and the alternative hypothesis, H_A.
    (ii) Use a hypothesis test at the 5% level of significance to decide if the new drug is different from its old counterpart. State your conclusion clearly.

6. A soccer manager has a hypothesis that young European soccer players born in the first three months of the year have an advantage in being selected to represent their country at the under-17 level over players born later in the same year.
    (i) Estimate the expected percentage of players born in the first three months of the year.
    (ii) Find the margin of error, at the 95% confidence level, for a sample size of 400.
    (iii) A survey of 400 players, selected at random, who played soccer at the under-17 level for their country showed that 35% of these players were born in the first three months of the year.

    Use a hypothesis test at the 5% level of significance to decide whether there is sufficient evidence to justify the manager's claim. State the null hypothesis and state your conclusion clearly.

Sampling distribution of the mean (distributions of the sample means)

Suppose a large number of different random samples, each of the same size, n, are selected independently from a population with mean μ and standard deviation σ.

Each of these samples will have its own mean, $\bar{x}$, and standard deviation, s. The set of these different sample means, $\{\bar{x}_1, \bar{x}_2, \bar{x}_3, \ldots\}$ are called the **sample means**.

If these sample means are represented with a curve, they have a distribution with the following properties, called the **central limit theorem**.

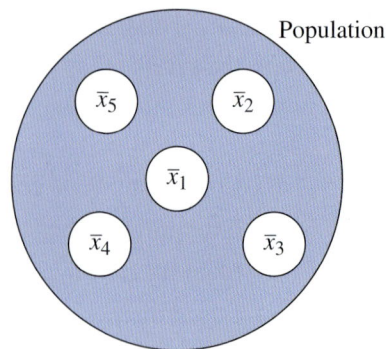

Population

$\bar{x}_5$ $\bar{x}_2$ $\bar{x}_1$ $\bar{x}_4$ $\bar{x}_3$

Central limit theorem

1. The distribution of the sample means is always normal.

2. $$\mu_{\bar{x}} = \mu$$
   Mean of the sample means = Means of the population

3. $$\sigma_{\bar{x}} = \frac{\sigma}{\sqrt{n}}$$
   Standard deviation of the sample means = (standard deviation of the population) $\div \sqrt{n}$

What is remarkable about the central limit theorem is that regardless of the shape of the original distribution, taking averages of samples results in a normal curve. To find the distribution of $\bar{x}$, the sample means, we need to know only the original population mean and standard deviation.

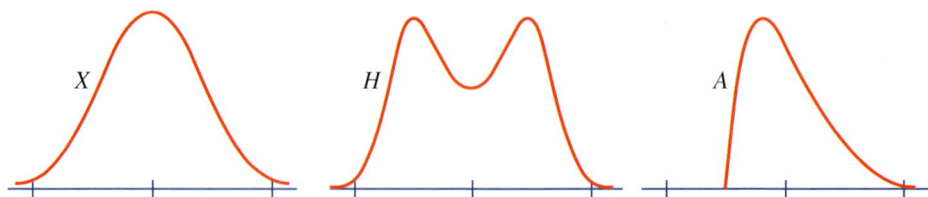

X   H   A

The three probability densities above all have the same mean and standard deviation. Despite their different shapes, when $n = 10$ (or more), the sampling distributions of the mean, $\bar{x}$, are nearly identical and in the shape of a normal curve.

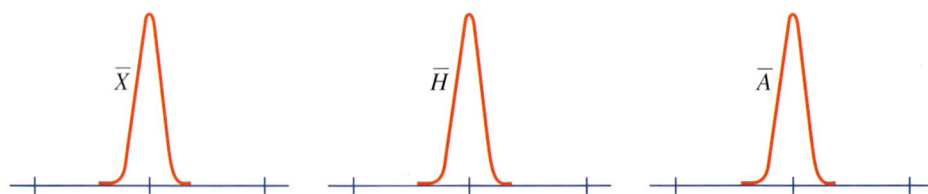

$\bar{X}$ $\bar{H}$ $\bar{A}$

Standard error of the mean

$$\sigma_{\bar{x}} = \frac{\sigma}{\sqrt{n}} = \text{standard error of the mean}$$

The standard deviation of the sample means is called the standard error and is denoted by $\dfrac{\sigma}{\sqrt{n}}$.

The standard error is precisely that. It is the standard distance, or error, that a sample mean is from the population mean. On our course, we want to know how good an estimate the sample mean is from the population mean. The standard error gives us just that. The standard error is also a standard deviation.

Note: As the sample size, n, gets larger, the standard error gets smaller. In other words, the approximation gets better and better with increasing sample size.

The distribution of the sample means is normal. Thus, we can use the Standard Normal Tables to calculate the probability that the mean of a sample of a certain size differs from the mean of the population by a given amount. Later on we will see how the distribution of the sample means is extremely useful to hypothesis testing when we consider a sample from a population rather than a single value.

Testing the null hypothesis using z-values

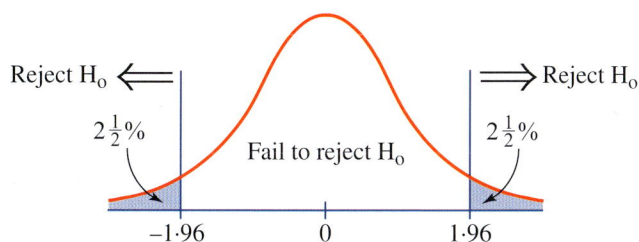

At the 5% level of significance for a two-tailed test:

$$-1 \cdot 96 \leq z \leq 1 \cdot 96$$

If the value of z lies outside the range $-1 \cdot 96 \leq z \leq 1 \cdot 96$, we reject H_0. The area outside the range is called the critical region (the shaded regions in the diagram above).

For z-values, the steps involved in hypothesis testing are:

1. Write down the null hypothesis, H_0, and the alternative hypothesis, H_A.

2. Convert the observed results into z units. (This is sometimes referred to as the test statistic.)

3. Reject H_0 if z is outside the range $-1 \cdot 96 \leq z \leq 1 \cdot 96$. Otherwise, we fail to reject H_0. (A diagram will help.)

4. State the conclusion in words.

EXAMPLE

A tyre company claims that the mean life of tyres that it produces is 11,000 km with a standard deviation of 240 km. An independent supplier of tyres wants to investigate the company's claim. A test on a random sample of 144 tyres from the company gave a mean life of 10,963 km. Carry out a hypothesis test at the 5% level of significance to see if there is evidence to support the company's claim.

Solution

1. State the null and alternative hypotheses.

   Null hypothesis, H_0:

   The company produces tyres with a mean life of 11,000 km. $\mu = 11,000$.

   Alternative hypothesis, H_A:

   The company produces tyres whose mean life is not 11,000 km. $\mu \neq 11,000$.

2. Convert the given results into z units (the test statistic):

$$z = \frac{\dfrac{\bar{x} - \mu}{\sigma}}{\sqrt{n}} = \frac{10,963 - 11,000}{\dfrac{240}{\sqrt{144}}} = -1 \cdot 85$$

3.

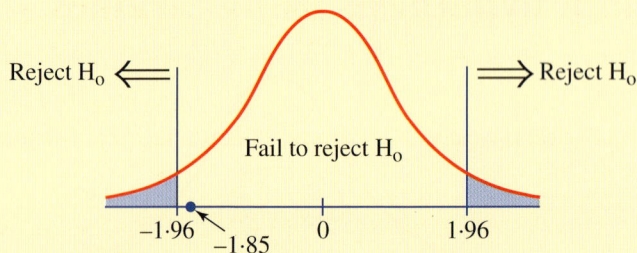

We fail to reject H_0, as $-1 \cdot 85$ is not in the critical regions.

4. Hence we fail to reject the company's claim.

   In the above example, we used:

   H_0: $\mu = 11,000$

   H_A: $\mu \neq 11,000$

   In these situations, because we do not use $\mu > 11,000$ or $\mu < 11,000$, no direction is stipulated. Therefore, this is a two-tailed test. (Only two-tailed tests are used on our course.) Also, H_0 always has an equal sign and uses population parameters.

Hypothesis testing – A summary

In the final analysis, testing the null hypothesis, H_0 simply involves a confidence interval and a red dot

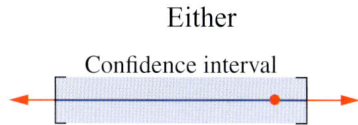

Either

Confidence interval

If the red dot is inside the confidence interval we fail to reject H_0.

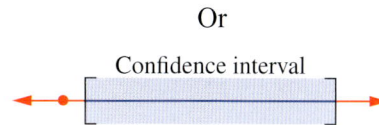

Or

Confidence interval

If the red dot is outside the confidence interval we reject H_0.

Exercise 3.18

1. A company manufactures pens with a mean writing life of 600 hours and a standard deviation of 12 hours.

   A retailer examines a sample of 98 pens from a supplier who claims to only sell pens from this company and finds their mean life is 597 hours.

   (i) State the null and alternative hypotheses.

   (ii) Hence, decide whether these pens are genuine products from the company at the 5% level of significance.

2. In an examination taken by a large number of students, the mean mark was 60·5 with a standard deviation of 9 marks. In a random sample of 43 students in a particular school, it was found that the mean mark was 63.

   At the 5% level of significance, investigate if there is evidence to conclude that the students of this school did as well as students in general.

3. The marks awarded in an examination are normally distributed with a mean mark of 60 and a standard deviation of 10.

   A sample of 50 students has a mean mark of 63.

   Test, at the 5% level of significance, the hypothesis that this is a random sample from the population.

4. The distribution of the weights of muffins produced in the EU by all Bakewell automated baking systems is shown in the diagram. It can be seen that the distribution is slightly skewed.

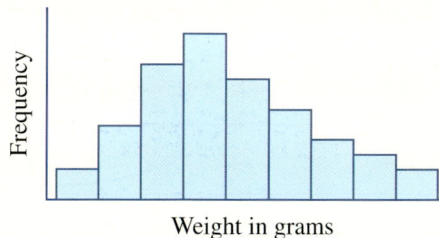

Weight in grams

The mean is 80 grams.

The standard deviation is 6 grams.

In one bakery using the Bakewell automated baking system, random samples of 50 muffins are selected for quality control purposes. The mean of each sample is recorded. 300 such sample means are recorded.

(i) State which way the given diagram is skewed.

(ii) Describe the expected distribution of these sample means. Your description should refer to the shape of the distribution and to its mean and standard deviation.

(iii) How many of the sample means would you expect to be greater than 81 grams?

5. (i) Assume that the duration of human pregnancies can be described by a normal model with a mean of 270 days and a standard deviation of 15 days.

(a) What percentage of pregnancies should last between 270 and 290 days?

(b) Using the empirical rule, write down the 95% confidence interval for the mean pregnancy duration.

(c) At least how many days should the upper quartile of all pregnancies last?

(d) Suppose a certain doctor is currently providing prenatal care to 48 pregnant women. Let $\bar{h}$ represent the mean length of their pregnancies. According to the central limit theorem, what is the distribution of this sample mean? Specify the model, mean and standard deviation.

(e) What is the probability that the mean duration of these patients' pregnancies will be more than 275 days?

(ii) The duration of human pregnancies may not actually follow a normal model as described in part (i).

(a) Explain why it may be somewhat skewed to the left.

(b) If the correct model is in fact skewed, does that change your answers to parts (a), (b), (c) and (d) of part (i)? Explain why or why not for each of the four parts.

6. The distribution of the hourly earnings of all employees in Ireland in October 2009 is shown in the diagram. It can be seen that the distribution is positively skewed.

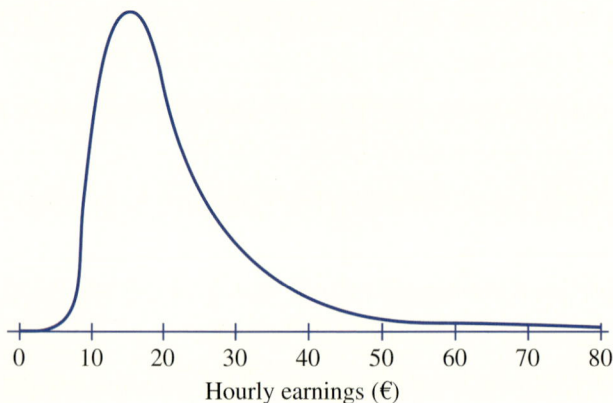

Hourly earnings (€)

The mean is €22·05.

The median is €17·82.

The standard deviation is €10·64.

The lower quartile is €12·80.

The upper quartile is €26·05.

(i) If six employees are selected at random from this population, what is the probability that exactly four of them had hourly earnings of more than €12·80?

(ii) In a computer simulation, random samples of size 200 are repeatedly selected from this population and the mean of each sample is recorded. 1,000 such sample means are recorded. Describe the expected distribution of these sample means. Your description should refer to the shape of the distribution and to its mean and standard deviation.

(iii) How many of the sample means would you expect to be greater than €23?

p-values

A *p*-value is used as an alternative method to make a decision on the null hypothesis.
A *p*-value is a probability. It is a measure of the strength of evidence to reject, or fail to reject, the null hypothesis. The smaller the *p*-valuc, the less likely the null hypothesis is true and vice versa.

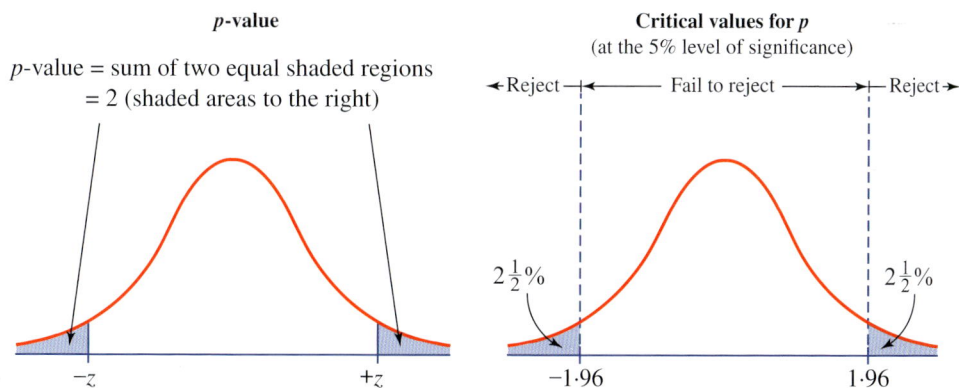

p-value

p-value = sum of two equal shaded regions
= 2 (shaded areas to the right)

$-z$ $+z$

Critical values for *p*
(at the 5% level of significance)

◄─Reject ─┤◄──── Fail to reject ────►├─ Reject ►

$2\frac{1}{2}\%$ $2\frac{1}{2}\%$

$-1\cdot96$ $1\cdot96$

The decision to reject, or fail to reject, H_0 is based on the comparison of the *p*-value with the level of significance. On our course we only use a two-tailed test at the 5% level of significance.

Critical p-value $= 0.05$ at the 5% significance level.

If $p \leq 0.05$, there is strong evidence to reject H_0.

If $p > 0.05$, there is strong evidence to fail to reject H_0.

Memory aid: If p is low, H_0 must go.

The lower the p-value, the stronger the evidence against H_0. The larger the sample size, the more precise the estimates.

p-value approach to perform a hypothesis test

1. State H_0 and H_A.
2. Calculate the z score (this is often called the test statistic, T).
3. Determine the p-value (a diagram is useful).
4. If $p \leq 0.05$, reject H_0. If $p > 0.05$, do not reject H_0.
5. State the conclusion in words.

Type I and type II errors

Type I error: Rejecting H_0 when it is true.

Type II error: Failing to reject H_0 when it is false.

Note: The strength of evidence using a p-value is enhanced by also including a 95% confidence interval for the population mean, μ.

EXAMPLE

A coal merchant sells coal in bags marked '50 kg'. The merchant claims that the bags have a mean weight of 50 kg with a standard deviation of 1·2 kg. To test this claim, a random selection of 72 of these bags was weighed and found to have a mean weight of 49·7 kg.

  (i) Write down H_0 and H_A.

  (ii) Calculate the test statistic for the sample mean.

 (iii) Calculate a p-value for this sample mean.

 (iv) At the 5% level of significance, is there evidence to show that the mean weight of the bags of coal is not 50 kg? Justify your answer.

Solution

  (i) $H_0 : \mu = 50$ and $H_A : \mu \neq 50$.

  (ii) $\bar{x} = 49.7$, $\mu = 50$, $\sigma = 1.2$ and $n = 72$.

The test statistic is given by:

$$T = \frac{\bar{x} - \mu}{\frac{\sigma}{\sqrt{n}}} = \frac{49{\cdot}7 - 50}{\frac{1{\cdot}2}{\sqrt{72}}} = -2{\cdot}12$$

(iii)

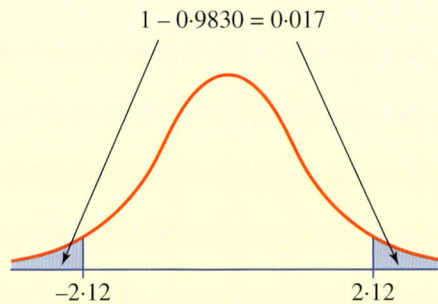

$1 - 0{\cdot}9830 = 0{\cdot}017$

$-2{\cdot}12 \qquad 2{\cdot}12$

p-value

$P(T < -2{\cdot}12)$

$= 1 - P(z \le -2{\cdot}12)$

$= 1 - P(z \le 2{\cdot}12) = 1 - 0{\cdot}9830 = 0{\cdot}017$ (tables)

$\therefore$ p-value $= 2(0{\cdot}017) = 0{\cdot}034 = 3{\cdot}4\%$

(iv) $0{\cdot}034 < 0{\cdot}05$ or $3{\cdot}4\% < 5\%$

Thus, there is strong evidence to reject the null hypothesis, H_0. Therefore, we conclude there is strong evidence to reject the claim by the coal merchant that the average weight of these bags of coal is 50 kg.

Exercise 3.19

Copy and complete the following table.

	H_0	H_A	μ	σ	$\bar{x}$	n	T	p	Reject, or fail to reject, H_0
1.	$\mu = 500$	$\mu \ne 500$	500	15	504	64	2·13	0·0332	Reject H_0
2.			120	3	120·85	36			
3.			210	6	211·5	100			
4.			80	18	77·3	144			
5.			150	20	153·8	200			
6.			70	6	68	40			
7.			60	10	62	50			
8.			90	14·3	87·6	110			

9. A company claims that the average weight of the packets of porridge it produces is 400 g with a standard deviation of 12 g. To test this claim, a random sample of 64 of these packets was weighed and found to have a mean value of 403 g.

   (i) Write down H_0 and H_A.

   (ii) Calculate the test statistics for this sample mean.

   (iii) Calculate a p-value for this sample mean.

   (iv) At the 5% level of significance, is there evidence to show that the mean weight of the packets of porridge is not 400 g? Justify your answer.

10. A machine produces metal rods which have a mean length of 600 cm with a standard deviation of 4 cm. After a service to the machine, it is claimed that the machine now produces rods with lengths that are not equal to 600 cm. To test the claim, a random sample of 100 rods from the serviced machine are measured and found to have a mean length of 600·6 cm.

    (i) Write down H_0 and H_A.

    (ii) Calculate the test statistic for this sample mean.

    (iii) Calculate a p-value for this sample mean.

    (iv) At the 5% level of significance, is there evidence to show that the mean length of the metal rods from the serviced machine is not 600 cm? Justify your answer.

11. An internet provider claims that the mean speed of its internet connection is 50 MB/s, with a standard deviation of 5 MB/s. To test this claim, a random sample of 72 customers of this internet provider was found to have a mean speed of 49 MB/s.

    (i) Write down H_0 and H_A.

    (ii) Calculate the test statistic for this sample mean.

    (iii) Calculate a p-value for this sample mean.

    (iv) At the 5% level of significance, is there evidence to show that the internet provider's claim is true? Justify your answer.

12. A manufacturer of car batteries claims that the average life of the batteries they manufacture is 3·8 years with a standard deviation of 0·6 years. To test this claim, a random sample of 50 batteries was tested and their average life was found to be 3·6 years.

    At the 5% level of significance, is there evidence to show that the claim made by this manufacturer is true? Justify your answer.

13. The mean national hourly rate of pay of employees in an EU country is €32. A random sample of 45 employees in the capital city of this country was found to have a mean hourly rate of €34 with a standard deviation of €6.

    (i) Construct a 95% confidence interval for the mean hourly rate of pay in the capital city. Interpret this result.

4. The pie chart displays data on the percentages of students studying different disciplines available in a university. Find two aspects of the pie chart that are incorrect.

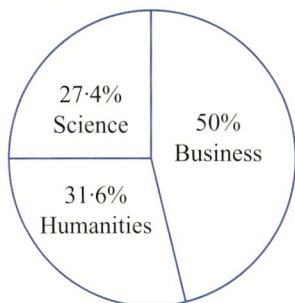

5. A manufacturer of footballs has determined that a newly developed process results in a new ball that lasts twice as long as the old ball. To illustrate this, he designs a brochure showing the new ball with twice the radius of the old ball.

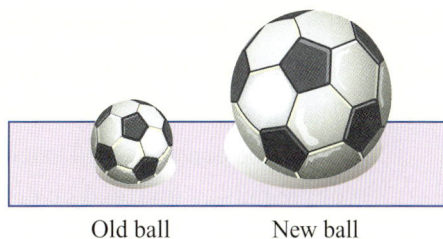

Old ball   New ball

   (i) What is wrong with the diagram?

   (ii) How can the diagram accurately illustrate that the new ball will last twice as long as the old ball?

6. A professor of economics once said, 'In the future, we hope that economic growth rates in all countries will be above the average.' What is wrong with his statement?

7. The bar chart shows the number of drunk driver court convictions by year. Comment on the following.

   (i) The false depth in the chart

   (ii) Pairs of years against single years and why this error might occur

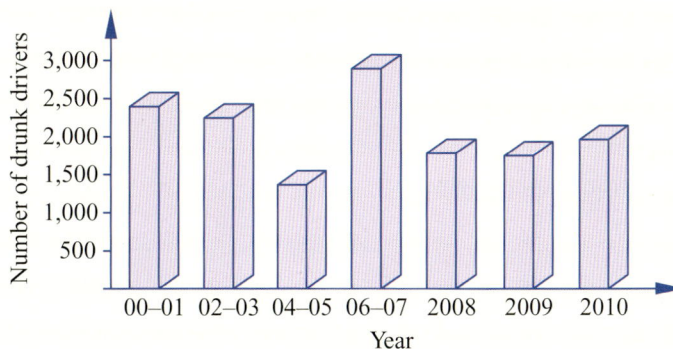

8. **Upper and middle-income area**

   35% of the city population lives here.
   Of them, 65% own a swimming pool.
   20% are in favour of building a public
   swimming pool.

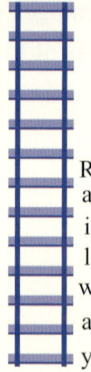

   Lower-income area

   65% of the city population lives here.
   Of them, 2% own a swimming pool.
   80% are in favour of building a
   public swimming pool.

   Railway

   (i) A city is physically divided by a railway line in two sections, as shown in the diagram.
   The city council proposes to conduct a survey to decide if a public swimming pool
   should be constructed. The council decides to survey 400 households, 200 on each side
   of the railway line, and gives each of these households one vote. Comment on the
   proposal of the council.

   (ii) Describe how you would conduct such a survey.

   (iii) Given that everyone in the city voted and voted exactly in line with the given
   percentages in the diagram, calculate the overall percentage in favour of the
   construction of the public swimming pool.

9. An Post commissioned a survey to find the mean
   number of letters delivered per day to family
   households. The results are shown in the diagram.

   The mean, μ, number of letters received was
   1·6 with a standard deviation, σ, of 1·2.

   It was decided to calculate the standard normal
   z-scores using

   $$z = \frac{x - \mu}{\sigma}.$$

   This was a big error. Explain why.

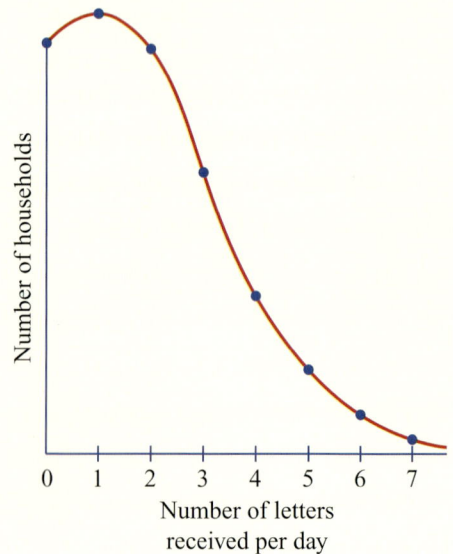

Number of households (vertical axis)

Number of letters
received per day (horizontal axis)

10. Some data are reported as a set of scores, and are presented in the table below. The scores are experimental observations, rounded off to the nearest integer.

Score	6	7	8	9	10	11	12	13	14
Frequency	2	5	13	16	20	18	15	7	4

A research assistant thinks that the scores are a random variable which has a normal distribution with parameters μ and σ.

   (i) Show that the mean of the data is $\mu = 10 \cdot 2$.

  (ii) Calculate σ, the standard deviation.

 (iii) To help in forming an opinion about the suitability of the normal model, compare the observed percentage of scores less than or equal to 8 with an appropriate probability.

 (iv) To help in forming an opinion about the suitability of the normal model, compare the observed percentage of scores greater than 12 with an appropriate probability.

  (v) The researcher used a normal model to analyse the data. Is this plausible? Use your answers from (ii) and (iii) to justify your answer.

Patterns

A significant part of mathematics is the discovery and analysis of patterns in a variety of situations. Once a pattern has been identified, the next step is to use that pattern to predict the future or to create the past. This is usually done by describing the pattern as a formula in terms of the stages of that pattern.

EXAMPLE

A sequence of arrowheads constructed from squares is shown:

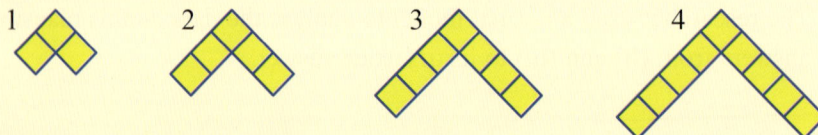

(i) Write down the number of squares as a sequence.

(ii) Write down the constant difference.

(iii) Derive a formula for the number of squares in the nth arrowhead.

(iv) Use your formula to calculate the number of squares in the 28th arrowhead.

Solution:

(i) 3, 5, 7, 9

(ii) 2

(iii) As the differences are 2, the formula will be of the form $2n \pm k$.

Pattern number	1	2	3	4
Difference × position	$2 \times 1 = 2$	$2 \times 2 = 4$	$2 \times 3 = 6$	$2 \times 4 = 8$
Original sequence	3	5	7	9

By inspection, we can see we need to add 1.

Thus, the numbers in the sequence 3, 5, 7, 9, . . . can be found by multiplying the position by 2 and adding 1. This can be written as $2n + 1$.

(iv) The 28th arrowhead will contain $2(28) + 1 = 57$ squares.

Exercise 4.1

1. A pattern of squares is made from matchsticks.

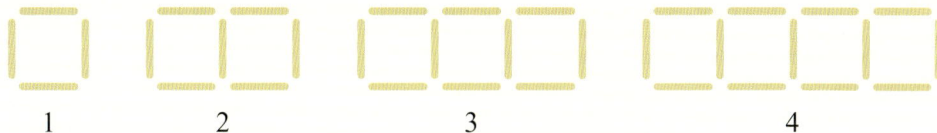

1   2   3   4

   (i) Copy and complete the table.

Pattern	1	2	3	4	5
Number of matchsticks					

   (ii) How many matchsticks would be needed for the 6th pattern?

   (iii) Derive a formula to calculate the number of matchsticks needed for the nth pattern.

   (iv) Hence or otherwise, calculate the number of matchsticks used to form the 12th pattern.

2. Red square tiles are placed to form U-shaped patterns.

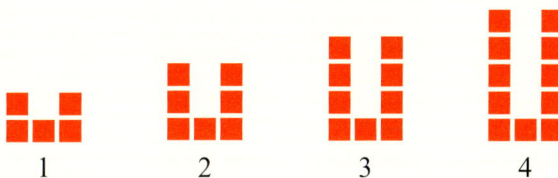

1   2   3   4

   (i) How many tiles will be used in pattern 5?

   (ii) Derive a formula to calculate the number of tiles needed for the nth pattern.

   (iii) Hence or otherwise, calculate the number of tiles used to form the 50th pattern.

   (iv) Which pattern will have 345 tiles?

3. A design is made from green and purple squares.

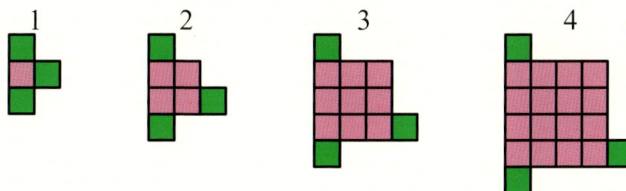

1   2   3   4

   (i) Copy and complete the table.

Pattern	1	2	3	4	5	6
Number of green squares						
Number of purple squares						
Total number of squares						

    (ii) Derive the formula for the number of purple squares.

    (iii) Derive the formula for the total number of squares in the nth pattern.

    (iv) Hence or otherwise, calculate the total number of squares used in the 18th pattern.

4. A pattern of pentagons is made from matchsticks.

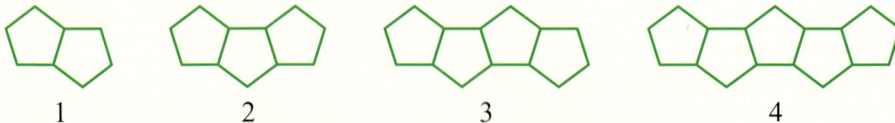

    1   2   3   4

    (i) How many matchsticks would be needed for the 6th pattern?

    (ii) Derive a formula to calculate the number of matchsticks needed for the nth pattern.

    (iii) Hence or otherwise, calculate the number of matchsticks used to form the 50th pattern.

5. A pattern of buildings consists of a number of doors and windows.

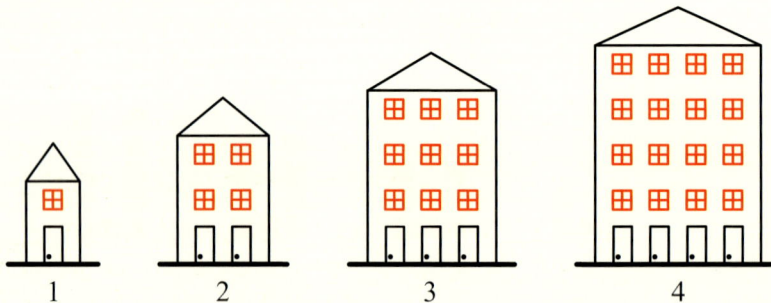

    1   2   3   4

    (i) How many doors will be in the 5th building?

    (ii) How many windows will be in the nth building?

    (iii) If each door and window needs a security lock, how many locks are needed for the nth building?

Sequences

A **sequence** is a set of numbers, separated by commas, in which each number after the first is formed by some definite rule.

Each number in a sequence is a **term** of that sequence. The first number is the **first term** and is denoted by T_1. Similarly, the second term is denoted by T_2 and so on.

T_n represents the nth term.

- 3, 7, 11, 15, . . .

    Each number after the first is obtained by adding 4 to the previous number.
    In this example, 3 is called the **first term**, 7 the **second term** and so on.

- 1, 3, 9, 27, . . .

    Each number after the first is obtained by multiplying the previous number by 3.
    In this example, 1 is called the **first term**, 3 the **second term** and so on.

Alternative notation

In the chapter on indices in Book 4, recurrence equations were described.

The equation $u_{n+1} = 2u_n + 4^n$ was given as an example.

In this case, u_n represented the nth term.

While u_n and T_n are usually interchangeable, it is not unusual to see a reference to u_0, as under some circumstances, the expression for u_n can be more easily understood when zero may be substituted to generate the first term. Consider this sequence:

$$1, x, x^2, x^3, \ldots$$

Expressing its rule as $u_n = x^n$ for $n \geq 0$ is neater than $T_n = x^{n-1}$ for $n \geq 1$.

The T_n notation should always begin with T_1. Both notations will be used in this chapter.

EXAMPLE 1

A sequence is given by $T_n = n^2 - 3n$, where $n \in \mathbb{N}$.

(i) Find T_{10}. **(ii)** For what value of $n \in \mathbb{N}$ is $u_n = 40$?

Solution:

(i) $T_n = n^2 - 3n$
    $T_{10} = (10)^2 - 3(10)$
    $= 100 - 30$
    $= 70$

(ii) Given: $T_n = 40$
    $\therefore \quad n^2 - 3n = 40$
    $n^2 - 3n - 40 = 0$
    $(n + 5)(n - 8) = 0$
    $n = -5$ or $n = 8$

Thus, $n = 8$, as $n \in \mathbb{N}$.

EXAMPLE 2

If $T_n = \dfrac{n}{n+1}$, show that $T_{n+1} > T_n$.

Solution:

$$T_n = \frac{n}{n+1} \qquad \Rightarrow \qquad T_{n+1} = \frac{n+1}{(n+1)+1} = \frac{n+1}{n+2}$$

$$T_{n+1} > T_n$$

$$\frac{n+1}{n+2} > \frac{n}{n+1}$$

$$(n+1)(n+1) = n(n+2) \qquad \left(\begin{array}{l}\text{multiply both sides by } (n+2) \text{ and } (n+1); \\ (n+2) \text{ and } (n+1) \text{ are both positive as } n \in \mathbb{N}\end{array}\right)$$

$$n^2 + 2n + 1 > n^2 + 2n$$

$$1 > 0 \quad \text{true} \qquad \text{(subtract } n^2 \text{ and } 2n \text{ from both sides)}$$

$$\therefore \ T_{n+1} > T_n$$

Notes: If $T_{n+1} > T_n$ for all $n \in \mathbb{N}$, then the sequence T_n is (monotonic) increasing.

If $T_{n+1} < T_n$ for all $n \in \mathbb{N}$, then the sequence T_n is (monotonic) decreasing.

Exercise 4.2

1. **(i)** If $u_n = 3n + 2$, find u_1 and u_2. **(ii)** Show that $u_{n+1} - u_n = 3$.

2. **(i)** If $u_n = n^2 - 3$, find u_1, u_2 and u_{n+1}.
   (ii) If $u_{n+1} - u_n = an + b$, where $a, b \in \mathbb{R}$, find the value of a and the value of b.
   (iii) If $u_n = 222$, find the value of n, $n \in \mathbb{N}$.

3. **(i)** If $u_n = n^2 + 5n$, find u_1, u_2 and u_{n+1}.
   (ii) If $u_{n+1} - u_n = pn + q$, where $p, q \in \mathbb{R}$, find the value of p and the value of q.
   (iii) If $u_n = 66$, find the value of n, where $n \in \mathbb{N}$.
   (iv) Show that $u_{n+1} > u_n$.

4. $T_n = an^2 + bn$, where $a, b \in \mathbb{R}$. If $T_1 = 7$ and $T_2 = 20$, find the following.
   (i) The value of a and the value of b
   (ii) The value of $n \in \mathbb{N}$ if $T_n = 64$

5. **(i)** If $T_n = 2^n + 1$, find T_1, T_2 and T_{n+1}. **(ii)** Show that $T_{n+1} > T_n$.

6. If $u_n = (5n - 2)3^n$, show that $u_{n+1} - 3u_n = 5(3)^{n+1}$.

7. If $u_n = (n + 1)5^n$, show that $u_{n+2} - 10u_{n+1} + 25u_n = 0$.

8. If $u_n = \frac{1}{3}(9^n - 3^n)$, show that $u_{n+1} = 3u_n + 2(9)^n$.

9. If $u_n = 2^{2n-1} + 2^{n-1}$, show that $u_{n+1} - 2u_n - 2^{2n} = 0$.

10. If $u_n = 3 + n(n - 1)^2$, show that $u_{n+1} - u_n = 3n^2 - n$.

11. **(i)** If $u_n = n^2 + 4n$, find u_1 and u_2.

   (ii) Simplify $(u_{n+2} - u_{n+1}) - (u_{n+1} - u_n)$.

12. If $u_n = 4(n + 1)!$, show that $u_{n+1} - nu_n = 2u_n$.

13. If $T_n = \dfrac{1}{n}$, show that $T_{n+1} < T_n$, where $n \in \mathbb{N}$.

14. If $T_n = \dfrac{1}{n^2}$, show that $T_{n+1} < T_n$, where $n \in \mathbb{N}$.

15. If $T_n = \dfrac{1}{2^n}$, show that $T_{n+1} < T_n$, where $n \in \mathbb{N}$.

16. If $T_n = \dfrac{n + 3}{2n + 1}$, show that $T_{n+1} < T_n$, where $n \in \mathbb{N}$.

17. The nth term of a sequence is given by $T_n = a(2)^n + bn + c$, where $a, b, c \in \mathbb{R}$.
   If $T_1 = 0$, $T_2 = 10$ and $T_3 = 26$, find the following.

   (i) The value of a, b and c **(ii)** T_4

Series

A **series** is a sum of numbers where each number after the first is formed by some definite rule.

S_n represents the sum of the first n terms.

For example:

$$\text{Sequence:} \qquad 1, 4, 7, 10, \ldots$$
$$\text{Series:} \qquad 1 + 4 + 7 + 10 + \cdots$$

The commas are replaced by plus signs to form the series.

The sum of the series is the result of adding the terms.

The sum of the first n terms of a series is denoted by S_n.

$$\therefore S_n = T_1 + T_2 + T_3 + \cdots + T_n$$

Note: Even though each term is separated by a plus sign rather than a comma, we still write
$T_1 = 4$, $T_2 = 7$, $T_3 = 10$, etc.

From this we have:

$$S_1 = T_1$$
$$S_2 = T_1 + T_2$$
$$S_3 = T_1 + T_2 + T_3, \text{ etc.}$$

Series and sigma (Σ) notation

A **finite series** is one which ends after a finite number of terms.

An **infinite series** is one that continues indefinitely.

The sum of the first n terms of a series is denoted by S_n, where:

$$S_n = T_1 + T_2 + \cdots + T_n$$

This is an example of a finite series, as there is a finite number of terms.

The finite series S_n can be expressed more concisely using sigma (Σ) notation.

$$S_n = \sum_{r=1}^{n} T_r = T_1 + T_2 + \cdots + T_n$$

Notes: The letter r (called a dummy variable) does not appear when u_r is written out.

$$\sum_{r=1}^{n} u_r = u_1 + u_2 + u_3 + \cdots + u_n.$$

Any other letter could also have been used, for example $\sum_{i=1}^{n} u_i$ or $\sum_{k=1}^{n} u_k.$

$\sum_{r=1}^{n} u_r$ is read as:

'the sum of u_r from $r = 1$ to $r = n$'   or   'sigma u_r from $r = 1$ to $r = n$'.

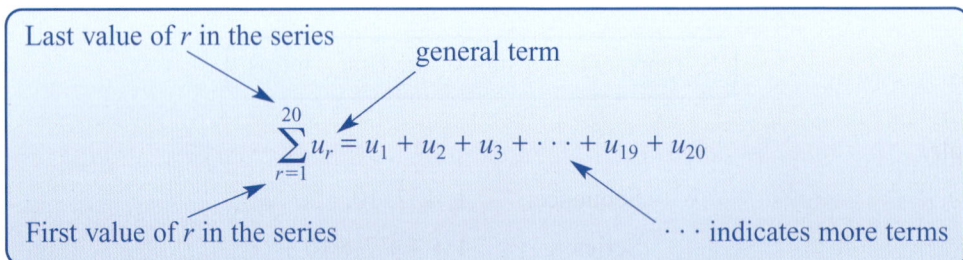

Last value of r in the series

general term

$$\sum_{r=1}^{20} u_r = u_1 + u_2 + u_3 + \cdots + u_{19} + u_{20}$$

First value of r in the series

$\cdots$ indicates more terms

The values of r increase in steps of 1 from the first term to the last term.

The notation can also be used to describe an infinite series.

There is no last value of r in this series

$$\sum_{r=1}^{\infty} u_r = u_1 + u_2 + u_3 + \cdots$$

$\cdots$ indicates that the series continues indefinitely

EXAMPLE

Evaluate: **(i)** $\displaystyle\sum_{r=0}^{4}(2r + 1)$ **(ii)** $\displaystyle\sum_{r=3}^{6}(-1)^{r+1}2^r$

Solution:

(i) $\displaystyle\sum_{r=0}^{4}(2r + 1) = [2(0) + 1] + [2(1) + 1] + [2(2) + 1] + [2(3) + 1] + [2(4) + 1]$

$\qquad\qquad = 1 + 3 + 5 + 7 + 9$

$\qquad\qquad = 25$

(ii) $\displaystyle\sum_{r=3}^{6}(-1)^{r+1}2^r = (-1)^{3+1}(2)^3 + (-1)^{4+1}(2)^4 + (-1)^{5+1}(2)^5 + (-1)^{6+1}(2)^6$

$\qquad\qquad\qquad = (1)(8) + (-1)(16) + (1)(32) + (-1)(64)$

$\qquad\qquad\qquad = 8 - 16 + 32 - 64$

$\qquad\qquad\qquad = -40$

Notice that in the second example the series alternates between positive and negative terms.

$(-1)^k = 1$ when k is even.

$(-1)^k = -1$ when k is odd.

Find T_n when given S_n

Since $S_4 = T_1 + T_2 + T_3 + T_4$ and $S_3 = T_1 + T_2 + T_3$, we can see that $T_4 = S_4 - S_3$.

> If $S_n = T_1 + T_2 + T_3 + \cdots + T_n$,
> then $T_n = S_n - S_{n-1}$ for all series.

EXAMPLE

If $S_n = 2n^2 - 3n$, find an expression for T_n and hence find T_{10}.

Solution:

$$S_n = 2n^2 - 3n$$
$$S_{n-1} = 2(n-1)^2 - 3(n-1) \qquad \text{(replace } n \text{ with } (n-1))$$
$$= 2(n^2 - 2n + 1) - 3n + 3$$
$$= 2n^2 - 4n + 2 - 3n + 3$$
$$= 2n^2 - 7n + 5$$

$$T_n = S_n - S_{n-1}$$
$$= (2n^2 - 3n) - (2n^2 - 7n + 5)$$
$$= 2n^2 - 3n - 2n^2 + 7n - 5$$
$$T_n = 4n - 5$$

Thus, $T_{10} = 4(10) - 5 = 35$.

Exercise 4.3

In questions 1–9, evaluate the series.

1. $\displaystyle\sum_{r=1}^{6}(2r + 1)$

2. $\displaystyle\sum_{r=0}^{5}(3r - 2)$

3. $\displaystyle\sum_{r=1}^{6}r^2$

4. $\displaystyle\sum_{r=1}^{5}r(r + 1)$

5. $\displaystyle\sum_{r=1}^{4}(-1)^{r+1}r^3$

6. $\displaystyle\sum_{r=0}^{6}(-1)^r 2^r$

7. $\displaystyle\sum_{r=2}^{5}(-1)^r(r + 1)(r + 3)$

8. $\displaystyle\sum_{r=3}^{7}\frac{(-1)^r}{r - 1}$

9. $\displaystyle\sum_{r=0}^{6}(-1)^r 2^r$

10. For a sequence, $u_n = 2n + 5$. Find **(i)** S_1 **(ii)** S_4.

11. For a sequence, $u_n = 3(2)^n$. Find **(i)** S_2 **(ii)** S_3.

12. For a sequence, $u_n = \dfrac{n}{n + 1}$. Find the value of S_3.

In questions 13–15, find T_n, given $S_n = T_1 + T_2 + \cdots + T_n$.

13. $S_n = n^2 + 2n$

14. $S_n = n^2 - 5n$

15. $S_n = 2n^2 + 2n$

16. For the series $S_n = T_1 + T_2 + \cdots + T_n$, $\quad S_n = \dfrac{n(n + 1)}{2}$.
Find **(i)** S_{n-1} **(ii)** T_n **(iii)** T_{20}.

17. For the series $S_n = T_1 + T_2 + \cdots + T_n$, $S_n = 2_n$.

    Find (i) S_{n-1} (ii) T_n (iii) T_{20} (iv) $\sqrt{T_9}$.

18. For the series $S_n = T_1 + T_2 + \cdots + T_n$, $S_n = 2(2)^n + n^2$.

    Find an expression for T_n and hence evaluate T_8.

19. $S_n = \dfrac{n(n + 1)(n + 2)}{6}$

    (i) By using a simpler notation or otherwise, evaluate $\displaystyle\sum_{r=1}^{10} T_r$.

    (ii) Hence or otherwise, evaluate $\displaystyle\sum_{r=11}^{20} T_r$.

Progressions

As sequences and series are closely linked, we use the term **progression** to refer to both. In the following sections, we will learn about arithmetic progressions. These will cover both arithmetic sequences and arithmetic series.

Arithmetic progressions (APs)

Arithmetic sequences 1

Consider the sequence of numbers 2, 5, 8, 11, . . .

Each term after the first can be found by adding 3 to the previous term.

This is an example of an arithmetic sequence.

> A sequence in which each term after the first is found by adding a constant number is called an **arithmetic sequence**.

The first term of an arithmetic sequence is denoted by a. In other words, $a = T_1$.

The constant number that is added to each term is called the **common difference** and is denoted by d.

Consider the arithmetic sequence 3, 5, 7, 9, 11, . . .

$$a = 3 \text{ and } d = 2$$

Each term after the first is found by adding 2 to the previous term.

Consider the arithmetic sequence 7, 2, −3, −8, . . .

$$a = 7 \text{ and } d = -5$$

Each term after the first is found by subtracting 5 from the previous term.
In an arithmetic sequence, the difference between any two consecutive terms is always the same.

$$\text{any term} - \text{previous term} = T_n - T_{n-1} = \text{constant} = d$$

If three terms, T_n, T_{n+1} and T_{n+2}, are in arithmetic sequence, then

$$T_{n+1} - T_n = T_{n+2} - T_{n+1}.$$

General term of an arithmetic sequence

In an arithmetic sequence, a is the first term and d is the common difference.
Thus, in an arithmetic sequence:

$T_1 = a$

$T_2 = a + d$

$T_3 = a + 2d$

$T_4 = a + 3d$, etc.

Notice the coefficient of d is always one less than the term number.

Examples:

$T_{10} = a + 9d$

$T_{15} = a + 14d$

$T_{50} = a + 49d$

To go from one term, just add on another d.

$$T_n = a + (n - 1)d$$

Note: Once we find a and d we can answer any question about an arithmetic progression.

EXAMPLE

The first three terms of an arithmetic sequence are 5, 8, 11, ...

(i) Find the first term, a, and the common difference, d.

(ii) Find, in terms of n, an expression for T_n, the nth term.

(iii) Hence or otherwise, find T_{17}.

(iv) Which term of the sequence is 122?

Solution:

  (i) Find a and d. The first three terms are 5, 8, 11, . . .

$$a = T_1 = 5 \qquad\qquad d = T_2 - T_1 = 8 - 5 = 3$$

  (ii)
$$
\begin{aligned}
T_n &= a + (n - 1)d \\
&= 5 + (n - 1)3 \\
&= 5 + 3n - 3 \\
&= 3n + 2
\end{aligned}
$$

(iii) Find T_{17}.

Method 1:

$$T_n = a + (n - 1)d$$
$$T_{17} = 5 + (17 - 1)(3)$$
(put in $n = 17$, $a = 5$ and $d = 3$)
$$T_{17} = 5 + 16(3)$$
$$T_{17} = 53$$

Method 2:

$$T_n = 3n + 2 \quad \text{(from part (ii))}$$
$$T_{17} = 3(17) + 2$$
(put in $n = 17$)
$$T_{17} = 53$$

(iv) Which term of the sequence is 122?

Method 1:

Equation given in disguise
$$T_n = 122$$
$$a + (n - 1)d = 122$$
(we know a and d, find n)
$$5 + (n - 1)(3) = 122$$
$$5 + 3n - 3 = 122$$
$$3n + 2 = 122$$
$$3n = 120$$
$$n = 40$$
Thus, the 40th term is 122.

Method 2:

Equation given in disguise
$$T_n = 122$$
$$(T_n = 3n + 2, \text{ find } n)$$
$$3n + 2 = 122$$
$$3n = 120$$
$$n = 40$$

Consecutive terms in an AP

If we need to find three consecutive terms of an arithmetic sequence, let the numbers be:

$$a - d, \quad a, \quad a + d.$$

If we need to find five consecutive terms of an arithmetic sequence, let the numbers be:

$$a - 2d, \quad a - d, \quad a, \quad a + d, \quad a + 2d.$$

Keep a in the middle of the sequence.

EXAMPLE 1

Three numbers are in arithmetic sequence. Their sum is 24 and their product is 494. Find the three numbers.

Solution:

Let the three terms be $a - d$, a and $a + d$, which are in arithmetic sequence.

$$\text{Given: } \quad \text{Sum of the three terms} = 24$$
$$(a - d) + a + (a + d) = 24$$
$$3a = 24$$
$$a = 8$$

$$\text{Given: } \quad \text{Product of the three terms} = 494$$
$$(a - d)(a)(a + d) = 494$$
$$(8 - d)(8)(8 + d) = 494 \qquad \text{(put in } a = 8\text{)}$$
$$8(8 - d)(8 + d) = 494$$
$$8(64 - d^2) = 494$$
$$512 - 8d^2 = 494$$
$$-8d^2 = -18$$
$$4d^2 = 9$$
$$d^2 = \tfrac{9}{4}$$
$$d = \pm\sqrt{\tfrac{9}{4}} = \pm\tfrac{3}{2}$$

$$a - d = 8 - \tfrac{3}{2} = \tfrac{13}{2} \qquad\qquad a = 8 \qquad\qquad a + d = 8 + \tfrac{3}{2} = \tfrac{19}{2}$$

Thus, the three terms are $\tfrac{13}{2}$, 8 and $\tfrac{19}{2}$.

EXAMPLE 2

The first three terms in an arithmetic sequence are $k + 2$, $2k + 3$, $5k - 2$, where $k \in \mathbb{R}$. Find the value of k and write down the first three terms.

Solution:

We use the fact that in an arithmetic sequence, the difference between any two consecutive terms is always the same. We are given the first three terms.

$$\therefore \quad T_2 - T_1 = T_3 - T_2 \quad \text{(common difference)}$$
$$(2k+3)-(k+2)=(5k-2)-(2k+3) \quad \text{(put in given values)}$$
$$2k+3-k-2=5k-2-2k-3$$
$$k+1=3k-5$$
$$-2k=-6$$
$$k=3$$

$T_1 = k+2 = 3+2 = 5$
$T_2 = 2k+3 = 2(3)+3 = 9$
$T_3 = 5k-2 = 5(3)-2 = 13$

Thus, the first three terms are 5, 9, 13.

Exercise 4.4

In questions 1–9, find a and d for the arithmetic sequence and find, in terms of n, an expression for T_n, the nth term.

1. 1, 3, 5, . . .
2. 2, 5, 8, . . .
3. 3, 7, 11
4. 6, 11, 16, . . .
5. 9, 7, 5, . . .
6. 4, 1, –2, . . .
7. 8, 3, –2, . . .
8. 4, –2, –8, . . .
9. –5, –3, –1, . . .

10. The first three terms of an arithmetic sequence are 1, 4, 7.

    (i) Find the first term, a, and the common difference, d.
    (ii) Find, in terms of n, an expression for T_n, the nth term. Hence or otherwise, find T_{50}.
    (iii) Which term of the sequence is 88?

11. The first three terms of an arithmetic sequence are 4, 9, 14.

    (i) Find the first term, a, and the common difference, d.
    (ii) Find, in terms of n, an expression for T_n, the nth term. Hence or otherwise, find T_{45}.
    (iii) Which term of the sequence is equal to 249?

12. The first three terms of an arithmetic sequence are 40, 36, 32.

    (i) Find the first term, a, and the common difference, d.
    (ii) Find, in terms of n, an expression for T_n, the nth term. Hence or otherwise, find T_{15}.
    (iii) Which term of the sequence is 0?

13. 5, 8, 11, . . . is an arithmetic sequence. Which term of the sequence is 179?

14. 3, 8, 13, 18, . . . is an arithmetic sequence. Which term of the sequence is 198?

15. The first three terms in an arithmetic sequence are $2k - 1$, $2k + 1$, $3k$, where $k \in \mathbb{R}$. Find the value of k and write down the first three terms.

16. The first three terms in an arithmetic sequence are $k - 1$, $2k - 1$, $4k - 5$, where k is a real number. Find the value of k and write down the first three terms.

17. The first three terms in an arithmetic sequence are $k + 6$, $2k + 1$, $k + 18$, where k is a real number. Find the value of k and write down the first four terms.

18. The first three terms in an arithmetic sequence are $k - 2$, $2k + 1$, $k + 14$, where k is a real number.

   (i) Find the value of k and write down the first four terms.

   (ii) Find, in terms of n, an expression for T_n. Hence or otherwise, find T_{21}.

   (iii) Which term of the sequence is 243?

Arithmetic sequences 2

In some questions we are given two terms of an arithmetic sequence. In this case, we use the method of simultaneous equations to find a and d.

EXAMPLE

In an arithmetic sequence, the fifth term, T_5, is 19 and the eighth term, T_8, is 31. Find the first term, a, and the common difference, d.

Solution:

We are given two equations in disguise and we use these to find a and d.

$$T_n = a + (n - 1)d$$

Given: $T_5 = 19$ Given: $T_8 = 31$
$\therefore a + 4d = 19$ ① $\therefore a + 7d = 31$ ②

Now solve the simultaneous equations ① and ② to find a and d.

$$\begin{aligned} a + 7d &= 31 \quad ② \\ -a - 4d &= -19 \quad ① \times -1 \\ \hline 3d &= 12 \\ d &= 4 \end{aligned}$$

Put $d = 4$ into ① or ②
$a + 4d = 19$ ①
$a + 4(4) = 19$
$a = 3$

Thus, $a = 3$ and $d = 4$.

Exercise 4.5

1. In an arithmetic sequence, the third term, T_3, is 7 and the fifth term, T_5, is 11. Find the first term, a, and the common difference, d.

2. In an arithmetic sequence, the fifth term, T_5, is 13 and the eighth term, T_8, is 22. Find the first term, a, and the common difference, d.

3. In an arithmetic sequence, the fourth term, T_4, is 19 and the seventh term, T_7, is 31. Find the first term, a, and the common difference, d.

4. In an arithmetic sequence, the fifth term, T_5, is 23 and the ninth term, T_9, is 43. Find the first term, a, and the common difference, d.

5. In an arithmetic sequence, the sixth term, T_6, is 35 and the eighth term, T_8, is 47. Find the first term, a, and the common difference, d.

6. In an arithmetic sequence, the first term, T_1, is 7 and the fifth term, T_5, is 19.

   (i) Find the common difference, d.
   (ii) Find, in terms of n, an expression for T_n. Hence or otherwise, find T_{20}.
   (iii) Which term of the sequence is 100?

7. In an arithmetic sequence, the sum of the third term, T_3, and the seventh term, T_7, is 38. The sixth term, T_6, is 23.

   (i) Find the first term, a, and the common difference, d.
   (ii) Find, in terms of n, an expression for T_n, the nth term.
   (iii) Show that $T_{19} = 5T_4$.
   (iv) For what value of n is $T_n = 99$?

8. The first four terms of an arithmetic sequence are $5, p, q, 11$.

   (i) Find the value of p and the value of q.
   (ii) Find T_{10}, the tenth term.

9. The first five terms of an arithmetic sequence are $p, q, 4, r, -2$.

   (i) Find the value of p, the value of q and the value of r.
   (ii) Find T_{20}, the twentieth term.

10. p, q and r are three numbers in an arithmetic sequence. Prove that $p^2 + r^2 \geq 2q^2$.

Arithmetic sequences 3

Verifying a sequence is arithmetic

To verify that a sequence is arithmetic, we must show the following:

$$T_n - T_{n-1} = \text{constant}$$

Verifying a sequence is not arithmetic

This time, we have two possible solutions. We can show that $T_n - T_{n-1} \neq$ constant or we can show that the differences between any two consecutive pairs of terms are not the same. In practice, this usually involves showing that $T_2 - T_1 \neq T_3 - T_2$ or similar.

EXAMPLE 1

The nth term of a sequence is $T_n = 3n - 2$. Verify that the sequence is arithmetic.

Solution:

$T_n = 3n - 2$

$T_{n-1} = 3(n-1) - 2$

$\quad = 3n - 3 - 2$

$\quad = 3n - 5$

$T_n - T_{n-1}$

$= (3n - 2) - (3n - 5)$

$= 3n - 2 - 3n + 5$

$= 3$ \quad (a constant)

Thus, T_n **is** an arithmetic sequence.

EXAMPLE 2

The nth term of a sequence is $T_n = n^2 - 2n + 5$. Verify that the sequence is not arithmetic.

Solution:

Method 1: Find a formula for T_n

$T_n = n^2 - 2n + 5$

$T_{n-1} = (n-1)^2 - 2(n-1) + 5$

$\quad = n^2 - 2n + 1 - 2n + 2 + 5$

$\quad = n^2 - 4n + 8$

$T_n - T_{n-1}$

$= (n^2 - 2n + 5) - (n^2 - 4n + 8)$

$= n^2 - 2n + 5 - n^2 + 4n - 8$

$= 2n - 3$ \quad (not a constant)

Thus, T_n **is not** an arithmetic sequence.

Method 2: Check some consecutive terms

$T_1 = (1)^2 - 2(1) + 5$

$\quad = 1 - 2 + 5$

$\quad = 4$

$T_2 = (2)^2 - 2(2) + 5$

$\quad = 4 - 4 + 5$

$\quad = 5$

$T_3 = (3)^2 - 2(3) + 5$

$\quad = 9 - 6 + 5$

$\quad = 8$

$T_2 - T_1 = 5 - 4 = 1$ \qquad $T_3 - T_2 = 8 - 5 = 3$

$$T_2 - T_1 \neq T_3 - T_2$$

Thus, T_n **is not** an arithmetic sequence.

Exercise 4.6

In questions 1–12, you are given the nth term, T_n, of a sequence. Show that the sequence is arithmetic.

1. $T_n = 2n + 3$
2. $T_n = 3n + 1$
3. $T_n = 4n + 5$
4. $T_n = 5n$
5. $T_n = 2n$
6. $T_n = 3n - 2$
7. $T_n = n - 4$
8. $T_n = 2n - 5$
9. $T_n = 7n + 1$
10. $T_n = 3 - n$
11. $T_n = 5 - 2n$
12. $T_n = 4 - 3n$

In questions 13–18, you are given the nth term, T_n, of a sequence. Show that the sequence is not arithmetic.

13. $T_n = n^2 + 2n$
14. $T_n = n^2 + 5n$
15. $T_n = n^2 - 3n$
16. $T_n = 2n^2 + n$
17. $T_n = 2n^2 - 1$
18. $T_n = n^2 - 4n + 3$

Arithmetic series

> An **arithmetic series** is the sum of the terms of an arithmetic sequence.

The sum of the first n terms of an arithmetic series is denoted by S_n.
The formula for S_n can be written in terms of n, a and d.

$$S_n = \frac{n}{2}[2a + (n - 1)d]$$

Note: Once we find a and d we can answer any question about an arithmetic series.

EXAMPLE 1

The first three terms of an arithmetic series are $4 + 7 + 10 + \cdots$

(i) Find, in terms of n, an expression for S_n, the sum to n terms.
(ii) Find S_{20}, the sum of the first 20 terms.

Solution:

(i) $4 + 7 + 10 + \cdots$

$a = T_1 = 4 \qquad d = T_2 - T_1 = 7 - 4 = 3$

$S_n = \frac{n}{2}[2a + (n - 1)d]$

$ = \frac{n}{2}[2(4) + (n - 1)(3)] \qquad$ (put in $a = 4$ and $d = 3$)

$$= \frac{n}{2}[8 + 3n - 3]$$

$$S_n = \frac{n}{2}(3n + 5)$$

(ii) Find S_{20}.

Method 1:

$$S_n = \frac{n}{2}[2a + (n - 1)d]$$

$$S_{20} = \frac{20}{2}[2(4) + (20 - 1)(3)]$$

(put in $n = 20$, $a = 4$ and $d = 3$)

$$S_{20} = 10(65) = 650$$

Method 2:

$$S_n = \frac{n}{2}(3n + 5) \quad \text{(from part (i))}$$

$$S_{20} = \frac{20}{2}(3(20) + 5)$$

$$= 10(65) = 650$$

In some questions we have to solve an equation in disguise to find the value of n.

EXAMPLE 2

Find the sum of the arithmetic series $7 + 9 + 11 + \cdots + 55$.

Solution:

The first step is to find the number of terms, n, that are in the series.

$$a = T_1 = 1 \qquad\qquad d = T_2 - T_1 = 9 - 7 = 2$$

Equation given in disguise:

Given: $\qquad\qquad T_n = 55$

$$\therefore a + (n - 1)d = 55$$

$$7 + (n - 1)(2) = 55$$

(put in $a = 7$ and $d = 2$)

$$7 + 2n - 2 = 55$$

$$2n + 5 = 55$$

$$2n = 50$$

$$n = 25$$

$$S_n = \frac{n}{2}[2a + (n - 1)d]$$

$$S_{25} = \frac{25}{2}[2(7) + (25 - 1)(2)]$$

(put in $n = 25$, $a = 7$ and $d = 2$)

$$= \frac{25}{2}[14 + (24)(2)]$$

$$= \frac{25}{2}[14 + 48]$$

$$= \frac{25}{2}(62)$$

$$S_{25} = 775$$

Thus, there are 25 terms.

In some questions we are given values of S_n and T_n for two values of n. In this case, we use the method of simultaneous equations to find a and d.

EXAMPLE 3

In an arithmetic series, the fifth term is 14 and the sum of the first six terms is 57.

(i) Find the first term, a, and the common difference, d.

(ii) Show that **(a)** $T_n = 3n - 1$ **(b)** $2S_n = 3n^2 + n$.

Solution:

(i) We are given two equations in disguise and we use them to find a and d.

$$T_n = a + (n - 1)d$$

$$S_n = \frac{n}{2}[2a + (n - 1)d]$$

Given: $\quad T_5 = 14$

$$\therefore a + (5 - 1)d = 14$$

$$a + 4d = 14 \quad \text{①}$$

Given: $\quad S_6 = 57$

$$\therefore \frac{6}{2}[2a + (6 - 1)d] = 57 \quad (n = 6)$$

$$3(2a + 5d) = 57$$

$$2a + 5d = 19 \quad \text{②}$$

(divide both sides by 3)

Now solve equations ① and ② to find the value of a and the value of d.

$$\begin{array}{ll} 2a + 8d = 28 & \text{①} \times 2 \\ -2a - 5d = -19 & \text{②} \times -1 \\ \hline 3d = 9 & \\ d = 3 & \end{array}$$

Put $d = 3$ into ① or ②

$$a + 4d = 14 \qquad \text{①}$$

$$a + 4(3) = 14$$

$$a + 12 = 14$$

$$a = 2$$

The next step is to find a.

Thus, $a = 2$ and $d = 3$.

(ii) We replace a with 2 and d with 3 in the formulas for T_n and S_n.

(a)

$$T_n = a + (n - 1)d$$

$$= 2 + (n - 1)(3)$$

(put in $a = 2$ and $d = 3$)

$$T_n = 2 + 3n - 3$$

$$T_n = 3n - 1$$

(b)

$$S_n = \frac{n}{2}[2a + (n - 1)d]$$

$$= \frac{n}{2}[2(2) + (n - 1)(3)]$$

(put in $a = 2$ and $d = 3$)

$$S_n = \frac{n}{2}[4 + 3n - 3]$$

$$S_n = \frac{n}{2}(3n + 1)$$

$$2S_n = n(3n + 1)$$

(multiply both sides by 2)

$$2S_n = 3n^2 + n$$

Exercise 4.7

1. The first three terms of an arithmetic series are $3 + 5 + 7 + \cdots$.
   Find S_{10}, the sum of the first 10 terms.

2. The first three terms of an arithmetic series are $4 + 7 + 10 + \cdots$.
   Find S_{12}, the sum of the first 12 terms.

3. The first three terms of an arithmetic series are $1 + 5 + 9 + \cdots$.
   Find S_{18}, the sum of the first 18 terms.

4. The first three terms of an arithmetic series are $3 + 8 + 13 + \cdots$.

   (i) Find, in terms of n, an expression for S_n, the sum to n terms.
   (ii) Find S_{20}, the sum of the first 20 terms.

5. The first three terms of an arithmetic series are $10 + 13 + 16 + \cdots$.

   (i) Find, in terms of n, an expression for S_n, the sum to n terms.
   (ii) Find S_{30}, the sum of the first 30 terms.

6. The nth term of an arithmetic series is given by $2n + 3$.

   (i) Write down the first four terms.
   (ii) Write down the common difference.
   (iii) Find S_{16}, the sum of the first 16 terms.

7. In an arithmetic series, the fifth term, T_5, is 22 and the sum of the first four terms, S_4, is 38.

   (i) Find the first term, a, and the common difference, d.
   (ii) Show that **(a)** $T_n = 5n - 3$ **(b)** $2S_n = 5n^2 - n$.

8. In an arithmetic series, the eighth term is 21 and the sum of the first six terms is 18.

   (i) Find the first term, a, and the common difference, d.
   (ii) Show that **(a)** $T_n = 4n - 11$ **(b)** $S_n = 2n^2 - 9n$.
   (iii) Find **(a)** T_{20} **(b)** S_{30}.

9. In an arithmetic series, the seventh term, T_7, is 20 and the sum of the first five terms, S_5, is 40.

   (i) Find the first term, a, and the common difference, d.
   (ii) Show that **(a)** $T_n = 3n - 1$ **(b)** $2S_n = 3n^2 + n$.
   (iii) Find **(a)** T_{30} **(b)** S_{30}.

10. In an arithmetic series, the eighth term, T_8, is 27 and the sum of the first 10 terms, S_{10}, is 120.

    (i) Find the first term, a, and the common difference, d.
    (ii) Show that **(a)** $T_n = 3(2n - 7)$ **(b)** $S_n = 3(n^2 - 6n)$.
    (iii) Find **(a)** T_{25} **(b)** S_6.

11. In an arithmetic series, the sum of the first four terms, S_4, is 44 and the sum of the first six terms, S_6, is 102.

    (i) Find the first term, a, and the common difference, d.

    (ii) Find **(a)** T_{20} **(b)** S_{20}.

12. Find the sum of the arithmetic series $2 + 5 + 8 + \cdots + 59$.

13. Find the sum of the arithmetic series $1 + 5 + 9 + \cdots + 117$.

14. Find the sum of the arithmetic series $3 + 8 + 13 + \cdots + 248$.

15. The nth term of a series is given by $T_n = 3n + 2$.

    (i) Write down, in terms of n, an expression for T_{n-1}, the $(n-1)$st term.

    (ii) Show that the series is arithmetic.

    (iii) Find S_{20}, the sum of the first 20 terms.

16. The first three terms of an arithmetic series are $10 + 20 + 30 + \cdots$.

    (i) Find, in terms of n, an expression for T_n, the nth term.

    (ii) Find, in terms of n, an expression for S_n, the sum to n terms.

    (iii) Using your expression for S_n, find the sum of the natural numbers that are both multiples of 10 and smaller than 2,001.

17. The first three terms in an arithmetic series are $1 + 3 + 5 + \cdots$

    (i) Show that **(a)** $T_n = 2n - 1$ **(b)** $S_n = n^2$.

    (ii) Hence or otherwise, evaluate **(a)** T_{20} **(b)** S_{20}.

    (iii) How many terms need to be added to give a sum of 225?

18. The first three terms of an arithmetic series are $3a + 4a + 5a + \cdots$ where $a \in \mathbb{R}$.

    (i) Find, in terms of a, an expression for T_{10}, the tenth term.

    (ii) Find, in terms of a, an expression for S_{10}, the sum of the first 10 terms.

    (iii) If $S_{10} - T_{10} = 126$, find the value of a.

    (iv) Write down the first four terms of the series.

    (v) Write down, in terms of n, expressions for **(a)** T_n **(b)** S_n.

    (vi) Hence or otherwise, evaluate **(a)** T_{20} **(b)** S_{20}.

19. The general term, T_n, of an arithmetic series is given by $T_n = 2n + 5$.

    (i) Find the first term, a, and the common difference, d.

    (ii) For what value of n is the sum of the first n terms, S_n, equal to 160?

20. A pupil saves money each week. The pupil saves 40c in the first week, 60c in the second week, 80c in the next week, continuing this pattern for 50 weeks.

    (i) How much will the pupil save in the 50th week?

    (ii) How much will the pupil have saved after 50 weeks?

21. A woman accepted a post with a starting salary of €30,000. In each following year she received an increase in salary of €2,000. What were her total earnings in the first 12 years?

22. In a potato race, 10 potatoes are placed 8 metres apart in a straight line. The object of the race is to pick up the first potato and place it in a basket 20 m in front of the first potato, then run to the second potato, pick it up and place it in the basket and so on.

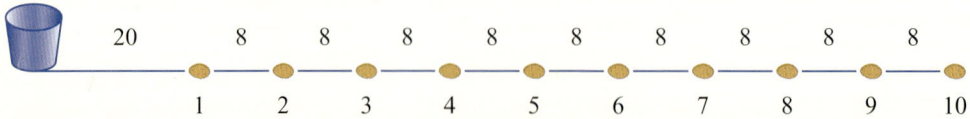

The race begins at the basket. Find the total distance covered by a contestant who finishes the race.

23. A display in a grocery store will consist of cans stacked as shown.

The first row is to have 18 cans and each row after the first is to have 2 cans fewer than the preceding row. How many cans will be needed in the display?

24. A man is given an interest-free loan. He repays the loan in monthly instalments. He repays €40 at the end of the first month, €44 at the end of the second month, €48 at the end of the third month, continuing the pattern of increasing the monthly repayments by €4 a month until the loan is repaid. The final monthly repayment is €228.

    (i) Show that it will take the man 48 months to repay the loan.

    (ii) Calculate the amount of the loan.

25. A ball rolls down a slope. The distances it travels in successive seconds are 2 cm, 6 cm, 10 cm, 14 cm and so on. How many seconds elapse before it has travelled a total of 18 metres?

26. An arithmetic progression has a first term of 5 and a common difference of 1·5.
    Find the greatest number of terms in the arithmetic progression if the sum of the terms must not exceed 400.

27. An arithmetic series has a common difference, d. If the sum of the first 20 terms is 25 times the first term, find, as an expression in d, the sum of the first 30 terms.

28. (i) Show that the series $\ln 3 + \ln 3^2 + \ln 3^3 + \cdots$ is arithmetic.

    (ii) Find the exact value of the common difference.

    (iii) Find an expression for S_n.

29. Amelia suggests an alternative form of the formula for the sum of the first n terms of an arithmetic progression:

$$S_n = n \left(\frac{a + l}{2} \right),$$

where l represents the last term. Investigate her formula.

30. Claire recently visited the Pyramids of Giza.
    She noticed that each face of the pyramid has 1 brick at its top and each row has an extra brick compared to the row above it.

    (i) How many bricks are in the tenth row from the top?
    (ii) Claire estimates that there are no more than 2,000 bricks on a face. How many rows of bricks must there be?

31. While at a lecture at university, Jakim investigated the number of students who could fit into a lecture theatre. Because the rows were curved, the number of seats per row increased by 2 as the rows went further from the front.

    (i) If there were 12 seats in the front row, how many seats were there in the 5th row?
    (ii) Given that the back row was the 18th, what was the seating capacity of the theatre?

Given S_n of an arithmetic series in terms of n

If we are given an expression for S_n in terms of n, then we use the fact that for all types of series:

$$T_n = S_n - S_{n-1}$$ and $$T_1 = S_1$$

Examples: $T_2 = S_2 - S_1$, $T_3 = S_3 - S_2$, $T_9 = S_9 - S_8$ and so on.

EXAMPLE

The sum of the first n terms, S_n, of an arithmetic series is given by $S_n = 2n^2 + n$. Find the first term, a, and the common difference, d.

Solution:

$$S_n = 2n^2 + n$$
$$S_1 = 2(1)^2 + (1)$$
$$= 2 + 1 = 3$$
$$S_2 = 2(2)^2 + (2)$$
$$= 2(4) + 2 = 10$$

$$T_2 = S_2 - S_1$$
$$= 10 - 3 = 7$$
$$a = T_1 = S_1 = 3$$
$$d = T_2 - T_1 = 7 - 3 = 4$$
Thus, $a = 3$ and $d = 4$.

Exercise 4.8

1. The sum of the first n terms, S_n, of an arithmetic series is given by $S_n = n^2 + 2n$. Use S_1 and S_2 to find the first term, a, and the common difference, d.

2. The sum of the first n terms, S_n, of an arithmetic series is given by $S_n = n^2 + 3n$. Find the first term, a, and the common difference, d.

3. The sum of the first n terms, S_n, of an arithmetic series is given by $S_n = 3n^2 - 2n$. Find the first term, a, and the common difference, d.

4. The sum of the first n terms, S_n, of an arithmetic series is given by $S_n = 2n^2 - 3n$. Find the first term, a, and the common difference, d.

5. The sum of the first n terms, S_n, of an arithmetic series is given by $S_n = \dfrac{n(3n + 1)}{2}$.

   (i) Calculate the first term of the series.
   (ii) By calculating S_8 and S_7, find T_8, the eighth term of the series.

6. The sum of the first n terms, S_n, of an arithmetic series is given by $S_n = 2n^2 + n$.

   (i) Calculate the first term of the series and the common difference.
   (ii) Find, in terms of n, an expression for T_n, the nth term.
   (iii) Hence, calculate T_{10}.
   (iv) Show that $T_{10} = S_{10} - S_9$.

7. The sum of the first n terms, S_n, of an arithmetic series is given by $S_n = 2n^2 - 4n$.

   (i) Find the first term, a, and the common difference, d.
   (ii) Find, in terms of n, an expression for T_n, the nth term.
   (iii) Find T_{20} and verify that $T_{20} = S_{20} - S_{19}$.
   (iv) Starting with the first term, how many terms of the series must be added to give a sum of 160?

Geometric progressions (GPs)

Geometric sequences

Consider the sequence of numbers 4, 12, 36, 108, . . .

Each term after the first can be found by multiplying the previous term by 3.

This is an example of a geometric sequence.

> A sequence in which each term after the first is found by multiplying the previous term by a constant number is called a **geometric sequence**.

The first term in a geometric sequence is denoted by a. So, as before, $a = T_1$.

The constant number by which each term is multiplied is called the **common ratio** and is denoted by r.

Note: When $r = -1$, 0 or 1, the progression becomes trivial to study. To see why, choose a (non-zero) first term and apply the ratio to form the next few terms.

- Consider the geometric series 3, 6, 12, 24, . . .

$$a = 3 \text{ and } r = 2$$

Each term after the first is found by multiplying the previous term by 2.

- Consider the geometric series 27, 9, 3, 1, . . .

$$a = 27 \text{ and } r = \frac{1}{3}$$

Each term after the first is found by multiplying the previous term by $\frac{1}{3}$.

Note: Multiplying by $\frac{1}{3}$ is the same as dividing by 3.

In a geometric sequence, the common ratio, r, between any two consecutive terms is always the same.

> $$\frac{\text{any term}}{\text{previous term}} = \frac{T_n}{T_{n-1}} = \text{constant} = r$$

> If three terms, T_n, T_{n+1} and T_{n+2}, are in geometric sequence, then:
> $$\frac{T_{n+1}}{T_n} = \frac{T_{n+2}}{T_{n+1}}$$

General term of a geometric sequence

$T_1 = a$
$T_2 = ar$
$T_3 = ar^2$
$T_4 = ar^3$, etc.

Notice the power of r is always one less than the term number.

Examples:
$T_{10} = ar^9$
$T_{15} = ar^{14}$
$T_{50} = ar^{49}$

Note: If $T_n = pq^n$, where p and q are constants, the sequence is geometric.

EXAMPLE 1

$2, 6, 18, \ldots, 486$ is a geometric sequence.
Find: **(i)** The nth term **(ii)** The number of terms in the sequence

Solution:

(i) $a = 2$ (given)

$r = \dfrac{T_2}{T_1} = \dfrac{6}{2} = 3$

$T_n = ar^{n-1}$

$T_n = 2(3)^{n-1}$

(ii) Given: $T_n = 486$

$2(3)^{n-1} = 486$

$3^{n-1} = 243$

$3^{n-1} = 3^5$

$n - 1 = 5$

$n = 6$

Thus, there are 6 terms in the sequence.

EXAMPLE 2

Three terms in geometric sequence are $x - 3$, x, $3x + 4$, where $x \in \mathbb{R}$.
Find two possible values of x.

Solution:

We use the fact that in a geometric sequence, any term divided by the previous term is always a constant.

Thus, $\dfrac{T_2}{T_1} = \dfrac{T_3}{T_2}$ (common ratio)

$\dfrac{x}{x - 3} = \dfrac{3x + 4}{x}$ (put in given values)

$(x)(x) = (3x + 4)(x - 3)$ (multiply both sides by $(x)(x - 3)$)

$x^2 = 3x^2 - 5x - 12$

$0 = 2x^2 - 5x - 12$

$2x^2 - 5x - 12 = 0$

$(2x + 3)(x - 4) = 0$

$2x + 3 = 0$ or $x - 4 = 0$

$x = -\dfrac{3}{2}$ or $x = 4$

EXAMPLE 3

In a geometric sequence, the second term is 8 and the fifth term is 64.
Find the first term, a, and the common ratio, r.

Solution:

$$T_n = ar^{n-1}$$

Given: $T_2 = 8$ Given: $T_5 = 64$

$\therefore ar = 8$ ① $\therefore ar^4 = 64$ ②

We now divide ② by ① to eliminate a and find r.

② ÷ ① gives: Put $r = 2$ into ① or ② to find a.

$$\frac{ar^4}{ar} = \frac{64}{8}$$

$$r^3 = 8$$

$$r = 2$$

$ar = 8$ ①

$a(2) = 8$

$a = 4$

Thus, the first term is $a = 4$ and the common ratio is $r = 2$.

Note: If the index of r is even, we get two values for r, one positive and the other negative.

Verifying a sequence is geometric

To verify that a sequence is geometric, we must show the following:

$$\frac{T_n}{T_{n-1}} = \text{constant}$$

Verifying a sequence is not geometric

As before, we have two solutions. We can show that $\dfrac{T_n}{T_{n-1}} \neq$ constant or we can show that the ratios of any two pairs of consecutive terms are not the same. In practice, this usually involves showing that $\dfrac{T_2}{T_1} \neq \dfrac{T_3}{T_2}$ or similar.

EXAMPLE

(i) Write down the first four terms of the sequence $T_n = 8\left(\dfrac{3}{4}\right)^n$.

(ii) Show that the sequence is geometric.

Solution:

(i) $T_n = 8\left(\dfrac{3}{4}\right)^n$

$$T_1 = 8\left(\dfrac{3}{4}\right)^1 = 8\left(\dfrac{3}{4}\right) = 6$$

$$T_2 = 8\left(\dfrac{3}{4}\right)^2 = 8\left(\dfrac{9}{16}\right) = \dfrac{9}{2}$$

$$T_3 = 8\left(\dfrac{3}{4}\right)^3 = 8\left(\dfrac{27}{64}\right) = \dfrac{27}{8}$$

$$T_4 = 8\left(\dfrac{3}{4}\right)^4 = 8\left(\dfrac{81}{256}\right) = \dfrac{81}{32}$$

Thus, the first four terms are:

$$6, \dfrac{9}{2}, \dfrac{27}{8}, \dfrac{81}{32}.$$

(ii) $T_n = 8\left(\dfrac{3}{4}\right)^n \Rightarrow T_{n-1} = 8\left(\dfrac{3}{4}\right)^{n-1}$

$$\dfrac{T_n}{T_{n-1}} = \dfrac{8\left(\frac{3}{4}\right)^n}{8\left(\frac{3}{4}\right)^{n-1}}$$

$$= \left(\dfrac{3}{4}\right)^1 \qquad \left(\dfrac{x^n}{x^{n-1}} = x\right)$$

$$= \dfrac{3}{4} \qquad \text{(a constant)}$$

$$\therefore \dfrac{T_n}{T_{n-1}} = \text{a constant.}$$

Thus, T_n is a geometric sequence.

Exercise 4.9

In questions 1–6, find T_n, the nth term in the geometric sequence.

1. 5, 10, 20, . . .
2. 4, 12, 36, . . .
3. 27, 18, 12, . . .
4. 50, −20, 8, . . .
5. $1, 2a, 4a^2, \ldots$
6. $\dfrac{5}{a}, \dfrac{10}{a^2}, \dfrac{20}{a^3}, \ldots$

7. Verify that the sequence $T_n = 5^n$ is geometric.
8. Verify that the sequence $T_n = 2(3)^{n+1}$ is geometric.
9. Verify that the sequence $T_n = n^2 - 3$ is not geometric.
10. The sum to n terms of a series is given by $3(2^n - 1)$.

    (i) Find T_n, the nth term.

    (ii) Verify that the series is geometric.

In questions 11–16, you are given the first three terms of a geometric sequence. Find the value(s) of x, where $x \in \mathbb{R}$.

11. $x - 2, x, x + 3$
12. $x - 1, 2x + 1, 4x + 17$
13. $4x + 36, 2x + 6, x$
14. $x - 6, 2x, 8x + 20$
15. $x + 1, x + 4, 3x + 2$
16. $3x - 5, x - 1, x - 2$

17. The lengths of the sides of a triangle are in geometric sequence. The length of the shortest side is 4 cm and the perimeter of the triangle is 19 cm. Find the lengths of the other sides.

18. $x + 1, x - 1$ and $2x - 5$ are the first three terms of a geometric sequence.

    (i) Find two values for x.

    (ii) Write down the first four terms of the two resulting sequences.

19. Four terms in geometric sequence are $6, a, b, \frac{3}{4}$.
Find the value of a and the value of b.

20. p, 10 and q are consecutive terms of an arithmetic sequence.
1, p and q are consecutive terms of a geometric sequence.
Find the value of p and the value of q, where $p, q \in \mathbb{R}$.

21. A geometric sequence has a first term a and common ratio r. It contains 21 terms.

   (i) Write down the last term in terms of a and r.

   (ii) Write down the middle term in terms of a and r.

   (iii) Show that the product of all the terms in the sequence is equal to the middle term raised to the power of 21.

   (iv) Write out the first five terms and test parts **(i)** to **(iii)** for a similar result.

22. a, b, c and d are, respectively, the first four terms of a geometric sequence.
Prove that $a^2 - b^2 - c^2 + d^2 \geq 0$.

Geometric series

If the sequence $T_1, T_2, T_3, \ldots, T_n$ is geometric, then the corresponding series

$$T_1 + T_2 + T_3 + \cdots + T_n$$

is a geometric series.

The formula for S_n of a geometric series can be written in terms of the first term, a, and the common ratio, r.

> If $S_n = T_1 + T_2 + T_3 + \cdots + T_n$ is a geometric series, then
> $$S_n = \frac{a(1 - r^n)}{1 - r} \text{ when } |r| < 1 \quad \text{or} \quad S_n = \frac{a(r^n - 1)}{r - 1} \text{ when } |r| > 1.$$

Note: In practice it does not matter which form is used.

To derive this result:

$$
\begin{aligned}
S_n &= a + ar + ar^2 + \cdots + ar^{n-1} \\
rS_n &= ar + ar^2 + \cdots + ar^{n-1} + ar^n \\
\hline
S_n - rS_n &= a \phantom{+ ar + ar^2 + \cdots + ar^{n-1}} - ar^n \quad \text{(subtract)} \\
S_n(1 - r) &= a(1 - r^n) \\
S_n &= \frac{a(1 - r^n)}{1 - r}
\end{aligned}
$$

Note: Once we find the first term, a, and the common ratio, r, we can answer any question about a geometric sequence or series.

EXAMPLE 1

The nth term of a geometric sequence is $T_n = \left(\dfrac{2}{3}\right)^n$.

(i) Find the first three terms.   **(ii)** Find S_5, the sum of the first five terms.

Solution:

(i) $T_n = \left(\dfrac{2}{3}\right)^n$

$$T_1 = \left(\dfrac{2}{3}\right)^1 = \dfrac{2}{3}$$

$$T_2 = \left(\dfrac{2}{3}\right)^2 = \dfrac{4}{9}$$

$$T_3 = \left(\dfrac{2}{3}\right)^3 = \dfrac{8}{27}$$

Thus, the first three terms are

$$\dfrac{2}{3}, \ \dfrac{4}{9}, \ \dfrac{8}{27}.$$

(ii) $S_n = \dfrac{a(1 - r^n)}{1 - r}$

$$S_5 = \dfrac{\frac{2}{3}\left(1 - \left(\frac{2}{3}\right)^5\right)}{1 - \frac{2}{3}}$$

$$= \dfrac{\frac{2}{3}\left(1 - \frac{32}{243}\right)}{\frac{1}{3}}$$

$$= \dfrac{422}{243}$$

EXAMPLE 2

In a geometric sequence, the sum of the first and third terms is $\dfrac{20}{3}$ and the sum of the second and fourth terms is $\dfrac{20}{9}$. Find the first term, a, and the common ratio, r.

Solution:

Given: $T_1 + T_3 = \dfrac{20}{3}$

$$\therefore a + ar^2 = \dfrac{20}{3}$$

$$a(1 + r^2) = \dfrac{20}{3} \quad \text{①}$$

Given: $T_2 + T_4 = \dfrac{20}{9}$

$$\therefore ar + ar^3 = \dfrac{20}{9}$$

$$ar(1 + r^2) = \dfrac{20}{9} \quad \text{②}$$

We now divide ② by ① to eliminate a and find r.

② ÷ ① gives:

$$\frac{ar(1 + r^2)}{a(1 + r^2)} = \frac{\frac{20}{9}}{\frac{20}{3}}$$

$$r = \frac{1}{3}$$

Put $r = 2$ into ① or ② to find a.

$$a(1 + r^2) = \frac{20}{3} \quad ①$$

$$a\left(1 + \frac{1}{9}\right) = \frac{20}{3}$$

$$a\left(\frac{10}{9}\right) = \frac{20}{3}$$

$$a = \frac{20}{3} \div \frac{10}{9} = 6$$

Thus, the first term is $a = 6$ and the common ratio is $r = \frac{1}{3}$.

Consecutive terms in a GP

If we need to find three unknown consecutive terms in geometric sequence, we let the terms be $\frac{a}{r}$, a and ar.

EXAMPLE

In an arithmetic sequence, the sum of the first term and the third term is 15. The first, third and seventh terms of the arithmetic sequence are the first three terms of a geometric sequence.

(i) Find the first term and the common difference of the arithmetic sequence, where the common difference is positive.

(ii) Find the first three terms and the common ratio of the geometric sequence.

Solution:

(i) For the arithmetic sequence, $T_n = a + (n - 1)d$

$T_1 = a$ $\qquad T_3 = a + 2d$ $\qquad T_7 = a + 6d$

Given: $\qquad T_1 + T_3 = 15$

$$a + (a + 2d) = 15$$

$$2a + 2d = 15 \quad ①$$

T_1, T_3 and T_7 are the first three terms in a geometric sequence.

$$\frac{T_3}{T_1} = \frac{T_7}{T_3} \qquad \text{(common ratio)}$$

$$\frac{a + 2d}{a} = \frac{a + 6d}{a + 2d}$$

$$(a + 2d)(a + 2d) = a(a + 6d) \qquad \text{(multiply both sides by } a(a + 2d))$$

$$a^2 + 4ad + 4d^2 = a^2 + 6ad$$

$$4d^2 - 2ad = 0$$

$$2d^2 - ad = 0$$

$$d(2d - a) = 0$$

$$d = 0 \text{ or } 2d - a = 0$$

$$a = 2d$$

As we are given $d > 0$, our second equation is $a = 2d$. ②

We now solve between the simultaneous equations ① and ②.

$$2a + 2d = 15 \qquad\qquad\qquad a = 2d$$

$$2(2d) + 2d = 15 \quad (a = 2d) \qquad = 2\left(\frac{5}{2}\right)$$

$$6d = 15$$

$$d = \frac{5}{2} \qquad\qquad\qquad\qquad a = 5$$

(ii) For the geometric sequence, we calculate the first, third and seventh terms of the arithmetic sequence.

$$T_1 = a = 5$$

$$T_3 = a + 2d = 5 + 2\left(\frac{5}{2}\right) = 10$$

$$T_7 = a + 2d = 5 + 6\left(\frac{5}{2}\right) = 20$$

$$r = \frac{T_2}{T_1} = \frac{10}{5} = 2$$

Thus, the first three terms of the geometric sequence are 5, 10 and 20 and the common ratio is 2.

Exercise 4.10

1. The first three terms of a geometric series are $2 + 6 + 18 + \cdots$.

   (i) Express in terms of n **(a)** T_n **(b)** S_n.

   (ii) Find **(a)** T_8 **(b)** S_8.

2. The first three terms of a geometric series are $64 - 32 + 16$.

   (i) Find in terms of n **(a)** T_n **(b)** S_n.

   (ii) Find **(a)** T_{10} **(b)** S_{10}.

In questions 3–5, find, in terms of n, the sum of the first n terms of the geometric series.

3. $6 + 12 + 24 + \ldots$ 4. $6 + 4 + \frac{8}{3} + \ldots$ 5. $63 - 21 + 7 \ldots$

6. Peter invests €200 in a saving scheme which gives 5% interest annually.

    (i) How much will his investment be worth after 1 year?

    (ii) Peter allows his investment to grow for 5 years.
        Will his investment grow arithmetically or geometrically? Justify your answer.

    (iii) How much will Peter's investment be worth after 5 years, to the nearest euro?

7. **(i)** Find, in terms of n, the sum of the first n terms of the geometric series $18 + 12 + 8 + \cdots$.

    (ii) If $S_n = \frac{1{,}330}{27}$, find the value of n.

8. If $\displaystyle\sum_{r=1}^{n} 2^{r+1} = 508$, find the value of n.

9. A geometric series has six terms, a common ratio of $\frac{1}{2}$ and a sum of $\frac{189}{8}$.
   Find **(i)** the first term   **(ii)** the nth term.

10. The third term, T_3, of a geometric series is -63. The fourth term, T_4, is 189.
    (i) Find **(a)** the common ratio   **(b)** the first term.
    (ii) Express in terms of n **(a)** T_n **(b)** S_n.

11. In a geometric series, the fourth term is 12 and the seventh term is 324.
    Find **(i)** the nth term   **(ii)** S_7, the sum of the first seven terms.

12. $S_n = a + ar + ar^2 + \cdots + ar^{n-1}$ is a geometric series.
    $T_3 - T_2 = 5$ and $T_4 - T_3 = 6$.
    Find the common ratio, r, and the first term, a.

13. A geometric series has a common ratio, r.
    The first three terms of the series are $\frac{a}{r}$, a and ar.
    The product of the three terms is 216 and the sum of the three terms is 21.

    (i) Find **(a)** the value of a **(b)** the values of r.

    (ii) Write down the first three terms.

14. The product of the first three terms of a geometric series is 27 and the sum of these terms is 13. Find the first four terms of the series.

15. Three terms, a, b and $a + b$, are in arithmetic sequence.
    Three terms, a, b and ab, are in geometric sequence.
    Find the value of a and the value of b, where $a, b \in \mathbb{R}$ and $a, b \neq 0$.

16. The first, fifth and seventeenth terms of an arithmetic series are the first three terms of a geometric series. The sum of the first four terms of the arithmetic series is 28. Find the common difference of the arithmetic series and the common ratio of the geometric series.

17. The first, fifth and twenty-first terms of an arithmetic sequence are the first three terms of a geometric sequence. Find the common ratio of the geometric sequence.

18. p, m and q are three consecutive terms of an arithmetic sequence.
    p, n and q are three consecutive terms of a geometric sequence, where p, q, $n > 0$.
    Show that $m \geq n$.

Infinite progressions

Infinite sequences cannot have a last term, but sometimes it is possible to predict what the last term might be. For example, consider this sequence:

$$\frac{1}{2}, \frac{2}{3}, \frac{3}{4}, \frac{4}{5}, \ldots, \frac{n}{n+1}, \ldots$$

Although the terms are increasing, they are all below 1, but as the sequence progresses, the terms are getting closer to 1. The more terms we calculate, the closer we get to 1.

Other sequences behave differently. For example:

$$1, 2, 4, 8, \ldots$$

In this sequence, the terms are increasing without limit. We cannot suggest a *finite number* that we are approaching.

We will also look at the behaviour of terms in an infinite series later.

Limits of sequences

In Book 4, we defined the limit of a function. Its definition included two important points:

• If a limit exists, its value will be a (finite) number.
• ∞ (infinity) is not a number.

A formal method was given to evaluate limits such as $\lim\limits_{n \to \infty} \dfrac{4n-1}{3n+2}$.

We will now consider a method of evaluating such limits **by inspection**.

To do this, we will need to establish some key points.

• When we see $n \to \infty$, we will think of n as being a very large number (perhaps 1 million).
• As $n \to \infty$, the value of n and $n + 8$ are almost the same.
• As $n \to \infty$, the value of $4n$ will always be twice the value of $2n$.
• As $n \to \infty$, the value of n^2 will be significantly greater than n.
• As $n \to \infty$, the value of terms such as n^2, n and constants are very small compared to n^3.

EXAMPLE

Find $\lim\limits_{n\to\infty} T_n$ for the following.

(i) $T_n = \dfrac{4n-1}{3n+2}$ (ii) $T_n = \dfrac{2n+9}{n^2-3n+7}$ (iii) $T_n = \dfrac{3n^2+1}{5n-2}$

Solution:

(i) $\lim\limits_{n\to\infty} \dfrac{4n-1}{3n+2}$

$= \lim\limits_{n\to\infty} \dfrac{4n}{3n}$

$= \lim\limits_{n\to\infty} \dfrac{4}{3}$

$= \dfrac{4}{3}$

(ii) $\lim\limits_{n\to\infty} \dfrac{2n+9}{n^2-3n+7}$

$= \lim\limits_{n\to\infty} \dfrac{2n}{n^2}$

$= \lim\limits_{n\to\infty} \dfrac{2}{n}$

$= 0$

(iii) $\lim\limits_{n\to\infty} \dfrac{3n^2+1}{5n-2}$

$= \lim\limits_{n\to\infty} \dfrac{3n^2}{5n}$

$= \lim\limits_{n\to\infty} \dfrac{3n}{5}$

$=$ no limit

Note: Although you may see it written, it is incorrect to give ∞ as the answer to a limit. A limit, if it exists, must be a finite number; otherwise the limit does not exist.

Exercise 4.11

In questions 1–18, find $\lim\limits_{n\to\infty} T_n$.

1. $T_n = \dfrac{2n-1}{n+1}$

2. $T_n = \dfrac{4n+1}{3n-2}$

3. $T_n = \dfrac{2n+1}{3n+5}$

4. $T_n = \dfrac{4n^2+2n}{5n^2-3}$

5. $T_n = \dfrac{3n^2-4n}{7n^2+2n}$

6. $T_n = \dfrac{4}{3n+1}$

7. $T_n = \dfrac{n}{n+2}$

8. $T_n = \dfrac{1}{5} - \dfrac{1}{n+1}$

9. $T_n = \dfrac{3}{4} - \dfrac{5}{n+2}$

10. $T_n = \dfrac{1}{2} - \dfrac{1}{2(2n+1)}$

11. $T_n = \dfrac{3}{2} - \dfrac{1}{n+1} - \dfrac{1}{n+2}$

12. $T_n = \dfrac{4}{5} - \dfrac{1}{n} - \dfrac{1}{n+3}$

13. $T_n = \sqrt{\dfrac{25n+2}{n-3}}$

14. $T_n = \dfrac{\sqrt{n-1}}{\sqrt{9n+4}}$

15. $T_n = \dfrac{\sqrt{4n^2-1}}{n+3}$

16. $T_n = \dfrac{1}{\sqrt{n^2+2}}$

17. $T_n = \dfrac{\sqrt{2n^2+3}}{n}$

18. $T_n = \dfrac{\sqrt{3n^2-1}}{2n+3}$

19. (i) $1+3+5+7+\ldots$ is an arithmetic series.
    Find in terms of n (a) T_n (b) S_n.
    (ii) Evaluate $\lim\limits_{n\to\infty} \dfrac{\sqrt{1+3+5+7+\cdots+T_n}}{2n}$.

Convergent, divergent

When the $\lim_{n\to\infty} T_n$ exists, we can say that the sequence is **convergent**. In the sequence

$$\frac{1}{2}, \frac{2}{3}, \frac{3}{4}, \frac{4}{5}, \ldots, \frac{n}{n+1}, \ldots$$

we can show that $T_n \to 1$ as $n \to \infty$. So we can say that this sequence is convergent and, furthermore, that it converges to 1.

Any sequence (or series) that is not convergent must be described as **divergent**.

The sequence

$$1, 2, 4, 8, \ldots$$

is divergent as its T_n has no limit as $n \to \infty$.

The rules for convergence are quite strict. For example,

$$1, -1, 1, -1, 1, -1, \ldots$$

is very predictable, but $\lim_{n\to\infty} T_n$ does not exist as there is no (single) value that T_n approaches as $n \to \infty$. So the sequence is divergent.

Infinite geometric series

When a series has an infinite number of terms, it is called an **infinite series** and the sum of the series is called the **sum to infinity** of the series.

Let us consider the value of a proper fraction (between 0 and 1) if we keep multiplying it by itself. Take, for example, $\frac{1}{4}$ and keep multiplying it by itself, i.e. $\left(\frac{1}{4}\right)^n$, as n increases indefinitely.

We can represent this situation in a table using a calculator.

n	1	2	3	$\cdots$	10
$\left(\frac{1}{4}\right)^n$	0·25	0·0625	0·015625	$\ldots$	0·0000009537

From the table we can see that as $n \to \infty$, the value of $\left(\frac{1}{4}\right)^n$ converges to 0.

This will happen for any proper fraction, positive or negative. So $\lim_{n\to\infty} \left(\frac{1}{4}\right)^n = 0$.

Symbolically:

$$\lim_{n\to\infty} (\text{proper fraction})^n = 0$$

In general, for the infinite geometric series:

$$a + ar + ar^2 + ar^3 + \cdots$$

If r is a proper fraction, then the terms will get closer to zero.

For r to be a proper fraction it must be between -1 and 1, i.e. $-1 < r < 1$.

$$\text{If } -1 < r < 1,$$
$$\text{then } \lim_{n \to \infty} r^n = 0.$$

Notes: If $r > 1$ or $r < -1$, then $\lim\limits_{n \to \infty} r^n$ does not exist.

The sum to infinity, S_∞, of a series is denoted by $\lim\limits_{n \to \infty} S_n$.

If $\lim\limits_{n \to \infty} S_n$ exists, the series is said to be **convergent**.

If $\lim\limits_{n \to \infty} S_n$ does **not** exist, the series is said to be **divergent**.

Let us now develop the general formula for the sum to infinity of a geometric series in which $-1 < r < 1$.

$$S_n = \frac{a(1 - r^n)}{1 - r}$$

The only part of this formula that changes as n increases is r^n.

As $n \to \infty$, $r^n \to 0$, because r is a proper fraction.

$$\therefore\ S_\infty = \frac{a(1 - 0)}{1 - r} = \frac{a}{1 - r}$$

Sum to infinity of a geometric series:
$$S_\infty = \frac{a}{1 - r} = \frac{\text{first term}}{1 - \text{common ratio}}$$
$$\text{if } -1 < r < 1.$$

Note: $-1 < r < 1$ is often written $|r| < 1$.

EXAMPLE 1

(i) Find the sum to infinity of the geometric series $1 + \left(\dfrac{2}{5}\right) + \left(\dfrac{2}{5}\right)^2 + \left(\dfrac{2}{5}\right)^3 + \cdots$.

(ii) Evaluate $\displaystyle\sum_{n=0}^{\infty} \left(\dfrac{5}{2x+1}\right)^n$ in terms of x, where $x > 2$.

Solution:

(i) $1 + \left(\dfrac{2}{5}\right) + \left(\dfrac{2}{5}\right)^2 + \left(\dfrac{2}{5}\right)^3 + \cdots$.

This is an infinite geometric series with first term $a = 1$ and common ratio $r = \dfrac{2}{5}$.

$$S_\infty = \frac{a}{1-r} = \frac{1}{1-\frac{2}{5}} = \frac{5}{5-2} = \frac{5}{3}$$

(ii) $\displaystyle\sum_{n=0}^{\infty} \left(\dfrac{5}{2x+1}\right)^n = 1 + \left(\dfrac{5}{2x+1}\right) + \left(\dfrac{5}{2x+1}\right)^2 + \left(\dfrac{5}{2x+1}\right)^3 + \cdots$

This is an infinite geometric series with first term $a = 1$ and common ratio $r = \dfrac{5}{2x+1}$.

$$S_\infty = \frac{a}{1-r} = \frac{1}{1-\frac{5}{2x+1}} = \frac{2x+1}{2x+1-5} = \frac{2x+1}{2x-4}.$$

EXAMPLE 2

$\displaystyle\sum_{n=0}^{\infty} (2x-3)^n = 1 + (2x-3) + (2x-3)^2 + (2x-3)^3 + \cdots$ is a geometric series.

(i) Find, in terms of x, the sum to infinity.
(ii) If the sum to infinity is $\frac{5}{4}$, find the value of x.
(iii) Find the range of values of x for which the sum to infinity exists.

Solution:

This is an infinite geometric series with first term $a = 1$ and common ratio $r = (2x-3)$.

(i) $S_\infty = \dfrac{a}{1-r}$

$= \dfrac{1}{1-(2x-3)}$

$= \dfrac{1}{1-2x+3}$

$= \dfrac{1}{4-2x}$

(ii) Given: $S_\infty = \dfrac{5}{4}$

$\therefore \dfrac{1}{4-2x} = \dfrac{5}{4}$

$4 = 20 - 10x$

$10x = 16$

$x = \dfrac{8}{5}$

(iii) S_∞ exists if $-1 < r < 1$ (i.e. $|r| < 1$)

$\qquad\qquad\qquad -1 < 2x - 3 < 1$ $(r = 2x - 3)$

$\qquad\qquad\qquad\quad 2 < 2x < 4$ (add 3 to each part)

$\qquad\qquad\qquad\quad\ \ 1 < x < 2$ (divide each part by 2)

Thus, the sum to infinity exists for $1 < x < 2$.

EXAMPLE 3

The sum to infinity of a geometric series is 36 and the second term of the series is 8. Find two possible series.

Solution:

Let the series be $a + ar + ar^2 + \cdots$

Given: $S_\infty = 36$ $\qquad$ Given: $T_2 = 8$

$\qquad \dfrac{a}{1-r} = 36$ $\qquad\qquad\qquad\quad$ $ar = 8$ ②

$\qquad\quad a = 36(1 - r)$ ①

We now solve between ① and ②.

Given: $S_\infty = 36$ $\qquad\qquad$ Put $r = \frac{2}{3}$ and $r = \frac{2}{3}$ into ① or ② to find the

$\qquad\qquad ar = 8$ ② $\qquad$ value of a.

$\quad 36(1 - r)r = 8$ $\qquad\qquad\qquad\qquad\qquad a = 36(1 - r)$

$\quad (36 - 36r)r = 8$

$\quad\ 36r - 36r^2 = 8$ $\qquad\qquad\qquad$ $r = \dfrac{1}{3}$ $\qquad\qquad$ $r = \dfrac{2}{3}$

$36r^2 - 36r + 8 = 0$

$\quad\ 9r^2 - 9r + 2 = 0$ $\qquad\qquad$ $a = 36\left(1 - \dfrac{1}{3}\right)$ $\qquad$ $a = 36\left(1 - \dfrac{2}{3}\right)$

$(3r - 1)(3r - 2) = 0$

$\quad 3r - 1 = 0$ or $3r - 2 = 0$ $\qquad\quad = 36\left(\dfrac{2}{3}\right)$ $\qquad\quad = 36\left(\dfrac{1}{3}\right)$

$\qquad 3r = 1$ or $3r = 2$

$\qquad\quad r = \dfrac{1}{3}$ or $r = \dfrac{2}{3}$ $\qquad\quad a = 24$ $\qquad\qquad\quad a = 12$

Thus, we have two series which obey the two given conditions:

(i) $a = 24$, $r = \frac{1}{3}$. The series is $24 + 8 + \frac{8}{3} + \cdots$

(ii) $a = 12$, $r = \frac{2}{3}$. The series is $12 + 8 + \frac{16}{3} + \cdots$

Recurring decimals

An application of the sum of infinite geometric series is expressing non-terminating, recurring decimals as rational numbers.

Note: The first five letters in the word 'rational' spell 'ratio'. In other words, a rational number is any number that can be written as a ratio (i.e. a fraction).

Recurring decimals can be expressed neatly by placing a dot over the first and last figures which repeat. This is called the **dot notation**. For example:

$0 \cdot \dot{4} = 0 \cdot 44444 \ldots = \frac{4}{9}$ $\qquad$ $0 \cdot 1\dot{6} = 0 \cdot 166666 \ldots = \frac{1}{6}$

$1 \cdot \dot{2}\dot{5} = 1 \cdot 252525 \ldots = 1 + \frac{25}{99} = \frac{124}{99}$ $\qquad$ $0 \cdot \dot{1}8\dot{5} = 0 \cdot 185185185 \ldots = \frac{5}{27}$

EXAMPLE

Express the recurring decimal $0 \cdot 7\dot{3}$ in the form $\dfrac{a}{b}$ where $a, b \in \mathbb{N}$.

Solution:

$$0 \cdot 7\dot{3} = 0 \cdot 733333 \ldots$$
$$= 0 \cdot 7 + 0 \cdot 03 + 0 \cdot 003 + 0 \cdot 0003 + \cdots$$
$$= \frac{7}{10} + \left[\frac{3}{100} + \frac{3}{1,000} + \frac{3}{10,000} + \cdots \right]$$

The series in the brackets is an infinite geometric series, with $a = \dfrac{3}{100}$ and $r = \dfrac{1}{10}$.

$$S_\infty = \frac{a}{1 - r} = \frac{\frac{3}{100}}{1 - \frac{1}{10}} = \frac{1}{30}$$

Thus, $0 \cdot 7\dot{3} = \dfrac{7}{10} + \dfrac{1}{30} = \dfrac{11}{15}$.

Exercise 4.12

In questions 1–9, find the sum of the infinite geometric series.

1. $1 + \dfrac{1}{2} + \dfrac{1}{4} + \cdots$

2. $2 + \dfrac{2}{3} + \dfrac{2}{9} + \cdots$

3. $5 + 1 + \dfrac{1}{5} + \cdots$

4. $2 + 1 \cdot 8 + 1 \cdot 62 + \cdots$

5. $3 - \dfrac{3}{2} + \dfrac{3}{4} - \cdots$

6. $\dfrac{3}{2} - \dfrac{1}{4} + \dfrac{1}{24} - \cdots$

7. $0 \cdot 2 - 0 \cdot 1 + 0 \cdot 005 - \cdots$

8. $1 + x + x^2 + \cdots$

9. $2 + \dfrac{2a}{3} + \dfrac{2a^2}{9} + \cdots$

10. Evaluate: **(i)** $\displaystyle\sum_{n=0}^{\infty}\left(\frac{1}{3}\right)^n$ **(ii)** $\displaystyle\sum_{n=0}^{\infty}3\left(\frac{1}{2}\right)^n$ **(iii)** $\displaystyle\sum_{n=0}^{\infty}x(1-x)^n$

11. **(i)** Find the sum to infinity of the geometric series $\frac{5}{10}+\frac{5}{100}+\frac{5}{1,000}+\cdots$.

    (ii) Using this series, show that $1\cdot\dot{5}=\frac{14}{9}$.

In questions 12–17, express the recurring decimal in the form $\dfrac{a}{b}$ where $a, b \in \mathbb{N}$.

12. $0\cdot\dot{4}$ 13. $2\cdot\dot{2}$ 14. $0\cdot\dot{7}\dot{2}$ 15. $0\cdot2\dot{7}$ 16. $0\cdot1\dot{2}$ 17. $1\cdot8\dot{3}$

18. The sum to infinity of a geometric series is 20 and the common ratio is $\frac{2}{5}$. Find the first term.

19. The sum to infinity of a geometric series is 4 and the first term is 6. Find the common ratio.

20. The sum to infinity of a geometric series is 5. The common ratio and the first term of the series are equal. Find the common ratio.

21. If the sum to infinity of a geometric series is five times the first term, find the common ratio.

22. $24x - 5$, $6x - 1$ and x are the first three terms of a geometric series.

    Find two values for **(i)** x **(ii)** the common ratio   **(iii)** the sum to infinity.

23. In a geometric series, $T_1 = a$ and $T_2 = a^2 - 2a$, $a \neq 0$.

    (i) Write down, in terms of a, the common ratio of the series.

    (ii) If the sum to infinity is 5, find the value of a.

    (iii) Find the range of values of $a \in \mathbb{R}$ for which the series has a sum to infinity.

24. $\displaystyle\sum_{n=0}^{\infty}x^2\left(\frac{1}{1-x}\right)^n = x^2 + \frac{x^2}{1-x} + \frac{x^2}{(1-x)^2} + \frac{x^2}{(1-x)^3} + \cdots$ is an infinite geometric series.

    (i) Find in terms of x **(a)** the common ratio **(b)** the sum to infinity.

    (ii) If the sum to infinity is 30, find the values of x.

25. **(i)** Factorise $1 - r^2$.

    (ii) $a + ar + ar^2 + ar^3 + \cdots$ is an infinite geometric series with $|r| < 1$.

    The sum to infinity is 8 and the sum to infinity of the even terms is 2.

    Find the value of the common ratio.

26. The sum to infinity of a geometric series is 27 and the second term of the series is 6. Find two possible series.

27. The sum to infinity of a geometric series is 2. When the terms of this geometric sequence are squared, a new geometric sequence is obtained whose sum to infinity is 12. Find the first term, a, and the common ratio, r, where $|r| < 1$.

28. A ball is dropped onto level ground.

It takes 1 second to hit the ground and 80% of that time to rise to its new height.

It continues to bounce at this rate until the ball comes to rest.

   (i)   How long does it take to hit the ground for the second time?
   (ii) Write the times for each individual bounce as an infinite series.
   (iii) How long does the ball take to come to rest?

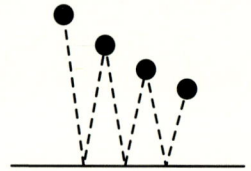

CHAPTER 5

THEOREMS

Glossary of examinable terms

Axiom:	An axiom is a statement which is assumed to be true. It can be accepted without a proof and used as a basis for an argument.
Converse:	The converse of a theorem is formed by taking the conclusion as the starting point and having the starting point as the conclusion.
Corollary:	A corollary follows after a theorem and is a statement which must be true because of that theorem.
If and only if:	Often shortened to 'iff'. One statement is true if and only if the second statement is true, so both statements must be true or both statements must be false.
Implies:	Implies indicates a logical relationship between two statements, such that if the first is true then the second must be true.
Is congruent to:	Two things are said to be congruent if they are identical in size and shape.
Is equivalent to:	Two things are said to be equivalent if they have the same value but different forms.
Proof:	A proof is a sequence of statements (made up of axioms, assumptions and arguments) that follow logically from the preceding one, starting at an axiom or previously proven theorem and ending with the statement of the theorem to be proven.
Proof by contradiction:	A proof by contradiction is a proof which establishes the truth of a statement by proving that the statement being false leads to a contradiction. Proving its falsity to be impossible proves that the statement must be true.
Theorem:	A theorem is a statement which has been proved to be true, deduced from axioms by logical argument.

You are required to know the following axioms, theorems and corollaries and must be able to apply them in answering geometric questions.

Axioms

Axiom 1: There is exactly one line through any two given points.

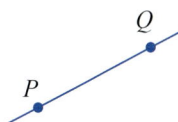

Axiom 2: **Ruler axiom**

The distance between points A and B has the following properties:

1. The distance $|PQ|$ is never negative

2. The distance between two points is the same, whether we measure from P to Q or from Q to P.

3. If there exists some point R between P and Q, then the distance from P to Q is equal to the sum of the distances from P to R and R to Q.

   $$|PR| + |RQ| = |PQ|$$

4. Marking off a distance

   Given any ray from P, and given any real number $k \geq 0$, there is a unique point Q on the ray whose distance from P is k.

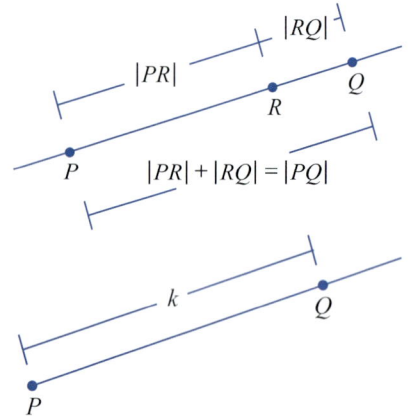

Axiom 3: **Protractor axiom**

The number of degrees in an angle (also known as its degree-measure) is always a number between $0°$ and $360°$. It has these properties:

1. A straight angle has $180°$.

2. If we know the angle $A°$, opened up at a point P, then there are two possible rays from P that form that angle.

3. If an angle is divided into two, then that angle is equal to the sum of the two angles that make it up.

   $$|\angle QPR| = |\angle QPS| + |\angle SPR|$$
   $$|\angle QPR| = A° + B°$$

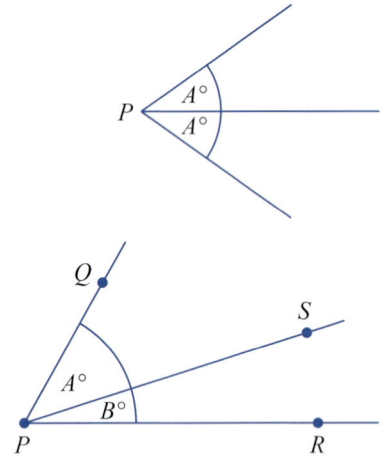

Axiom 4: **Congruent triangles**

We can say that two triangles are congruent if:

1. SAS: Two sides and the angle in between are the same in both.

2. ASA: Two angles and a side are the same in both.

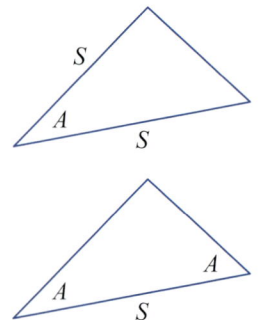

3. SSS: All three sides are the same in both.

4. RHS: Right angle, hypotenuse and another side.

Axiom 5: Given any line *l* and a point *P*, there is exactly one line through *P* that is parallel to *l*.

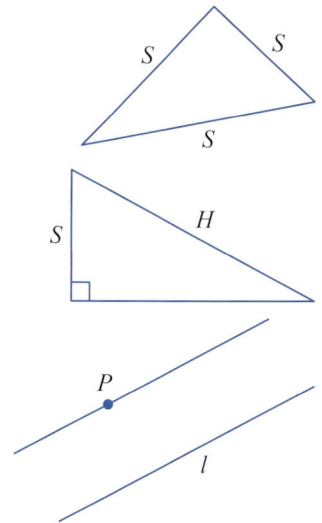

Theorems

- The application of all theorems can be examined.
- Only proofs for theorems 11, 12 and 13 are examinable (marked with *).
- You will be presented with the worded statement of theorem, without reference to the theorem number.
- Proofs are expected to begin with a diagram, followed by the following headings: 'Given', 'To prove', 'Construction' and 'Proof'.
- You must explain all construction steps fully.
- You may be asked for an example of 'proof by contradiction'.

Theorem 1: **Vertically opposite angles**

Vertically opposite angles are equal in measure.

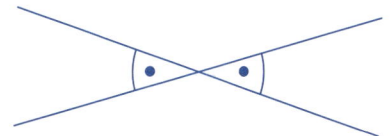

Theorem 2: **Isosceles triangles**

1. In an isosceles triangle, the angles opposite the equal sides are equal.

2. Conversely, if two angles are equal, then the triangle is isosceles.

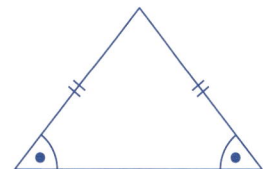

Theorem 3: **Alternate angles**

If a transversal makes equal alternate angles on two lines, then the lines are parallel (and converse).

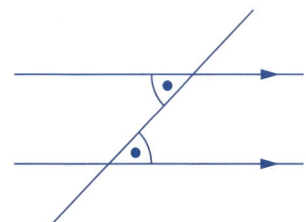

Theorem 4: **Angles in a triangle**

The angles in any triangle add to 180°.

$$A° + B° + C° = 180°$$

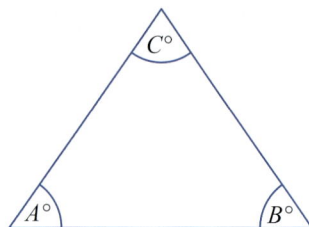

Theorem 5: **Corresponding angles**

Two lines are parallel if, and only if, for any transversal, the corresponding angles are equal.

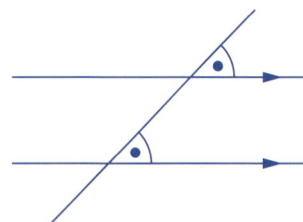

Theorem 6: **Exterior angle**

Each exterior angle of a triangle is equal to the sum of the interior opposite angles.

$$E° = A° + B°$$

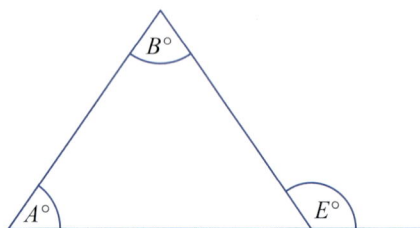

Theorem 7: **Angle-side relationship**

1. In a triangle, the angle opposite the greater of two sides is greater than the angle opposite the lesser side.

2. Conversely, the side opposite the greater of two angles is greater than the side opposite the lesser angle.

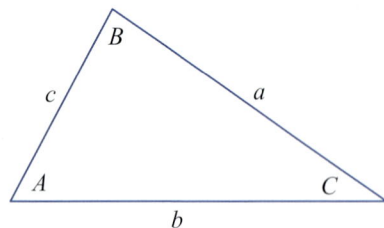

Theorem 8: **Triangle inequality**

Two sides of a triangle are together greater than the third.

$$a + b > c$$
$$b + c > a$$
$$a + c > b$$

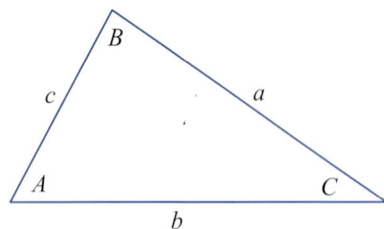

Theorem 9: **Parallelograms**

In a parallelogram, opposite sides are equal and opposite angles are equal.

Two converses of this theorem are true:

1. If the opposite angles of a quadrilateral are equal, then it is a parallelogram.

2. If the opposite sides of a quadrilateral are equal, then it is a parallelogram.

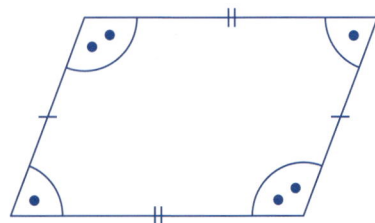

Corollary: A diagonal divides a parallelogram into two congruent triangles.

Theorem 10: **Diagonals of a parallelogram**

The diagonals of a parallelogram bisect each other.

Converse:

If the diagonals of a quadrilateral bisect one another, then it is a parallelogram.

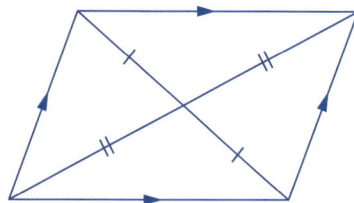

*Theorem 11: **Transversals**

If three parallel lines cut off equal segments on some transversal line, then they will cut off equal segments on any other transversal.

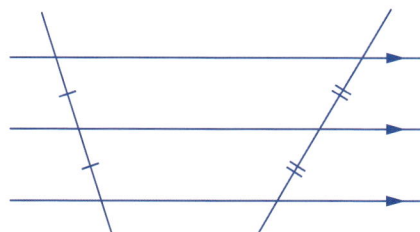

*Theorem 12: **Proportional sides**

Let *ABC* be a triangle. If a line *XY* is parallel to *BC* and cuts [*AB*] in the ratio *s* : *t*, then it also cuts [*AC*] in the same ratio.

Converse:

If a line *XY* cuts the sides *AB* and *AC* in the same ratio, then it is parallel to *BC*.

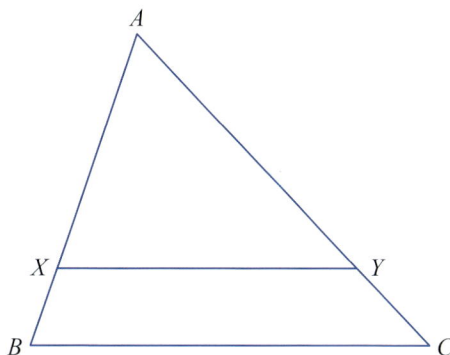

*Theorem 13: **Similar triangles**

If two triangles are similar, then their sides are proportional, in order.

$$\frac{|PQ|}{|AB|} = \frac{|PR|}{|AC|} = \frac{|QR|}{|BC|}$$

Converse:

If the corresponding sides of two triangles are proportional, then they are similar.

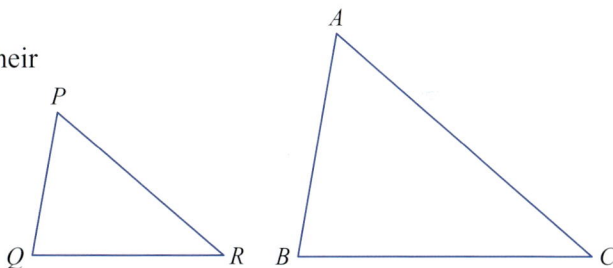

Theorem 14: **Theorem of Pythagoras**

In a right-angled triangle, the square of the hypotenuse is the sum of the squares of the other two sides.

$$|AC|^2 = |AB|^2 + |BC|^2$$

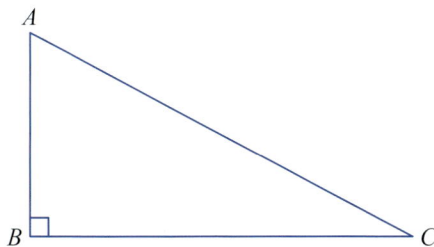

Theorem 15: **Converse to Pythagoras**

If the square of one side is the sum of the squares of the other two, then the angle opposite the first side is a right angle.

Theorem 16: **Area**

For a triangle, base × height does not depend on the choice of base.

Definition:

The area of a triangle is half the base by the height, regardless of which side you choose as the base.

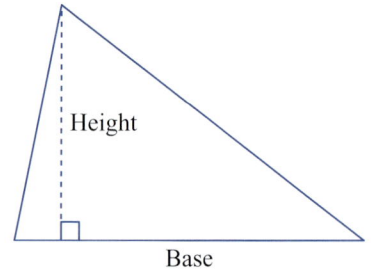

Theorem 17: **Parallelogram bisector**

A diagonal of a parallelogram bisects the area.

Area △*ABD* = Area △*CDB*

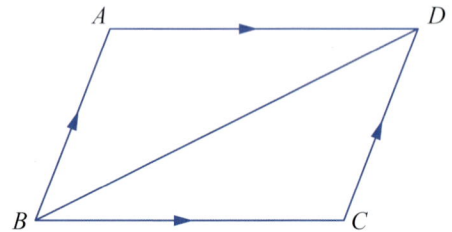

Theorem 18: **Area of a parallelogram**

The area of a parallelogram is the base × height.

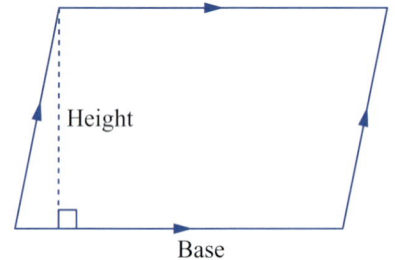

Theorem 19: **Circle theorem**

The angle at the centre of a circle standing on a given arc is twice the angle at any point of the circle standing on the same arc.

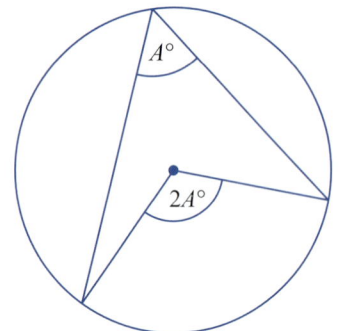

Corollary 1: All angles at points of a circle standing on the same arc are equal.

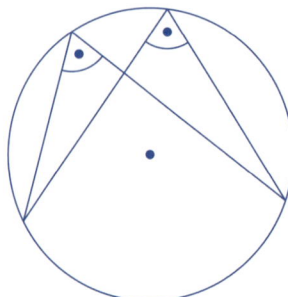

Corollary 2: Each angle in a semi-circle is a right angle.

Corollary 3: If the angle standing on a chord [BC] at some point on the circle is a right angle, then [BC] is a diameter.

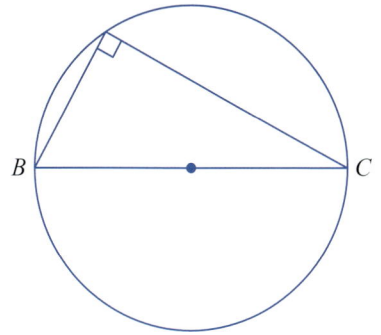

Corollary 4: If ABCD is a cyclic quadrilateral, then opposite angles sum to 180°.

$$A° + C° = 180°$$
$$B° + D° = 180°$$

Converse:

If the opposite angles of a quadrilateral sum to 180°, the quadrilateral is cyclic.

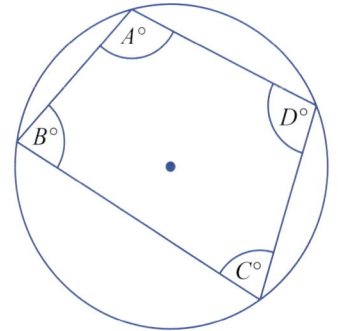

Theorem 20: **Tangents**

1. Each tangent is perpendicular to the radius that goes to the point of contact.
2. If P lies on the circle S, and a line l is perpendicular to the radius at P, then l is a tangent to S.

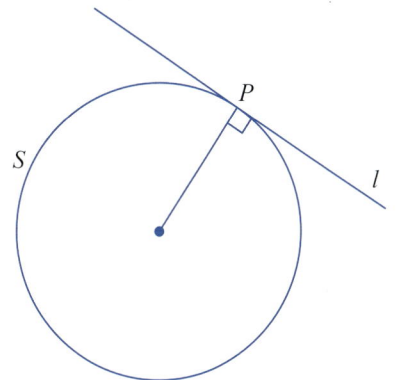

Corollary: If two circles intersect at one point only, then the two centres and the point of contact are collinear.

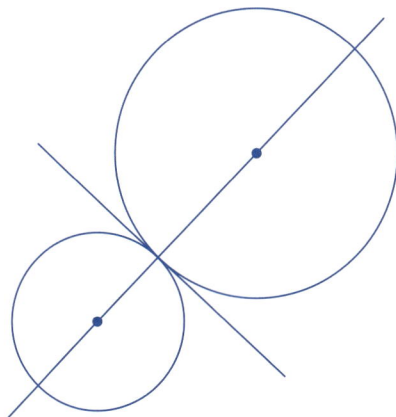

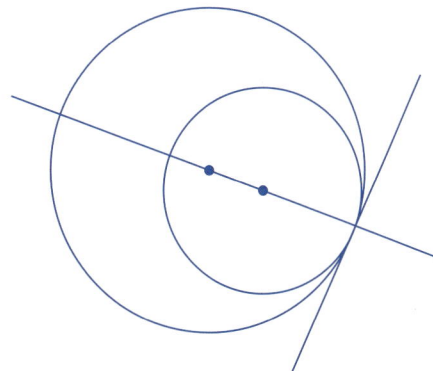

Theorem 21: Perpendicular bisector of a chord

1. The perpendicular from the centre of a circle to a chord bisects the chord.

2. The perpendicular bisector of a chord passes through the centre of the circle.

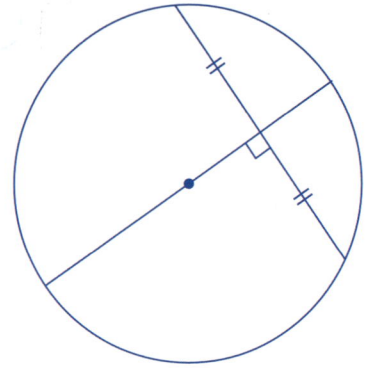

Proof of theorems

Theorem 11: If three parallel lines cut off equal segments on some transversal line, then they will cut off equal segments on any other transversal.

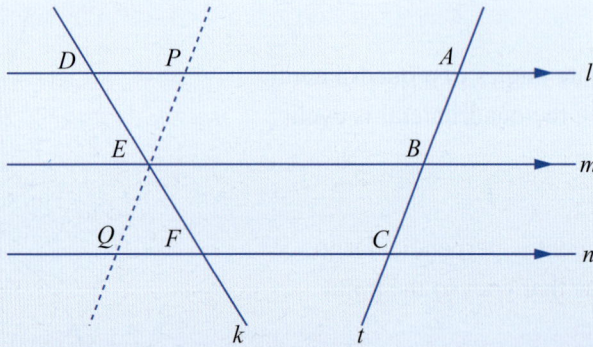

Given: Three parallel lines, l, m and n, intersecting the transversal t at the points A, B and C such that $|AB|=|BC|$. Another transversal, k, intersects the lines at D, E and F.

To prove: $|DE|=|EF|$

Construction: Through E, construct a line parallel to t and intersecting l at the point P and n at the point Q.

Proof: $PEBA$ and $EQCB$ are parallelograms.

Then $|PE|=|AB|$ and $|EQ|=|BC|$. (Opposite sides)

But $|AB|=|BC|$.

So, $|PE|=|EQ|$.

In $\triangle DEP$ and $\triangle FEQ$:

$|PE|=|EQ|$

$|\angle PED|=|\angle FEQ|$ (Vertically opposite angles)

$|\angle DPE|=|\angle FQE|$ (Alternate angles)

$\therefore \triangle DEP$ and $\triangle FEQ$ are congruent. (ASA rule)

$\therefore |DE|=|EF|$

Theorem 12: Let ABC be a triangle. If a line XY is parallel to BC and cuts $[AB]$ in the ratio $s : t$, then it also cuts $[AC]$ in the same ratio.

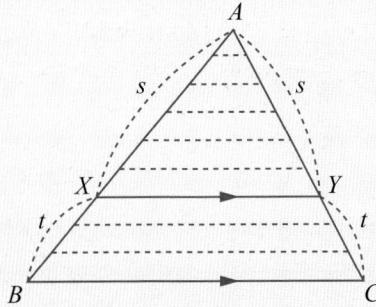

Given: The triangle ABC with XY parallel to BC.

To prove: $\dfrac{|AX|}{|XB|} = \dfrac{|AY|}{|YC|}$

Construction: Divide $[AX]$ into s equal parts and $[XB]$ into t equal parts.

Draw a line parallel to BC through each point of the division.

Proof: The parallel lines make intercepts of equal length along the line $[AC]$.

(Converse of transversal theorem)

$\therefore$ $[AY]$ is divided into s equal intercepts and $[YC]$ is divided into t equal intercepts.

$\therefore \dfrac{|AY|}{|YC|} = \dfrac{s}{t}$

But $\dfrac{|AX|}{|XB|} = \dfrac{s}{t}$

$\therefore \dfrac{|AX|}{|XB|} = \dfrac{|AY|}{|YC|}$

Theorem 13: If two triangles, *ABC* and *DEF*, are similar, then their sides are proportional in order:

$$\frac{|AB|}{|DE|} = \frac{|BC|}{|EF|} = \frac{|AC|}{|DF|}$$

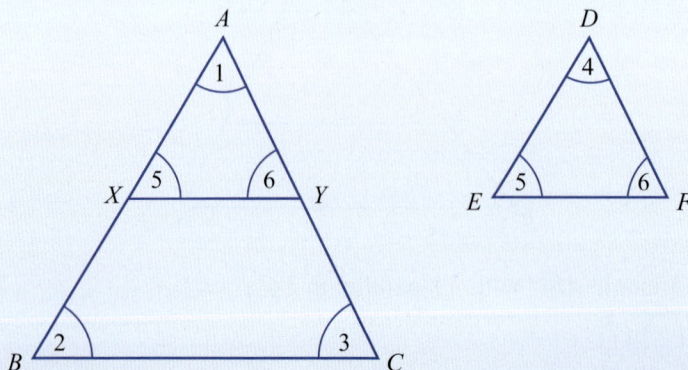

Given: The triangles *ABC* and *DEF* in which $|\angle 1| = |\angle 4|$, $|\angle 2| = |\angle 5|$ and $|\angle 3| = |\angle 6|$.

To prove: $\dfrac{|AB|}{|DE|} = \dfrac{|BC|}{|EF|} = \dfrac{|AC|}{|DF|}$

Construction: Mark the point *X* on [*AB*] such that $|AX| = |DE|$.

Mark the point *Y* on [*AC*] such that $|AY| = |DF|$.

Join *XY*.

Proof: The triangles *AXY* and *DEF* are congruent.   (SAS)

$\therefore |\angle AXY| = |\angle DEF| = |\angle 5|$ (Corresponding angles)

$\therefore |\angle AXY| = |\angle ABC|$

$\therefore XY \parallel BC$ (Corresponding angles)

$\therefore \dfrac{|AB|}{|AX|} = \dfrac{|AC|}{|AY|}$ (A line parallel to one side divides the other side in the same ratio)

$\therefore \dfrac{|AB|}{|DE|} = \dfrac{|AC|}{|DF|}$

Similarly, it can be proven that $\therefore \dfrac{|AB|}{|DE|} = \dfrac{|BC|}{|EF|}$.

$\therefore \dfrac{|AB|}{|DE|} = \dfrac{|BC|}{|EF|} = \dfrac{|AC|}{|DF|}$

Proof by contradiction

This method of proof takes a proposition of the form:

> **If** certain conditions, **then** a result will follow.

And examines the consequences of assuming that:

> **If** certain conditions, **then** the *opposite* result will follow.

To prove: A triangle has at most one obtuse angle.

Proof: Consider a triangle with angles A, B and C.
Assume that the opposite of the 'to prove' statement is true, i.e. the triangle has more than one obtuse angle.

Suppose A and B are both obtuse.

$\therefore$ A is more than 90° and B is more than 90°.

$\therefore$ $A + B$ is more than 90° + 90°, which is more than 180°.

But this is impossible, as the *three* angles must add up to 180°.

Therefore, it is not possible for the triangle to have two obtuse angles.

Therefore, a triangle has at most one obtuse angle.

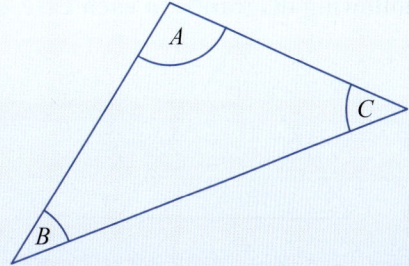

The following exercise is a revision of the Geometry material covered at Junior Cert Higher Level.

Exercise 6.1

In questions 1–4, calculate the value of the letter representing the angle in each of the following diagrams. In each case, give a reason for your answer.

1.

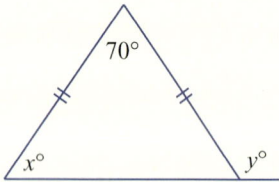

2.

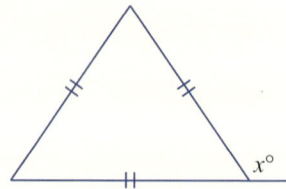

In questions 3–4, parallel lines are indicated with arrows.

3.

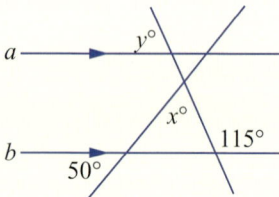

4.

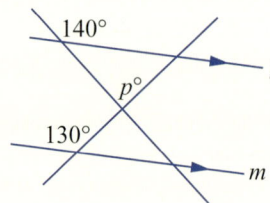

5. In the diagram, $|PQ| = |PR|$.

Find the value of:

(i) x (ii) y (iii) z

In each case, give a reason for your answer.

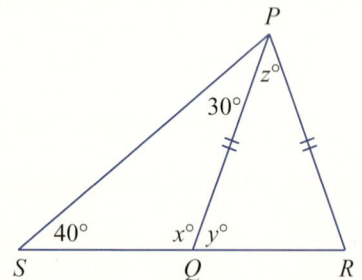

6. The diagram shows a parallelogram $PQRS$ with diagonal $[PR]$ and $|\angle PRS| = 45°$. T is a point on the ray $[PS]$ such that $|\angle RST| = 130°$.

Find the measure of the following.

(i) $|\angle PSR|$ (ii) $|\angle PQR|$

(iii) $|\angle PRQ|$ (iv) $|\angle QPR|$

In each case, justify your answer.

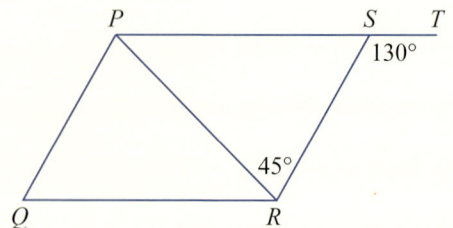

7. In the diagram, AC is parallel to DE.
   $|\angle CAB| = 135°$ and $|\angle EDB| = 147°$.
   Find $|\angle ABD|$.

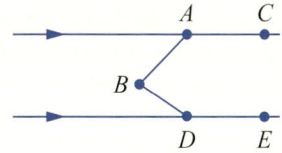

8. In the following diagrams, l, m and n are parallel lines. They cut equal intercepts on the transversals. In each case, calculate the value of the variables x, y, a and b.

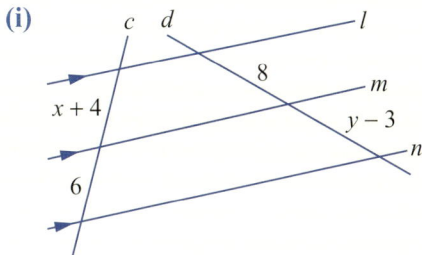

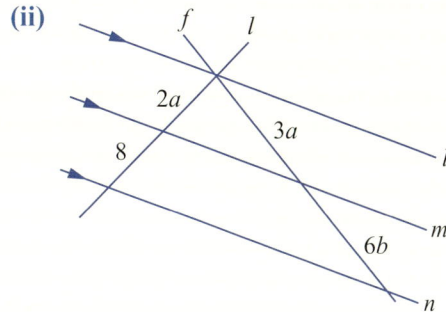

   (i)

   (ii)

9. The diagram shows three parallel lines, l, m and n. They cut equal intercepts on the line u, such that $u \perp l$.

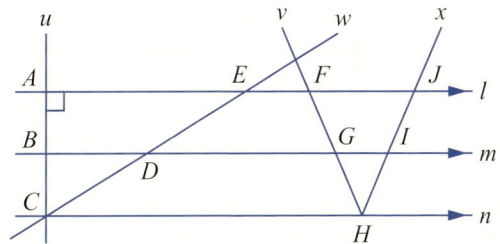

   (i) Is $u \perp n$? Give a reason for your answer.
   (ii) If $|AC| = 18$ cm, find $|BC|$.
   (iii) If $|\angle BCD| = 60°$, calculate $|DC|$.
   (iv) If $|AC| + |FH| = 40$ cm, find $|FH|$.
   (v) If $\triangle GHI$ is isosceles, find $|HI|$.
   (vi) Is $\triangle FHJ$ isosceles? Give a reason for your answer.
   (vii) Calculate $|FJ|$ in surd form.
   (viii) A point K is drawn such that $FJHK$ is a parallelogram. Illustrate K on the diagram.
   (ix) Calculate the area of the parallelogram $FJHK$ to the nearest whole number.
   (x) Hence or otherwise, calculate the perpendicular distance between $[FK]$ and $[JH]$ to the nearest whole number.

10. The diagram shows three parallel lines, l, m and n. They cut equal intercepts on the line u. The line v makes a $60°$ angle with the vertical, as shown in the diagram.

    (i) If $|AC| = 16$ cm, find $|DE|$.
    (ii) If $|GH| = 22$ cm, calculate $|\angle HEF|$.
    (iii) Find the area of $\triangle HEF$.

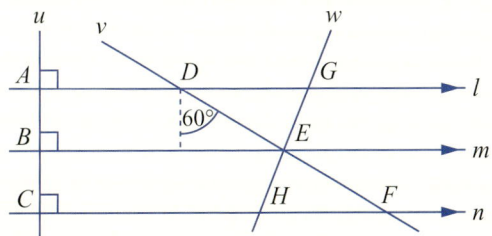

(iv) Using this area or otherwise, find $|HF|$.

(v) Using the formula $A = \sqrt{s(s-a)(s-b)(s-c)}$, where $s = \dfrac{a+b+c}{2}$, verify your answer for part **(iii)**.

11. Find the value of the letter representing the angles in each of the following. In each case, give a reason for your answer. Where necessary, the centre of the circle is indicated by O and tangents are indicated by t.

(i)

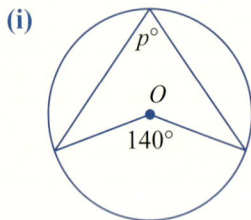

(ii)

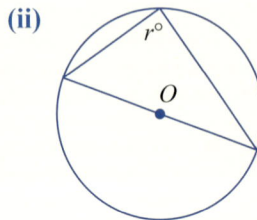

(iii)

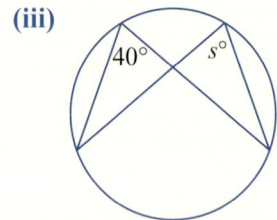

(iv)

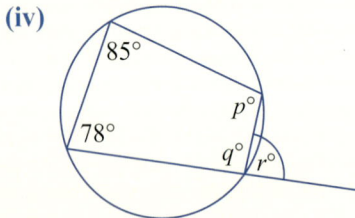

(v)

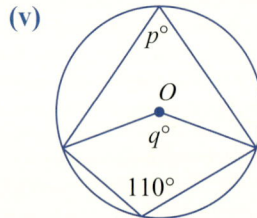

(vi)

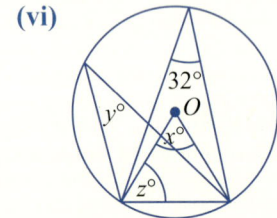

(vii)

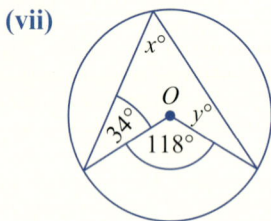

(viii)

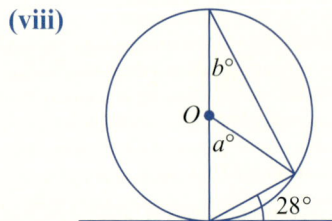

(ix)

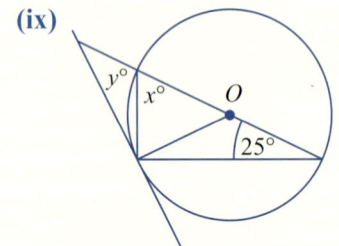

12. In the diagram, O is the centre of the circle. PT is a tangent, $|PQ| = |RQ|$ and $|\angle SPT| = 38°$. Calculate $|\angle QRS|$.

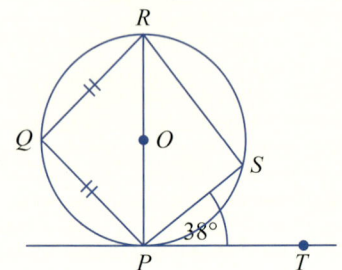

13. In the diagram, $|\angle XCB| = 54°$ and O is the centre of the circle. Calculate $|\angle BOD|$, where $\angle BOD$ is obtuse.

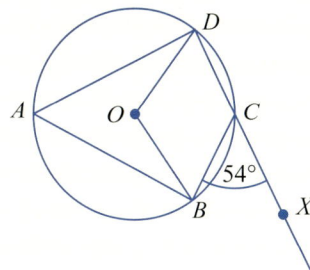

14. R is a point on a circle, centre C, and $|\angle CPQ| = 40°$. Calculate:
    (i) $|\angle PCQ|$
    (ii) $|\angle PQR|$
    (iii) If $|\angle PCR| = 200°$, calculate $|\angle CRP|$.

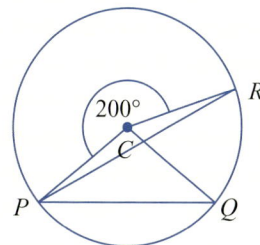

15. $PQRS$ is a cyclic quadrilateral such that $|\angle SPQ| = x$, $|\angle PQR| = 4x - 2$ and $|\angle QRS| = 8x$, all angles in degrees. Calculate (i) x (ii) $|\angle RSP|$.

16. O is the centre of the circle c and $OM \perp AB$. $|OM| = 5$ cm and the radius is 13 cm.
    Find $|AB|$.

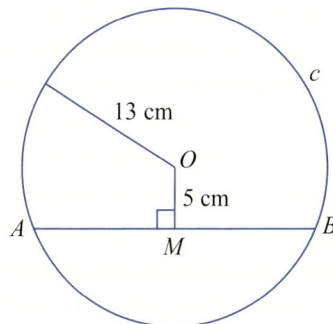

17. B is the centre of the circle of radius 4·5 cm. PT is a tangent and T is a point on the circle. If $|PA| = 3$ cm, calculate $|PT|$.

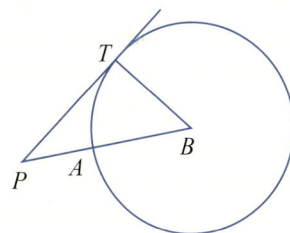

18. In the diagram, O is the centre of the circle of radius 17 cm. X is a point on $[PQ]$ such that $|OX| = 15$ cm. $[AB]$ is a chord through X perpendicular to PQ.
    (i) Find $|AB|$.
    (ii) Find $|AQ|$, correct to one decimal place.

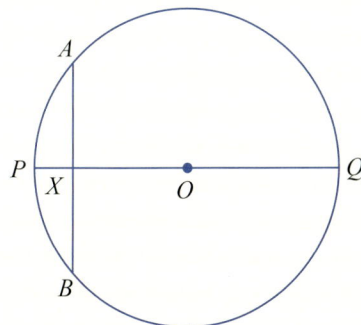

273

19. Calculate the value of x, where O is the centre.

(i)

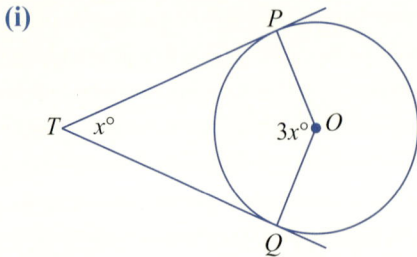

(ii)

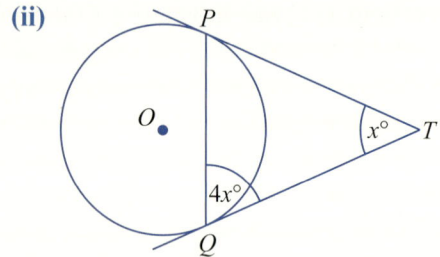

20. The diagram shows two circles, h and k, intersecting externally at one point. The radius of h is 6 cm and the radius of k is 4 cm. P is any point on h and Q is any point on k.

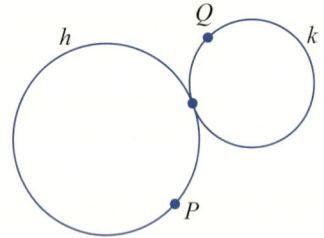

    (i) Calculate the maximum value of $|PQ|$.

    (ii) If the circles touched at one point internally, calculate the maximum value of $|PQ|$.

21. A circle, centre X, of radius 12 cm, touches another circle, centre Y, of radius 3 cm, at the point W. The circles also touch the sides of a rectangle at the points P, Q, R, S and T, as shown, and $YZ \parallel QP$. Calculate the following.

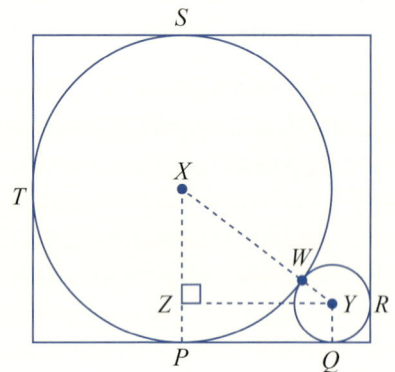

    (i) $|XY|$

    (ii) $|XZ|$

    (iii) $|ZY|$

    (iv) The area of the rectangle $ZYQP$

    (v) Is $|\angle ZXY| > |\angle ZYX|$? Justify your answer.

22. The circles p and q have radii of 18 cm and 8 cm, respectively, and touch externally, as shown. The line AB is a tangent to both circles at points A and B, respectively. Calculate $|AB|$.

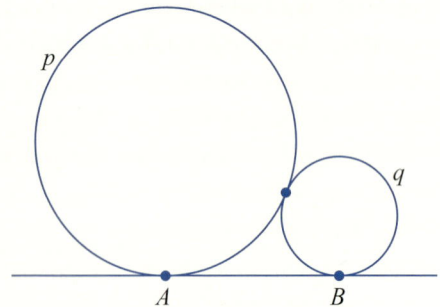

23. The diagram shows the side view of a wedge. The wedge is 112 mm long and 30 mm high. The top part of the wedge is 40 mm long. Calculate the length of the sloping part of the wedge.

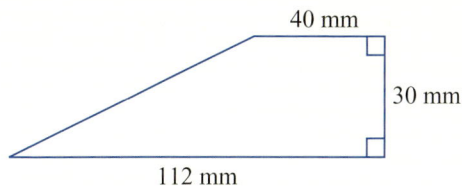

40 mm

30 mm

112 mm

24. Andrew and Brian are in the All-Ireland conkers competition in Freshford, Co. Kilkenny. Andrew's conker, C, is tied to the end of a string 34 cm in length. He pulls it back from its vertical position until it is 30 cm horizontal from its original position. Calculate h, the vertical distance that the conker has risen.

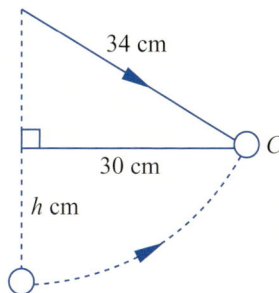

34 cm

30 cm

C

h cm

25. Consider $\triangle ABC$. Using **acute angle**, **right angle** or **obtuse angle**, name the type of angle that $\angle ACB$ makes if:

(i) $c^2 = a^2 + b^2$

(ii) $c^2 > a^2 + b^2$

(iii) $c^2 < a^2 + b^2$

In each case, explain your answer.

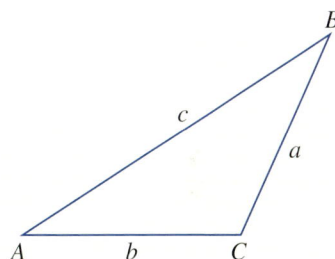

B

c

a

A b C

26. The diagram shows a cuboid wooden model of a room with diagonal struts $[QW]$, $[PV]$ and $[PW]$.
$|PQ| = 9$ cm, $|QV| = 12$ cm and $|WV| = 5$ cm.

Calculate (i) $|QW|$ (ii) $|PV|$ and (iii) $|PW|$, correct to two decimal places.

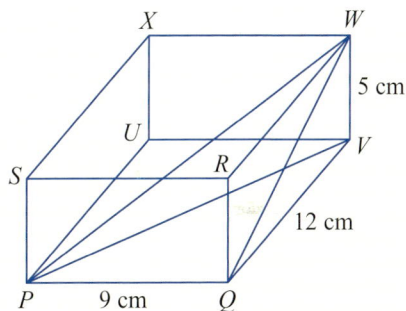

X W

5 cm

U

V

S R

12 cm

P 9 cm Q

27. The diagram shows a rectangular box. Prove that $|PQ| = \sqrt{a^2 + b^2 + c^2}$.

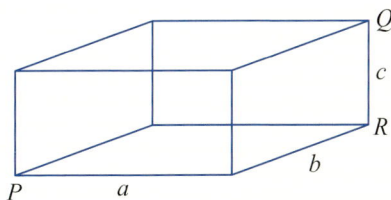

Q

c

R

P a b

275

28. The lengths of the sides of an isosceles triangle are $\sqrt{x^2 + 1}$, $\sqrt{x^2 + 1}$ and $2x$.
Taking $2x$ as the base, find the perpendicular height of the triangle.

29. A rectangle has length $2\sqrt{x}$ cm and width $\sqrt{x}$ cm.
The length of a diagonal of the rectangle is $\sqrt{45}$ cm.

   (i) Find the area of the rectangle.

   (ii) The area of a square is twice the area of the rectangle.
Find the length of a side of the square.

30. The diagram shows a piece of metal which has broken off from a
circular disc, where PTQ is part of the original circle.

   If $|PQ| = 36$ cm and $|TM| = 12$ cm where $|PM| = |MQ|$,
calculate the length of the radius of the disc.

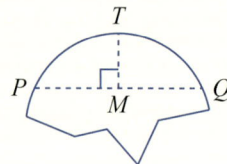

31. A 4 m-wide crosswalk
diagonally crosses a street,
as shown. The curbs are 8 m
apart. The crosswalk
intersects the opposite curb
with a 6 m displacement.
Find the area of the
crosswalk.

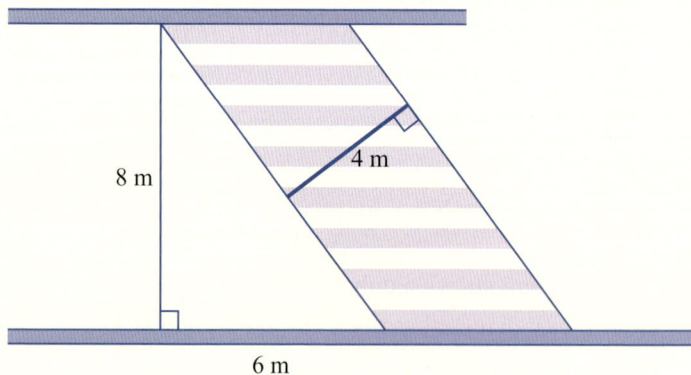

32. In the diagram, $ABCF$, $ABFE$
and $ACDE$ are parallelograms.
The area of $\triangle AFE$ is
15 square units.

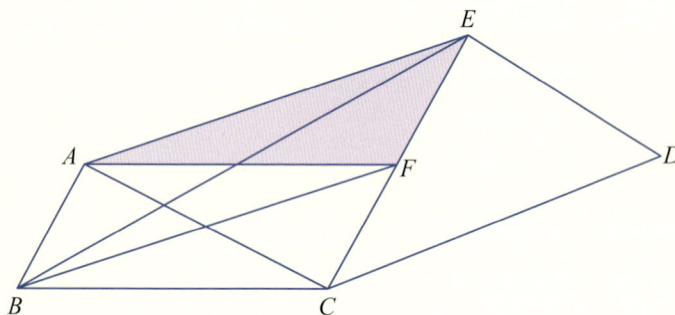

   (i) State clearly why the area of $\triangle AFB$ must also be 15 square units.

   (ii) Find the area of the whole figure $ABCDE$. Show your work.

   (iii) If the perpendicular distance from D to the line EC is 6, find $|AB|$. Show your work.

33. Using the formula area of a triangle, $A = \sqrt{s(s-a)(s-b)(s-c)}$, where $s = \dfrac{a+b+c}{2}$, calculate the area of the following triangles.

(i)

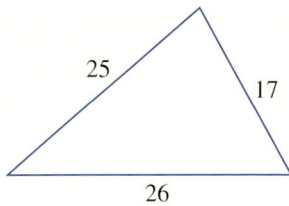

(ii)

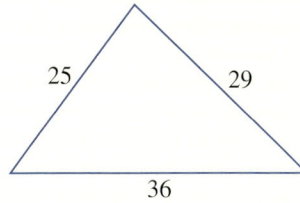

34. **(i)** Using the formula $A = \sqrt{s(s-a)(s-b)(s-c)}$, where $s = \dfrac{a+b+c}{2}$, find the area of an equilateral triangle that has sides equal to 10 cm. Leave your answer in surd form.

(ii) Hence, using the formula $A = \frac{1}{2}bh$, find the vertical height of the triangle in the form of $a\sqrt{b}$.

(iii) Using the formula $A = \frac{1}{2}ab \sin C$ or otherwise, verify that any of the angles is 60°.

35. The diagram shows a porthole on a ship. C_1 represents the outside of the porthole and C_2 represents the glass. If the square $ABCD$ is inscribed inside the larger circle C_1 and the smaller circle C_2 is inscribed inside the same square, show that the area of the outside circle (C_1) is exactly twice the area of the glass (C_2).

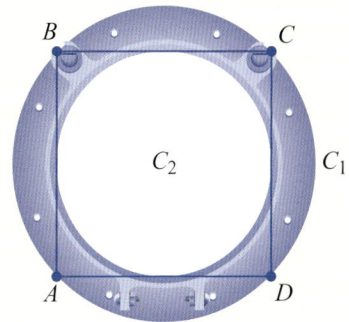

36. A rectangular block of cheese measures 8 cm × 8 cm × 4 cm. One corner is cut away from the block in such a way that three of the edges are cut through their midpoints A, B and C.

(i) Find the lengths of the sides $[AB]$, $[AC]$ and $[BC]$ in surd form.

(ii) Find the area of the triangular face ABC created by the cut.

Give all answers exactly.

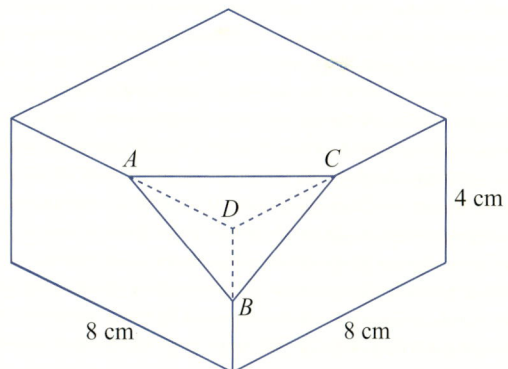

37. A two-person tent has a rectangular base of 6·3 m by 3·2 m. The vertical height of the tent is 7 m.

   (i) Calculate the slant length of the tent, $|EC|$, correct to two decimal places.

   (ii) Using the formula $A = \sqrt{s(s-a)(s-b)(s-c)}$, where $s = \dfrac{a+b+c}{2}$, or otherwise, calculate, to the nearest square metre, the minimum amount of canvas needed to make this tent (including the base).

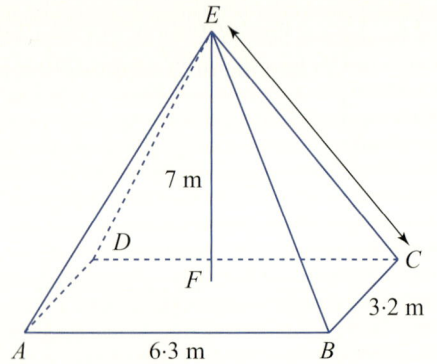

38. The diagram shows a crystal pyramid of rectangular base and slant height of 28 mm.

   (i) Clearly outline the steps required for finding the vertical height of this crystal.

   (ii) Calculate the vertical height of the crystal, correct to one decimal place.

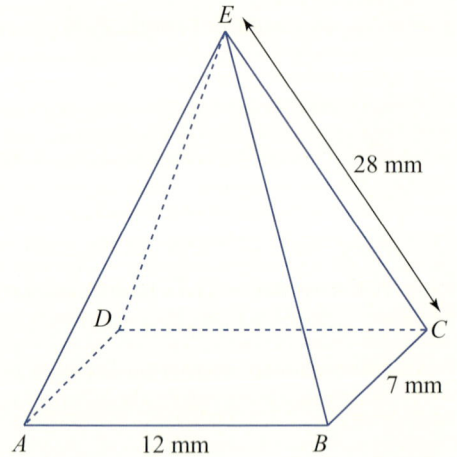

39. State the four cases of similar triangles.

40. Show that each pair of triangles below are similar.

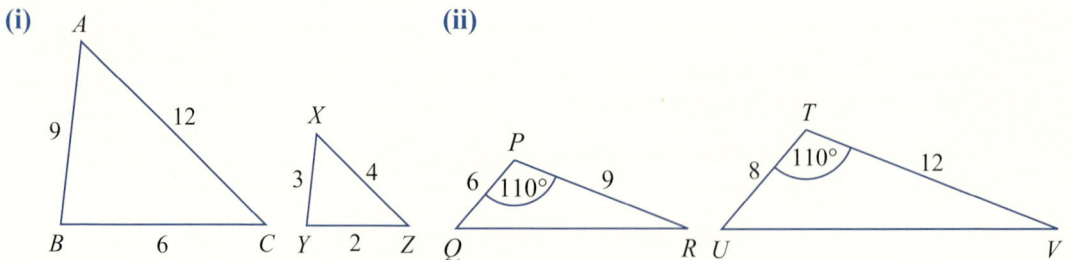

   (i)

   (ii)

41. Give one reason why each pair of triangles is not similar.

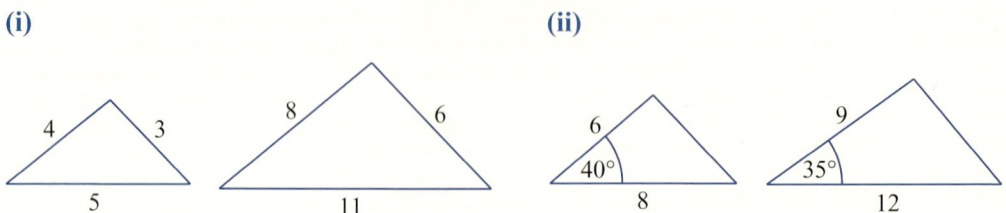

   (i)

   (ii)

42. Each pair of triangles are similar, with equal angles marked. In each case, calculate the lengths p and q (all dimensions are in centimetres and diagrams are not drawn to scale).

(i)

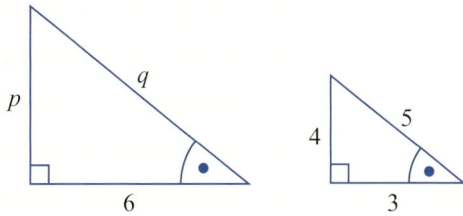

(ii)

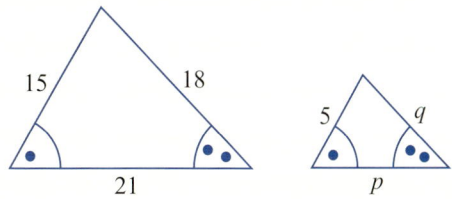

(iii)

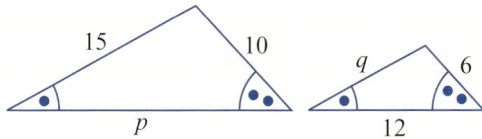

(iv)

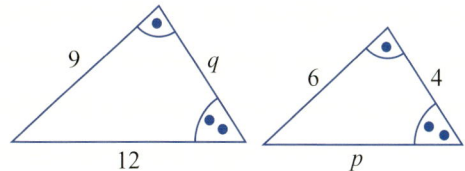

43. **(i)** In $\triangle ABC$, $XY \parallel BC$. Prove that $\triangle ABC$ and $\triangle AXY$ are similar.

(ii) If $|AX| = 4$ cm, $|XB| = 2$ cm, $|AY| = 6$ cm and $|BC| = 12$ cm, find **(a)** $|YC|$ and **(b)** $|XY|$.

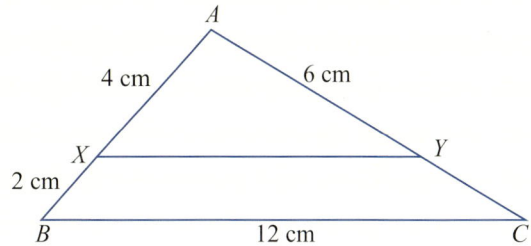

44. In $\triangle STR$, $XY \parallel ST$.

(i) Explain why $\triangle STR$ and $\triangle XYR$ are similar.

(ii) $|SX| = 4$ cm, $|RY| = 12$ cm and $|SR| = 12$ cm. Calculate $|XR|$.

(iii) Calculate **(a)** $|TR|$ **(b)** $|YT|$.

(iv) If $|XY| = 6$ cm, calculate $|ST|$.

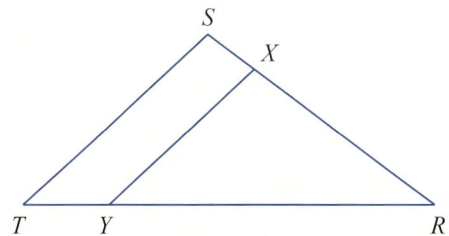

45. In $\triangle ABC$, $XY \parallel BC$ and $|AX| = 3\,|XB|$. $|AB| = 20$ cm, $|AY| = 24$ cm and $|BC| = 36$ cm. Calculate the following.

(i) $|AX|$

(ii) $|YC|$

(iii) $|AC|$

(iv) $|XY|$

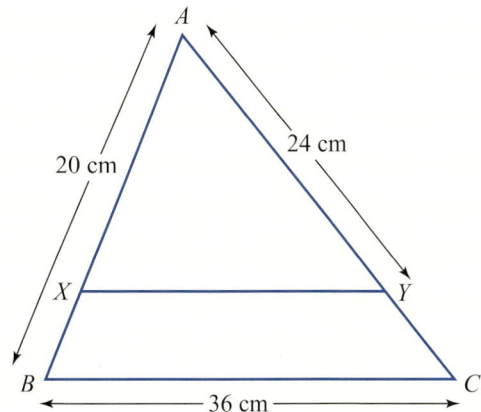

46. In the diagram,

$|\angle BAC| = |\angle DEC|, |AB| = 3$ cm,

$|BC| = 6$ cm, $|CD| = 4$ cm

and $|CE| = 5$ cm.

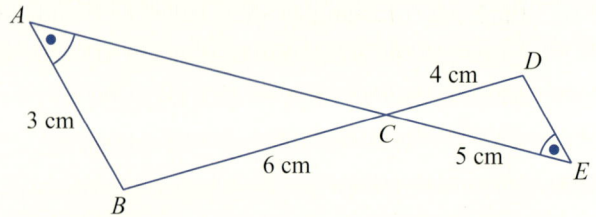

(i) Explain why $\triangle ABC$ and $\triangle EDC$ are similar.

(ii) Calculate **(a)** $|DE|$ **(b)** $|AC|$.

47. A 15 m ladder leans against a vertical wall. The foot of the ladder is 4·2 m from the base of the wall on level ground.

(i) How far up the wall is the ladder?

(ii) A person is two-thirds of the way up the ladder.

(a) How far above the ground is the person?

(b) How far away from the wall is the person?

48. The diagram shows how a camera lens works. Two similar triangles are formed. The actual height of the man is 180 cm. His image in the camera is 4·5 cm tall. Calculate:

(i) The distance the man is from the camera (X)

(ii) The distance the image is from the lens

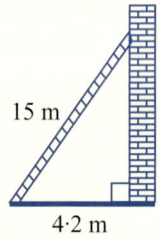

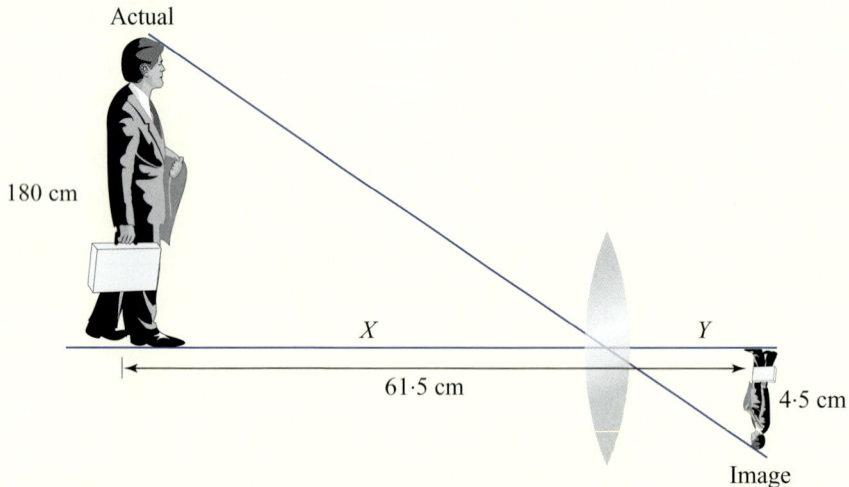

49. A vertical wall 6 m high casts a shadow 180 cm wide on level ground. If Carol is 160 cm tall, how far away from the wall can she stand and still be entirely in the shade?

50. Jane is a distance of 800 m from a cliff. She holds a ruler 60 cm in front of her eyes, as illustrated in the diagram.

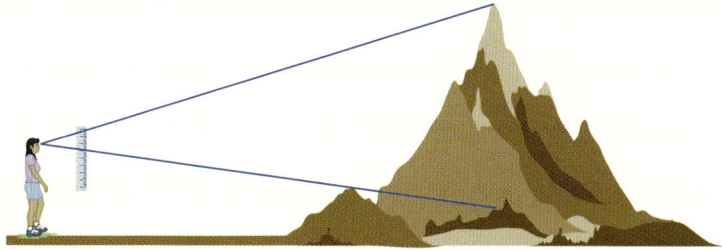

Jane sees that the top and bottom points of the cliff line up with marks separated by 9 cm on the ruler.

What is the approximate height of the cliff?

51. A swimming pool is being filled. Find the length, l m, of the surface of the water when the pool has been filled to a depth of 3 m.

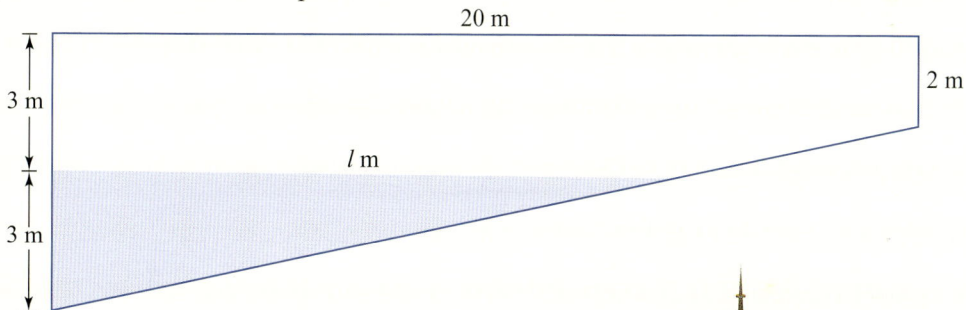

20 m

2 m

3 m

l m

3 m

52. A park wishes to build a bandstand, similar to the one shown.

The bandstand is to be octagonal in shape and therefore the roof consists of two similar regular octagons.

The length of the diagonal of the larger octagon is 20 m.
The reduction factor is $\frac{3}{5}$.

Diagram of the structure of the roof:

    (i) Use trigonometry to calculate the length of one side of the larger octagon to the nearest cm.

  (ii) Using similar triangles or otherwise, calculate the length of one side of the smaller octagon to the nearest cm.

 (iii) What length of wood, to the nearest metre, is required to construct both octagons and the diagonals?

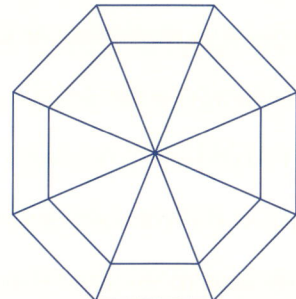

53. A research team wishes to determine the altitude of a mountain as follows. They use a light source at L, mounted on a structure of height 2 m, to shine a beam of light through the top of a pole P' through the top of the mountain M'.

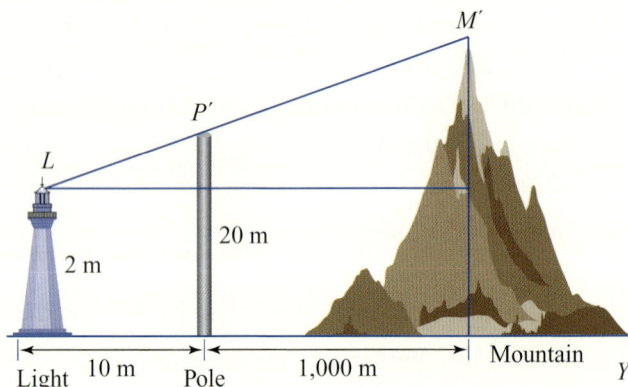

The height of the pole is 20 m. The distance between the altitude of the mountain and the pole is 1,000 m. The distance between the pole and the light is 10 m.

We assume that the light source mount, the pole and the altitude of the mountain are in the same plane.

Find the altitude, h, of the mountain.

Proofs: If a question says 'prove', 'verify' or 'show', then each statement made must be justified with a comment.

54. The line l bisects $\angle ABD$ and the line k bisects $\angle CBD$.
Prove that $l \perp k$.

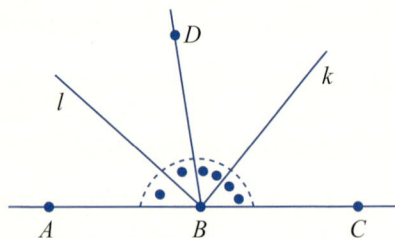

55. In the diagram, $|\angle QPR| = 2x°$ and $|\angle PQR| = (90 - x)°$.
Prove that $|PQ| = |PR|$.

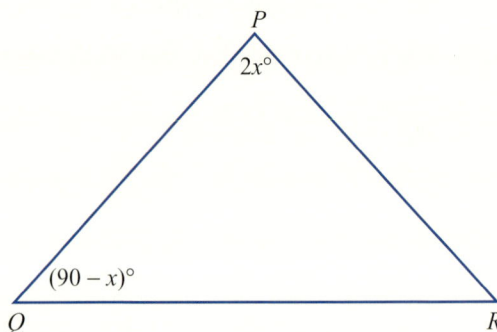

56. In the diagram, $PQ \perp QR$ and $|\angle APB| = |\angle CRQ| = 75°$.

Prove that $PS \perp RS$.

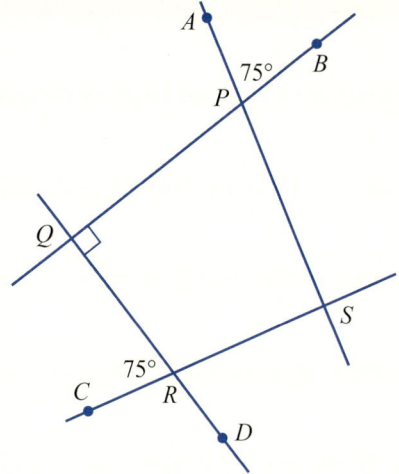

57. $[DM]$ and $[CB]$ are diameters of a circle, centre O.

AB and PM are tangents at B and M, respectively.

Show that $|\angle PMC| = |\angle ABD|$.

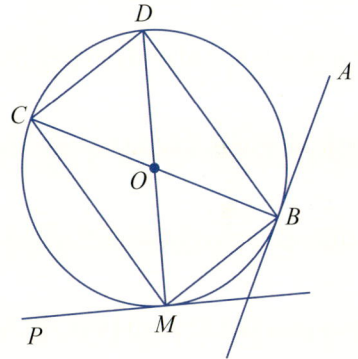

58. The indicated angles in the diagram are equal.

Prove that $[PR]$ is a diameter of the circle.

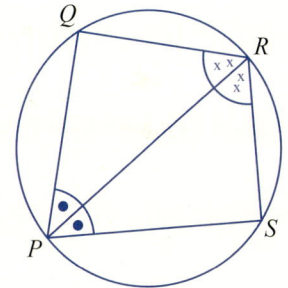

59. The circles h and k have diameters $[AB]$ and $[AC]$, respectively. Prove that EB is parallel to DC.

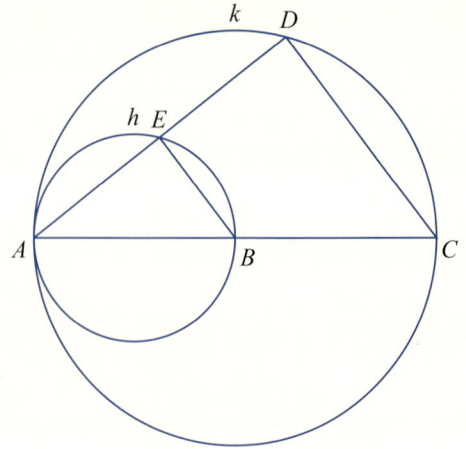

60. P, Q, R and S are points on a circle. If $PQ \parallel SR$, prove that $|\angle PSR| = |\angle QRS|$.

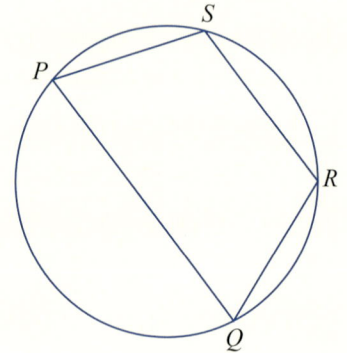

61. State the four cases for congruent triangles.

62. **(i)** Is $\triangle ABC \equiv \triangle PQR$?

   Explain your answer.

   (ii) If the triangles are not congruent, write down one extra piece of information you would need to be given for the triangles to be congruent.

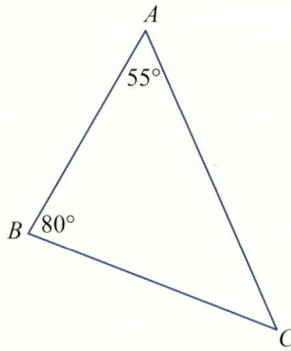

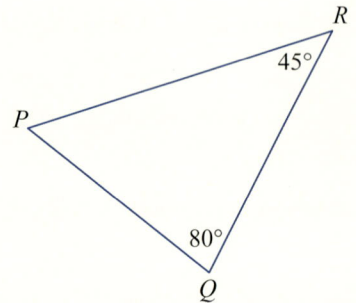

63. $PQRS$ is a parallelogram with diagonals intersecting at T.

   (i) Prove that diagonal $[PR]$ bisects the area of parallelogram $PQRS$.

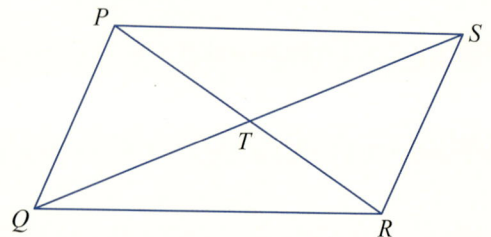

   (ii) Prove that $|QT| = |ST|$.

64. In the diagram, $|PS| = |RS|$ and $|\angle PSQ| = |\angle RSQ|$.

    (i) Prove that $\triangle PQS \equiv \triangle RQS$.

    (ii) Hence, show that $\triangle PQR$ is isosceles.

    (iii) Prove that $PR \perp QS$.

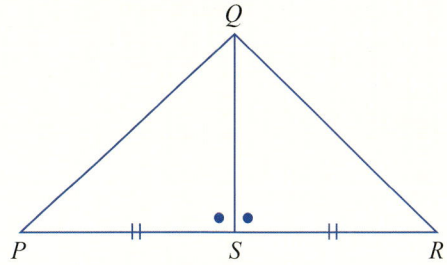

65. In $\triangle ABC$, $|DC| = |EC|$ and $|\angle 1| = |\angle 2|$.
Prove that $|AC| = |BC|$.

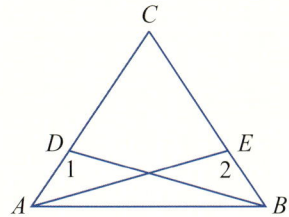

66. PQ is a diameter of a circle K. R is a point such that $|PR| = |PQ|$.

    Prove that K bisects $[RQ]$ at S.

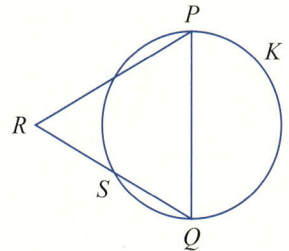

67. In $\triangle PQR$, MN is drawn such that $|\angle PQR| = |\angle PNM|$.

    (i) Prove that $\triangle PQR$ and $\triangle PNM$ are similar.

    (ii) Prove that $\dfrac{|PQ|}{|PN|} = \dfrac{|PR|}{|PM|}$.

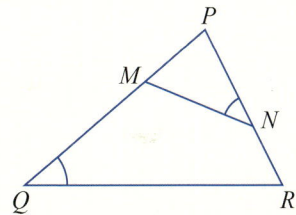

68. $|\angle ABC| = |\angle RST| = 40°$ and $|\angle BCA| + |\angle STR| = 140°$.

    (i) Show that $|\angle BAC| = |\angle STR|$.

    (ii) Hence or otherwise, show that $\dfrac{|AB|}{|TS|} = \dfrac{|BC|}{|RS|}$.

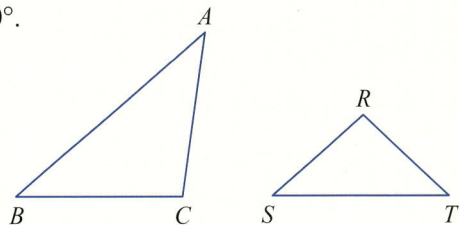

69. $[PQ]$ is the diameter of circle k_1.

$[PS]$ is the diameter of circle k_2.

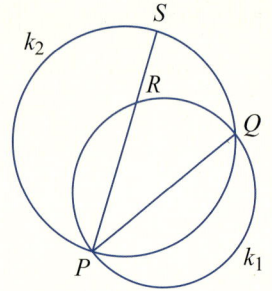

    (i) Explain why $|\angle PRQ| = |\angle PQS|$.

    (ii) Show that $\triangle PQR$ and $\triangle PSQ$ are similar.

    (iii) Redraw $\triangle PQR$ and $\triangle PSQ$ so that corresponding angles or sides match each other.

    (iv) Prove that $|PQ|^2 = |PR| \times |PS|$.

70. Two chords, PQ and RS, of a circle meet in T such that $|\angle SRP| = |\angle QRT|$.

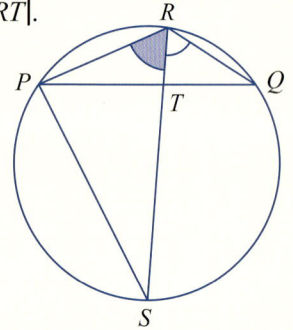

    (i) Explain why the triangles SRP and QRT are equiangular.

    (ii) Complete the ratio $\dfrac{|PR|}{|RS|} = \dfrac{|RT|}{|??|}$.

    (iii) Prove that $|PR| \times |RQ| = |RT|^2 + |PT| \times |TQ|$.

71. In the $\triangle PQR$, $BC \parallel QR$ and $AC \parallel BR$.

Prove that $\dfrac{|PB|}{|BQ|} = \dfrac{|PA|}{|AB|}$.

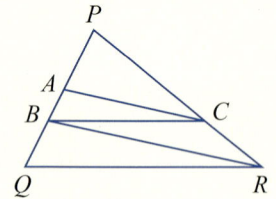

72. c_1 and c_2 are two circles. O is the centre of c_1 and $[OA]$ is the diameter of c_2. The chord $[AB]$ intersects c_2 at X.

Prove that $|AX| = |XB|$.

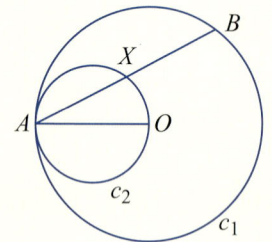

73. $ABCD$ and $BDEF$ are rectangles and ECF is a straight line.

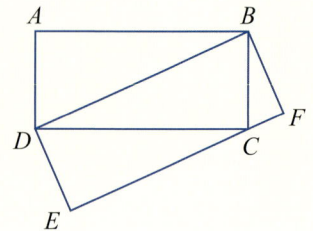

Prove that:

    (i) $|\angle ADB| = |\angle CDE|$

    (ii) Triangles ABD, ECD and FBC are similar

    (iii) The rectangles are equal in area

    (iv) $\dfrac{|CE|}{|CF|} = \dfrac{|AB|^2}{|AD|^2}$

74. $[PQ]$ is the diameter of circle K_1 and $[PS]$ is the diameter of circle K_2.

Prove that $|PR| \times |PS| = |PQ|^2$.

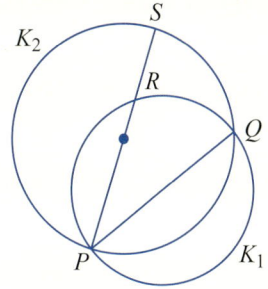

75. The $\triangle PQR$ has lengths of sides as shown, where $[PR]$ is the largest side.

Prove that $[PQ] \perp [QR]$.

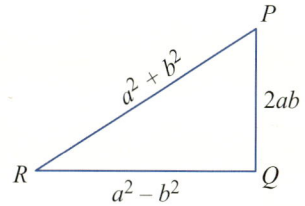

76. $ABCD$ is a quadrilateral in which
AC is perpendicular to BD.

  (i) Why is $|AB|^2 = |AM|^2 + |BM|^2$?

  (ii) Hence, prove that $|AB|^2 + |CD|^2 = |AD|^2 + |BC|^2$.

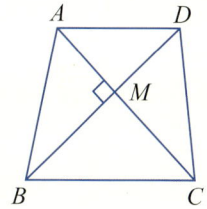

77. In $\triangle ABC$, $|\angle BAC| = 90°$ and $AD \perp BC$.

  (i) Using equiangular triangles or otherwise, prove that $|AB|^2 = |BD| \times |BC|$.

  (ii) Write down two ratios equal to $\dfrac{|AD|}{|BD|}$.

  (iii) If $|AC| = 2|AB|$ and $|AD| = 4$, find the value of $|AB|$.

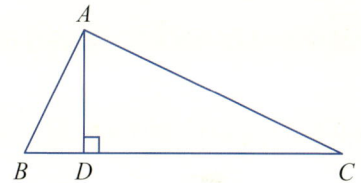

78. In $\triangle PQR$, $PS \perp RQ$.

  (i) Use $|RS| = |RQ| - |QS|$ to write an expression for $|RS|^2$.

  (ii) Deduce that $|RP|^2 = |RQ|^2 + |QP|^2 - 2|QR| \times |QS|$.

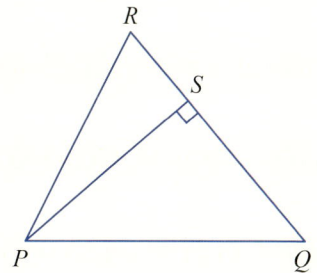

79. The diagram shows two circles. The larger circle has centre a and radius R. The smaller circle has centre b and radius r.

Show that the distance X is $2\sqrt{Rr}$.

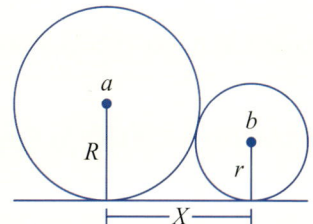

Angle-side relationship in a triangle and triangle inequality

Angle-side relationship in a triangle

> In a triangle, the angle opposite the greater of two sides is greater than the angle opposite the lesser side.

In $\triangle ABC$,

if $\qquad |AC| > |AB|$,

then $\qquad |\angle B| > |\angle C|$.

Conversely,

if $\qquad |\angle B| > |\angle C|$,

then $\qquad |AC| > |AB|$.

In other words, the greatest angle is opposite the longest side and the smallest angle is opposite the shortest side and vice versa. What can you say about the other angle and the other side?

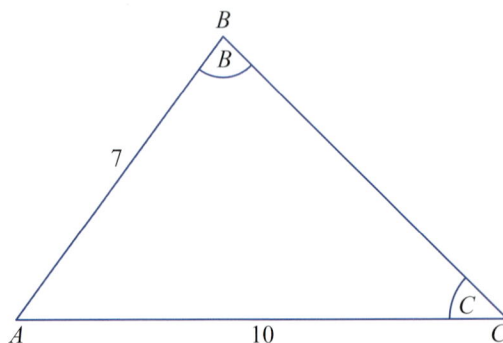

EXAMPLE 1

In $\triangle ABC$, $|AB| = 10$, $|AC| = 8$ and $|BC| = 7$.

(i) Which angle is the greatest?

(ii) Which angle is the smallest?

(iii) What can you say about the remaining angle?

Solution:

Label angles A, B and C.

(i) $\angle C$ is the greatest angle because it is opposite the longest side.

(ii) $\angle A$ is the smallest angle because it is opposite the shortest side.

(iii) $\angle B$ is less than $\angle C$ and $\angle B$ is greater than $\angle A$. Alternatively, $|\angle C| < |\angle B| < |\angle A|$.

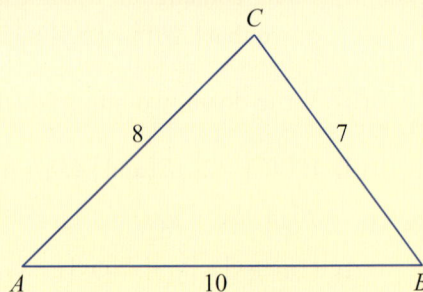

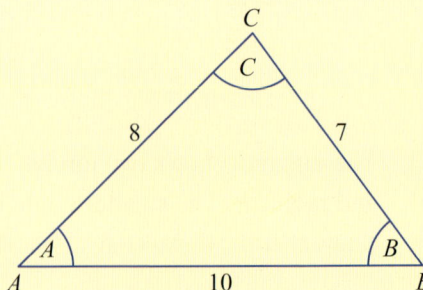

Triangle inequality

The lengths of any two sides of a triangle added together are **always** greater than the length of the third side.

The converse is also true:

If two lengths added together are less than or equal to a third length, then the three lengths **cannot** form a triangle.

Quick check: The two shorter sides added together must be greater than the longest side, otherwise a triangle **cannot** be drawn.

For the triangle on the right:
- $a + b > c$
- $a + c > b$
- $b + c > a$

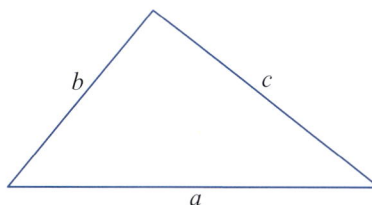

EXAMPLE 2

Find the range of values of k for which $\triangle ABC$ can be constructed.

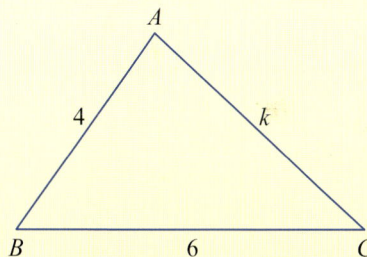

Solution:

The triangle inequality gives us three separate inequalities to solve:

1. $k + 4 > 6$
   $k > 2$

2. $k + 6 > 4$
   $k > -2$
   (length can't be negative)

3. $6 + 4 > k$
   $10 > k$
   $k < 10$

Combining **1** and **3**: $2 < k < 10$.
The length k is greater than 2 and less than 10.

Exercise 6.2

1. Copy and complete each of the following.

   (i) If one side of a triangle is longer than a second side, then the larger angle is opposite the _____ side.

   (ii) The sum of the lengths of any two sides of a triangle is _____ than the length of the third side.

2. In $\triangle ABC$, $|\angle BAC| = 56°$ and $|\angle ABC| = 72°$. Which is the shortest side? Justify your answer.

3. In $\triangle PQR$, $|\angle RPQ| = 54°$ and $|\angle RPQ| > |\angle PQR|$. Name the shortest side. Justify your answer.

Is it possible for a triangle to have the sides with the given lengths in questions 4–9? In each case, justify your answer.

4. 2, 6, 7	5. 2, 3, 7	6. 5, 12, 8
7. 9, 6, 2	8. 9, 8, 7	9. 1, 1, 3

10. A woman wants to build a triangular-shaped rockery in her back garden. To fit in with the rest of her garden, she wants the measurements of the rockery to be 6 m by 10 m by 3 m. Is it possible to construct this rockery to the given dimensions? Justify your answer.

11. Two sides of an isosceles triangle measure 3 cm and 10 cm. What is the possible length of the third side? Justify your answer.

12. Two sides of an isosceles triangle measure 4 cm and 9 cm. What is the possible length of the third side? Justify your answer.

13. In each of the following, find the range of values of k for which the triangle can be constructed.

   (i)
   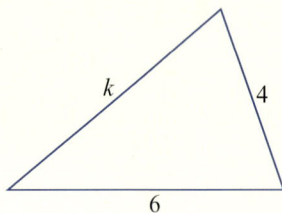

   (ii)
   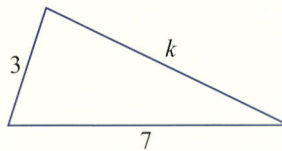

   (iii)
   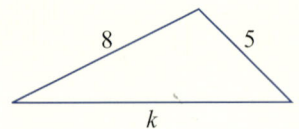

14. **(i)** Two sides of a triangle have lengths 8 cm and 10 cm. The length of the third side can be any length between a cm and b cm. Find the value of a and the value of b.

   (ii) If the third side must be a whole number, find the minimum value and the maximum value.

15. You live 6 km from the shopping centre, S, and 4 km from your friend's house, F. The distance from your friend's house to the shopping centre is x km.

   (i) Write an inequality in terms of x that describes the distance between the shopping centre and your friend's house.

   (ii) Write an inequality in terms of x that describes the distance you travel if you go to your friend's house first and then to the shopping centre.

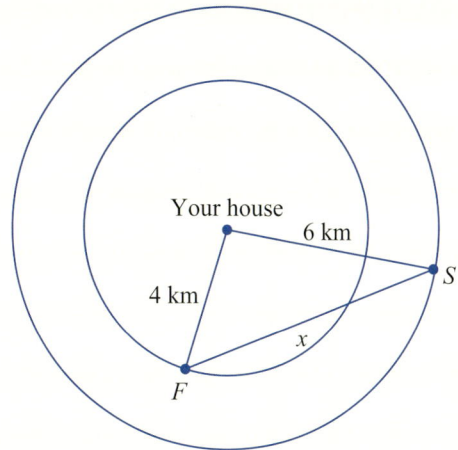

16. A bird is perched on a wire such that it is 14 m from its nest and 25 m from a bird feeder.

   (i) Write down an inequality that describes the distance, X, between the nest and the bird feeder.

   (ii) Write an inequality that describes the total distance travelled, D, if the bird flies to the bird feeder and takes the food directly back to his nest.

   (iii) Draw a diagram showing the relative positions of the bird feeder, the nest and the bird if the distance X is at its maximum value. What one word could you use to describe their relative positions in this case?

17. A ship at sea is 22 km from port A and 15 km from a lighthouse.

   (i) Write down an inequality that describes the distance, D, between port A and the lighthouse.

   (ii) After moving for 2 hours at 5 km/hr, the ship is now 14 km from port A and 8 km from the lighthouse. Write down a new inequality that describes the distance, D, between port A and the lighthouse.

   (iii) Using the cosine rule three times, calculate the distance, D, between port A and the lighthouse to the nearest kilometre.

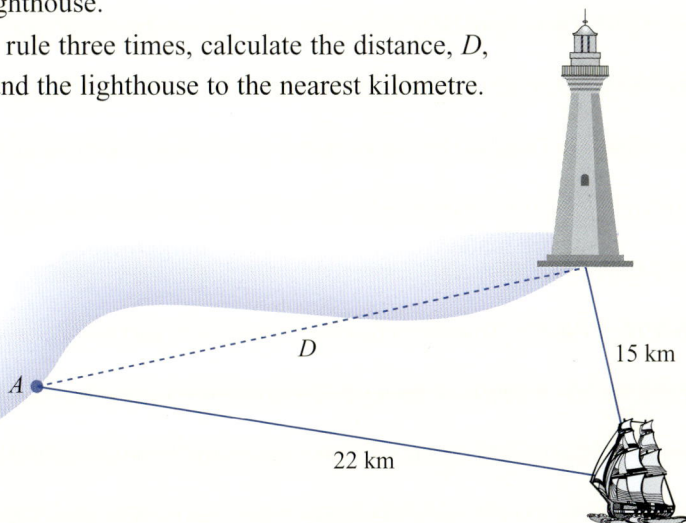

Enlargements

An **enlargement** changes the size of a shape to give a similar image. To enlarge a shape, we need:

1. A centre of enlargement.   **2.** A scale factor.

When a shape is enlarged, all lengths are multiplied by the scale factor and all angles remain unchanged. A slide projector makes an enlargement of a shape. In this case, the light bulb is the **centre of enlargement**.

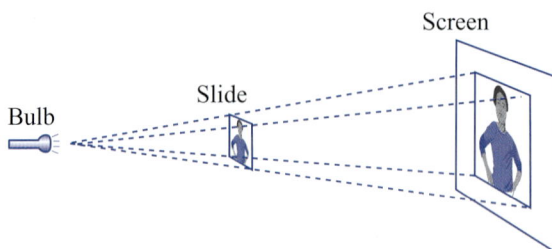

Ray method

In the diagram below, the triangle ABC is the **object** (the starting shape) and the triangle $A'B'C'$ is the **image** (the enlarged shape) under an enlargement, centre O, and a scale factor of 2.

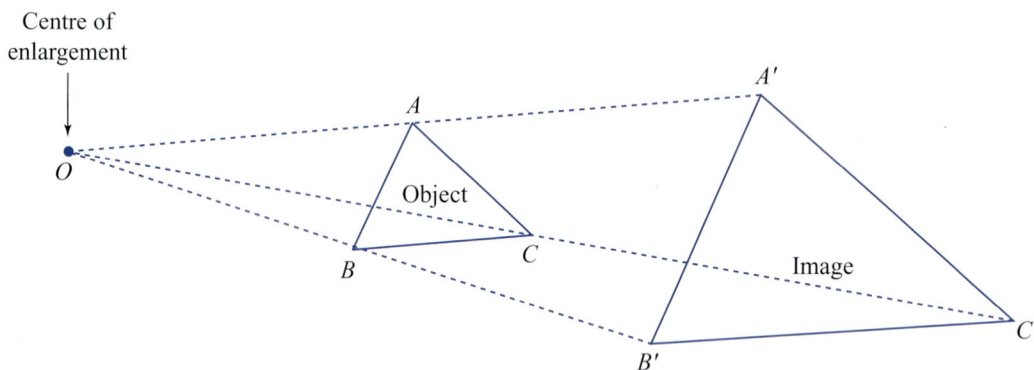

The rays have been drawn from the centre of enlargement, O, to each vertex and beyond. The distance from the centre of enlargement, O, to each vertex on triangle ABC was measured and multiplied by 2. Thus, $|OA'| = 2|OA|$, $|OB'| = 2|OB|$ and $|OC'| = 2|OC|$.

Note: All measurements are made from the centre of enlargement, O.

Properties of enlargements:

1. The shape of the image is the same as the shape of the object (only the size has changed).
2. The amount by which a figure is enlarged is called the **scale factor** and is denoted by k.
3. Image length = k(object length)   or $k = \dfrac{\text{image length}}{\text{object length}}$.
4. Area of image = k^2(area object)   or $k^2 = \dfrac{\text{area of image}}{\text{area of object}}$.

Notes:
1. The scale factor can be less than 1 (i.e. $0 < k < 1$). In these cases, the image will be smaller than the object. Though smaller, the image is still called an enlargement.
2. The centre of enlargement can be a vertex on the object figure, inside it or outside.

To find the centre of enlargement, do the following.

1. Choose two points on the image and their corresponding points on the original figure.
2. From each of these points on the larger figure, draw a line to the corresponding point on the smaller figure.
3. Produce these lines until they intersect at the point that is the centre of enlargement.

EXAMPLE 1

Triangle PQR is the image of triangle ABC under an enlargement. $|AB| = 8$ and $|PR| = 24$. The scale factor of enlargement is 1·5.

(i) Copy the diagram and show how to find the centre of enlargement, O.

(ii) Find **(a)** $|PQ|$ **(b)** $|AC|$.

(iii) If the area of $\triangle ABC$ is 16·4 square units, calculate the area of $\triangle PQR$.

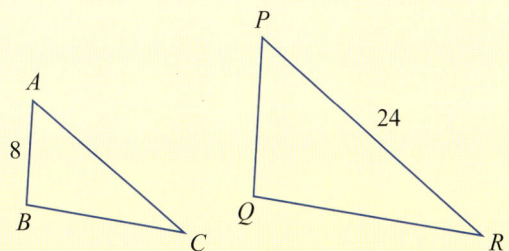

Solution:

(i) Join P to A and continue beyond.
Join R to C and continue beyond.
Continue these lines until they meet.
This is the centre of enlargement, O.

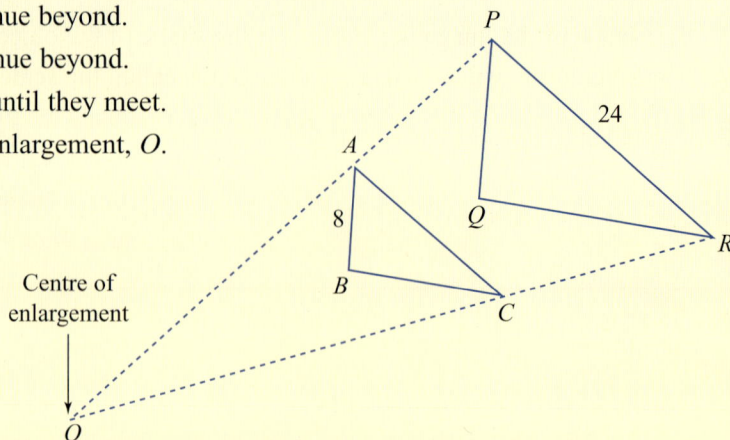

Centre of enlargement

(ii)

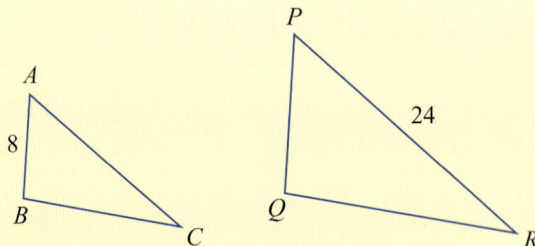

Image length = k(object length)

(a) $|PQ| = k|AB|$
$|PQ| = 1 \cdot 5(8)$
$|PQ| = 12$

(b) $|PR| = k|AC|$
$24 = 1 \cdot 5|AC|$
$16 = |AC|$
(divide both sides by $1 \cdot 5$)

(iii) $\therefore$ Area of image = k^2(area of object)
Area of $\triangle PQR = (1 \cdot 5)^2$ (area of $\triangle ABC$)
Area of $\triangle PQR = (2 \cdot 25)\,(16 \cdot 4)$
Area of $\triangle PQR = 36 \cdot 9$

EXAMPLE 2

The triangle *ORS* is the image of the triangle *OPQ* under an enlargement. $|OP| = 6$ and $|PR| = 7 \cdot 5$.

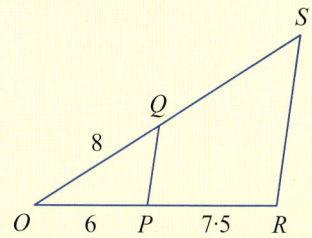

(i) Write down the centre of enlargement.

(ii) Find *k*, the scale factor of enlargement.

(iii) If $|OQ| = 8$, find $|QS|$.

Solution:

(i) The centre of enlargement is the point *O* (as *O* is common to both triangles). Divide the figure into two separate similar triangles. Mark in known lengths.

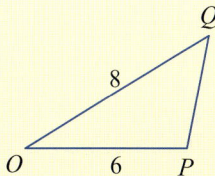

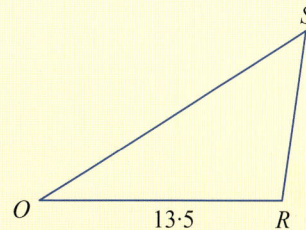

(ii) Scale factor $= k = \dfrac{\text{image length}}{\text{object length}}$

$$= \frac{|OR|}{|OP|}$$

$$= \frac{13 \cdot 5}{6} = 2 \cdot 25$$

(iii) Image length $= k(\text{object length})$

$$|OS| = k|OQ|$$

$$= 2 \cdot 25(8) = 18$$

$$|QS| = |OS| - |OQ| = 18 - 8 = 10$$

EXAMPLE 3

The rectangle *PQRS* is the image of the rectangle *ABCD* under an enlargement, centre *O*. If the area of *PQRS* is 121 cm² and the area of *ABCD* is 25 cm², find the scale factor of enlargement, *k*.

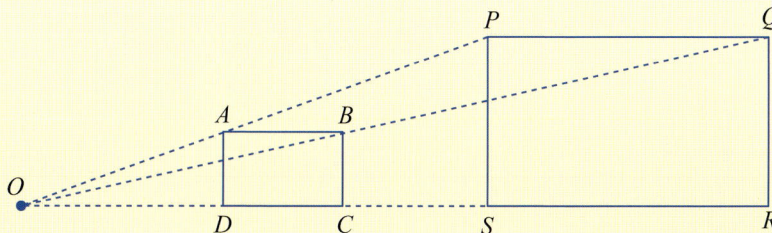

Solution:

$$(\text{Area of image}) = k^2(\text{area of object})$$

$$\therefore \text{Area of rectangle } PQRS = k^2(\text{area of rectangle } ABCD)$$

$$121 = k^2(25) \quad \text{(put in known values)}$$

$$4{\cdot}84 = k^2 \quad \text{(divide both sides by 25)}$$

$$\sqrt{4{\cdot}84} = k \quad \text{(take the square root of both sides)}$$

$$2{\cdot}2 = k$$

Thus, the scale factor of enlargement is 2·2.

Exercise 6.3

1. Triangle PQR is the image of triangle ABC under an enlargement.
   $|PR| = 8, |AC| = 4, |AB| = 3$ and $|QR| = 4$.

   (i) Write down the centre of enlargement.

   (ii) Find the scale factor of enlargement, k.

   (iii) Find **(a)** $|PQ|$ **(b)** $|BC|$.

   (iv) If the area of triangle ABC is 3 square units, find the area of triangle PQR.

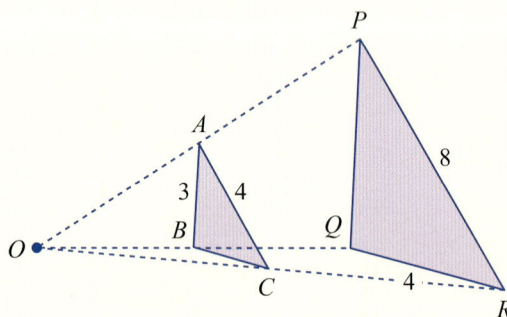

2. Triangle XYZ is the image of triangle ABC under the enlargement, centre O, with $|AB| = 4$ and $|XZ| = 12$. The scale factor of the enlargement is 1·5.

   (i) Find $|XY|$.

   (ii) Find $|AC|$.

   (iii) If the area of triangle ABC is 12·2 square units, calculate the area of triangle XYZ.

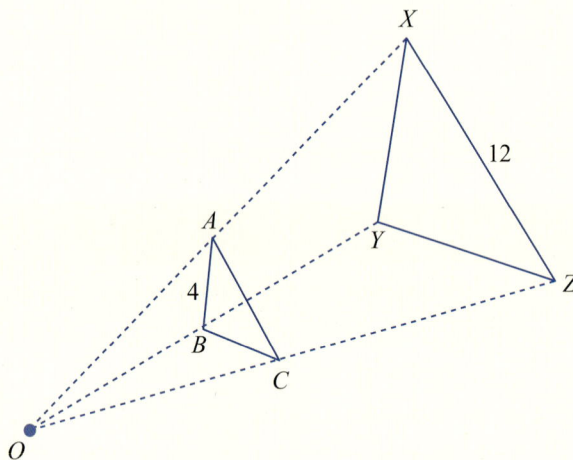

3. Triangle *OCD* is the image of triangle *OAB* under an enlargement, centre *O*, with $|OA| = 2$ and $|AC| = 3$.

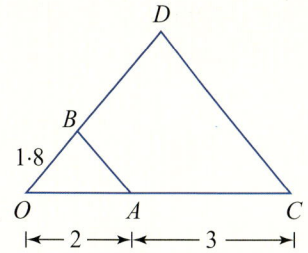

(i) Find the scale factor of the enlargement.

(ii) If $|OB| = 1\cdot8$, find $|BD|$.

(iii) Calculate $|AB| : |CD|$.

(iv) If the area of triangle *OCD* is 12·5 square units, find the area of triangle *OAB*.

4.

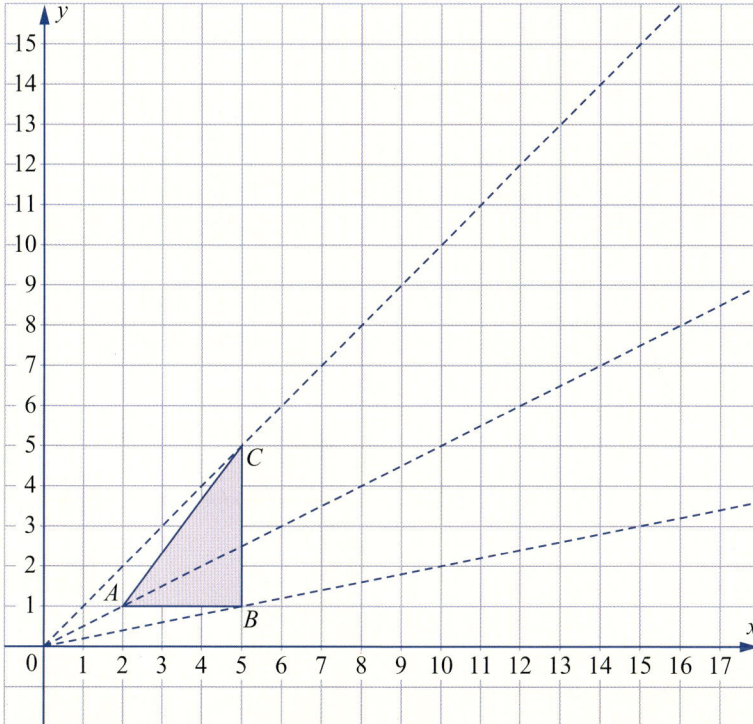

(i) Write down the coordinates of the points *A*, *B* and *C*.

(ii) Triangle *PQR* is the image of triangle *ABC* by a scale factor of 3 from the centre of enlargement *O* (0, 0). Using the rays or otherwise, find the coordinates of *P*, *Q* and *R*.

(iii) Calculate (a) $|AC|$ (b) $|PR|$ (c) $|AC| : |PR|$.

(iv) Calculate the ratio of the area of $\triangle PQR$: area of $\triangle ABC$.

5. Triangle *OAB* is the image of triangle *OXY* under the enlargement, centre *O*, with $|XY| = 8, |OX| = 10$ and $|AB| = 18$.

   (i) Find the scale factor of the enlargement.

   (ii) Find $|XA|$.

   (iii) The area of triangle *OAB* is 101·25 square units. Find the area of triangle *OXY*.

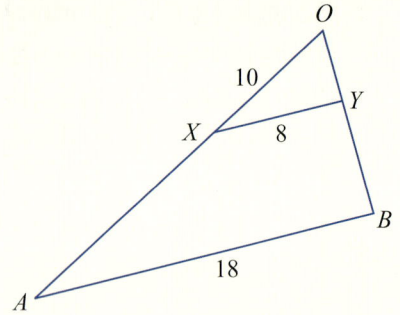

6. A woman spent €400 on a carpet for a bedroom. The cost is proportional to the area of the floor. She wants to carpet the living room in the house. Both the bedroom and the living room floors have the same shape. Each length of the living room is 1·6 times larger than the corresponding length in the bedroom. Calculate how much it will cost to carpet the living room.

7. Kenny painted two similar rooms with the same paint. One tin of paint can cover roughly 10 m². The smaller of the two rooms needed exactly two tins of paint. Each length in the larger room is 1·5 times larger than the corresponding length in the smaller room. How many tins of paint did Kenny need to paint the larger room?

8. The sauce bottles are similar, with heights as shown. The smaller bottle has a label of area 50 cm². What is the area of the label on the larger bottle? Show your work.

9. Vase *A* and vase *B* are similar.
   Vase *A* is 8 cm in height.
   The total surface of vase *A* is 60 cm².
   The total surface of vase *B* is 375 cm².
   Find the height of vase *B*.

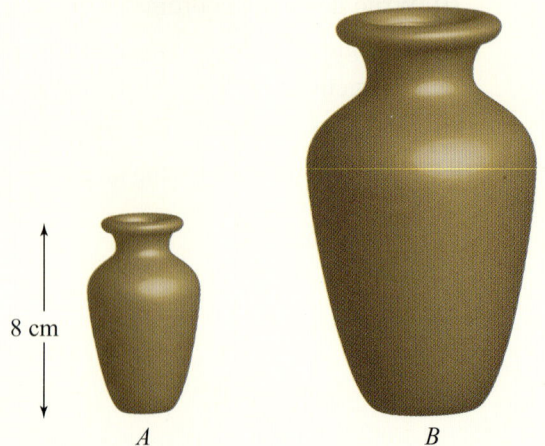

10. Russian dolls are wooden dolls that fit inside each other. All dolls are similar.

The smallest Russian doll out of a set of three is 6 cm tall and the medium doll is 9 cm tall.

  (i) Find the scale factor, K.

  (ii) Find the height of the tallest doll if the scale factor is consistent.

 (iii) If the surface area of the smallest doll is 75 cm^2, find the surface area of the two larger dolls.

11. These two milk jugs are similar. Jug A is 28 cm tall and jug B is 17·5 cm tall.

If jug A has a surface area of 1,100 cm^2, find the surface area of jug B to the nearest square centimetre.

12. The enlargement reading on a photocopier is 100% when the copy is to be the same size as the original. When the reading is 110%, then each length is increased by 10%.

  (i) What enlargement reading do you use if you want:

   (a) Each length decreased by 30%

   (b) An 8 cm line increased to 12 cm

   (c) A 15 cm line reduced to 9 cm

  (ii) A shaded area on the original is 50 cm^2. What is the shaded area on the copy when the enlargement reading is **(a)** 120% **(b)** 60%?

 (iii) The ratio 120 : 60 is equal to 2 : 1. Explain why the answers in part **(ii)** are not in the ratio 2 : 1.

  (iv) What percentage, correct to the nearest whole number, would you use on the photocopier to double the size of a document? Justify your answer.

  (v) To exactly double the size of a document, the scale factor of enlargement is $\sqrt{k}$. What is the value of k? Justify your answer in conjunction with the answer in part **(iv)**.

13. The ray method was used to enlarge a design for a Valentine card. The original is labelled A and the image is labelled B.

   (i) Find the centre of enlargement.

   (ii) Find the scale factor of the enlargement. Show your work.

   (iii) Calculate the ratio $\dfrac{\text{Area of drawing } B}{\text{Area of drawing } A}$.

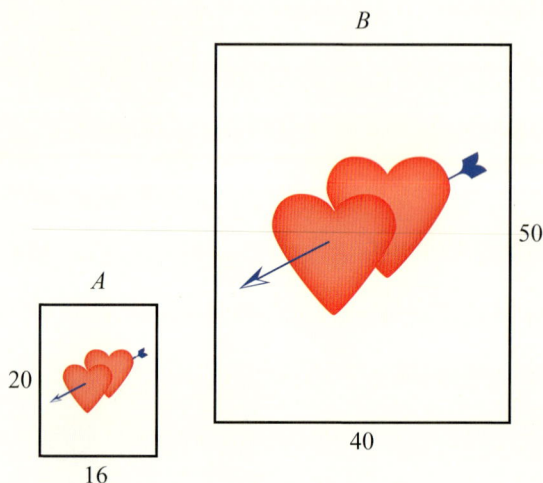

B

A

50

20

40

16

14. (i) Enlarge the rectangle X by scale factor $\frac{2}{3}$ about the origin. Label the image Y.

   (ii) Write down the ratio of the lengths of the sides of rectangle X to the lengths of the sides of rectangle Y.

   (iii) Work out the ratio of the perimeter of rectangle X to the perimeter of rectangle Y.

   (iv) Work out the ratio of the area of rectangle X to the area of rectangle Y.

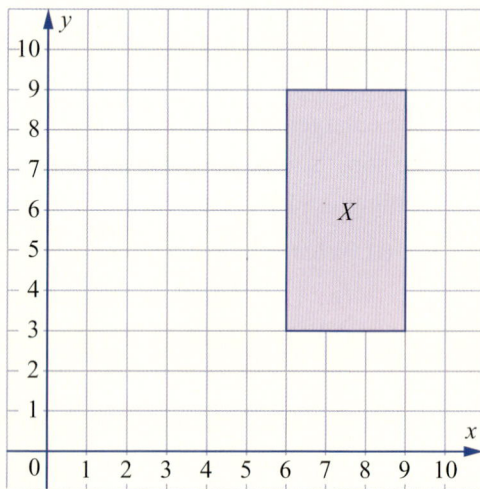

15. A triangle T is drawn on graph paper, as shown.

   (i) Calculate the area of triangle T.

   (ii) Enlarge triangle T by scale factor 2 with (0, 0) as the centre of enlargement. Call this enlarged triangle S.

  (iii) Find the area of triangle S.

  (iv) Find the ratio of the area of triangle S to the area of triangle T.

   (v) Comment on the significance of your answer from part **(iv)**.

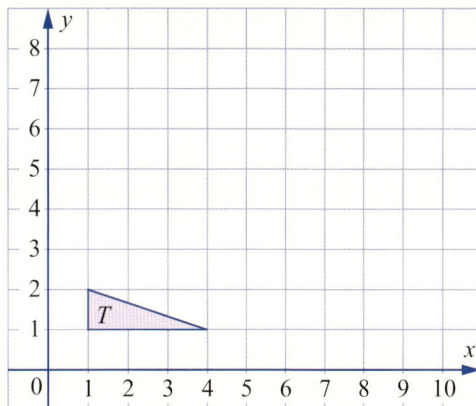

16. The diagram shows shape A, drawn on graph paper.

   (i) Draw the enlargement of shape A with scale factor $K = \frac{1}{3}$ and centre of enlargement (0, 0). Call this new shape B.

  (ii) Calculate the area of shape A.

  (iii) Calculate the area of shape B.

  (iv) Verify that the ratio of the area of shape B to the area of shape A is k^2.

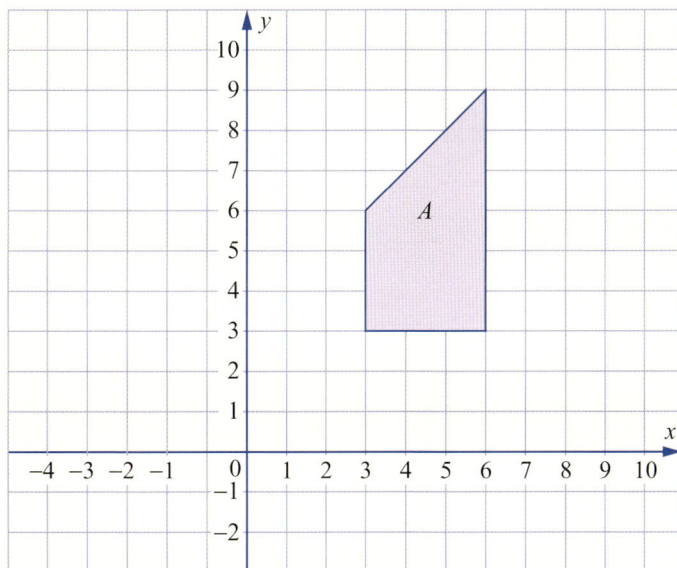

17. Triangle P is an enlargement of the shaded triangle.

    (i) What is the scale factor of the enlargement?
    (ii) What is the centre of the enlargement?

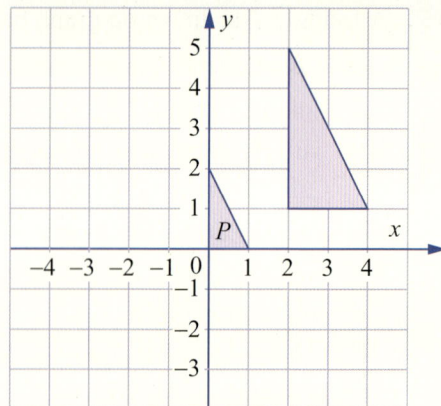

18. If the sides of a rectangular flowerbed measuring 35 m by 40 m are reduced by a scale factor of $\frac{1}{5}$, show that its perimeter is reduced by a scale factor of $\frac{1}{5}$ and that its area is reduced by a scale factor of $\frac{1}{25}$.

19. If the dimensions $L \times W$ of a rectangular card are increased by a scale factor of $\frac{1}{K}$, show that its area is increased by a factor of $\frac{1}{K^2}$.

20. If the dimensions, 10 cm by 12 cm by 16 cm, of a rectangular box are increased by a scale factor of 2, show that its surface area has increased by a scale factor of 4.

21. If the dimensions $L \times W \times H$ of a rectangular box are increased by a factor of K, show that the total surface area is increased by a factor of K^2.

There are 22 constructions on the course.

1. Bisector of an angle, using only a compass and straight edge.
2. Perpendicular bisector of a segment, using only a compass and straight edge.
3. Line perpendicular to a given line *l*, passing through a given point not on *l*.
4. Line perpendicular to a given line *l*, passing through a given point on *l*.
5. Line parallel to given line, through a given line.
6. Division of a line segment into two or three equal segments without measuring it.
7. Division of a line segment into any number of equal segments without measuring it.
8. Line segment of a given length on a given ray.
9. Angle of a given number of degrees with a given ray as one arm.
10. Triangle, given length of three sides (SSS).
11. Triangle, given two sides and the included angle (SAS).
12. Triangle, given two angles and the common side (ASA).
13. Right-angled triangle, given length of hypotenuse and one other side (RHS).
14. Right-angled triangle, given one side and one of the acute angles.
15. Rectangle, given side lengths.
16. Circumcentre and circumcircle of a given triangle, using only a straight edge and compass.
17. Incentre and incircle of a given triangle, using only a straight edge and compass.
18. Angle of 60° without using a protractor or set square.
19. Tangent to a given circle at a given point on it.
20. Parallelogram, given the length of the sides and the measure of the angles.
21. Centroid of a triangle.
22. Orthocentre of a triangle.

You will have completed constructions 1 to 15 on your Higher Level Junior Certificate course. The steps required for constructions 16 to 22 are given below.

Any work involving accurate constructions requires a good pencil, a compass, a ruler and a protractor. It is important not to rub out any construction lines or marks you make at any stage during a construction. All construction lines or marks should **always** be left on the diagram.

Notes:

- A straight edge is like a ruler without any numbers or markings.
- A ruler is a straight edge but has numbers and markings on it.
- When a question requires a straight edge, you can use your ruler but not the numbers or markings on it.

Locus

A locus is a set of points that obey a certain rule. For example:

A circle is the set of points that are the same distance from the centre.	The bisector of an angle is the set of points that are the same distance from the arms of the angle.	A point moves so that it is always the same distance from a line segment.

The following exercise is a revision of the Geometry material covered at Junior Cert Higher Level.

Exercise 7.1

1. Copy these angles into your copybook and using only a compass and straight edge, construct the angle bisector of each of these angles, showing all your construction lines. In each case, use your protractor to check your work.

   (i) 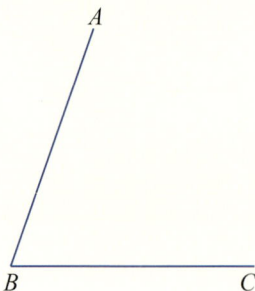 **(ii)** 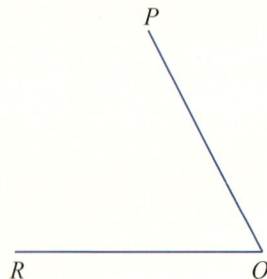 **(iii)**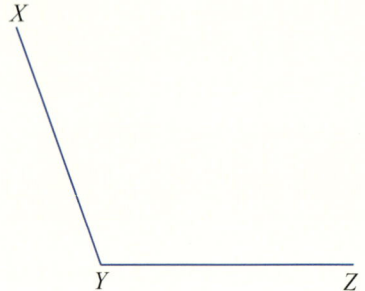

2. Construct each of the following line segments exactly. Using only a compass and straight edge, construct the perpendicular bisector of each line segment, showing all your construction lines. In each case, use your ruler to check your work.

   (i) $|AB| = 8$ cm   **(ii)** $|PQ| = 7$ cm   **(iii)** $|XY| = 64$ mm   **(iv)** $|RS| = 85$ mm

3. (i) Using a compass and straight edge only, construct the perpendicular bisector of the line segment [AB].

   (ii) Mark any point, C, on the perpendicular bisector.
   What is the relationship between the point C and the points A and B?

   (iii) If C is **not** a point on [AB], what type of triangle is $\triangle ABC$?

   (iv) If C is a point on [AB], complete the following: $|AC| + |CB| = |\quad|$.

4. In each of the following, draw a line through the given point, perpendicular to the line that contains the point.

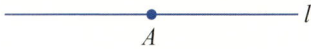

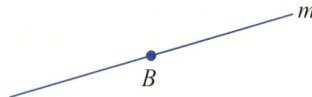

5. In each of the following, draw a line through the given point, not on the line, perpendicular to the line.

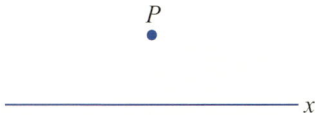

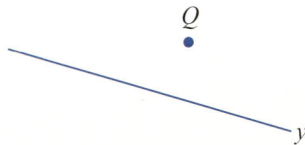

6. In each of the following, draw a line through the given point, not on the line, parallel to the line.

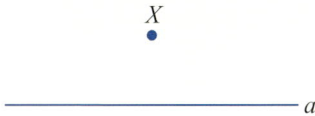

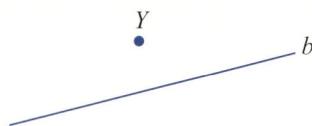

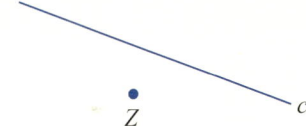

7. The diagram shows an island.
   There is treasure buried at the point T.
   T is equidistant from A and B and is also equidistant from C and D.
   Using only a compass and straight edge, locate the point T.

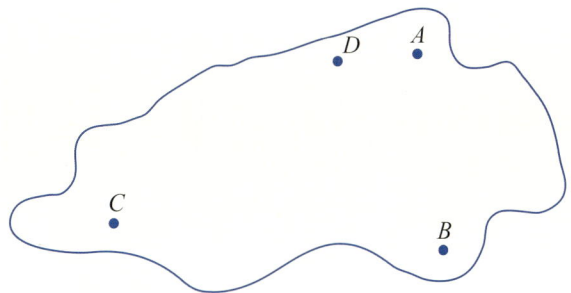

8. The diagram shows two straight roads connecting three towns A, B and C. A gas pipe was laid that is equidistant from towns B and C. Using a scale of 1 cm to 1 km, copy the diagram.

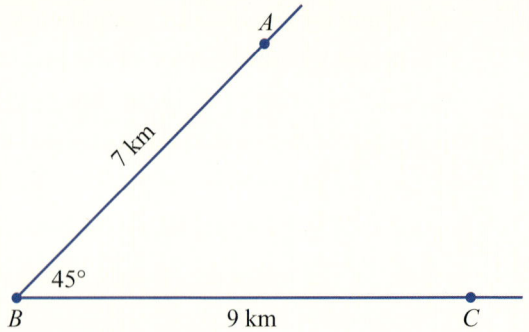

   (i) On your diagram, construct the path of the gas pipe.

   (ii) A new gas pipe is to be laid from town B that is to be equidistant from towns A and C. This new gas pipe is to connect to the older gas pipe at the point X. On your diagram, construct the path of the new gas pipeline and indicate the point X.

9. An electrical firm is asked to fit an outdoor spotlight in a rectangular garden measuring 16 m by 10 m. The light must be the same distance from the two corners, P and Q, of the back wall of the house, but also has to be the same distance from the fence RS at the end of the garden and the side of the garden, PS. Using a scale of 1 cm to 2 m, draw a scale drawing of the garden and find the position of the spotlight. Mark its position T.

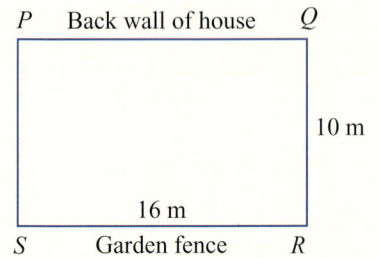

10. Construct each of the following line segments exactly. Using only a compass, straight edge and set square, show how to divide each of the line segments into three equal parts, showing all your construction lines. In each case, use your ruler to check your work.

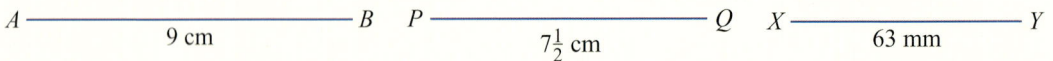

    A ———— 9 cm ———— B P ———— $7\frac{1}{2}$ cm ———— Q X ———— 63 mm ———— Y

11. Draw the line segment $[AB]$ such that $|AB| = 10$ cm. Using only a compass, straight edge and set square, show how to divide $[AB]$ into four equal parts, showing all your construction lines.

12. A farmer wants to erect four more posts equally spaced between the posts A and B, as shown. Using a scale of 1 cm = 10 m, construct an accurate diagram for the farmer. Show all construction lines, using only a compass, straight edge and set square.

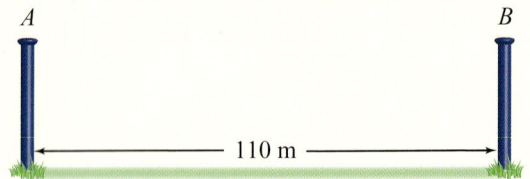

13. The diagram shows a rectangular garden, *PQRS*. Copy the diagram using a scale of 1 cm to 1 m. A concrete path is to be laid. The centre of the path runs diagonally from *P* to *R*.

    The width of the concrete path is to be 1 m. On your diagram, shade in the concrete path. A circular flowerbed is to be planted in this garden. The flowerbed will cover the area of the garden that lies within 3 m from the point *Q*. On your diagram, shade in the region that the flowerbed occupies.

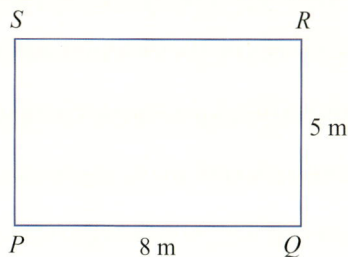

14. The diagram shows a circle with centre *O* and two chords, [*PQ*] and [*RS*]. Copy the diagram. Using only a compass and straight edge, construct the perpendicular bisectors of both chords. Show all your construction lines clearly. Comment on the point of intersection of the two bisectors.

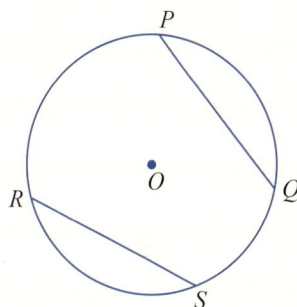

15. A part of a machine uses cylindrical cams (wheels). However, the centres are not marked on them. The exact centre of each wheel is required in order to drill holes in them.

    (i) State a theorem from your course that could be used to locate the centre of a circle with geometrical instruments.

    (ii) Find the centre of the circle on the right by applying the theorem you mentioned above. Show all your construction lines clearly.

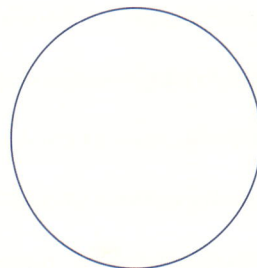

    (iii) Describe another method that could be used to locate the centre of the circle.

16. The diagram shows the circle *k* of radius 3 cm. The point *P* lies on the circle, as shown.

    Accurately draw the circle *k* and construct a tangent to *k* at the point *P*.

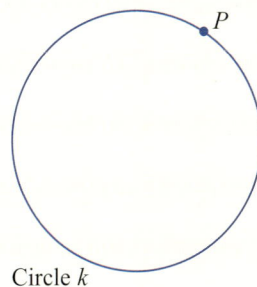

    Circle *k*

307

17. A landscape architect is designing a garden and wants to construct a straight pathway so that it passes exactly along the edge of a circular pond at a point X (as marked in the diagram).

Clearly outline the steps the architect must follow in order to be able to draw the exact position of the pathway on his plan of the garden.

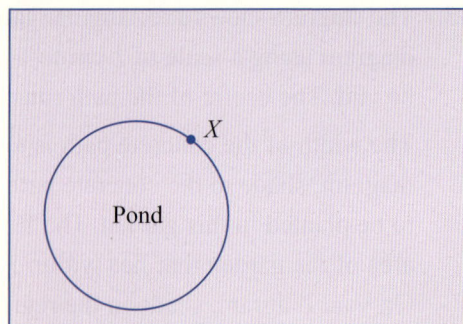

18. Accurately construct each of the following triangles, with all dimensions in centimetres (the diagrams are not drawn to scale).

(i)

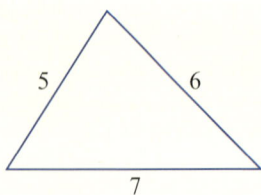

(ii)

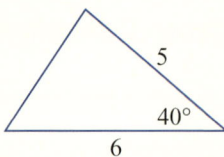

(iii)

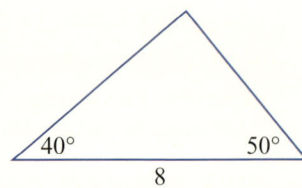

(iv)

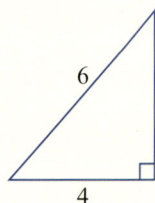

(v)

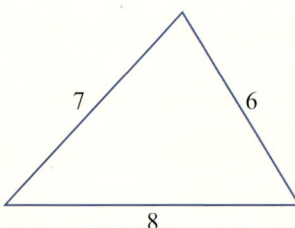

(vi)

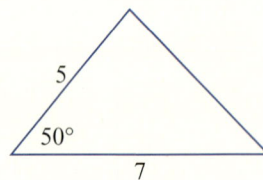

In questions 19–24, it is good practice to draw a rough sketch first and to draw one side as a horizontal base at the beginning.

19. Construct triangle ABC with $|AB| = 9$ cm, $|AC| = 8$ cm and $|BC| = 7$ cm.

20. Construct triangle PQR with $|PQ| = 8$ cm, $|QR| = 6$ cm and $|\angle PQR| = 30°$.

21. Construct triangle PQR with $|PQ| = 5$ cm, $|\angle RPQ| = 60°$ and $|\angle RQP| = 45°$.

22. Construct triangle XYZ with $|XY| = 8$ cm, $|XZ| = 6$ cm and $|\angle YXZ| = 90°$. Write down $|YZ|$.

23. (i) Construct triangle ABC with $|AB| = 1$ cm, $|AC| = 2$ cm and $|\angle ABC| = 90°$.

(ii) Use Pythagoras' theorem to find $|BC|$, leaving your answer in surd form.

(iii) Use a ruler to verify your answer for (ii).

24. Construct an isosceles right-angled triangle with hypotenuse equal to $\sqrt{2}$.

25. The diagram shows a rectangular garden, 24 m by 18 m. A tree is to be planted in the garden. The tree must be 12 m from P and the tree must be the same distance from SR and RQ. Copy the diagram using a scale of 1 cm to 3 m. Using only a compass and straight edge, construct the position of the tree.

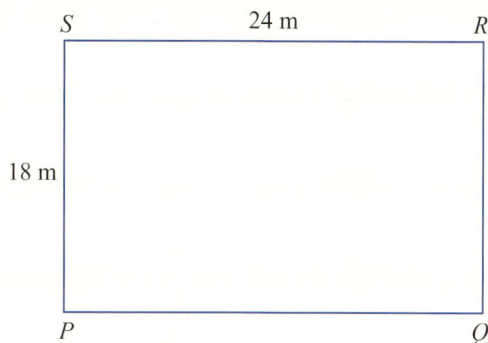

26. In a garden, a dog is on a lead that is 3 m in length. The lead is connected with a metal loop to a 10 m metal rail fixed horizontally to the ground so that the lead can slide easily along its length, as shown. Using a scale of 1 cm to 1 m, draw a diagram of the rail and shade the area of the garden that the dog can play on.

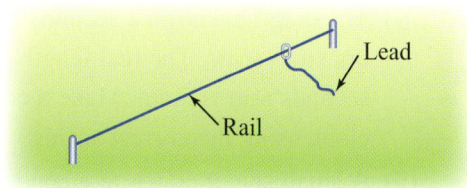

27. Following a storm, the direct route from Huntsville to Newtown is blocked by a felled tree. While the tree is blocking the road, drivers are forced to re-route via Edendale (see diagram.)

    (i) Using a scale of 1 cm = 1 km, redraw this diagram accurately.

    (ii) How much further did the drivers have to travel to get from Huntsville to Newtown while the road was blocked?

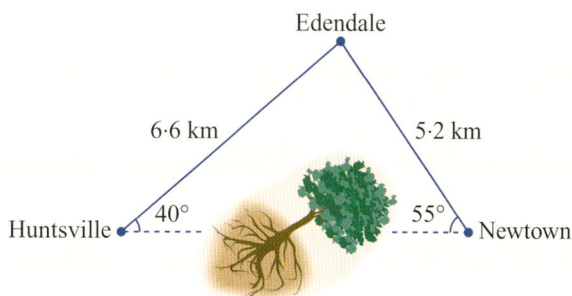

28. The diagram shows the sketch of a large office.

    (i) Construct an accurate scale drawing of the office. Use a scale of 1 cm to represent 10 m.

    (ii) A new printer is going to be installed in the office. The new printer must be the same distance from A and B. Construct the set of points in the office equidistant from A and B.

    (iii) The printer must also be within 45 m of point C. Construct the set of points which are exactly 45 m from C.

    (iv) Show on your diagram all possible positions for the printer.

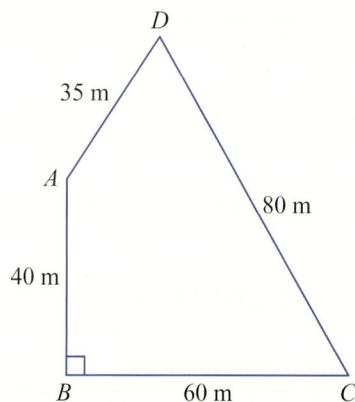

29. On a page, indicate the point A. Construct an accurate diagram to indicate the set of all points such that each point is less than or equal to 4 cm from A.

30. On a page, indicate the point B. Construct an accurate diagram to indicate the set of all points such that each point is greater than or equal to 3 cm from B and less than or equal to 6 cm from B.

31. The two points P and Q are such that $|PQ| = 6$ cm. Construct the points. On your diagram, shade the region which contains all the points that satisfy both conditions:

    (i) The distance from P is less than or equal to 4 cm.

    (ii) The distance from P is greater than or equal to the distance from Q.

32. **(i)** The diagram shows a seconds clock, not drawn to scale. The real length of the seconds arm is 5 cm. Make a copy of the clock using the correct scale.

    (ii) A small spider crawls at a constant speed along the seconds hand as it rotates. It starts at the centre when the hand is pointing to 60. It reaches the end of the hand 50 seconds later. By drawing lines from the centre to 5, 10, 15 and so on, find points on the spider's path and draw as accurately as you can the path (locus) of the spider's journey.

33. The diagram shows a plan of a rectangular garden with a rectangular building, where all dimensions are in metres. A 20 m rope is attached to a point A and the other end of the rope is attached to a dog. Using an accurate scaled diagram shade in the area of the garden which can be reached by the dog.

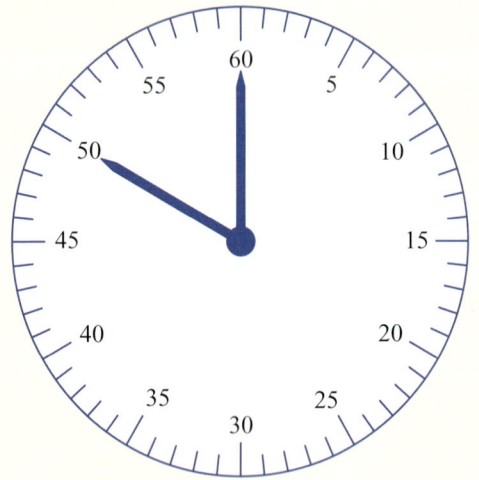

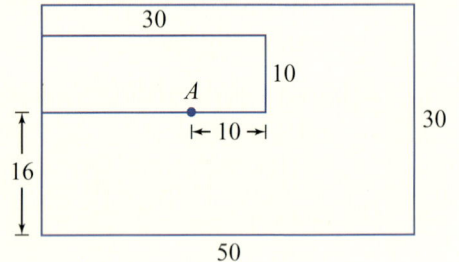

Constructions 16–22

16. Circumcentre and circumcircle of a triangle

The three perpendicular bisectors of the sides of a triangle meet at one point called the **circumcentre**, K, in the diagram. The **circumcircle** of a triangle is a circle that passes through the three vertices of the triangle. The radius of the circumcircle is $r = |KA|$. ($|KB|$ or $|KC|$ could also be used as a radius.) If the triangle has an obtuse angle, then the circumcentre is **outside** the triangle. If the triangle is a right-angled triangle, then the circumcentre is the **midpoint of the hypotenuse**.

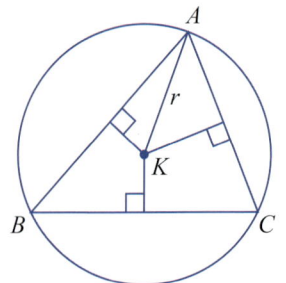

Steps to construct the circumcentre and circumcircle of triangle ABC

1. Construct the perpendicular bisector of $[AB]$.

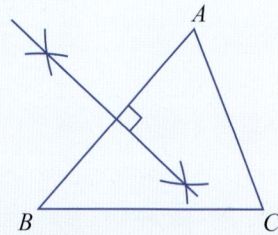

2. Construct the perpendicular bisector of $[AC]$ to meet the other perpendicular bisector at K.
   K is the circumcentre.

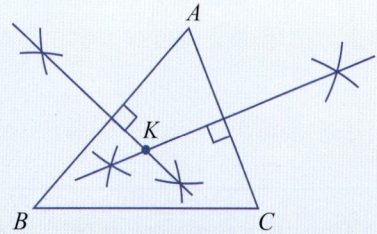

3. With K as the centre and radius $r = |KA|$, draw a circle. This circle will pass through the three vertices of the triangle.
   The circle drawn is the circumcircle.
   ($|KB|$ or $|KC|$ could also be used as a radius.)

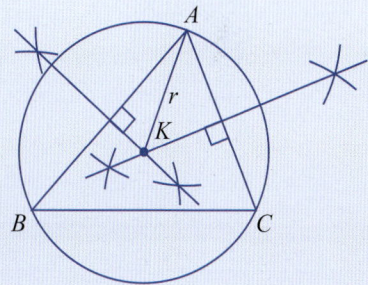

Note: The perpendicular bisector of $[BC]$ would also contain K.

17. Incentre and incircle of a triangle

The three angle bisectors of a triangle meet at one point called the **incentre**, K, in the diagram. The **incircle** of a triangle is a circle that touches the three sides of a triangle. r is the radius of the incircle.

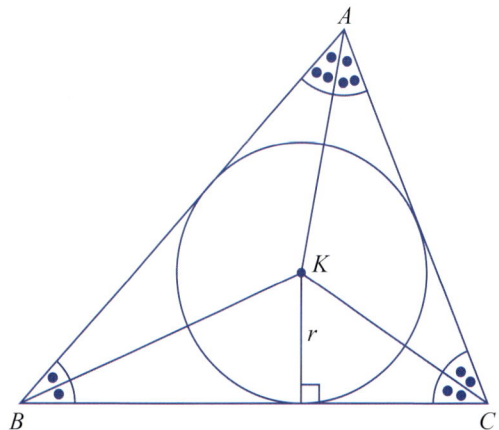

Steps to construct the incentre and incircle of triangle *ABC*

1. Construct the bisector of ∠*ABC*.

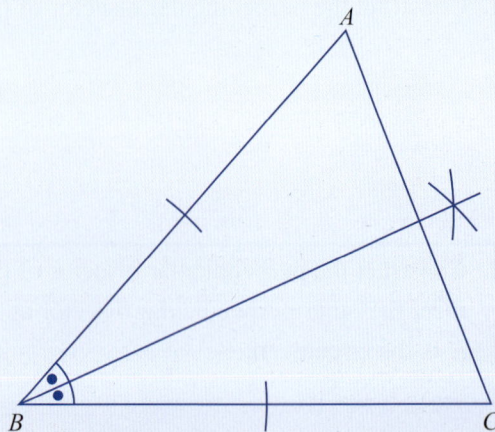

2. Construct the bisector of ∠*ACB* to meet the other angle bisector at *K*.
   K is the incentre.

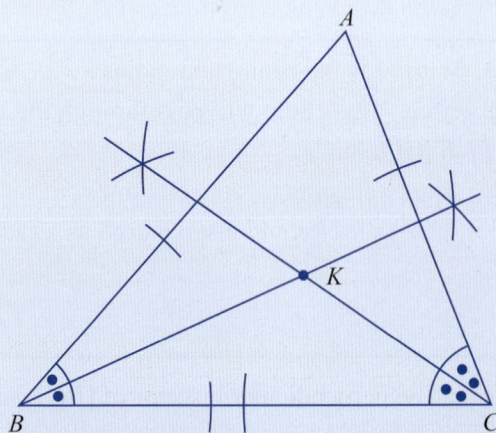

3. With *K* as the centre and radius *r*, draw a circle.
   This circle will touch the three sides of the triangle.
   The circle drawn is the incircle.

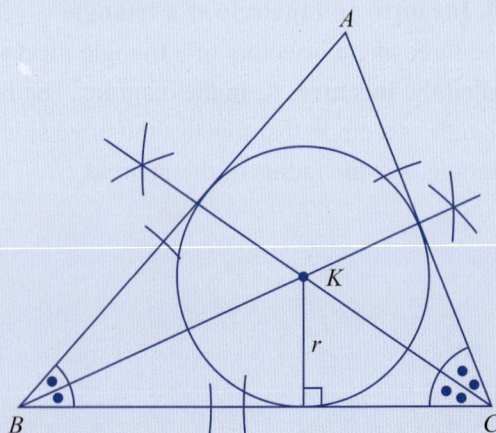

Note: The bisector of ∠*BAC* would also contain *K*.

18. Construct an angle of 60° without using a protractor or set square

Given a line *AB*.

A   B

Steps in constructing an angle of 60° without using a protractor or set square

1. Set your compass to a sensible radius. Place the compass point on *A*. Draw an arc from above *A* to intersect the line *AB*. Where the arc meets the line *AB*, label this point *C*.	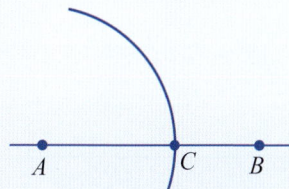
2. Keep the same radius as in step 1. Place the compass point on *C*. Draw an arc to meet the other arc. Where these arcs meet, label this point *D*.	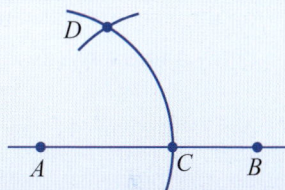
3. Using your ruler, draw the line *AD*. $|\angle DAC| = 60°$.	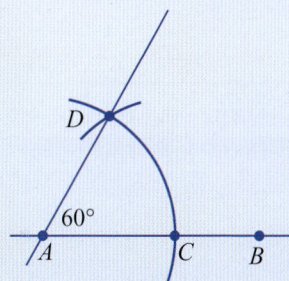

19. Tangent to a circle at a given point on the circle

A **tangent to a circle** is a line that touches a circle at one point only.
A tangent is perpendicular to the radius at the point of contact.

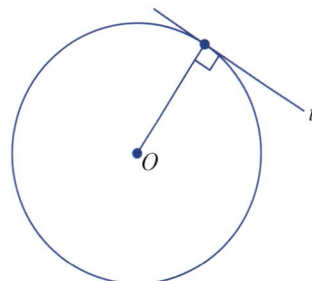

Given a circle, centre *O*, and a point *P* on the circumference.
(We need to construct a line through *P* perpendicular to *OP*.)

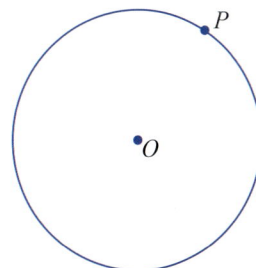

Steps to construct a tangent to a circle at a given point on the circle

Method 1:

1. Draw the line *OP*.

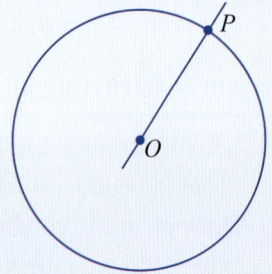

2. Place one of the **shorter** edges of the 45° set square
   on the line *OP* with the 90° vertex on point *P*.
   Draw a line towards *P*.

   Note: You can also use the 30°/60° set square.

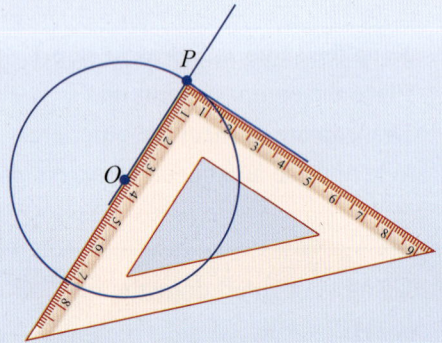

3. Using your ruler or set square, continue the line
   through *P*. This line is a tangent to the circle at the
   point *P*.

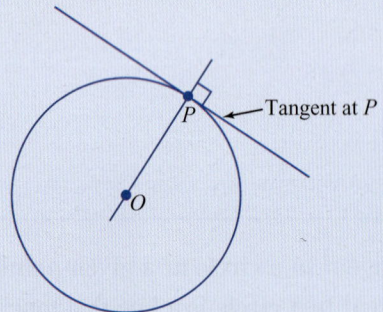

Method 2:

1. Draw the line *OP.*

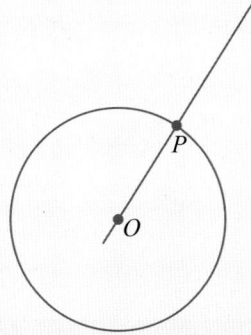

2. Set the compass to a sensible radius (usually a little less than *OP*). Place the compass point on *P*. Draw two arcs to intersect the line *OP* at *X* and *Y*.

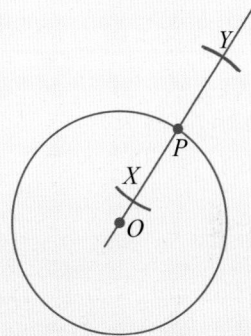

3. Place the compass point on *X*. Draw an arc. Keep the same radius. Place the compass point on *Y* and draw an arc to intersect the other arc. Where the arcs intersect, label the point *Z*.

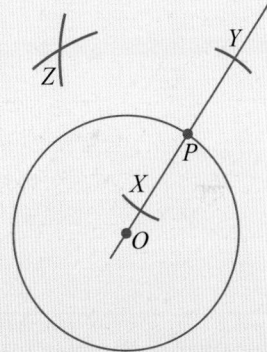

4. Draw the line *ZP*. The line *ZP* is a tangent to the circle at the point *P*.

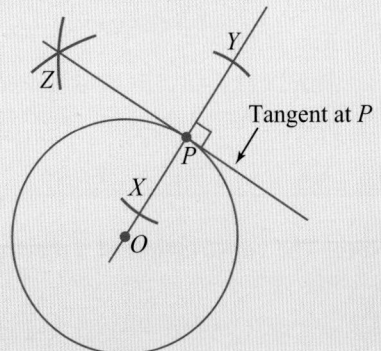

Tangent at *P*

20. Parallelogram

Construct parallelogram $ABCD$ such that $|AB| = 8$ cm, $|BC| = 5$ cm and $|\angle BAD| = 70°$.

1. A rough sketch with the given information is shown on the right.

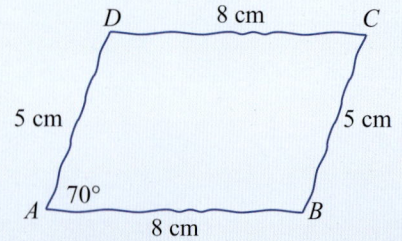

2. Using a ruler, draw a horizontal line segment 8 cm in length. Label the end points A and B.

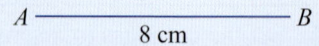

3. Place your protractor on point A. Draw an angle of $70°$.

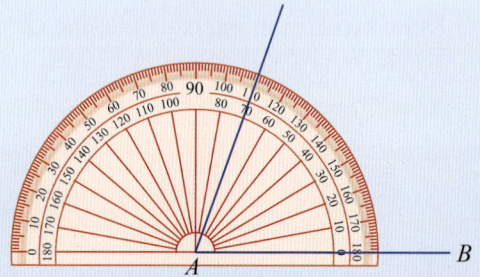

4. Place your protractor on point B. Draw an angle of $70°$.

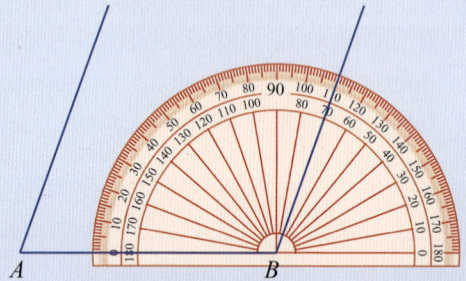

5. Use your ruler or compass to mark the points D and C such that $|AD| = 5$ cm and $|BC| = 5$ cm. Join D to C. Parallelogram $ABCD$ is now drawn.

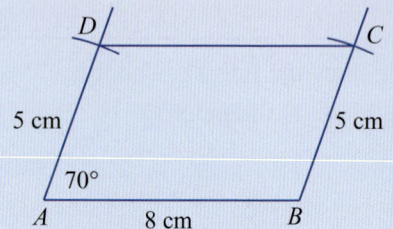

Note: The construction of a rectangle is the same as a parallelogram, but all angles are $90°$.

21. Centroid of a triangle

A line drawn from a vertex of a triangle to the midpoint of the opposite side is called a **median**. The three medians of a triangle meet at one point called the **centroid** (K in the diagram). The centroid divides each median in the ratio 2 : 1. K is also the centre of gravity of the triangle.

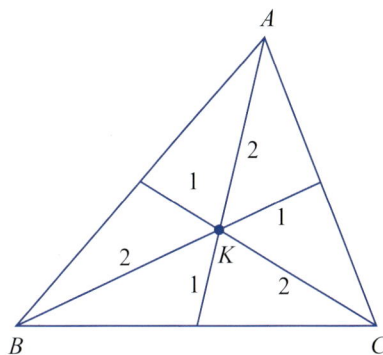

Steps in constructing the centroid of triangle ABC

1. Construct the perpendicular bisector of [AB]. Label the midpoint S.
   Join S to C (median).

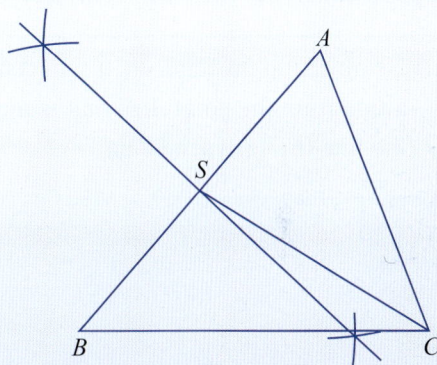

2. Construct the perpendicular bisector of [AC].
   Label the midpoint T.
   Join T to B (median).
   The two medians intersect at K.
   K is the centroid of the triangle.

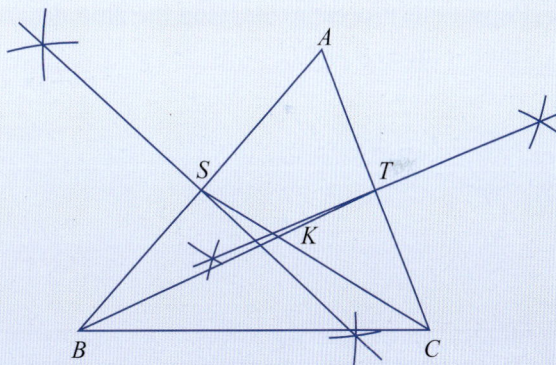

Note: The third median from A to the midpoint of [BC] would also contain K.

22. Orthocentre of a triangle

An altitude is a line that goes through the vertex of a triangle and is perpendicular to the opposite side.

The orthocentre of a triangle is the point where the three altitudes of a triangle meet.

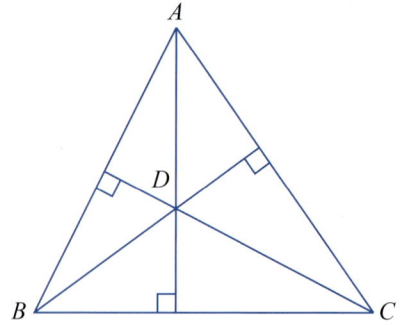

Steps to construct the orthocentre of triangle *ABC*

1. Using a straight edge and a set square, draw a line from the point *A* so that is meets the line [*BC*] perpendicularly.	
2. Repeat this procedure, drawing the altitudes from vertices *B* and *C*.	
3. The point where the three altitudes intersect is the orthocentre of the triangle, *D*.	

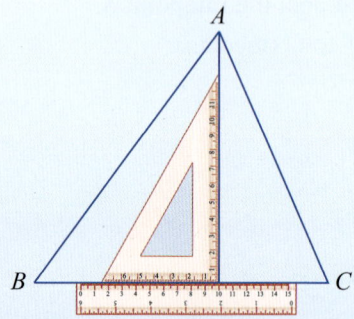

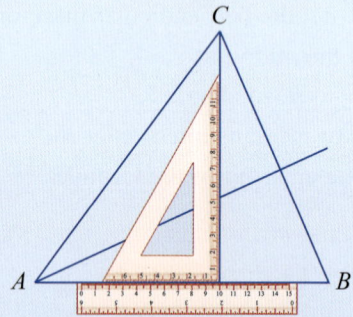

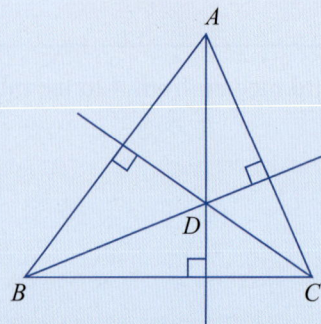

Properties of the orthocentre

Acute triangle	Right-angled triangle	Obtuse triangle
If a triangle is acute, the orthocentre is inside the triangle.	If a triangle is right-angled, the orthocentre is at the vertex with the right angle.	If one of the angles is an obtuse angle, then the orthocentre will lie outside of the triangle.

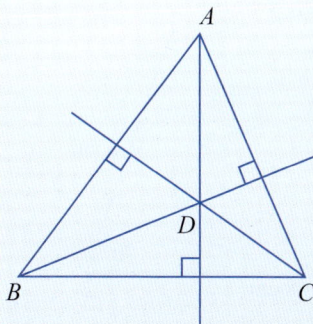 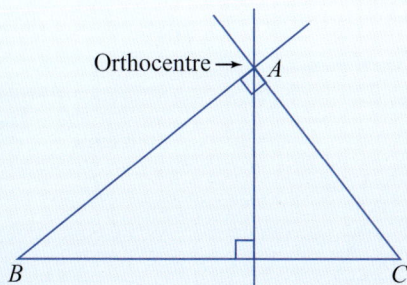

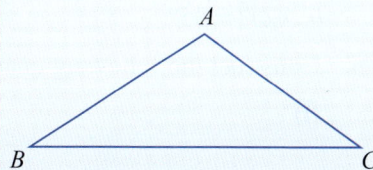

Note: To construct the orthocentre in this case, you must extend out the sides of the triangle. Use a dotted line when doing this.

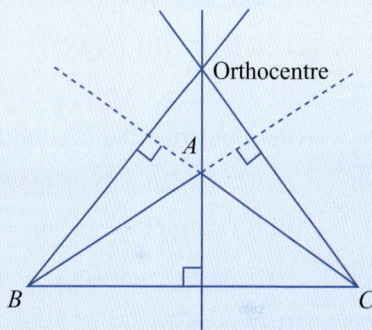

Note: If we construct the centroid, circumcentre and orthocentre of a triangle on the one diagram, we will see that the three points are collinear. The line joining these three points is known as **Euler's line**.

Exercise 7.2

1. Using only a compass and straight edge, construct an angle of 60°.

2. Construct the following parallelograms.

(i)

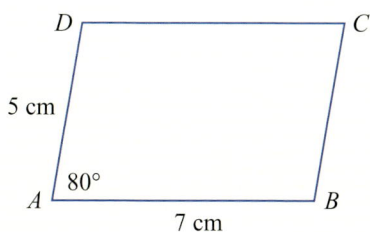

(ii)

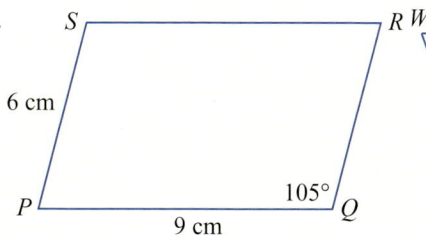

(iii)

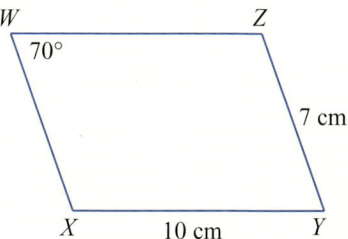

In questions 3–5, it is good practice to draw a rough sketch first and to draw one side as a horizontal base at the beginning.

3. Construct parallelogram $ABCD$ such that $|AB| = 6$ cm, $|\angle BAD| = 50°$ and $|AD| = 4$ cm.

4. Construct parallelogram $PQRS$ such that $|SR| = 8$ cm, $|\angle QPS| = 75°$ and $|QR| = 6$ cm.

5. Construct parallelogram $XYZW$ such that $|XY| = 9$ cm, $|YZ| = 7$ cm, $|\angle YXZ| = 30°$ and $|\angle XZY| = 35°$.

6. Construct the following quadrilaterals.

    (i)

    (ii)

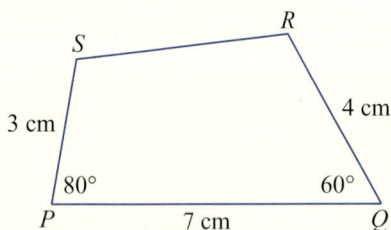

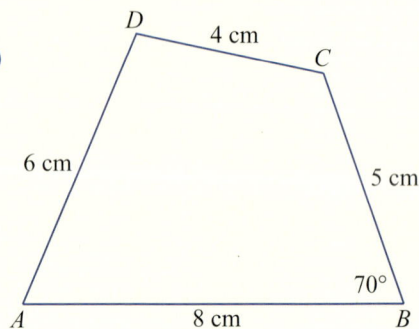

    Measure and write down:

    (a) $|RS|$ (b) $|\angle QRS|$

    Measure and write down:

    (a) $|\angle ADC|$ (b) $|\angle BCD|$

7. (i) Construct a triangle of sides 8 cm, 7 cm and 6 cm.
    (ii) Construct the (a) circumcentre and (b) circumcircle of the triangle.

8. (i) Construct a triangle of sides 11 cm, 8 cm and 6 cm.
    (ii) Construct the (a) incentre and (b) incircle of the triangle.

9. (i) Construct a triangle of sides 10 cm, 9 cm and 7 cm.
    (ii) Construct the centroid of the triangle.

10. (i) Accurately construct the triangle ABC such that $|AB| = 10$ cm, $|BC| = 12$ cm and $|AC| = 8$ cm.
    (ii) Construct the centroid of this triangle, showing all construction lines.

11. (i) Accurately construct the triangle UVW such that $|VW| = 12$ cm, $|\angle UVW| = 65°$ and $|\angle UWV| = 75°$.
    (ii) Construct the incircle of this triangle.

12. (i) Accurately construct the triangle ABC such that $|AB| = 5$ cm, $|AC| = 12$ cm and $|BC| = 13$ cm.
    (ii) What type of triangle is this? Justify your answer.
    (iii) Construct the circumcircle of this triangle.
    (iv) What word would you use to describe the line segment $[BC]$? Give a reason for your answer.

13. **(i)** Accurately construct the triangle UVW such that $|UV| = 15$ cm, $|UW| = 8$ cm and $|VW| = 9$ cm.

(ii) Construct the circumcircle of this triangle.

(iii) Comment on the position of the circumcircle relative to the triangle.

14. **(i)** Accurately construct the triangle PQR such that $|PQ| = 9$ cm, $|QR| = 10\cdot5$ cm and $|\angle PQR| = 60°$.

(ii) Construct the orthocentre of this triangle.

15. **(i)** Accurately construct the triangle PQR where $|PQ| = 8$ cm, $|QR| = 7$ cm and $|RP| = 6$ cm.

(ii) Construct the orthocentre of triangle PQR.

16. **(i)** Accurately construct the triangle ABC where $|AB| = 5$ cm, $|BC| = 4$ cm and $|AC| = 3$ cm.

(ii) Construct the orthocentre of triangle ABC. Comment on the position of the orthocentre.

17. **(i)** Accurately construct the triangle RST where $|RS| = 10$ cm, $|RT| = 7$ cm and $|ST| = 5$ cm.

(ii) Construct the orthocentre of triangle RST. Comment on the position of the orthocentre.

18. Copy and complete the following three sentences.

(i) For a triangle with all acute angles, the orthocentre is _____.

(ii) For a triangle with a right angle, the orthocentre is _____.

(iii) For a triangle with an obtuse angle, the orthocentre is _____.

19. In a certain area, there are two mobile phone transmitters, C and D, where $|CD| = 8$ km. Signals from transmitter C can reach 6 km and signals from transmitter D can reach 4 km. Using a scale of 1 cm = 1 km, indicate, by shading, the region in which signals can be reached from both transmitters.

20. P, Q and R represent three radio masts, where $|PQ| = 225$ km, $|PR| = 200$ km and $|QR| = 175$ km. Using a scale of 1 cm = 25 km, represent the situation on an accurate diagram. Signals from mast P can be received 125 km away, from mast Q 150 km away and from mast R 175 km away. Shade in the region in which signals can be received from all three masts.

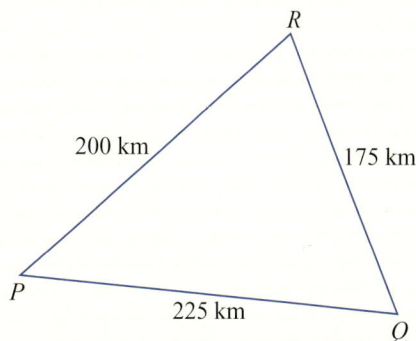

21. A graphic artist wants to design a logo which consists of a circle fitting exactly inside a triangle such that the circle touches all three sides of the triangle.

(i) What would such a circle be called?

(ii) Outline the steps involved in constructing this circle.

(iii) Accurately draw the designer's logo if the triangle is to be an isosceles triangle of sides 11 cm, 11 cm, 15 cm.

22. (i) Construct a triangle XYZ in which $|XY| = 10$ cm, $|YZ| = 8$ cm and $|XZ| = 6$ cm. Is the triangle a right-angled triangle? Justify your answer.

(ii) Construct the circumcircle of the triangle, showing all your construction lines clearly. Explain why the centre of the circumcircle is the midpoint of $[XY]$.

(iii) Calculate the area of the triangle using $\frac{1}{2}$ base × height.

(iv) Show that the area of the circle is greater than three times the area of the triangle.

(v) Let $|XY| = a$, $|YZ| = b$ and $|XZ| = c$.

Verify that the area of $\triangle XYZ$ is given by $A = \sqrt{s(s-a)(s-b)(s-c)}$ cm^2,

where $s = \dfrac{a+b+c}{2}$.

23. The diagram shows three villages, A, B and C, and the road distances, in km, between each. Using a scale of 1 cm = 1 km, construct an accurate triangle to represent the three towns. It is planned that the three towns will pool their resources to build a recreation centre. A vote was taken and it was decided to build the recreation centre in a place such that it is equidistant from each of the three villages. Using a compass and straight edge, construct on your diagram the position where the recreation centre should be built.

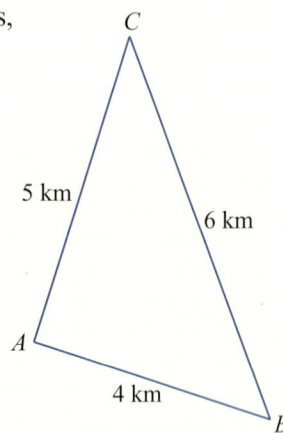

(i) In geometry, what is the position of the recreation centre called?

(ii) Is the position of the recreation centre fair to all three towns? Justify your answer.

(iii) If the triangular road connecting the towns was a right-angled triangle or an obtuse triangle, would this make any difference? Discuss.

24. (i) Using graph paper and starting with the point (6, 2) as the bottom left corner, construct a rectangle that is 4 units wide and 3 units high.

(ii) Using (0, 0) as the centre of enlargement and a scale factor of $\frac{1}{2}$, construct the scaled image of the rectangle in part (i).

25. (i) Construct $\triangle ABC$, with $|BC| = 10$ cm, $|AB| = 9$ cm and $|AC| = 7$ cm, as shown. Construct the incircle of $\triangle ABC$, with centre K. Show all your construction lines clearly.

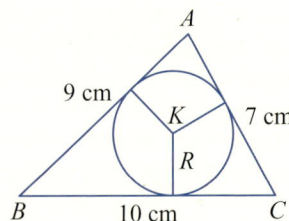

(ii) If R cm is the length of the radius of the circle, prove that:

(a) The area of $\triangle KBC$ is $5R$ cm^2

(b) The area of $\triangle ABC$ is $13R$ cm^2

26. **(i)** In $\triangle ABC$, O is the incentre and R is the radius of the incircle. $|AC| = 3$ cm, $|\angle ACB| = 90°$ and $|CB| = 4$ cm. Construct $\triangle ABC$.

(ii) Calculate **(a)** $|AB|$ and **(b)** the area of $\triangle ABC$.

(iii) Explain why the area of $\triangle AOC = \frac{3}{2} R$.

(iv) Hence or otherwise, show that R, the radius of the incentre, is 1 cm.

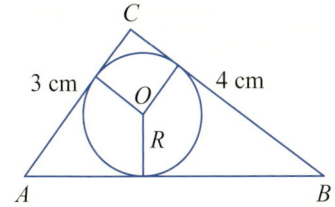

27. Construct triangle PQR such that $|PQ| = 5$ cm, $|QR| = 12$ cm and $|PR| = 13$ cm.

Prove: **(i)** $|\angle PQR| = 90°$

(ii) The radius of the circumcircle is $6\frac{1}{2}$ cm

(iii) The area of the triangle is 30 cm^2

(iv) The radius of the incircle is 2 cm

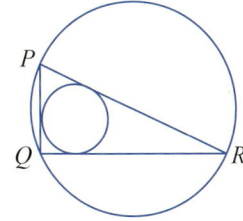

28. There are three satellites orbiting the Earth over the equator. They are equally spaced around a circular orbit. In the diagram, you are looking down on the North Pole of the Earth, with the equator running around the edge of the earth's disk. In order that any point on the equator is visible by at least one satellite, their positions form an equilateral triangle. If the satellites are in the lowest orbit possible, the Earth is the incircle of the triangle and the orbit is the circumcircle. Assume the Earth has a circumference of 40,000 km.

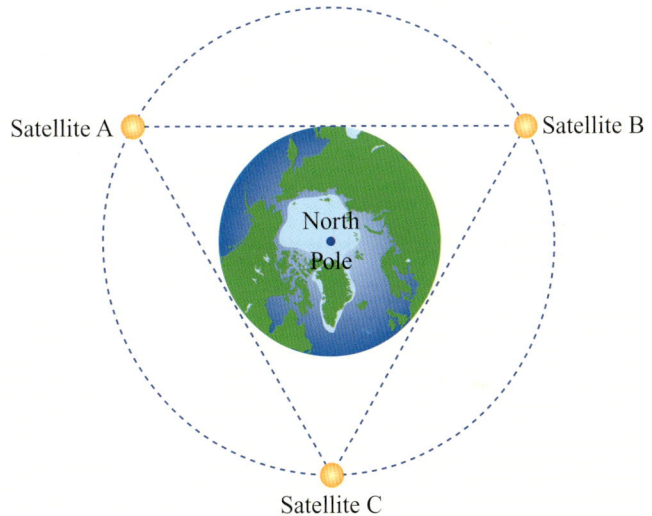

(i) What is the radius of the Earth, to the nearest kilometre?

(ii) What is the length of one side of the equilateral triangle linking the three spacecraft?

(iii) What is the radius of the orbit?

(iv) How high above the Earth's surface are the spacecraft flying?

(v) From the above results, can you see a connection between the answers to **(i)** and **(iv)**? What does this mean in mathematical terms?

Ratio and proportion

The following exercise is a revision of material covered at Junior Certificate Higher Level.

Exercise 8.1

1. There are three red marbles in a bag containing 12 marbles. Express the proportion of the red marbles as a (simplified) fraction and as an exact percentage.

2. In a survey, the proportion of people who watched a rugby match on television was $\frac{2}{7}$.

   (i) What proportion did not watch the match?

   (ii) If 240,000 watched the match, how many people were surveyed?

3. Divide **(i)** €504 in the ratio 3 : 4 : 5   **(ii)** 336 cm in the ratio 2 : 5 : 7

4. Divide **(i)** €210 in the ratio $1 : 2 : \frac{1}{2}$ **(ii)** 585 cm in the ratio $\frac{1}{2} : 2 : 5$

5. A and B share a sum of money such that B receives 60% of the sum. If A's share is €72, calculate B's share.

6. In a competition, team A scored $22\frac{1}{2}$ points and team B scored $17\frac{1}{2}$ points. The two teams share a prize of €28,000 in proportion to the number of points they scored. How much money does each team receive?

7. The angles of a triangle are in the ratio 2 : 3 : 4. What is the size of the smallest angle?

8. P, Q and R share a sum of money in the ratio 2 : 4 : 5, respectively. If Q's share is €60, find:

   (i) P's share

   (ii) The total sum of money shared

9. The ratio of the cost of a calculator to the cost of the batteries it needs to operate is 33 : 7. What percentage of the total cost do the batteries represent?

10. What length on a map should represent a distance of 279 km when the scale used is 1 cm = 18 km?

11. The floor plan of a building is drawn using a scale in which $\frac{3}{4}$ cm corresponds to 1 m. Determine the actual length of a room that measures $6\frac{3}{4}$ cm on the floor plan.

12. A glass rod falls and breaks into three pieces whose lengths are in the ratio 8 : 9 : 5. If the sum of the lengths of the two larger pieces is 119 cm, find the length of the third side.

13. Roy and Sam share €440 in the ratio of 8 : 3.
    (i) How much does each get?
    (ii) If Roy gives €45 of his share to Sam, what ratio is the money in now?

14. At a certain school, the ratio of the number of second year students to the number of fourth years is 8 to 5, and the ratio of the number of first year students to the number of second years is 3 to 4. If the ratio of the number of third year students to the number of fourth years is 3 to 2, what is the ratio of the number of first years to the number of third years?

15. In the rectangle $ABCD$, P is a point on AB such that $AP = \frac{1}{4} AB$. Calculate the ratio of the area of the triangle PBC to that of the rectangle $ABCD$.

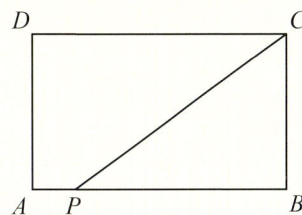

Percentages

The following exercise is a revision of material covered at Junior Certificate Higher Level.

Exercise 8.2

1. Calculate (i) 8% of €120 (ii) 12% of €216 (iii) 21% of 124 cm

2. One litre of water is added to four litres of milk in a container. Calculate the percentage of water in the container.

3. A solicitor's fee for the sale of a house is $1\frac{1}{2}$% of the selling price. If the fee is €3,480, calculate the selling price.

4. A salesperson's income for a year was €59,000. This was made up of a basic pay of €45,000 plus a commission of 4% on sales. Calculate the amount of the sales for the year.

5. Adam's pay went from €20 per hour to €25 per hour after his first evaluation. After his second evaluation his pay was raised to €33 per hour. When comparing the percentage increases, what per cent more than the first raise was the second?

6. A musical shop owner pays €2,800 for a set of drums and marks it up so that he makes a profit of 35%. Then 21% VAT is added on. Calculate the selling price.

7. An antiques dealer bought three chairs at an auction. He sold them later for €301·60, making a profit of 16% on their total cost.

    (i) Calculate the total cost of the chairs.

    (ii) The first chair cost €72 and it sold at a profit of 15%. Calculate its selling price.

    (iii) The second chair cost €98 and it was sold for €91. Find the percentage profit made on the sale of the third chair.

8. A bill for €58·08 includes VAT at 21%. Calculate the amount of VAT in the bill.

9. A bill for €96·76 includes VAT at 18%. Calculate the amount of the bill before VAT is added.

10. The purchase price of a TV increases by €20 when the rate of VAT is increased from 12% to 20%. Find the price of the TV before any VAT was added.

11. When the rate of VAT was increased from 18% to 21%, the price of a guitar increased by €81. Calculate the price of the guitar, inclusive of VAT at 21%.

12. A shop pays €240 for a bicycle and marks it up so that they makes a profit of 20%.

    (i) Find the selling price.

    During a sale the price of the bicycle is reduced by 15%. Calculate:

    (ii) The sale price

    (iii) The percentage profit on the bicycle during the sale

13. A €480 washing machine was put on sale for 30% off. It didn't sell, so the price was lowered an additional per cent off the sale price, making the new price €285·60. What was the second per cent discount that was given?

14. Donal has a mobile phone contract, which has a standing charge of €12·50 per month. His tariff then charges 8c per text message sent and 22c per minute for phone calls. These charges are all exclusive of VAT. At the end of the month his bill shows that he has sent 231 text messages and spent 128 minutes on phone calls. If VAT is charged at 21%, calculate Donal's bill.

15. A shop's electricity meter shows a reading of 12,854 units at the start of February and 15,238 at the start of April. The electricity provider has a standing charge of €8·96 per month and charges 12·5c per unit of electricity used. If these charges are exclusive of VAT and VAT is charged at a rate of 19%, calculate the total electricity bill for the two-month period of February and March.

16. Anne hires a plumber to repair her shower. The repair involves the purchase of €190 worth of goods and 4 hours of labour, billed at €55 per hour. If VAT is charged at 21% on goods and 13·5% on labour, calculate how much Anne owes the plumber.

17. During 1908, the population of a small town rose by 6%. The following year, the population declined by 6%. Would the population at the start of 1910 be less than, equal to or greater than the population two years earlier? Explain your answer.

Foreign exchange

The following exercise is a revision of material covered at Junior Certificate Higher Level.

Exercise 8.3

1. A train ticket costs $54. If €1 = $1·08, calculate the cost of the ticket in euro.

2. Dollars were bought for €8,000 when the exchange rate was €1 = $1·02. A commission was charged for this service. If the person received $7,956, calculate the percentage commission charged.

3. A supplier agrees to buy 100 computers for ¥75,600 (Japanese yen) each. He plans to sell them for a total of €80,000.

   (i) If the exchange rate is €1 = ¥108, calculate the percentage profit, to two decimal places, on the cost price.

   (ii) If the exchange rate changes to €1 = ¥110, calculate the percentage profit, to two decimal places, on the cost price.

4. Exchange rates for GBP£1:

US dollar (2003) = $1·60	US dollar (2002) = $1·45
Australian dollar (2003) = $2·55	Australian dollar (2002) = $2·71

   How many more Australian Dollars could you purchase in 2002 than in 2003 with $2,000 US dollars?

5. Michelle wants to buy a new MP3 player. She can buy it in a local shop for €180. Alternatively, she can order it from a website in the UK for GBP£120 plus £10·50 delivery. If the exchange rate is €1 = £0·85, which way would it be cheaper for Michelle to buy the MP3 player and by how much less, in euro, would it cost?

6. An Irish company imports goods from the US and exports them to the UK. In a particular week the company imported US$13,550 worth of goods and exported them for GBP£9,200. If the exchange rates during the week of the transaction were €1 = US$1·38 and GBP£1 = €1·16, calculate the percentage profit that the company makes on the transaction.

7. On a certain day in the foreign exchange markets, one euro (EUR) was worth 136·8 Japanese yen (JPY) and one euro was worth 9·66 Hong Kong dollars (HKD).

   (i) Find the value of JPY 10,000 in EUR, giving your answer correct to the nearest 10 cent.

   (ii) Convert HKD 65 into JPY, giving your answer correct to the nearest whole number.

8. A company in Cork specialises in custom-made furniture. A customer commissions a dining suite for €2,150. In order to make the furniture, the company imported the wood from Canada for $650 and then paid 17% importation tax. The craftsman took 30 hours to complete the work and he charged €24 per hour plus an extra €120 for materials. The rate of exchange at the time of importation of the wood was €1 = $1·34.

   (i) Calculate the percentage profit the company made on the sale.

   (ii) A week after importing the wood, the exchange rate changed to €1 = $1·39. Calculate the percentage profit that the company would have made had they imported the wood a week later.

9. Chris wants to buy a used car. He has found the car that he wants and it is available for purchase in Cork, Ireland for €11,500 or Manchester, England for GBP£7,900. Chris lives in Dublin and must work out which is the cheaper option for him.

   (i) Calculate how much the car will cost Chris if he buys it in Cork, given that he will need to get a train to Cork, which costs €55, and then drive the car the 261 km home. Petrol for the car is €1 for every 9 km.

   (ii) Given that the exchange rate at the time is €1 = GBP 0·87p, calculate how much the car will cost him if he buys it in Manchester, given that he will have to pay for a flight, which costs €70, then drive the car the 190 km from Manchester to Holyhead, getting 10 km per GBP£1 of petrol. The price of the ferry home is €160. Once in Dublin, the car will be subject to a 24% charge on the purchase price for import and re-registration.

   (iii) Which option is cheaper for Chris and by how much?

   (iv) Do you think Chris should take the cheaper option? Give a reason for your answer.

10. The table shows part of a currency conversion chart. For example, GBP 1 is equivalent to FFR 8·33.

	GBP	USD	FFR
GBP 1	1	p	8·33
USD 1	0·64	1	q
FFR 1	0·12	0·19	1

(i) Correct to two decimal places, calculate the value of:

(a) p

(b) q

(ii) Sadbh has USD 1,500 to exchange at a bank.

(a) Assuming no commission is charged, how much in GBP will Sadbh receive from the bank?

(b) Assuming the bank charges 1·5% commission:

(1) How much in GBP does Sadbh pay in commission?

(2) How much in GBP does Sadbh actually receive for her USD 1,500?

Index notation

The following exercise is a revision of material covered at Junior Certificate Higher Level.

Exercise 8.4

In questions 1–15, express your answer in the form $a \times 10^n$, where $1 \leq a < 10$ and $n \in \mathbb{Z}$.

1. 0·0007

2. 0·0035

3. 2,470,000

4. $\dfrac{1,512}{0·36}$

5. $\dfrac{0·0048}{0·15}$

6. $\dfrac{0·0099}{2·2}$

7. $(1·7 \times 10^3) \times (2 \times 10^4)$

8. $(5·3 \times 10^2) \times (1·8 \times 10^4)$

9. $(9·85 \times 10^5) \times (2·3 \times 10^{-3})$

10. $(3·91 \times 10^5) \div (2 \times 10^3)$

11. $(5·04 \times 10^7) \div (3 \times 10^{-2})$

12. $(4·2 \times 10^{-3}) \div (7 \times 10^2)$

13. $\dfrac{2·45 \times 10^5 - 1·8 \times 10^3}{1·6 \times 10^3}$

14. $\dfrac{1·4 \times 10^3 + 5·6 \times 10^2}{7 \times 10^{-1}}$

15. $\dfrac{2·8 \times 10^4 + 4·2 \times 10^5}{2·24 \times 10^6}$

16. If $f = 7·5 \times 10^{-5}$, express $\frac{1}{f}$ in the form $a \times 10^n$, where $1 \leq a < 10$ and $n \in \mathbb{Z}$.

17. The population density of a country is the average number of people per square kilometre. Norway has a population of $4·9 \times 10^6$ and an area of $3·25 \times 10^5$ square kilometres. Calculate the population density of Norway.

18. In 1981 the population of Peru was approxiamately $1·8 \times 10^7$. By 1988 the population had increased by 2·5 million. What was the approximate population of Peru in 1988?

19. A postage stamp weighs $3·2 \times 10^{-5}$ kg. A speck of dust weighs $1·6 \times 10^{-7}$ kg. How many specks of dust weigh the same as a stamp?

20. **(i)** A packet of A4 paper contains 5×10^2 sheets of paper. The packet is 6 cm in height. Calculate the thickness of one sheet of paper.

(ii) A magazine is made from 54 sheets of these A4 sheets of paper. The number of magazines printed is $6\cdot48 \times 10^7$. Calculate the number of sheets of paper needed to print these magazines.

(iii) If all the magazines were piled up on top of each other, how high would the pile be? Give your answer to the nearest kilometre.

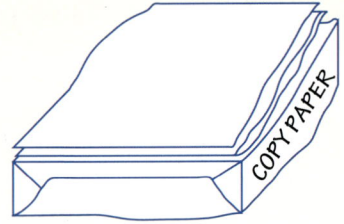

21. The circumference of the Earth at the equator is about 4×10^4 km. Calculate the length of the radius at the equator. Express your answer in the form $a \times 10^n$, where $1 \leq a < 10$ and $n \in \mathbb{Z}$, correct to three significant figures.

22. Express 2^{27} in the form $a \times 10^n$, where $1 \leq a < 10$ and $n \in \mathbb{N}$, correct to three decimal places.

23. The surface area of the Earth is approximately $5\cdot2 \times 10^{14}$ m^2. Approximately 29% of the surface area is land. What is the approximate area of the Earth that is covered by water?

24. Calculate h, the length of the hypotenuse of the right-angled triangle shown.

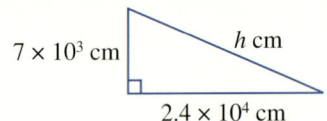

7×10^3 cm

h cm

2.4×10^4 cm

25. The density of an object is found by dividing its mass by its volume. A proton is considered to be spherical in shape. Given that the mass of a proton is $1\cdot67 \times 10^{-27}$ kg and its radius is $8\cdot768 \times 10^{-14}$ m, find its density.

Relative error and percentage error

When calculations are being made, errors can occur, especially calculations which involve rounding. It is important to have a measure of the error.

Definitions

Error = | true value – estimate value | and is always considered positive.

$$\text{Relative error} = \frac{\text{Error}}{\text{True value}}$$

$$\text{Percentage error} = \frac{\text{Error}}{\text{True value}} \times 100\%$$

Accumulated error: the collected inaccuracy that can occur when multiple errors are combined.

EXAMPLE

The answer to $5\cdot6 + 7\cdot1$ was given as $12\cdot5$.

What was the percentage error, correct to two decimal places?

Solution:

True value $= 5\cdot6 + 7\cdot1 = 12\cdot7.$ Estimated value $= 12\cdot5.$

Error $= |\text{true value} - \text{estimated value}| = |12\cdot7 - 12\cdot5| = |0\cdot2| = 0\cdot2$

$$\text{Percentage error} = \frac{\text{Error}}{\text{True value}} \times 100\% = \frac{0\cdot2}{12\cdot7} \times 100\% = 1\cdot57\% \text{ (correct to two decimal places)}$$

Exercise 8.5

1. The estimate for repairing a car was €3,325. The actual cost was €3,500. Calculate the percentage error.

2. The value of $\dfrac{30\cdot317}{\sqrt{24\cdot7009}}$ was estimated to be 6. Calculate:

   (i) The error

   (ii) The percentage error, correct to two decimal places

3. The value of $\dfrac{48\cdot27 + 12\cdot146}{14\cdot82 - 3\cdot02}$ was estimated to be 5. Calculate the percentage error, correct to one decimal place.

4. (i) Calculate the volume of a solid cylinder of radius 6 cm and height 14 cm $\left(\text{assume } \pi = \frac{22}{7}\right)$.

   (ii) When doing this calculation, a student used $\pi = 3$. Calculate the student's percentage error in the calculation, assuming that $\pi = \frac{22}{7}$ is the exact value, correct to one decimal place.

5. A food manufacturer sells carrots in 500 g tins. For two hours, a faulty machine filled 12,500 tins with only 495 g of carrots.

   (i) Calculate the percentage error.

   (ii) How many kg of carrots were used during the two hours?

   (iii) How many tins would usually be filled with the quantity used?

   (iv) If the tins had been sold at the usual price of 50c, how much profit would the manufacturer have made because of the fault?

6. The recorded value of the atomic mass of an isotope of nickel is $57\cdot9$ g/mol. If a scientist in her laboratory determined the mass to be $59\cdot6$ g/mol, what is the percentage error?

7. At 20°C, the solubility of potassium chloride is actually 34·7 grams per 100 cm^3 water. A laboratory experiment yielded 30·3 grams per 100 cm^3 water at that temperature. What is the percentage error?

8. David is given a sphere of true diameter 4·50 cm. If he made a 5% error when measuring the diameter, what percentage error will this cause in the volume of the sphere?

9. A surveyor standing 30 metres from the base of a building measures the angle of elevation to the top of the building. If the true angle of elevation from this point is 75°, how accurately must the angle be measured for the percentage error in estimating the height of the building to be less than 4%?

10. A statement arrives at an office showing three invoices that need to be paid:

   Invoice 1: €421·76   Invoice 2: €315·97   Invoice 3: €1,273·12

   The accountant's assistant checks the statement quickly to estimate how much is owed. He rounds each figure to the nearest euro and adds them.

   (i) What is the total he comes to?
   (ii) What is the true total?
   (iii) What is the accumulated error?

Tolerance and wastage

Modern machines are manufactured from hundreds of components which need to fit together accurately. For that reason, the various parts must be made to exact measurements, although the level of exactness can vary. For example, the parts which make up a cruise ship might not need to be manufactured as accurately as parts of a watch.

Objects which must be made very accurately (such as a watch) would have a very low tolerance value. For example, a small circular cog for a watch might need to be 8 mm in diameter. If it was 10 mm in diameter, it would be unlikely to fit. The watchmaker could describe the part as needing a diameter of 8 mm ± 0·5 mm.

This would mean that the smallest acceptable diameter is 8 − 0·5 mm = 7·5 mm and the largest acceptable diameter is 8 + 0·5 mm = 8·5 mm.

EXAMPLE

A shipbuilder needs sheets of metal to be 2 m long by 1 m wide but will accept sheets which are 2 m ± 3 mm by 1 m ± 2 mm.

(i) What are the dimensions (in mm) of the largest sheets and the smallest within the given tolerances?

(ii) Calculate, in m², the difference between the area of the largest and the smallest sheets.

Solution:

Draw a sketch:

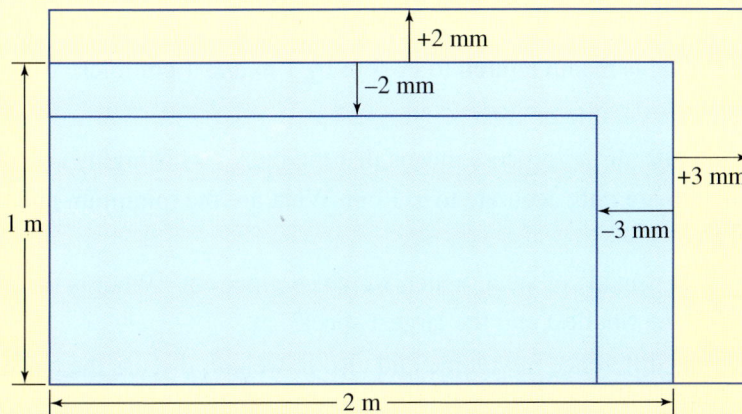

The shaded part shows the desired sheet. The larger outline shows the maximum sheet, while the smaller outline shows the minimum.

(i) Maximum length: 2 m + 3 mm = 2,000 mm + 3 mm = 2,003 mm

Maximum width: 1 m + 2 mm = 1,000 mm + 4 mm = 1,002 mm

Maximum dimensions: 2,003 mm × 1,002 mm

Minimum length: 2 m − 3 mm = 2,000 mm − 3 mm = 1,997 mm

Minimum width: 1 m − 2 mm = 1,000 mm − 4 mm = 998 mm

Minimum dimensions: 1,997 mm × 998 mm

(ii) Convert: 2,003 mm = 2·003 m;   1,002 mm = 1·002 m

Maximum area: 2·003 m × 1·002 m = 2·007 006 m²

Convert: 1,997 mm = 1·997 m;   998 mm = 0·998 m

Maximum area: 1·997 m × 0·998 m = 1·993 006 m²

∴ The difference in the areas = $(2 \cdot 007006 - 1 \cdot 993006)\,\text{m}^2 = 0 \cdot 014\,\text{m}^2$

Exercise 8.6

1. A packet of peanuts describes the contents as containing $300 \pm 2\%$ peanuts. What is the tolerance in terms of peanuts?

2. A bridge over a motorway needs to span a distance of 40 m. After some consultation, the specification for the bridge requires a width of $39 \cdot 9 \pm 0 \cdot 1$ m.

   (i) By how much can the bridge vary?

   (ii) Why would the bridge need to be shorter than the distance it needs to span?

3. The length of a table is measured with an accuracy of $0 \cdot 15$ cm. The observed measurement is 65 cm. What is the tolerance interval on this measurement?

4. A person travels 800 m ± 4 m in a time of 3 minutes 12 seconds ± 2 sec. What are the largest and smallest possible values for the speed in metres per second?

5. A sheet of metal is manufactured to be 3 m by 1 m and 1 cm thick.

   (i) What is its volume in cm^3?

   (ii) The manufacturing process means that the thickness is highly accurate but the length and width are only accurate to ± 1 cm. What are the minimum and maximum volumes?

   (iii) The sheet is made of steel, which weighs 8 g per cm^3. What is the difference in weight between the smallest and the largest sheet?

   (iv) Given the difference in volume and also in weight, discuss the consequences of this tolerance.

6. A baker recently received an order for 126 cupcakes.

   (i) If wastage of the finished product is assumed to be 10%, how many cupcakes should the baker prepare?

   The production costs of the batch of cupcakes are as follows:

Cost of labour	€9·50 per hour
Labour hours required	6 hours
Direct materials	€80
Bakery overheads allocated to this job	€30

   (ii) Calculate the cost of the batch (based on the number of units calculated in (i)).

   (iii) Calculate the cost per unit.

   (iv) If the baker wishes to make a profit of 20%, what price should they charge per cupcake?

7. A catering company receives an order for an event. The order is for 76 lasagnes and 115 quiches.

   (i) If the wastage of the finished products are assumed to be 5% on the lasagnes and 8% on the quiches, how many of each would the caterer need to make?

The production costs of each item is as follows:

	Per lasagne	Per quiche
Cost of labour	€9·00 per hour	€10·50 per hour
Labour hours required	0·2 hours	0·16 hours
Direct materials	€1·70	€0·95
Bakery overheads	€0·75	€1·05

   (ii) Calculate the unit cost per lasagne and per quiche.
   (iii) Calculate the cost of the batch (based on the number of units calculated in (i)).
   (iv) If the caterer wishes to make a profit of 22%, what should they charge for the entire order?

Income tax

The following is called the income tax equation:

Gross tax − tax credit = tax payable

Gross tax is calculated as follows:

Standard rate on all income up to the standard rate cut-off point + A higher rate on all income above the standard rate cut-off point

EXAMPLE 1

A woman has a gross yearly income of €48,000. She has a standard rate cut-off point of €27,500 and a tax credit of €3,852. The standard rate of tax is 18% of income up to the standard rate cut-off point and 37% on all income above the standard rate cut-off point. Calculate:

(i) The amount of gross tax for the year

(ii) The amount of tax paid for the year

Solution:

(i) Gross tax = 18% of €27,500 + 37% of €20,500

$\qquad$ = €27,500 × 0·18 + €20,500 × 0·37

$\qquad$ = €4,950 + €7,585

$\qquad$ = €12,535

> Income above the standard rate cut-off point
>
> = €48,000 − €27,500
>
> = €20,500

(ii) Income tax equation:

$\qquad$ Gross tax − tax credit = tax payable

$\qquad$ €12,535 − €3,852 = €8,683

$\qquad$ Therefore, she paid €8,683 in tax.

Note: If a person earns less than their standard rate cut-off point, then they pay tax only at the standard rate on all their income.

EXAMPLE 2

A man paid €10,160 in tax for the year. He had a tax credit of €3,980 and a standard rate cut-off point of €26,000. The standard rate of tax is 17% of income up to the standard rate cut-off point and 36% on all income above the standard rate cut-off point. Calculate:

(i) The amount of income taxed at the rate of 36%

(ii) The man's gross income for the year

Solution:

(i) Income tax equation:

Gross tax − tax credit = tax payable

17% of €26,000 + 36% of (income above cut-off point) − €3,980 = €10,160

€4,420 + 36% of (income above cut-off point) − €3,980 = €10,160

36% of (income above cut-off point) + €440 = €10,160

36% of (income above cut-off point) = €9,720

1% of (income above cut-off point) = €270

(divide both sides by 36)

100% of (income above cut-off point) = €27,000

(multiply both sides by 100)

Therefore, the amount of income taxed at the higher rate of 36% was €27,000.

(ii) Gross income = standard rate cut-off point + income above the standard rate cut-off point

= €26,000 + €27,000 = €53,000

Exercise 8.7

1. A woman has a gross yearly income of €39,500. She has a standard rate cut-off point of €23,600 and a tax credit of €3,950. The standard rate of tax is 20% of income up to the standard rate cut-off point and 42% on all income above the standard rate cut-off point. Calculate:

   (i) The amount of gross tax for the year

   (ii) The amount of tax paid for the year

2. A man has a gross yearly income of €48,750. He has a standard rate cut-off point of €29,250 and a tax credit of €3,150. The standard rate of tax is 16% of income up to the standard rate cut-off point and 38% on all income above the standard rate cut-off point. Calculate:

   (i) The amount of gross tax for the year

   (ii) The amount of tax paid for the year

3. A woman has a gross yearly income of €57,600. She has a standard rate cut-off point of €31,600 and a tax credit of €4,250. The standard rate of tax is 22% of income up to the standard rate cut-off point and 43% on all income above the standard rate cut-off point. Calculate:

   (i) The amount of gross tax for the year
   (ii) The amount of tax paid for the year

4. Jeremy has a gross yearly income of €26,000. He has a standard rate cut-off point of €28,000 and a tax credit of €1,800. If he pays tax of €3,400, calculate the standard rate of tax.

5. Eileen has a standard rate cut-off point of €37,500. The standard rate of tax is 18% and the higher rate is 41%. If Eileen's gross tax is €15,975, what is her gross income?

6. Rebecca paid €10,280 in tax for the year. She had a tax credit of €2,540 and a standard rate cut-off point of €29,000. The standard rate of tax is 18% of income up to the standard rate cut-off point and 40% on all income above the standard rate cut-off point. Calculate:

   (i) The amount of income taxed at the rate of 40%
   (ii) Rebecca's gross income for the year

7. Oisin paid €10,775 in tax for the year. He had a tax credit of €1,960 and a standard rate cut-off point of €28,500. The standard rate of tax is 15% of income up to the standard rate cut-off point and 36% on all income above the standard rate cut-off point. Calculate:

   (i) The amount of income taxed at the rate of 36%
   (ii) Oisin's gross income for the year

Further deductions on income

All deductions can be divided into two categories: statutory and non-statutory.

Statutory deductions:	Non-statutory deductions:
Compulsory deductions, which must be paid.	Voluntary deductions, which the worker can choose to pay or not pay.
Examples:	Examples:
Income tax	Pension contributions
Pay-Related Social Insurance (PRSI)	Trade union subscriptions
Universal Social Charge (USC)	Health insurance payments

Pay-related social insurance (PRSI)

PRSI is made up of social insurance and health contributions. The social insurance part goes to funds to pay for social welfare and benefits in Ireland. The health contribution part goes to the Department of Health and Children to help fund health services in Ireland. The amount of PRSI an employee pays depends on how much they earn and is calculated as a percentage of their earnings. The employer will also pay a contribution to the employee's PRSI payment.

Universal social charge (USC)

The Universal Social Charge is a tax payable on gross income. This additional tax was introduced in 2011 and it provides income for the state. The rates for USC as of 2012 are as follows, but it is important to note that these rates are set by the government and can be changed in the annual budget.

If a worker earns under €10,036 in total, then they do not pay USC.

If a worker earns over €10,036, USC is charged as follows:

2%	On the first €10,036
4%	On the next €5,980
7%	On the balance

EXAMPLE

Aisling has a gross income of €92,500. Her standard rate cut-off point is €33,500. The standard rate of tax is 18% and the higher rate is 43%. She has a tax credit of €5,300. Aisling is in PRSI class A1, which means that she does not pay PRSI on the first €127 earned per week, but she pays it at a rate of 4% on all income above that amount (assume a 52-week year). Aisling pays trade union subscriptions of €15 every two weeks, health insurance of €85 a month and a pension contribution of €350 per month.

  (i) Calculate the total amount of income tax Aisling must pay for the year.
 (ii) Calculate her USC payment for the year.
(iii) Calculate her PRSI contribution per week, to the nearest cent.
(iv) What is Aisling's weekly net income after all deductions?

Solution:

  (i) Gross tax = 18% of €33,500 + 43% of €59,000
            = €33,500 × 0·18 + €59,000 × 0·43
            = €6,030 + €25,370
            = €31,400

Income above the standard rate cut-off point
= €92,500 − €33,500
= €59,000

Income tax equation:

Gross tax − tax credit = tax payable

$$€31,400 − €5,300 = €26,100$$

Therefore, she pays €26,100 in tax.

(ii) USC = 2% of €10,036 + 4% of €5,980 + 7% of €76,484

$$= €10,036 × 0·02 + €5,980 × 0·04 + €76,484 × 0·07$$

$$= €200·72 + €239·20 + €5,353·88$$

$$= €5,793·80$$

(iii) Gross pay per week = €92,500 ÷ 52

$$= €1,778·85$$

PRSI due = 0% on first €127 + 4% on €1,651·85

$$= €0 + €66·07$$

$$= €66·07 \text{ per week}$$

(iv)

Deductions:	**Total**
Income tax	€26,100
USC	€5,793·80
PRSI = €66·07 × 52 =	€3,435·64
Trade union subscriptions = €15 × 26 =	€390
Health insurance = €85 × 12 =	€1,020
Pension contributions = €350 × 12 =	€4,200
Total deduction in one year:	€40,939·44

Annual net income = gross income − total deductions

$$= €92,500 − €40,939·44$$

$$= €51,560·56$$

Weekly net income = €51,560·56 ÷ 52 = €991·55

Exercise 8.8

1. Charlie has a gross income of €81,000. His standard rate cut-off point is €38,500. The standard rate of tax is 21% and the higher rate is 42%. He has a tax credit of €4,200.

   (i) Calculate the total amount of income tax Charlie must pay for the year.

   (ii) Calculate Charlie's USC payment for the year.

   Charlie is in PRSI class A1, which means that he does not pay PRSI on the first €127 earned per week, but he pays it at a rate of 4% on all income above that amount (assume a 52-week year).

   (iii) Calculate Charlie's PRSI contribution per week, to the nearest cent.

   (iv) What is Charlie's weekly net income after all deductions?

2. Hannah has a gross income of €61,500. Her standard rate cut-off point is €27,000. The standard rate of tax is 18% and the higher rate is 39%. She has a tax credit of €3,600.

   (i) Calculate the total amount of income tax Hannah must pay for the year.

   (ii) Calculate Hannah's USC payment for the year.

   Hannah is in PRSI class B1, which means that she does not pay PRSI on the first €26 earned per week, but she pays it at a rate of 2% on all income above that amount (assume a 52-week year).

   (iii) Calculate Hannah's PRSI contribution per week, to the nearest cent.

   (iv) What is Hannah's weekly net income after all deductions?

3. Mairead has a gross income of €76,000. Her standard rate cut-off point is €25,500. The standard rate of tax is 19% and the higher rate is 41%. She has a tax credit of €4,100. Mairead is in PRSI class D2, which means that she does not pay PRSI on the first €26 earned per week, but she pays it at a rate of 2·35% on all income above that amount (assume a 52-week year). Mairead pays trade union subscriptions of €13 every two weeks and health insurance of €100 a month.

   (i) Calculate the total amount of income tax Mairead must pay for the year.

   (ii) Calculate her USC payment for the year.

   (iii) Calculate her PRSI contribution per week, to the nearest cent.

   (iv) What is Mairead's weekly net income after all deductions?

4. Graham has a gross income of €70,000. His standard rate cut-off point is €28,200. The standard rate of tax is 19% and the higher rate is 41%. He has a tax credit of €3,750. Graham is in PRSI class A1, which means that he does not pay PRSI on the first €127 earned per week, but he pays it at a rate of 4% on all income above that amount (assume a

52-week year). Graham pays trade union subscriptions of €17 every two weeks, health insurance of €99 a month and a pension contribution of €375 per month.

   (i) Calculate the total amount of income tax Graham must pay for the year.

  (ii) Calculate his USC payment for the year.

 (iii) Calculate his PRSI contribution per week, to the nearest cent.

 (iv) What is Graham's weekly net income after all deductions?

5. Ian has a gross income of €81,500. His standard rate cut-off point is €31,000. The standard rate of tax is 20% and the higher rate is 40%. He has a tax credit of €3,750. Ian is in PRSI class B1, which means that he does not pay PRSI on the first €26 earned per week, but he pays it at a rate of 2% on all income above that amount (assume a 52-week year). Ian pays trade union subscriptions of €17 every two weeks, health insurance of €79 a month, a pension contribution of €320 per month and a salary protection insurance payment of €41 every two weeks.

   (i) Calculate the total amount of income tax Ian must pay for the year.

  (ii) Calculate his USC payment for the year.

 (iii) Calculate his PRSI contribution per week, to the nearest cent.

 (iv) What is Ian's weekly net income after all deductions?

People advertising loans and investment product want to make their products seems as attractive as possible. They may have different ways of calculating the interest and the products might involve different periods of time. This makes it difficult for consumers to compare the products. Therefore, governments have rules about what information must be provided in advertisements for financial products and in the agreements that businesses make with their customers.

Time value of money

This is the value of money when factoring in a given amount of interest earned over a given time period. This is a concept which says it is more valuable to receive a sum of money now than in a year or two, as if you receive it now you can invest it and earn interest on it. For example, if you had €100 today and invested it at an interest rate of 3%, it would be worth €103 in a year's time. So, €100 now has the same value as €103 one year from now, given a 3% interest (growth) rate.

Present value

Also known as present discounted value, this is the value on a given date of a future payment or series of future payments, discounted to reflect the time value of money and other factors such as investment risk, etc. Present value calculations are used, for example, to find the fair market value of a bond, the amount of each regular payment for a given loan, how much money to invest now to receive a specific cash amount in the future and the size of a pension fund required on the date of retirement to give a fixed income every year for a certain number of years.

Discount rate

When future values are brought back to present values at a given rate of interest, the interest rate is referred to as the discount rate.

Annual equivalent rate (AER) and annual percentage rate (APR)

Nowadays, if you put your money into a savings account or into an investment, you should be given the annual equivalent rate (AER). The AER can also be referred to as the equivalent annual rate (EAR) or the compound annual rate (CAR). You may have invested your money for any period of time, but the AER tells you how much your money would earn in **exactly one year**. For example, suppose a bank offers you a five-year deal: 4% interest for the first six months followed by 2% for the remainder of the time. It will be much simpler to compare this deal with others if you can compare them on some common standard. The AER would, in this case, give you one simple annual percentage to use for comparison.

When borrowing money, there are often other costs involved, such as a set-up fee. Because these other costs can be significant, lenders are expected to tell the borrower the annual percentage rate (APR). This again allows a potential borrower to compare different loans to see which is more expensive.

Bonds

A bond is a certificate issued by a government or a public company promising to repay borrowed money at a fixed rate of interest at a specified time.

Interest

Interest is the sum of money that you pay for borrowing money or that is paid to you for lending money.

When dealing with interest, we use the following symbols.

> P = the **principal**, the sum of money borrowed or invested at the beginning of the period.
>
> t = the **time**, the number of weeks/months/years for which the sum of money is borrowed or invested.
>
> i = the **interest rate**, the percentage rate per week/month/year expressed as a fraction or a decimal at which interest is charged.
>
> A = the **amount** of money, including interest, at the end of a week/month/year.
>
> F = the **final amount**, i.e. the final sum of money, including interest, at the end of the period.

Note: per annum = per year.

Compound interest

When a sum of money earns interest, this interest is often added to the principal to form a new principal. This new principal earns interest in the next year and so on. This is called **compound interest**.

When calculating compound interest, do the following.

Method 1:

> Calculate the interest for the **first** year and add this to the principal to form the new principal for the next year. Calculate the interest for **one** year on this new principal and add it on to form the principal for the next year, and so on. The easiest way to calculate each stage is to multiply the principal at the beginning of each year by the factor:
>
> $$(1 + i)$$
>
> This will give the principal for the next year, and so on.

Method 2:

If the number of years is greater than three, then using a formula and a calculator will be much quicker.

> Use the formula: $F = P(1 + i)^t$

Note: The formula does not work if:

> the interest rate, i, is changed during the period
>
> **or**
>
> money is added or subtracted during the period.

EXAMPLE 1

Calculate the compound interest on €10,000 for three years at 4% per annum.

Solution:

$$1 + i = 1 + \frac{4}{100} = 1 + 0\cdot04 = 1\cdot04$$

Method 1:

$P_1 = 10{,}000$	(principal for the first year)
$A_1 = 10{,}000 \times 1\cdot04 = 10{,}400$	(amount at the end of the first year)
$P_2 = 10{,}400$	(principal for the second year)
$A_2 = 10{,}400 \times 1\cdot04 = 10{,}816$	(amount at the end of the second year)
$P_3 = 10{,}816$	(principal for the third year)
$A_3 = 10{,}816 \times 1\cdot04 = 11{,}248\cdot64$	(amount at the end of the third year)

Compound interest $= A_3 - P_1 = €11{,}248\cdot64 - €10{,}000 = €1{,}248\cdot64$.

The working can also be shown using a table:

Year	Principal	Amount
1	10,000	$10{,}000 \times 1{\cdot}04 = 10{,}400$
2	10,400	$10{,}400 \times 1{\cdot}04 = 10{,}816$
3	10,816	$10{,}816 \times 1{\cdot}04 = 11{,}248{\cdot}64$

Compound interest $= A_3 - P_1 = €11{,}248{\cdot}64 - €10{,}000 = €1{,}248{\cdot}64$.

Method 2:

Given: $P = 10{,}000, \quad i = \dfrac{4}{100} = 0{\cdot}04, \quad t = 3$. Find F.

$$F = P(1 + i)^t$$
$$= 10{,}000(1{\cdot}04)^3$$
$$F = 11{,}248{\cdot}64$$

Compound interest $= F - P = €11{,}248{\cdot}64 - €10{,}000 = €1{,}248{\cdot}64$.

EXAMPLE 2

€12,000 was invested at a rate of 4.5% per annum. If the future value of the investment is €14,954, calculate the number of year, t, that the money had been invested for.

Solution:

Given: $P = 12{,}500$, rate $= 4.5\%$, $t = $ t years.

$$F = P(1 + i)^t$$
$$14{,}954 = 12{,}000(1 + 0.045)^t \quad \text{(divide both sides by 12,000)}$$
$$1{\cdot}246167 = (1.045)^t \quad \text{(} \log_e \text{ both sides)}$$
$$\log_e 1{\cdot}246167 = \log_e (1.045)^t$$
$$\log_e 1{\cdot}246167 = t \log_e (1.045)$$
$$\frac{\log_e 1.246167}{\log_e (1.045)} = t \quad \text{(divide both sides by } \log_e (1.045))$$
$$4.999 = t$$

Therefore, $t = 5$ years.

EXAMPLE 3

An investment bond offers a 15% return at the end of 4 years. Calculate the AER for this bond.

Solution:

Formula: $F = P(1 + i)^t$

Where:

F = final value	P = principal
F = principal + interest	P = 100%
F = 100% + 15%	P = 1
F = 115%	
F = 1·15	

t = No. of years	i = AER
t = 4 years	

$$F = P(1 + i)^t$$
$$1·15 = 1(1 + i)^4$$
$$\sqrt[4]{1·15} = 1 + i$$
$$1·035558 = 1 + i$$
$$0·035558 = i$$
$$3·56\% = i$$

Continuous compounding

Sometimes the interest is compounded continuously. In this case, the compounding period becomes infinitesimally small and so the growth rate is exponential.

The formula for calculating the final value is:

$$F = Pe^{rt}$$

Where:

F = final value	P = principal
r = nominal annual rate	t = number of years

EXAMPLE 4

€2,250 is invested in a savings account where the interest is compounded continuously with a nominal annual rate of 3·5%. Calculate the future value of this investment in three years.

Solution:

Given: $P = 2{,}250$, rate = 3·5%, so $r = \dfrac{3{\cdot}5}{100} = 0{\cdot}035$, $t = 3$ years.

$$F = Pe^{rt}$$
$$F = (2{,}250)e^{(0{\cdot}035)(3)}$$
$$F = (2{,}250)e^{0{\cdot}105}$$
$$F = 2{,}499{\cdot}10$$

Thus, after three years, the investment is worth €2,499·10

Exercise 9.1

1. Calculate the compound interest on €750 for 3 years at 10% per annum.

2. Calculate the compound interest on €12,400 for 2 years at 6·5% per annum.

3. A painting was purchased for €33,000. If it appreciates in value by 4·5% per annum, what would be its value in 5 years time, correct to the nearest euro?

4. A sum of €5,000 is invested with an annual equivalent rate (AER) of 6%. Find the value of the investment when it matures in eight years' time.

5. €20,000 was invested for three years at compound interest. The rate for the first year was $3\frac{1}{2}$%, the rate for the second year was 5%, and the rate for the third year was 4%. Calculate the amount after three years.

6. €8,500 is invested in a savings account where the interest is compounded continuously with a nominal annual rate of 2·8%. Calculate the future value of this investment in three years.

7. €15,000 is invested in a savings account where the interest is compounded continuously with an annual rate of 3·5%. Calculate the future value of this investment in four and a half years.

8. If $F = P(1 + i)^t$, express P in terms of F, I and T. Hence, or otherwise, find what sum of money will have a future value of €88,578·05 in 6 years at 10% per annum compound interest.

9. What sum of money, to the nearest euro, will have a future value of €4,116·69 in 4 years at 6·5% per annum compound interest?

10. What sum of money, to the nearest euro, will have a future value of €2,036·53 in five years at 2·5% AER?

11. What sum of money, to the nearest euro, will have a future value of €1,300 in two years at an AER of 4% if the interest is compounded continuously?

12. What sum of money, to the nearest euro, will earn €402.25 interest in four years at 3·8% per annum compound interest?

13. **(i)** A sum of €4,500 is invested with an AER of 5%. Find the value of the investment in six years' time.
   (ii) A different investment account gives a lump sum of 20% interest after six years. Calculate the AER for this bond, to two decimal places.

14. €15,500 was invested at a rate of r% per annum. If the future value of the investment in five years' time was €21,236·34, calculate the value of r, to one decimal place.

15. €8,000 was invested at a rate of r% per annum. If the future value of the investment in three years' time was €8,741·82, calculate the value of r.

16. Janet invests in a bond which will pay out 12% at the end of three years. Calculate the AER for this bond, to two decimal places.

17. €12,000 was invested at a rate of r% per annum, compounded continuously. If the future value of the investment in two and a half years' time was €13,195·91, calculate the value of r.

18. €7,500 was invested at a rate of r% per annum, compounded continuously. If the future value of the investment in four years' time was €9,345·58, calculate the value of r.

19. David invests in a bond which will pay out 16% at the end of five years. Calculate the AER for this bond, to two decimal places.

20. A government bond offers 50% gross return after 10 years. Calculate the EAR for the bond, to two decimal places.

21. A woman borrowed €30,000 at 6% per annum compound interest. She agreed to repay €5,000 at the end of the first year, €5,000 at the end of the second year and to clear the debt at the end of the third year. How much was paid to clear the debt?

22. A man borrowed €15,000. He agreed to repay €2,000 after one year, €3,000 after two years and the balance at the end of the third year. If the interest was charged at 8% in the first year, 5% in the second year and 6% in the third year, how much was paid to clear the debt?

23. €75,000 was invested for three years at compound interest. The rate for the first year was 3%. The rate for the second year was $2\frac{1}{2}$ %. At the end of the second year, €10,681·25 was withdrawn.
   (i) Find the principal for the third year.
   (ii) The rate for the third year was r%. The total investment at the end of the third year was €70,897·50. Calculate the value of r.

24. A person invested €30,000 for three years at 5% AER.

    (i) Calculate the amount after two years.

    (ii) After two years, a sum of money was withdrawn. The money which remained amounted to €26,250 at the end of the third year. Calculate the amount of money withdrawn after two years.

25. €45,000 was invested for three years at compound interest. The AER for the first year was 6%, the AER for the second year was 4% and the AER for the third year was 3%. At the end of the first year, €7,700 was withdrawn. At the end of the second year, €W was withdrawn. At the end of the third year, the investment was worth €37,080. Find the value of W.

Depreciation

Over time, material goods (e.g. machinery, vehicles, etc.) lose value as a result of wear and tear, age or obsolescence. This loss of value is known as depreciation.

Reducing balance method

Using the reducing balance method, the cost of the asset is depreciated at a constant rate each year. This method is based on the principle that an asset is more useful in its initial years than in its later years. So, instead of spreading the total cost of the asset over its productive lifespan, it is expensed at a constant rate. The depreciated value of an asset can be found by calculating the value at the end of each year or by using the depreciation formula.

Depreciation formula

$$F = P(1 - i)^t$$

Where: F = final value (net book value, NBV)
P = original value at the start of the period
i = rate, in decimal form
t = number of years

EXAMPLE

A company buys a machine for €12,000. They estimate that it will depreciate at a rate of 9% per annum. Find the value of the machine, to the nearest euro, after four years by:

(i) Calculating the net book value at the end of each year

(ii) Using the depreciation formula

Solution:

(i)

Year	Value at the start of the year	Depreciation	Value at the end of the year
1	12,000	12,000 × 9% = 1,080	12,000 − 1,080 = 10,920
2	10,920	10,920 × 9% = 982·80	10,920 − 982·80 = 9,937·20
3	9,937·20	9,937·20 × 9% = 894·348	9,937·20 − 894·348 = 9,042·852
4	9,042·852	9,042·852 × 9% = 813·85668	9,042·852 − 813·85668 = 8,228·99532

So the value at the end of the 4th year is 8,228·995 = €8,229.

(ii) $P = 12,000$, rate = 9%, so $i = \dfrac{9}{100} = 0·09$, $t = 4$ years.

$F = P(1 - i)^t$

$F = 12,000(1 - 0·09)^4$

$F = 12,000(0·91)^4$

$F = 8,228·995$

Thus, after four years, the machine is worth €8,229.

Continuously declining value

Sometimes the depreciation is compounded continuously. In this case, the compounding period becomes infinitesimally small and so the depreciation rate is exponential.

Formula for continuous depreciation

$$F = Pe^{-rt}$$

Where:

F = final value (net book value, NBV)

P = original value at the start of the period

r = nominal annual rate

t = number of years

Exercise 9.2

1. A machine depreciates at 10% per annum. It was bought for €55,000.

   (i) Use a table to calculate the value of the machine at the end of each year over a three-year period.

   (ii) Use the formula for depreciation to check your answer for the net book value of the machine at the end of the third year.

2. A car depreciates at 15% per annum. It was bought for €30,000. Find the value of the car after three years.

3. A machine costs €100,000 when new. In the first year it depreciates by 15%. In the second year it depreciates by 8% of its value at the end of the first year. In the third year it depreciates by 5% of its value at the end of the second year.

New price	€100,000
Value after 1 year	
Value after 2 years	
Value after 3 years	

   (i) Copy and complete the table to calculate the machine's value after three years.

   (ii) Calculate its total depreciation after three years.

4. Robert bought a new car for €36,500. If the rate of depreciation on the car is 6% the first year and then 4% for every year after that, what would be the value of the car after five years?

5. A company buys a photocopier for €2,800 and four new computers at €950 each. After four years the company runs into financial difficulty and so must sell off its assets. The photocopier depreciated at a rate of 4% per annum and the computers depreciated at a rate of 9% the first year and then 7·5% per annum after that.

   (i) Calculate how much money the company can sell these items for after the four years.

   (ii) What was the total percentage loss that the company experienced on these goods?

6. Joanne's car depreciated at the rate of 16% per annum. If she sold it for €4,500, how much did Joanne pay for the car when she bought it seven years ago, to the nearest euro?

7. David bought a car for €9,000. After how many years will the value of the car fall below €3,000 if the annual rate of depreciation is 16.7%?

8. A company buys a computer for €1,600. If the computer depreciates by 10% per annum, how long is it before the computer loses half its value? Give your answer correct to the nearest year.

9. The NBV of an asset is €110,086 and the depreciation rate for this asset is 6%. If the original cost was €150,000, how many years' depreciation have been written off this asset?

10. A fleet of trucks was purchased at the start of January 2001 for €1·2 million. The NBV of the fleet was €425,000 at the end of December 2011.

   (i) Find the annual rate of depreciation.

   (ii) Hence, find the value of the fleet at the end of 2005, correct to the nearest €10,000.

11. A car was bought for €24,000 in January 2006 and depreciates at a rate of $r\%$ per annum. If the NBV of the car at the end of 2009 was €18,738, calculate the value of r.

12. A computer is bought for €1,250. If it depreciates continuously with a nominal annual rate of 8%, calculate the NBV of the computer after three years.

13. A tractor is bought for €12,500. If it depreciates continuously with a nominal annual rate of 7·5%, calculate the NBV of the tractor after five years.

14. A helicopter is bought for €110,000. It depreciates continuously with a nominal annual rate of $r\%$. If its future value after seven years is €72,275, calculate the nominal annual rate.

15. A bus is bought for €85,000. It depreciates continuously with a nominal annual rate of $r\%$. If its net book value after five years is €67,874, calculate the nominal annual rate, to one decimal place.

Other situations of growth or decline

The compound formula does not only apply to financial situations; it can be used in any situation where the value is increasing or decreasing at a steady rate (e.g. population growth, bacteria growth).

EXAMPLE

(i) If there are 120 bacteria at 0 hours and the bacteria grows at 5% per hour, how many bacteria will there be at 24 hours?

(ii) If the growth continues at this rate, how many bacteria will be present in one week?

Solution:

(i) $F = P(1 + i)^t$

$F = 120(1 + 0.05)^{24}$

$F = 387.01$ bacteria

(ii) We must first work out how many hours are in one week:

1 week = 7 days × 24 hours = 168 hours

$F = P(1 + i)^t$

$F = 120(1 + 0.05)^{168}$

$F = 435,495.32$ bacteria

Exercise 9.3

1. The present population of a country is 23·7 million people. If this is expected to increase by 1·8% per annum over the next decade, find the population of the country in 10 years' time.

2. A farmer has 6,000 sheep on his property. During a drought, 6% of the herd dies each month. How many sheep died during the first year?

3. A town had a population of 45,000 people. 53% of the population were men and the remainder were women. During the Black Plague, 12% of the men and 8% of the women died each month.

   (i) After the first year of the plague, what was the population of the town?

   (ii) At the end of the first year, what percentage of the population was male?

4. (i) In city A, house prices have increased by 3% each year for the last three years. If a house cost €180,000 three years ago, calculate, to the nearest euro, its value today.

   (ii) In city B, a house worth €100,000 three years ago is now valued at €119,102. Calculate the yearly percentage increase in the value of this house.

5. The diameter of a tree trunk increases by 2% of its previous year's value each year that the weather is good and by 0·7% of its previous year's value each year when the weather is bad.

   2001 and 2004 were years when the weather was good. 2002 and 2003 were years when the weather was bad.

   At the end of 2000, the diameter of a tree trunk was 81·8 cm. What was its diameter, to one decimal place, at the end of:

   (i) 2001   (ii) 2004

6. Under certain conditions, the number of bacteria in a particular culture doubles every 10 seconds. If a sample of this bacteria contains 20 bacteria at the start of observation, how many bacteria will be present after:

   (i) One minute   (ii) One hour

   (iii) After how long, to the nearest second, will the culture contain 26,000 bacteria?

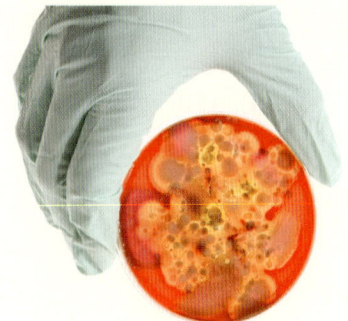

7. A biologist is researching a species of bacteria. At time $t = 0$ hours, she puts 100 bacteria into what she has determined to be a favourable growth medium. Six hours later, she measures 450 bacteria. Assuming continuous growth, what is the growth rate, k, for the bacteria? (Round k to two decimal places.)

8. A certain type of bacteria, given a favourable growth medium, doubles in population every 6·5 hours. Given that there were approximately 100 bacteria to start with, how many bacteria will there be in a day and a half?

Net present value

This concept is used to determine whether or not something would be a good investment.

> Net present value (NPV) = present value of all cash inflows − present value of all cash outflows.
> If NPV > 0, the investment will yield a profit and so would be a good investment.
> If NPV ≤ 0, the investment will make a loss and so would be a bad investment.

EXAMPLE

Colm is setting up a new company and he is looking for investors. He outlines the projected cash outflows and inflows for the first five years of business.

Year	0	1	2	3	4
Cash flow (€)	−25,000	−10,000	12,000	18,000	21,000

If a potential investor was to apply a discount rate of 4%, would it be worthwhile for them to invest in this company?

Solution:

We must calculate the present value of each of these future values, based on a discount rate of 4%, using the formula $P = \dfrac{F}{(1 + i)^t}$.

Note: The initial outflow is not discounted, as it is already at its present value.

Year 0	−25,000	−25,000·00
Year 1	$\dfrac{-10,000}{(1 + 0·04)^1}$	−9,615·38
Year 2	$\dfrac{12,000}{(1 + 0·04)^2}$	11,094·67
Year 3	$\dfrac{18,000}{(1 + 0·04)^3}$	16,001·93
Year 4	$\dfrac{21,000}{(1 + 0·04)^4}$	17,950·89
	Net present value:	€10,432·11

Since NPV > 0, the investors should invest in Colm's company.

Exercise 9.4

1. Janet is setting up a new company and she is looking for investors. She outlines the projected cash outflows and inflows for the first five years of business.

Year	0	1	2	3	4
Cash flow (€)	−21,000	−13,000	−2,500	15,000	24,000

If a potential investor was to apply a discount rate of 6%, would it be worthwhile for them to invest in this company? Justify your answer.

2. Howard is setting up a new company and he is looking for investors. He outlines the projected cash outflows and inflows for the first five years of business.

Year	0	1	2	3	4
Cash flow (€)	−12,000	−7,500	1,500	8,250	11,300

If a potential investor was to apply a discount rate of 4·5%, would it be worthwhile for them to invest in this company? Justify your answer.

3. Jake is an investor. He is presented with the following investment options:

Year	0	1	2	3	4
Cash flow (€) company A	−9,500	−4,000	3,600	8,200	11,750
Cash flow (€) company B	−14,500	−7,600	2,000	10,500	16,250

Applying a discount rate of 5%, which company would you advise Jake to invest in? Justify your answer.

4. The marketing section of Harvey Inc. proposed a new advertising campaign which will cost the company €40,000 to set up in the first year. However, it is projected that this new campaign will generate a cash inflow of €12,000 per year over the following four years. Applying a discount rate of 4%, should the company invest in this new campaign?

5. Pat is presented with an investment opportunity. If he invests €12,000 now, he will receive a payment of €4,500 at the end of each year for the next three years. Growth over this period is estimated to be 4·5%. Use present values to determine whether Pat should invest in this scheme.

6. A company is trying to raise capital. They offer an investment opportunity where if an investor pays them €25,000 now, the investor will receive €6,500 at the end of each year for the next four years. The growth over this period is estimated to be 3·8%.

    (i) Do you think the company will get many people investing in this scheme? Justify your answer.

    (ii) Suggest a way that the company could make this investment scheme more attractive for potential investors.

Applications of geometric series

Some saving schemes require the investor to save a fixed amount at regular intervals (e.g. to save €100 per month). Certain loan repayment schedules will require the borrower to make regular payments at fixed intervals of time. Calculations involving regular payments require the summation of a geometric series.

Annuities

An annuity is a form of investment involving a series of periodic equal contributions made by an individual to an account for a specified term. The term 'annuity' is also used for a series of regular payments made to an individual for a specified time.

Pension funds involve making contributions to an annuity before retirement and receiving contributions from an annuity after retirement. Other examples of annuities are monthly rent payments, social welfare benefits, annual premium for life insurance, loan repayments and regular deposits into a savings account.

Payments in periods other than annually

Calculations are the same as for annual payments, but the AER or APR must be treated appropriately.

Method 1	Method 2
• Leave time in years. • Do not change the APR/AER. • Use fractional units of time.	• Switch to a different time period. • Adjust the APR/AER accordingly. • Use whole number units of time.

EXAMPLE 1

A credit union offers a special savings account with an AER of 3.5%. Natalie deposits €100 at the start of each month for a three-year period. How much will her investment be worth at the end of the three years?

Solution:

Method 1: Leave time in years, use fraction units of time.

Use the formula: $F = P(1 + i)^t$ Let: $P = 100$, $i = 0 \cdot 035$

The first €100 deposit will be in the account for 36 months $\left(\frac{36}{12}\text{ years}\right)$, the second €100 deposit will be in the account for 35 months, etc.

$$F = 100(1 \cdot 035)^{\frac{36}{12}} + 100(1 \cdot 035)^{\frac{35}{12}} + 100(1 \cdot 035)^{\frac{34}{12}} + \cdots + 100(1 \cdot 035)^{\frac{1}{12}}$$

$$F = 100[(1 \cdot 035)^{\frac{36}{12}} + (1 \cdot 035)^{\frac{35}{12}} + (1 \cdot 035)^{\frac{34}{12}} + \cdots + (1 \cdot 035)^{\frac{1}{12}}]$$

Rewriting the series in ascending order:

$$F = 100[(1 \cdot 035)^{\frac{1}{12}} + (1 \cdot 035)^{\frac{2}{12}} + (1 \cdot 035)^{\frac{3}{12}} + \cdots + (1 \cdot 035)^{\frac{36}{12}}]$$

The part in the squared brackets is a geometric series, where: $a = (1 \cdot 035)^{\frac{1}{12}}$

$$r = (1 \cdot 035)^{\frac{1}{12}}$$

$$S_n = \frac{a(r^n - 1)}{(r - 1)}$$

$$S_{36} = \frac{(1 \cdot 035)^{\frac{1}{12}}\left[\left((1 \cdot 035)^{\frac{1}{12}}\right)^{36} - 1\right]}{\left((1 \cdot 035)^{\frac{1}{12}} - 1\right)}$$

$$S_{36} = \frac{1 \cdot 00287[0 \cdot 1087]}{(0 \cdot 00287)}$$

$$S_{36} = 37 \cdot 9833$$

So,

$$F = 100(37 \cdot 9833)$$
$$F = €3,798 \cdot 33$$

Method 2: Change time to months and adjust AER.

Adjust AER to find monthly percentage rate:

$$F = P(1 + i)^t$$
$$1 \cdot 035 = 1(1 + i)^{12}$$
$$\sqrt[12]{1 \cdot 035} = 1 + i$$

$$1\cdot00287 = 1 + i$$
$$0\cdot00287 = i$$

The first €100 deposit will be in the account for 36 months, the second €100 deposit will be in the account for 35 months, etc.

$$F = 100(1\cdot00287)^{36} + 100(1\cdot00287)^{35} + 100(1\cdot00287)34 + \cdots + 100(1\cdot00287)^{1}$$
$$F = 100[(1\cdot00287)^{36} + (1\cdot00287)^{35} + (1\cdot00287)^{34} + \cdots + (1\cdot00287)^{1}]$$

Rewriting the series in ascending order:

$$F = 100[(1\cdot00287)^{1} + (1\cdot00287)^{2} + (1\cdot00287)^{3} + \cdots + (1\cdot00287)^{36}]$$

The part in the squared brackets is a geometric series, where: $a = (1\cdot00287)^{1}$
$$r = 1\cdot00287$$

$$S_n = \frac{a(r^n - 1)}{(r - 1)}$$

$$S_{36} = \frac{1\cdot00287[(1\cdot00287)^{36} - 1]}{(1\cdot00287 - 1)}$$

$$S_{36} = \frac{1\cdot00287[0\cdot1087]}{(0\cdot00287)}$$

$$S_{36} = 37\cdot9833$$

So,

$$F = 100(37\cdot9833)$$
$$F = €3{,}798\cdot33$$

EXAMPLE 2

A company wishes to raise capital to expand their business. They offer a 10-year €2,500 bond that will pay €100 every year, at the **end** of each year, for 10 years. Given an APR of 4·5%, calculate a fair market value for this bond.

Solution:
First, calculate the present value of a future payment of €2,500, in 10 years' time, at a rate of 4·5% per annum.

$$F = P(1 + i)^t$$
$$2{,}500 = P(1 + 0\cdot045)^{10}$$
$$\frac{2{,}500}{(1\cdot045)^{10}} = P$$
$$€1{,}609\cdot82 = P$$

Secondly, calculate the cost of a payment of €100 at the end of each year at a rate of 4·5% per annum.

Cost = (present value of €100 at end of yr 1) + … + (present value of €100 at end of yr 10)

$$\text{Cost} = \frac{100}{(1\cdot045)^1} + \frac{100}{(1\cdot045)^2} + \frac{100}{(1\cdot045)^3} + \cdots + \frac{100}{(1\cdot045)^{10}}$$

This is the sum of a geometric series where $a = \dfrac{100}{(1\cdot045)^1} = 95\cdot6937799$ and $r = \dfrac{1}{1\cdot045}$.

$$S_n = \frac{a(1-r^n)}{(1-r)}$$

$$S_{10} = \frac{95\cdot6937799\left(1 - \left(\dfrac{1}{1\cdot045}\right)^{10}\right)}{\left(1 - \dfrac{1}{1\cdot045}\right)}$$

$$S_{10} = \frac{95\cdot6937799(0\cdot356072318)}{\left(\dfrac{0\cdot045}{1\cdot045}\right)} = 791\cdot27$$

So the total cost of this bond is €1,609·82 + €791·27 = €2,401·09.

This means that if an investor purchases this bond now at a fair market value of €2,401·09, they will receive a payment of €100 at the end of each year for the next 10 years as well as a payment of €2,500 at the end of the 10th year.

EXAMPLE 3

Craig needs €8,000 in four years. How much should he deposit at the **end** of each month in an account that pays 6% (AER) in order to achieve his goal?

Solution:

Use the formula: $F = P(1+i)^t$ Let: $F = 8{,}000$ $P = x$ $i = 0\cdot06$

Since he is making the deposit at the end of each month, the first deposit will be in the account for 47 months ($\frac{47}{12}$ years), the second deposit will be in the account for 46 months, etc.

$$8{,}000 = x(1\cdot06)^{\frac{47}{12}} + x(1\cdot06)^{\frac{46}{12}} + x(1\cdot06)^{\frac{45}{12}} + \cdots + x(1\cdot06)^{\frac{1}{12}} + x$$

$$8{,}000 = x[1 + (1\cdot06)^{\frac{1}{12}} + (1\cdot06)^{\frac{2}{12}} + (1\cdot06)^{\frac{3}{12}} + \cdots + (1\cdot06)^{\frac{47}{12}}]$$

The part in the squared brackets is a geometric series, where:

$$a = 1 \quad r = (1 \cdot 06)^{\frac{1}{12}}$$

$$S_n = \frac{a(r^n - 1)}{(r - 1)}$$

$$S_{48} = \frac{1\left[\left((1 \cdot 06)^{\frac{1}{12}}\right)^{48} - 1\right]}{\left((1 \cdot 06)^{\frac{1}{12}} - 1\right)}$$

$$S_{48} = \frac{1[0 \cdot 26247696]}{(0 \cdot 00486755)}$$

$$S_{48} = 53 \cdot 9238$$

So,

$$8{,}000 = x(53 \cdot 9238)$$
$$€148 \cdot 36 = x$$

Craig should deposit €148·36 at the end of each month for the next four years to achieve his goal of having €8,000 in four years' time.

EXAMPLE 4

Stuart is 35 years old and is planning for his pension. He intends to retire in 30 years' time, when he is 65. First, he calculates how much he wants to have in his pension fund when he retires. Then, he calculates how much he needs to invest in order to achieve this. He assumes that in the long run, money can be invested at an inflation adjusted annual rate of 3%, so all calculations should therefore be based on a 3% annual growth rate.

  (i) Write down the present value of a future payment of €25,000 in one year's time (i.e. if Stuart wants to receive €25,000 in one year's time, how much should he invest now, given that the interest rate is 3%?).

  (ii) Write down, in terms of t, the present value of a future payment of €25,000 in t years' time.

 (iii) Stuart wants to have a fund that could, from the date of his retirement, give him a payment of €25,000 at the start of each year for 25 years. Show how to use the sum of a geometric series to calculate the value on the date of retirement of the fund required.

(iv) Stuart plans to invest a fixed amount of money every month in order to generate the fund calculated in part **(iii)**. His retirement is $30 \times 12 = 360$ months away.

    (a) Find, correct to four significant figures, the rate of interest per month that would, if paid and compounded monthly, be equivalent to an effective annual rate of 3%.

    (b) Write down, in terms of n and P, the value on the retirement date of a payment of €P made n months before the retirement date.

    (c) If Stuart makes 360 equal payments of €P from now until his retirement, what value of P will give the fund he requires?

    (d) If Stuart waits five years before starting his pension investments, how much will he then have to pay each month in order to generate the same pension fund?

Solution:

(i) $P = \dfrac{F}{(1+i)^r} = \dfrac{25{,}000}{(1+0\cdot03)^1} = €24{,}271\cdot8447$

(ii) $P = \dfrac{F}{(1+i)^r} = \dfrac{25{,}000}{(1\cdot03)^t}$

(iii) The amount of money required in the fund at the start of the retirement must equal the sum of the present values of all the payments from the date of the retirement.

$$\text{Retirement fund} = \frac{25{,}000}{(1\cdot03)^0} + \frac{25{,}000}{(1\cdot03)^1} + \frac{25{,}000}{(1\cdot03)^2} + \frac{25{,}000}{(1\cdot03)^3} + \cdots + \frac{25{,}000}{(1\cdot03)^{24}}$$

This is the sum of a geometric series, where $a = 25{,}000$ and $r = \dfrac{1}{1\cdot03}$.

$$S_{25} = \frac{a(1 - r^n)}{1 - r}$$

$$S_{25} = \frac{25{,}000\left(1 - \left(\dfrac{1}{1\cdot03}\right)^{25}\right)}{1 - \dfrac{1}{1\cdot03}}$$

$$S_{25} = €448{,}388\cdot5531$$

(iv) (a)

$$F = P(1+i)^t$$
$$1\cdot03 = 1(1+i)^{12}$$
$$\sqrt[12]{1\cdot03} = 1+i$$
$$1\cdot00246627 = 1+i$$
$$0\cdot00246627 = i$$

So the rate of interest per month that would give an AER of 3% = 0.2466%.

(b) $F = P(1 + i)^n$

$\quad F = P(1 + 0.002466)^n$

(c) €448,388·5531 $= P(1 + i)^1 + P(1 + i)^2 + P(1 + i)^3 + \ldots + P(1 + i)^{360}$

€448,388·5531 $= P(1.002466)^1 + P(1.002466)^2 + \ldots + P(1.002466)^{360}$

€448,388·5531 $= P[(1.002466)^1 + (1.002466)^2 + (1.002466)^3 + \ldots + (1.002466)^{360}]$

This is the sum of a geometric series, where $a = 1.002466$ and $r = 1.002466$.

$$S_n = \frac{a(r^n - 1)}{r - 1}$$

$$S_{360} = \frac{1.002466(1.002466^{360} - 1)}{1.002466 - 1}$$

So,

$$€448,388\cdot5531 = P\left[\frac{1.002466(1.002466^{360} - 1)}{1.002466 - 1}\right]$$

€448,388·5531 $= P\,[580\cdot1080215]$

€772·94 $= P$: Monthly Payments

(d) If Stuart waits five years, then he will have 25 years to contribute. So the number of monthly contributions $= 25 \times 12 = 300$.

€448,388·5531 $= P[(1.002466)^1 + (1.002466)^2 + (1.002466)^3 + \ldots + (1.002466)^{300}]$

This is the sum of a geometric series, where $a = 1.002466$ and $r = 1.002466$.

$$S_n = \frac{a(r^n - 1)}{r - 1}$$

$$S_{300} = \frac{1.002466(1.002466^{300} - 1)}{1.002466 - 1}$$

So,

$$€448,388\cdot5531 = P\left[\frac{1.002466(1.002466^{300} - 1)}{1.002466 - 1}\right]$$

€448,388·5531 $= P\,[444\cdot5684266]$

€1,008·59 $= P$: Monthly Payments

Exercise 9.5

1. A bank offers a special savings account with an AER of 4·2%. A man deposits €250 at the start of each month for a two-year period. How much will his investment be worth at the end of the two years?

2. A building society offers a special savings account with an AER of 5·5%. A woman deposits €120 at the start of each month for a three-year period. How much will her investment be worth at the end of the three years?

3. A credit union offers a savings account with an EAR of 3·6%. A man deposits €175 at the end of each month, starting 31 January 2008. How much will his investment be worth on 31 December 2012?

4. A company plans to issue an eight-year €2,500 bond that will pay €150 at the end of every year. Based on an interest rate of 4% per annum, what is a fair market value for this bond?

5. The government plans to issue a 10-year €3,000 bond that will pay €100 at the start of every year (so you receive the first €100 immediately). Based on an interest rate of 6·5% per annum, what is a fair market value for this bond?

6. At the end of each month, a deposit of €400 is made into an account that pays an AER of 7%. What will the final amount be after six years?

7. At the end of each quarter (three months), a deposit of €280 is made into an account that pays an EAR of 5·5%. What will the final amount be after four years?

8. Khassim needs €5,000 in three years. How much should he deposit at the **end** of each month in an account that pays an AER of 4·8% in order to achieve his goal?

9. Judith needs €7,500 in four years. How much should she deposit at the **start** of each month in an account that pays an EAR of 3·75% in order to achieve her goal?

10. Grandparents Mairead and Jim want to start a regular savings account for their new grandchild so that on his 18th birthday he will have €24,000 to help fund his education. How much will they deposit at the end of each month to achieve this target if they avail of a regular savings scheme at 3·25% EAR?

11. Eddie plans to deposit €400 at the end of each month for three years in an account earning 3·25% AER. What single sum of money would Eddie need to invest now to achieve the same future value?

12. You have won a prize in a lottery. The prize entitles you to €1,500 per month, paid at the end of each month, for the next 20 years. However, you would prefer to have the entire amount now, in a lump sum. If the EAR is 5·5%, how much will you accept as a lump sum?

13. Aisling won a prize in a lottery. She has
    been given a choice of two options.

    Option A: Receive an annuity of €1,200 at
    the beginning of each month for
    25 years.

    Option B: Take a lump sum instead.

    Aisling decides to take Option B.

    (i) What lump sum should she accept assuming an AER of 6%?

    (ii) She invests the lump sum she receives, for 20 years, in an account that pays an AER of
    4·5%. How much will Aisling's investment have amounted to after the 20 years?

14. Una won €1,200,000 in a lottery, to be received in four annual payments of €300,000. She
    will receive the first payment exactly one year from now.

    (i) What is the present value of the four payments if the interest rate is 5·4% AER?

    (ii) Did it cost the lottery €1,200,000 to pay Una her prize money? Explain.

15. A1 Software Company needs to raise money to expand. It issues a 12-year bond of €1,500
    that pays €50 at the end of every six-month period for the 12 years. If the current market
    annual EAR is 6·75%, with interest added at six-month intervals, what is the fair market
    value of the bond?

16. The management company of an apartment
    block estimates that they will need €22,000 in
    three years' time to repaint the outside of the
    building and common areas.

    If regular payments are made to an investment
    fund earning 4·25% EAR, calculate:

    (i) The rate of interest per month that would,
    if paid and compounded monthly, be
    equivalent to an effective annual rate
    of 4·25%

    (ii) How much must be deposited at the end
    of each month to meet this target

    (iii) How much interest will be earned in the three years

17. Terry is planning for his pension. He intends to retire in 35 years' time. He assumes that money can be invested at an inflation adjusted annual rate of 4·2%, so all calculations should therefore be based on a 4·2% annual growth rate.

   (i) Terry wants to have a fund that could, from the date of his retirement, give him a payment of €30,000 at the start of each year for 25 years. Use the sum of a geometric series to calculate the value of the fund required on the date of retirement.

   (ii) Terry plans to invest a fixed amount of money at the start of every month in order to generate the fund calculated in part (i). His retirement is $35 \times 12 = 420$ months away.

       (a) If Terry makes 420 equal payments of €P from now until his retirement, what value of P will give the fund he requires?

       (b) If Terry waits seven years before starting his pension investments, how much will he then have to pay each month in order to generate the same pension fund?

18. Grainne is planning for her pension. She intends to retire in 38 years' time. She assumes that money can be invested at an inflation adjusted annual rate of 3·8%, so all calculations should therefore be based on a 3·8% annual growth rate.

   (i) Grainne wants to have a fund that could, from the date of her retirement, give her a payment of €35,000 at the start of each year for 27 years. Use the sum of a geometric series to calculate the value on the date of retirement of the fund required.

   (ii) Grainne plans to invest a fixed amount of money at the start of every month in order to generate the fund calculated in part (i). Her retirement is 38 years away.

       (a) If Grainne makes 456 equal payments of €P from now until her retirement, what value of P will give the fund she requires?

       (b) If Grainne waits four years before starting her pension investments, how much will she then have to pay each month in order to generate the same pension fund?

19. Marian contributed €100 at the end of each week for 20 years to a pension fund earning 4·6% AER. Take one year to be 52 weeks.

   (i) Find the rate of interest per week which would, if paid and compounded weekly, be equivalent to an effective annual rate of 4·6%.

   (ii) How much was in her pension fund (to the nearest euro) when she retired?

   (iii) Find the rate of interest per month which would, if paid and compounded monthly, be equivalent to an effective annual rate of 3·8%.

   (iv) Marian used her lump sum to buy an annuity at 3·8% AER giving her an allowance at the end of each month for the next 20 years. How much is her monthly allowance to the nearest euro?

Amortised loans

An amortised loan is one which involves paying back a fixed amount at regular intervals over a fixed period of time. Term loans and mortgages are examples of amortised loans. A mortgage is a loan drawn down for the purchase of property. Typically a mortgage is taken out over a very long period of time (20–30 years) and paid back in equal monthly repayments. Amortisation is the process by which the loan principal decreases over the life of the loan. With each mortgage payment made, a portion of the payment is applied towards reducing the principal and another portion of the payment is applied towards paying the interest on the loan. At the start of the life of the mortgage, the majority of the repayment will go towards paying the interest and only a small amount will go towards reducing the principal.

As the life of the mortgage increases, the principal decreases and hence the interest on the loan decreases. Therefore, the proportion will change and towards the end of the term of the mortgage the majority of the repayment will go towards the principal.

Showing principal and interest portions of the payments

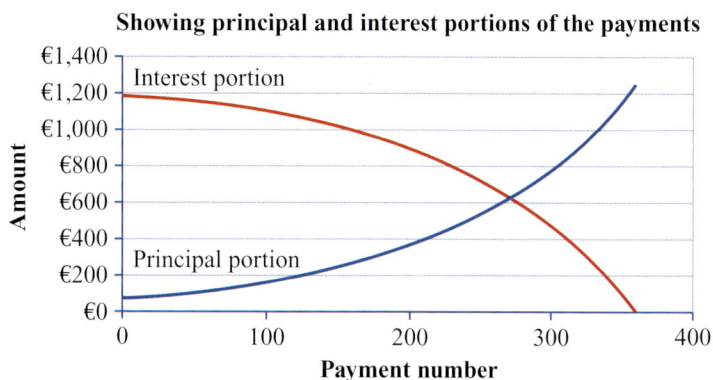

The graph shows the amortisation schedule for a loan paid back monthly over 360 months.

To calculate the annual amortisation (repayment) on a mortgage if the interest is compounded annually:

$$A = P \frac{i(1 + i)^t}{(1 + i)^t - 1}$$

Where:

A = annual repayment i = annual rate, in decimals
P = principal t = number of years

1. **Note:** This formula can only be used on loans.
2. For monthly replacements, adjust i and accordingly.

EXAMPLE

A couple wants to buy a house and needs to borrow a mortgage of €300,000 over a period of 30 years. They are able to obtain a fixed rate mortgage of 3·5% per annum. The bank requires them to pay the mortgage back in equal monthly instalments.

  (i) Use the formula for amortisation to work out what the monthly repayment amount will be.

 (ii) If the couple decides to take out the mortgage over 25 years instead of 30 years, how much extra will they pay per month?

(iii) If the couple opts for the 25-year mortgage, how much less will they pay back in total?

Solution:

  (i) Adjust the APR:

$$F = P(1 + i)^t$$
$$1{\cdot}035 = 1(1 + i)^{12}$$
$$\sqrt[12]{1{\cdot}035} = 1 + i$$
$$1{\cdot}00287 = 1 + i$$
$$0{\cdot}00287 = i$$

$$P = 300{,}000 \quad i = 0{\cdot}00287 \quad t = 30 \times 12 = 360$$

$$A = P\,\frac{i(1 + i)^t}{(1 + i)^t - 1}$$

$$A = 300{,}000\left(\frac{0{\cdot}00287(1 + 0{\cdot}00287)^{360}}{(1 + 0{\cdot}00287)^{360} - 1}\right)$$

$$A = 300{,}000\left(\frac{0{\cdot}00287(1{\cdot}00287)^{360}}{(1{\cdot}00287)^{360} - 1}\right)$$

$$A = 300{,}000\,(0{\cdot}004459)$$

Monthly repayments: €1,337·77

 (ii) $P = 300{,}000 \quad i = 0{\cdot}00287 \quad t = 25 \times 12 = 300$

$$A = 300{,}000\left(\frac{0{\cdot}00287(1 + 0{\cdot}00287)^{300}}{(1 + 0{\cdot}00287)^{300} - 1}\right)$$

$$A = 300{,}000\left(\frac{0{\cdot}00287(1{\cdot}00287)^{300}}{(1{\cdot}00287)^{300} - 1}\right)$$

$$A = 300{,}000\,(0{\cdot}004976)$$

Monthly repayments: €1,492·88

So if the couple opts for the 25-year mortgage, they will pay back

€1,492·88 − €1,337·77 = €155·11 extra per month.

(iii) With the 30-year mortgage, they will repay €1,337·77 × 360 = €481,597·20.

With the 25-year mortgage, they will repay €1,492·88 × 300 = €447,864·00.

Difference: €481,597·20 − €447,864·00 = €33,733·20 less will be repaid if the couple opts for the 25-year mortgage

Exercise 9.6

1. Delrick borrows €20,000 to purchase a new car. The APR on the loan is 6·5%. He must repay the loan in equal monthly instalments over five years. **(i)** Calculate his monthly repayments. **(ii)** Calculate the total interest paid.

2. Shannon borrows €32,000 to build an extension onto her house. The APR on the loan is 7·2%. She must repay the loan in equal monthly instalments over six years. **(i)** Calculate her monthly repayments. **(ii)** Calculate the total interest paid.

3. Tim draws down a mortgage of €200,000 over 25 years. He secures an APR of 4% from the bank.

   (i) Calculate Tim's annual repayments.

   (ii) Calculate the total interest repaid as a percentage of the original borrowings.

4. In order to buy an apartment, Robert needs a mortgage of €120,000 over 20 years. He secures a fixed annual rate from the bank of 4%, compounded annually.

   (i) Calculate Robert's monthly repayments.

   (ii) Calculate the total interest repaid as a percentage of the original borrowings.

5. A couple wants to buy a house and needs to borrow a mortgage of €270,000 over a period of 30 years. They are able to obtain a fixed rate mortgage of 4·25% per annum. The bank requires them to pay the mortgage back in equal monthly instalments.

   (i) Use the formula for amortisation to work out what the monthly repayment amount will be.

   (ii) If the couple decides to take out the mortgage over 27 years instead of 30 years, how much extra will they pay per month?

   (iii) If the couple opts for the 27-year mortgage, how much less will they pay back in total?

6. Daire and Jenny get a loan of €225,000 to be repaid at the end of each month in a series of equal payments over 26 years. The interest rate for the loan is 7·2% APR. Calculate:

   (i) The rate of interest per month that would, if paid and compounded monthly, be equivalent to an effective annual rate of 7·2%

   (ii) The amount of each monthly repayment

   (iii) The total amount repaid

   (iv) The total interest to be paid

(v) If they had paid fortnightly, what would the repayment amount be and what would the total interest paid be in this case? (Assume 1 year = 52 weeks)

(vi) How much would Daire and Jenny save by paying every fortnight instead of every month?

7. Graham paid €380 at the end of each month for four years to pay back a loan he borrowed for a car at an APR of 7·28%. How much did he borrow?

8. Doireann paid €400 at the end of each month for six and a half years to pay back a loan she borrowed while in college at an APR of 6·2%. How much did she borrow?

9. A loan of €P is drawn down over t years at a rate of i per annum. An amount €A is repaid annually.

(i) Find the present value, at the start of the loan, of the repayment made at the end of year 1.

(ii) Find the present value, at the start of the loan, of the repayment made at the end of year 2.

(iii) The sum of all present values of the payment made from year 1 until the final year equal the amount of the loan drawn down, €P. Use this information to write an expression for P in terms of A, i and t.

(iv) Use the sum of a geometric series to show that

$$A = P \frac{i(1 + i)^n}{(1 + i)^n - 1}.$$

CHAPTER 10

METHODS OF PROOF

Axioms

Statements that are assumed to be true, and which form the basis of further work, are called **axioms**. In the past, some axioms were accepted which were later shown to be wrong:

- The Earth is flat.
- The sun rotates around the Earth.

By accepting these statements as facts, further logical deductions were made and these were also false.

> An **axiom** is a statement which is assumed to be true and is used as a basis for developing a system.

Conjecture

In mathematics, some of the important results have come about from experimentation which led to an ability to predict further results. However, this is not the same as a proof. If we find a pattern, how can we be sure that the pattern will always be true?

Consider the conjecture that the expression $n^2 - n + 17$ is prime for all $n \in \mathbb{N}$.

We can test this conjecture by putting in $n = 1, 2, 3, \ldots$

$$n^2 - n + 17$$
$$n = 1: \quad 1^2 - 1 + 17 = 17, \text{ a prime number.}$$
$$n = 2: \quad 2^2 - 2 + 17 = 19, \text{ a prime number.}$$
$$n = 3: \quad 3^2 - 3 + 17 = 23, \text{ a prime number.}$$

If we put in 4, 5, 6, 7, 8, . . . we continue to get a prime number. This suggests that the conjecture could be true. In the next chapter, we will return to this conjecture.

> A **conjecture** is a statement which may be true but has not been proven.

EXAMPLE

Examine the expression $n^2 + n + 1$ for $n \in \mathbb{N}$. Form a conjecture from the results.

Solution:

$n = 1$: $1^2 + 1 + 1 = 3$

$n = 2$: $2^2 + 2 + 1 = 7$

$n = 3$: $3^2 + 3 + 1 = 13$

$n = 4$: $4^2 + 4 + 1 = 21$

$n = 5$: $5^2 + 5 + 1 = 31$

From the 5 tests:

Conjecture:

$n^2 + n + 1$ is odd for all $n \in \mathbb{N}$.

Exercise 10.1

1. Examine the expression $n^2 + 3n - 1$ for $n \in \mathbb{N}$. Form a conjecture from the results.

2. Examine the expression $n^3 - n$ for $n \in \mathbb{N}$. Form a conjecture (involving divisibility) from the results.

3. Tom has been drawing points on a circle. By joining the dots, he breaks the circle into a number of separate sections.

   The diagram shows the result of choosing four points and joining them. There are eight sections.

   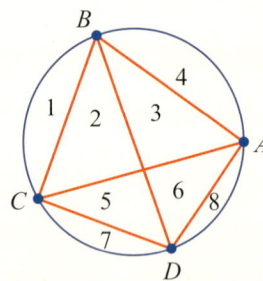

   (i) Based on this result, Tom's first conjecture is that if there are n points, then there are $2n$ sections. By drawing a diagram with just three points, show that this conjecture is false.

   (ii) Copy and complete the following table.

Number of points	1	2	3	4
Number of sections	1			8

   (iii) Suggest Tom's second conjecture.

   (iv) Predict the number of sections using five points and confirm your answer with a diagram.

   (v) It can be shown that using six points, there are 30 or 31 sections, depending on how the points are placed. What does this mean for Tom's second conjecture?

4. The Fibonacci sequence (F_n) and the Lucas sequence (L_n) are shown in the table.

n	0	1	2	3	4	5	6	7	8	9	10
F_n	0	1	1	2	3	5	8	13	21		
L_n	2	1	3	4	7	11	18	29	47		

(i) Copy and complete the table.

(ii) Form a conjecture between a Lucas number, L_k, and the previous and next Fibonacci numbers (F_{k-1} and F_{k+1}). An example is shown in the green cells.

(iii) Form a conjecture between a Fibonacci number, F_k, and the previous and next Lucas numbers (L_{k-1} and L_{k+1}). An example is shown in the orange cells.

Notation and terminology

In formal proofs, you will meet symbols which join the statements. It is important to realise that a proof should become 'good English' when all these symbols are converted to words.

Symbol	Definition	Example
$\therefore$	therefore	$2x = 6 \therefore x = 3$
$\Rightarrow$	implies	$x^2 = 9 \Rightarrow x = \pm 3$
$\Leftrightarrow$	implies and is implied by	$(n + 1)^2 - n^2 > 0 \Leftrightarrow 2n + 1 > 0$

Never use $\Rightarrow$ as = as they have very different meanings.

Remember that $\Rightarrow$ works in one direction and is used to build up to a conclusion.

For example, $x > 2 \Rightarrow x^2 > 4$, but $x^2 > 4 \nRightarrow x > 2$.

While 'if and only if' is usually abbreviated to iff, $\Leftrightarrow$ is sometimes read as 'if and only if'.

Methods of proof

There are many ways that mathematical statements can be proved (or disproved). These include:

1. Direct proof

   Using definitions, axioms and previous results in a sequential argument.

2. Reductio ad absurdum

   A proposition is disproved by deducing logically that it leads to an absurd result.

   One common type of this is **proof by contradiction**, where a statement is proved true because it cannot be false.

3. Induction

4. Graphical

Direct proof

All proofs are a sequence of statements leading to the conclusion, but some rely more on words than mathematical symbols.

EXAMPLE

Prove that the expression $n^2 + n + 1$ is odd for all $n \in \mathbb{N}$.

Solution:

$n^2 + n + 1 = n(n + 1) + 1$

n and $(n + 1)$ are consecutive integers, so one of them must be even and the other is odd.

$\therefore$ $n(n + 1)$ must be even (the product of an even number by any integer is an even number).

$\therefore$ $n(n + 1) + 1$ must be odd.

This is one of the theorems you learned previously. It uses a definition and the result of a previous proof.

Theorem 6: Each exterior angle of a triangle is equal to the sum of the two interior opposite angles.

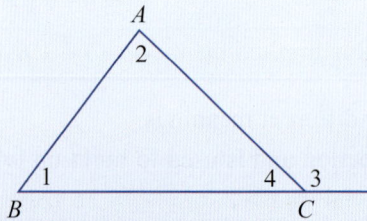

Given:	$\triangle ABC$ with interior opposite angles 1 and 2 and exterior angle 3
To prove:	$|\angle 1| + |\angle 2| = |\angle 3|$
Construction:	Label angle 4.
Proof:	$|\angle 1| + |\angle 2| + |\angle 4| = 180°$ (three angles in a triangle)
	$|\angle 3| + |\angle 4| = 180°$ (straight angle)
	$\therefore$ $|\angle 1| + |\angle 2| + |\angle 4| = |\angle 3| + |\angle 4|$
	$\therefore$ $|\angle 1| + |\angle 2| = |\angle 3|$

Exercise 10.2

1. Give an example of x such that $x^2 > 4$ but $x \not> 2$.

2. (i) Under what condition does $2n$ represent an even number?
   (ii) Write down a corresponding expression which represents an odd number.
   (iii) Prove that the square of an even number is an even number.
   (iv) Prove that the square of an odd number is an odd number.

3. Prove that the sum of two even numbers is another even number.

4. Conjecture: the sum of two odd numbers is an even number. Prove it.

5. Prove that the sum of two rational numbers is a rational number.

6. Show that there is no solution to $\dfrac{x^2 + 3x + 1}{x + 3} = x$.

7. (i) Using a table, show the sample space for rolling two six-sided dice and calculating the sum of the results.

   (ii) Copy and complete the following table.

Sum	2	3	4	5	6	7	8	9	10	11	12
Number of ways											

   (iii) Colonel George Sicherman proposes that a pair of six-sided dice numbered 1, 2, 2, 3, 3, 4 and 1, 3, 4, 5, 6, 8 offer the same results. Prove this conjecture.

Reductio ad absurdum

Sometimes, when we are asked to show a problem has no solution, we go ahead and try to solve it as normal. When we get an absurd answer, we then state that the question has no solution. Absurd answers include statements such as '1 = 0' or values such as $\sqrt{-4}$ when solutions must be real.

Rather than give a mathematical example, here is a hypothetical conversation:

Parent: Why haven't you tidied your room?
Child: My friends told me they don't have to.
Parent: So if your friends told you to jump off a cliff, you'd do that too?

Exercise 10.3

1. Show that there is no point of intersection of the lines $2x - y - 8 = 0$ and $2y = 4x + 9$.

2. Using simultaneous equations, show that the line $x + y = 4$ does not intersect $x^2 + y^2 = 6$.

3. Show that $f(x) = \dfrac{x}{x - 2}$, $x \neq 2$ has no turning points.

Proof by contradiction

This method of proof takes a proposition of the form

If certain conditions **then** a result will follow.

and examines the consequences of assuming that

If certain conditions **then** the *opposite* result will follow.

EXAMPLE 1

An equilateral triangle is also an acute-angled triangle.

Proof:
Assume that the opposite is true: an equilateral triangle is **not** an acute-angled triangle.
A triangle which is not acute-angled much have an angle greater than 90°.
But if the triangle is equilateral, then all the angles must be equal.
$\Rightarrow$ Each of the angles must be greater than 90°.
$\Rightarrow$ The sum of the angles is greater than 3(90°).
But this sum is greater than 180°, which is impossible.

In the next example we will use one of Euclid's axioms: the whole is greater than the part.

EXAMPLE 2

Prove that in a triangle with two equal angles, the sides opposite these angles are equal.

Proof:
We are given a triangle ABC with $|\angle B| = |\angle C|$.
Let us assume that the opposite is true: the sides opposite these angles are **not** equal in measure.
This creates two possibilities: $|AB| > |AC|$ or $|AB| < |AC|$.
Taking the first case, we find a point D on $[AB]$ such that $|BD| = |AC|$ and join $[DC]$.
Compare $\triangle DBC$ and $\triangle ABC$:

$$|BD| = |AC| \qquad \text{[S] (construction)}$$
$$|\angle DBC| = |\angle ACB| \qquad \text{[A] (given)}$$
$$|BC| = |BC| \qquad \text{[S] (common side)}$$
$$\therefore \triangle DBC \equiv \triangle ABC \qquad \text{(SAS)}$$

But $\triangle DBC$ is part of $\triangle ABC$ and therefore cannot equal it.
This is a contradiction, so the sides opposite these angles must be equal in measure.
If $|AB| < |AC|$, a similar argument can be made, thus completing the proof.

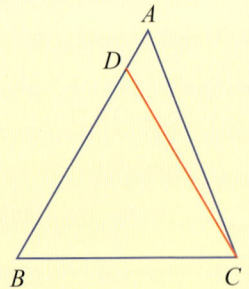

EXAMPLE 3

Prove that $\sqrt{2}$ is irrational.

Proof:

Let us assume that the opposite is true: $\sqrt{2}$ is **not** irrational.

Thus, $\sqrt{2}$ is rational and can be written as a fraction.

$$\text{Let} \qquad \sqrt{2} = \frac{a}{b} \qquad\qquad \text{where } a \text{ and } b \text{ have no common factor}$$

$$\Rightarrow \qquad 2 = \frac{a^2}{b^2} \qquad\qquad \text{squaring both sides}$$

$$\Rightarrow \qquad 2b^2 = a^2$$

Since $2b^2$ is even, a^2 must also be even. So a must be even and can be written as $a = 2k$.

$$\text{So} \qquad 2b^2 = (2k)^2$$

$$\Rightarrow \qquad 2b^2 = 4k^2$$

$$\Rightarrow \qquad b^2 = 2k^2$$

Since $2k^2$ is even, b^2, and therefore b, must be even.

But now we have a and b both even, so they have a common factor of 2.

This is a contradiction so we **cannot** say that $\sqrt{2}$ is rational.

Thus, $\sqrt{2}$ is irrational.

For the next example, you need to be aware that every whole number greater than 1 can be divided by at least one prime number.

EXAMPLE 4

There is an infinite number of primes.

Proof:

Let us assume that the opposite is true: there is a finite number of primes $p_1, p_2, p_3, \ldots, p_n$.

Let $x = p_1 p_2 p_3 \ldots p_n + 1$.

Dividing x by each of the known primes will leave a remainder of 1.

Thus, x must be divisible by a prime number not in the list $p_1, p_2, p_3, \ldots, p_n$.

This is a contradiction so we **cannot** say that there is a finite number of primes.

Thus, there is an infinite number of primes.

Exercise 10.4

1. Prove by contradiction that there is no greatest even integer.

2. The average of three different numbers is μ. Prove by contradiction that at least one of the numbers must be greater than μ.

3. Prove by contradiction that there are no positive integer solutions to $x^2 - y^2 = 8$.

4. Two shirts together cost more than €50.

   Prove that at least one costs more than €25.

5. If a and b are non-zero positive real numbers, prove by contradiction that $\dfrac{a}{b} + \dfrac{b}{a} > 2$.

6. In a right-angled triangle with sides of length a, b and c, prove by contradiction that $a + b > c$, where c is the length of the hypotenuse.

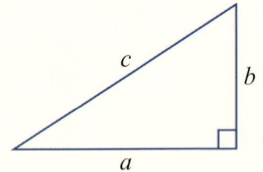

Induction

This form of proof takes a statement and establishes that it is true for a given range of values. It is an unusual procedure as it needs the result in order to proceed.

This method is described in the next chapter.

Graphical

It is unusual to find proofs that contain few words, but some clever examples exist.

EXAMPLE 1

Show that the area of a circle with radius length r is πr^2.

Proof:

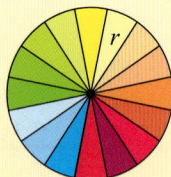

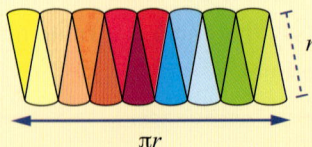

Explanation

You must imagine the slices being very thin so that they almost form a rectangle. As a limit, it **is** a rectangle whose area is $\pi r \times r = \pi r^2$.

EXAMPLE 2

Show that $1 + 2 + \cdots + n = \begin{pmatrix} n + 1 \\ 2 \end{pmatrix}$.

Proof:

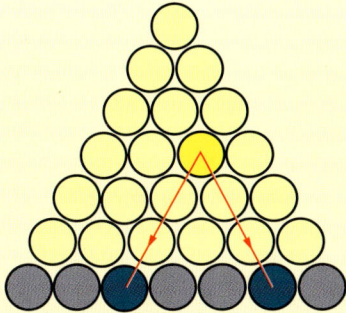

Explanation

The yellow discs represent

$$1 + 2 + \cdots + n$$

while the bottom row has $n + 1$ grey discs. Each yellow disc has a direct path to a unique pair of grey discs. There are $\begin{pmatrix} n + 1 \\ 2 \end{pmatrix}$ such pairs.

EXAMPLE 3

There are as many points on a line segment as there are on the real number line.

Proof:

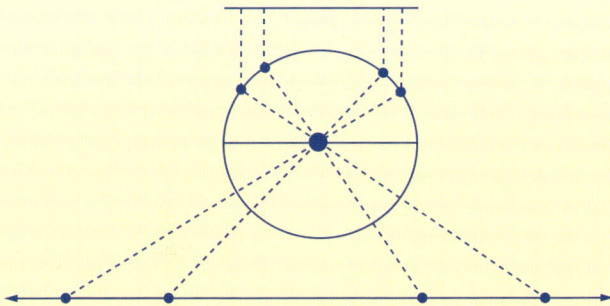

Explanation

Each point on the line segment is uniquely linked to a point on the number line. Therefore, there are as many points on one as on the other. This is an example of a bijection.

The discovery of a formula

In the previous chapter, we showed how experimentation can lead to a conjecture, which is turn might lead to a formula. We considered the conjecture that the expression $n^2 - n + 17$ is prime for all $n \in \mathbb{N}$. We had tested this proposition by putting in $n = 1, 2, 3, 4, 5, \ldots$ and found it to be true.

$$n^2 - n + 17$$

For example, $n = 2$: $2^2 - 2 + 17 = 19$, a prime number.

However, if $n = 17$, $17^2 - 17 + 17 = 289 = 17^2$ which is not prime.

Hence, the conjecture is **false**.

Another remarkable result comes from a series of odd natural numbers:

1 odd number	$1 = 1^2$
2 odd numbers	$1 + 3 = 2^2$
3 odd numbers	$1 + 3 + 5 = 3^2$

It appears that the sum of the first n odd numbers will be n^2. Having discovered a formula, we can test it for any number of values but this is not a proof. We need a method of proving the correctness of a formula, not just for some values but for **all** values.

Inductive principle

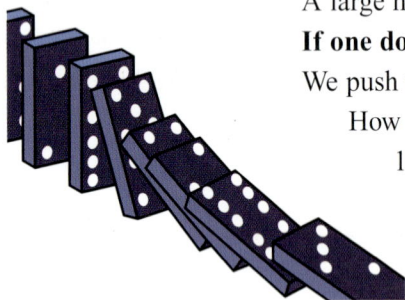

A large number of dominoes are set up in a line close together.

If one domino falls over, then the next one will also fall over.

We push the first one over.

How many will now fall over?

1?

6?

20?

All of them?

Proof by induction

Many propositions, or statements, which we may develop from simple cases, can be proved using the **principle of mathematical induction**.

Proof by induction involves two steps:

1. Proving that the proposition is true for the smallest value of n given in the question. If that number is 1, then we call this P(1).

2. Assuming the proposition is true for $n = k$, show that the proposition is true for $n = k + 1$. In other words: $P(k) \Rightarrow P(k + 1)$.

Note: If it is true for $n = 1$, then step 2 ensures that it is true for $n = 2$. If it is true for $n = 2$, then step 2 ensures that it is true for $n = 3$ and so on.

We will use **proof by induction** to prove propositions in three areas:

1. **Divisibility**   2. **Series**   3. **Inequalities**

Notes: 1. Proof by induction applies only to propositions that are stated to be true for whole numbers greater than or equal to zero.

2. The proposition is often denoted by P(n). The assumption P(k) must **always** be used in proving that P($k + 1$) is true.

Divisibility

There are a number of approaches to handling the checking of P($k + 1$). In the first method, we encourage the inclusion of P(k) by factorising and compensating for extra terms added.

Suppose we have an expression $6^{k+1} - 1$ and we wish to incorporate $6^k - 1$ into it. We could take the following steps:

$6^{k+1} - 1 = 6(6^k) - 1$ (now we have the 6^k term)

But we really want $6^k - 1$ as the factor:

$= 6(6^k - 1) \ldots$ (now we have an extra -6 and the -1 is missing)

$= 6(6^k - 1) + 6 - 1$ ($+6$ solves the problem and remember the -1)

$= 6(6^k - 1) + 5$ (now, hopefully, we can proceed)

EXAMPLE 1

Prove by induction that $3^n - 1$ is divisible by 2 for all $n \in \mathbb{N}$.

Solution:

P(n): $3^n - 1$ is divisible by 2 for all $n \in \mathbb{N}$.

Step 1: $P(1) = 3^1 - 1 = 3 - 1 = 2$, which is divisible by 2.

∴ P(1) is true.

Step 2: Assume P(k) is true, i.e. $3^k - 1$ is divisible by 2.

Test P($k + 1$): $\qquad$ $3^{k+1} - 1$ is divisible by 2

$$3^{k+1} - 1$$
$$= 3(3^k - 1) + 3 - 1$$
$$= 3(3^k - 1) + 2$$

We assumed $(3^k - 1)$ was divisible by 2 and 2 is divisible by 2.

∴ P($k + 1$) is divisible by 2.

∴ P($k + 1$) is true if P(k) is true.

Hence, by the principle of mathematical induction, P(n) is true.

An alternative approach involves splitting one of the extra factors into a sum involving the divisibility value.

EXAMPLE 2

Prove by induction that $9^n - 5^n$ is divisible by 4 for all $n \in \mathbb{N}$.

Solution:

P(n): $9^n - 5^n$ is divisible by 4 for all $n \in \mathbb{N}$.

Step 1: P(1) $= 9^1 - 5^1 = 9 - 5 = 4$, which is divisible by 4.

∴ P(1) is true.

Step 2: Assume P(k) is true, i.e. $9^k - 5^k$ is divisible by 4.

Test P($k + 1$): $\qquad$ $9^{k+1} - 5^{k+1}$ is divisible by 4

Test $\qquad$ P($k + 1$) $= 9^{k+1} - 5^{k+1}$

$$= 9 \times 9^k - 5 \times 5^k$$
$$= (4 + 5) \times 9^k - 5 \times 5^k \qquad \text{(split 9 into 4 + 5)}$$
$$= 4 \times 9^k + 5 \times 9^k - 5 \times 5^k$$
$$= 4 \times 9^k + 5(9^k - 5^k)$$

4×9^k is divisible by 4 and we assumed $(9^k - 5^k)$ was divisible by 4.

∴ P($k + 1$) is divisible by 4.

∴ P($k + 1$) is true if P(k) is true.

Hence, by the principle of mathematical induction, P(n) is true.

Exercise 11.1

In questions 1–17, prove the statement by induction.

1. $5^n - 1$ is divisible by 4 for all $n \in \mathbb{N}$.

2. $4^n - 1$ is divisible by 3 for all $n \in \mathbb{N}$.

3. $9^n + 3$ is divisible by 4 for all $n \in \mathbb{N}$.

4. $7^n - 2^n$ is divisible by 5 for all $n \in \mathbb{N}$.

5. $13^n - 5^n$ is divisible by 8 for all $n \in \mathbb{N}$.

6. $5^n - 2^n$ is divisible by 3 for all $n \in \mathbb{N}$.

7. $3^{2n} - 1$ is divisible by 8 for all $n \in \mathbb{N}$.

8. $2^{3n-1} + 3$ is divisible by 7 for all $n \in \mathbb{N}$.

9. $5^{2n} - 3^{2n}$ is divisible by 8 for all $n \in \mathbb{N}$.

10. $n^2 + 3n + 2$ is even (divisible by 2) for all $n \geq 0$, $n \in \mathbb{Z}$.

11. $n(n + 1)(2n + 1)$ is divisible by 6 for all $n \in \mathbb{N}$.

12. $n^3 + 6n^2 + 8n$ is divisible by 3 for all $n \in \mathbb{N}$.

13. $5^n - 4n + 3$ is divisible by 4 for all $n \in \mathbb{N}$.

14. $5^{2(n+1)} - 4^{n+1}$ is divisible by 21 for all $n \in \mathbb{N}$.

15. $7^k + 4^k + 1$ is divisible by 6 for all $n \in \mathbb{N}$.

16. $2^{6n} + 3^{2n-2}$ is divisible by 5 for all $n \in \mathbb{N}$.

17. $9(4^{2n}) - 5^{n-1}$ is divisible by 11 for all $n \in \mathbb{N}$.

18. $P(n) = 8^{2n} - 3^{2n}$

    (i) Evaluate $P(1)$ and $P(2)$.

    (ii) Express $P(n + 1)$ in the form $a(8^{2n}) - b(3^{2n})$.

    (iii) Show that $P(n + 1) - 9P(n) = 55(8^{2n})$.

    (iv) Hence or otherwise, show that 5 is a factor of $P(n)$ for all $n \in \mathbb{N}$.

Series

In the following example, we must show that one side of a proposition is equal to the other side. To do this, we will take the left-hand side (LHS) and after some manipulations, we will transform it into the expression on the right-hand side (RHS), thus proving that the LHS = the RHS.

EXAMPLE

Prove by induction that $1^2 + 2^2 + 3^2 + \cdots + n^2 = \dfrac{n}{6}(n + 1)(2n + 1)$, $n \in \mathbb{N}$.

Solution:

$$P(n): 1^2 + 2^2 + 3^2 + \cdots + n^2 = \frac{n}{6}(n + 1)(2n + 1)$$

Step 1: $P(1)$:   LHS $= 1^2 = 1$ RHS $= \frac{1}{6}(1 + 1)(2 + 1) = 1$

$\therefore P(1)$ is true.

Step 2: Assume $P(k)$ is true, i.e. $1^2 + 2^2 + 3^2 + \cdots + k^2 = \dfrac{k}{6}(k + 1)(2k + 1)$.

Test $P(k + 1)$: $1^2 + 2^2 + 3^2 + \cdots + k^2 + (k + 1)^2 = \dfrac{k + 1}{6}(k + 2)(2k + 3)$

$$\begin{aligned}
\text{LHS} &= 1^2 + 2^2 + 3^2 + \cdots + k^2 + (k + 1)^2 \\
&= (1^2 + 2^2 + 3^2 + \cdots + k^2) + (k + 1)^2 \\
&= \frac{k}{6}(k + 1)(2k + 1) + (k + 1)^2 &&\text{(using our assumption)} \\
&= \frac{k(k + 1)(2k + 1) + 6(k + 1)^2}{6} &&\text{(use common denominator 6)} \\
&= \frac{(k + 1)}{6}[k(2k + 1) + 6(k + 1)] &&\left(\text{take out common factor } \left(\frac{k + 1}{6}\right)\right) \\
&= \frac{(k + 1)}{6}[2k^2 + k + 6k + 6] \\
&= \frac{(k + 1)}{6}[2k^2 + 7k + 6] \\
&= \frac{(k + 1)}{6}(k + 2)(2k + 3)
\end{aligned}$$

LHS $=$ RHS

$\therefore P(k + 1)$ is true if $P(k)$ is true.

Hence, by the principle of mathematical induction, $P(n)$ is true.

Note: This question could have been asked using series notation,

i.e. prove by induction that $\displaystyle\sum_{r=1}^{n} r^2 = \frac{n}{6}(n + 1)(2n + 1)$.

Exercise 11.2

In questions 1–13, prove the statement by induction.

1. $1 + 2 + 3 + \cdots + n = \frac{n}{2}(n + 1)$ for all $n \in \mathbb{N}$.

2. $2 + 4 + 6 + \cdots + 2n = n(n + 1)$ for all $n \in \mathbb{N}$.

3. $1 + 3 + 5 + \cdots + (2n - 1) = n^2$ for all $n \in \mathbb{N}$.

4. $1^3 + 2^3 + 3^3 + \cdots + n^3 = \frac{n^2}{4}(n + 1)^2$ for all $n \in \mathbb{N}$.

5. $(1 \times 2) + (2 \times 3) + (3 \times 4) + \cdots + n(n + 1) = \frac{n}{3}(n + 1)(n + 2)$ for all $n \in \mathbb{N}$.

6. $\dfrac{1}{1 \times 3} + \dfrac{1}{3 \times 5} + \dfrac{1}{5 \times 7} + \cdots + \dfrac{1}{(2n - 1)(2n + 1)} = \dfrac{n}{2n + 1}$ for all $n \in \mathbb{N}$.

7. $\displaystyle\sum_{r=1}^{n} (3r - 2) = \frac{n}{2}(3n - 1)$.

8. $\displaystyle\sum_{r=1}^{n} r(r + 3) = \frac{n}{3}(n + 1)(n + 5)$.

9. $a + (a + d) + (a + 2d) + \cdots + [a + (n - 1)d] = \frac{n}{2}[2a + (n - 1)d]$ for all $n \in \mathbb{N}$, $a, d \in \mathbb{R}$.

10. $a + ar + ar^2 + \cdots + ar^{n-1} = \dfrac{a(1 - r^n)}{1 - r}$, $r \neq 1$, $n \in \mathbb{N}$, $a, r \in \mathbb{R}$.

11. $\displaystyle\sum_{r=1}^{n} (r + 1)2^r = n2^{n+1}$

Hint for questions 12 and 13: $\quad 5 \times 4! = 5!$ $\quad\quad 10 \times 9! = 10!$ $\quad\quad (k + 1)k! = (k + 1)!$

12. $1 \times 1! + 2 \times 2! + 3 \times 3! + \cdots + n \times n! = (n + 1)! - 1$ for all $n \in \mathbb{N}$.

13. $\displaystyle\sum_{r=1}^{n} (r^2 + 1)r! = n(n + 1)!$

14. A sequence is defined as follows:
$$T_1 = 7 \text{ and } T_{n+1} = \frac{n}{n + 1} T_n \text{ for all } n \in \mathbb{N}.$$

   (i) Write down the first three terms in the sequence.

   (ii) Deduce an expression, in terms of n, for T_n.

   (iii) Prove your expression using induction.

Inequalities

EXAMPLE 1

Prove by induction that $(1 + r)^n \geq 1 + nr$, $r > -1$ and $n \in \mathbb{N}$.

Solution:

$$P(n): (1 + r)^n \geq 1 + nr, \; r > -1 \text{ and } n \in \mathbb{N}$$

Step 1: P(1): LHS $= (1 + r)^1 = 1 + r$ RHS $= 1 + (1)r = 1 + r$

$\therefore$ LHS $\geq$ RHS

$\therefore$ P(1) is true.

Step 2: Assume P(k) is true, i.e. $(1 + r)^k \geq (1 + kr)$.

Test P(k + 1): $(1 + r)^{k+1} \geq 1 + (k + 1)r$

$$
\begin{aligned}
\text{LHS} &= (1 + r)^{k+1} \\
&= (1 + r)^k(1 + r)^1 \\
&\geq (1 + kr)(1 + r) && \text{(using our assumption)} \\
&= 1 + r + kr + kr^2 \\
&= 1 + (k + 1)r + kr^2 && \text{(common factor } r\text{)} \\
&\geq 1 + (k + 1)r && \text{(as } kr^2 > 0\text{)}
\end{aligned}
$$

$\therefore$ LHS $\geq$ RHS

$\therefore$ P(k + 1) is true if P(k) is true.

Hence, by the principle of mathematical induction, P(n) is true.

Not all of the inequality propositions can be solved as easily as the last example. For others, we can use a transitive approach.

Procedure for proving an inequality proposition using a transitive relation

> If $A > B$ and $B > C$,
> then $A > C$.

We will take P(k), which is in the form $A > C$, and deduce a statement in the form $A > B$.
We will then state that $B > C$ and proceed to prove that this is true.
From this we can deduce that $A > C$.

Because we use a different process for these two stages, the example uses $\Rightarrow$ ('implies') as statements are deduced in the first stage and uses $\Leftrightarrow$ ('if and only if') as statements are assumed in the second.

We should try to use the symbols to produce a proof which can be read out loud and still be coherent.

EXAMPLE 2

Prove by induction that $2^n \geq n^2$ where $n \in \mathbb{N}$ and $n \geq 4$.

Solution:

$P(n)$: $2^n \geq n^2$ where $n \in \mathbb{N}$ and $n \geq 4$.

Step 1: $P(4)$: LHS $= 2^4 = 16$ \qquad RHS $= 4^2 = 16$

$\therefore$ LHS $\geq$ RHS

$\therefore P(4)$ is true.

Step 2: Assume $P(k)$ is true, i.e. $2^k \geq k^2$

Test $P(k + 1)$: \qquad $2^{k+1} \geq (k + 1)^2$

$$2^k \geq k^2 \qquad\qquad\qquad 2k^2 \geq (k + 1)^2$$
$$\Rightarrow \quad 2(2^k) \geq 2(k^2) \qquad \Leftrightarrow \quad 2k^2 \geq k^2 + 2k + 1$$
$$\Rightarrow \quad 2^{k+1} \geq 2k^2 \qquad \Leftrightarrow \quad k^2 \geq 2k + 1$$
$$\Leftrightarrow \quad k^2 - 2k \geq 1$$
$$\Leftrightarrow \quad k^2 - 2k + 1 \geq 1 + 1$$
$$\Leftrightarrow \quad (k - 1)^2 \geq 2 \qquad \text{(true for } k \geq 4)$$
$$\therefore \quad 2k^2 \geq (k + 1)^2$$
$$\therefore \quad 2^{k+1} \geq (k + 1)^2$$

$\therefore P(k + 1)$ is true if $P(k)$ is true.

Hence, by the principle of mathematical induction, $P(n)$ is true.

Exercise 11.3

In questions 1–9, prove the statement by induction.

1. $2n^2 > (n + 1)^2$ where $n \geq 3$, $n \in \mathbb{N}$.

2. $2^n > n$, \qquad $n \in \mathbb{N}$.

3. $(a + b)^n > a^n + b^n$ for all $a, b > 0$, where $a, b \in \mathbb{R}$ and $n \in \mathbb{N}$.

4. $n! > 2^n$ for $n \geq 4$, $n \in \mathbb{N}$.

5. $3^n > 2n + 1$ for $n > 1$, $n \in \mathbb{N}$.

6. $3^n > n^2$ for all $n \in \mathbb{N}$.

7. $4^n \geq 3n^2 + 1$ for all $n \in \mathbb{N}$.

8. $1 + \dfrac{1}{\sqrt{2}} + \dfrac{1}{\sqrt{3}} + \cdots + \dfrac{1}{\sqrt{n}} > \sqrt{n}$ for $n > 1$, $n \in \mathbb{N}$.

9. $\dfrac{1}{(1 + r)^n} \leq \dfrac{1}{1 + nr}$, \quad $r > 0$, for all $n \in \mathbb{N}$.

De Moivre's theorem

You are required to be able to prove De Moivre's theorem for powers of natural numbers.

$$(\cos \theta + i \sin \theta)^n = \cos n\theta + i \sin n\theta, \qquad \forall n \in \mathbb{N}$$

Proof for De Moivre's theorem for $n \in \mathbb{N}$ (using induction)

$P(n)$: $(\cos \theta + i \sin \theta)^n = \cos n\theta + i \sin n\theta$

Step 1: $P(1)$:   LHS $= (\cos \theta + i \sin \theta)^1$ RHS $= \cos 1\theta + i \sin 1\theta$

$\qquad\qquad\qquad\qquad = \cos \theta + i \sin \theta \qquad\qquad\qquad = \cos \theta + i \sin \theta$

$\qquad \therefore$ $P(1)$ is true.

Step 1: Assume $P(k)$ is true, i.e. $(\cos \theta + i \sin \theta)^k = \cos k\theta + i \sin k\theta$.

$\qquad\quad$ Test $P(k + 1)$: $\qquad\qquad (\cos \theta + i \sin \theta)^{k+1} = \cos(k + 1)\theta + i \sin(k + 1)\theta$

$\qquad\qquad\qquad (\cos \theta + i \sin \theta)^{k+1}$

$\qquad\qquad = (\cos \theta + i \sin \theta)^k (\cos \theta + i \sin \theta)^1$

$\qquad\qquad = (\cos k\theta + i \sin k\theta)(\cos \theta + i \sin \theta)$

$\qquad\qquad = \cos k\theta \cos \theta + i \cos k\theta \sin \theta + i \sin k\theta \cos \theta + i^2 \sin k\theta \sin \theta$

$\qquad\qquad = \cos k\theta \cos \theta - \sin k\theta \sin \theta + i(\sin k\theta \cos \theta + \cos k\theta \sin \theta)$

$\qquad\qquad = \cos(k\theta + \theta) + i \sin(k\theta + \theta)$

$\qquad\qquad = \cos(k + 1)\theta + i \sin(k + 1)\theta$

$\qquad \therefore \quad (\cos \theta + i \sin \theta)^{k+1} = \cos(k + 1)\theta + i \sin(k + 1)\theta$

$\qquad \therefore \quad P(k + 1)$ is true if $P(k)$ is true.

Hence, by the principle of mathematical induction, $P(n)$ is true.

A very useful piece of mathematical information

If the three angles in one triangle are equal in measure to the three angles in a second triangle, then the triangles are similar and the sides are in the same proportion.

If two chords, AB and CD, of a circle intersect at the point K, as in the diagram, then $|AK|\,|KB| = |CK|\,|KD|$
or alternatively, $|AK|\,|BK| = |CK|\,|DK|$. The K is positioned last in each of the pairs as a memory aid.

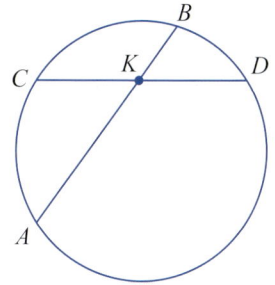

EXAMPLE 1

Two chords, PQ and XY, in a circle centre O intersect at the point W, as in the diagram. Given $|PQ| = 7$ cm, $|PW| = 3$ cm and $|WY| = 6$ cm. Calculate:

(i) The length of the radius

(ii) The area of the circle in terms of π

Solution:

(i) We know

$$|PW|\,|QW| = |XW|\,|YW|$$
$$(3)(7-3) = |XW|(6)$$
$$12 = 6\,|XW|$$
$$2 = |XW|$$

Since $O \in XY$, then $|XY| = $ diameter $= 2 + 6 = 8$ cm $\Rightarrow$ radius $= 4$ cm.

(ii) Area circle $= \pi r^2 = \pi(4)^2 = 16\pi$ cm^2.

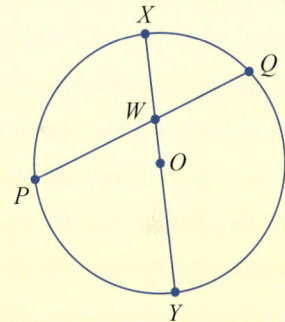

EXAMPLE 2

A chord [AB] divides a circle with centre O into two regions whose areas are in the ratio 2 : 1. If angle $AOB = \theta$ radians, show that $3\theta - 3\sin\theta = 2\pi$.

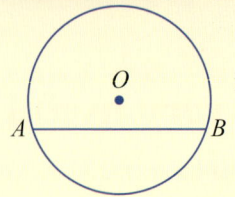

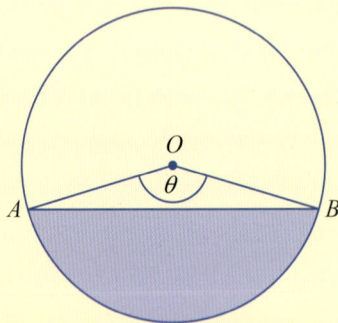

Solution:

Let r = radius of circle

Area circle = πr^2

Shaded region = $\frac{1}{3}(\pi r^2)$

Area $\triangle AOB = \frac{1}{2}(r)(r)\sin\theta = \frac{1}{2}r^2\sin\theta$

Area (small) sector $AOB = \frac{1}{2}r^2\theta$

Area (small) sector AOB − area $\triangle AOB$ = shaded region

$$\frac{1}{2}r^2\theta - \frac{1}{2}r^2\sin\theta = \frac{1}{3}\pi r^2$$

$$\frac{1}{2}\theta - \frac{1}{2}\sin\theta = \frac{1}{3}\pi$$

$$3\theta - 3\sin\theta = 2\pi$$

EXAMPLE 3

In the diagram, $ABCD$ is a square with $|AB| = 1$. M is the midpoint of [CD] and $|\angle APB| = 90°$.

   (i) Find $|MB|$ in surd form.

   (ii) Hence, find $|BP|$ and $|PA|$ in surd form.

   (iii) Find the ratio $\dfrac{\text{area of triangle } APB}{\text{area of triangle } BCM}$.

   (iv) Hence or otherwise, find the area of the shaded region.

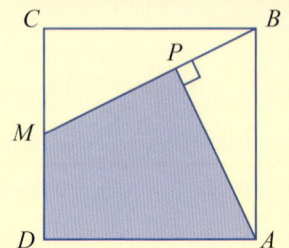

Solution:

(i) $|MB|^2 = (1)^2 + \left(\frac{1}{2}\right)^2 = 1 + \frac{1}{4} = \frac{5}{4}$

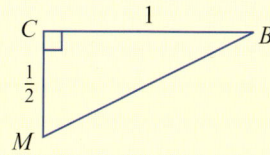

$|MB| = \sqrt{\frac{5}{4}} = \frac{\sqrt{5}}{2} = \frac{1}{2}\sqrt{5}$

(ii) Label angles 1, 2, 3 and 4 as in the diagram.

$\angle 1 + \angle 2 = 90°$

$\angle 1 + \angle 3 = 90°$

By comparison, $\angle 2 = \angle 3$.

$\therefore \triangle BCM$ is equiangular to $\triangle PBA$.

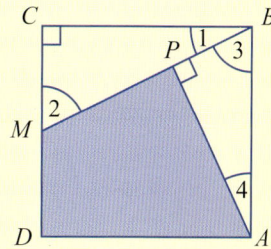

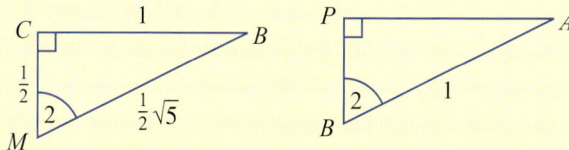

We can state (by theorem)

$$\frac{|CB|}{|PA|} = \frac{|CM|}{|PB|} = \frac{|MB|}{|BA|}$$

$$\frac{1}{|PA|} = \frac{\frac{1}{2}}{|PB|} = \frac{\frac{1}{2}\sqrt{5}}{1}$$

$\dfrac{1}{|PA|} = \dfrac{\frac{1}{2}\sqrt{5}}{1}$ $\qquad$ $\dfrac{\frac{1}{2}}{|PB|} = \dfrac{\frac{1}{2}\sqrt{5}}{1}$

$1 = \frac{1}{2}\sqrt{5}\,|PA|$ $\qquad$ $\frac{1}{2} = \frac{1}{2}\sqrt{5}\,|PB|$

$\dfrac{2}{\sqrt{5}} = |PA|$ $\qquad$ $\dfrac{1}{\sqrt{5}} = |PB|$

(iii) Area $\triangle APB = \frac{1}{2}$ (base)(perpendicular height)

$= \frac{1}{2}|PB|\,|PA|$

$= \frac{1}{2}\left(\frac{1}{\sqrt{5}}\right)\left(\frac{2}{\sqrt{5}}\right)$

$= \frac{1}{5}$

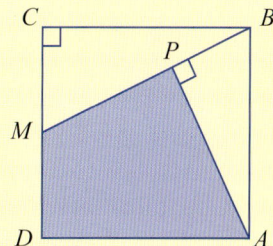

$$\text{Area } \triangle BCM = \tfrac{1}{2} \text{ (base)(perpendicular height)}$$
$$= \tfrac{1}{2}|BC||CM|$$
$$= \tfrac{1}{2}(1)\left(\tfrac{1}{2}\right)$$
$$= \tfrac{1}{4}$$
$$\therefore \frac{\text{Area } \triangle APB}{\text{Area } \triangle BCM} = \frac{\tfrac{1}{5}}{\tfrac{1}{4}} = \frac{4}{5}$$

(iv) Area shaded region = area square $ABCD$ − area $\triangle APB$ − area $\triangle BCM$
$$= (1)(1) - \tfrac{1}{5} - \tfrac{1}{4}$$
$$= 1 - \tfrac{1}{5} - \tfrac{1}{4} = \tfrac{11}{20}$$

Exercise 12.1

1. Find the area of the triangle shown, correct to the nearest m^2.

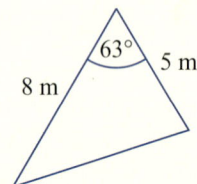

2. The isosceles triangle shown has an area of 100 cm^2. Find x, correct to one decimal place.

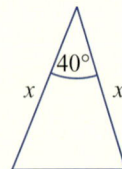

3. Find the area, in surd form, of an equilateral triangle of side 10 cm.

4. A rectangle is 7 cm longer than it is wide. Its perimeter is 182 cm. Showing your method clearly, find the length of the rectangle.

5. (i) For any triangle with sides of length a, b and c, Heron's formula states that the area, A, is given by
$$A = \sqrt{s(s-a)(s-b)(s-c)}$$
   where $s = \dfrac{a+b+c}{2}$.

   Check that these formulae for s and A are dimensionally sound.

   (ii) Find, in surd form, the area of the triangle with sides of length 5, 7 and 9 cm.

6. (i) Find the area of the parallelogram $ABCD$ with $|AB| = 8$ cm, $|AD| = 5$ cm and $|\angle BAD| = 74°$. Give your answer correct to two decimal places.

(ii) The trapezium shown has a perpendicular height of 3·5 cm. Find its area.

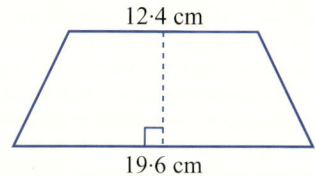

12·4 cm

19·6 cm

7. Nina is studying drama and wants to determine how brightly to illuminate her stage. She looks in her textbook and comes across this formula:

stage width (in metres) × stage length (in metres) × 110 = total watts for stage

If her stage is 7·25 metres wide and 11·5 metres long:

(i) Calculate the **exact** number of watts needed to illuminate the stage

(ii) Calculate the number of watts needed to illuminate the stage, **rounded to the nearest 10 watts**

(iii) Write the answer to part **(ii)** in the form $a \times 10^k$ where $1 \le a < 10$ and $k \in \mathbb{Z}$

8. Find the area of a regular hexagon of side 8 cm. Give your answer in surd form.

9. The area of an equilateral triangle is 50 cm². Find the length of a side of the triangle correct to one decimal place.

10. Find the length of a side of an equilateral triangle of area 212 m², correct to the nearest integer.

11. The area of a regular pentagon is 150 cm². Calculate the length of one side of the pentagon correct to one decimal place.

12. The photograph shows the Dockland building in Hamburg, Germany.
The diagram below is a side view of the building. It is a parallelogram.
The parallelogram is 29 metres high. The top and bottom edges are 88 metres long.

(i) Find the area of this side of the building.

(ii) If $|BD| = |AD|$, find $|BC|$.

(iii) The lines BC and AD are parallel. Find the distance between these parallel lines.

A B

D C

13. Leonardo has a cylindrical block of wood of diameter
6 cm and height 18 cm. He glues the base to a board, but
wants to paint the rest of the block. He wants to paint the
bottom half of the wood blue and the top half white.

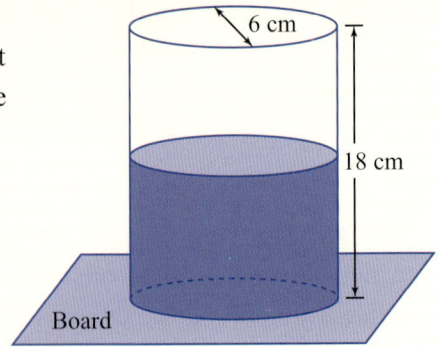

6 cm

18 cm

Board

   (i) Calculate the surface area of the block that
   Leonardo will paint blue in terms of π.

   (ii) Calculate the surface area of the block that
   Leonardo will paint white in terms of π.

The blue paint will cost Leonardo €0·03 for every
12 cm² painted and the white paint will cost Leonardo €0·04 for every 15 cm² painted.

   (iii) If b represents the area of the blue surface and w represents the white surface, write an
   expression for the cost, C, of painting the block in terms of b and w.

   (iv) Calculate the value of C for Leonardo's block correct to three decimal places.

   (v) Determine whether or not Leonardo could paint his entire block white for less than or
   equal to €1·00.

14. A field of gas off the west coast of Ireland has an area of 20 km² with an uncertainty of
$\pm 20\%$ in the area of the field. Calculate the maximum and minimum area of the field in m².

15. Sally makes bolts. The bolts have lengths with tolerance $4 \cdot 2 \pm 0 \cdot 05$ cm and diameters with
tolerance $1 \cdot 4 \pm 0 \cdot 05$ cm.

Wendy sells drills. All the drills she sells have a tolerance of $\pm 0 \cdot 025$ cm.

   (i) If Sally buys a drill from Wendy with a nominal diameter of 1·4 cm for use with the
   bolts that she makes, what problems may she experience?

   (ii) What can Sally do to solve any problems that she may have?

16. The tables in a primary school classroom are like the one in the
drawing. The top of the table is in the shape of a trapezium, as
shown in the diagram below the drawing.

The measurements are as follows:

$$|AD| = 140 \text{ cm}$$
$$|BC| = 70 \text{ cm}$$
$$|AB| = |DC|$$
$$|\angle ADC| = |\angle DAB| = 60°$$

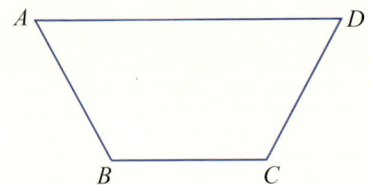

A   D

B   C

   (i) Show that $|AB| = 70$ cm.

   (ii) Find the distance between the parallel sides $[AD]$ and
   $[BC]$. Give your answer in centimetres correct to one
   decimal place.

(iii) Some of the tables are painted with a yellow and blue pattern as shown. What fraction of the surface is yellow? Show your work.

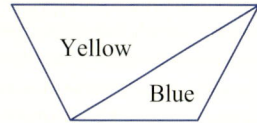

(iv) Two of the tables, painted as in part **(iii)** above, are arranged to form a hexagon. Prove that the yellow area is a rectangle.

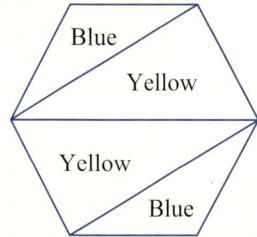

(v) Twelve of the tables are arranged as six hexagons in a classroom, as shown in the diagram. The clearance between neighbouring tables is 2 metres and the clearance to the side walls is 1·5 metres, as shown.

Find the total width of the classroom, in metres, correct to two decimal places.

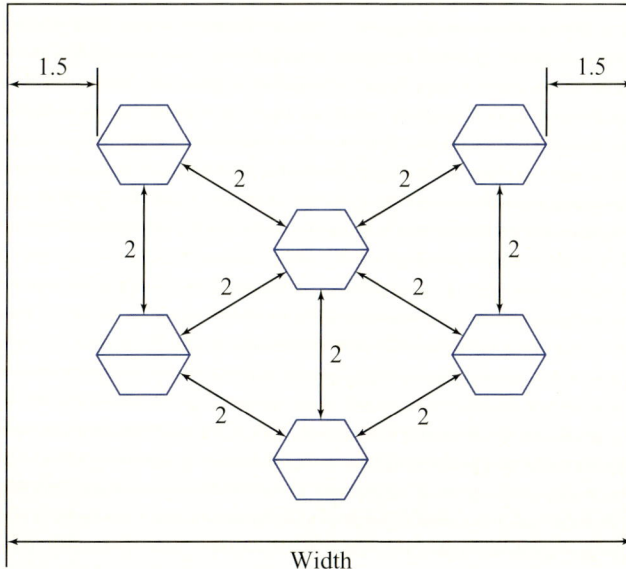

(vi) The tops of the trapezium tables are made of wood. The wood is 1·6 cm thick. Each cubic centimetre of the wood weighs 0·75 grams. Each table also has a metal frame weighing 6 kilograms. How much does each table weigh? Give your answer in kilograms, correct to one decimal place.

17. The diagram represents a large symmetrical arrow
ABCD that is painted on the ground at one end of a
runway.

The distance *BD* is 5 metres and the distance *CA* is
2·5 metres, as shown. The angle *BCD* measures 126°.

(i) Find the length of the perimeter of the arrow.
Give your answer correct to one decimal place.

(ii) Cat's eyes are reflective devices used in road
markings. They are being laid along the
perimeter of the arrow. One is placed at each
vertex and others are placed at intervals of no
more than half a metre along the perimeter.
How many are needed?

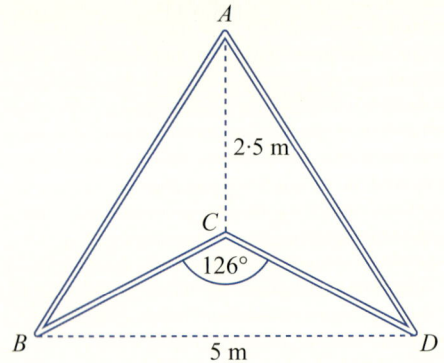

18. The diagram shows two concentric circles with radii of 1 and 4.
If $|\angle AOB| = \dfrac{\pi}{3}$, find in terms of π:

(i) The area of the shaded region

(ii) The perimeter of the shaded region

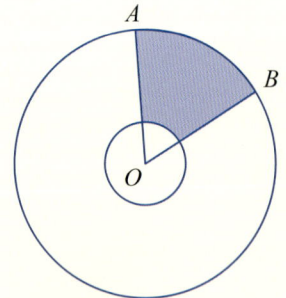

19. The international radiation symbol (known as a trefoil)
first appeared in 1946. It is coloured black. The symbol
consists of a central circle of radius *r*, an internal radius
of 1·5 *r* and an external radius of 5 *r* for the blades,
which are separated from each other by 60°.
Calculate, in terms of π and *r*, the black area.

20. An architect has designed an eco-friendly
theatre in the shape of a rectangle
inscribed in a circle, as shown in the
diagram.

(i) Given that E is the centre of the
circle, find the radius of the circle
correct to the nearest metre.

(ii) The shaded area represents the
entrance hall within the building.
Calculate this area correct to the
nearest square metre.

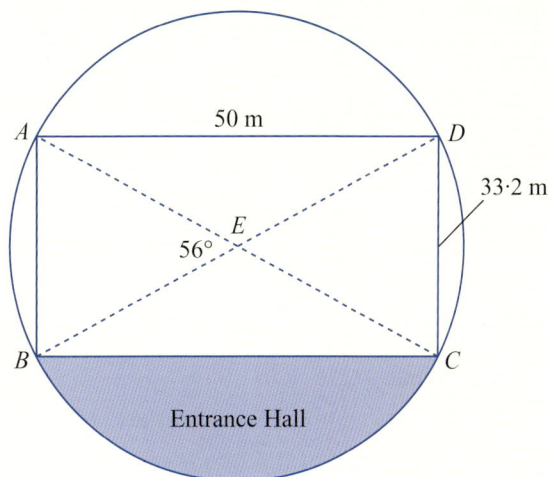

21. A part of a track is shown in the diagram. The radius of the
inner circle is 60 m and the width of the track is 3 m. The
length of the inner arc is 20π and the outer arc is 21π. Find
the area of the track.

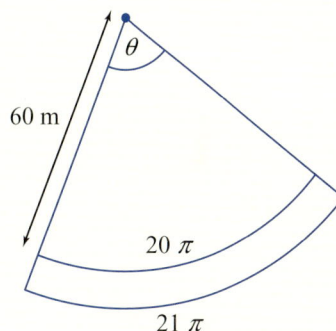

22. The diagram shows two straight lines intersecting at O and
two circles, each with centre O.

The outer circle has radius R and the inner circle has
radius r.

Consider the shaded regions with areas A and B. Given that
$A : B = 2 : 1$, find the exact value of the ratio $R : r$.

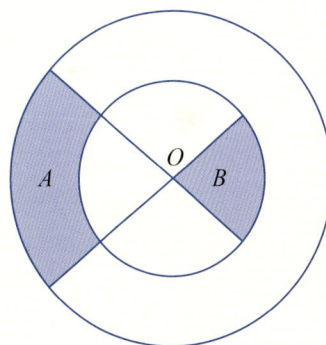

23. The radius of the circle is 35 cm. AB and CD are perpendicular
and $|AB| = 56$ cm. Find the length of $|CD|$.

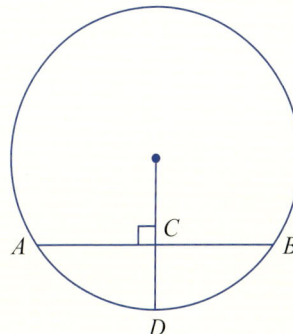

24. Given $|AB| = 20$ cm and $|PQ| = 5$ cm.

   The circle k has radius r and centre O, as shown in the diagram.

   Calculate the following correct to one decimal place.

   (i) The length of the radius of k

   (ii) The area of k

   (iii) The area of $\triangle AOB$

   (iv) The angle AOB

   (v) The length of the minor arc AB

   (vi) The area of the minor sector AOB

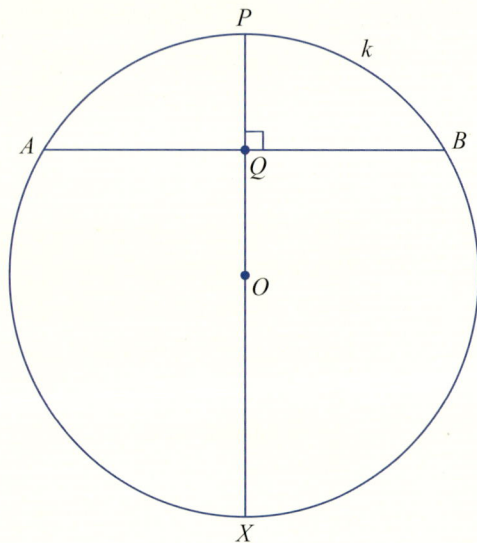

25. Triangle ABC has $AB = 9$ cm, $BC = 10$ cm and $CA = 5$ cm.

   A circle, centre A and radius 3 cm, intersects AB and AC at P and Q respectively, as shown in the figure.

   (i) Show that, to three decimal places, $|\angle BAC| = 1{\cdot}504$ radians.

   (ii) Calculate the area, in cm^2, of the sector APQ.

   (iii) Calculate the area, in cm^2, of the shaded region $BPQC$.

   (iv) Calculate the perimeter, in cm, of the shaded region $BPQC$.

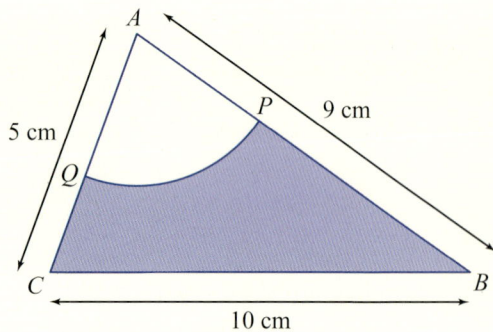

26. A pyramid has a square base of side 20 m and a perpendicular height of $13{\cdot}5$ m.

   (i) Using a suitable scale, draw the net of the pyramid. (Clearly indicate the scale you use.)

   (ii) Hence or otherwise, show that the total surface area of the five sides equals 1,072 m^2, correct to the nearest integer.

27. The end view of a polytunnel is shown in the diagram. Calculate:

    (i) The radius of the arc with centre at the point O

    (ii) The angle θ correct to one decimal place

    (iii) The length of the arc correct to one decimal place

    (iv) The amount of covering needed to fully cover this end of the tunnel correct to the nearest square metre

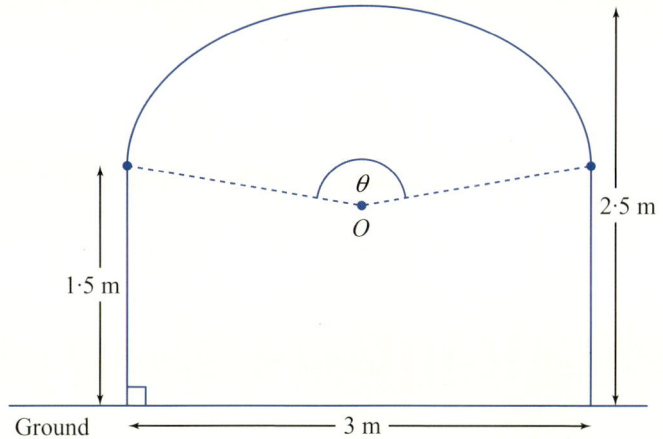

28. The Wonder Building is an arched building that does not need any support inside, due partly to the fact that its shape is an arc of a circle.

    The arc for a Wonder Building can be a full semicircle or less than a semicircle. It cannot be more than a semicircle. The span of the building is the total width from one side of the arch to the other.

    (i) A particular Wonder Building has a span of 30 metres and a height of 10 metres. Find the radius of the arc.

    (ii) A customer wants a building with a span of 18 metres and a height of 10 metres.

        (a) What arc radius would be required to give such a building?

        (b) Explain why the Wonder Building that the customer wants is not possible.

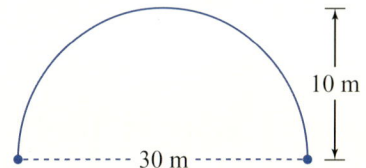

    (iii) An air force needs a Wonder Building to house a *Tornado* military jet. The dimensions of the aircraft are as follows:

        • Wingspan: 14 metres
        • Height: 6 metres
        • Height of wingtips above ground: 2 metres

The shelter must be at least 0·5 metres above the top of the tail and at least 1 metre clear horizontally of the wingtips.

For the shelter to have the exact clearance required, find the radius of the arc.

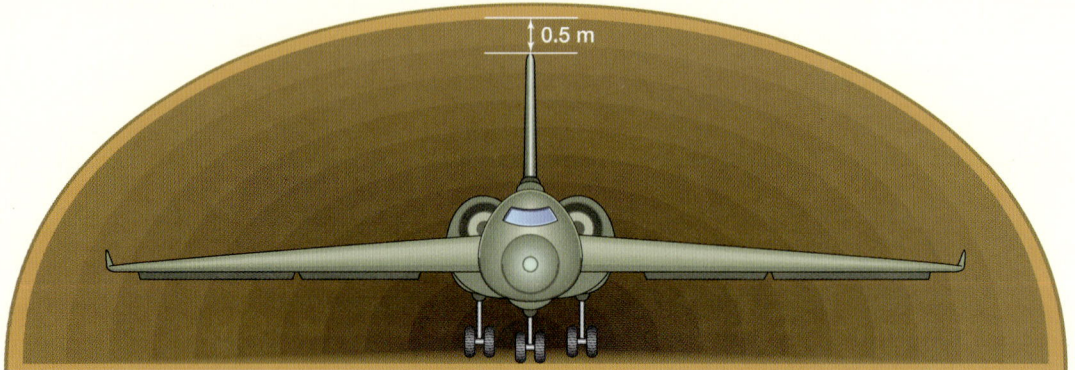

0.5 m

29. The equilateral triangle *DEF* contains three circles each of radius *r* with centres *A*, *B*, *C*, as shown in the diagram. Each circle touches the other circle at one point and the sides of the triangle form tangents to the circles.

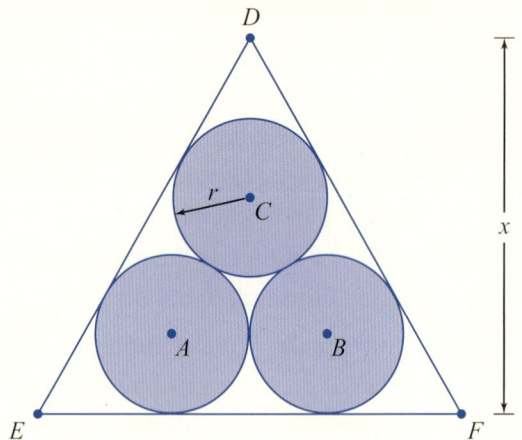

   (i) Write down $|\angle DEF|$.

   (ii) Show that $|EF| = 2r(\sqrt{3} + 1)$.

   (iii) Hence or otherwise, write *x*, the perpendicular height of $\triangle DEF$ in terms of *r*.

   (iv) Find the area of $\triangle DEF$ in terms of *r*.

   (v) Find, correct to one decimal place, the percentage area of $\triangle DEF$ that is occupied by the circles.

Trapezoidal rule

The trapezoidal rule gives a concise formula to enable us to make a good approximation of the area of an irregular shape.

Consider the diagram below.

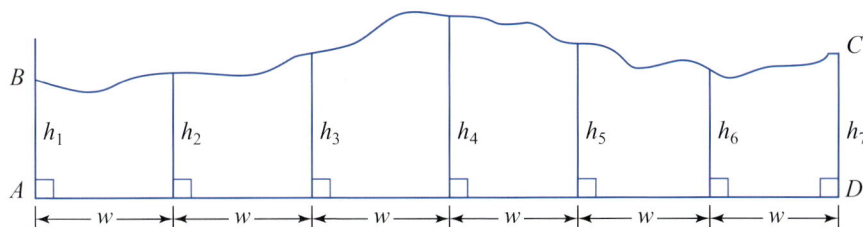

To find the area of the figure *ABCD*, do the following.

1. Divide the figure into a number of strips of equal width. (Note: The number of strips can be even or odd.)
2. Number and measure each height, *h*.
3. Use the following formula:

$$\text{Area} = \frac{W}{2}\left[h_1 + h_7 + 2(h_2 + h_3 + h_4 + h_5 + h_6)\right]$$

$$\text{Area} = \frac{\text{Width}}{2}\left[\text{first height} + \text{last height} + 2(\text{sum of all remaining heights})\right]$$

Note: The greater the number of strips taken, the greater the accuracy.

EXAMPLE 1

Use the trapezoidal rule to estimate the area of the figure below.

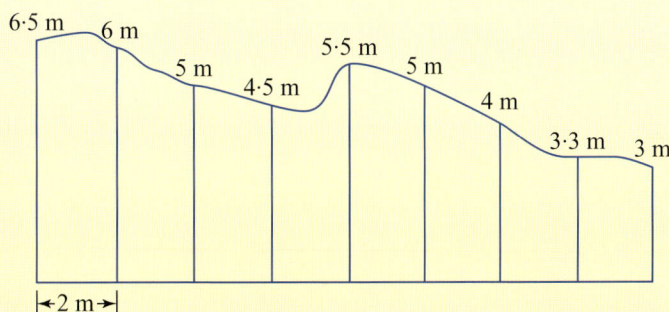

Solution:

$$\text{Area} = \frac{W}{2}[\text{first height} + \text{last height} + 2(\text{sum of all remaining heights})]$$

$$\text{Area} = \frac{W}{2}[h_1 + h_9 + 2(h_2 + h_3 + h_4 + h_5 + h_6 + h_7 + h_8)]$$

Now $h_1 = 6\cdot5$, $h_2 = 6$, $h_3 = 5$, $h_4 = 4\cdot5$, $h_5 = 5\cdot5$, $h_6 = 5$, $h_7 = 4$, $h_8 = 3\cdot3$, $h_9 = 3$

$$\text{Area} = \frac{2}{2}[6\cdot5 + 3 + 2(6 + 5 + 4\cdot5 + 5\cdot5 + 5 + 4 + 3\cdot3)]$$

$$\text{Area} = 1[9\cdot5 + 2(33\cdot3)]$$

$$\text{Area} = 76\cdot1 \text{ m}^2$$

If an irregular shape has no straight edge, it can be broken up into two regions, each with its own straight edge, as in the diagram. We then apply the trapezoidal rule in the normal way, except we treat both heights on each side of the line as one height in using the formula (see the next example).

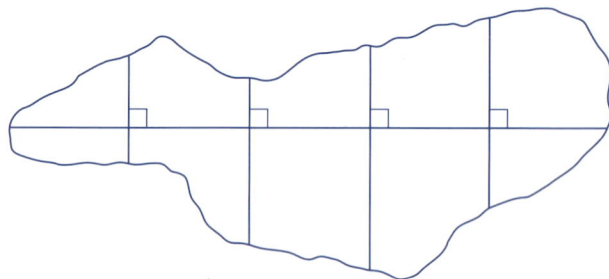

Sometimes we also have to deal with an equation in disguise.

EXAMPLE 2

A surveyor makes the following sketch in estimating the area of a building site, where k is the length shown. Using the trapezoidal rule, she estimates that the area of the site is 175 m². Find k.

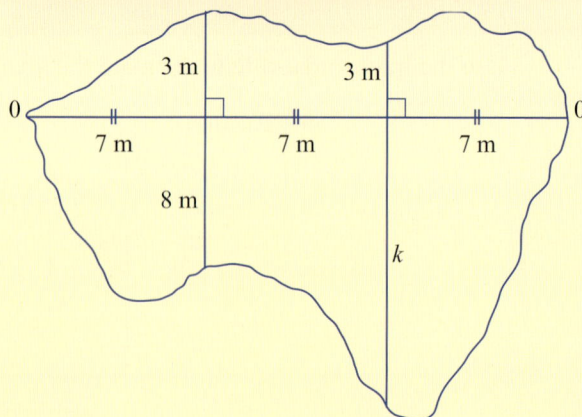

0

3 m   3 m

7 m   7 m   7 m

8 m

k

0

Solution:

Estimated area of building site = 175 m^2.

$$\therefore \frac{W}{2}[h_1 + h_4 + 2(h_2 + h_3)] = 175 \text{ m}$$

$$h_1 = 0$$
$$h_2 = 3 + 8 = 11$$
$$h_3 = 3 + k$$
$$h_4 = 0$$

$$\frac{7}{2}[0 + 0 + 2(11 + 3 + k)] = 175$$

$$\frac{7}{2}[22 + 6 + 2k] = 175$$

$$77 + 21 + 7k = 175$$

$$7k = 175 - 77 - 21$$

$$7k = 77$$

$$k = 11 \text{ m}$$

Exercise 12.2

Use the trapezoidal rule to estimate the area of the following figures in questions 1 and 2 (all dimensions are in m).

1.

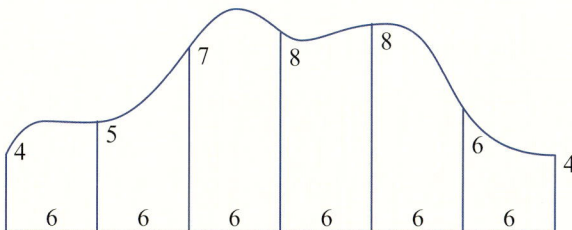

2.

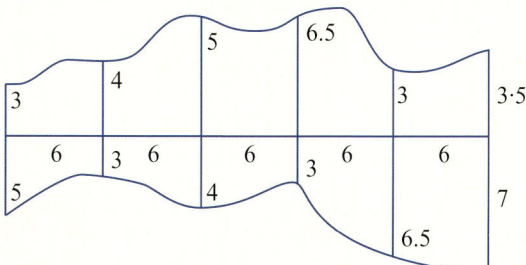

3. The sketch shows a field *ABCD* which has one uneven edge. At equal intervals of 6 m along [*BC*], perpendicular measurements of 7 m, 8 m, 10 m, 11 m, 13 m, 15 m and x m are made to the top of the field.

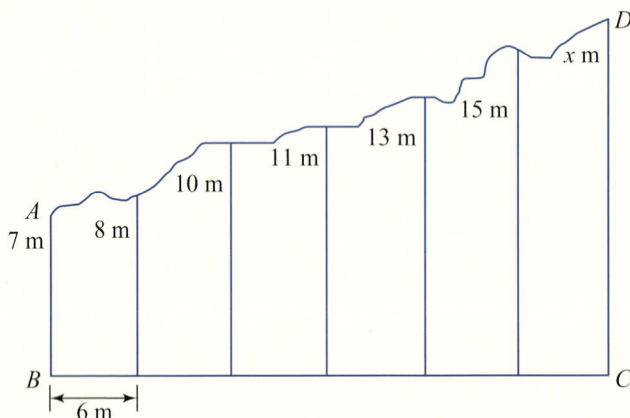

Using the trapezoidal rule, the area of the field is calculated to be 410 m². Calculate the value of x.

4. In order to estimate the area of the irregular shape below, a horizontal line is drawn across the widest part of the shape and three offsets (perpendicular line) are drawn at equal intervals along this line.

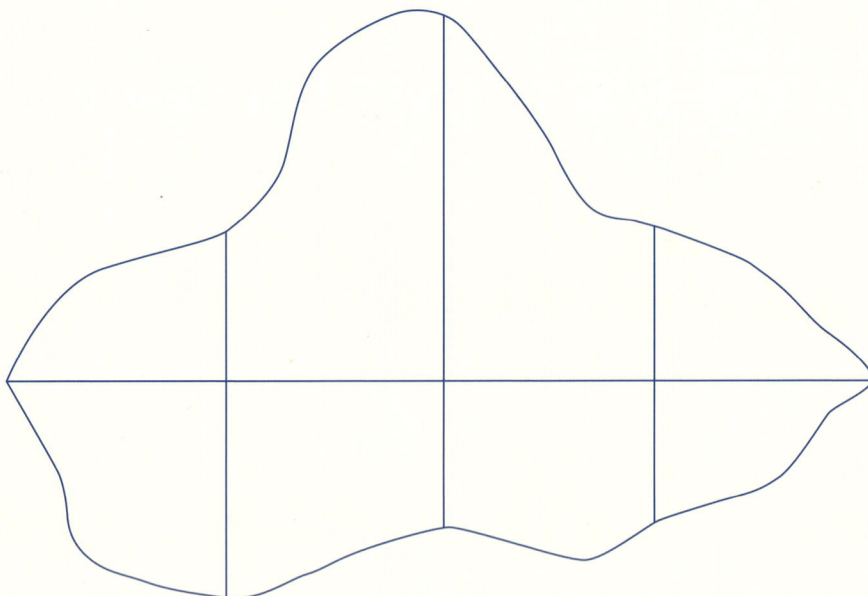

(i) Measure the horizontal line and the offsets in centimetres.

(ii) Make a rough sketch of the shape in your answerbook and record the measurements on it. Use the trapezoidal rule with these measurements to estimate the area of the shape.

5. The sketch shows a flood caused by a leaking underground pipe that runs from A to B.

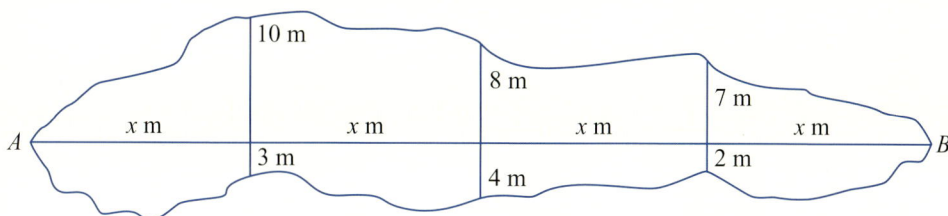

At equal intervals of x m along $[AB]$, perpendicular measurements are made to the edges of the flood. The measurements to the top edge are 10 m, 8 m and 7 m. The measurements to the bottom edge are 3 m, 4 m and 2 m. At A and B, the measurements are 0 m.

Using the trapezoidal rule, the area of the flood is estimated to be 672 m². Find x correct to the nearest cm and hence write down the length of the pipe.

6. Archaeologists excavating a rectangular plot $ABCD$ measuring 120 m by 60 m divided the plot into eight square sections, as shown on the diagram. At the end of the first phase of the work, the shaded area had been excavated. To estimate the area excavated, perpendicular measurements were made to the edge of the excavated area, as shown.

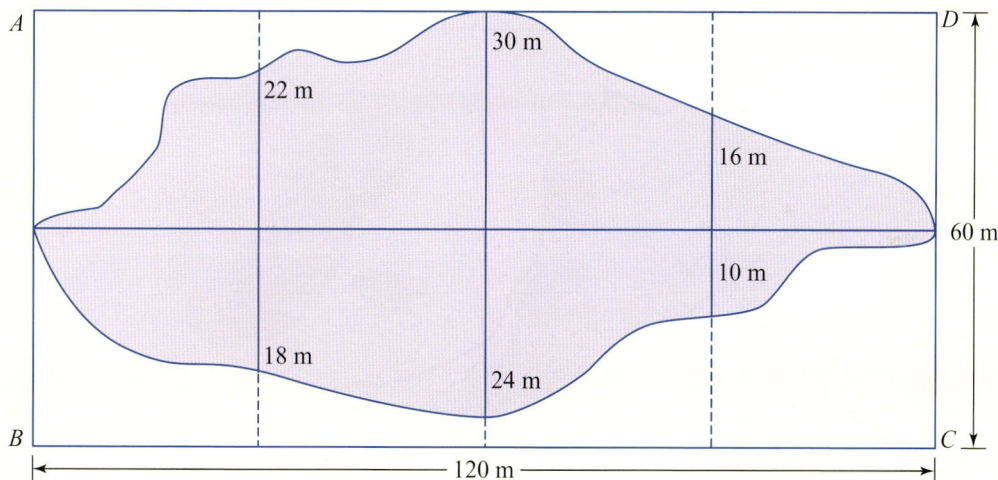

(i) Use the trapezoidal rule to estimate the area excavated.

(ii) Express the excavated area as a percentage of the total area.

7. The depth of the water in a river of width 20 m was measured at intervals of 4 m, starting from one bank and ending at the other. The results are recorded in the following table.

Distance from the bank (m)	0	4	8	12	16	20
Depth (m)	0·6	0·8	1·4	2·1	1·9	0·7

(i) Use the trapezoidal rule to estimate the area of a cross-section of the water at this point.

(ii) At this point of the river, it was calculated that the water was flowing at a speed of $\frac{1}{2}$ m per second. Find the volume of water passing this point each minute (a) in cubic metres (b) in litres.

8. A Geography class is required to estimate the area of Carlingford Lough from a map with a scale of 1 : 70,000.

An axis line *ABCDEF* is drawn and divided into five equal segments (of 3 cm each), as shown.

(i) Complete the following table by writing down the values of *x* and *y* by measuring from the map. Give your answers correct to the nearest half centimetre.

Through the point	*A*	*B*	*C*	*D*	*E*	*F*
Perpendicular distance from shore to shore in cm	0	$3\frac{1}{2}$	$3\frac{1}{2}$	*x*	*y*	$2\frac{1}{2}$

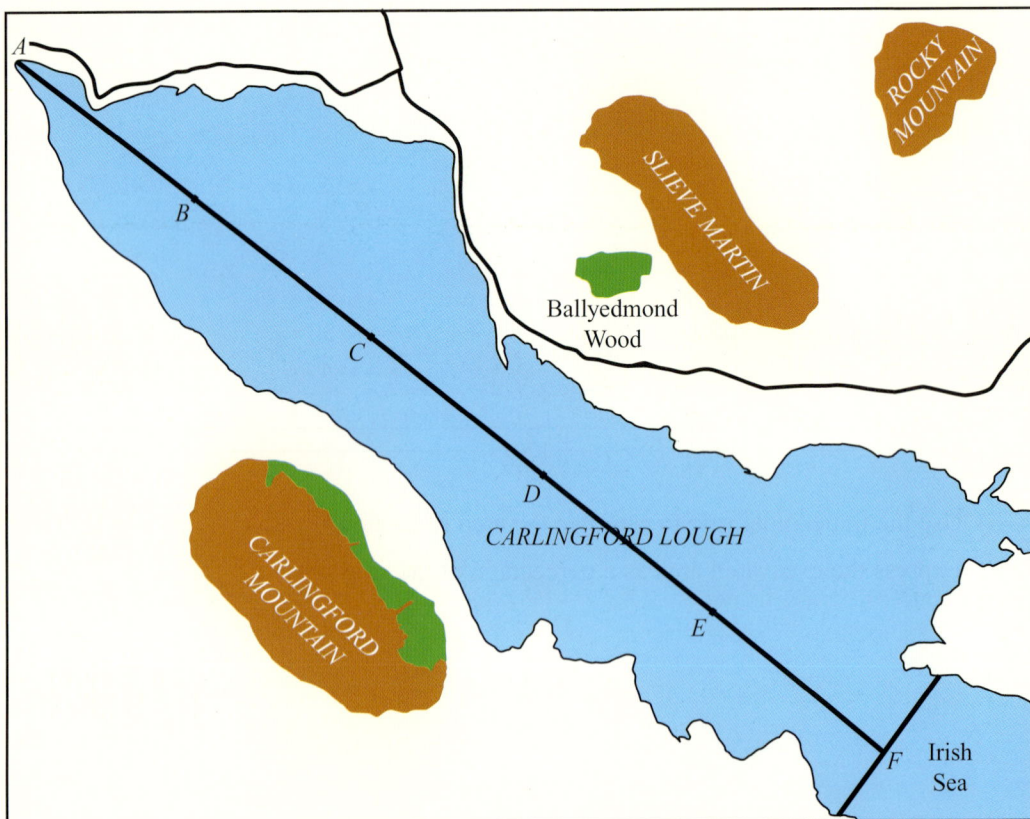

(ii) Use the trapezoidal rule to estimate the following.

    (a) The area in cm^2 of Carlingford Lough as outlined on the map, correct to the nearest cm^2.

    (b) The actual area in km^2 of Carlingford Lough as outlined, correct to the nearest km^2.

    (c) Comment on the accuracy or otherwise of the trapezoidal rule in this situation. Justify your comment.

Volume

EXAMPLE 1

The relationship between the volumes of similar solids.

A cuboid measuring 1 unit by 1 unit by 2 units has been enlarged by a scale factor 4 to give a similar cuboid which measures 4 units by 4 units by 8 units.

The volume of the smaller cuboid is 2 cubic units.
The volume of the larger cuboid is 128 cubic units.

The ratio of these volumes is

$$\frac{\text{Volume of larger cuboid}}{\text{Volume of smaller cuboid}} = \frac{128}{2} = 64 = 4^3.$$

So the ratio of the volumes = (scale factor)^3.

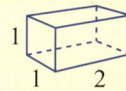

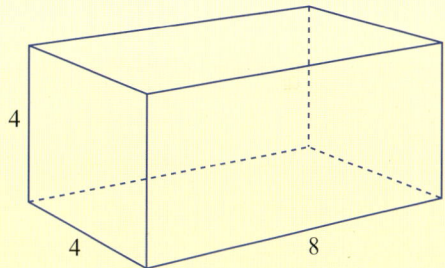

EXAMPLE 2

The diagram shows a cuboid $ABCDEFGH$
Given $|FC| = 2\sqrt{61}$ cm and $|FB| = 6\sqrt{5}$ cm.

    (i) When $|FH| = 4\sqrt{13}$ cm. Find $|BC|$

    (ii) Show that $|FG| = 12$ cm.

    (iii) Hence, calculate $|BG|$.

    (iv) Calculate the volume of the cuboid, giving your answers in litres.

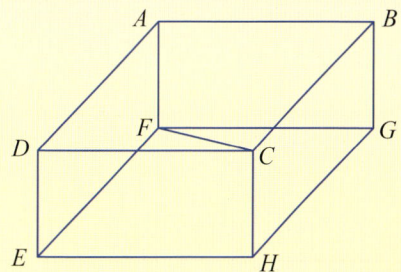

Solution:

(i) $\triangle FBC$ is right angled at B.

$\Rightarrow |FC|^2 = |FB|^2 + |BC|^2$

$(2\sqrt{61})^2 = (6\sqrt{5})^2 + |BC|^2$

$244 = 180 + |BC|^2$

$64 = |BC|^2$

$8 \text{ cm} = |BC|$

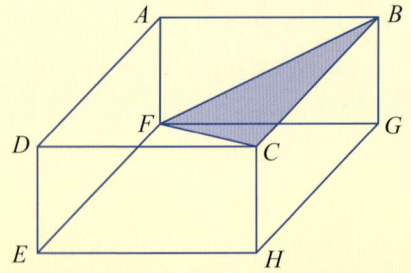

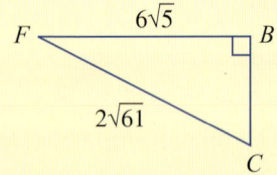

(ii) $\triangle FGH$ is right angled at G.

$\Rightarrow |FH|^2 = |FG|^2 + |GH|^2$

$(4\sqrt{13})^2 = |FG|^2 + (8)^2$

$208 = |FG|^2 + 64$

$144 = |FG|^2$

$12 \text{ cm} = |FG|$

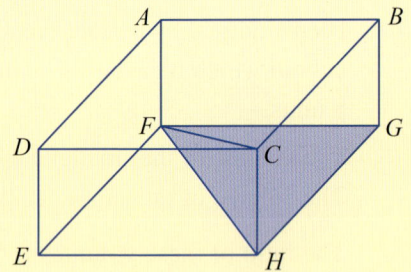

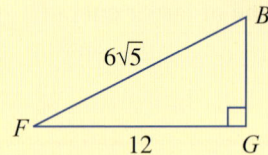

(iii) $|FB|^2 = |BG|^2 + |FG|^2$

$(6\sqrt{5})^2 = |BG|^2 + (12)^2$

$180 = |BG|^2 + 144$

$36 = |BG|^2$

$6 = |BG|$

(iv) Volume cuboid $= (l)(b)(h)$

$= (12)(8)(6)$

$= 576 \text{ cm}^3$

$= 0 \cdot 576 \, l$

EXAMPLE 3

A cylinder is cut from a solid wooden sphere of radius 8 cm, as shown in the diagram. The height of the cylinder is $2h$ cm.

(i) Find $|AE|$ (the radius of the cylinder) in terms of h.

(ii) Show that the volume (V) of the cylinder may be written as $V = 2\pi h(64 - h^2)$ cm^3.

Given $h = \dfrac{8}{\sqrt{3}}$ cm, find:

(iii) The radius of the cylinder

(iv) The volume of the cylinder

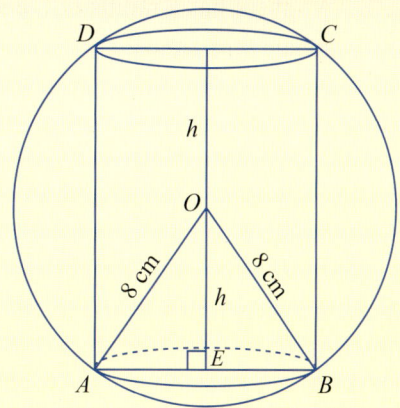

Solution:

(i) $\triangle OEA$ is right angled at E.

Using the theorem of Pythagoras, we write

$$(8)^2 = h^2 + r^2$$
$$64 - h^2 = r^2$$
$$\sqrt{64 - h^2} = r$$

(ii) Volume of cylinder $= \pi r^2 h$

$$\therefore V = \pi(64 - h^2)(2h)$$
$$V = 2\pi h(64 - h^2) \text{ cm}^3$$

(iii) $h = \dfrac{8}{\sqrt{3}} \Rightarrow r = \sqrt{64 - h^2}$

Becomes $r = \sqrt{64 - \left(\dfrac{8}{\sqrt{3}}\right)^2}$

$$r = \sqrt{64 - \dfrac{64}{3}}$$

$$r = \sqrt{\dfrac{128}{3}} = \sqrt{\dfrac{64(2)}{3}} = 8\sqrt{\dfrac{2}{3}} \text{ cm}$$

(iv) Volume cylinder $= \pi r^2(2h)$

$$= \pi\left(8\sqrt{\dfrac{2}{3}}\right)^2 2\left(\dfrac{8}{\sqrt{3}}\right)$$

$$= \pi(64)\left(\dfrac{2}{3}\right)\left(\dfrac{16}{\sqrt{3}}\right)$$

$$= \dfrac{2048\pi}{3\sqrt{3}} \text{ cm}^3$$

Exercise 12.3

1. A sphere has a radius of 8 cm. Find the volume of the smallest (rectangular) box that the sphere will fit in.

2. Calculate the area of a triangle with sides of length 3 cm, 5 cm and 7 cm. Hence, calculate the volume of the wedge shown.

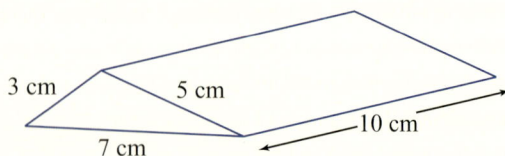

3. A megaphone in the shape of a cone has a vertical angle of $60°$ and a slant height of 45 cm, as shown in the diagram.

   (i) Determine the diameter of the megaphone.

   (ii) Determine the volume of the megaphone in litres correct to two significant figures.

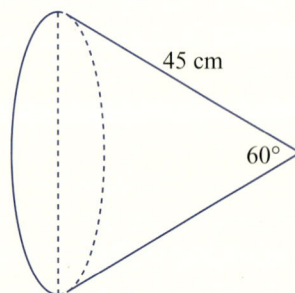

4. A cone has a radius $3r$ cm and a vertical height $\frac{h}{\pi}$ cm. If the volume of this cone is r^2 cm^3, find the value of h.

5. The volume of a sphere in cubic centimetres is numerically equal to its surface area in square centimetres. Show that the radius of the sphere is equal to 3 cm.

6. The vertical height of a cylinder is $\frac{h}{3}$ cm and the radius of its base is $h\sqrt{3}$ cm. If the volume of the cylinder is 64π cm^3, find the value of h.

7. A hollow cylindrical metal can (including a top) of uniform thickness has an external radius of 5 cm and an external height of 15 cm.

   (i) Find the external volume of the can in terms of π.

   (ii) Find the (external) area of metal required to make the can.

   (iii) Assuming wastage of 33%, how many complete cans could be made from 1 m^2 of metal sheet?

8. The diagrams show a sketch of a house and its cross-section.

   The house consists of a cuboid and a wedge-shaped roof.

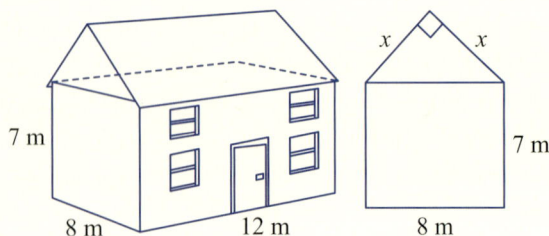

   (i) Show that $x = 5.66$ m, correct to two decimal places.

   (ii) Hence, calculate the volume of the house. Give your answer to the nearest cubic metre.

9. A test tube is in the shape of a cylinder standing on a hemisphere, as in the diagram. The height of the cylinder is 8 cm and the radius of the hemisphere is 3 cm.

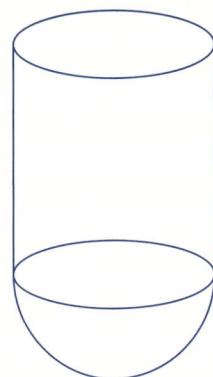

    (i) Write down the height of the test tube.

   (ii) The volume of the test tube is $k\pi$ cm^3. Find the value of k.

  (iii) The test tube is filled with 250 ml of water. Calculate the height of the water in the test tube correct to the nearest integer.

10. **(i)** Find the volume of a cylinder of radius 6 mm and height 20 mm. Give your answer in two forms, as follows **(a)** in terms of π, and **(b)** correct to two decimal places.

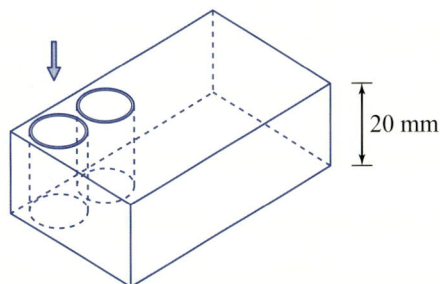

   (ii) A solid rectangular block measures 60 mm × 35 mm × 20 mm.

     Cylindrical holes of radius 6 mm are drilled, one at a time, through the block, in the direction shown.

     After how many holes will more than half of the original block have been removed?

20 mm

11. A cylindrical coronary stent of length 20 mm and radius 1·5 mm is inserted to unblock an artery. The stent is inserted using a device called a balloon catheter. Once in position, the catheter is inflated and opens the stent by a scale factor of 2·1.

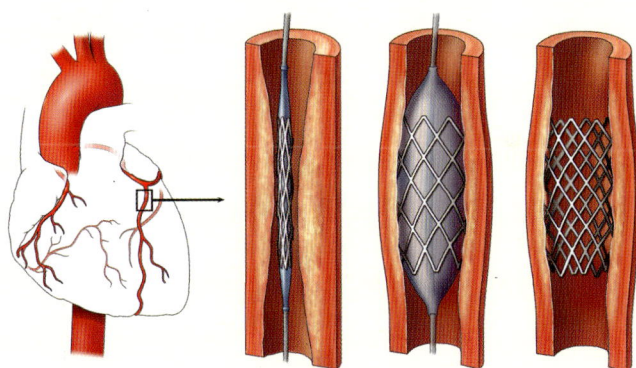

    (i) Write down the radius of the stent after it is inflated.

   (ii) Given the length of the stent is not changed with the inflation, find the volume of the stent after it is inflated.

  A coronary stent is a metal tube used to unblock the arteries, whose insertion can help prevent a heart attack.

  (iii) Hence or otherwise, find the ratio

$$\frac{\text{Volume of inflated stent}}{\text{Volume of stent before procedure}}.$$

12. **(i)** A model of a car is made to a
scale of 1 : 50. The length of
the real car is 4·3 metres.
Calculate the length of the
model car.

(ii) The volume of the model car
is 54 cubic centimetres.
Calculate the volume of the
real car in litres.

13. Four identical solid chocolate spheres, each
of radius r cm, are to fit exactly into a
presentation pack in the shape of a cylinder.
The production manager considers two
possible cylinders A or B, for the presentation pack.
The diagram shows the two cylinders.

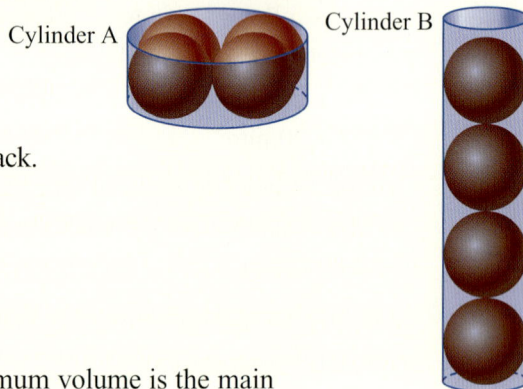

Cylinder A

Cylinder B

Find, in terms of π and r, the volume of:

(i) Cylinder A

(ii) Cylinder B

(iii) Given that a presentation pack with minimum volume is the main
consideration, which presentation pack should the production
manager choose?

14. A scoop in the shape of a wedge is made by cutting two equal
squares of length x cm from the corners of a rectangular sheet
of thin metal which measures 30 cm by 20 cm.

|← 30 cm →|

20 cm

x

x

(i) Show that V, the volume of the scoop in cm³, can be
expressed as $V = 2x(30 - x)(10 - x)$.

(ii) Draw a graph of V against x for values of x from
0 to 10.

(iii) Use your graph to estimate:

(a) The value of V when $x = 2.5$ cm

(b) The values of x when $V = 900$ cm³

(c) The maximum value of V and the value of x which gives the maximum value

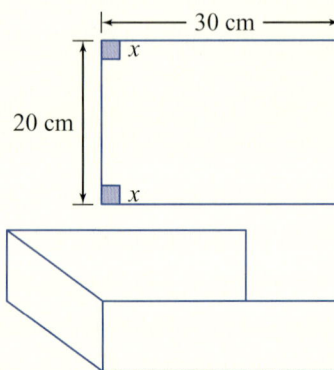

15. The diagram shows a model of a water storage facility.

The facility consists of the base of a truncated inverted cone (frustrum) on top of a cylinder on level ground.

The total height of the structure above ground is 40 m. The heights of the cylinder and frustrum are in the ratio 3 : 2 respectively. Other measurements are given in the diagram.

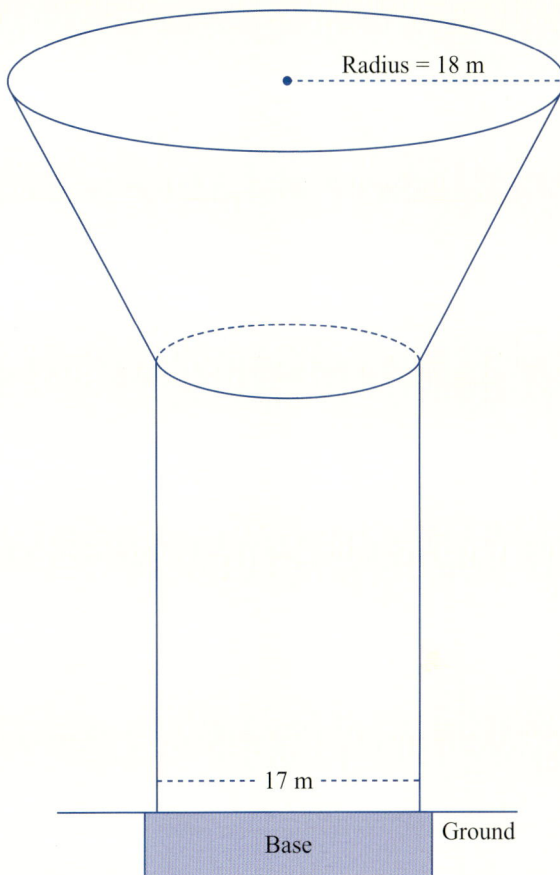

(i) Calculate, in m^3, the volume of the frustrum.

(ii) The frustrum stores a maximum of 6·1 million litres of water. Find the volume of water stored at maximum as a percentage of the volume of the frustrum. Give your answer to the nearest per cent.

(iii) 30% of the structure is below ground. Find the total volume of the structure above and below ground.

(iv) The structure below ground is a cuboid with a square base and depth of 13 m. Find the length of the square base, correct to the nearest metre.

Radius = 18 m

17 m

Base

Ground

16. A packaging company makes boxes for chocolates. An example of a box is shown. This box is closed and the top and bottom of the box are identical regular hexagons of side x cm.

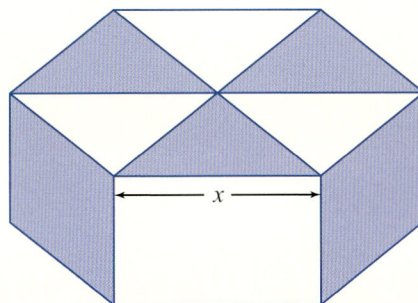

(i) Show that the area of each hexagon is $\dfrac{3\sqrt{3}x^2}{2}$ cm^2.

(ii) Hence, write an expression for the volume of the box.

x

(iii) Given that the volume of the box is $1l$ and the height is $h = \dfrac{16x}{3\sqrt{3}}$, find the value of x.

17. A slice is taken out of a cylindrical cake of height 6 cm such that the angle of the slice is $\frac{\pi}{3}$.

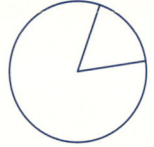

   (i) If the radius of the cake is r cm, find an expression for the total surface area of the slice.

   (ii) If the total surface area of the slice is 200 cm^2, then write down a quadratic equation involving r.

   (iii) Use the quadratic formula to find r (to one decimal place).

18. The Earth can be regarded as a sphere of radius 6,378 km.

   (i) Show clearly that $1 \cdot 087 \times 10^{12}$ km^3 is an approximate value for Earth's volume.

   (ii) It is estimated that two-thirds of Earth's surface is covered by water. The area covered by water can be written as $3 \cdot 41 \times 10^n$ km^2. Find the value of n.

   (iii) Given the mean depth of water in the oceans is 3,800 m, show that the volume of water in the oceans is approximately $1 \cdot 3 \times 10^9$ km^3.

   (iv) In a simulated study on global warming, the melting of the ice caps on Greenland and Antarctica used the following figures.

   The total volume of land ice in these polar areas is 30 million cubic km.

   Since ice is an expanded form of water, the conversion ratio volume ice : volume water = 100 m^3 : 90 m^3 was used.

ANTARCTICA

● South Pole

The study considered two cases:

(a) A melting of 15% of the total polar land ice

(b) A melting of 25% of the total polar land ice

Calculate the mean rise in sea level for Earth in both cases. Give both answers correct to the nearest metre.

19. A rectangular sheet of metal, with dimensions shown, is folded along the centre line to create a guttering.

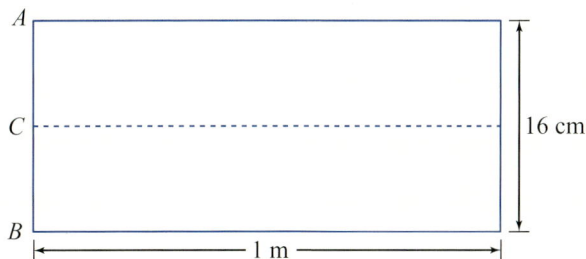

(i) Show clearly that the area of $\triangle ABC = 32 \sin \theta$ cm^2.

(ii) Hence, write down the volume of the guttering in the form $k \sin \theta$ cm^3 where $k \in N$.

(iii) Investigate (by trial and error) the relationship between the angle at the fold, shown as θ, and the volume of the guttering.

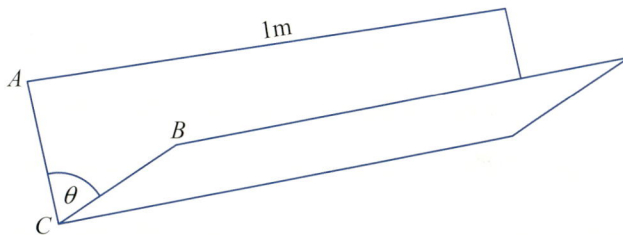

(iv) Find the angle for which the volume of guttering is greatest.

(v) Explain how the angle in (iv) can be found without guesswork.

20. The figure $ABCDEFGH$ is a cube with side W cm. P is the centre of face $EFGH$.

(i) Show that $|PF| = \dfrac{w}{\sqrt{2}}$.

(ii) Hence, write $|PB|$ in the form $w\sqrt{\dfrac{x}{y}}$, where $x, y \in N$.

(iii) Given the area of $\triangle PBC = \frac{3}{2}\sqrt{5}$ cm^2, by finding the perpendicular height of $\triangle PBC$ or otherwise, find the value of w. Write your answer in surd form.

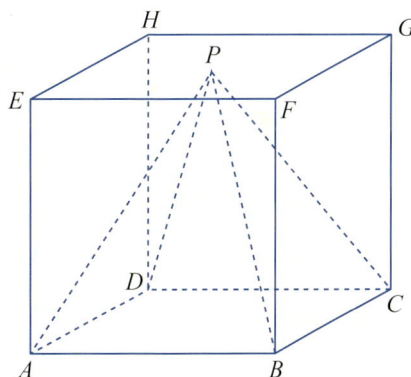

(iv) Hence, write the volume of the figure in the form $V\sqrt{V}$ cm^3 where $V \in N$.

21. A regular tetrahedron has four faces, each of which is an equilateral triangle.

 The tetrahedron is placed inside a cylindrical container with one face flat against the bottom, as in the diagram.

 Given the length of one edge of the tetrahedron is $2x$, show that the volume of the smallest possible cylindrical container

 is $\left(\dfrac{8\sqrt{6}}{9}\right)\pi x^3$.

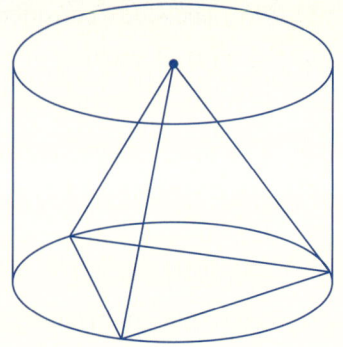

22. The diagram shows a solid with volume V, obtained from a cube with edge $a > 1$ when a smaller cube with edge $\dfrac{1}{a}$ is removed.

 (i) Let $x = a - \dfrac{1}{a}$. Find V in terms of x.

 (ii) Hence or otherwise, show that the only value of a for which $V = 4x$ is $a = \dfrac{1 + \sqrt{5}}{2}$.

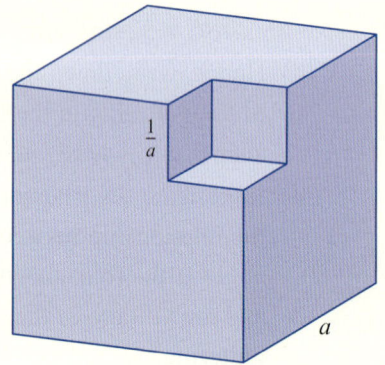

1.   **(i)** Cyril has drawn three scatter graphs but he has forgotten to label them.

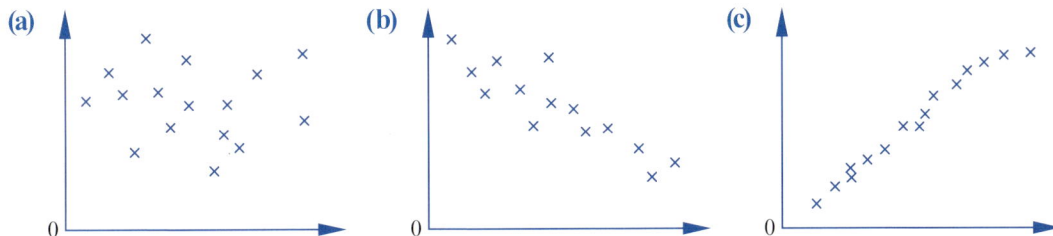

(a)   **(b)**   **(c)**

Which label is most likely to belong to each graph?

Label X hours spent playing computer games vs. hours spent reading books

Label Y age vs. hours of homework set

Label Z weight vs. IQ

(ii) The dot plots below are drawn on the same scale. They show the class scores in tests taken before and after a unit of work was completed.

Before

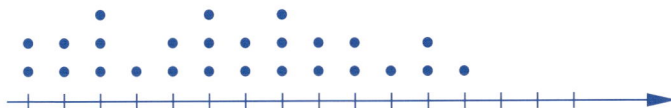

After

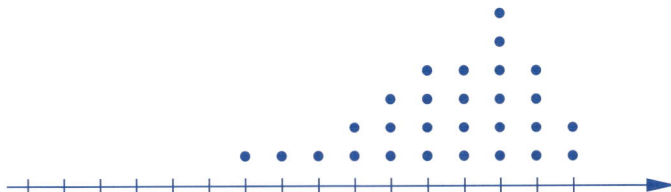

Which statement about the change in scores is correct?

A The mean increased and the standard deviation decreased.

B The mean increased and the standard deviation increased.

C The mean decreased and the standard deviation decreased.

D The mean decreased and the standard deviation increased.

(iii) Out of 50 men in a room, 10 are left handed and six are deaf. Two of them are both left handed and deaf. If a man in the room is chosen at random, find, giving your answers as fractions in their simplest forms, the probability that:

(a) He is neither deaf nor left handed

(b) He is not deaf given that he is not left handed

2. **(i)** Show that the point $(1, 5)$ is on the line $2x - 5y + 23 = 0$.
    If $2x - 5y + 23 = 0$, express y in terms of x.

    (ii) A triangle ABC lies entirely in the first quadrant and has an area of $4\frac{1}{2}$ square units.
    The equation of one side of the triangle is $2x - 5y + 23 = 0$ and the vertices of A and B
    are $(1, 5)$ and $(3, 4)$, respectively. Find the coordinates of the point C.

3. **(i)** Verify that $x(x - a) + y(y - b) = k(bx + ay - ab)$ is the equation of a circle passing through
    the points $(a, 0)$ and $(0, b)$ for $k \in \mathbb{R}$.

    (ii) Find the equation of the circle through the points $(1, 0)$ and $(0, 2)$ which has its centre on
    the line $x + 3y - 11 = 0$.

4. In the diagram, P, Q and R are points on the equator. N is the
    North Pole, S is the South Pole and O is the centre of the Earth.

    NQS is the prime meridian ($0°$), NPS is a line of longitude $4°$W and
    NRS is a line of longitude $117°$E.

    Madrid and Beijing are situated at ($40°$N $4°$W) and at ($40°$N $117°$E)
    respectively.

    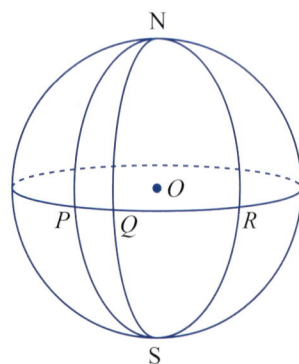

    (i) On the diagram, draw the circle of latitude $40°$N and show the
    positions of Madrid and Beijing.

    (ii) What is the size of the angle POR?

    (iii) Calculate the distance between Madrid and Beijing measured along their common circle of
    latitude (give your answer correct to three significant figures). Take the radius of the earth
    to be 6,400 km.

5. In a two-person game, players Buzz and Woody have cards of different colours, numbered as shown
    below.

    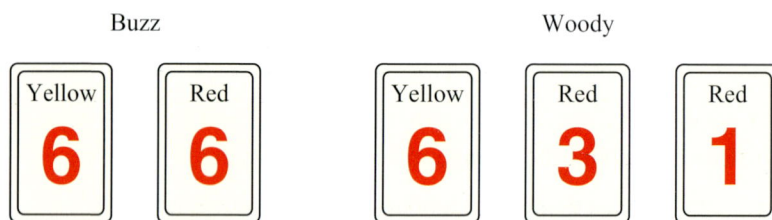

    The game they are to play is as follows:

    At a given signal, the players *simultaneously* turn over one of their cards. If the cards match in
    colour, Buzz wins the difference between the numbers on the cards; if the cards do not match in
    colour, Woody wins the difference between the numbers on the cards played.

(i) Copy and complete this table to show the outcomes of the game, i.e. to show the wins made by the players.

Woody (W)

		Yellow 6	Red 3	Red 1
Buzz (B)	Yellow 6		(B,W) (0, 3)	
	Red 6			

(ii) A player's best or optimal strategy is the one he uses to ensure that he does not lose.

    (a) What is Buzz's best or optimal strategy?

    (b) What is Woody's best or optimal strategy?

    (c) If both players use their optimal strategies, who wins and how much does he win?

(iii) Is the game fair? Give a reason for your answer.

6. **Answer either 6A or 6B.**

6A.   **(i)** State if $\triangle PQR$ is similar to $\triangle XYZ$. Justify your statement.

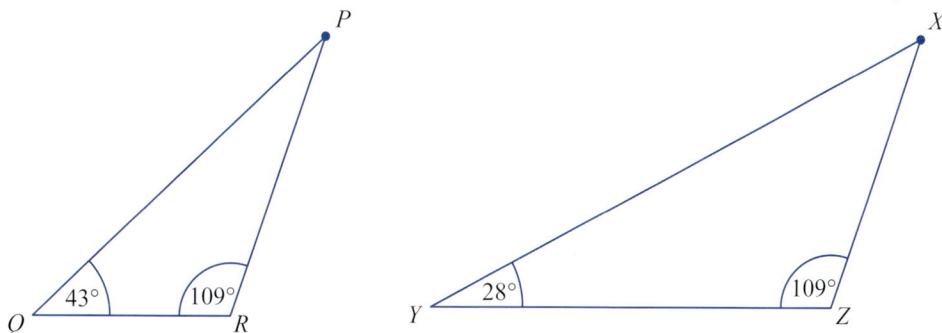

(ii) The $\triangle ABC$ and $\triangle XYZ$ have three measures equal:

$|AB| = |XY|$, $|BC| = |YZ|$ and $|\angle BAC| = |\angle YXZ|$.

Is $\triangle ABC$ congruent to $\triangle XYZ$? Justify your answer.

(iii) State the conditions under which the circumcircle of a triangle will lie:

    (a) Inside   **(b)** Outside   **(c)** On the triangle

6B.   **(i)** $ABCD$ is a parallelogram in which $|AD| = 2|AB|$ and $|CX| = |XB|$.

Prove that AX is perpendicular to XD.

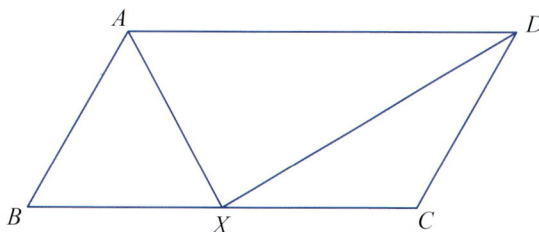

419

(ii) *PQR* is a triangle and *XYT* is its incircle.

(a) Prove that $|PX| = |PT|$.

(b) Hence, deduce that $2[|PT| + |QR|]$ is the perimeter of the triangle *PQR*.

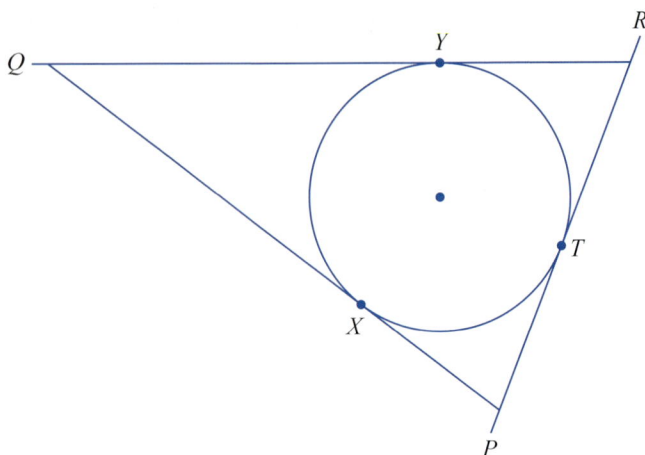

7. An office tower is in the shape of a cuboid with a square base. The roof of the tower is in the shape of a square-based right pyramid.

The diagram shows the tower and its roof with dimensions indicated. The diagram is not drawn to scale.

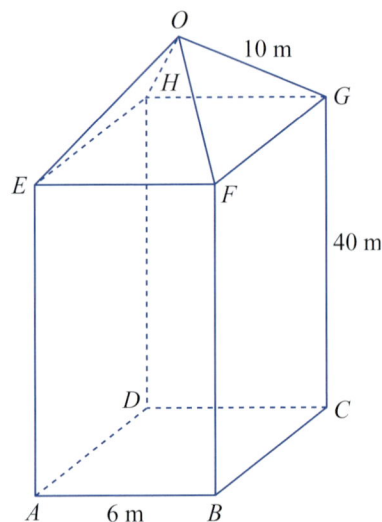

Calculate, correct to three significant figures:

   (i) The size of the angle between *OF* and *FG*

   (ii) The shortest distance from *O* to *FG*

   (iii) The total surface area of the four triangular sections of the roof

   (iv) The size of the angle between the slant height of the roof and the plane *EFGH*

   (v) The height of the tower from the base to *O*

   (vi) A gull's nest is perched at a point, *P*, on the edge, *BF*, of the tower. A person at the point *A*, outside the building, measures the angle of elevation to point *P* to be 79°. Find, correct to three significant figures, the height of the nest from the base of the tower.

8. The diagram shows a large wheel moving slowly on level ground. *P* is a fixed point on the inner part of the wheel. The height, *h* cm, of *P* above the ground at time *t* seconds is given by the formula $h = 70 + 30 \sin 60t$.

(i) Sketch the graph of $h = 70 + 30 \sin 60t$ for $0 \leq t \leq 6$.

(ii) Write down the maximum and minimum values of h.

(iii) At what time will P first reach its minimum height?

(iv) Calculate the values of h at **(a)** $t = 2 \cdot 5$ **(b)** $t = 3 \cdot 7$.

(v) Explain why the outer radius of the wheel must be 70 cm.

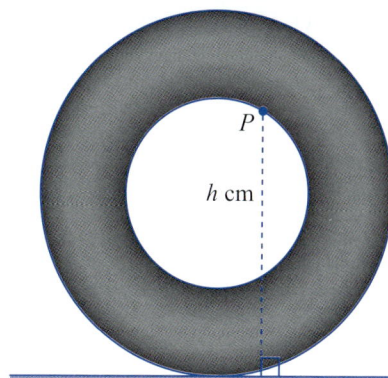

9. Is there any pattern to the locations of the planets in our solar system? The table shows the average distance of each of the eight planets from the sun.

Planet	Position number	Distance from sun (million kilometres)
Mercury	1	60
Venus	2	110
Earth	3	150
Mars	4	230
Jupiter	5	770
Saturn	6	1,400
Uranus	7	2,850
Neptune	8	4,470

(i) Make a scatterplot and describe the association.

(ii) Why would you not want to talk about the correlation between planets' *position* and *distance* from the sun?

(iii) Make a scatterplot showing the logarithm of *distance* vs. *position*. What is better about this scatterplot?

(iv) Find the mean distance of the planets from the sun. (Answer to the nearest million.)

(v) Calculate the standard deviation for the data. (Answer to the nearest million.)

(vi) Analyse your answers to parts **(iv)** and **(v)**. What information can we deduce about our solar system from the calculations?

(vii) Another solar system was also found to have eight planets. In this new system, the mean planetary distance was 550 million km from its sun and a standard deviation of 1,250 million km. Use the results from **(iv)** and **(v)** to describe differences between the two solar systems.

(viii) A planet is selected at random from our solar system. What is the probability that it is more than the mean distance from the sun?

(ix) Three planets are selected from our solar system. What is the probability that:

    (a) All three are less than the mean distance from the sun?

    (b) Exactly one is less than the mean distance from the sun?

10. In a city with a large population, 65% of the population are vaccinated against infection by a certain disease. However, about 5% of those vaccinated nevertheless eventually acquire the disease, while about 20% of those unvaccinated acquire it.

    (i) Show that the probability that a person has the disease is just over 10%.

    (ii) Show that the probability that an infected person is vaccinated is about 0·32.

    If five unvaccinated people are selected at random from the city, find the probability that:

    (iii) None of them has the disease

    (iv) Exactly two of them have the disease

    (v) At least three of them have the disease

11. Two standard six-sided dice are tossed. A diagram representing the sample space is shown below.

Score on second die

	1	2	3	4	5	6
1	•	•	•	•	•	•
2	•	•	•	•	•	•
3	•	•	•	•	•	•
4	•	•	•	•	•	•
5	•	•	•	•	•	•
6	•	•	•	•	•	•

Score on first die

Let X be the sum of the scores on the two dice.

    (i) Find:

        (a) $P(X = 6)$

        (b) $P(X > 6)$

        (c) $P(X = 7 | X > 5)$

    (ii) Elena plays a game where she tosses two dice.

        If the sum is 6, she wins 3 points.

        If the sum is greater than 6, she wins 1 point.

        If the sum is less than 6, she loses k points.

        Find the value of k for which Elena's expected number of points is zero.

12. k_1 is a circle $x^2 + y^2 - 8x + 11 = 0$.

k_2 is another circle whose radius is twice that of k_1. If the circles touch at the point $(6, 1)$, find the equations of k_2.

13. **(i)** *OPQR* is a parallelogram and *O* is the origin.

The equation of *OP* is $3y = x$ and the equation of *OR* is $y = 3x$.

If the coordinates of *Q* are $(4, 3)$, find the coordinates of *P* and *R*.

(ii) In the given diagram, the triangles *ABC* and *DEF* are equiangular, with $AB \parallel FE$, $AC \parallel DF$ and $BC \parallel DE$. Find the coordinates of the point *F*.

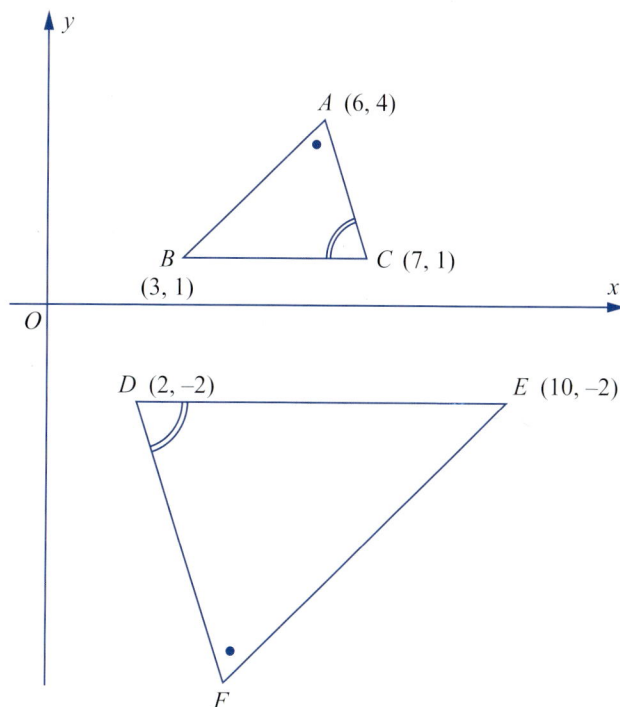

14. **(i)** A game is played in which a fair die is thrown nine times. What is the mean number of sixes obtained per game?

(ii) If the probability of obtaining exactly *t* sixes in a game is denoted by $p(t)$, determine the value of $p(2)/p(1)$.

15. *A* and *B* are two independent events with $p(A) = \frac{1}{15}$ and $p(B) = \frac{1}{10}$. Calculate:

(i) $p(A \cap B)$ **(ii)** $p(A \cup B)$ **(iii)** $p(A \cap B \,|\, A \cup B)$.

Give your answers as fractions in their lowest terms.

16. The diagram below shows the graphs of $y = f(x)$ and $y = g(x)$.

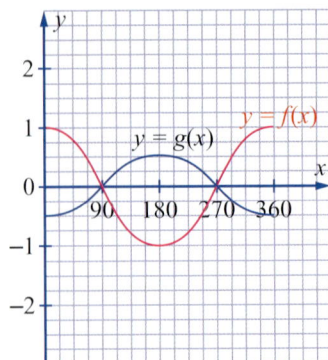

(i) Write down the equations of the graphs shown by:

    (a) $y = f(x)$

    (b) $y = g(x)$

(ii) On the grid above, sketch graphs of:

    (a) $y = f(x) + 1$

    (b) $y = f(2x)$

(iii) Solve the equation $\sin 2\theta = \frac{1}{2}$ for $\theta \in \mathbb{R}$ (where θ is in radians).

17. Answer either 17A or 17B.

17A. (i) Explain fully, with the aid of an example, what is meant by *proof by contradiction*.

(ii) In the diagram, all horizontal lines are parallel and equal distances apart.

Given $\dfrac{|AX|}{|XB|} = \dfrac{h}{k}$ where $k, h \in \mathbb{N}$:

    (a) Write down a value for $\frac{h}{k}$

    (b) Write down another pair of line segments with the same ratio as $h : k$

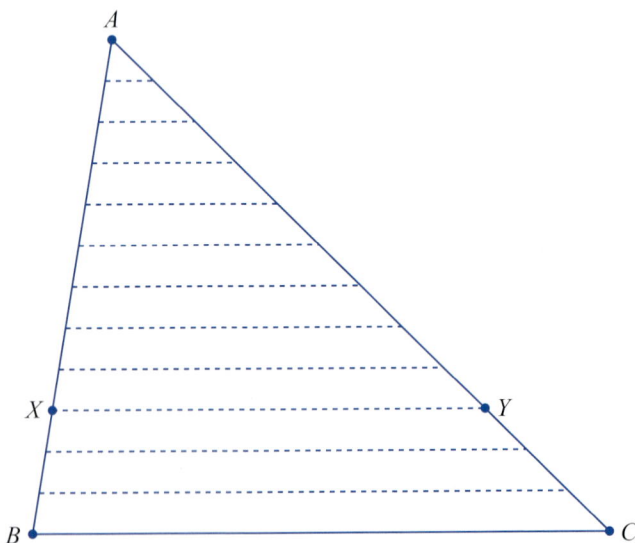

17B. **(i)** A, B, C and D are points on a circle as in the diagram.

Name an angle in the diagram equal to $|\angle BAC|$.

Justify your answer.

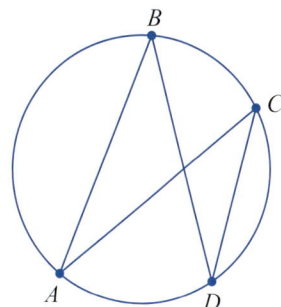

(ii) E, F, G and H are points on the circle k as in the diagram.

Prove that $|\angle HGF| + |\angle HEF| = 180°$.

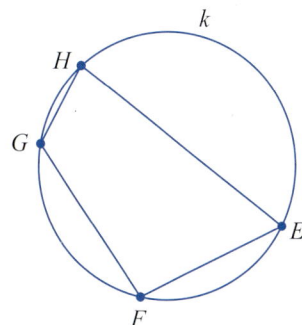

(iii) XYZ is a triangle.

P is the point on YZ such that XP is perpendicular to YZ.

Q is the point on XZ such that YQ is perpendicular to XZ.

Prove that $|\angle POZ| = |\angle PQZ|$.

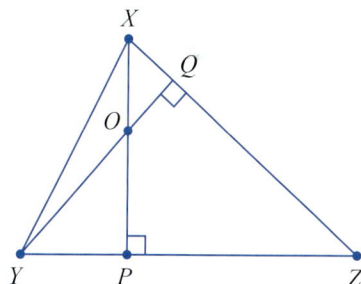

18. Ernie and Bert have been chosen to represent their countries in the rubber duck throw. Assume that the distance thrown by each athlete is normally distributed. The mean distance thrown by Ernie in the past year was 60·33 m with a standard deviation of 1·95 m.

(i) In the past year, 90% of Ernie's throws have been longer than x metres. Find x, correct to two decimal places.

(ii) In the past year, 90% of Bert's throws have been longer than 56·52 m. If the mean distance of his throws was 59·39 m, find the standard deviation of his throws, correct to two decimal places.

425

(iii) This year, Bert's throws have a mean of 59·50 m and a standard deviation of 3·00 m. Ernie's throws still have a mean of 60·33 m and a standard deviation of 1·95 m. In a competition, an athlete must have at least one throw of 65 m or more in the first round to qualify for the final round. Each athlete is allowed three throws in the first round.

(a) Determine which of these two athletes is more likely to qualify for the final on their first throw.

(b) Find the probability that both athletes qualify for the final.

19. The following table shows the cost in euro of seven paperback books chosen at random, together with the number of pages in each book.

Book	1	2	3	4	5	6	7
Number of pages (x)	50	120	200	330	400	450	630
Cost (y, euro)	6·00	5·40	7·20	4·60	7·60	5·80	5·20

(i) Using a suitable scale, plot these pairs of values on a scatter diagram.

(ii) Write down the linear correlation coefficient, r, for the data.

(iii) Stephen wishes to buy a paperback book which has 350 pages in it. He plans to draw a line of best fit to determine the price. State whether or not this is an appropriate method in this case and justify your answer.

20. A ferris wheel with centre O and a radius of 15 metres is represented in the diagram below. Initially seat A is at ground level. The next seat is B, where $AOB = \frac{\pi}{6}$.

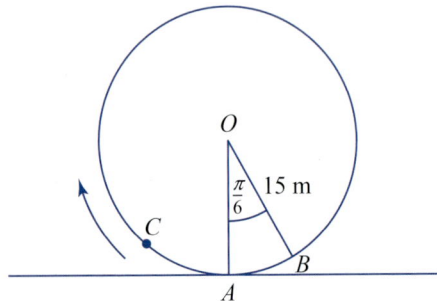

(i) Find the length of the arc AB.

(ii) Find the area of the sector AOB.

(iii) The wheel turns clockwise through an angle of $\frac{2\pi}{3}$. Find the height of A above the ground.

The height, h metres, of seat O above the ground after t minutes can be modelled by the function:

$$h(t) = 15 - 15\cos\left(2t + \frac{\pi}{4}\right)$$

    (iv) Find the height of seat C when $t = \dfrac{\pi}{4}$.

    (v) Find the initial height of seat C.

    (vi) Find the time at which seat C first reaches its highest point.

21.   **(i)** Consider the equation $4x^2 + kx + 1 = 0$. For what values of k does this equation have two equal roots?

    Let f be the function $f(\theta) = 2 \cos 2\theta + 4 \cos \theta + 3$, for $-360 \leq \theta \leq 360$.

  (ii) Show that this function may be written as $f(\theta) = 4 \cos^2 \theta + 4 \cos \theta + 1$.

 (iii) Consider the equation $f(\theta) = 0$ for $-360 \leq \theta \leq 360$.

    (a) How many distinct values of $\cos \theta$ satisfy this equation?

    (b) Find all values of θ which satisfy this equation.

  (iv) Given that $f(\theta) = c$ is satisfied by only three values of θ, find the value of c.

Hint: Sketch $f(\theta)$ in the domain $-360 \leq \theta \leq 360$.

22.   **(i)** Calculate the mean, μ, and the standard deviation of the population of the four numbers 2, 3, 7, 8.

  (ii) A sample of three numbers is to be drawn at random from this population (without replacement). Let $\bar{x}$ be the mean of this sample. List all such possible samples and calculate the value of $\bar{x}$ in each case.

    Hence, find the expected value of $\bar{x}$, $E(\bar{x})$ and the standard deviation of $\bar{x}$.

 (iii) Explain how your work in **(i)** and **(ii)** satisfies the formula $\mu = E(\bar{x})$.

  (iv) If the samples were drawn with replacement, would you expect the standard deviation of $\bar{x}$ to be smaller than, equal to or larger than the previous value? Justify your answer.

23. A group of 25 females was asked how many children they each had. The results are shown in the diagram below.

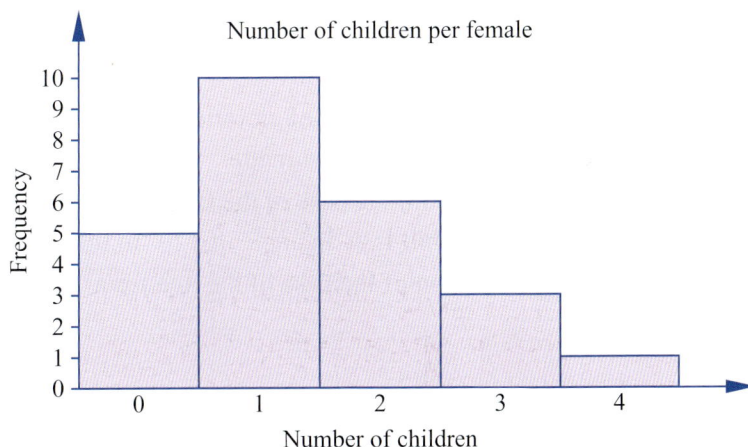

(i) Show that the mean number of children per female is 1·4.

(ii) Show clearly that the standard deviation for this data is approximately 1·06.

(iii) Another group of 25 females was surveyed and it was found that the mean number of children per female was 2·4 and the standard deviation was 2. Use the results from parts (i) and (ii) to describe the differences between the number of children the two groups of females have.

(iv) A female is selected at random from the first group. What is the probability that she has more than two children?

(v) Two females are selected at random from the first group. What is the probability that:

(a) Both females have more than two children?

(b) Only one of the females has more than two children?

(c) The second female selected has two children given that the first female selected had no children?

24. Jonathan is sitting in the middle of a 10 m path, $|HB|$, between a hill and a building. He has a 10-metre tape measure and a clinometer.

The hill and a building are directly opposite each other.

A tree (T) is growing vertically, 3 m from the base of the hill.

A goose is perched on the edge of the building at G.

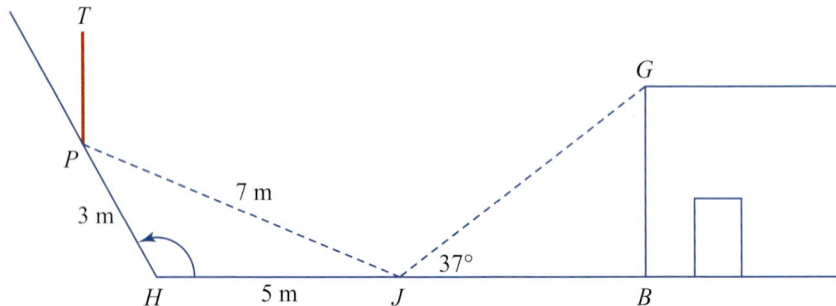

(i) Using his clinometer he measures the angle of elevation of the top of the building as 67°. Find the height of the building, to the nearest metre.

(ii) Jonathan measures the distance from the base of the tree to where he is sitting and finds it to be 7 m exactly. Verify that the hill is at an angle of 120° to the path.

(iii) Find $|\angle HJP|$, the angle of elevation of the base of the tree from Jonathan's position, to the nearest degree.

(iv) Deduce the value of $|\angle JPT|$.

(v) The goose flies from its perch, G, to the top of the tree, T.

Jonathan would like to calculate the distance $|GT|$.

Outline a set of steps Jonathan could take to find $|GT|$. With each step, give the method, rule or equipment used. No actual calculations are required.

25. When geese fly in formation they form an inverted V-shape.

(i) If the lines of geese can be represented by the equations $x + 2y - 10 = 0$ and $3x - 2y - 6 = 0$, find the coordinates of the leading goose.

(ii) Find the angle, to the nearest degree, formed by the formation of geese.

(iii) After 1 hour, the leading goose has flown to a point $(37, 67)$.

Assuming the geese flew in a straight line and taking each unit to represent 1 km, find the distance travelled by the geese to the nearest km.

(iv) Hence, find the average flying speed in m/s.

26. A spacecraft is launched towards the moon. When it reaches a point R above the moon's surface, a landing craft will attempt to land on the moon at L.

The radius of the moon is 20 units and its centre, O, is $(10, 6)$.

Assume the moon is a perfect sphere.

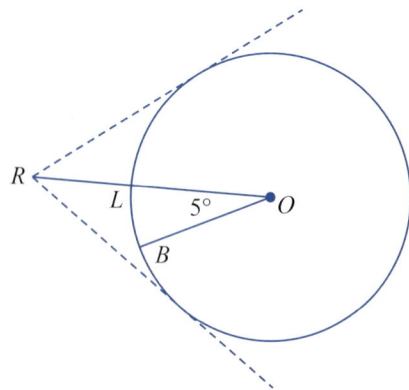

(i) Write down the equation of the surface of the moon.

(ii) The rendezvous point, R, is at $(25, 26)$. How far is R from the centre of the moon?

(iii) Hence or otherwise, find the coordinates of L, the landing point.

(iv) A radio transmitter is to be set up at a point $5°$ from the landing point, L.
How far would an astronaut have to travel to reach B from the landing point?
Give your answer correct to one decimal place.

(v) If each unit represents 100 km, is this a feasible task for an astronaut? Justify your answer.

(vi) From the point R, the astronauts can see the edges of the moon.
Find the equations of the two lines shown on the diagram.

(vii) A comet is due to fly past the dark side of the moon. Its path can be represented by the line $x + 2y + 35 = 0$. At its nearest point, how close is it to the moon's surface?
Give your answer to the nearest km.

27. The diagram is a representation of a robotic arm that can move in a vertical plane. The point P is fixed, and so are the lengths of the two segments of the arm. The controller can vary the angles α and β from $0°$ to $180°$.

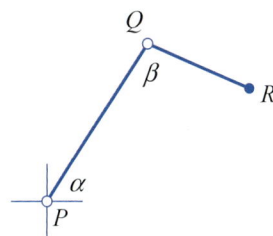

   (i) Given that $|PQ| = 20$ cm and $|QR| = 12$ cm, determine the values of the angles α and β so as to locate R, the tip of the arm, at a point that is 24 cm to the right of P and 7 cm higher than P. Give your answers correct to the nearest degree.

  (ii) In setting the arm to the position described in part **(i)**, which will cause the greater error in the location of R: an error of $1°$ in the value of α or an error of $1°$ in the value of β? Justify your answer. You may assume that if a point moves along a circle through a small angle, then its distance from its starting point is equal to the length of the arc travelled.

 (iii) The answer to part **(ii)** above depends on the particular position of the arm. That is, in certain positions, the location of R is more sensitive to small errors in α than to small errors in β, while in other positions, the reverse is true. Describe, with justification, the conditions under which each of these two situations arises.

  (iv) Illustrate the set of all possible locations of the point R on the coordinate diagram below. Take P as the origin and take each unit in the diagram to represent a centimetre in reality. Note that α and β can vary only from $0°$ to $180°$.

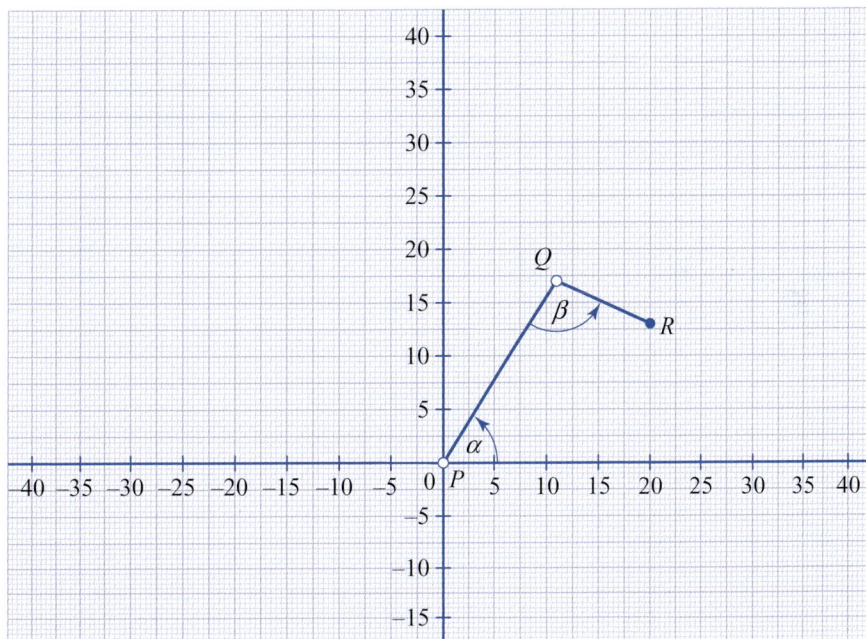

431

28. **(i)** Calculate, correct to one decimal place, the area of the trapezium using the measurements in the diagram.

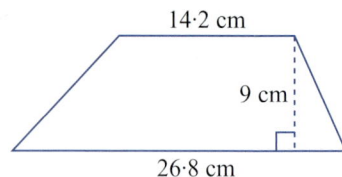

14·2 cm

9 cm

26·8 cm

(ii) **(a)** Evaluate $\displaystyle\int_0^{\frac{\pi}{2}} \cos x \, dx$.

(b) Use the trapezoidal rule to find an approximation for the shaded region in the diagram using the two indicated intervals. Answer correct to two decimal places.

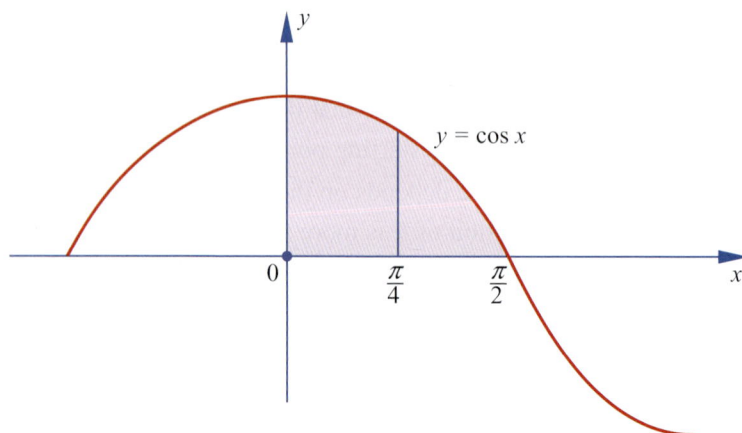

$y = \cos x$

$\dfrac{\pi}{4}$ $\dfrac{\pi}{2}$

(c) Find the error between **(a)** and **(b)**.

(d) Which answer is more accurate, **(a)** or **(b)**? Justify your answer.

(e) Hence, calculate the percentage error.

29. **(i)** In Turlough Hill, a pumped storage hydroelectric power station, water issues from a cylindrical pipe of internal diameter 2·4 m at a rate of 29,000 *l* per second. At what speed is the water flowing through the pipe? Give your answers:

(a) In m/sec correct to one decimal place

(b) In km/hour correct to the nearest km

(c) Hence, or otherwise, if the diameter of the pipe was doubled, find the new speed of the water in m/sec correct to one decimal place.

(ii) Andy is an artist commissioned to make a visual display to promote a new type of conical container. He decides on a linear display, as in the diagram.

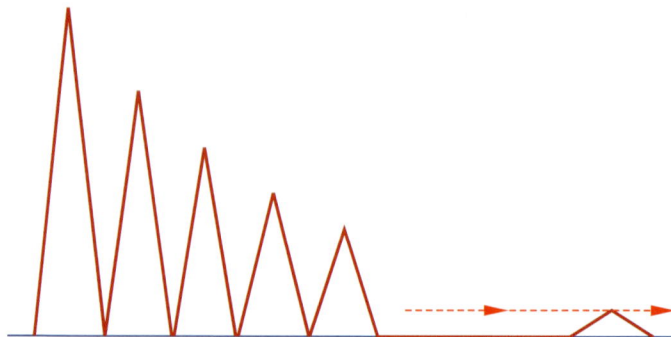

The first conical container is 8 m tall. The display attempts to convey an infinite number of containers. The height of each container is $\frac{3}{4}$ of the previous one. The diameter of each container is a constant 1 m.

Where relevant, give your answers in terms of π.

(a) Calculate the volume of the fifth conical container.

(b) Find the theoretical maximum volume required by Andy for an infinite display.

(c) The height, h, of the cones can be modeled by the graph $h = a(b)^{x-1}$. Where $a, b \in \mathbb{R}$. Write down the value of a and b.

(d) Find $\frac{dh}{dx}$ and use it to verify that the height is always decreasing.

30. (i) A regular tetrahedron (four equal equiangular triangular sides), as in the diagram, has sides of length 5 cm. Find:

(a) The area of the triangular face ABC in the form $\frac{p}{q}\sqrt{3}$ where $p, q \in \mathbb{N}$

(b) The total surface area of the tetrahedron correct to one decimal place

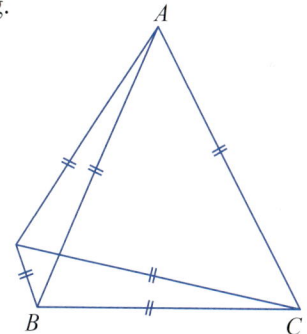

(ii) In Roswell, USA, a mission to the edge of space using a helium-filled balloon was carried out.

The balloon was required to carry a payload of 1,400 kg into the stratosphere.

The balloon changes shape (and volume) as it ascends. At the halfway stage the compound shape of the balloon is a hemisphere, radius 30 m, and cone as indicated in diagram.

At this height each kg of payload requires 100 m^3 of volume. Find at this halfway stage:

(a) The height of the conical section in metres correct to the nearest m

(b) The total surface area of the balloon in hectares correct to two decimal places.

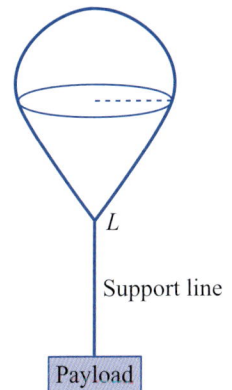

31. (i) By considering each strip to approximate to a trapezium, prove the trapezoidal rule for the following irregular shape.

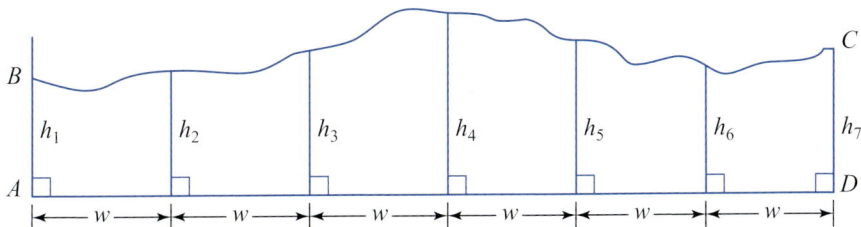

(ii) (a) Evaluate $\displaystyle\int_3^\infty \frac{1}{x^3}\,dx$.

(b) The diagram shows part of the graph of $y = \dfrac{1}{x^3}$ together with line segments parallel to the coordinate axes.

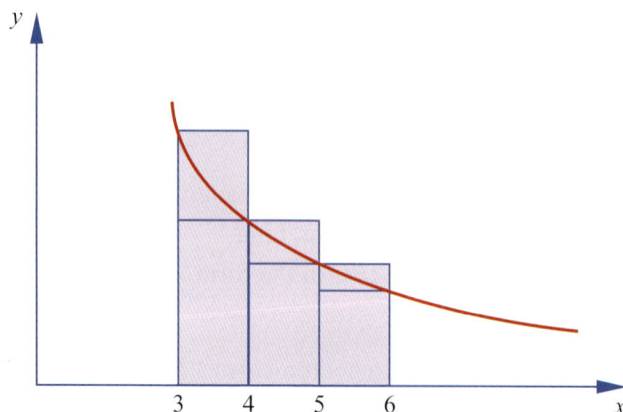

Using the diagram, show that:

$$\frac{1}{4^3} + \frac{1}{5^3} + \frac{1}{6^3} + \cdots < \int_3^\infty \frac{1}{x^3}\,dx < \frac{1}{3^3} + \frac{1}{4^3} + \frac{1}{5^3} + \cdots.$$

32. **(i)** In the statistics of the normal distribution, it can be shown that approximately 95% of the distribution lies within ± 2 standard deviations of the mean.

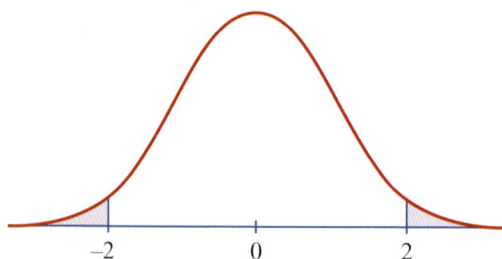

This is given by the integral:

$$\int_{-2}^{2} \frac{1}{\sqrt{2\pi}}\, e^{-\frac{x^2}{2}}\,dx \approx 0.95$$

Use the trapezoidal rule with four strips to estimate the value of the integral.

(ii) (a) Differentiate $p = \sin^3 x$ with respect to x.

(b) Hence or otherwise, write down the antiderivative of $\dfrac{dy}{dx} = \cos x \sin^2 x$.

33. **(i)** Express $i^{30} - 2i^{11}$ in the form $a + bi$.

(ii) Let $u = a + bi$, where $a, b \in \mathbb{R}$.

If $u\bar{u} + 4i = 7 + 2iu$, find two possible values of u.

(iii) Express $\left(1 + \sqrt{3}i\right)^{14}$ in the form $2^k(-1 + \sqrt{3}i)$, where $k \in \mathbb{N}$.

(iv) Part of the graph of the function

$f(z) = z^3 + kz^2 + z + 5$ is shown here.

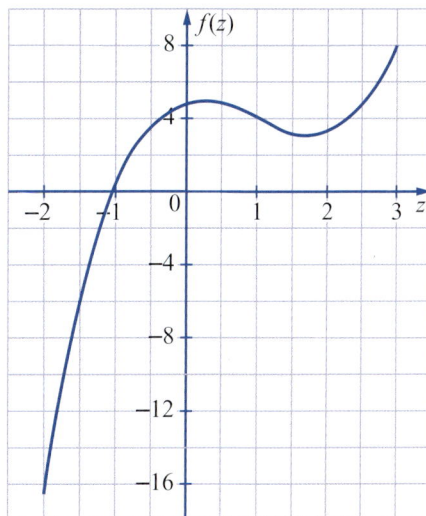

(a) Write down the coordinates of the two points where the graph of $f(z)$ crosses the axes.

(b) Write down the real root of $f(z) = 0$.

(c) Find the value of k, where $k \in \mathbb{N}$.

(d) $f(z) = (z - a)(z^2 + bz + c)$.

Find the value of a, b and c.

(e) Solve $f(z) = 0$.

34. **(i)** Evaluate $(-1 + i)^{20}$.

(ii) (a) Find the two complex numbers $a + bi$ for which $(a + bi)^2 = 15 - 8i$.

(b) Hence, solve the equation $z^2 - (2 + 3i)z + 5(i - 1) = 0$.

(iii) Use De Moivre's theorem to find the three roots of the equation $z^3 + 8 = 0$ and graph your solutions on the Argand diagram. What is the equation of the curve on which the three solutions lie?

(iv) Three complex numbers, z, z^2 and z^3, are shown on the Argand diagram where the same scale is used on both axes. They satisfy the following conditions:

$|z| > 1$

One of them lies on the real axis.

(a) Identify each number on the diagram.

(b) Find θ_1, the argument of z, θ_2, the argument of z^2, and θ_3, the argument of z^3.

(c) If $|z| = 2$, express z, z^2 and z^3 in the form $a + bi$.

(d) If $z^4 = kz^2$, find the value of k.

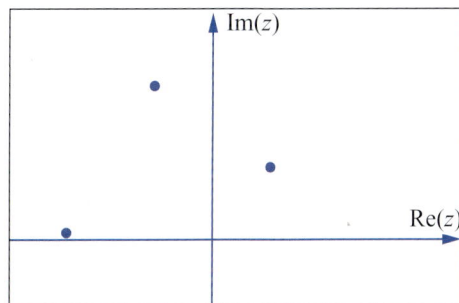

35. **(i)** $z = -\sqrt{3} + i$ and $w = -1 + \sqrt{3}i$. Show that:

(a) $\dfrac{z}{w} = 2\sqrt{3} + 2i$

(b) $\arg\left(\dfrac{z}{w}\right) = \arg(z) - \arg(w)$

(ii) $1 + 2i$ is a root of the equation $z^2 + (i - p)z + (q - i) = 0$, where $p, q \in \mathbb{R}$.

   (a) Give a reason why the roots do **not** occur in conjugate pairs.

   (b) Find **(1)** the value of p and the value of q **(2)** the other root of the equation.

(iii) (a) $(2 + 3i)(a + bi) = -1 + 5i$. Express $a + bi$ in the form $r(\cos\theta + i\sin\theta)$.

   (b) Hence or otherwise, calculate $(a + bi)^{11}$.

(iv) Let $z = x + yi$.

   p is the set of points that satisfy $|z - 4 + 2i| = 4$.

   q is the set of points that satisfy $|z - 2i| = |z|$.

   (a) Find the equation of p and the equation of q.

   (b) Graph p and q on the same Argand diagram.

   (c) Shade in the region where $|z - 4 + 2i| \le 4$ and $|z - 2i| \le z$.

36. **(i)** $u = a + bi$ and $w = c + di$, where $i^2 = -1$. Show that $\overline{u + w} = \overline{u} + \overline{w}$.

(ii) Let $z = -2\sqrt{3} + ai$ and $w = k + ki$.

   (a) If $\arg(z) = \dfrac{7\pi}{6}$, find **(1)** a **(2)** $|z|$.

   (b) If $|w| = 5\sqrt{2}$, find two possible values of $\arg(w)$.

(iii) Evaluate $\dfrac{[\cos\frac{2\pi}{5} + i\sin\frac{2\pi}{5}]^8}{[\cos(-\frac{3\pi}{5}) + i\sin(-\frac{3\pi}{5})]^3}$.

(iv) The complex number z has modulus $3\dfrac{3}{8}$ and argument $\dfrac{2\pi}{3}$. Find, in polar form, the complex third roots of z. (That is, find the three values of w for which $w^3 = z$.)

(v) Let $z = 1 + \sqrt{3}i$ and $w = 1 + i$.

   (a) Express $\dfrac{z}{w}$ in the form $\left(\dfrac{\sqrt{p}+1}{2}\right) + \left(\dfrac{\sqrt{p}-1}{2}\right)i$, where p is a prime number.

   (b) Show that $\arg\left(\dfrac{z}{w}\right) = \arg(z) - \arg(w)$.

   (c) Express $\dfrac{z}{w}$ in the form $r(\cos\theta + i\sin\theta)$.

   (d) Hence, find expressions in surd form for $\cos\theta$ and $\sin\theta$.

37. The diagram shows the graph of the function
$y = f(x)$ for $-2 \le x \le 6$.

Estimate the values of x for which:

   (i) $f'(x) = 0$

   (ii) $f'(x) < 0$

   (iii) $f'(x) > 0$

   (iv) $f''(x) = 0$

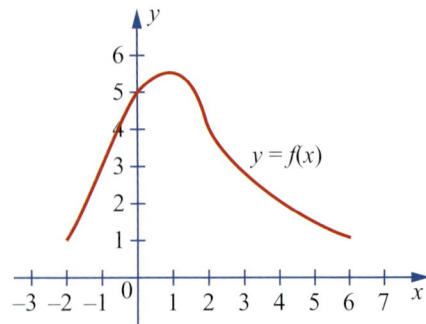

38. The diagram shows the graph of the function
$y = f(x)$ for $0 \leq x \leq 7$.

Estimate the values of x for which:

(i) $f'(x) = 0$

(ii) $f'(x) < 0$

(iii) $f'(x) > 0$

(iv) $f''(x) = 0$

(v) $f''(x) < 0$

(vi) $f''(x) > 0$

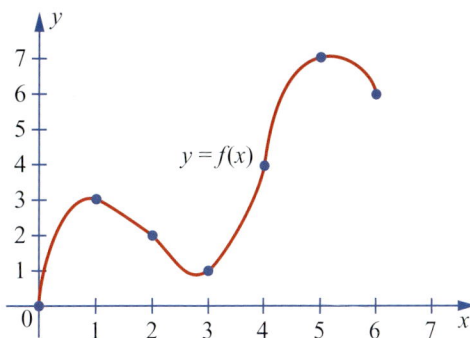

39. The diagram shows the graph of $y = x^2 - 3$ and its derivative. Which is which?

Give at least two reasons to support your choice.

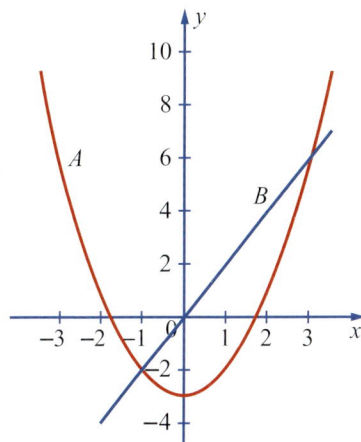

40. The diagram shows the function $y = f(x)$.

Which of the graphs below, A, B, C or D, shows the derivative of $f(x)$?

Give three reasons for your answer.

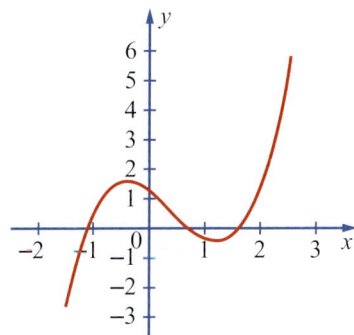

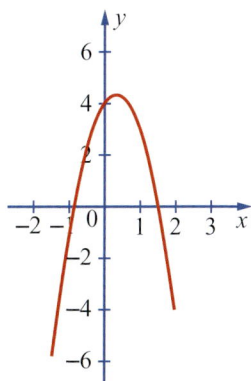

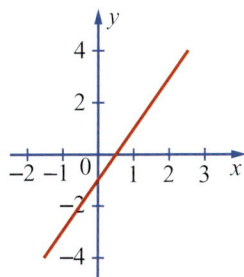

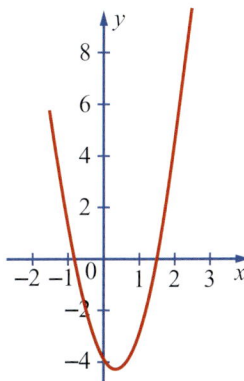

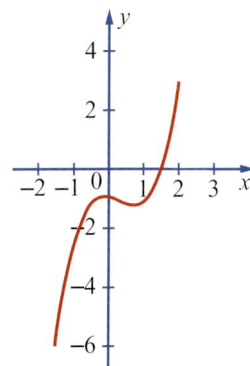

41.   **(i)** Draw the sketch of $y = \sin x$ for $-\pi \le x \le \pi$.

    (ii) Draw the sketch of its derivative on the same graph.

    (iii) Suggest a simple transformation which maps (moves) $\sin x$ onto its derivative.

42.   **(i)** Draw the sketch of $y = |\sin x|$ for $0 \le x \le 2\pi$.

    (ii) Using your graph, what unusual phenomenon occurs when $x = \pi$?
      If you do not see anything out of the ordinary, you should use GeoGebra.
      Type $y = \text{abs}(\sin(x))$ as the function.

43.   **(i)** Find the points where $y = x^2 - 6x - 16$ crosses the x-axis.

    (ii) Choosing a suitable range of values of x, draw the graph of $y = x^2 - 6x - 16$.

    (iii) Show the derivative of the curve on the same graph.

    (iv) Find the point(s) where the derivative crosses the x-axis.

    (v) How is this point related to the graph of $y = x^2 - 6x - 16$?

44. The diagram shows the graph of $y = x^3 + 3x^2 - 24x - 10$.

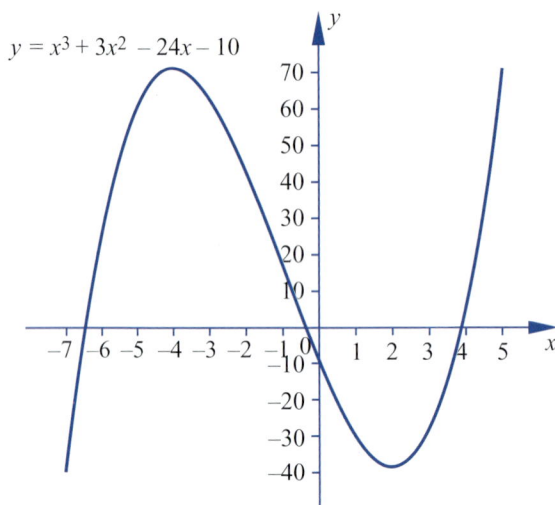

  (i) Estimate the values of x for which $y = 30$.
  (ii) Show that the local maximum is $(-4, 70)$.
  (iii) Make a sketch of the graph shown and on it draw the line $y = 70$.
  (iv) Algebraically solving $x^3 + 3x^2 - 24x - 10 = 70$ should produce three roots.
     Graphically, the line meets the curve at only two points.
     Explain these different results.

45.   **(i)** Find the stationary points on the curve $y = x^4 - 4x^3$.
    (ii) Find any points of inflection.
    (iii) Find the coordinates of the points where the curve intersects the x-axis and the y-axis.
    (iv) Sketch the curve.

(v) Find the range of values of x for which the curve is:

    (a) Decreasing

    (b) Increasing

46. Prove by induction that:

$$3 + 9 + 18 + \cdots + \frac{3}{2}n(n+1) = \frac{1}{2}n(n+1)(n+2)$$

47.   **(i)** **(a)** Show that if $P(k) = 4^k + 6k$ is divisible by 6, then $P(k+1)$ is also divisible by 6.

      (b) Investigate whether $4^n + 6n$ is divisible by 6 for $n \geq 1$.

    (ii) Investigate whether $4^n + 6n$ is divisible by 5 for $n \geq 1$.

    (iii) Investigate whether $4^n + 6n - 1$ is divisible by 9 for $n \geq 1$.

48.   **(i)** Write $\displaystyle\sum_{i=1}^{n} r^{i-1}$ as a sum of terms, where $r \neq 1$.

    (ii) Prove, by induction, that:

$$\sum_{i=1}^{n} r^{i-1} = \frac{r^n - 1}{r - 1}, \text{ where } r \neq 1$$

49.   **(i)** Differentiate $\sin x - x \cos x$.

    (ii) Hence or otherwise, find $\displaystyle\int x \sin x \, dx$.

50.   **(i)** Differentiate $xe^x - e^x$.

    (ii) Hence or otherwise, find the anti-differentiation of xe^x.

51. Find the area bounded by the curves $y = x^2 + 5x$ and $y = 3 - x^2$.

52. The velocity, in metres per second, of an object in motion is given by $24 + 2t$ where t is measured in seconds.

    (i) What was the initial velocity?

    (ii) Use differentiation to show that the acceleration of the object is constant.

    (iii) Use anti-differentiation to find an expression for the distance travelled by the object.

    (iv) If the object started at the origin, find the formula for the distance, s, travelled and use it to find how far the object had moved after 10 seconds.

    (v) If the object started 25 metres behind the origin, find the formula for s. In this case, what does s represent?

53.   **(i)** Find the sum of the first 1,000 natural numbers.

    (ii) Find the sum of the first 500 natural numbers.

    (iii) Hence or otherwise, find the sum of the first 500 even natural numbers.

    (iv) Hence or otherwise, find the sum of the first 500 odd natural numbers.

54. Determine whether the following sequence is arithmetic, geometric or neither. Give an explanation for your answer.

$$3, 15, 75, 375, \ldots$$

55. Convert $4\cdot\dot{2} = 4\cdot222 \ldots$ to a fraction without using a calculator.

56. Matt intends on retiring in 25 years' time.

(i) What would the value of a fund need to be in order to provide an annual salary of €40,000 for 20 years? Assume that investments will grow by 3% annually.

(ii) If Matt makes monthly contributions for 25 years up to his retirement, what will he pay per month to generate the required fund?

57. **(i)** g, h and k are three functions where

$g: x \to \sin x^{\circ}$, $h: x \to 15x$ and $k: x \to x^{\frac{1}{2}}$, where $x \in \mathbb{R}$.

f is the composite function $f: x \to g \circ h \circ k(x)$. Evaluate $f(4)$.

(ii) The diagram shows part of the curve with equation $y = f(x)$.
On separate diagrams, sketch:

(a) $y = |f(x)|$ **(b)** $y = -|f(x)|$

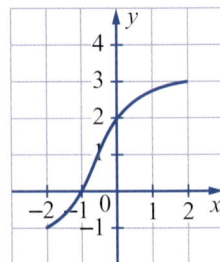

58. **(i)** A shop offers a 10% discount during a sale. The shop must charge VAT at 10% on all sales.

(a) Does it matter to the customer whether the discount applies first and then the VAT, or vice versa? Explain with the use of composite functions.

(b) Does it matter to the government which order is used in the transaction?

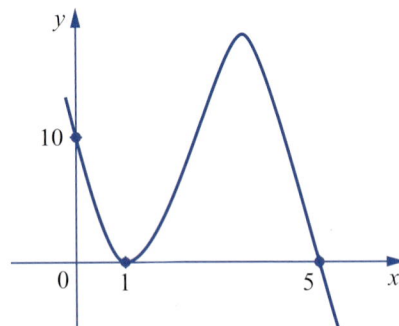

(ii) The diagram shows the graph with equation $y = k(x - 1)^2(x + t)$.

What are the values of k and t?

(iii) The diagram shows a sketch of the function $y = g(x)$, where $x \in \mathbb{R}$ and $0 \le x \le 5$.

(a) Write down the range of $g(x)$.

(b) Write down $g^{-1}(2)$ and $g^{-1}(2\cdot5)$.

(c) Copy the diagram and sketch $g^{-1}(x)$.

(d) Explain why $g(5)$ is not defined.

(e) Find $g^{10}(2)$.

(iv) A student is drawing graphs of the form $f(x) = ax^2 + bx + c$ and solving equations of the form $ax^2 + bx + c = 0$, where a, b and $c \in \mathbb{R}$ and a, b and c have no common factors. For one equation she uses the $-b$ or

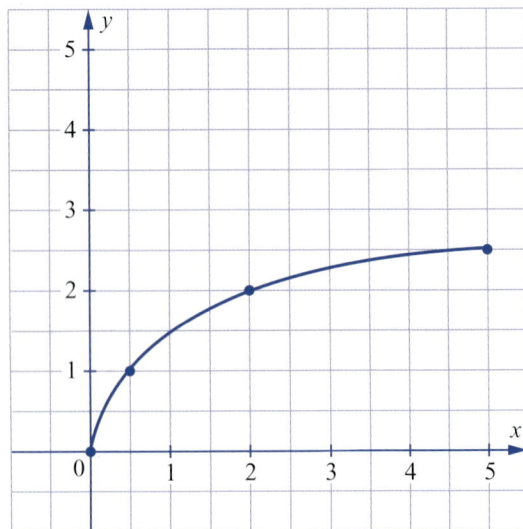

quadratic formula and correctly substitutes the values to get:

$$x = \frac{-12 \pm \sqrt{8}}{4}$$

(a) Calculate the value of a, the value of b and the value of c.

(b) Find the minimum value of $f(x)$.

(c) Make a sketch of $f(x)$.

(d) Is $f(x)$ a function? Justify your answer.

(e) Explain why $f(x)$ is (1) not injective (2) not surjective.

(f) What restriction can be placed on the domain to ensure $f(x)$ is injective?

59. (i) Let $f(n + 1) = 3f(n) + 4$. If $f(1) = 2$, find $f(3)$.

(ii) The diagram shows part of the graph whose equation is of the form $y = 2m^x$. What is the value of m?

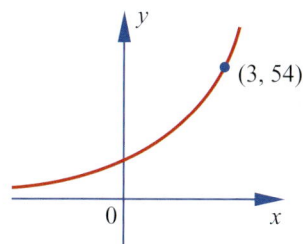

(iii) $f(x) = 2x + 1$ for $x \in \mathbb{R}$.

Show that there exists a real number k such that for all x, $f(x + f(x)) = kf(x)$.

(iv) The graph of the function $f : x \rightarrow ax^3 + bx^2 + cx + d$, where $x \in \mathbb{R}$, is shown.

(a) Write down the value of d.

(b) Find the values of a, b and c.

(c) Hence, calculate the values of p, q and r.

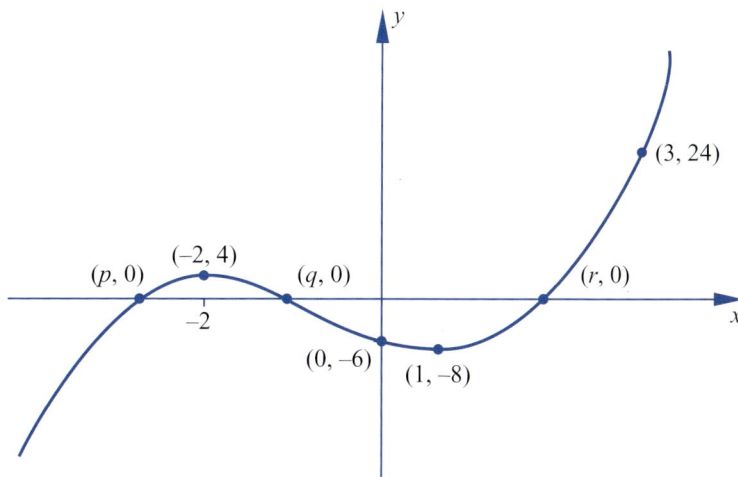

(v) A liquid cools is such a way that at n minutes, its temperature, $T(n)°C$, can be modelled by the formula $T(n) = 20 + 60e^{-0.1n}$, where $n \geq 0$.

  (a) Write down the initial temperature.

  (b) Sketch the graph of $T(n)$.

  (c) Explain why the temperature is always above 20°C.

  (d) Find, correct to one decimal place, the value of n when $T(n) = 60$.

  (e) Find $T^1(n)$.

  (f) Hence, find the value of $T(n)$ at which the temperature is decreasing at a rate of $1.8°C$ per minute.

60. **(i)** A function f is given by $f(x) = \sqrt{9 - x^2}$, where $x \in \mathbb{R}$. What is a suitable domain of f?

  (ii) The diagram shows parts of the graph of the functions $f(x)$ and $g(x)$. Find:

  (a) $f \circ g(1)$

  (b) $g \circ f(-2)$

  (c) $f \circ g \circ f(2)$

  (d) $[gf(0)]^9$

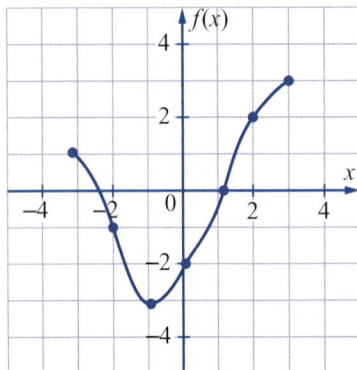

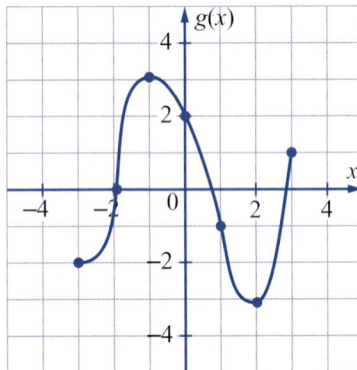

  (iii) $f(x) = x^2 + 5$ and $g(x) = x + 3$, where $x \in \mathbb{R}$.

  (a) Find expressions for **(1)** $f[g(x)]$ **(2)** $g[f(x)]$.

  (b) Solve $f[g(x)] = g[f(x)]$ and verify your answer.

  (iv) $f(x) = \dfrac{3x - 5}{x - 3}$

  (a) Find $f^{-1}(x)$.

  (b) Verify that $f(x)$ and $f^{-1}(x)$ are self inverse.

(v) A company has to design a rectangular box for a new range of jellybeans. The box is to be assembled from a single piece of cardboard, cut from a rectangular sheet measuring 31 cm by 22 cm. The box is to have a capacity (volume) of 500 cm^3.

The net for the box is shown below. The company is going to use the full length and width of the rectangular piece of cardboard. The shaded areas are flaps of width 1 cm which are needed for assembly. The height of the box is h cm, as shown on the diagram.

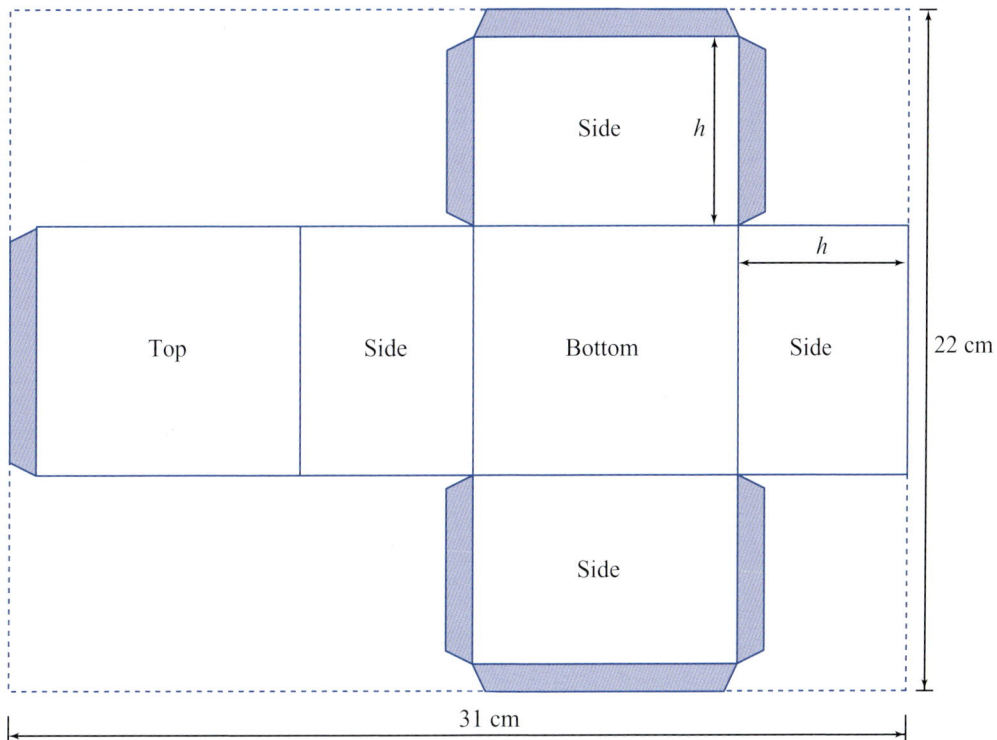

(a) Write the dimensions of the box, in centimetres, in terms of h.

(b) Write an expression for the capacity of the box in cubic centimetres, in terms of h.

(c) Show that the value of h that gives a box with a square bottom will give the correct capacity.

(d) Find, correct to one decimal place, the other value of h that gives a box of the correct capacity.

(e) The client is planning a special '10% extra free' promotion and needs to increase the capacity of the box by 10%. The company is checking whether they can make this new box from a piece of cardboard the same size as the original one (31 cm × 22 cm). They draw the graph below to represent the box's capacity as a function of h. Use the graph to explain why it is *not* possible to make the larger box from such a piece of cardboard.

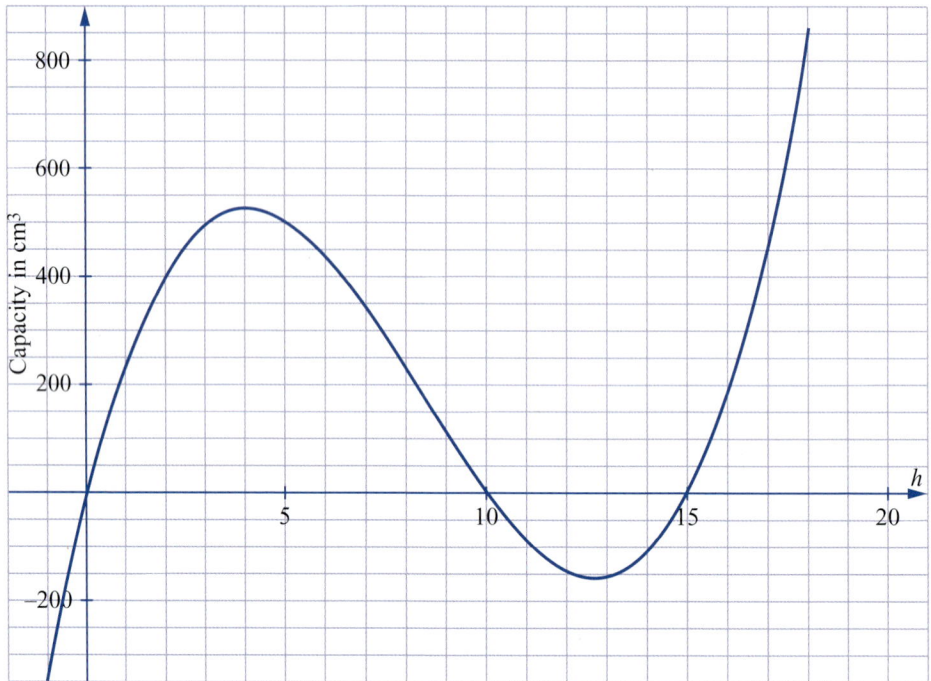

61. **(i)** **(a)** Given that $f(x) = \dfrac{1}{x^a}$, find the value of a for which $f(x) = f\left(\dfrac{1}{x}\right)$.

(b) Show that $f(a) - f(b) = f\left(\dfrac{ab}{b-a}\right)$.

(c) Given $f(x) = \dfrac{x^2 + 1}{2x}$. If $f(a) = f(b)$ and $a \neq b$, show that $ab = 1$.

(ii) The function f is given by $f(x) = x^2 - 6x + 10$ for $x \geq 3$.
(a) Write $f(x)$ in the form $(x - p)^2 + q$.
(b) Find the inverse function $f^{-1}(x)$.
(c) State the domain of $f^{-1}(x)$.

(iii) A parabola has equation $y = ax^2 + bx + c$, where a, b and $c \in \mathbb{R}$. Sketch the following six parabolas, where:
(a) $a > 0$ and $b^2 - 4ac > 0$ **(b)** $a < 0$ and $b^2 - 4ac > 0$
(c) $a > 0$ and $b^2 - 4ac = 0$ **(d)** $a < 0$ and $b^2 - 4ac = 0$
(e) $a > 0$ and $b^2 - 4ac < 0$ **(f)** $a < 0$ and $b^2 - 4ac < 0$

(iv) Graph the function $y = g(x)$, where:

$$g(x) = \begin{cases} x + 6 & \text{for} & -6 \leq x < -2 \\ x^2 & \text{for} & -2 \leq x \leq 2 \\ 4 & \text{for} & 2 < x \leq 6 \end{cases}$$

(v) Let $f(x) = -0{\cdot}5x^2 + 5x - 0{\cdot}98$, where $x \in \mathbb{R}$.

(a) Find the value of $f(0{\cdot}2)$.

(b) Show that f has a local maximum point at $(5, 11{\cdot}52)$.

A sprinter's velocity over the course of a particular 100-metre race is approximated by the following model, where v is the velocity in metres per second and t is the time in seconds from the starting signal:

$$v(t) = \begin{cases} 0 & \text{for} & 0 \leq t < 0{\cdot}2 \\ -0{\cdot}5t^2 + 5t - 0{\cdot}98 & \text{for} & 0{\cdot}2 \leq t < 5 \\ 11{\cdot}52 & \text{for} & t \geq 5 \end{cases}$$

Note that the function in part **(a)** and **(b)** above is relevant to $v(t)$ above.

(c) Sketch the graph of v as a function of t for the first 7 seconds of the race.

(d) Find the distance travelled by the sprinter in the first 5 seconds of the race.

(e) Find the sprinter's finishing time for the race. Give your answer correct to two decimal places.

62. **(i)** Solve the simultaneous equations:

$$p^2 + pq + q^2 = 91$$
$$p + q - 11 = 0$$

(ii) Find the set of all real values of x for which $\dfrac{2 - 3x}{1 - 2x} < 5$, for $x \in \mathbb{R}$.

63. **(i) (a)** The cubic function $f: x \to 5x^3 - 8x^2 + 6x - 20$ has one integer root and two complex roots. Find all three roots.

(b) Using part **(a)** or otherwise, solve the equation:

$$5(k - 3)^3 - 8(k - 3)^2 + 6(k - 3) - 20 = 0$$

(ii) The length of a rectangular room is 9 m less than the square of its width. If the perimeter of the room is 42 m, find the dimensions of the room.

64. **(i)** Solve the equation $x^2 + 4\sqrt{2}x - 42 = 0$, giving your answers in the form $a\sqrt{2}$, where $a \in \mathbb{Q}$.

(ii) $(x - 2)$ and $(x + 1)$ are factors of $x^3 + bx^2 + cx + d$.

(a) Express c in terms of b.

(b) Express d in terms of b.

(c) Given that b, c and d are three consecutive terms in an arithmetic sequence, find their values.

65. **(i)** Find the value of $\dfrac{x}{y}$ when $\dfrac{2x + 3y}{x + 6y} = \dfrac{4}{5}$.

(ii) **(a)** Solve the simultaneous equations:

$$2x + y - z = 3$$
$$3x + 2y + 2z = 13$$
$$x - 3y + z = -6$$

(b) Hence or otherwise, deduce the solutions of:

$$\frac{2}{a - 1} + \frac{1}{b + 3} - \frac{1}{3 - c} = 13$$
$$\frac{3}{a - 1} + \frac{2}{b + 3} + \frac{2}{3 - c} = 13$$
$$\frac{1}{a - 1} - \frac{3}{b + 3} + \frac{1}{3 - c} = -6$$

66. **(i)** Solve for x.

(a) $8^{4+3x} = 32^{1+2x}$

(b) $64^{x-3} = 16^{2x+1}$

(c) $\sqrt{\dfrac{1}{8^{x+1}}} = 4^x$

(ii) Solve for x: $2^{2x+8} - 32(2^x) + 1 = 0$.

(iii) pH is a measure of acidity. The pH is defined as follows:

$pH = -\log_{10}[H^+]$ where $[H^+]$ is the hydrogen ion concentration in an aqueous solution.

A pH of 7 is considered neutral. For bases, $pH > 7$. For acids, $pH < 7$ (at 25°C).

Determine the pH of the following substances and hence classify each substance as an acid or a base:

(a) A substance whose $[H^+] = 2 \cdot 7 \times 10^{-5}$ moles/litre

(b) A substance whose $[H^+] = 1 \cdot 25 \times 10^{-9}$ moles/litre

(c) A substance whose $[H^+] = 1 \cdot 0 \times 10^{-7}$ moles/litre

67. **(i)** Solve for x: $x - 2 = \sqrt{3x - 2}$.

(ii) Solve the simultaneous equations:

$$\log_3 x + \log_3 y = 2$$
$$\log_3(2y - 3) - 2\log_9 x = 1$$

(iii) The function A (blue) is defined by the equation $y = x^2$. By observation or otherwise, write down the equation of the functions B, C and D.

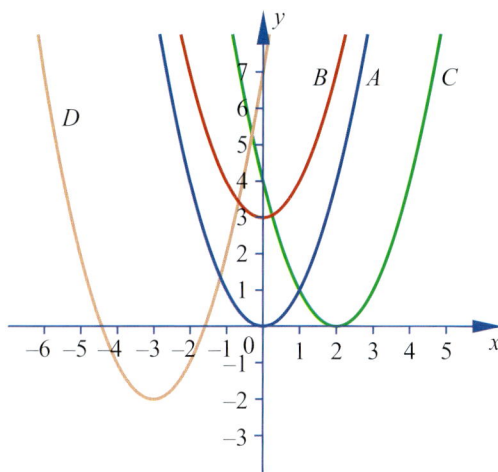

68. **(i)** Simplify fully $\dfrac{x^2 + 4}{x^2 - 4} - \dfrac{x}{x + 2}$.

(ii) Two of the roots of the equation $ax^3 + bx^2 + cx + d = 0$ are p and $-p$. Show that $bc = ad$.

69. **(i)** A cubic function f is defined as $x \in \mathbb{R}$ as

$$f: x \to x^3 + (1 - k^2)x + k, \text{ where } k \text{ is a constant.}$$

  (a) Show that $-k$ is a root of f.

  (b) Find, in terms of k, the other two roots of f.

  (c) Find the set of values of k for which f has exactly one real root.

(ii) Sound levels are measured in decibels (dB).

The following formula is used to compare two sound levels, B_1 and B_2, measured in dB, where their respective sound intensities are I_1 and I_2:

$$B_1 - B_2 = 10\log_{10}\left(\frac{I_1}{I_2}\right)$$

The sound level at a concert at distance of 25 m in front of the speakers was measured as B_1 = 115 dB. What is the ratio (to the nearest whole number) of the intensity, I_1 of the concert sound at that spot compared with the intensity (I_2) from a jackhammer, operating at a sound level of B_2 = 91 dB, at the same spot?

70. **(i) (a)** Find the roots of the function $f: x \to 6x^3 + 5x^2 - 12x + 4$.

  (b) Hence or otherwise, draw a sketch of the function $f(x)$.

(ii) $x^2 - px + q$ is a factor of $x^3 + 3px^2 + 3qx + r$.

    (a) Show that $q = -2p^2$.

    (b) Show that $r = -8p^3$.

    (c) Find the three roots of $x^3 + 3px^2 + 3qx + r = 0$ in terms of p.

71. (i) Solve for x:

    (a) $\log_{\sqrt{2}} x = 4$

    (b) $\log_4(6x + 1) - 2 = 2\log_4 x$

(ii) The graph shows the cubic function $f(x) = 3x^3 + ax^2 - 22x - 8$.

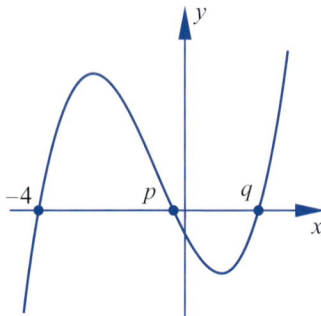

    (a) Find the value of a.

    (b) Hence, find the value of p and the value of q.

72. (i) Express $x^2 + 8x + 10$ in the form $(x + a)^2 + b$.

(ii) Prove that $x + \dfrac{9}{x + 2} \geq 4$, where $x + 2 > 0$.

(iii) (a) Graph $f(x) \to |x - 2|$ for $-2 \leq x \leq 6$.

    (b) On the same diagram, draw $g(x) = 3$.

    (c) At what points do $f(x)$ and $g(x)$ intersect?

    (d) Use your graph to determine the values of x for which $|x - 2| < 3$.

    (e) Use your graph to determine the values of x for which $|x - 2| > 3$.

    (f) At the points of intersection of $f(x) = g(x)$, is $|x - 2| > 3$, $|x - 2| < 3$ or $|x - 2| = 3$?

73. The following shows the graph of a polynomial.

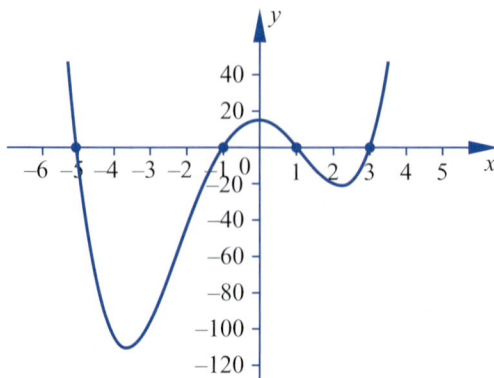

    (i) By observing the shape of this curve, what is the highest power of x in this polynomial?

    (ii) What are the roots of this function?

    (iii) Hence or otherwise, form the function.

74.   **(i)** Four vegetable plots of unequal lengths and of equal widths are arranged as shown.

1	2	3	4

    The length of the third plot is one-quarter the length of the second plot. The length of the fourth plot is one half the length of the second plot. The length of the first plot is 10 metres more than the length of the fourth plot. If the total length of the four plots is 100 metres, find the length of each plot.

  (ii) (a) Solve the equation $\sqrt{2x + 7} = 2 + \sqrt{x}$.

      (b) For $a > 1$ and $b > 1$, prove:

$$\log_b a \, \log_a b = 1$$

75.   **(i)** Solve the equation: $\log_2 x - \log_2(x - 1) = 4\log_4 2$.

  (ii) Solve the equation: $3^{2x+1} - 17(3^x) - 6 = 0$.

    Give your answer correct to two decimal places.

  (iii) The length of Natalie's rectangular garden is 4 metres greater than its width. The width of Jemma's rectangular garden is equal to the length of Natalie's and its length is 18 metres. The two gardens are similar rectangles, that is, the ratio of the length to the width of Natalie's garden equals the ratio of the length to the width of Jemma's garden. Find the possible dimensions of each garden. (Two answers are possible.)

76.   **(i)** Find the range of values of x that satisfy the inequality:

$$x^2 - 3x - 10 \leq 0.$$

  (ii) (a) Solve the equation: $2^{x^2} = 8^{2x+9}$.

      (b) Solve the equation: $\log(2x + 3) + \log(x - 2) = 2 \log(x + 4)$ for $x > 2$.

77.   **(i) (a)** Given two real numbers a and b, where $a > 1$ and $b > 1$, prove that:

$$\frac{1}{\log_b a} + \frac{1}{\log_a b} \geq 2$$

      (b) Under what condition is $\dfrac{1}{\log_b a} + \dfrac{1}{\log_a b} = 2$?

  (ii) A rectangular swimming pool is 14 m long and 6 m wide. It is surrounded by a pebble path of uniform width x m. If the area of the path is 96 m², find the width.

78. 500 mg of a medicine enters a patient's bloodstream at noon and its mass reduces at a rate of 15% per hour.

  (i) Write an equation to express the mass remaining in the patient's bloodstream after t hours.

  (ii) Find the time, correct to one decimal place, when only 25 mg of the medicine remains active.

79. M_1 and M_2 are the magnitudes of two earthquakes on the Richter magnitude scale. If A_1 and A_2 are their corresponding amplitudes, measured at an equal distance from the earthquakes, then:

$$M_1 - M_2 = \log_{10}\left(\frac{A_1}{A_2}\right)$$

An earthquake rated 6·3 on the Richter magnitude scale in Iran on 26 December 2003 killed 40,000 people. The earthquake on Banda Aceh on 26 December 2004 was rated 9·2 on the Richter magnitude scale.

How many times greater (to the nearest whole number) in amplitude of ground motion was the earthquake in Banda Aceh compared to the earthquake in Iran?

80. When a microwave oven is turned on for t minutes, the relationship between the temperature, C, inside the oven is given by $C(x) = 500 - 480(0.9)^t$ where $t \geq 0$.

    (i) Find the value of $C(0)$.

    (ii) Explain the meaning of $C(0)$.

    (iii) Find the value of $C(15)$.

    (iv) Can the temperature inside the microwave oven reach 550°C?

    (v) What is the maximum temperature the inside of the oven can reach?
        (Hint: as time tends towards infinity)

81.   **(i)** James invested a sum of money in 7% bonds. He invested €400 more than this sum in 8% bonds. If the total annual interest from these two investments is €257, how much did he invest at each rate?

    (ii) A car was bought for €24,000 in January 2006 and depreciates at a rate of r% per annum. If the NBV (net book value) of the car at the end of 2009 was €18,738, calculate the value of r, to the nearest percentage.

82. €140,000 was deposited at the beginning of January 2005 into an account earning 7% compound interest annually. When, to the nearest month, will the investment be worth €200,000?

83. €45,000 was invested for three years at compound interest. The AER for the first year was 6%, the AER for the second year was 4% and the AER for the third year was 3%. At the end of the first year €7,700 was withdrawn. At the end of the second year €W was withdrawn. At the end of the third year the investment was worth €37,080. Find the value of W.

84.   **(i)** A bus is bought for €16,500. If it depreciates continuously with a nominal annual rate of 7·5%, calculate the NBV of the bus after 4 years.

    (ii) David borrowed a sum of money at 10% interest. He borrowed a second sum, which was €1,500 less than the first sum, at 11% interest. If the annual interest on these two loans is €202·50, how much did he borrow at each rate?

85. Carl sees a car on a car dealer's website. He clicks on the section saying 'Finance this car' and finds out how much it would cost him to borrow €5,000.

The details are shown in the table.

Loan Calculator				
Over 5 Years	APR	Monthly Repayment	Total Repayable	Total Cost of Credit
€5,000	14·9%	A	B	C

Calculate the values A and B and C.

86. A certain type of bacteria, given a favourable growth medium, doubles in population every 3 hours. Given that there were approximately 20 bacteria to start with, how many bacteria will there be in a day and a half?

87. Tom wants to buy a car in three years' time. He estimates the car will cost €10,000 so he decides to put a certain amount of money into a special savings deposit account that pays 4% AER compounded monthly. If this is to give him €10,000 in three years' time, how much would he need to save each month?

88. **(i)** At the end of each month, Mary makes a deposit of €350 into an account that pays an AER of 7%. What will the final amount be after 5 years?

(ii) Mary decides instead to deposit €500 at the start of each month into a different savings account. If the account earns 2·5% AER compounded monthly, how much will she have in 5 years?

89. John purchases a house, which is financed with a 20-year loan of €200,000 at a rate of 3% APR. On the property website where he saw the ad for the house, the mortgage calculator showed the following repayments.

Loan Information

Loan Amount (€):	200,000	(90% of price)
Nominal Interest Rate:	3	%
Repayment Term:	20	years

Calculate

Results: Mortgage Affordability Information

Monthly Payments:	240
Total Monthly Payment:	A
Total Interest:	B

(i) Find the value of the monthly repayment A.

(ii) Find the total interest B John will pay over the 20 years.

90. Caitlin won €1,600,000 in a lottery, to be received in four annual payments of €400,000. She will receive the first payment exactly one year from now.

(i) What is the present value of the four payments if the interest rate is 4·8% AER?

(ii) Did it cost the lottery €1,600,000 to pay Caitlin her prize money? Explain.

91. Sarah has €30,000 in a deposit account that pays 6% AER. Sarah believes that after 15 years this investment will be worth treble its present value.

(i) Is this true?

(ii) If not, find the amount of years correct to the nearest year for this investment to treble.

92. Melanie is planning for her pension. She intends to retire in 36 years' time. She assumes that money can be invested at an inflation adjusted annual rate of 3·6%, so all calculations should therefore be based on a 3·6% annual growth rate.

(i) Melanie wants to have a fund that could, from the date of her retirement, give her a payment of €36,000 at the start of each year for 29 years. Use the sum of a geometric series to calculate the value, on the date of retirement, of the fund required.

(ii) Melanie plans to invest a fixed amount of money every month in order to generate the fund calculated in part (i). Her retirement is 36 years away.

   (a) If Melanie makes 432 equal payments of €P from now until her retirement, what value of P will give the fund she requires?

   (b) If Melanie waits for 4 years before starting her pension investments, how much will she then have to pay each month in order to generate the same pension fund?

93. In order to buy an apartment, Craig needs a 20-year mortgage of €175,000. He secures a fixed annual rate from the bank of 6%, compounded annually.

(i) Calculate Craig's monthly repayments.

(ii) Calculate the total interest repaid as a percentage of the original borrowings.

94. Eamon and Sile have just had their first child, Donal. They are planning for his education in 18 years' time. First, they calculate how much they would like to have in the education fund when Donal is 18. Then, they calculate how much they need to invest in order to achieve this. They assume that in the long run, money can be invested at an inflation-adjusted annual rate of 2%. Your answers throughout this question should therefore be based on a 2% annual growth rate.

(i) Write down the present value of a future payment of €5,000 in 1 year's time.

(ii) Write down, in terms of t, the present value of a future payment of €5,000 in t years' time.

(iii) Eamon and Sile want to have a fund that could, from the date of his eighteenth birthday, give Donal a payment of €5,000 at the start of each year for 5 years. Show how to use the sum of a geometric series to calculate the value on the date of his eighteenth birthday of the fund required.

(iv) Eamon and Sile plan to invest a fixed amount of money every month in order to generate the fund calculated in part (iii). Donal's eighteenth birthday is $18 \times 12 = 216$ months away.

(a) Find, correct to four significant figures, the rate of interest per month that would, if paid and compounded monthly, be equivalent to an effective annual rate of 2%.

(b) Write down, in terms of n and P, the value on the maturity date of an education plan of €P made n months before that date.

(c) If Eamon and Sile make 216 equal monthly payments of €P from now until Donal's eighteenth birthday, what value of P will give the fund he requires?

(v) If Eamon and Sile wait for 10 years before starting Donal's education fund, how much will they then have to pay each month in order to generate the same education fund?

95. (i) A group of four boys and three girls are to stand in a row for a photograph. How many different ways can they be arranged if

(a) It does not matter who they stand next to

(b) The girls have to stand beside each other

(c) All three girls cannot stand beside each other

(d) No two boys can stand beside each other

(e) The three girls must stand in the middle

(ii) A ball enters a chute at S.

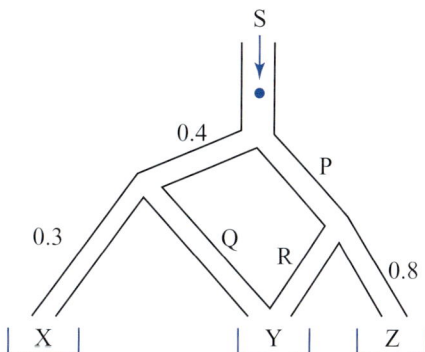

(a) What are the probabilities of the ball going down each of the chutes labelled P, Q and R?

(b) Calculate the probability of the ball landing in tray:

(1) X   (2) Y   (3) Z

(iii) The spinner shown has ten equal sectors. Each sector contains an integer power of i and was designed by a maths teacher. The proposal is to charge €5 to spin the wheel.

(a) Copy and complete the probability distribution below.

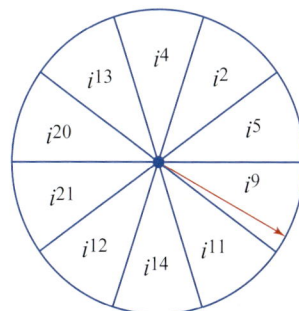

Outcome	i	-1	$-i$	1
Payout	€0	€1	€20	€2
Probability				

453

(b) Calculate the expected value to the school for each spin.

(c) Is this a fair game? Justify your answer.

96. **(i)** A group consists of eight women and seven men. A quiz team of four people is chosen from this group of 15 people.

(a) How many different quiz teams can be chosen?

(b) In how many of these quiz teams are there exactly three men?

(c) In how many of these quiz teams are there more women than men?

(ii) The probability that a biased spinner will land on each of the numbers 1 to 5 is given in the probability distribution table.

Number	1	2	3	4	5
Probability	3 W	2 W	W	3 W	W

(a) Calculate the value of W.

(b) Hence, find the probability that on one spin the result will be a number less than 3.

(c) If the spinner is spun 800 times, estimate the number of times it will show:

(1) the number 4   **(2)** an odd number.

(d) Calculate the expected value.

(iii) Two events A and B are such that $P(A) = 0.6$, $P(A \cap B) = 0.18$ and $P[(A \cup B)'] = 0.28$.

(a) Complete the Venn diagram.

(b) Find $P(B)$.

(c) Find the conditional probability $P(A|B)$.

(d) Are A and B independent events? Justify your answer.

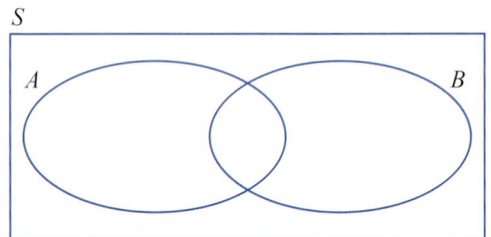

97. **(i)** Solve:

(a) $\binom{n}{2} = 28$ **(b)** $\binom{n}{2} = 10\binom{n}{1}$

(ii) The amounts due on monthly mobile phone bills are normally distributed with a mean of €54 and a standard deviation of €15. If a bill is chosen at random, find the probability that the amount due is between €51 and €75.

(iii) A discrete random variable x has the following probability distribution, where $a \in \mathbb{Q}$.

x	1	2	3
$P(x)$	a	$4a$	$2a$

(a) Find the value of *a*.   (b) Find $P(x) > 1$.

(iv) A certain basketball player scores 60% of the free-throw shots she attempts. During a particular game, she gets six free throws.

(a) What assumption(s) must be made in order to regard this as a sequence of Bernoulli trials?

(b) Based on such assumption(s), find, correct to three decimal places, the probability that:

(1) she scores on exactly four of the six shots

(2) she scores for the second time on the fifth shot.

98. (i) *z* is a random variable with standard normal distribution.

Calculate $P(-2 \cdot 13 \leq z \leq 1 \cdot 46)$.

(ii) Events *E* and *F* are such that $P(E) = 0 \cdot 6$ and $P(F) = 0 \cdot 3$.

(a) If *E* and *F* are mutually exclusive, what is $P(E \cup F)$?

(b) If *E* and *F* are independent, what is $P(E \cup F)$?

(iii) In a certain type of archery competition, Laura hits the target with an average of two out of every three shots. The shots are independent of each other. During one such competition, she has 10 shots at the target.

(a) Find the probability that Laura hits the target exactly nine times. Give your answer correct to three decimal places.

(b) Find the probability that Laura hits the target fewer than nine times. Give your answer correct to three decimal places.

(iv) 20% of the bolts produced by a machine are defective.

(a) Find the probability that in a group of five bolts randomly selected from a batch produced by the machine, at most two are defective.

(b) A shipment of 250 packets of five bolts produced by this machine is inspected. A packet is rejected if it has more than two defective bolts. Show that approximately 14 packets are expected to be rejected.

99. (i) *Z* is a random variable with standard normal distribution.

Use the tables to find the value of z_1 for which $P(Z \geq z_1) = 0 \cdot 0778$.

(ii) Cereal packets filled by a machine have a mean of 200 grams with a standard deviation of 10 grams.

(a) In a sample of 300 packets, how many can be expected to weigh more than 215 grams? Show all your work.

(b) The machine is adjusted and another sample of 300 is checked. If the expected value of the number of packets that weigh more than 215 grams is now 10, calculate the new mean, assuming that the standard deviation after adjustment is the same as before.

(iii) To enter a particular college course, candidates must complete an aptitude test. The mean score was 490 with a standard deviation of 100. The distribution of the scores on the aptitude test is a normal distribution.

(a) What percentage of candidates scored between 390 and 590 on this aptitude test?

(b) One student scored 731 on this test. How does this student's score compare to the rest of the scores?

(c) The college admits only students who were among the highest 33% of the scores on this test. What score would a student need on this test to be qualified for admission to this college? Explain your answer.

(d) Tom is preparing to sit the aptitude test the following year. He heard that a score of over 650 would guarantee him a place on the course. He knew 20 people who were going to take the test. Based on this year's mean and standard deviation, approximately how many of the people he knew were likely to get a score of above 650 and secure a place on the course? Justify your answer.

100. When building a road beside a vertical rockface, engineers often use wire mesh to cover the rockface. This helps to prevent rocks and debris from falling onto the road. The shaded region of the diagram below represents a part of such a rockface.

This shaded region is bounded by a parabola and a straight line.

The equation of the parabola is $y = 4 + \frac{5}{3}x - \frac{1}{6}x^2$ and the equation of the line is $y = 4 - \frac{1}{3}x$.

(i) Find algebraically the area of wire mesh required for this part of the rockface.

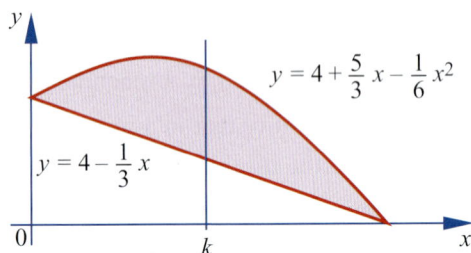

(ii) To help secure the wire mesh, weights are attached to the mesh along the line $x = h$ so that the area of mesh is bisected.

By using your answer to part (a), or otherwise, show that

$$h^3 - 18h^2 + 432 = 0.$$

(iii) (a) Verify that $h = 6$ is a solution of this equation.

(b) Find algebraically the other two solutions of this equation.

(c) Explain why $h = 6$ is the only valid solution to this problem.

Arithmetic mean
A measure of central tendency that sums all the scores in the data sets and divides by the number of scores.

Asymptotic
The quality of the normal curve such that the tails never touch the horizontal axis.

Bell-shaped curve (see normal curve)
A distribution of scores that is symmetrical about the mean, median and mode and has asymptotic tails.

Bias
Systematic errors in the way the sample represents the population. It can be caused by poorly worded surveys, non-response or undercoverage.

Bimodal
A bimodal data set (distribution) has two peaks of data.

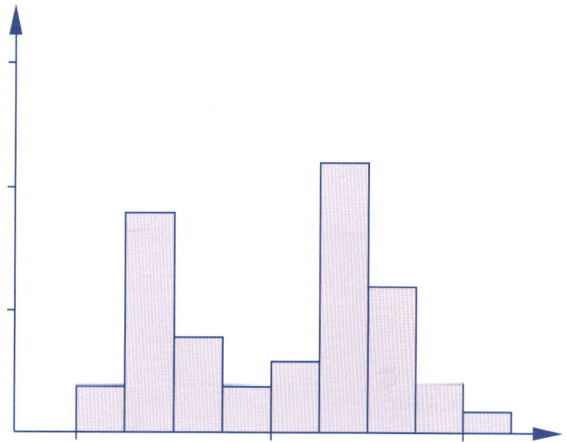

Bivariate data
A survey that examines the relationship between two variables (data sets). In our course, the two variables are usually quantitative variables.

Categorical data
Non-numerical data that can be counted but only described in words. Such data may be ordered or unordered.

Causality
The relationship between an event (the cause) and a second event (the effect).

Class interval
The upper and lower boundary of a set of scores used in the creation of a frequency distribution.

Confidence interval
A range around a measurement that conveys how precise the measurement is.

Confidence level
A measure of the reliability of a result. A confidence level of 95% (0·95) means we are 95% sure the result is reliable. Some confusion is caused by the use of the term 5% level to represent the 95% level.

Continuous numerical data
Data which can take any numerical value within a certain range.

Correlation coefficient (*r*)
A numerical index that reflects the relationship between two variables, constant between −1 and 1.

Critical value
The value necessary for rejection (or non-acceptance) of the null hypothesis.

Cumulative frequency distribution
A frequency distribution that shows frequencies for class intervals along with the cumulative frequency for each.

Data
An item, or items, of factual information derived from measurement or research.

Data point
An observation.

Data set
A set of data points.

Dependent variable
Often denoted by *y*, whose value depends on another variable. It is usually represented on the vertical axis.

Descriptive statistics
Values that describe the characteristics of a sample or population.

Direct correlation
A positive correlation where the values of both variables change in the same direction.

Discrete numerical data
Data which can only have certain values.

Frequency distribution
A method for illustrating the distribution of scores within class intervals. Often given in tabular form (frequency distribution table).

Frequency polygon
A graphical representation of a frequency distribution.

Histogram
A graphical representation of a frequency distribution.

Hypothesis
An if-then statement of conjecture that relates variables to one another.

Independent variable
Often denoted by x, whose variation does not depend on another variable. It is usually represented on the horizontal axis.

Indirect correlation
A negative correlation where the values of variables move in opposite directions.

Inferential statistics
Tools that are used to infer the results based on a sample to a population.

Line of best fit (regression line)
The line that best fits the actual scores and minimises the error in prediction.

Margin of error
The extent of the interval on either side of the sample proportion.

Mean
The value where scores are summed and divided by the number of observations.

Measures of central tendency
The mean, median and mode.

Median
The point at which 50% of the cases in a distribution fall below and 50% fall above.

Mid-interval value
The central value in a class interval.

Mode
The most frequently occurring score in a distribution.

Multimodal
A distribution is said to be multimodal if it has three or more peaks.

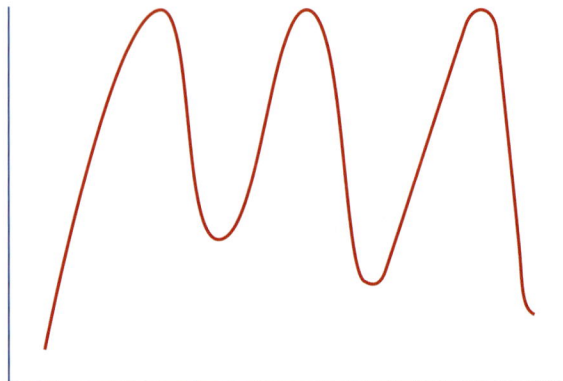

Normal curve
See *bell-shaped curve.*

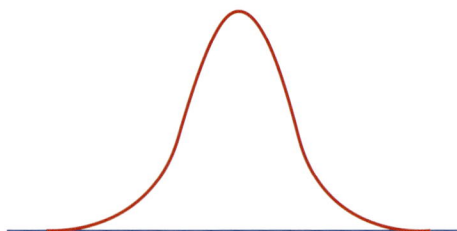

Null hypothesis (H_0)
The statement being tested in a test of significance is called the null hypothesis. The test of significance is designed to assess the strength of the evidence against the null hypothesis. Usually the null hypothesis is a statement of 'no effect' or 'no difference.'

Observed score
The score that is recorded or observed.

Obtained value
The value that results from the application of a statistical test.

One-tailed test
Applies when interested only in extreme values on one side of the mean, i.e. one tail of the distribution.

Outliers
Those scores in a distribution that are noticeably much more extreme than the majority of scores. Exactly what score is an outlier is usually an arbitrary decision made by the researcher.

Parameter
The term used to identify a characteristic, feature or measureable factor that can help understand/interpret a particular system.

Percentile point
The point at or below where a score appears.

Platykurtic
The quality of a normal curve that defines its flatness.

Population
All the possible subjects or cases of interest.

Primary data
First-hand data that you collect yourself or are collected by someone under your direct supervision.

Predictor
The variable that predicts an outcome.

Qualitative data
A type of information that describes or characterises, but does not measure, data. Often referred to as non-numerical data.

Quantitative data
A type of information that can be counted or expressed numerically.

Range
The highest score minus the lowest score.

Reliability
The quality of a test such that it is consistent.

Sample
A subset of a population.

Sampling error
The difference between sample and population values.

Scatter plot

A plot of paired data points.

Secondary data

Second-hand data that have already been collected and made available from an external source such as newspapers, government departments or the internet.

Significance level

The risk set by the researcher for rejecting a null hypothesis when it is true.

Skew or skewness

The quality of a distribution that defines the disproportionate frequency of certain scores. A longer right tail than left corresponds to a smaller number of occurrences at the high end of the distribution; this is a *positively* skewed distribution. A shorter right tail than left corresponds to a larger number of occurrences at the high end of the distribution; this is a *negatively* skewed distribution.

Standard deviation (σ)

A measure of dispersion (spread) of a set of values from their mean.

Standard error

The standard deviation of the sample means. $\left(\dfrac{\sigma}{\sqrt{n}}\right)$

Standard score

See *z-score*.

Statistics

A set of tools and techniques used to collect, organise, represent and interpret information.

Two-tailed test

A test that applies when interested in the corresponding *z*-score on both sides of the mean, i.e. both tails of the distribution. Sometimes called two-sided tests.

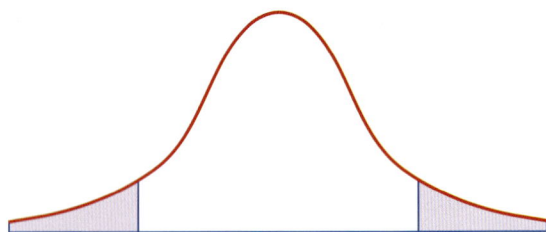

Type I error

The probability of rejecting a null hypothesis when it is true.

Type II error

The probability of accepting a null hypothesis when it is false.

Unbiased estimate

A conservative estimate of a population parameter.

Unimodal
A unimodal data set (distribution) has one peak of data.

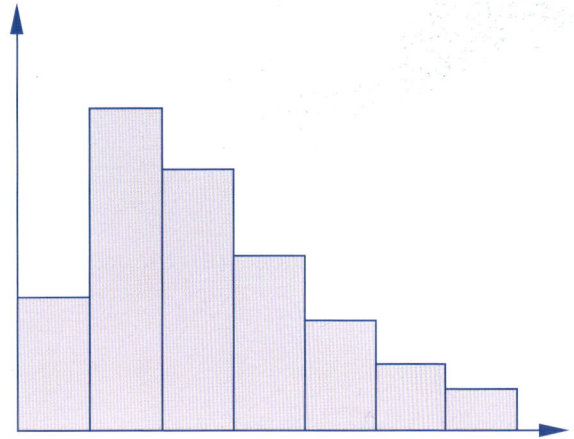

Univariate data
A survey that looks at only one variable (data set). The variable may be either qualitative or quantitative.

Validity
The quality of a test such that it measures what it says it does.

Variability
The amount of spread or dispersion in a set of scores.

Variance
The square of the standard deviation, and another measure of a distribution's spread or dispersion.

Z-score
Indicates the number of standard deviations that a value is above or below the mean:

$$z = \frac{x - \mu}{\sigma}$$

Exercise 1.1

1. **(i)** 18　**(ii)** 22　**(iii)** 24
2. **(i)** 10; underestimation　**(ii)** 14; overestimation　**(iii)** 20; underestimation

Exercise 1.2

1. **(i)**

(ii) 45　**(iii)** 8·8%　2. $\dfrac{25}{8}$

3. **(i)**

x	0	1	2	3	4	5
y	5	4·90	4·58	4	3	0

; 18·98　**(ii)** Underestimation

(iii)

x	0	0·5	1	1·5	2	2·5	3	3·5	4	4·5	5
y	5	4·97	4·90	4·77	4·58	4·33	4	3·57	3	2·18	0

(iv) $\dfrac{25}{4}\pi$　**(v)** 3·1　4. 46 units^2　5. 67·5　6. **(i)** $\dfrac{\pi}{4}\left(1+\sqrt{2}\right)$　**(ii)** 5·19%

7. **(i)** $\dfrac{5}{2}$　**(ii)** 0·08%　**(iv)** 20·42%

8. **(i)** Between 5 and 15 minutes

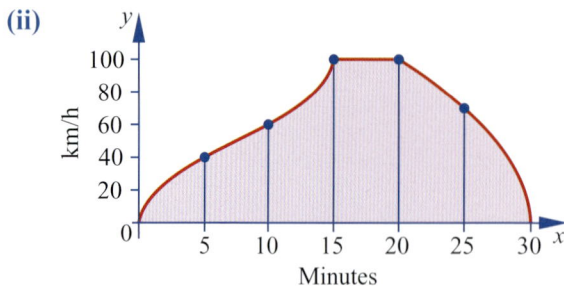

(ii)

(iii) Area = Time × Speed = Distance

9. **(i)** 1　**(ii)**

x	−3	−2	−1	0	1	2	3
y	0·004	0·054	0·242	0·399	0·242	0·054	0·004

(iii) 0·995　**(iv)** 0·9974　**(v)** 0·24%

Exercise 1.3

1. $\dfrac{x^4}{4} + c$ **2.** $\dfrac{x^3}{3} + c$ **3.** $x^5 + c$ **4.** $-\dfrac{1}{2}x^2 + c$ **5.** $-\dfrac{2}{3}x^3 + c$ **6.** $5x + c$

7. $-2x + c$ **8.** $-\dfrac{1}{x} + c$ **9.** $\dfrac{2}{3}x^{\frac{3}{2}} + c$ **10.** $4\sqrt{x} + c$ **11.** $x^3 + 4x^2 + c$

12. $\dfrac{1}{3}x^3 + x^2 + c$ **13.** $\dfrac{2}{3}x^3 - \dfrac{5}{2}x^2 + c$ **14.** $\dfrac{1}{3}x^3 + \dfrac{1}{x} + c$ **15.** $x^4 + \dfrac{1}{x^2} + c$

16. $\dfrac{2}{3}x^{\frac{3}{2}} + 2\sqrt{x} + c$ **17.** $x^2 + \dfrac{1}{3}x^3 + c$ **18.** $\dfrac{1}{4}x^4 + \dfrac{5}{3}x^3 + c$ **19.** $\dfrac{2}{5}x^{\frac{5}{2}} + \dfrac{2}{3}x^{\frac{3}{2}} + c$

20. $x - \dfrac{3}{x} + c$ **21.** $-\dfrac{1}{x} - \dfrac{1}{2x^2} + c$ **22.** $\dfrac{6}{5}x^{\frac{5}{2}} - 10\sqrt{x} + c$ **23.** $\dfrac{1}{4}x^4 - \dfrac{2}{3}x^3 + \dfrac{1}{2}x^2 + c$

24. $\dfrac{1}{3}x^3 - 2x - \dfrac{1}{x} + c$ **25.** $\dfrac{1}{5}x^5 + x^2 - \dfrac{1}{x} + c$ **26.** $x^3 - x^2 + 5$ **27.** $x^3 - \dfrac{2}{3}x^{\frac{3}{2}} + 4$

28. $t^4 - 3t^2 + 4$ **29.** $4x^4 + x^2 + x + 2$ **30.** $x^3 + 4x + 2$

Exercise 1.4

1. 7 **2.** 16 **3.** $\dfrac{15}{4}$ **4.** $\dfrac{14}{3}$ **5.** $\dfrac{32}{3}$ **6.** -18 **7.** $\dfrac{16}{3}$ **8.** $\dfrac{1}{6}$ **9.** 0

10. $\dfrac{25}{4}$ **11.** -1 **12.** 7 **13.** $\dfrac{29}{6}$ **14.** -9 **15.** $\dfrac{7}{8}$ **16.** 5 **17.** $\dfrac{1}{2}(2x+3); 5$

18. $x^2 + 2x + 4; \dfrac{16}{3}$ **19.** 3 **20.** 2 **21.** 5

Exercise 1.5

1. $2\ln x + c$ **2.** $\dfrac{3x^2}{2} - 5\ln x + c$ **3.** $\dfrac{x^3}{3} + \dfrac{7}{2}\ln x + c$ **4.** $\dfrac{1}{3}\ln(3x+5) + c$

5. $\dfrac{5}{4}\ln(4x-2) + c$ **6.** $\dfrac{3}{5}\ln(5x+7) + c$ **7.** $\dfrac{62}{3} + 3\ln 5$ **8.** $15 + \ln\dfrac{2}{7}$ **9.** $4 - 2\ln 4$

Exercise 1.6

1. $\dfrac{1}{2}\sin 2x + c$ **2.** $-\dfrac{1}{4}\cos 4x + c$ **3.** $\sin 3x + c$ **4.** $\dfrac{1}{4}\sin 4\theta + \dfrac{1}{2}\cos\theta + c$

5. $4\sin 2\theta + \cos 8\theta + c$ **6.** $-\dfrac{1}{5}\cos 5\theta + \dfrac{1}{7}\sin 7\theta + c$ **7.** $\sin 6x + \sin 2x; -\dfrac{1}{6}\cos 6x - \dfrac{1}{2}\cos 2x + c$

8. $\sin 7x - \sin 5x; -\dfrac{1}{7}\cos 7x + \dfrac{1}{5}\cos 5x + c$ **9.** $\dfrac{1}{2}(\cos 2x - \cos 8x); \dfrac{1}{4}\sin 2x - \dfrac{1}{16}\sin 8x + c$

10. $\dfrac{1}{2}(\cos 5x + \cos x); \dfrac{1}{10}\sin 5x + \dfrac{1}{2}\sin x + c$ **11.** $\dfrac{1}{\sqrt{2}}$ or $\dfrac{\sqrt{2}}{2}$ **12.** 0 **13.** $\dfrac{3}{2}$

14. (i) $\dfrac{1}{2}(\cos 5x + \cos x)$ (ii) $\dfrac{3}{5}$ **15.** (i) $\dfrac{1}{2}(\sin 6x + \sin 2x)$ (ii) $\dfrac{7}{24}$

Exercise 1.7

1. $\dfrac{1}{3}e^{3x} + c$ **2.** $\dfrac{1}{2}e^{2x+3} + c$ **3.** $-\dfrac{1}{4}e^{-4x} + c$ or $-\dfrac{1}{4e^{4x}} + c$ **4.** $-\dfrac{1}{3}e^{1-3x} + c$

5. $-\dfrac{1}{2e^{2x}} + c$ **6.** $4e^{\frac{x}{2}} + c$ **7.** $\dfrac{1}{2}e^{2x} + e^x + c$ **8.** $\dfrac{1}{3}\left(e^{3x} + \dfrac{1}{e^{3x}}\right) + c$

9. $\dfrac{1}{2}(e^2 - 1)$ **10.** $\dfrac{1}{3}\left(e^2 - \dfrac{1}{e^4}\right)$ **11.** $\dfrac{1}{4}\left(e^7 - \dfrac{1}{e}\right)$ **12.** $\dfrac{4^x}{\ln 4} + c$ **13.** $\dfrac{7^{x+3}}{\ln 7} + c$

14. $\dfrac{6^x}{\ln 6} + c$ **15.** $\dfrac{2^{x-2}}{\ln 2} + c$ **16.** $\dfrac{24}{\ln 5}$ **17.** $\dfrac{990}{\ln 10}$ **18.** $\dfrac{3}{8 \ln 2}$

Exercise 1.8

1. $\dfrac{21}{2}$ **2.** 9   **3.** 120   **4.** 13   **5.** $\dfrac{37}{12}$ **6.** $\dfrac{32}{3}$ **7.** 9   **8.** 10   **9.** $\dfrac{39}{4}$

10. 18   **11.** $\dfrac{9}{2}$ **12.** $\dfrac{32}{3}$ **13. (i)** 2; 4   **(ii)** $\dfrac{4}{3}$

14. (i) $A(1, 4)$; $B(2, 7)$ **(iii)** $\dfrac{1}{6}$

(ii)

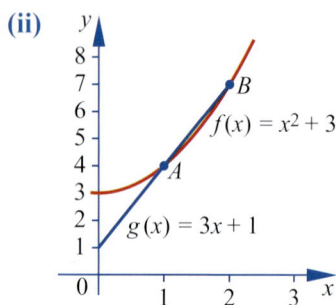

15. 13   **16.** $\dfrac{8}{3}$ **17.** $\dfrac{9}{2}$ **18.** $\dfrac{32}{3}$ **19.** $\dfrac{28}{3}$

20. $6 - \ln 2$ **21.** $k = 6$ **22.** $p = 6$ **23. (i)** $A(2, 0)$;

$B(4, 8)$ **(ii)** $\dfrac{32}{3}$ **24. (i)** $(2, 32)$ **(ii)** 105   **(iii)** 108

25. (i) $x = \sqrt[3]{y}$ **26.** $\dfrac{41}{3}$ **27.** $\dfrac{15}{2} - 4 \ln 4$

28. $\dfrac{16}{3}$ **29. (i)** $A(-2, 0)$; $B(4, 0)$ **31.** $2\sqrt{2} - 2$

32. (i) $(-3, 9)$; $(-1, 2)$ **(ii)** 1·34

Exercise 1.9

1. 11   **2.** 20   **3.** $\dfrac{2}{\pi}$ **4.** $\dfrac{1}{3}(e^3 - 1)$ **5. (i)** 160,000 m³   **(ii)** 40 min   **(iii)** $53,333\dfrac{1}{3}$ m³

6. (i) After 1 and 5 seconds   **(ii)** −8 m/s

7. (i)   **(ii)** 4   **(iii)** 0   **(iv)** $\dfrac{8}{3}$ **8. (i)** 0400 hrs or 4 a.m.   **(ii)** 21° C

Exercise 1.10

1. (i) 22 m/s²   **(ii)** $s = t^3 + 2t^2 - 5t + 6$ **(iii)** 36 m   **2. (i)** $N = 2e^{3t} - 5t + c$

(ii) 16,224 bacteria   **3. (i)** $\dfrac{25,000}{49}$ m   **(ii)** $\dfrac{1,000}{49}$ sec

Exercise 1.11

1. (i) $2xe^{x^2}$ (ii) $e^{x^2} + c$ **2.** (i) $xe^x + e^x$ (ii) $xe^x - e^x + c$ **3.** (i) $1 + \ln x$ (ii) 1

4. (i) $8xe^{2x} + 4e^{2x}$ (ii) $2(e^2 + 1)$ **5.** (i) $9x \cos 3x + 3 \sin 3x$ (ii) $\dfrac{\pi - 2}{2}$ **6.** 2 **7.** 2

8. (i) 0 or $\dfrac{\pi}{2}$ (ii) $-4x \sin 2x + 2 \cos 2x$; $\sin 2x - 2x \cos 2x + c$ (iii) π square units

Exercise 2.1

1. $2i$ **2.** $5i$ **3.** $7i$ **4.** $10i$ **5.** $4i$ **6.** $12i$ **7.** $3i$ **8.** $11i$ **9.** $20i$

10. $14i$ **11.** $13i$ **12.** $17i$ **13.** $2\sqrt{2}i$ **14.** $2\sqrt{3}i$ **15.** $3\sqrt{2}i$ **16.** $5\sqrt{2}i$

17. $4\sqrt{5}i$ **18.** $3\sqrt{7}i$ **19.** -1 **20.** $-i$ **21.** 1 **22.** i **23.** 1 **24.** -1

25. $-i$ **26.** -1 **27.** i **28.** -1 **29.** $-i$ **30.** 1 **31.** (i) 1 (ii) i (iii) -1

(iv) $-i$ **32.** (i) $-1 - 4i$ (ii) $-1 + 2i$ (iii) $3 - 4i$ **34.** $-7 + 10i$ **35.** $-2 + 15i$

36. $-18 - i$ **37.** $-1 - 17i$ **38.** $-5 + 5i$ **39.** $0 - 12i$ **40.** $17 + 17i$ **41.** $8 - 64i$

42. $-13 + 10i$ **43.** 1 **44.** $-11 + 3i$ **45.** (i) $-16 - 11i$ (ii) $-5 + 12i$ (iii) $2 + 5i$

(iv) $11 - 16i$ **48.** $\dfrac{2}{3}$ **49.** $-\dfrac{5}{2}$ **50.** -2 **51.** (i) -2 (ii) 1 **52.** (i) -1 (ii) 4

53. $z_1 = 1 + i$, $z_2 = 3 - 2i$

Exercise 2.2

1. $2 + i$ **2.** $2 + 3i$ **3.** $1 + i$ **4.** $2 - 3i$ **5.** $\dfrac{1}{2} + \dfrac{1}{2}i$ **6.** $\dfrac{4}{5} - \dfrac{3}{5}i$ **7.** $\dfrac{4}{13} - \dfrac{7}{13}i$

8. $-\dfrac{1}{2} + \dfrac{7}{2}i$ **9.** $a = 3, b = 1$ **10.** 1 **11.** 1 **12.** i **13.** $i; -3$ **14.** (i) $-8i$ (ii) $-\dfrac{1}{9}$

(iii) -1 **15.** $i; 1$ **16.** i **17.** -1 **18.** 1 **19.** (i) 1 (ii) -1 **20.** $z_1 = 2 + i$,

   $z_2 = -1 + 3i$

Exercise 2.3

1. $x = 2, y = 1$ **2.** $x = 3, y = 2$ **3.** $x = 15, y = -21$ **4.** $x = -5, y = 5$

5. $h = 3, k = 2$ **6.** $p = 4, q = -1$ **7.** $t = \dfrac{3}{5}, k = 7$ **8.** $t = 10, k = 2$

9. $a = -\dfrac{4}{3}, b = \dfrac{4}{3}$ **10.** $l = -2, k = -3$ **11.** $l = -2, p = 7$ **12.** (i) $3 - 3i$ (ii) $a = 0, b = -3$

13. $4 + 3i; 4 - 3i$ **14.** $2 - 3i; 2 + i$ **15.** $3 + 2i; 3 - i$ **16.** $a = 1, b = -3$

17. $1 - 2i$ **18.** (i) $a = -10, b = 8$ (ii) $8 + 24i$ **19.** $k = -\dfrac{1}{5}$ **20.** $8\sqrt{3}$

21. (i) $5 + 3i; 5 - 3i$ **22.** $a = -2, b = 2$ or $a = -4, b = 1$

Exercise 2.4

12. (i) 5 (ii) 13 (iii) 17 (iv) 25 (v) 2 (vi) 4 (vii) 16 (viii) 1 (ix) 1

(x) $\sqrt{2}$ (xi) $\sqrt{13}$ (xii) 1 **13.** 5 **14.** (i) $\dfrac{6}{5} - \dfrac{8}{5}i$ (ii) 2 **16.** (i) $\dfrac{1}{5}$ (ii) 1

17. $3 - 4i$ **(ii)** $h = 2, k = -\dfrac{2}{5}$ 18. ± 6 19. ± 5 20. $11, -9$ 21. $15 + 8i, -15 + 8i$

22. $\sqrt{2} + i$ 23. ± 2 25. **(i)** $s = 3, t = 1$ **(ii)** $x^2 + y^2 = 10$

Exercise 2.5

1. $1 \pm i$ 2. $1 \pm 2i$ 3. $-5 \pm 3i$ 4. $\dfrac{1}{2} \pm \dfrac{1}{2}i$ 5. $-\dfrac{3}{2} \pm \dfrac{1}{2}i$ 6. $\dfrac{1}{5} \pm \dfrac{7}{5}i$ 7. $\pm 2i$

8. $\pm 3i$ 9. $\pm 10i$ 10. **(i)** $p = 2, k = 3$ **(ii)** yes   11. $-2 + i; -2 - i$ 12. $1 + 3i; 1 - i$;
not all coefficients are real   13. $2 + 2i, -1 + 2i$ 14. $3 - i, -i$ 15. $1 + 3i, 1 + 2i$

16. $z^2 + 4z + 5 = 0$ 17. $z^2 - 6z + 13 = 0$ 18. $z^2 + 2z + 26 = 0$ 19. $z^2 + 9 = 0$

20. $z^2 + 2z + 3 = 0$ 21. $z^2 - 4z + 9 = 0$ 22. $2z^2 + 2z + 1$ 23. $9z^2 + 6z + 5 = 0$

24. $p = -6, q = 34$ 25. $m = 6, n = 18$ 26. $k = 26$ 27. $a = -4, b = 13$ 28. **(i)** $a = 5$,
$b = 2$ **(iii)** $5 - i, 5 - 5i$ 29. -4 30. 17 31. $p = 2, q = 7; 1 - 3i$ 32. $\dfrac{1}{2} + \dfrac{3}{2}i, -\dfrac{3}{2} + \dfrac{3}{2}i$

Exercise 2.6

1. $1 + 4i, -1 - 4i$ 2. $1 - 2i, -1 + 2i$ 3. $3 - i, -3 + i$ 4. $2 + 3i, -2 - 3i$

5. $4 - i, -4 + i$ 6. $2 + 5i, -2 - 5i$ 7. $3 - 4i, -3 + 4i$ 8. $4 - 5i, -4 + 5i$

9. $1 + i, -1 - i$ 10. **(i)** $1 + 2i, -1 - 2i$ **(ii) (a)** $2 + i, 1 - i$ **(b)** $i, -1 - i$

11. **(i)** $1 + 5i, -1 - 5i$ **(ii)** $2 + 4i, 1 - i$ 12. **(i)** $\pm(4 + i)$ **(ii)** $1; -3 - i$

13. **(i)** $\pm(2 + i)$ **(ii)** $-2; i$ 14. **(i)** $\pm(3 - 2i)$ **(ii) (a)** $-2 + i, 1 - i$ **(b)** $3 + 4i, -1 - 2i$

15. **(i)** $\pm(4 + i)$ **(ii)** $2 - i, 1 + 3i$ 16. $\pm\left(\sqrt{3} - i\right)$ 17. **(i) (a)** $\pm(2 + i)$ **(b)** $\pm(2 - i)$
(ii) $\pm(2 + i), \pm(2 - i)$

Exercise 2.7

1. **(ii)** $3 \pm i$ 2. **(ii)** $-2 \pm 3i$ 3. **(i)** $-3, -2 \pm i$ **(ii)** $-1, \pm i$ 4. **(i) (a)** $2i$ **(b)** $-2 + 2i$
(ii) $3, 1 - i$ 5. $-4, 1 \pm 2i$ 6. $5, -2 \pm 3i$ 7. $0, 1 \pm i$ 8. **(i)** $4, 2 \pm i$ **(ii)** $4 - 3i, 2 - 2i$,
$2 - 4i$ 9. **(i)** -4 **(ii)** $2, 1 \pm i$ **(iii)** $0, -1 + i, -1 - i$ 10. **(i)** -3 **(ii)** $1, 1 \pm 2i$ **(iii)** $1 + 2i$,
$1 + 4i, 1$ 11. **(i)** $i, \pm 3$ **(ii)** $3i, 3 + 2i, -3 + 2i$ 12. **(i)** $a = -4, b = 6$ **(ii) (a)** $-2, 1 \pm i$
(b) $-3, \pm i$ 13. **(i)** $p = -6, q = 34$ **(ii) (a)** $-2, 4 \pm i$ **(b)** $-2 + 2i, 4 + 3i, 4 + i$

14. **(i)** $a = -2, b = 2$ **(ii)** $2, 1 \pm i$ 15. $a = 4, b = 5$ 16. $a = -10, b = 29$

17. **(i)** $(z - 3)(z - 2)$ **(iii)** $2, 3, -1 - i$ 18. **(i)** $(z - 2)(z + 2); \pm 2$ **(iii)** $\pm 2, -3 - i$

19. $\pm 4, -1 - i$ 20. **(i)** $z^2 - 6z + 10 = 0$ **(ii) (a)** 8 **(b)** $2, 3 - i$

21. **(i)** $(1, 0), (0, -8)$ **(ii)** 1 **(iii)** 4 **(iv)** $a = 1, b = 4, c = 8$ **(v)** $1, -2 \pm 2i$

22. **(i)** 3 **(ii)** -1 **(iii)** $a = 3, b = 2, c = 5$ **(iv)** $3, -1 \pm 2i$

23. **(i)** $-1, 3$ **(ii)** $\pm 2i$ **(iii)** $\pm 2i$ 24. $k = \pm 3; \dfrac{1}{2}, \pm 3i$

Exercise 2.8

1. $\sqrt{2}(\cos 45° + i \sin 45°)$ 2. $2(\cos 30° + i \sin 30°)$ 3. $4(\cos 60° + i \sin 60°)$

4. $(\cos 90° + i \sin 90°)$ 5. $2(\cos 0° + i \sin 0°)$ 6. $2(\cos 300° + i \sin 300°)$

7. $\sqrt{2}(\cos 315° + i \sin 315°)$ **8.** $2(\cos 135° + i \sin 135°)$ **9.** $2\sqrt{2}(\cos 225° + i \sin 225°)$

10. $2(\cos 150° + i \sin 150°)$ **11.** $8(\cos 240° + i \sin 240°)$ **12.** $2(\cos 330° + i \sin 330°)$

13. $2(\cos 90° + i \sin 90°)$ **14.** $\sqrt{2}(\cos 45° + i \sin 45°)$ **15.** $2(\cos 210° + i \sin 210°)$

16. $(\cos 60° + i \sin 60°)$ **17.** $0 + i$ **18.** $1 + i$ **19.** $-3 - 3\sqrt{3}i$

20. $-5\sqrt{3} + 5i$ **21.** $-2 - 2\sqrt{3}i$ **22.** $2 - 2i$ **23.** (i) $315°$ (ii) $45°$

25. (i) 5 (ii) $5\sqrt{2}$ **26.** (i) (a) $a = -8$ (b) $|z_1| = 8\sqrt{2}$ (ii) (a) $b = -3$ (b) $|z_2| = 3\sqrt{2}$

(iii) (a) $c = -\sqrt{3}$ (b) $|z_3| = 2$ (iv) (a) $d = -6$ (b) $|z_4| = 4\sqrt{3}$ **27.** $30°$ or $330°$

Exercise 2.9

1. i **2.** -1 **3.** $8i$ **4.** 15 **5.** $-12i$ **6.** $16i$ **7.** $20i$ **8.** -6 **9.** i

10. -2 **11.** $-3i$ **12.** $-4\sqrt{3} + 4i$ **13.** $5 + 5\sqrt{3}i$ **14.** $0 + i$ **15.** $-2 + 0i$

16. $0 - 3i$ **17.** (i) (a) $\cos 9x + i \sin 9x$ (b) $\cos x + i \sin x$ (ii) (a) $-i$ (b) $\dfrac{\sqrt{3}}{2} + \dfrac{1}{2}i$

18. 12 **19.** (i) $0 + 6i$ (ii) $z^2 + 36 = 0$

Exercise 2.10

1. $1 + 0i$ **2.** $-1 + 0i$ **3.** $0 + i$ **4.** $-1 + 0i$ **5.** $-64 + 0i$ **6.** $0 - 6i$

7. $16 - 16\sqrt{3}i$ **8.** $-1 + 0i$ **9.** $-16\sqrt{2} - 16\sqrt{2}i$ **10.** (i) (a) 2 (b) $30°$

(ii) $2(\cos 30° + i \sin 30°)$ (iii) $8i$ **11.** $16 + 0i$ **12.** $-4 + 0i$ **13.** $0 - 8i$

14. $128 + 128i$ **15.** $0 + 64i$ **16.** $-128 + 128\sqrt{3}i$ **17.** $0 - i$ **18.** $-\dfrac{1}{2} - \dfrac{\sqrt{3}}{2}i$

19. (i) $\sqrt{2}(\cos 45° + i \sin 45°)$ (ii) $32i$ **20.** (i) $1 - i$ (ii) $8i$

21. (i) $\left(\sqrt{2}, 135°\right); \sqrt{2}(\cos 135° + i \sin 135°)$ **22.** $\sqrt{2}(\cos 45° + i \sin 45°); -32 + 32i$

23. $2^9\left(1 - \sqrt{3}i\right)$ **24.** (i) -1 (ii) $-\dfrac{1}{4}$ **25.** 1 **26.** (i) -1 (ii) i

27. 1 (real) **28.** (i) $-\dfrac{\sqrt{3}}{2} + \dfrac{1}{2}i$ (ii) $-1 + 0i$ **29.** (i) 9 (ii) 6θ **30.** $8 + 8\sqrt{3}i$

Exercise 2.11

1. (ii) $\dfrac{2\tan\theta}{1 - \tan^2\theta}$ **2.** (ii) $\dfrac{3\tan\theta - \tan^3\theta}{1 - 3\tan^2\theta}$ **3.** (ii) $\dfrac{4\tan\theta - 4\tan^3\theta}{1 - 6\tan^2\theta + \tan^4\theta}$

5. (iv) (f) $\dfrac{1}{8}(\cos 4\theta - 4\cos 2\theta + 3)$

Exercise 2.12

1. (i) $2(\cos 90° + i \sin 90°)$ (ii) $\pm(1 - i)$ **2.** (i) $\cos 0° + i \sin 0°$ (ii) $\pm 1, \pm i$ (iii) 4

3. (i) $8(\cos 270° + i \sin 270°)$ (ii) $2i, \sqrt{3} + i, \sqrt{3} - i$ (iii) $3i, \pm\sqrt{3}$

4. (i) (a) $64(\cos 270° + i \sin 270°)$ (b) $64(\cos(270° + n\,360°) + i \sin(270° + n\,360°))$

(ii) $4i, 2\sqrt{3} - 2i, -2\sqrt{3} - 2i$ (iii) 0

5. (i) $4(\cos 300° + i \sin 300°)$ (ii) $\pm\left(\sqrt{3} - i\right)$

6. (i) $16(\cos 240° + i \sin 240°)$ **(ii)** 4096 **(iii)** $\pm(1 + \sqrt{3}i), \pm(\sqrt{3} - i)$ **(iv)** $x^2 + y^2 = 4$

(v)

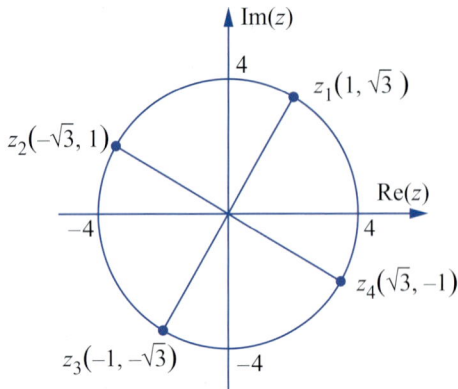

(vi) A square **7.** $\pm 2i, \pm(\sqrt{3} + i), \pm(-\sqrt{3} + i)$

8. (i) $\cos 0° + i \sin 0°$, $\cos 72° + i \sin 72°$, $\cos 144° + i \sin 144°$, $\cos 216° + i \sin 216°$, $\cos 288° + i \sin 288°$ **(ii)** $-2 \cos 36°$ (real) **(iii)** -1 **9. (i)** $\cos 300° + i \sin 300°$ **(ii)** $\pm i$

10. (i) $4(\cos 120° + i \sin 120°)$ **(ii)** ± 8 **11. (i)** $4(\cos 90° + i \sin 90°)$ **(ii)** $\pm(16\sqrt{2} + 16\sqrt{2}i)$

12. (i) $27(\cos 180° + i \sin 180°)$ **(ii)** $-3, \dfrac{3}{2} + \dfrac{3\sqrt{3}}{2}i, \dfrac{3}{2} - \dfrac{3\sqrt{3}}{2}i$ **(iii)** $x^2 + y^2 = 9$

(iv) **(v)** Each length is $3\sqrt{3}$ units or all angles are $60°$

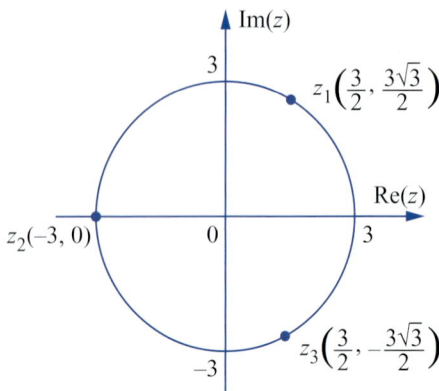

13. $\dfrac{3}{2}(\cos 20° + i \sin 20°)$, $\dfrac{3}{2}(\cos 110° + i \sin 110°)$, $\dfrac{3}{2}(\cos 200° + i \sin 200°)$, $\dfrac{3}{2}(\cos 290° + i \sin 290°)$

14. (i) $1, -\dfrac{1}{2} + \dfrac{\sqrt{3}}{2}i, -\dfrac{1}{2} - \dfrac{\sqrt{3}}{2}i$ **(ii) (a)** 1 **(b)** 32 **15.** $a = 4, b = -2$

Exercise 2.13

1. yes, both the same distance, 5, from the origin **2. (ii)** same as z **(iii)** central symmetry in the origin, $0(0, 0)$ **(iv)** z **(v)** rotation of $90°$ and $450°$ about the origin, $0(0, 0)$, maps (moves) a point to the position **(vi)** rotate by $90°$ and double its distance from the origin (in a straight line from the origin) or vice versa **(vii)** $5 > \sqrt{5}$ **3. (i)** $u = 4 + 2i, v = 2 + i$ **(i)** $k = 2$ **(iii)** $l = \dfrac{1}{2}$ **(iv)** on the same straight line through the origin with $2i^3v$ twice as far as $-iv$ from the origin, $0(0, 0)$;

$(2 - 4i = 2(1 - 2i))$ **4. (ii)** rotation of $360°$ about the origin maps (moves) a point to it original position   **(iii)** yes; rotation of $180° =$ rotation of $-180°$ about the origin, $0(0, 0)$ **(iv)** rotate by $90°$ and treble its distance from the origin (in a straight line from the origin) or vice versa

5. (i) yes. The three points $z_1(-1, 10)$, $z_2(3, 2)$ and $z_3(4, 0)$ are on the line $2x + y - 8 = 0$. Or slope of $z_1 z_2 =$ slope of $z_2 z_3$ ($=$ slope of $z_1 z_3$). Or, $|z_1 z_2| + |z_2 z_3| = |z_1 z_3|$ **(ii)** Any point on the line $2x + y - 8 = 0$. For example, $z_4 = 5 - 2i$ or $z_4 = 8i$.   **6. (iv)** circle; centre $= (2, 1)$ and radius $= 5$ **(v)** yes   **(vi)** $5 + 5i$ **7. (i)** $1 + 2i$ **7. (i)** $z^2 = 0 + 2i$, $z^3 = -2 + 2i$

(iii)

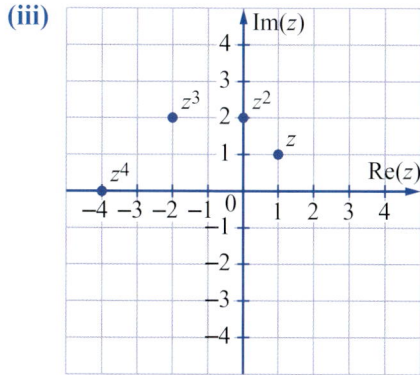

(iv) Each time z is multiplied by itself it rotates by $45°$ about the origin and it also moves further away from the origin by $\sqrt{2}$ each time. If we keep multiplying z by itself and join the points the curve will look like a spiral.   **(v)** $z^8 = 16$, $z^{12} = -64$, $z^{16} = 256$ **(vi)** $z^{40} = (z^4)^{10} = (-4)^{10} = 1{,}048{,}572$ positive number. Alternatively, (-4) to an even exponent (power) will always be positive.   **(vii)** $z^{40} = (-2)^{20}$ **(viii)** $z^{41} = 1{,}048{,}576(1 + i)$ or $1{,}048{,}576 + 1{,}048{,}576i$

(ix) $\left(\sqrt{2}\right)^{41}$ or $2^{20}\sqrt{2}$ or $1{,}048{,}576\sqrt{2}$ or $1{,}482{,}910{\cdot}4$

8. (i) (a) $\text{Re}(z_1) = 3$ **(b)** $\text{Re}(z_1) = 4$ **(ii) (a)** Mary   **(b)** $\text{Im}(z) = 4$, a real number **(iii)** Plot the point $(4, 0)$ (not $(0, 4)$)

9.

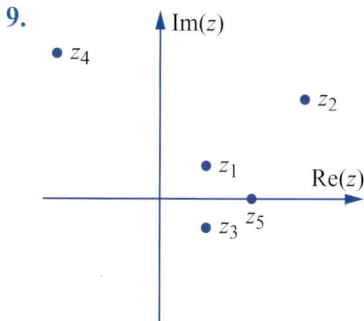

10.

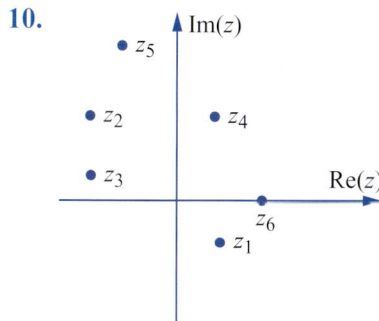

11. (i)

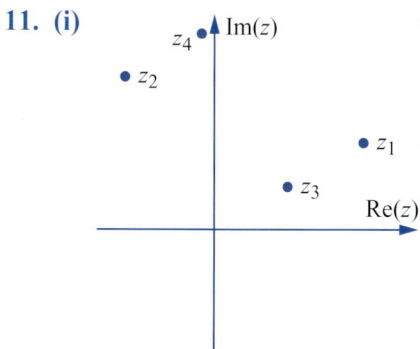

(ii) $k = \dfrac{1}{2}$ **12. (i)**

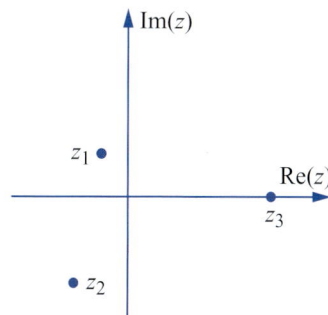

(ii) $120°, 240°, 0°$ **(iii)** $-1 + \sqrt{3}i, -1 - \sqrt{3}i, 8 + 0i$ **(iv)** 16

13. (i) All lie on the same straight line **(ii)** 1 **(iii)**

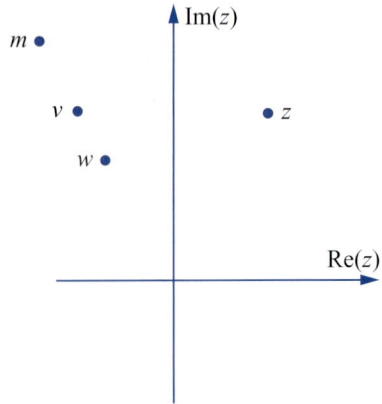

If $|z| < 1$, then z^2 must be closer to the origin.

14. (i) (a) $135°$ **(b)** $225°$ **(ii) (a)** $0 + i$ **(b)** $-1 + 0i$ **(c)** $\dfrac{1}{\sqrt{2}} + \dfrac{1}{\sqrt{2}}i$ **(d)** $-\dfrac{1}{\sqrt{2}} + \dfrac{1}{\sqrt{2}}i$

(iv) (a) $\cos 0 + i \sin 0$ **(b)** $\cos 45° + i \sin 45°$ **(c)** $\cos 90° + i \sin 90°$ **(d)** $\cos 135° + i \sin 135°$

(v) $\cos n(45°) + i \sin n(45°)$ **(vi)** 0 **(vii)** 15

15. (ii) $y = \pm\sqrt{3}$

(iii) 4

(iv) $n = 3$

$\cos 300° = \cos 720°$

and

$\sin 360° = \sin 720°$

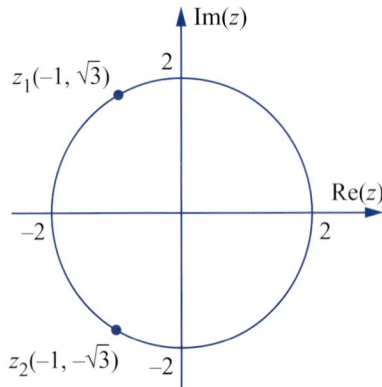

16.

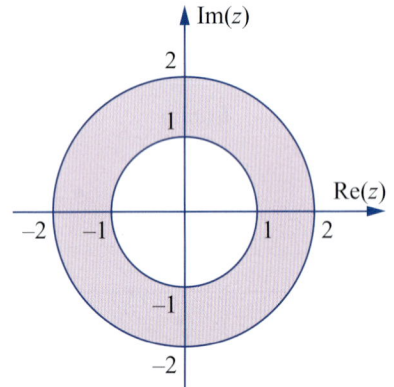

17. (i) $0°, 180°$ **(ii)** $90°, 270°$ **18.** $p = -1, q = 1$ **19. (i)** $x = y$, where $x, y \geq 0$

(ii) $x = \sqrt{3}y$, where $x, y \geq 0$ **(iii)** circle, centre $(2, 0)$ and radius 4. $(x - 2)^2 + y^2 = 16$ or

$x^2 + y^2 - 4x - 12 = 0$

20. (i) $x - y - 1 = 0$

(ii) $f(z) = x - y$, a real number

Every complex number of the form $x + yi$ will be mapped onto the real axis at the point $(x - y, 0)$

(iii) (a) 7   **(b)** 3

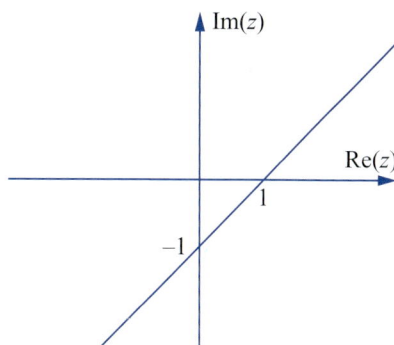

Exercise 3.1

1. **(i)** Inferential   **(ii)** Descriptive   **(iii)** Inferential

2. **(ii)** 5 variables:

Rent – continuous

Electricity – categorical

Pets – categorical

No. of rooms – discrete

Beach distance – continuous

4. Time of day to study using morning, afternoon, evening, night would be categorical.
No. of subjects studied per day, discrete; amount of time studying, continuous.

5. **(i)** Sample: 800 individuals, pop: total who watch TV.

(ii) Sample: 210 athletes, pop: all athletes at the event.

(iii) Sample: 40 random calls, pop: all Cork city + county emergency calls made in the time period

6. **(i)** 40, no. of children per household attending primary school

(ii) 660, no. of hours studying

(iii) 2,805, no. of pets per household

7. (i) Discrete   **(ii)** Continuous   **(iii)** Discrete   **8. (i)** $\{0, 1, 2, 3 \ldots\}$ **(ii)** Discrete

Exercise 3.3

1. **(i) (a)** 8   **(b)** 8   **(c)** Cannot tell   **(ii)** 8, 8 or 6, 10 or 3, 13 or greatest range $= 15 - 1 = 14$

(iii) 5, 11

2. (i) F   **(ii)** F   **3.** $x = 14$ and $y = 30$ **4. (i)** Two possible values   **(ii)** $x = 3$

5. Median $= 7$ is highest

6. (i) 35 k (low)   **(ii)** Mean $= 121{\cdot}3$ k (distorted by extreme values)   **(iii)** Median $= 65$ k

7. (i) 14   **(ii)** 13   **(iii)** 24 or 1

8. 8   **9.** 11   **10. (i)** 4   **(ii)** $W \geq 14$ **(iii)** $\dfrac{58 + 5W}{17 + W}$ **(iv)** 7, $\dfrac{31}{8}$ **11.** 9, 10, 10, 15

12. (i) $49{\cdot}6$ **(ii)** 49

Exercise 3.4

1. (i) 3 **(ii)** 4 **(iii)** 5 **(iv)** 3·25 **(v)** 3·3
2. (ii) 4 **(iii)** 4 **(iv)** 5 **(v)** 40% **(vi)** 200 **(vii)** 6
4. (i) 36 **(ii)** 31 **(iii)** 90 **(iv)** 30–40 **(v)** 40–50
5. (i) 8 **(ii)** 30 **(iii)** Discrete   **6. (i)** $x = 6$ **7. (i)** $x = 2$ **(ii)** Discrete

Exercise 3.5

1. 1·41   **2.** 3·06   **3.** 1·87   **4.** 1·63   **5.** 2·45   **6.** 4·24   **7.** 3·87   **8.** 2·65
9. 2·73   **10.** $k = 2$ **14. (i)** 2·37, 4·86   **15. (i)** Q, R **(ii)** P **(iii)** P
    (iv) {4, 4, 4, 4, 4, 4, 4, 4, 4, 4, 4} **(v)** 4   **17. (iii)** {9, 9, 9, 9, 9, 9}
18. (i) $\sigma_{age} = 9·24$, $\sigma_{income} = 8,967$ **(ii)** $\sigma_{age} = 9·24$, $\sigma_{income} = (8,967)(1·5)$

Exercise 3.6

1. 3, 1·21   **2.** 8, 3·02   **3.** 11, 4·36   **4.** 35, 20·37   **5. (i)** 12, 13, 20, 45, 30 **(ii) (a)** 4 **(b)** 2·3
6. (i) 6·7 **(ii)** 0·93 **(iii)** 4·84, 8·56 and 95% **7. (i)** 48·75, 13·3 **(ii)** 75·35
8. (i) 18 **(ii)** 6·4 **(iii)** 11·6, 24·4 **(iv)** 5 **(v)** 83·3% **(vi)** 20 **(vii)** 6·4
9. (i) 13·4, 0·6 (mean + 1 year, spread of ages shows no change) **(ii)** 12·9 **(iii)** $> 0·6$ because
    data are more spread out   **10. (i)** 39, 14·55 **(ii)** Five journeys
11. (i) 6–8 **(ii)** Continuous **(iii)** 6 and 2·9 **(iv)** 78
12. (ii) $\sigma_{men} = 6·4$, $\sigma_{women} = 8·8$ **(iii)** Men = (8·6, 21·4), women = (13·2, 30·8)
13. (i) Mean = 0 **(ii)** $\sqrt{\dfrac{5}{2}}$ **14. (i) (a)** 34 **(b)** 65 **(ii)** 17 **(iii)** 17

Exercise 3.7

1. (i) 5, 10, 60, 50, 25, 20 **(ii)** 170 **(iii)** 103 **2. (i)** 24, 16, 42, 40, 12 **(ii)** 40–60
    (iii) 6,700,000   **3. (i)** (12, 30, 12, 27, 9) **(ii) (a)** 24 **(b)** 12 **(iv)** 108
4. Q is larger than P in (a) and (d)
    P is larger than Q in (b), (e) and (f)
    Both are the same in (c)

Exercise 3.8

1. (i) (e) **(ii)** (d) **(iii)** (b) **(iv)** (c) **(v)** (a)
2. (iii) Positively/right skewed
3. (i) Negatively/left skewed **(ii)** (b)   **4. (i)** Positively/right skewed **(ii)** (a)
5. (i) Mean = 36·2, median = 35 **(ii)** Close to symmetric
6. (i) 25, 23, 22 **(iii)** 5·53 **(iv)** Gym members probably not representative
7. (ii) Mean $>$ median **(iii)** Range   **9. (ii)** S is more spread out from the mean and has the
    largest standard deviation.

Exercise 3.9

1. (i) Positively skewed (ii) (b) (iii) 12·5 (iv) 63   2. (i) 121, 113 and 74, 13
3. (i) 8 (ii) 8 (iii) 4 (iv) 6   4. (i) $A = 29$ (ii) $B = 33$ (iii) $C = 33$
5. (i) $W = 1, Q = 8$ (ii) $x = 6, y = 2$ (iii) $B = 3$ (iv) $R = 2, V = 9$
6. (ii) (a) 74 (b) 96·5 (iii) (a) 63 (b) 76
7. (ii)

Girls		Boys
5 5 5 4	2	4 5 5
7 7 6 6 6 6	2	6 6 6 6 7 7 7 7
9 9 8	2	9 9
10	3	0 1 1 1
3 3 3 2	3	2 2 2 2
4	·3	

$4/2 = 24$ for girls   Key $2/4 = 24$ for boys
(iii) Similar means, similar medians.
Range for girls = 10, for boys = 8
8. (i) 17·6% Leitrim 5·9% Dublin (ii) Close to normal distribution, centre at 12% and spread 7%
9. No key; both sides have 21 students; 62 and 66 not ordered; which group is which?

Exercise 3.10

1. (i) None, zero (ii) Strong, positive (iii) Moderate, positive (iv) Weak, moderate
(v) Strong, negative (vi) None, zero (vii) Strong, positive (viii) Moderate, positive
2. (ii) (11, 65) definite and (17, 30) marginal (iii) Moderate to strong positive correlation
3. (ii) Yes, graph shows positive correlation (iii) €105
5. (i) B (ii) E (iii) C (iv) A
6. P—B   Q—A   R—C   7. (iii) B

Exercise 3.11

1. (iii) outlier at (10, 1)   2. (ii) negative correlation, might surprise you
(iii) several points e.g. (25, 92) (iv) −0·796   3. (ii) 0·56 (iv) 1
5. (ii) (a) 1,700 (b) 175   6. (ii) $\bar{x} = 170, \bar{y} = 72$ (iii) A = 29, F = 24·6
7. (i) (90, 8) (iii) −0·11   8. (i) (10, 9) (ii) (4, 6)
9. (i) $r = 0·87$ in both cases   Slope AB = 2, Slope PQ = $\dfrac{1}{2}$

Exercise 3.12

1. (iii) 32 (iv) 223   2. (i) 42·3 (ii) 9·3 (iv) Strong negative (vii) (a) 5 g (b) 26 years
3. (i) Negative; data more reliable for 35-year-olds
4. (i) 17 (ii) 3 (iii) 0   6. (ii) (70, 21) (v) 0·86

Exercise 3.13

1. **(i)** Q_1 and Q_3

   (ii) Positively skewed

   (iii) Lowest salary = €1,600

   Mean salary = €3,200

   Median salary = €2,400

   Range = €5,000, no change

   Interquartile range = €2,600, no change

   First quartile = €1,600

   Standard deviation = €1,600, no change

   (iv) Lowest salary = €1,610

   Mean salary = €3,450

   Median salary = €2,530

   Range = €5,750

   Interquartile range = €2,990

   First quartile = €1,840

   Standard deviation = €1,840

2. **(i)** 62 **(ii)** 74 **(iii)** 56 **(iv)** 44   3. **(i)** $B = 48$, $K = 54$ **(ii)** 200   4. **(i)** $\mu = 12$

6. **(i)** 80 **(ii)** 77·3 **(iii)** 82·7 **(iv)** 5·4   7. **(i)** 0·8159 **(ii)** 0·0885 **(iii)** 0·1151

   (iv) 0·7257   8. **(i)** 1·2 **(ii)** 0·4 **(iii)** −1·6 **(iv)** −0·2   9. 6,000

10. **(ii) (a)** 50% **(b)** $97\frac{1}{2}$% **(c)** 16% **(d)** 84% **(e)** $97\frac{1}{2}$%

11. Music $= \dfrac{10}{7}$, Home Economics $= \dfrac{12}{7}$

12. **(ii)** Never Stop z-score $= -1\cdot11$

    Always Go z-score $= -1\cdot07$

13. **(i)** 124 **(ii)** 94%   14. **(i)** 28 **(ii)** 28 **(iii)** 544   15. **(i)** 1·5 **(ii)** Both the same

16. **(i)** 0·75% **(ii)** 43% **(iii)** 91% 17. **(ii)** 39·6 18. **(i) (a)** 16% **(b)** 0·025 **(c)** [68,132]

    (ii) (a) 175 **(b)** 175 **(c)** 25

Exercise 3.14

2. **(i)** 3, 6, 4, 3, 2, 2 **(ii)** $\mu = 169\cdot7$, $\sigma = 2\cdot5$

   75% within $\mu \pm \sigma$ ∴ Reject H_0

3. **(ii) (c) (iv)** −0·86, strong negative correlation   4. **(ii)** $0\cdot80 = r$ **(iv)** $0\cdot67 = r$

5. $z = 0\cdot9901$. Lisa is in the top 1% of her age group.

Exercise 3.15

1. **(i)** 1% **(ii)** 2·3% **(iii)** 3·2% **(iv)** 3·5% **(v)** 4·8%

2. **(i)** 400 **(ii)** 625 **(iii)** 2,500 **(iv)** 4,444 **(v)** 6,944   3. [25% − 35%]   4. [68% − 76%]

5. [24% – 44%]   **6.** [69% – 81%]   **7.** [18% – 28%]   **8.** [50·8% – 57·2%]; yes, there is significant evidence   **9. (i)** No, this is a sample mean   **(ii)** 10%   **(iii)** [€3,150, €3,850]   **(iv)** 400   **10. (i) (a)** 5%   **(b)** [13% – 23%]   **(ii)** Would reject the architect's assumption

Exercise 3.16

2. $31·4\% \leq p \leq 36·6\%$ **3.** Yes, because the confidence intervals overlap

4. From 52·6% to 59·4%

5. (i) From 63·58% to 66·36%   **(ii)** We are 95% confident that between 63·58% and 66·36% of EU citizens drink beer, wine or spirits at least occasionally.

6. (i) 0·062   **(ii)** 0·05, smaller   **(iii)** 616

7. (i) 0·4   **(ii)** $0·2481 \leq p \leq 0·5519$ **(iii)** Increase the number of employees selected.   **(iv)** $n = 93$ **8. (i)** 278   **(ii) (c)** True

Exercise 3.17

1. (i) 0·77   **(ii)** 0·021   **(iii)** $0·749 \leq p \leq 0·791$ **(iv)** Reject H_0

2. (i) $0·832 \leq p \leq 0·908$

   (ii) We are 95% certain that the proportion of satisfied customers is between 83·2% and 90·8%.

   (iv) Fail to reject the null hypothesis   **(v)** Increase the sample size

3. (ii) Claim is within the confidence interval, fail to reject H_0

4. H_0: coin is not biased

   H_A: coin is biased

   Since 50% is not within the confidence interval, reject H_0. Coin is biased.

5. (ii) 72% is inside the confidence interval, fail to reject H_0

6. (i) 25%   **(ii)** 4·2%

   (iii) Since 35% is outside the confidence interval, reject H_0 and accept the manager's claim

Exercise 3.18

1. (i) $H_0 = 600$; $H_A \neq 600$ **(ii)** Test statistic/z unit $= -2·47 \Rightarrow$ Reject H_0

2. $H_0 = 60·5$; $H_A \neq 60·5$ Test statistic/z unit $= 1·82 \Rightarrow$ Fail to reject H_0

3. Test statistic/z unit $= 2·18 \Rightarrow$ Reject H_0 **4. (i)** Positively skewed

   (ii) Normal distribution, $\mu = 80$, and $\sigma_{\bar{x}} = 0·85$ **(iii)** Expect 35 samples with means > 81 g

5. (iii) Approximately normal $(3, 0·26)$

   (i) (a) 41%   **(b)** 240–300   **(c)** 281   **(d)** Normal $(270, 2·16)$ **(e)** 0·01

   (ii) (a) There are more premature births than very long pregnancies

       (b) For **(i) (a)** and **(b)** and **(c)** yes, cannot use the normal model if it is very skewed

           (i) (d) No, as CLT guarantees a normal model for this large sample size

6. (i) $\left(\dfrac{6}{4}\right)\left(\dfrac{1}{4}\right)^2\left(\dfrac{3}{4}\right)^4 = 0·29663$ **(ii)** Normal $(\mu = 22·05, \sigma = 0·75)$ **(iii)** 103

Exercise 3.19

	H_0	H_A	μ	σ	$\bar{x}$	n	T	p	Reject, or fail to reject, H_0
1.	$\mu = 500$	$\mu \neq 500$	500	15	504	64	2·13	0·0332	Reject H_0
2.	$\mu = 120$	$\mu \neq 120$	120	3	120·85	36	1·7	0·0892	Fail to reject H_0
3.	$\mu = 210$	$\mu \neq 210$	210	6	211·5	100	2·5	0·0124	Reject H_0
4.	$\mu = 80$	$\mu \neq 80$	80	18	77·3	144	−1·8	0·0718	Fail to reject H_0
5.	$\mu = 150$	$\mu \neq 150$	150	20	153·8	200	2·68	0·0074	Reject H_0
6.	$\mu = 70$	$\mu \neq 70$	70	6	68	40	−2·11	0·0348	Reject H_0
7.	$\mu = 60$	$\mu \neq 60$	60	10	62	50	1·41	0·1586	Fail to reject H_0
8.	$\mu = 90$	$\mu \neq 90$	90	14·3	87·6	110	−1·76	0·0784	Fail to reject H_0

9. (i) H_0: $\mu = 400g$; H_A: $\mu \neq 400g$ (ii) $T = 2$ (iii) $p = 4·56\%$ (iv) Yes. Reject H_0.

10. (i) H_0: $\mu = 600g$; H_A: $\mu \neq 600g$ (ii) $T = 1·5$ (iii) $p = 13·36\%$ (iv) No. Fail to reject H_0.

11. (i) H_0: $\mu = 50$ MB/s; H_A: $\mu \neq 50$ MB/s (ii) $T = -1·70$ (iii) $p = 8·92\%$ (iv) Yes. Fail to reject H_0.

12. Yes. $1·82\% < 5\%$, therefore reject H_0. There is evidence that the average life of the batteries is **not** 3·8 years.

13. (i) [€32·25, €35·75]. Evidence to suggest that the national and capital city hourly rates of pay are different.

   (ii) H_0: $\mu = $ €32; H_A: $\mu \neq$ €32 $T = 2·24$ and $p = 2·25\%$ Yes. $2·25\% < 5\%$, $\therefore$ reject H_0. Thus, there is evidence to suggest that the national and capital city hourly rates of pay are different.

14. H_0: $\mu = 750$ ml; H_A: $\mu \neq 750$ ml $T = -1·46$ and $p = 14·42\%$ Yes. $14·42\% > 5\%$, $\therefore$ reject H_0. Evidence to suggest that the machine will not deliver, on average, 750 ml of water to each bottle.

15. (i) H_0: $\mu = 3·5$ kg; H_A: $\mu \neq 3·5$kg (ii) $T = -1·46$ (iii) $p = 14·42\%$
   (iv) Yes. $14·42\% > 5\%$, $\therefore$ fail to reject H_0. Thus, there is evidence to suggest that smoking during pregnancy has an effect on the weights of newborn babies.

Exercise 3.20

2. Mean is misleading, better to use mode

3. (i) Vertical axis not scaled (ii) No, data sums to 101%

4. Business not 50% of pie, data sums to 109%

8. (i) A survey of 200 households on each side of the rail line is not representative (iii) 59%

9. The curve is not a normal curve, hence it is not suitable to use z-scores

10. (ii) 1·86 (iii) 0·2 and 0·119 (iv) 0·11 and 0·0655 (v) Model not plausible as probabilities very different

Exercise 4.1

1. (i)

Pattern	1	2	3	4	5
Number of matchsticks	4	7	10	13	16

(ii) 19　**(iii)** $3n + 1$　**(iv)** 37

2. (i) 13　**(ii)** $2n + 3$　**(iii)** 103　**(iv)** 171

3. (i)

Pattern	1	2	3	4	5	6
Number of green squares	3	3	3	3	3	3
Number of purple square	1	4	9	16	25	36
Total number of squares	4	7	12	19	28	39

(ii) n^2　**(iii)** $n^2 + 3$　**(iv)** 327

4. (i) 29　**(ii)** $4n + 5$　**(iii)** 205　　　　**5. (i)** 5　**(ii)** n^2　**(iii)** $n^2 + n$

Exercise 4.2

1. (i) 5; 8　　　**2. (i)** −2; 1; $n^2 + 2n - 2$　**(ii)** $a = 2$; $b = 1$　**(iii)** 15　　**3. (i)** 6; 14; $n^2 + 7n + 6$

(ii) $p = 2$; $q = 6$　**(iii)** 6　　**4. (i)** $a = 3$; $b = 4$　**(ii)** 4　　**5. (i)** 3; 5; 2^{n+1}　　**11. (i)** 5; 12; 2

17. (i) $a = 3$; $b = 4$; $c = -10$　**(ii)** 54

Exercise 4.3

1. 48　　**2.** 33　　**3.** 91　　**4.** 70　　**5.** −44　　**6.** 43　　**7.** −22　　**8.** $-\dfrac{23}{60}$

9. 43　　**10. (i)** 7　**(ii)** 40　　**11. (i)** 18　**(ii)** 42　　**12.** $\dfrac{23}{12}$　　**13.** $2n + 1$　　**14.** $2n - 6$

15. $4n - 1$　　**16. (i)** $\dfrac{(n-1)(n)}{2}$　**(ii)** n　**(iii)** 20　　**17. (i)** 2^{n-1}　**(ii)** 2^{n-1}　**(iii)** 512　**(iv)** 16

18. $2^n + 2n - 1$; 271　　**19. (i)** 220　**(ii)** 1,320

Exercise 4.4

1. $a = 1$; $d = 2$; $T_n = 2n - 1$　　　**2.** $a = 2$; $d = 3$; $T_n = 3n - 1$　　　**3.** $a = 3$; $d = 4$; $T_n = 4n - 1$

4. $a = 6$; $d = 5$; $T_n = 5n + 1$　　　**5.** $a = 9$; $d = -2$; $T_n = 11 - 2n$　　**6.** $a = 4$; $d = -3$; $T_n = 7 - 3n$

7. $a = 8$; $d = -5$; $T_n = 13 - 5n$　　**8.** $a = 4$; $d = -6$; $T_n = 10 - 6n$　　**9.** $a = -5$; $d = 2$; $T_n = 2n - 7$

10. (i) $a = 1$, $d = 3$　**(ii)** $T_n = 3n - 2$; $T_{50} = 148$　**(iii)** T_{30}　　**11. (i)** $a = 4$, $d = 5$

(ii) $T_n = 5n - 1$; $T_{45} = 224$　**(iii)** T_{50}　　**12. (i)** $a = 40$, $d = -4$　**(ii)** $T_n = 44 - 4n$; $T_{15} = -16$

(iii) T_{11}　　　**13.** T_{59}　　**14.** T_{30}　　**15.** $k = 3$; 5, 7, 9　　**16.** $k = 43$; 3, 7, 11

17. $k = 11$; 17, 23, 29, 35　　**18. (i)** $k = 5$; 3, 11, 19, 27　**(ii)** $T_n = 8n - 5$; $T_{21} = 163$　**(iii)** T_1

Exercise 4.5

1. $a = 3$, $d = 2$　　**2.** $a = 1$, $d = 3$　　**3.** $a = 7$, $d = 4$　　**4.** $a = 3$, $d = 5$　　**5.** $a = 5$, $d = 6$

6. (i) $d = 3$　**(ii)** $3n + 4$; 64　**(iii)** T_{24}　　**7. (i)** $a = 3$, $d = 4$　**(ii)** $4n - 1$　**(iv)** $n = 25$

8. (i) $p = 7$, $q = 9$　**(ii)** 23　　**9. (i)** $p = 10$, $q = 7$, $r = 1$　**(ii)** −47

Exercise 4.7

1. 120   2. 246   3. 603

4. (i) $\dfrac{n}{2}(5n + 1)$ (ii) 1,010   5. (i) $\dfrac{n}{2}(3n + 17)$ (ii) 1,605   6. (i) 5, 7, 9, 11 (ii) 2 (iii) 320

7. (i) $a = 2$, $d = 5$ 8. (i) $a = -7$, $d = 4$ (iii) (a) 69 (b) 1,530   9. (i) $a = 2$, $d = 3$

   (iii) (a) 89 (b) 1,365   10. (i) $a = -15$, $d = 6$ (iii) (a) 129 (b) 0   11. (i) $a = 2$, $d = 6$

   (ii) (a) 116 (b) 1,180   12. 610   13. 1,770   14. 6,275   15. (i) $3n - 1$ (iii) 620

   16. (i) $10n$ (ii) $5n(n + 1)$ (iii) 201,000   17. (ii) (a) 39 (b) 400 (iii) 15   18. (i) $12a$

   (ii) $75a$ (iii) $a = 2$ (iv) 6, 8, 10, 12 (v) (a) $2n + 2$ (b) $n(n + 5)$ (vi) (a) 42 (b) 500

19. (i) $a = 7$, $d = 2$ (ii) 10

20. (i) €10.20 (ii) €265   21. €492,000   22. 1,120m   23. 90   24. (ii) €6,432

25. 30 seconds   26. 20   27. 1,575d 28. (ii) ln 3 (iii) $\dfrac{n(n + 1) \ln 3}{2}$

29. It is an alternative formula.   30. (i) 10 (ii) 60   31. (i) 20 (ii) 522

Exercise 4.8

1. $a = 3$, $d = 2$ 2. $a = 4$, $d = 2$ 3. $a = 1$, $d = 6$ 4. $a = -1$, $d = 4$

5. (i) 2 (ii) 23   6. (i) 3; 4 (ii) $4n - 1$ (iii) 39   7. (i) $a = -2$, $d = 4$ (ii) $4n - 6$

   (iii) 74 (iv) 10

Exercise 4.9

1. $5(2)^{n-1}$ 2. $4(3)^{n-1}$ 3. $27\left(\dfrac{2}{3}\right)^{n-1}$ 4. $50\left(-\dfrac{2}{5}\right)^{n-1}$ 5. $(2a)^{n-1}$ 6. $\dfrac{5}{a}\left(\dfrac{2}{a}\right)^{n-1}$

10. (i) $3(2)^{n-1}$ 11. 6   12. 2   13. 3   14. -3, 10   15. -2, $\dfrac{7}{2}$

16. $\dfrac{3}{2}$, 3   17. 6 cm, 9 cm   18. (i) -2, 3 (ii) -1, -3, -9, -27, … or 4, 2, 1, $\dfrac{1}{2}$

19. $a = 3$, $b = \dfrac{3}{2}$ 20. $p = -5$, $q = 25$ or $p = 4$, $q = 16$ 21. (i) a; ar^{20} (ii) ar^{10}

(iv) a, ar, ar^2, ar^3, ar^4; Result holds true.

Exercise 4.10

1. (i) (a) $2(3)^{n-1}$ (b) $3^n - 1$ (ii) (a) 4,374 (b) 6,560

2. (i) (a) $64\left(-\dfrac{1}{2}\right)^{n-1}$ (b) $\dfrac{128}{3}\left[1 - \left(-\dfrac{1}{2}\right)^n\right]$ (ii) (a) $-\dfrac{1}{8}$ (b) $\dfrac{341}{8}$

3. $6(2^n - 1)$ 4. $18\left[1 - \left(\dfrac{2}{3}\right)^n\right]$ 5. $\dfrac{189}{4}\left[1 - \left(-\dfrac{1}{3}\right)^n\right]$

6. (i) €210   (ii) Geometrically. Investment increases by a factor of 1·05   (iii) €255

7. (i) $54\left[1 - \left(\frac{2}{3}\right)^n\right]$ (ii) 6   **8.** 7   **9.** (i) 12   (ii) $12\left(\frac{1}{2}\right)^{n-1}$

10. (i) (a) −3   (b) −7   (ii) (a) $-7(-3)^{n-1}$

(b) $\frac{7}{4}[(-3)^n - 1]$ **11.** (i) $\frac{4}{9}(3)^{n-1}$ (ii) $485\frac{7}{9}$ **12.** $r = \frac{6}{5}, a = \frac{125}{6}$ **13.** (i) (a) 6 (b) $\frac{1}{2}$, 2

(ii) 12, 6, 3, or 3, 6, 12   **14.** 1, 3, 9, 27 or 9, 3, 1, $\frac{1}{3}$ **15.** $a = 2, b = 4$

16. $d = 2, r = 3$ **17.** 4

Exercise 4.11

1. 2   **2.** $\frac{4}{3}$ **3.** $\frac{2}{3}$ **4.** $\frac{4}{5}$ **5.** $\frac{3}{7}$ **6.** 0   **7.** 1   **8.** $\frac{1}{5}$ **9.** $\frac{3}{4}$ **10.** $\frac{1}{2}$

11. $\frac{3}{2}$ **12.** $\frac{4}{5}$ **13.** 5   **14.** $\frac{1}{3}$ **15.** 2   **16.** 0   **17.** $\sqrt{2}$ **18.** $\frac{\sqrt{3}}{2}$

19. (i) (a) $2n - 1$ (b) n^2 (ii) $\frac{1}{2}$

Exercise 4.12

1. 2   **2.** 3   **3.** $\frac{25}{4}$ **4.** 20   **5.** 2   **6.** $\frac{9}{7}$ **7.** $\frac{2}{15}$ **8.** $\frac{1}{1-x}$ **9.** $\frac{6}{3-a}$

10. (i) $\frac{3}{2}$ (ii) 6 (iii) 1   **11.** (i) $\frac{5}{9}$ **12.** $\frac{4}{9}$ **13.** $\frac{20}{9}$ **14.** $\frac{8}{11}$ **15.** $\frac{5}{18}$

16. $\frac{11}{90}$ **17.** $\frac{11}{6}$ **18.** 12   **19.** $-\frac{1}{2}$ **20.** $\frac{5}{6}$ **21.** $\frac{4}{5}$ **22.** (i) $\frac{1}{4}, \frac{1}{3}$ (ii) $\frac{1}{2}, \frac{1}{3}$

(iii) $2, \frac{9}{2}$ **23.** (i) $a - 2$ (ii) $\frac{5}{2}$ (iii) $1 < a < 3$ **24.** (i) (a) $\frac{1}{1-x}$ (b) $x^2 - x$ (ii) −5, 6

25. (i) $(1 - r)(1 + r)$ (ii) $\frac{1}{3}$ **26.** 18, 6, 2, ... or 9, 6, 4, ...   **27.** $a = 3, r = -\frac{1}{2}$

28. (i) 2·6 s   (ii) 1·8, 1·44, 1·152, ...   (iii) 9 s

Exercise 6.1

1. $x = 55; y = 125$ **2.** $x = 120$ **3.** $x = 65; y = 65$

4. $p = 90$ **5.** (i) 110 (ii) 70 (iii) 40   **6.** (i) 50° (ii) 50° (iii) 85° (iv) 45°

7. 78°   **8.** (i) $x = 2; y = 11$ (ii) $a = 4; b = 2$

9. (i) Yes (ii) 9 cm (iii) 18 cm (iv) 22 cm (v) 11 cm (vi) Yes

(vii) $8\sqrt{10}$ (ix) 455 cm² (x) 21 cm

10. **(i)** 16 cm **(ii)** 103·3° **(iii)** 85·6 cm^2 **(iv)** 21·4 cm

11. **(i)** 70 **(ii)** 90 **(iii)** 40 **(iv)** $p = 102$; $q = 95$; $r = 85$ **(v)** $p = 70$; $q = 140$

    (vi) $x = 64$; $y = 32$; $z = 58$ **(vii)** $x = 59$; $y = 25$ **(viii)** $a = 56$; $b = 28$ **(ix)** $x = 65$; $y = 40$

12. 83°   **13.** 108°   **14. (i)** 100° **(ii)** 100° **(iii)** 10°   **15. (i)** $x = 20°$ **(ii)** $y = 102°$

16. 24 cm   **17.** 6 cm   **18. (i)** 16 cm **(ii)** 33 cm   **19. (i)** 45° **(ii)** 20°

20. **(i)** 20 cm **(ii)** 8 cm   **21. (i)** 15 cm **(ii)** 9 cm **(iii)** 12 cm **(iv)** 36 cm^2 **(v)** yes

22. 24 cm   **23.** 78 mm   **24.** 18 cm

25. **(i)** Right angle **(ii)** Obtuse angle **(iii)** Acute angle

26. **(i)** 13 cm **(ii)** 15 cm **(iii)** 15·81 cm

28. 1   **29. (i)** 18 cm^2 **(ii)** 6 cm   **30.** 19·5 cm   **31.** 40 m^2

32. **(ii)** 75 square units **(iii)** 5   **33. (i)** 204 **(ii)** 360

34. **(i)** $25\sqrt{3}$ **(ii)** $5\sqrt{3}$

36. **(i)** $[AB] = 2\sqrt{5}$; $[AC] = 4\sqrt{2}$; $[BC] = 2\sqrt{5}$ **(ii)** $4\sqrt{6}$

37. **(i)** 7·84 m **(ii)** 90 m^2 **38. (ii)** 27·1 mm

39. **1.** If the length of corresponding sides are in proportion.

    2. If two pairs of matching angles are equal.

    3. Lengths of two sides are in proportion and the included angles are equal.

    4. In a right-angled triangle, if the length of the hypotenuse and another side are in proportion.

41. **(i)** Sides are not in proportion **(ii)** Included angle is not equal

42. **(i)** $p = 8$; $q = 10$ **(ii)** $p = 7$; $q = 6$ **(iii)** $p = 20$; $q = 9$ **(iv)** $p = 8$; $q = 6$

43. **(ii) (a)** 3 cm **(b)** 8 cm

44. **(i)** All angles are equal. **(ii)** 8 cm **(iii) (a)** 18 cm **(b)** 6 cm **(iv)** 9 cm

45. **(i)** 15 cm **(ii)** 8 cm **(iii)** 32 cm **(iv)** 27 cm

46. **(i)** Two pair of matching angles. **(ii) (a)** 2 cm **(b)** 7·5 cm

47. **(i)** 14·4 m **(ii) (a)** 9·6 m **(b)** 1·4 m   **48. (i)** 60 cm **(ii)** 1·5 cm   **49.** 1·32 m

50. 120 m   **51.** 15 m   **52. (i)** 7·65 cm **(ii)** 4·59 cm **(iii)** 178 m   **53.** 1,820 m

61. **1.** The three sides are equal in measure (SSS).

    2. Two sides and the included angle (SAS).

    3. One side and two angles (ASA).

    4. A right angle, the hypotenuse and another side (RHS).

77. **(ii)** $\dfrac{|AC|}{|BA|} = \dfrac{|DC|}{|DA|}$ **(iii)** $4\sqrt{5}$

Exercise 6.2

1. **(i)** Longer **(ii)** Greater   2. |AB| 3. |PR|

4. Yes   5. No   6. Yes

7. No   8. Yes   9. No

10. No   11. 10 cm   12. 9 am

13. **(i)** $2 < k < 10$ **(ii)** $4 < k < 10$ **(iii)** $3 < k < 13$

14. **(i)** $a = 2$ cm; $b = 18$ cm   **(ii)** Minimum = 3 cm; maximum = 17 cm

15. **(i)** $2 < x < 10$ **(ii)** $6 <$ distance < 10 16. **(i)** $11 < x < 39$ **(ii)** $36 < D < 64$ **(iii)** Collinear

17. **(i)** $7 < D < 37$ **(ii)** $6 < D < 22$ **(iii)** 19 km

Exercise 6.3

1. **(i)** O **(ii)** 2   **(iii) (a)** 6 **(b)** 2   **(iv)** 12

2. **(i)** 6   **(ii)** 8   **(iii)** 27·45 sq. units

3. **(i)** 2·5   **(ii)** 2·7   **(iii)** 2 : 5   **(iv)** 2 sq units

4. **(i)** $A = (2, 1)$, $B = (5, 1)$, $C = (5, 5)$ **(ii)** $P = (6, 3)$, $Q = (15, 3)$, $R = (15, 15)$

   (iii) (a) 5   **(b)** 15   **(c)** 1 : 3   **(iv)** 9 : 1

5. **(i)** 2·25   **(ii)** 12·5   **(iii)** 20 sq. units

6. €1,024   7. 4·5 tins   8. 72 cm^2 9. 20 cm

10. **(i)** 1·5   **(ii)** 13·5 cm   **(iii)** 168·75 cm^2; 379·6875 cm^2

11. 430 cm^2

12. **(i) (a)** 70%   **(b)** 150%   **(c)** 60%   **(ii) (a)** 72 cm^2 **(b)** 18 cm^2 **(iv)** 141%   **(v)** 2

13. **(ii)** 2·5   **(iii)** $\dfrac{25}{4}$

14. **(ii)** 3 : 2   **(iii)** 3 : 2   **(iv)** 9 : 4

15. **(i)** 1·5 sq. units   **(iii)** 6 sq. units   **(iv)** 4 : 1

16. **(ii)** 13·5 sq. units   **(iii)** 1·5 sq. units

17. **(i)** 2   **(ii)** $(-2, -1)$

Exercise 7.1

3. **(ii)** C is equidistant from A and B.   **(iii)** Isosceles   **(iv)** |AB|

23. **(ii)** $\sqrt{3}$ 25. **(ii)** 3·74 km

Exercise 7.2

12. **(ii)** Right-angled   **(iv)** Hypotenuse   13. **(iii)** Outside the triangle.   21. **(i)** Incircle

22. **(i)** Yes   **(iii)** 24 cm^2 23. **(i)** Circumcentre   26. **(ii) (a)** 5 cm   **(b)** 6 cm^2

28. (i) 6,366 km **(ii)** 22,053 km **(iii)** 12,732 km **(iv)** 6,366 km **(v)** Answers to (i) and (iv) are equal, so the satellite must be placed at a height equal to the radius of the Earth.

Exercise 8.1

1. $\frac{1}{4}$; 25%   **2. (i)** $\frac{5}{7}$ **(ii)** 840,000   **3. (i)** €126, €168, €210   **(ii)** 48 cm, 120 cm, 168 cm

4. (i) €60, €120, €30   **(ii)** 39 cm, 156 cm, 390 cm   **5.** €108   **6.** A: €15,750 B: €12,250

7. 40°   **8. (i)** €30   **(ii)** €165   **9.** 17.5%   **10.** 15.5 cm   **11.** 9 m   **12.** 35 cm

13. (i) Roy = €320 Sam = €120   **(ii)** 5 : 3   **14.** 4 : 5   **15.** 3 : 8

Exercise 8.2

1. (i) €9·60   **(ii)** €25·92   **(iii)** 26.04 cm   **2.** 20%   **3.** €232,000   **4.** €350,000

5. 7%   **6.** €4,573·80   **7. (i)** €260   **(ii)** €82·80   **(iii)** 42%   **8.** €10·08   **9.** €82

10. €250   **11.** €3,267   **12. (i)** €288   **(ii)** €244·80   **(iii)** 2%   **13.** 15%   **14.** €71·56

15. €365.28   **16.** €479·60

17. Less than in 1908. It would be 99.64% of the population in 1908

Exercise 8.3

1. €50   **2.** 2.5%   **3. (i)** 14.29%   **(ii)** 16.4%   **4.** Aus $550.43

5. From the UK by €26.47   **6.** 8.69%   **7. (i)** €73·10   **(ii)** 920 JPY

8. (i) 52.75%   **(ii)** 55%   **9. (i)** €11,584   **(ii)** €11,511·61   **(iii)** Going to the UK, by €72·39

10. (i) (a) $p = 1.56$ **(b)** $q = 5.26$ **(ii) (a)** £960   **(b) (1.)** £14·40   **(2.)** £945·60

Exercise 8.4

1. 7×10^{-4} **2.** $3\cdot5 \times 10^{-3}$ **3.** $2\cdot47 \times 10^{6}$ **4.** $4\cdot2 \times 10^{3}$

5. $3\cdot2 \times 10^{-2}$ **6.** $4\cdot5 \times 10^{-3}$ **7.** $3\cdot4 \times 10^{7}$ **8.** $9\cdot54 \times 10^{6}$

9. $2\cdot266 \times 10^{3}$ **10.** $1\cdot955 \times 10^{2}$ **11.** $1\cdot68 \times 10^{9}$ **12.** $6\cdot0 \times 10^{-6}$

13. $1\cdot52 \times 10^{2}$ **14.** $2\cdot8 \times 10^{3}$ **15.** $2\cdot0 \times 10^{-1}$ **16.** $1\cdot33 \times 10^{4}$

17. $1\cdot508 \times 10^{1}$ **18.** $2\cdot05 \times 10^{7}$ **19.** 200   **20. (i)** $1\cdot2 \times 10^{-2}$ cm

   (ii) $3\cdot499 \times 10^{9}$ **(iii)** 420 km   **21.** $6\cdot37 \times 10^{3}$ **22.** $1\cdot342 \times 10^{8}$

23. $3\cdot692 \times 10^{14}$ m^2 **24.** $2\cdot5 \times 10^{4}$ **25.** $5\cdot915 \times 10^{11}$ kg/m^3

Exercise 8.5

1. 5%   **2. (i)** 0·1   **(ii)** 1·64%   **3.** 2·3%   **4. (i)** 1584 cm^3 **(ii)** 4·5%

5. (i) 1%   **(ii)** 6187·5 kg   **(iii)** 12,375   **(iv)** €62·50   **6.** 2·94%   **7.** 12·68%

8. 14·3% error if he under-measured; 15·76% if he over-measured.

9. He must measure the angle as being between 75·55° and 74·4°.

10. (i) €2,011 **(ii)** €2,010·85 **(iii)** €0·15

Exercise 8.6

1. ±6 peanuts **2. (i)** 0·2 m **(ii)** The material in the bridge will expand when it gets warm

3. 64·85 cm − 65·15 cm **4.** 4·23 m/s ; 4·1 m/s **5. (i)** 30,000 cm^3 **(ii)** 29,601 cm^3; 30,401 cm^3

  (iii) 6,400 g **6. (i)** 140 **(ii)** €167 **(iii)** €1·19 **(iv)** €1·43

7. (i) 80 lasagnes, 125 quiches **(ii)** €4·25 per lasagne, €3·68 per quiche **(iii)** €800 **(iv)** €976

Exercise 8.7

1. (i) €11,398 **(ii)** €7,448 **2. (i)** €12,090 **(ii)** €8,940

3. (i) €18,132 **(ii)** €13,882 **4.** 20% **5.** €60,000

6. (i) €19,000 **(ii)** €48,000 **7. (i)** €23,500 **(ii)** €52,000

Exercise 8.8

1. (i) €21,735 **(ii)** €4,988·80 **(iii)** €57·23 **(iv)** €986·54

2. (i) €14,715 **(ii)** €3,623·80 **(iii)** €23·13 **(iv)** €806·89

3. (i) €21,450 **(ii)** €4,638·80 **(iii)** €33·74 **(iv)** €896·51

4. (i) €18,746 **(ii)** €4,218·80 **(iii)** €48·77 **(iv)** €737·87

5. (i) €22,650 **(ii)** €5,023·80 **(iii)** €30·83 **(iv)** €883·21

Exercise 9.1

  1. €248·25 **2.** €1,664·39 **3.** €41,124 **4.** €7,969·24 **5.** €22,604·40

  6. €9,244·85 **7.** €17,558·71 **8.** $P = \dfrac{F}{(1 + i)^t}$; €50,000 **9.** €3,200 **10.** €1,800

11. €1,202 **12.** €2,500 **13. (i)** €6,030·43 **(ii)** 3·09% **14.** 6·5% **15.** 3%

16. 3·85% **17.** 3·8% **18.** 5·5% **19.** 3·01% **20.** 4·14% **21.** €24,812·48

22. €12,624·60 **23. (i)** €68,500 **(ii)** 3·5% **24. (i)** €33,075 **(ii)** €8,075 **25.** €5,600

Exercise 9.2

  1. (ii) €40,095 **2.** €18,423·75 **3. (i)** €85,000; €78,200; €74,290 **(ii)** €25,710

  4. €29,141·08 **5. (i)** €5,115·02 **(ii)** 22·5% **6.** €15,250 **7.** 6 years **8.** 6·6 years

9. 5 years **10. (i)** 9% **(ii)** €750,000 **11.** 6% **12.** €983·28 **13.** €8,591·12

14. 6 years **15.** 4·5 years

Exercise 9.3

1. 28.33 million **2.** 3,144 **3. (i)** 12,920 **(ii)** 39.8% **4. (i)** €196,690·86 **(ii)** 6%

5. (i) 83·4 cm **(ii)** 86·3 cm **6. (i)** 1,280 **(ii)** $4·697 \times 10^{109}$ **(iii)** 103 secs **7.** $k = 0·25$

8. 4,648

Exercise 9.4

1. No, since the NPV $= -€3,884·60 < 0$. **2.** Yes, since the NPV $= €1,417·44 > 0$.

3. Company A. Company A : NPV $= €6,706·01$ Company B : NPV $= €2,515·17$

4. Yes, since the NPV $= €3,558·74$ **5.** Yes, since the NPV $= €370·33$

6. (i) No. The NPV $= -€1,294·05 < 0$ **(ii)** Reduce the initial cost or increase the annual payout.

Exercise 9.5

1. €6,264·49 **2.** €4,696·75 **3.** €11,468·14 **4.** €2,836·64 **5.** €2,363·79

6. €35,423·95 **7.** €4,962·52 **8.** €129·60 **9.** €144·81 **10.** €82·29

11. €13,712·45 **12.** €220,476·95 **13. (i)** €190,042·62 **(ii)** €458,328·45

14. (i) €1,053,974·73 **(ii)** No, as NPV < 0 **15.** €1,836·58 **16. (i)** 0·34745% **(ii)** €574·75

   (iii) €1,309·08 **17. (i)** €478,190·99 **(ii) (a)** €508·24 **(b)** €756·16

18. (i) €606,789·08 **(ii) (a)** €602·41 **(b)** €737·28 **19. (i)** 0·865% **(ii)** €168,661·79

   (iii) 0·311% **(iv)** €998·69

Exercise 9.6

1. (i) €389·58 **(ii)** €3,375 **2. (i)** €545·15 **(ii)** €7,250·81 **3. (i)** €12,802·39

   (ii) 60% **4. (i)** €722·66 **(ii)** 44.5%

5. (i) €1,315·53 **(ii)** €74·36 **(iii)** €23,266·44 **6. (i)** 0·581% **(ii)** €1,563·82

   (iii) €487,912·89 **(iv)** €262,912·89 **(v)** €720·69 **(vi)** €725·51 **7.** €15,854·18

8. €25,758·70 **9. (i)** $\dfrac{A}{1+i}$ **(ii)** $\dfrac{A}{(1+i)^2}$ **(iii)** $P = \dfrac{A}{1+i} + \dfrac{A}{(1+i)^2} + \dfrac{A}{(1+i)^3} + \cdots + \dfrac{A}{(1+i)^t}$

Exercise 11.1

18. (i) 55; 55 **(ii)** $64(8^{2n}) - 9(3^{2n})$

Exercise 11.2

14. (i) $7, \dfrac{7}{2}, \dfrac{7}{3}$ **(ii)** $T_n = \dfrac{7}{n}$

Exercise 12.1

1. 18 m^2 **2.** 17·6 cm **3.** $25\sqrt{3}$ cm^2 **4.** 49 cm **5. (ii)** $\dfrac{21}{4}\sqrt{11}$ cm^2

6. (i) 38·45 cm^2 **(ii)** 56 cm^2 **7. (i)** 9171·25 **(ii)** 9,170 **(iii)** $9·17 \times 10^3$ **8.** $96\sqrt{3}$ cm^2

9. 10·7 cm   **10.** 22 m   **11.** 9·3   **12. (i)** 2,552 m^2 **(ii)** 52·697 m **(iii)** 48·43 m

13. (i) 54π **(ii)** 63π **(iii)** $\dfrac{b}{400}$ and $\dfrac{w}{375}$ **(iv)** 0·9519 **(v)** Yes

14. 2·4 × 10^7 and 1·6 × 10^7

15. (i)

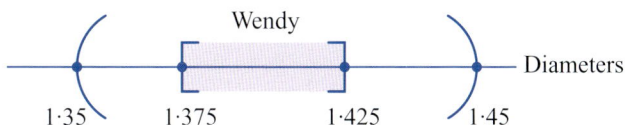

A significant proportion of bolts will not fit.

(ii) Change the tolerance levels of bolts or drill or both

16. (ii) 60·6 cm **(iii)** 2/3 **(v)** 9·96 m **(vi)** 13·6 kg   **17. (i)** 14·7 m **(ii)** 32

18. (i) $\dfrac{5\pi}{2}$ **(ii)** $\dfrac{5\pi}{3} + 6$ **19.** 12·375 πr^2 **20. (i)** 30 m **(ii)** 601 m^2

21. $\dfrac{123\pi}{2}$ **22.** $\sqrt{3} : 1$ **23.** 14 cm

24. (i) 12·5 cm **(ii)** 490·9 cm^2 **(iii)** 75 cm^2 **(iv)** 106·3° **(v)** 23·2 cm **(vi)** 144·9 cm^2

25. (ii) 6·8 cm^2 **(iii)** 15·6 cm^2 **(iv)** 22·5 cm

27. (i) 1·625 m **(ii)** 134·8° **(iii)** 3·8 m **(iv)** 7 m^2

28. (i) 16·25 m **(ii) (a)** 9·05 m **(b)** 10 > Radius **(iii)** 9·3611 m

29. (i) 60° **(iii)** $r(3 + \sqrt{3})$ or $\sqrt{3}\,r(\sqrt{3} + 1)$ **(iv)** $(4\sqrt{3} + 6)r^2$ **(v)** 72·9%

Exercise 12.2

1. 228 m^2 **2.** 265·5 m^2 **3.** $\dfrac{47}{3}$ m   **4. (i)** 12 cm **(ii)** (0, 5, 7, 4, 0); 48 cm^2

5. 1,976 cm; 7,904 cm   **6. (i)** 3,600 m^2 **(ii)** 50%

7. (i) 27·4 m^2 **(ii) (a)** 822 m^3 **(b)** 822,000 l

8. (i) $x = 3$, $y = 4\tfrac{1}{2}$ **(ii) (a)** 47 **(b)** 23

Exercise 12.3

1. 4,096 cm^3 **2.** $\dfrac{15\sqrt{3}}{4}$ cm^2; $\dfrac{75\sqrt{3}}{2}$ cm^3 **3. (i)** 45 **(ii)** 21 l   **4.** $\dfrac{1}{3}$

6. 4 cm   **7. (i)** 375π cm^3 **(ii)** 200π cm^2 **(iii)** 10   **8. (ii)** 864 m^3

9. (i) 11 cm **(ii)** 90 **(iii)** 10   **10. (i) (a)** 720π mm^3 **(b)** 2261·95 mm^3 **(ii)** 10

11. (i) 3·15 mm **(ii)** 198·45π mm^3 **(iii)** 4·41

12. (i) 8·6 cm **(ii)** 6750 l

13. (i) $2\pi r^3(3 + 2\sqrt{2})$ **(ii)** $8\pi r^3$ **(iii)** Since A = 11·65πr^3 > B, select pack B.

14. (iii) (a) 1000 **(b)** 2 and 7 **(c)** 1,250; 4·5

15. (i) 9,203 **(ii)** 66% **(iii)** 20930 **(iv)** 22

16. **(ii)** $\dfrac{3\sqrt{3}x^2 h}{2}$ cm³; 5 cm   17. **(i)** $\dfrac{\pi}{3}r^2 + 12r + 2\pi r$ **(ii)** $\dfrac{\pi}{3}r^2 + (12 + 2\pi)\,r - 200 = 0$

   (iii) 7·6

18. **(ii)** $n = 8$ **(iv) (a)** 12 m   **(b)** 20 m   19. **(ii)** 3200 sin θ **(iv)** $\theta = 90°$ **(v)** max value

   $\sin\theta = 1. \Rightarrow \theta = 90°$

20. **(ii)** $w\sqrt{\dfrac{3}{2}}$ **(iii)** $\sqrt{6}$ cm   **(iv)** $6\sqrt{6}$ cm³   22. **(i)** $V = x^3 + 3x.$

Exercise 13.1

1. **(i) (a)** z **(b)** X   **(c)** Y   **(ii)** A   **(iii) (a)** $\dfrac{18}{25}$ **(b)** $\dfrac{9}{10}$

2. **(i)** $y = \dfrac{2x + 23}{5}$ **(ii)** (6, 7)   3. **(ii)** $x^2 + y^2 - 7x - 5y + 6 = 0$ 4. **(ii)** 121°   **(iii)** 10,500 km

5. **(ii) (a)** Use red 6   **(b)** Use yellow 6   **(c)** Woody wins; he wins zero

6A. **(iii) (a)** Acute triangle   **(b)** Obtuse triangle   **(c)** Right-angled triangle

7. **(i)** 72·5°   **(ii)** 9·54 m   **(iii)** 114 m²   **(iv)** 71·7°   **(v)** 49·1 m; 30·9 m high

8. **(i)**

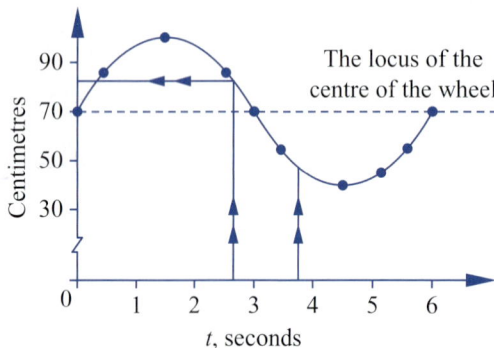

The locus of the centre of the wheel

   (ii) 100,40 cm   **(iii)** $4\dfrac{1}{2}$ secs   **(iv) (a)** 82 cm   **(b)** 48 cm   **(v)** The centre of the wheel does not move up or down. The path of the centre (locus) is indicated on the graph. The centre is always at 70 cm.

9. **(ii)** Position is not quantitative data   **(iii)** (Roughly) linear   **(iv)** 1,255 million km
   (v) 1,506 million km   **(vi)** can use $\mu \pm \sigma$ **(vii)** Our system's planets are more spread out and further from the sun   **(viii)** $\dfrac{3}{8}$ **(ix) (a)** $\dfrac{5}{28}$ **(b)** $\dfrac{15}{36}$

10. **(iii)** 0·33   **(iv)** 0·2   **(v)** 0·058   11. **(i) (a)** $\dfrac{5}{36}$ **(b)** $\dfrac{7}{12}$ **(c)** $\dfrac{3}{13}$ **(ii)** 3.6

12. $(x - 10)^2 + (y - 3)^2 = 20$ and $(x - 2)^2 + (y + 1)^2 = 20$ 13. **(i)** $\left(\dfrac{27}{8}, \dfrac{9}{8}\right)\left(\dfrac{5}{8}, \dfrac{15}{8}\right)$ **(ii)** (4, −8)

14. **(i)** 1·5   **(ii)** $\dfrac{4}{5}$ 15. **(i)** $\dfrac{1}{150}$ **(ii)** $\dfrac{12}{75}$ **(iii)** $\dfrac{1}{24}$ 16. **(i) (a)** cos x **(b)** $-\dfrac{1}{2}$ cos x

(iii) $\dfrac{\pi}{12} + n\pi$ and $\dfrac{5\pi}{12} + n\pi$ **17A. (ii) (a)** $\dfrac{3}{1}$ **(b)** $|AY|:|YC|$ **17B. (i)** $\angle BDC$

18. (i) 58·69 m   **(ii)** 3·41 m   **(iii) (a)** Bert   **(b)** 0·0024   **19. (ii)** $r = -0{\cdot}14$ **(iii)** r implies not appropriate   **20. (i)** 7·85 m   **(ii)** 58·9 m^2 **(iii)** $22\dfrac{1}{2}$ m   **(iv)** 25·61 m   **(v)** 4·39 m

(vi) $\dfrac{3\pi}{8}$ secs   **21. (i)** $k = \pm 4$ **(iii) (a)** Four values ± 120; ± 240 **(b)** $120 + 360n$ and $240 + 360n$ where $n \in z$ **(iv)** 9   **22. (i)** 5; 1·8   **(ii)** $\{2, 3, 7\}$ $\{2, 3, 8\}$ $\{2, 7, 8\}$ $\{3, 7, 8\}$ $\bar{x} = 4$; $\dfrac{13}{3}$; $\dfrac{17}{3}$; 6 $E(\bar{x}) = 5$ and $\sigma(\bar{x}) = 0.85$ **(iii)** $\mu = 5 = E(\bar{x})$ **(iv)** More samples indicates more spread out implies standard deviation larger   **23. (iii)** Original group had total 35 children

and was less spread out than the new group   **(iv)** $\dfrac{4}{25}$ **(v) (a)** $\dfrac{1}{50}$ **(b)** $\dfrac{7}{25}$ **(c)** $\dfrac{1}{4}$

24. (i) 12 m   **(iii)** 22°   **(iv)** 112°   **25. (i)** (4, 3)   **(ii)** 83°   **(iii)** 72 km   **(iv)** 20 m/sec
26. (i) $(x - 10)^2 + (y - 6)^2 = 400$ **(ii)** 25 units   **(iii)** (22, 22)   **(iv)** 1·7 units   **(v)** 170 km is too far
(vi) $y = 26$ and $24x + 7y - 782 = 0$ **(vii)** 549 km   **27. (i)** $\beta = 100$; $\alpha = 44$ **(ii)** Error of $\pm 1°$ on a smaller angle (α) will cause the greatest error in location of R **(iii)** When (PR) is the smallest side in $\triangle PQR$, then location of R will be more sensitive to small errors in β

(iv)

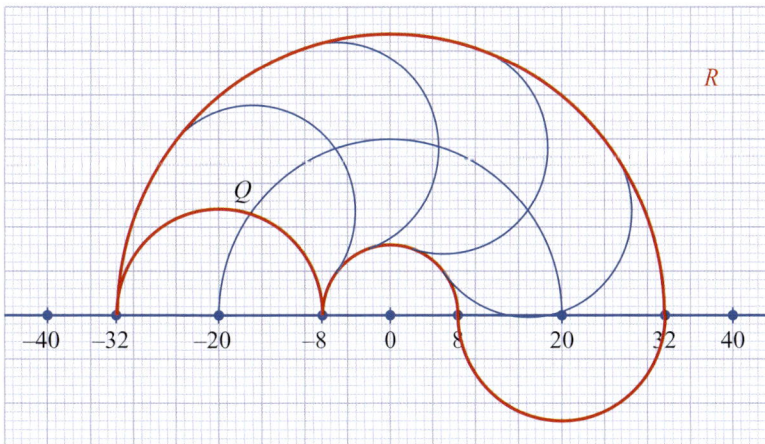

28. (i) 184·5 cm^2 **(ii) (a)** 1   **(b)** 0·95   **(c)** 5%   **29. (i) (a)** 6·4 m/sec   **(b)** 23 km/h
(c) 1·6 m/sec   **(ii) (a)** $\dfrac{27}{128}\pi\text{m}^3$ **(b)** $\dfrac{8\pi}{3}$ m^3 **(c)** $a = 8$, $b = \dfrac{3}{4}$ **(d)** $8\left(\dfrac{3}{4}\right)^{x-1}\ln\dfrac{3}{4}$

30. (i) (a) $\dfrac{25\sqrt{3}}{4}$ cm^2 **(b)** 43·3 cm^2 **(ii) (a)** 89 m   **(b)** 1·45 ha   **31. (ii) (a)** $\dfrac{1}{18}$

32. (i) 0·937   **(ii) (a)** $3\sin^2 x\cos x$ **(b)** $\dfrac{1}{3}\sin^3 x + $ constant

33. (i) $(-1 + 2i)$ **(ii)** $2 - 3i$, $2 + i$ **(iii)** $2^{13}(-1 + \sqrt{3}i)$ **(iv) (a)** $(-1, 0)$, $(0, 5)$ **(b)** -1 **(c)** -3
(d) $a = -1$, $b = -4$, $c = 5$ **(e)** -1, $2 + i$, $2 - i$ **34. (i)** $-1{,}024$ **(ii) (a)** $4 - i$, $-4 + i$

(b) $3 + i, -1 + 2i$ **(iii)** $-2, 1 + \sqrt{3}i, 1 - \sqrt{3}i, x^2 + y^2 = 4$

(iv) (a)

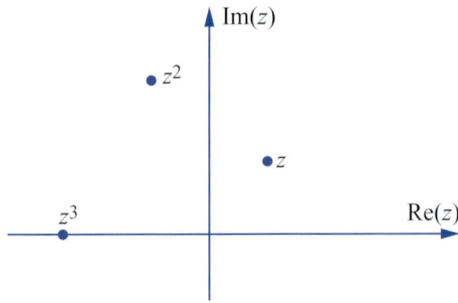

(b) $\theta_1 = 60°, \theta_2 = 120°$
(c) $z = 1 + \sqrt{3}i, z^2 = -2 - 2\sqrt{3}i, z^3 = -8$
(d) 4

35. (i) (a) $30° = 150° - 120°$ **(ii) (a)** Not all coefficients are real   **(b) (1)** $p = 2, q = 7$ **(2)** $1 - 3i$
(iii) (a) $\sqrt{2}(\cos 45° + i \sin 45°)$ **(b)** $2^5(-1 + i)$ or $-32 + 32i$ **(iv)** $p: (x - 4)^2 + (y + 2)^2 = 16, q: y = 1$

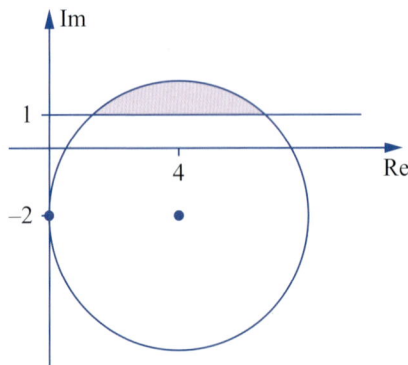

36. (ii) (a) 1. -2 **2.** 4 **(b)** $45°, 225°$ or $\dfrac{\pi}{4}, \dfrac{5\pi}{4}$ **(iii)** -1

(iv) $\dfrac{3}{2}(\cos 40° + i \sin 40°), \dfrac{3}{2}(\cos 160° + i \sin 160°), \dfrac{3}{2}(\cos 280° + i \sin 280°)$

(v) (a) $\left(\dfrac{\sqrt{3} + 1}{2}\right) + \left(\dfrac{\sqrt{3} - 1}{2}\right)i$ **(b)** $15° = 60° - 45°$ **(c)** $\sqrt{2}(\cos 15° + i \sin 15°)$

(d) $\dfrac{\sqrt{3} + 1}{2\sqrt{2}}, \dfrac{\sqrt{3} - 1}{2\sqrt{2}}$ **37. (i)** 1 **(ii)** $1 < x < 6$ **(iii)** $-2 < x < 1$ **(iv)** 2 **38. (i)** $1; 5$

(ii) $1 < x < 3, 5 < x < 6$ **(iii)** $0 < x < 1, 3 < x < 5$ **(iv)** $2, 4$ **(v)** $0 < x < 2; 4 < x < 6$

(vi) $2 < x < 4$ **39.** A: graph; B: derivative. A is a parabola and would have an equation of the
form $y = ax^2 + bx + c$. The derivation of $x^2 - 3$ is $2x$, which would be represented by a straight line.
40. C. The curve looks like a cubic function so its derivative must be a quadratic. The curve has a
local max and a local min, so its derivative must cross the x-axis at two points. The slope begins as
positive until the local max and then becomes negative. Its derivative should be decreasing at the
corresponding times.

41. (i) (ii)

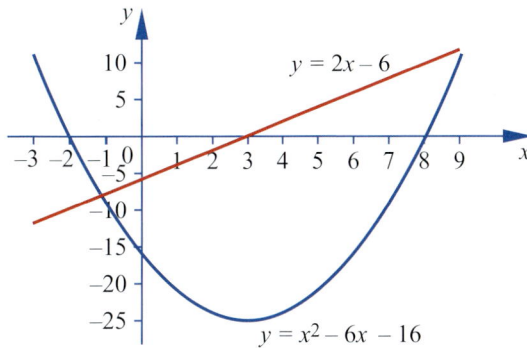

$\dfrac{dy}{dx} = \cos x$ $y = \sin x$

42. (i)

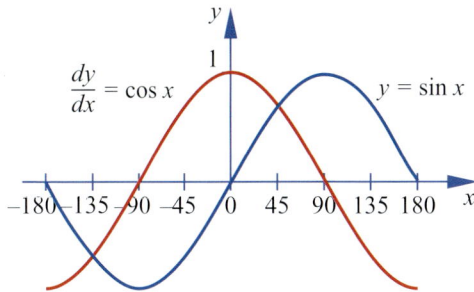

$y = |\sin x|$

(iii) Move (translate) sin x 90° to the left

(ii) It has a sharp corner

43. (i) (−2, 0), (8, 0) **(ii) and (iii)**

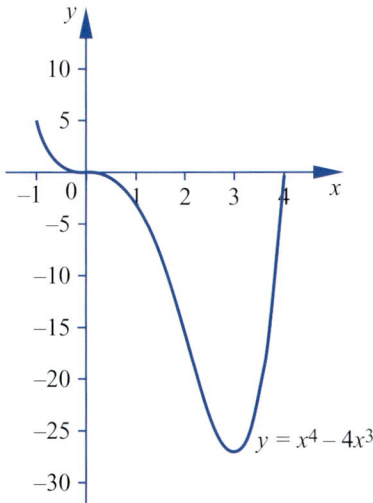

$y = 2x - 6$

$y = x^2 - 6x - 16$

(iv) (3, 0) **(v)** The x-coordinate is the same for the local maximum of the curve

44. (i) −5·9, −1·5 and 4·4

(iv) The three roots include the x-coordinate of the maximum twice

45. (i) (3, −27) **(ii)** (0, 0), (2, −16) **(iii)** (0, 0), (4, 0)

(iv)

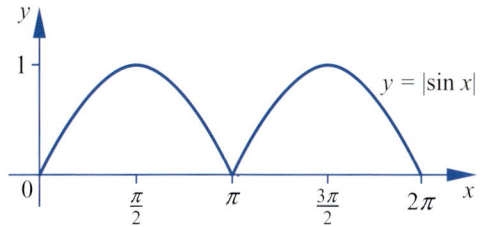

$y = x^4 - 4x^3$

(v) (a) $x < 0$; $0 < x < 2$ **(b)** $x > 2$

47. (i) (b) It is not **(ii)** It is not **(iii)** It is

48. (i) $1 + r + r^2 + \cdots + r^{n-1}$

49. (i) $x \sin x$ **(ii)** $\sin x - x \cos x + c$

50. (i) xe^x **(ii)** $xe^x - e^x + c$

51. $\dfrac{243}{24}$ **52. (i)** 24 m/s **(ii)** $a = 2$ m/s^2, which is a constant **(iii)** $s = t^2 + 24t + c$

(iv) $s = t^2 + 24t$; 340 m **(v)** $s = t^2 + 24t - 25$; the displacement from the origin at time t

53. (i) 500,500 **(ii)** 125,250 **(iii)** 250,500 **(iv)** 250,000 **54.** Geometric. Each term after the first is 5 times the previous term. **55.** $4\frac{2}{9}$ or $\frac{38}{9}$ **56. (i)** €273,575·32 **(ii)** €615·37

57. (i) 0·5 or $\frac{1}{2}$ **(ii) (a)**

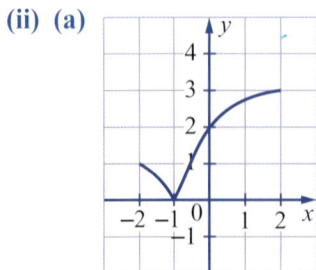

(b)

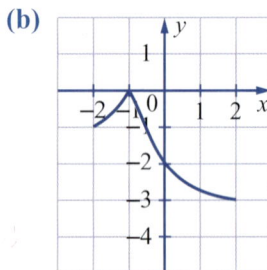

58. (i) (a) No **(b)** Yes **(ii)** $k = -2, t = -5$ **(iii) (a)** $0 \le y \le 3$ **(b)** 2, 5 **(d)** Outside domain $0 \le x \le 5$ **(e)** 2 **(iv) (a)** 2, 12, 17 **(b)** −1 **(c)**

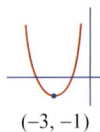

(−3, −1)

(d) Yes, any vertical line will cut the graph of $f(x)$ once **(e) (1)** $f(-4) = 1$ and $f(-2) = 1$, two different inputs have the same output or a horizontal line can intersect the graph more than once **(2)** Some horizontal lines will not intersect the curve. For example, $y = -2$ **(f)** $x \ge -3$ or $x \le -3$

59. (i) 34 **(ii)** $m = 3$ **(iii)** 3 **(iv) (a)** $d = -6$ **(b)** $a = 1, b = 2, c = -5$ **(c)** $p = -3, q = -1, r = 2$

(v) (a) 80°C **(b)**

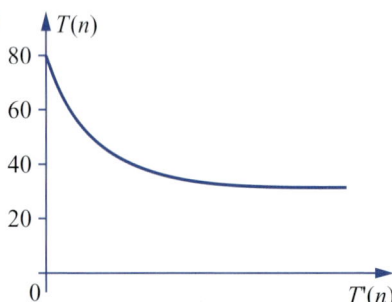

(c) $e^{-0.1n} \ge 0$ **(d)** 4·1 **(e)** $-6e^{-0.1n}$ **(f)** 38

60. (i) $-3 \le x \le 3$ **(ii) (a)** −3 **(b)** 3 **(c)** 1 **(d)** 0 **(iii) (a) (1)** $x^2 + 6x + 14$ **(2)** $x^2 + 8$ **(b)** −1 **(iv) (a)** $\dfrac{5 - 3x}{3 - x}$

(v) (a) $l = (15 - h)$ cm, $w = (20 - h)$ cm

(b) $v = (2h^3 - 50h^2 + 300h)$ cm³

(c) $l = w$ gives $h = 5$; $V(5) = 500$ cm³ **(d)** 2·9 cm

(e) New capacity is 500 cm³ + 10% of 500 cm³ = 600 cm³. The line V = 600 intersects the graph at about $h = 17\cdot3$. Can't have a negative length. Therefore, not possible to make this larger box from this piece of cardboard. **61. (i) (a)** 0 **(ii) (a)** $(x - 3)^2 + 1$ **(b)** $\sqrt{x - 1} + 3$ **(c)** $x \ge 1$

(iii) (a)

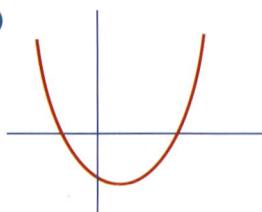

(b)

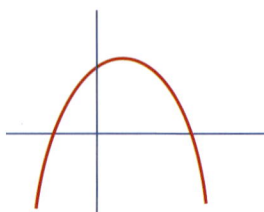

(c)

(d)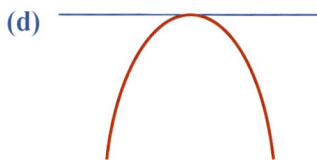

(e)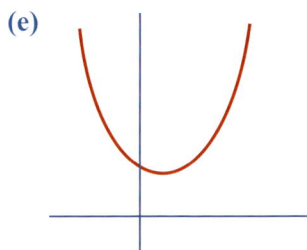

(f)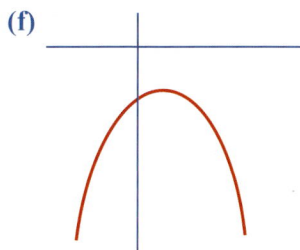

(iv)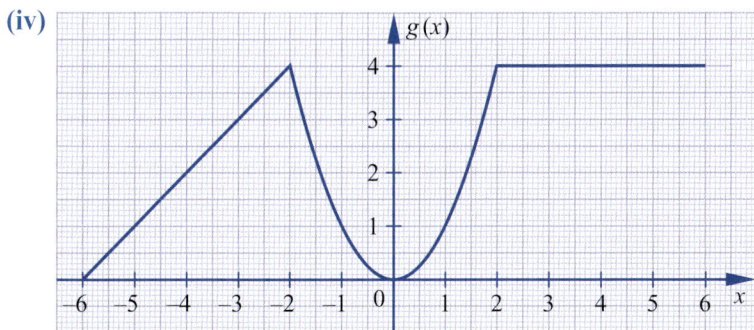

(v) (a) 0   **(d)** 36·6 m

    (e) 10·50 seconds

62. (i) $p = 5$, $q = 6$ or $p = 6$, $q = 5$ **(ii)** $x < \dfrac{3}{7}$, $x > \dfrac{1}{2}$

63. (i) (a) $x = 2$, $-\dfrac{1}{5} \pm \dfrac{7}{5}i$

    (b) $k = 5$, $\dfrac{14}{5} \pm \dfrac{7}{5}i$

(ii) Width = 5 cm, length = 16 m   **64. (i)** $x = 3\sqrt{2}, -7\sqrt{2}$

(ii) (a) $c = -3 - b$ **(b)** $d = -2 - 2b$ **(c)** $b = -4$, $c = 1$, $d = 6$ **65. (i)** $\dfrac{x}{y} = \dfrac{3}{2}$

(ii) (a) $x = 1$, $y = 3$, $z = 2$ **(b)** $a = 2$, $b = -\dfrac{8}{3}$, $c = \dfrac{5}{2}$ **66. (i) (a)** $x = 7$ **(b)** $x = -11$

(c) $x = -\dfrac{3}{7}$ **(ii)** $x = 4$ **(iii) (a)** pH = 4·57, acid   **(b)** pH = 8·9, base   **(c)** pH = 7, neutral

67. (i) $x = 6$ **(ii)** $x = 2$, $y = \dfrac{9}{2}$ **(iii)** B is $y = x^2 + 3$, C is $y = (x - 2)^2$, D is $y = (x + 3)^2 - 2$

68. (i) $\dfrac{2}{x - 2}$ **69. (i) (b)** $\dfrac{k \pm \sqrt{k^2 - 4}}{2}$ **(c)** $-2 < k < 2$ **(ii)** $I_1 : I_2 = 631{:}1$

70. (i) (a) $x = -2$, $\dfrac{1}{2}$, $\dfrac{2}{3}$ **(ii) (c)** $x = -4p$, $-p$, $2p$ **71. (i) (a)** $x = 4$ **(b)** $x = \dfrac{1}{2}$ **(ii) (a)** $a = 7$

(b) $p = -\dfrac{1}{3}$, $q = 2$ **72. (i)** $(x + 4)^2 - 6$ **(iii) (c)** $(-1, 3)$ and $(5, 3)$ **(d)** $-1 < x < 5$

(e) $x < -1$, $x > 5$ **(f)** $|x - 2| = 3$ **73. (i)** 4   **(ii)** -5, -1, 1, 3 **(iii)** $f(x) = x^4 + 2x^3 - 16x^2 - 2x + 15$

74. (i) First plot = 30 m, second plot = 40 m, third plot = 10 m, fourth plot = 20 m

(ii) (a) $x = 9$ **75. (i)** $x = \dfrac{4}{3}$ **(ii)** 1·63

(iii) Natalie: length = 6 m and width = 2 m, Jemma: $L = 18$ m and $W = 6$ m or
Natalie: $L = 12$ m and $W = 8$ m, Jemma: $L = 18$ m and $W = 12$ m   **76. (i)** $-2 \le x \le 5$
(ii) (a) $x = -3$, 9   **(b)** $x = 11$ **77. (i) (b)** When $a = b$ **(ii)** $x = 2$ m   **78. (i)** $A = 500(0.85)^t$

(ii) 18.4 hrs   **79.** $A_{Banda} = 794$ (A_{Iran})   **80. (i)** 20°C   **(ii)** This is the temperature the microwave
is before you switch it on. So this temperature is the room temperature.
(iii) 401°C   **(iv)** No. This would involve $(0.9)^x$ being a negative value, which is not possible.

(v) 500°C   **81. (i)** €1,500 in 7% bond and €1,900 in 8% bond **(ii)** 6%

82. 63 months, which brings the date to April 2010   **83.** €5,600   **84. (i)** €12,223·50

(b) €1,750 at 10% and €250 at 11%   **85.** A = €116·26, B = €6,975·60, C = €1,975·60

86. 81,920   **87.** €262·18   **88. (i)** €24,918·44   **(ii)** €31,963·44   **89. (i)** €1,015·15

(ii) €65,236   **90. (i)** €1,424,994·61   **(ii)** No. The value of the €1,600,000 at the time that Caitlin

won the lottery was only €1,424,994·61.   **91. (i)** No, not true. It amounts to €71,896·75

(ii) 19 years   **92. (i)** €664,527·35   **(ii) (a)** €760·27   **(b)** €930·79   **93. (i)** €1,237·76

(ii) €122,062·67   **94. (i)** €4,901·96   **(ii)** P = $\dfrac{5,000}{(1·02)^t}$ **(iii)** €24,038·64   **(iv) (a)** 0·1652%

(b) $p(1 + 0·0001652)^n$ **(c)** €92·55   **(v)** €230·90   **95. (i) (a)** 5,040   **(b)** 720

(c) 4,320   **(d)** 144   **(e)** 144   **(ii) (a)** P = 0·6, Q = 0·7, R = 0·2   **(b) (1)** 0·12

(2) 0·48   **(3)** 0·4

(iii) (a)

Outcome	i	−1	$-i$	1
Payout	€0	€1	€20	€2
Probability	0·4	0·2	0·1	0·3

(c) No. Gambled money – expected value ≠ 0 (€5 – €2·80 ≠ 0).

96. (i) (a) 1,365   **(b)** 280   **(c)** 462   **(ii) (a)** 0·1 or $\dfrac{1}{10}$ **(b)** 0·5   **(c) (1)** 240   **(2)** 400

(d) 2·7   **(iii) (a)**

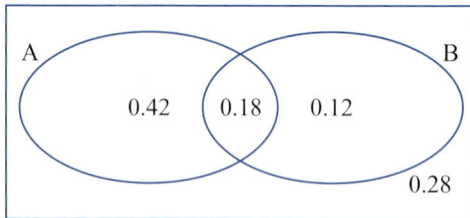

(b) 0·3   **(c)** 0·6 or $\dfrac{3}{5}$

(d) Yes. P(A) × P(B) = P(A ∩ B) or P(A | B) = P(A) or P(B | A) = P(B)

97. (i) (a) 8   **(b)** 21   **(ii)** 0·4985

(iii) (a) $\dfrac{1}{7}$ **(b)** $\dfrac{6}{7}$

(iv) (a) Trials are independent of each other. Probability of success and failure remains the same for each throw. Only two outcomes (given). Finite number of throws (given).

(b) (1) 0·311   **(2)** 0·092   **98. (i)** 0·9113   **(ii) (a)** 0·9   **(b)** 0·72   **(iii) (a)** 0·087

(b) 0·896   **(iv) (a)** 0·94208   **99. (i)** 1·42   **(ii) (a)** 20   **(b)** 196·6 g   **(iii) (a)** 68·26%

(b) 2·41 standard deviations above the mean, ∴ in the top 0·4%   **(c)** 534   **(d)** 1

100. (i) 48 m²   **(iii) (c)** k = −4.4 or k = 16.4 is outside the range 0 ≤ k ≤ 12. Thus, k = 6 is the only solution.

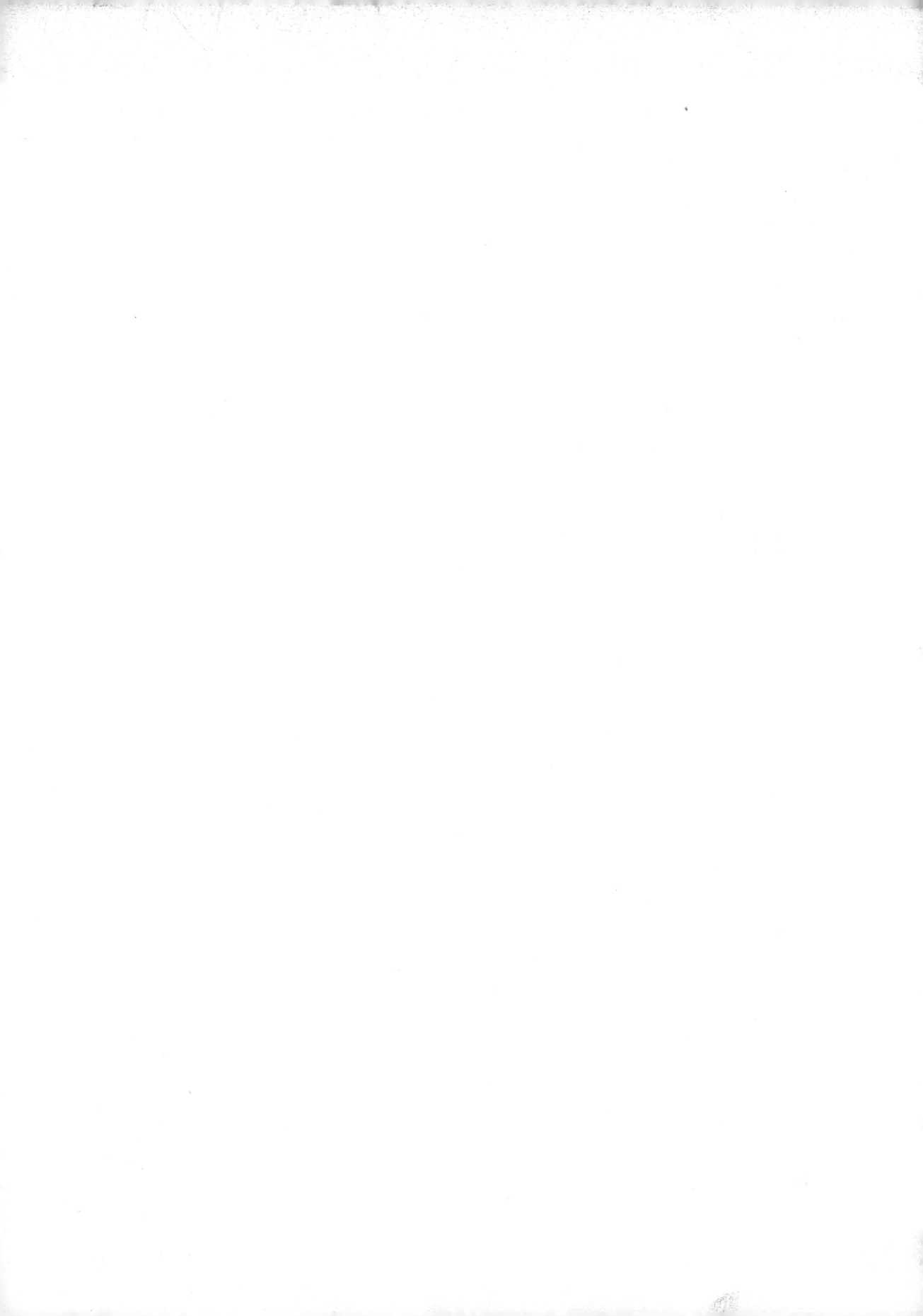